Marketing Across Cultures

Marketing Across Cultures
second edition
———— ◆◆◆ ————

formerly
International Marketing
A Cultural Approach

Jean-Claude Usunier

PRENTICE HALL

LONDON NEW YORK TORONTO SYDNEY TOKYO SINGAPORE

MADRID MEXICO CITY MUNICH

First published 1996 by
Prentice Hall Europe
Campus 400, Maylands Avenue
Hemel Hempstead
Hertfordshire, HP2 7EZ
A division of
Simon & Schuster International Group

© Prentice Hall Europe 1996

Typeset in 10/12 pt Times
by Photoprint, Torquay, Devon

Printed and bound in Great Britain by
MPG Books Ltd, Bodmin, Cornwall

Library of Congress Cataloging-in-Publication Data

Available from the publisher

British Library Cataloguing in Publication Data

A catalogue record for this book is available
from the British Library

ISBN 0–13–236175–2

3   4   5   6   00   99   98   97

Contents

Contents

Introduction

This book is not a classical text of consumer marketing with an emphasis on world markets. It adopts a cultural approach to international marketing, which has two main dimensions:

1. A cross-cultural approach which proceeds by *comparing* national marketing systems and local commercial customs in various countries. It aims to emphasize what is country-specific and what is universal. This type of analysis is essential for the preparation and implementation of marketing strategies in different national contexts.
2. An inter-cultural approach, which is centred on the study of *interaction* between business people, buyers and sellers (and their companies) who have different national/cultural backgrounds. This intercultural view extends further to the interaction between products (and their physical and symbolic attributes) from a definite nation-culture (i.e. a country with a definite and homogeneous national culture) and the consumers from a different nation-culture, and to the interaction between messages conveyed by marketing communications (brands, packaging and advertising) and consumers from a different culture. To this extent it is interaction in its broad sense: not only between people, but also between people and messages, and people and products. In this book commerce is emphasized as much as marketing. When the word *commerce* is used in this text, it refers to the complex dimensions of business relationships entwined with interpersonal relations.

The basic assumption behind this book is that culture penetrates our inner being subconsciously and at a deep level. World cultures share many common features. Nevertheless they all display a unique style when such common elements are combined: kinship patterns, education systems, valuation of the individual and the group, emphasis on economic activities, friendship patterns, time-related organization patterns, the criteria for aesthetic appreciation, and so on. The examples which are used in this book are by their very nature eclectic. I have chosen those examples that seem to be both the most striking and pertinent.

I have no wish to describe cultures, either from an insider's point of view, or exhaustively. What I have attempted to provide for the reader is *a method for dealing with intercultural situations in international marketing*. The underlying postulate of this book is, that international marketing relationships have to be built on solid foundations. Transaction costs in international trade are high: only a stable and firmly established link between business people may enable them to overcome disagreements and conflicts of interest. In international marketing it is advisable to be very methodical and long-term oriented, to select a limited number of partners and opportunities and to develop them to their fullest extent.

In Part 1, the first three chapters are devoted to the cultural variable. They try to define it, to delineate the components of culture, and finally to emphasize its dynamic nature. The last two chapters are devoted to consumer behaviour and international market research seen from a cross-cultural perspective.

Part 2 deals with the globalization of markets and its general impact on international marketing strategies, with special emphasis on the key issue for product policy, that is, the dilemma between adaptation and standardization. Part 3 presents further issues related to international marketing decisions: brand names for international markets, country of origin images and their possible use for supporting sales, pricing, the choice of distribution channels. Emphasis has deliberately been placed on the culture-based approaches to such decisions. That is why, for instance, I accentuate bargaining (with its cultural variations) in the chapter on pricing, and the Japanese *keiretsu* distribution system, in the chapter on distribution decisions.

Part 4 presents marketing communications in an intercultural environment. It starts by a general overview of language, culture and communication issues, which are applied in the following two chapters to advertising issues, personal selling, public relations, and to bribery and ethical issues in international marketing ; the two last chapters are devoted to international marketing negotiations. Table 1 describes basic contents, linking culture to marketing issues, in Chapters 4 to 16.

This book is written from a European viewpoint. No international marketing textbook may be considered universal, and this one is no exception. It is written certainly in a somewhat less pragmatic and issue-orientated style than most international marketing textbooks. Statements may sometimes be considered as value judgements, since they are not as frequently backed by facts and empirical evidence, as is the case in American textbooks. Therefore it may sometimes look unusual to native English-speaking readers. I believe they have to consider it as part of the message of the book: it is a more contextual, and therefore less explicit, relationship with the reader. The chapters are followed by questions, cases, exercises and critical incidents. An **instructor's manual** is available. Since different national versions of this book have been published (Dutch, English, French and German), it may be used in cross-cultural training settings.

I wish to acknowledge the help of various institutions which during the last ten years have provided me with the opportunity to teach international marketing, and colleagues who have encouraged me to put more and more emphasis on the cultural dimension of international marketing. I thank also Julia Helmsley and the whole team at Prentice Hall

Table 1   *The impact of cultural differences on selected aspects of marketing*

Area of marketing	Cultural differences influence . . .	Chapter
Consumer behaviour	Consumers' values, attitudes and decision-making	4
Market research	Equivalence and methods in cross-national market surveys	5
Overall marketing strategy	Global versus locally customized marketing strategies	6
Targeting market segments	Groups of countries or consumers sharing cultural traits	7
Defining regional market clusters	Organizing for marketing on a regional basis	7
Product policy	Adaptation or standardization of product attributes	8
Brand image	Brand and country-of-origin evaluations by consumers	9
Price policy	Bargaining rituals/price–quality evaluations / price strategies towards consumers, competitors and suppliers	10
Distribution channels	Channel style and service, producer–distributor relationships	11
Communication	World-views (through language) and communication styles	12
Advertising	Tailoring messages to audiences' cultural traits	13
Personal selling	Selling styles, sales force management, public relations, bribery and ethical issues in an international context	14
Marketing negotiations	Negotiation strategies, processes and outcomes	15
National style of marketing negotiation	Attitude, organization, scheduling, role of emotions and friendship, communication and interaction style, etc.	16

who have been instrumental in editing this book and Ann Bone for her insightful copy-editing. I remain responsible for any errors and shortcomings in the book.

Scanning the environment:
The cultural variable in international marketing

1

———◆◆◆———

The cultural process

Not everything is culture-based. It would be most dangerous to equate the behaviour of individuals entirely with that of the cultural grouping to which they belong. Furthermore, we often have a rather stereotyped perception of such behaviour, which provides only a shallow, imperfect picture of the operation of a cultural group. Interpretation is often defensive and the analysis neither comprehensive nor fully explicative.

International marketing automatically accords a prominent place to the cultural variable, despite the difficulties of isolating it for direct implementation. One of the principal aims is to identify, categorize, evaluate and finally select market segments. Nation-states are an enduring reality. In many cases, though not all, national territory and the concept of a nation are justified by the existence of groups that are relatively homogeneous on an ethnic, linguistic and religious level. Lack of homogeneity is often at the centre of disputes between different cultural communities. The cultural variable is complex, and the way in which it influences behaviour is difficult to analyze.

The objective of this chapter is to clear the way for the arguments that will be developed later in the book. Initially this involves the definition of culture and its major constituents, and an examination of its relations with nationality (i.e. the concept of national character) and individual psychology (that is, personality/individual character). Culture is not only used as a guide for communication and interaction, quite subconsciously, with others in one's own community, but also for rather more conscious interaction with people belonging to other cultural communities. I have borrowed from the field of anthropology, particularly cultural anthropology, and also from several other disciplines, sociology, social psychology and cross-cultural psychology.

I strongly urge interested readers to use the notes and bibliographical references at the end of this and the following two chapters, and to refer to the sources mentioned in their original form wherever possible.

1.1 Culture: definition(s)

In French the word *culture*, was defined by Emile Littré in his dictionary which appeared at the end of the nineteenth century, as 'cultivation, farming activity'. The abstract sense probably originated in Germany where the word *Kultur* was used as early as the eighteenth century to refer to civilization. In the Anglo-Saxon world the abstract notion of culture came into widespread use at the beginning of the twentieth century.

Many definitions have been formulated for culture: because it is a vague, abstract notion, there are many candidates for the ultimate definition. Kroeber and Kluckhohn (1952) even devoted an article to a review of the definitions of culture and listed no less than 164! This did not prevent them from adding their own. Most of these definitions were the work of anthropologists, generally those who had studied 'primitive' societies (American Indians, Pacific Islanders, African natives and so on). But their definitions also took into account our 'civilized' societies and 'modern' cultures. The use of several definitions, each one adding to the cultural jigsaw puzzle, will help to determine the main aspects of this abstract and elusive concept.

Particular solutions to universal problems

Kluckhohn and Strodtbeck (1961, p. 10) emphasize the following basic points:

1. '... there is a limited number of common human problems for which all peoples at all times must find some solution.'
2. 'While there is a variability in solutions of all the problems, it is neither limitless nor random but is definitely variable within a range of possible solutions.'
3. '... all alternatives of all solutions are present in all societies at all times, but are differentially preferred. Every society has, in addition to its dominant profile of value orientations, numerous variant or substitute profiles.'

How does culture link the individual to society?

Ralph Linton (1945, p. 21) advanced the following definition: 'A culture is the configuration of learned behaviour and results of behaviour whose component elements are shared and transmitted by the members of a particular society.' At a previous point in his book, Linton clearly indicates the limits of the cultural programming which the society can impose on the individual (1945, pp. 14–15, emphasis added):

> No matter how carefully the individual has been trained or how successful his conditioning has been, he remains a distinct organism with his own needs and with capacities for independent thought, feeling and action. Moreover *he retains a considerable degree of individuality*. . . . Actually, the role of the individual with respect to society is a double one. Under ordinary circumstances, the more perfect his conditioning and consequent integration into the social structure, *the more effective his contribution to the smooth functioning of the whole and the surer his rewards*. However societies have to exist and function in an ever-changing world. The unparalleled ability of our species to adjust to changing conditions and to develop ever more effective responses to familiar ones rests upon the residue of individuality which survives in every one of us after society and culture have done their utmost. As a simple unit in the social organism, the individual perpetuates the *status quo*. As an individual he helps to change the status quo when the needs arises.

What use is culture to the individual?

According to Goodenough (1971), culture is a set of beliefs or standards, shared by a group of people, which help the individual decide what is, what can be, how to feel, what to do and how to go about doing it. On the basis of this definition there is no reason for culture to be equated with the whole of one particular society. It may be more related to activities that are shared by a particular group of people. Thus individuals may share different cultures with several different groups. When in a particular cultural situation, they will 'switch into' the culture that is operational. The term 'operational' describes a culture that is shared by those among whom there must be cooperation and that is suitable for the task.

Goodenough's concept of 'operational culture' assumes that the individual can choose the culture in which to interact at any given moment or in any given situation. This is, of course, subject to the overriding condition that the culture has been correctly internalized from past experiences. Although the concept of operational culture is somewhat debatable, it does have the advantage of highlighting the multicultural nature of many individuals in today's societies (binationals, multilingual people, people who have a particular national identity and an international professional culture, employees influenced by corporate culture). It draws our attention to the important issue of the sources of the individual's acculturation.

How to define the 'borders' of a culture?

As Child and Kieser emphasize (1977, p. 2):

> Cultures may be defined as patterns of thought and manners which are widely shared. The boundaries of the social collectivity within which this sharing takes place are problematic so that it may make as much sense to refer to a class or regional culture as to a national culture.

In colloquial language, when we say 'Texans', or 'Parisians', or 'docs', or 'showbiz' we are referring to cultures as well as to the groups of people who share them. But it is important to consider the following issue: to what extent do the characteristics of these groups relating to certain patterns of thought, belief or behaviour, really differentiate them from other cultural groups?

1.2 Elements of culture

Culture is much more a process than a distinctive whole, which would be entirely identifiable by the sum of its elements. Its elements are organically interrelated and work as a coherent set. It is not only a 'toolbox' for it also provides people with some 'directions for use' in their daily life in the community. Nevertheless it may be interesting to identify some key elements of culture. Tylor (1913) describes culture as a complex and interrelated set of elements, comprising knowledge, beliefs and values, arts, law, manners and morals, and all other kinds of skills and habits acquired by a human being as a member of a particular society.

The biological foundations of culture

The anthropologist Bronislaw Malinowski has evidenced the relationship between the purely biological needs of people and the way in which they are organized and regulated within the framework of the cultural community. For Malinowski (1944, p. 75) there are clearly biological foundations to culture: 'We have to base our theory of culture on the fact that all human beings belong to an animal species. . . . No culture can continue if the group is not replenished continually and normally.' He develops the example of eating habits, which must be regarded as both biological *and* cultural:

> Cultural determination is a familiar fact as regards hunger or appetite, in short the readiness to eat. Limitations of what is regarded as palatable, admissible, ethical; the magical religious, hygienic and social taboos on quality, raw materials, and preparation of food; the habitual routine establishing the time and the type of appetite – all these could be exemplified from our civilization, from the rules and principles of Judaism, or Islam, Brahmanism or Shintoism, as well as from every primitive culture.

Malinowski (1944, pp. 86–7) also evokes the cultural relativity of sexual behaviour:

> The specific form in which the sexual impulse is allowed to occur is deeply modified by anatomical inroads (circumcision, infibulation, clitoridectomy, breast, foot and face lacerations); the attractiveness of a sex object is affected by economic status and rank; and the integration of the sex impulse involves the personal desirability of a mate as an individual and as a member of the group. It would be equally easy to show that fatigue, somnolence, thirst and restlessness are determined by such cultural factors as a call to duty, the urgency of a task, the established rhythm of activities.

Language

Language has a prominent role as an element of culture. A linguist and anthropologist, Benjamin Lee Whorf (Carroll, 1956, p. 65), a chemical engineer working for a fire insurance company, spent his spare time tracing back the origins and grammar of American Indian languages. He is the author of a seminal, and quite controversial, hypothesis, often referred to as the Whorfian hypothesis or Whorf–Sapir hypothesis. Aspects of this theory have been incorporated, either explicitly or implicitly, at many points in this book, particularly those chapters in which language and linguistic figure strongly: market research (Chapter 5) – because of questionnaires and interviews – brands (Chapter 9), marketing communication advertising (Chapters 14 and 15) and negotiation (Chapters 16 and 17). Whorf defines his basic tenet as follows:

> The ethnologist engaged in studying a living primitive culture must often have wondered: 'What do these people think? How do they think? Are their intellectual and rational

processes akin to ours or radically different?' But thereupon he has probably dismissed the idea as a psychological enigma and has sharply turned his attention back to more readily observable matters. And yet the problem of thought and thinking in the native community is not purely and simply a psychological problem. It is quite largely cultural. It is moreover largely a matter of one especially cohesive aggregate of cultural phenomena that we call a language.

In short, Whorf defends the idea that the language we learn in the community where we are born and raised shapes and structures our world-view and our social behaviour. It influences the way in which we address issues, select those we consider relevant, solve problems and finally act. Although the Whorfian hypothesis has been harshly criticized by many linguists, it remains a *fundamental metaphor*, though not a fully validated scientific theory. We will refer to it as a key issue when describing the pitfalls of intercultural communication (in Chapter 12). Language, especially through tenses and words, shapes time-related behaviour which has an influence on business attitudes (when negotiating or dealing with delivery times or appointments). African Bantu people, for instance, do not have a specific word (like most western cultures) which clearly differentiates the 'here' and the 'now'. They have a common time–space localizer (see reading A2.4).

Social institutions, material and symbolic productions

Language is an essential part of culture: it is regarded as a reflection of culture. It is the basic input of any culture-based communication process, because everyday life is mostly a matter of interaction through communication in a culturally homogeneous community. But obviously it is not the only element of the culture shared in the community. For instance, the Swiss use different languages but have shared a common culture for several centuries. Accordingly, three other types of element appear to be quite significant:

1. Institutions, broadly defined, because they are the 'spine' of the cultural process, in that they link the individual to the group. This area may include family as well as political institutions, or any kind of social organization within which the individual has to comply fairly obediently with rules in exchange for various rewards (e.g. being fed, loved, paid and so on). These rules are not static and an individual may also sometimes act as a proactive agent of change.
2. Productions (again, broadly defined): not only material productions, but also productions of intellect, artistry and service in so far as they transmit, reproduce, update and continuously attempt to improve the knowledge and skills in the community.[1]
3. Symbolic and sacred elements, because they are the basis for the description (and therefore management) of the relations between the physical and the metaphysical world. Cultures range from those where the existence of any kind of metaphysical world is completely denied to those where symbolic representations of the metaphysical world are present in everyday life. A central preoccupation of cultural communities is to define, through religious and moral beliefs, whether there is life after death and of what kind. The scientific movement, especially at the end of the nineteenth century, has seemed close to eliminating these questions by pushing back

the boundaries of the metaphysical world. Nowadays scientists recognize that the metaphysical question will never be resolved fully by scientific knowledge. What is in fact of interest to us is not the answers to these questions *per se*; it is the consequences of moral and religious assumptions, which differ widely across cultures, on individual and collective behaviours.

There is nothing to prevent a particular cultural item from belonging to these four elements of culture simultaneously, which then appear as different layers. For instance, music is at the same time a language, an institution, an artistic production, and also a symbolic element.

Productions are diverse: tools, machines, factories, paper, books, instruments and media of communication, food, clothing, ornaments, etc. As a result, we often confuse an influential civilization (which corresponds to the German word *Kultur*) with a cultural community which successfully produces many goods and services. But material consumption or wealth orientation is not definitive proof of cultural sophistication. *There is no hierarchy, apart from the purely subjective, between world cultures*. There are many different cultural attitudes to the material world, its importance and the level of priority in the community's resource allocation given to productions and material achievements.

In *A Scientific Theory of Culture* (1944), Bronislaw Malinowski compiled a list of universal types of institutions across cultures, to which the following refers. The first institution is based on the integrative principle of *reproduction*: it is underpinned by blood relationships and marriage as an established contractual framework. It covers all kinds of kinship patterns – the family as the basic institution formed by the parents and their children. The reproduction principle also incorporates the ways courtship and marriage are legally organized. The extended family must also be considered: clan organization and its nature (matrilineal, patrilineal); the regulation of interclan relationships, etc.

The second type of institution is based on the integrative principle of *territoriality*. Common interests are dictated by neighbourhood and vicinity. Cooperation may be enhanced by the commonly perceived threat of potential foes who are located outside the common territory. This type of institution may range from a horde of nomads to a village, a small town community, a region, a province, or, at the largest level, the 'mega-tribe' composed of all the people sharing the same nationality. Initially territoriality is concrete, based on physical space and some kind of fencing or borders. In the modern world, it may be extended to abstract territories (associations, clubs, alumni, and so on).

The third integrative principle is a *physiological* one: people in the community are basically characterized by their sex, age, physical traits or defects. This includes institutions such as the sexual division of labour, sex roles, the relationship patterns between age groups and the way minority members of the community are treated (asylums for the mentally ill, or special homes for the disabled).

The fourth principle deals with the *spontaneous tendency to join together*, in order to pursue common goals. This gives rise to various kinds of associations: primitive secret societies, clubs, artistic societies, mutual companies, etc.

The fifth principle is that of *occupational and professional activities*: it deals with the way labour is divided and the kinds of expertise that have been developed. In modern societies, this includes economic organization, the medical system, the legal system and other groups of experts; in fact all those institutions that maintain the fabric of a society: economic organizations, the medical system, the legal system, the police, the army, educational institutions and religious bodies.

The sixth principle relates to the inevitable *hierarchy* among any society: the existence of rank and status positions. This includes the following, *inter alia*: the nobility, the middle class and slaves, or more generally any kind of social class system or caste system. The social hierarchy may follow a variety of criteria: ethnicity, education or the level of riches, etc.

The seventh principle proposed by Malinowski corresponds to the necessity of gathering and coordinating, these diverse elements into a reasonably coherent whole, that is, *totality*. The political process, whatever it may be (feudal, democratic, theocratic, dictatorial, etc.), expresses the need for totality. It deals with the collective decision process at the highest level. The various strata of totality, such as the individual striving for identity and the community striving for coherence, may compete with each other: that of a minority, that of a state; more generally sub-groups of the mega-tribe of a nation-state. A minority, willing to practise its religion and mores (e.g. polygamy), may be opposed to the state which tries to maintain the global coherence by limiting social customs to the dominant solution (e.g. monogamy). More generally any sub-group of the 'mega-tribe', composed of all the nationals of a particular state, may feel that their particular interests are conflicting with those of the community as a whole. These oppositions will be stronger in 'simple' states (where the nationals are not necessarily homogeneous from a cultural point of view) than in a real 'nation-state' (where the nationals share a common linguistic and cultural background).

Culture as a collective fingerprint: are some cultures superior?

Culture is *the* domain of pure quality. There are no 'good' or 'bad' elements of a particular cultural group. Value judgements should be avoided as much as possible. In this respect culture is entirely qualitative. Culture is identity: a sort of collective fingerprint. Cultural differences exist, but this is no reason for judging a particular culture as *globally* superior or inferior to others. Cultures may be evaluated and indeed ranked, but only on the basis of facts and evidence according to precise criteria and for very specific segments of culture-related activities. Some people may be said to make better warriors, others to hold finer aesthetic judgement, or to be more gifted in the composition of music, and so on. But culture is a set of *coherent* elements: straightforward comparison might allow us to indulge in the rather dangerous illusion that it is possible to select the best from each culture and make an 'ideal' combination. However, as we will see later on, it is not quite that easy.

A joke about Europeans illustrates this. It goes: 'Heaven is where the cooks are French, the mechanics are German, the policemen are English, the lovers are Italian, and it is all organized by the Swiss. Hell is where the policemen are German, the mechanics are French, the cooks are British, the lovers are Swiss, and it is all organized by the Italians.'

It is easy to see that not only would it be difficult to take the best traits from a culture, while rejecting the worst, but also any attempt to combine the best of several cultures could eventually turn to be a disaster. This is because *coherence* is needed at the highest level (corresponding to *identity* at the individual level).

The importance of the symbolic dimension

Productions of culture cannot be described only by their physical attributes: they always contain a symbolic or sacred dimension. This is true also of many behavioural artefacts (see reading A1.3 'Body ritual among the Naciremas'). Mircea Eliade (1956, p. 79) describes how the arts of the blacksmith and the alchemist, the forerunners of modern metallurgy and chemistry, hold a powerful symbolic dimension:

> The alchemist, like the smith, and like the potter before him, is a 'master of fire'. It is with fire that he controls the passage of matter from one state to another. The first potter who, with the aid of live embers, was successful in hardening those shapes which he had given to his clay, must have felt the intoxication of the demiurge: he had discovered a transmuting agent. That which natural heat – from the sun or the bowels of the heart – took so long to ripen, was transformed by fire at a speed hitherto undreamed of. This demiurgic enthusiasm springs from that obscure presentiment that the great secret lay in discovering how to 'perform' faster than Nature, in other words (since it is always necessary to talk in terms of the spiritual experience of the primitive man) how, without peril, to interfere in the processes of the cosmic forces. Fire turned out to be the means by which man could 'execute' faster, but it could also do something other than what already existed in Nature. It was therefore the manifestation of a magico-religious power which could modify the world and which, consequently, did not belong to this world. This is why the most primitive cultures look upon the specialist in the sacred – the shaman, the medicine-man, the magician – as a 'master of fire'.

Numerous illustrations of the strength of symbolic dimensions are given throughout the book. In the area of marketing communication, symbolic dimension is of the utmost importance: products and their advertising communicate through the symbolism of colour, shape, label, brand name and so on. The interpretation of symbols is strongly culture-bound.

Traditional societies have always been more consciously involved in symbolic thought and behaviour than modern societies. Since less is *explained*, more must be *related*. For example: Why does the sun shine everyday? Should its disappearance be considered ominous? What should be done to satisfy it so that it goes on spreading its generous rays on the fields and rivers? The bloody ritual sacrifices in the pre-Colombian civilizations were heavily charged with symbolic content.[2] Human sacrifices were dedicated to the sun, as were the blood and the living heart which was pulled out of the bodies of living people. The Spanish conquerors were utterly horrified by these sacrifices because they did not understand their meaning. The Spaniards were helped in their conquest by a myth: Mayas and Aztecs were waiting for the return of Quetzalcoatl, a sort of man-god, who had been a benevolent ruler over his people and whose return was to herald a golden age. When the bearded Hernando Cortés landed in Mexico, accompanied by strange creatures (the Indians believed that horses and their riders were a single body), they saw him as Quetzalcoatl.

Of course, symbols are not only related to religious and metaphysical matters; they also extend into everyday life. It is a common mistake to believe that the symbolic dimension has largely disappeared in modern life, forgotten by the modern people who have progressed along the road towards science and knowledge, pushing back the boundaries of the metaphysical world, which will ultimately be eliminated. The illusion of the pre-eminence of science generated by technological breakthroughs in the nineteenth century, is now largely abandoned by today's top scientists. As Stephen Hawking points out (1988, p. 13):

> ... ever since the dawn of civilization, people have not been content to see events as unconnected and inexplicable. They have craved an understanding of the underlying order in the world. Today we still yearn to know why we are here and where we came from.

1.3 Culture and nationality

Nationality is one delimitation of individuals belonging to a large group; it is operational and obviously convenient. However, the direction of causality between these concepts of nationality and culture is not self-evident. It is likely that, historically, shared culture has been a fundamental building block in the progressive construction of modern nation-states. But as soon as these states began to emerge, they struggled against local particularisms, patois and customs, and tried to homogenize institutions. Conflicts in large countries have often had a strong cultural base: the War of Secession in the United States, the rivalry between the English and the Scots in the United Kingdom and the progressive elimination of local powers in the highly centralized French State, all have distinctive cultural elements at stake: language, values, religion, concepts of freedom, etc.

Nevertheless an attempt to equate culture directly with the nation-state, or country, would be misguided for a number of convergent reasons:

1. A country culture can only be defined by reference to other country cultures. India is a country culture in comparison with Italy or Germany, but the Indian subcontinent is made up of highly diversified ethnic and religious groups (Muslims, Hindus, Sikhs, etc.) and languages (there are more than twenty principal languages). India is a deeply multicultural country.
2. Some nation-states are explicitly multicultural – Switzerland, for instance. One of the basic levels of organization is the canton (*Gau* in German), which defends local particularisms. Precise staffing levels have been established in public bodies, companies and banks, which prevent discrimination between linguistic communities whose numbers are unequal: the German-speaking Swiss make up almost three-quarters of the total population, the French-speakers a little more than 20 per cent, Italian-speakers 3–4 per cent and Romansch-speakers about 1 per cent. However, there is a common misconception that Switzerland administers its multicultural-ism without encountering any difficulties.[3] The Swiss political system, which was

established more than seven centuries ago, enables the people to manage successfully the complex trade-off between an exacerbated compliance with local peculiarities and a common attitude towards anything that is not Swiss.

3. Political decisions, especially during the last century, have imposed the formation of new states, particularly through the processes of colonization and decolonization. The borders of these new states, sometimes straight lines on a map, were often fixed with little respect for cultural realities, and international negotiators obviously had very little in common with the people for whom they were making decisions. Many significant national cultures, such as that of the Kurds (split between the Iraqis, the Syrians, the Turks and the Iranians) have never been accorded the right to a territory or a state. The Eritreans (in Ethiopia) have been given such a possibility after seventy years of civil war.

Sources of culture

The national element is not always the main source of culture when regarded from an 'operational culture' perspective (Goodenough, 1971). Figure 1.1 shows the basic sources of cultural background at the level of the individual. For instance, medical researchers or computer hardware specialists, whatever their nationality, share a common specialized education, common interests and largely the same professional culture. This is developed through common training, working for the same companies, reading the same publications world-wide, and contributing to research where international cross-cultural comparability of purely scientific methods and results is fundamental.

Language(s)
Nationality
Education (general)
Profession (specialized education)
Group (ethnicity)
Religion
Family
Sex[a]
Social class[b]
Corporate or organizational culture

Sources of culture

[a] In 1948 the anthropologist Margaret Mead published *Male and Female* (William Morrow: New York), which draws on her in-depth knowledge of several South Pacific and Balinese cultures. It not only depicts their organization of relationships between men and women, the division of labour and roles in the community, but also explains how these patterns may be compared to those of contemporary American society. *Male and Female*, which has been a continuous best-seller, is an excellent and detailed introduction to sex cultures. Although rarely mentioned in this book, which is principally concerned with territory and national culture, the difference between masculine and feminine culture is in fact the most basic cultural distinction.

[b] Social class may be a distinctive source of culture, to a greater or lesser degree, depending on the country. For instance in France and England, where there are traditions of accepted birth inequalities and a strong historical orientation, social class is a very distinctive source of culture; the way one speaks immediately reveals one's social class. However in the United States, Japan or the Scandinavian countries, this is not so marked. But like sex, and unlike most other sources, social class is not a territory-based source of culture.

Figure 1.1   Sources of culture.

Likewise, the sense of belonging to an important ethnic group may override, and even nullify the feeling of belonging to a particular nation-state. The Tamil population in Sri Lanka, which makes up about 20 per cent of the total Sri Lankan population and is mostly centred around Jaffna in the north of the island, is strongly linked with the large Tamil community in southern India (numbering 55 million), which supports them in their claim for autonomy. The Tamils are involved in a brutal struggle with the Singalese community which accounts for the largest part of the population. The sense of belonging to a large ethnic group is, in this case, much stronger than the feeling of belonging to a national group.

National/cultural territories with specific, recognized borders are rarely fully homogeneous. The transition from one to another is often facilitated by 'cross-border' cultures. Examples of this are numerous. In the area around the border between France and Spain, for instance, two cultures, which are almost national cultures, exist side by side and offer continuity between the two countries: the Basque country to the west, Catalonia to the east. The painter Salvador Dali, a Catalan born in Figueras (Spain) which is 20 km from the French border, was fascinated by the train station at Perpignan in France – the French part of Catalonia. In reality these two places, on either side of the border, belong to the same Catalan culture, which is sustained by the use of the Catalan language. Other examples show that some people have been able to reach a compromise: the Swedish-speaking minority on the west coast of Finland, for instance, or the Alsatians in France. Alsatians speak a mostly German-based patois, behave in the workplace like Germans and traditionally lean towards a sense of French nationality and the adoption of the French lifestyle outside the workplace. People who belong to these 'cross-border' cultures generally have a privileged position as 'exporters' from one country to other.

Physical and climatic conditions are also a fairly systematic source of differentiation (subtle rather than fundamental). Hence almost every apparently unified country is made up of a 'North' and a 'South'. Even in a country that is homogeneous from a linguistic, ethnic, religious and institutional point of view, such as Sweden, there is a fairly marked difference, at least for the Swedes, between the culture and lifestyle of a southern city (say, Malmö) and a northern town (say, Luleå). This difference may not be so strongly perceived by foreigners, who initially appreciate only their own differences from Swedes and Sweden as a whole.

Cultural homogeneity and relevant segmentation

Most international market segments are based on geographical/geopolitical divisions, which may be also an efficient segmentation criteria in cultural terms. However, sociodemographic variables or lifestyles may also be relevant for international segmentation. Should one, for instance, target a transnational ethnic segment, a national segment or a cross-border regional segment? Chapters 5 and 7 examine the issue of regional versus national segmentation, which is particularly important in large countries like the United States and in economic areas such as the European Union (EU).

Homogeneity in certain fields is clearly favourable to the emergence of a coherent culture in a nation-state and hence to the possible confusion of culture and country and treatment of the latter as a culturally unified and coherent segment (which could be broken down into sociodemographic microsegments):

1. Linguistic homogeneity.
2. Religious homogeneity.
3. Ethnic homogeneity.
4. Climatic homogeneity.
5. Geographical homogeneity.
6. Institutional and political homogeneity.
7. Social/income homogeneity.

The word 'homogeneity' implies one of the following:

1. The existence, throughout the whole population, of a unique modality (that is, only one religion, or one language) or a reduced standard deviation (in per capita income, for instance, across all social strata) in comparison with the mean value of the characteristic across the whole population.
2. An accepted diversity, that is, an agreement for maintaining several languages, more or less spoken and/or understood by everybody, or several different religions (as in Germany), but all of them officially recognized and financed by the state.
3. 'Perceived homogeneity', that is, the perception of differences within a country as being acceptable within the national community. For instance, people may observe huge differences in wealth and income but consider it acceptable for various reasons: fatalism, indifference, or metaphysical justification.

The concept of national culture

The concept of national culture may seem dangerous in many respects, because it sums up a complex and multiform reality. In short, as a variable it is too artificial to avoid the traps of cliché and stereotype. The following two questions should give a better grasp of the concept:

1. Is this concept coherent and substantial enough to constitute an explanatory variable, not only in the scientific sense, but also from a pragmatic point of view?
2. How does it influence behaviour: can one speak of national character or national culture?

The answer to the first question is clear: the concept of national culture suffers a systematic lack of coherence. It is an 'intersection' of concepts, one being the result of the merging of culture (a mostly anthropology-based concept), and the other, more official, concept being that of the nation-state. As discussed earlier, cultures do not often correspond to nation-states but to linguistic, ethnic, religious or even organizational entities. This is due to the fact that in modern times, the most frequent mode of political organization of individuals within a particular society is that of the nation-state, hence the emergence of this 'intersection' concept of national culture. The vagueness of this concept probably explains why it has been systematically underestimated, especially in international trade theory. Theory-builders who generally seek to construct formally convincing theoretical explanations, tend to remove such vague variables from their models even if they are explanatory. However, the fact that a construct is not easily measurable is no justification for ignoring it. Despite its limitations, the concept of national culture can still be an interesting Pandora's box.

The second question merits consideration, but the two possible responses as to whether culture directly influences personality cannot be assessed on a scientific basis. Some people favour the idea that the cultural variable directly influences individual psychological characteristics, i.e. culture has a distinct imprint on personality. Personality traits exist for which the average individual in one culture scores significantly higher (or lower) than individuals belonging to another culture. This corresponds to the idea of national character or more precisely the concept of modal personality, which has been developed in greater detail by Inkeles and Levinson (1969).[4] This approach largely grew out of enquiries which now seem to have lost some of their relevance: why are certain people more violent, more aggressive, more domineering, collectively more prone to declare war on other nations or to organize and implement genocide? These questions stemmed from the Second World War, especially the Nuremberg trials. Numerous empirical studies have been undertaken, particularly during the 1950s and 1960s, taking as a starting point the formation process of national character (where there could be a divergence between nations): rearing practices, early childhood, education systems, the socialization process of children, etc. Generally the results neither prove nor disprove the existence of national character.

The second approach is that of the anthropologist Ralph Linton in his book, *The Cultural Background of Personality*. According to Linton, individual psychology and therefore personality traits are largely free from the influence of culture (1945, pp. 14–15): 'His [the individual's] integration into society and culture goes no deeper than his learned responses, and although in the adult the greater part of what we call the personality, there is still a good deal of the individual left over.' The question of whether personality is modal (culture-bound) or culture-free is not just academic. In Linton's view, individuals may have personalities quite separate from their cultural background. From a 'national character' perspective, one would expect to meet people with an average personality which reflects their culture.

1.4 Culture and competence

Some environmental predispositions

Some peoples are considered to be more work-oriented and more efficient when it comes to producing material goods. Among the most efficient peoples are those who lost the Second World War: Germany, Japan and Italy. Climate has often been considered an environmental variable which has a strong influence on performance. Box 1.1 contains the beginning of Montesquieu's theory of climates (1748). The physiological explanations are scarcely credible now; it is nevertheless a starting point for the north/south stereotype. The question is: do some countries/climates tend to harden (or soften) people, with the result that they become more (or less) inclined towards activities of war, commerce or industry,[5] and more (or less) efficient in pursuing these activities?

Box 1.1   *Of the difference of men in different climates*

A cold air* constringes the extremities of the external fibres of the body; this increases their elasticity, and favors the return of the blood from the extreme parts to the heart. It contracts+ those very fibres; consequently, it increases also their force and elasticity. People are therefore more vigorous in cold climates. Here the action of the heart and the reaction of the extremities of the fibres are better performed, the temperature of the humors is greater, the blood moves freer towards the heart, and reciprocally, the heart has more power. This superiority of strength must produce various effects; for instance, a greater boldness, that is, more courage; a greater sense of superiority, that is, more frankness, less suspicion, policy, and cunning. In short, this must be productive of very different tempers. Put a man into a close warm place, and, for the reasons above given, he will feel a great faintness. If, under this circumstance, you propose a bold enterprize to him, I believe you will find him very little disposed towards it: his present weakness will throw him into a despondency; he will be afraid of every thing, being in a state of total incapacity. The inhabitants of warm countries are, like old men, timorous; the people in cold countries are, like young men, brave. If we reflect on the late** wars, (which are more recent in our memory, and in which we can better distinguish some particular effects, that escape us as a greater distance of time), we shall find that the northern people, transplanted into southern regions++, did not perform such exploits as their countrymen who, fighting in their own climate, possessed their full vigor and courage.

*This appears even in the countenance: in cold weather people look thinner.
+We know it shortens iron.
**Those for the succession to the Spanish monarchy.
++For instance in Spain.

(Source: Montesquieu, 1748, vol. 1, book XIV, ch. 11, pp. 224–5.)

It is a different assumption to say that climate has either a direct influence, that heat physically discourages effort and action, or an indirect influence on skills, through cultural adaptation to climatic conditions. The indirect may be combined with the direct influence because climate may have had a long-term influence on the culture, which would in turn influence skills and behaviour. If the influence is purely direct, air conditioning is obviously a solution for some settings (for instance, one cannot have an air-conditioned battle). If climate has both a direct and an indirect influence, via progressive genetic adaptation and/or cultural traits acquired through education and socialization, then air conditioning is still necessary but not enough.

National character and educational practices

Research about national character has emphasized the influence of education practices on the development of adult personalities. Margaret Mead for instance, in her description of American character, notes that adult personality in the United States must be seen as an adolescent peer culture. In this setting, education favours diffuse, depersonalized author-ity where children face a demand for strong inner moral control. In many European countries, the cheerful, easy-going, informal Americans are often jokingly referred to as being big children.

One of the most efficient ways to study the formation process of national character is to observe education systems and rearing practices; particularly the rearing of small children, up to the age of 5 or 6. Some of the key elements of personality development are here: feeding and nourishing, weaning, personal hygiene and toilet training, the degree and modes of socialization into various parts of the community (with other children, with adults, with the opposite sex), the demands and prohibitions imposed on small children, and finally the reward/sanction systems which help to orientate their behaviour.[6]

Culture and skills

It seems that cultural background has an influence on perceptual and cognitive skills and their orientations and capacities. Segall *et al.* (1990) clearly demonstrate the existence of differences in perception of visual illusions. They base their findings on the following simple theory: if people belonging to various human groups differ in their visual inference systems,[7] this is because the physical environment at which they are used to looking may differ widely from group to group. Some people live in a constructed environment, based on straight lines and sharp angles (especially those of modern buildings and industrial objects), whereas other people live in a more rounded and curvilinear physical setting. The daily environment shapes people's visual inferences: the very same objects are seen differently (where vision is considered as a culturally built interpretation of specific retinal signals).

The variations in levels of competences and skills across cultural groups is another important issue. The first research on the intellectual abilities of non-European people has been undertaken by researchers such as Levy-Bruhl, who classified the thought patterns of primitives as 'pre-logical'. Little by little this somewhat extreme attitude, that 'primitives' could never conceive of anything in the way that we do (we being the modern, westernized people of European culture or origin), has given way to a more reasonable position. Franz Boas became interested in the idea of the psychic unity of mankind: every human group studied presents common traits such as the ability to remember, to generalize, to form concepts and to think and reflect logically on abstract concepts. In fact it seems more likely that differences in ability in specific activities should be attributed to the cultural relativity of skills and competences developed by the individuals in the specific cultural grouping where they have been raised. The scores on intelligence quotient (IQ) tests will always remain relative to the type of questions asked and to the situations evoked in the verbal part of the test (reading, memorization and understanding of texts); even that part of the test which is clearly quantitatively oriented (mathematics, geometry, statistics, logic) requires the handling of abstract and mathematical signs. One cannot claim that it encompasses all the possible facets of human intelligence, or even that it offers total objectivity in the experimental and empirical methods of evidencing them. It is therefore necessary to accept that definitions of intelligence are culturally contingent. This does not mean that all people are equally intelligent, or that IQ tests are of no interest or practical usefulness. It simply means that the results should be interpreted cautiously when tests are administered to people who do not originate from the culture where these tests were conceived and/or are not familiar with this culture.

1.5   Culture and social representations

The notion of social representation will be used throughout this book, even where there is no explicit reference to it. For instance, the acceptance (or prohibition in some countries) of comparative advertising across countries is related to social representations of the necessity to inform consumers, to allow price competition and even to risk the denigration of one company by another through a comparative advertising campaign (see Chapter 13).

Moscovici (1961) considers social representation (SR) a 'forgotten concept'. He traces it back to Durkheim, for whom it was a class of psychic and social phenomena that relate the individual to the social aspect of collective life. Social representations are miniatures of behaviour, copies of reality and forms of operational knowledge in order to reach and implement everyday decisions. For instance, people may use a combination of social representations in order to make their health-care decisions. Moscovici gives the following example that in the south-west of the United States Hispanic populations concurrently use four bases of knowledge for classifying and interpreting illnesses: the traditional popular medical knowledge, which relates mainly to pains and sufferance; the medical knowledge orally transmitted within Amerindian tribes; the modern (English) popular medical knowledge; and medical scientific knowledge (established and recognized). According to the seriousness of the illness and the availability of money for paying for the cure, Hispanic populations let themselves be guided either by collective representations or by scientific information in order to choose which one of these four sources should be pursued in search of a cure.

Social representations are collective images which are progressively formulated within a particular society. They may be surveyed by public opinion polls. Robert Farr (1988, p. 383) explains that social representations of health and sickness may have a strong influence on consumption patterns. Villagers in many European countries, for instance, tend to moan over the invasion of the countryside by urban development; the entire population compares the constraints of city life to the natural pace of country life. These social representations help to explain the development of natural and organic products, direct from the farm, with no additives or industrial processing, and the diffusion of ecological ideas in modern society.

Jodelet (1988, p. 360) posits social representations at the very intersection of the psychological/individual and social/collective levels. They serve as artificial reference images, as frameworks 'which enable us to interpret what happens to us, possibly even to give sense to the unexpected; categories which serve to classify circumstances, phenomena, individuals with whom we have to deal and theories which enable us to make a decision on these issues'.

The interpretation by people of their daily reality with this sort of preconceived

reference framework could be considered pejoratively as reflecting merely their prejudices. However, it would give but a scant idea of the dynamic, collectively verified and
validated nature of social representations, which are constantly updated through social
situations, individual behaviour and social activities. The media, public opinion polls,
news summaries, court decisions and sentences are all sources from which people derive
their opinions and stimulate debate and social information processes, which in turn
continuously update dynamic social representations.

Social representations do vary across societies. They therefore have a cultural value for
the individuals when they have to decide what is, what can be, how to feel, what to do,
and how to go about doing it (operating culture). Social representations are less profound,
as they alter within shorter time spans (ten to twenty years), than basic cultural
orientations which change over centuries – the latter are reviewed in the next chapter. But
social representations are none the less important – they may oppose basic cultural
orientations since their time-scale is short term and they are more suited to the urgent
need for collective and individual adaptation to reality.

Questions

1. Discuss cultural variation in solutions which have been found across societies to the
   four common problems listed below:
   (a) How to secure oneself (to feel secure, subjectively, and to protect oneself,
       objectively) against unforeseeable negative events (a grave illness, an incident,
       etc.).
   (b) How to treat the eldest in the community, when they cannot work anymore.
   (c) Who should have access to education, on what criteria, and how should its cost be
       financed, given that resources available for education, private and public, are not
       infinite? To what extent should education be given to *all* members of a particular
       society, irrespective of their age, social class and personal capacities? On which
       bases should access to education be organized?
   (d) How should couples, the basic unit for the reproduction of the species, be formed?
       What role should love, common ethnic or social belonging, age or (even) sex play
       in such a process?
2. Discuss the marketing implications of differing cultural solutions to points (a) and (b)
   in question 1, in terms of the existence of certain products or services, provided by the
   market, the state or mutual bodies, organized within the family group or by a
   traditional community.
3. A common problem, across cultures is to attract/be attractive for potential partners.
   Discuss how, in Kluckhohn and Strodtbeck's terms, there is a range of possible
   solutions, and how they are differentially preferred across societies (see p. 30). Outline
   possible consequences for marketing.
4. In light of the definitions of culture given in this chapter, is it possible for a culture to
   disappear? Why, or why not? Give an example.
5. Discuss the case of multi-language/multi-religion countries (e.g. India, Canada,

Switzerland): how can people in these countries share a common culture? On which segments of culture?

6. Discuss the role of education (at home, at school and elsewhere) in the transmission of culture.

7. What is *national character*?

Teaching materials

A1.1   Critical incident: An old lady from Malaysia

The frail, old, almost totally blind lady appeared at every clinic session and sat on the dirt floor enjoying the activity. She was dirty and dishevelled, and obviously had very little, even by Malaysian kampong (local village) standards.

One day the visiting nurse happened upon this woman in her kampong. She lived by herself in a rundown shack about 10 by 10 feet [3 × 3 m]. When questioned how she obtained her food, she said she was often hungry, as she only received food when she worked for others – pounding rice, looking after the children, and the like.

The nurse sought to obtain help for the woman. It was finally resolved that she would receive a small pension from the Department of Welfare which would be ample for her needs.

At each weekly clinic, the woman continued to appear. She had become a center of attention, laughed and joked freely, and obviously enjoyed her increased prestige. No change was noted in her physical status, however. She continued to wear the same dirty black dress and looked no better fed.

The nurse asked one of the rural health nurses to find out if the woman needed help in getting to a shop to buy the goods she seemed so sorely in need of.

In squatting near the woman, the rural health nurse noted a wad of bills in the woman's pocket. 'Wah,' she said, 'It is all here. You have spent nothing. Why is that?'

The woman laughed and then explained: 'I am saving it all for my funeral.'

(Source: Weeks *et al.*, 1987, pp. 24–5. Reproduced with the kind permission of the publisher.)

A1.2   Critical incident: The parable

The leader tells the following parable to the group, illustrating with rough chalkboard drawings if desired:

Rosemary is a girl of about 21 years of age. For several months she has been engaged to a young man named – let's call him Geoffrey. The problem she faces is that between her and her betrothed there lies a river. No ordinary river mind you, but a deep, wide river infested with hungry crocodiles.

Rosemary ponders how she can cross the river. She thinks of a man she knows who has a boat. We'll call him Sinbad. So she approaches Sinbad, asking him to take her across. He replies, 'Yes, I'll take you across if you'll spend the night with me.' Shocked at this offer, she turns to another acquaintance, a certain Frederick, and tells him her story. Frederick responds by saying, 'Yes, Rosemary, I understand your problem – but – it's your problem, not mine.' Rosemary decides to return to Sinbad, spends the night with him, and in the morning he takes her across the river.

Her reunion with Geoffrey is warm. But on the evening before they are to be married, Rosemary feels compelled to tell Geoffrey how she succeeded in getting across the river. Geoffrey responds by saying, 'I wouldn't marry you if you were the last woman on earth.'

Finally, at her wit's end, Rosemary turns to our last character, Dennis. Dennis listens to her story and says, 'Well, Rosemary, I don't love you . . . but I will marry you.' And that's all we know of the story.

(Source: Weeks *et al.*, 1987, pp. 25–6. Reproduced with the kind permission of the publisher.)

Discussion guide

1. Before any discussion, participants should be asked to write down individually on a piece of paper the characters of whose behaviour they most approve, plus a sentence or two explaining their first choice.
2. Participants may be split into small groups of four or five, to share their views and raise relevant issues.
3. The discussion should centre around the cultural relativity of values and their relation to one's own cultural background.

A1.3   Reading: Body ritual among the Nacirema

The anthropologist has become so familiar with the diversity of ways in which different peoples behave in similar situations that he is not apt to be surprised by even the most exotic customs. In fact, if all of the logically possible combinations of behavior have not been found somewhere in the world, he is apt to suspect that they must be present in some yet undescribed tribe. This point has, in fact, been expressed with respect to clan organization by Murdock (1949: 71). In this light, the magical beliefs and practices of the Nacirema present such unusual aspects that it seems desirable to describe them as an example of the extremes to which human behavior can go.

Professor Linton first brought the ritual of the Nacirema to the attention of anthropologists twenty years ago (1936: 326), but the culture of this people is still very poorly understood. They are a North American group living in the territory between the Canadian Cree, the Yaqui and Tarahumare of Mexico, and the Carib and Arawak of the Antilles. Little is known of their origin, although tradition states that they came from the east. According to Nacirema mythology, their nation was originated by a culture hero,

Notgnihsaw, who is otherwise known for two great feats of strength – the throwing of a piece of wampum across the river Pa-To-Mac and the chopping down of a cherry tree in which the Spirit of Truth resided.

Nacirema culture is characterized by a highly developed market economy which has evolved in a rich natural habitat. While much of the people's time is devoted to economic pursuits, a large part of the fruits of these labors and a considerable portion of the day are spent in ritual activity. The focus of this activity is the human body, the appearance and health of which loom as a dominant concern in the ethos of the people. While such a concern is certainly not unusual, its ceremonial aspects and associated philosophy are unique.

The fundamental belief underlying the whole system appears to be that the human body is ugly and that its natural tendency is to debility and disease. Incarcerated in such a body, man's only hope is to avert these characteristics through the use of the powerful influences of ritual and ceremony. Every household has one or more shrines devoted to this purpose. The more powerful individuals in the society have several shrines in their houses and, in fact, the opulence of a house is often referred to in terms of the number of such ritual centers it possesses. Most houses are of wattle and daub construction, but the shrine rooms of the more wealthy are walled with stone. Poorer families imitate the rich by applying pottery plaques to their shrine walls.

While each family has at least one such shrine, the rituals associated with it are not family ceremonies but are private and secret. The rites are normally only discussed with children, and then only during the period when they are being initiated into these mysteries. I was able, however, to establish sufficient rapport with the natives to examine these shrines and to have the rituals described to me.

The focal point of the shrine is a box or chest which is built into the wall. In this chest are kept the many charms and magical potions without which no native believes he could live. These preparations are secured from a variety of specialized practitioners. The most powerful of these are the medicine men, whose assistance must be rewarded with substantial gifts. However, the medicine men do not provide the curative potions for their clients, but decide what the ingredients should be and then write them down in an ancient and secret language. This writing is understood only by the medicine men and by the herbalists who, for another gift, provide the required charm.

The charm is not disposed of after it has served its purpose, but is placed in the charm-box of the household shrine. As these magical materials are specific for certain ills, and the real or imagined maladies of the people are many, the charm-box is usually full to overflowing. The magical packets are so numerous that people forget what their purposes were and fear to use them again. While the natives are very vague on this point, we can only assume that the idea in retaining all the old magical materials is that their presence in the charm-box, before which the body rituals are conducted, will in some way protect the worshipper.

Beneath the charm-box is a small font. Each day every member of the family, in succession, enters the shrine room, bows his head before the charm-box, mingles different sorts of holy water in the font, and proceeds with a brief rite of ablution. The holy waters are secured from the Water Temple of the community, where the priests conduct elaborate ceremonies to make the liquid ritually pure.

In the hierarchy of magical practitioners, and below the medicine men in prestige, are specialists whose designation is best translated 'holy-mouth-men.' The Nacirema have an almost pathological horror of and fascination with the mouth, the condition of which is believed to have a supernatural influence on all social relationships. Were it not for the rituals of the mouth, they believe that their teeth would fall out, their gums bleed, their jaws shrink, their friends desert them and their lovers reject them. They also believe that a strong relationship exists between oral and moral characteristics. For example, there is a ritual ablution of the mouth for children which is supposed to improve their moral fiber.

The daily body ritual performed by everyone includes a mouth-rite. Despite the fact that these people are so punctilious about care of the mouth, this rite involves a practice which strikes the uninitiated stranger as revolting. It was reported to me that the ritual consists of inserting a small bundle of hog hairs into the mouth, along with certain magical powders, and then moving the bundle in a highly formalized series of gestures.

In addition to the private mouth-rite, the people seek out a holy-mouth-man once or twice a year. These practitioners have an impressive set of paraphernalia, consisting of a variety of augers, awls, probes, and prods. The use of these objects in the exorcism of the evils of the mouth involves almost unbelievable ritual torture of the client. The holy-mouth-man opens the client's mouth and, using the above mentioned tools, enlarges any holes which decay may have created in the teeth. Magical materials are put into these holes. If there are no naturally occurring holes in the teeth, large sections of one or more teeth are gouged out so that the supernatural substance can be applied. In the client's views, the purpose of these ministrations is to arrest decay and to draw friends. The extremely sacred and traditional character of the rite is evident in the fact that the natives return to the holy-mouth-men year after year, despite the fact that their teeth continue to decay.

It is to be hoped that, when a thorough study of the Nacirema is made, there will be careful inquiry into the personality structure of these people. One has but to watch the gleam in the eye of a holy-mouth-man, as he jabs an awl into an exposed nerve, to suspect that a certain amount of sadism is involved. If this can be established, a very interesting pattern emerges, for most of the population shows definite masochistic tendencies. It was to these that Professor Linton referred in discussing a distinctive part of the daily body ritual which is performed only by men. This part of the rite involves scraping and lacerating the surface of the face with a sharp instrument. Special women's rites are performed only four times during each lunar month, but what they lack in frequency is made up in barbarity. As part of this ceremony, women bake their heads in small ovens for about an hour. The theoretically interesting point is that what seems to be a preponderantly masochistic people have developed sadistic specialists. The medicine men have an imposing temple, or *latipso*, in every community of any size. The more elaborate ceremonies required to treat very sick patients can only be performed at this temple. These ceremonies involve not only the thaumaturge but a permanent group of vestal maidens who move sedately about the temple chambers in distinctive costume and headdress.

The *latipso* ceremonies are so harsh that it is phenomenal that a fair proportion of the really sick natives who enter the temple ever recover. Small children whose indoctrination is still incomplete have been known to resist attempts to take them to the temple because 'that is where you go to die.' Despite this fact, sick adults are not only willing but eager to undergo the protracted ritual purification, if they can afford to do so. No matter how ill the supplicant or how grave the emergency, the guardians of many temples will not admit a client if he cannot give a rich gift to the custodian. Even after one has gained admission and survived the ceremonies, the guardians will not permit the neophyte to leave until he makes still another gift.

The supplicant entering the temple is first stripped of all his or her clothes. In everyday life the Nacirema avoids exposure of his body and its natural functions. Bathing and excretory acts are performed only in the secrecy of the household shrine, where they are ritualized as part of the body-rites. Psychological shock results from the fact that body secrecy is suddenly lost upon entry into the latipso. A man, whose own wife has never seen him in an excretory act, suddenly finds himself naked and assisted by a vestal maiden while he performs his natural functions into a sacred vessel. This sort of ceremonial treatment is necessitated by the fact that the excreta are used by a diviner to ascertain the course and nature of the client's sickness. Female clients, on the other hand, find their naked bodies are subjected to the scrutiny, manipulation and prodding of the medicine men.

Few supplicants in the temple are well enough to do anything but lie on their hard beds. The daily ceremonies, like the rites of the holy-mouth-men, involve discomfort and torture. With ritual precision, the vestals awaken their miserable charges each dawn and roll them about on their beds of pain while performing ablutions, in the formal movements of which the maidens are highly trained. At other times they insert magic wands in the supplicant's mouth or force him to eat substances which are supposed to be healing. From time to time the medicine men come to their clients and jab magically treated needles into their flesh. The fact that these temple ceremonies may not cure, and may even kill the neophyte, in no way decreases the people's faith in the medicine men.

There remains one other kind of practitioner, known as a 'listener.' This witch-doctor has the power to exorcise the devils that lodge in the heads of people who have been bewitched. The Nacirema believe that parents bewitch their own children. Mothers are particularly suspected of putting a curse on children while teaching them the secret body rituals. The counter-magic of the witch-doctor is unusual in its lack of ritual. The patient simply tells the 'listener' all his troubles and fears, beginning with the earliest difficulties he can remember. The memory displayed by the Nacirema in these exorcism sessions is truly remarkable. It is not uncommon for the patient to bemoan the rejection he felt upon being weaned as a babe, and a few individuals even see their troubles going back to the traumatic effects of their own birth.

In conclusion, mention must be made of certain practices which have their base in native esthetics but which depend upon the pervasive aversion to the natural body and its functions. There are ritual fasts to make fat people thin and ceremonial feasts to make thin people fat. Still other rites are used to make women's breasts larger if they are small, and smaller if they are large. General dissatisfaction with breast shape is symbolized in the fact that the ideal form is virtually outside the range of human variation. A few women afflicted with almost inhuman hypermammary development are so idolized that they make a handsome living by simply going from village to village and permitting the natives to stare at them for a fee.

Reference has already been made to the fact that excretory functions are ritualized, routinized and relegated to secrecy. Natural reproductive functions are similarly distorted. Intercourse is taboo as a topic and scheduled as an act. Efforts are made to avoid pregnancy by the use of magical materials or by limiting intercourse to certain phases of the moon. Conception is actually very infrequent. When pregnant, women dress so as to hide their condition. Parturition takes place in secret, without friends or relatives to assist, and the majority of women do not nurse their infants.

Our review of the ritual life of the Nacirema has certainly shown them to be a magic-ridden people. It is hard to understand how they have managed to exist so long under the burdens which they have imposed upon themselves. But even such exotic customs as these take on real meaning when they are viewed with the insight provided by Malinowski when he wrote (1948: 70):

> Looking from far and above, from our high places of safety in the developed civilization, it is easy to see all the crudity and irrelevance of magic. But without its power and guidance early man could not have mastered his practical difficulties as he has done, nor could man have advanced to the higher stages of civilization.

References cited

LINTON, RALPH,
    1936, The Study of Man. New York, D. Appleton-Century Co.
MALINOWSKI, BRONISLAW,
    1948, Magic, Science, and Religion. Glencoe, The Free Press.
MURDOCK, GEORGE P.,
    1949, Social Structure. New York, The Macmillan Co.

(Source: Miner, 1956. Reproduced with the permission of the review and Mrs Agnes Miner.)

Notes

1. One may be wary of the ethnocentric (western/modern) bias of the author, i.e. an overemphasis on culture as striving only for the improvement of material productions; in some cultures, the dominant values may be extremely antagonistic towards material preoccupations.
2. The conquest of Mexico by Hernando Cortés is a fascinating example of the almost total destruction of a culture heavily loaded with symbolism (mostly that of the Aztecs and the Mayas) by only a very small group of Spanish invaders. When Cortés's army left the island of Cuba, sailing to Mexico, it numbered only 508 soldiers, 100 sailors and 10 horses. At that time Mexico City had half a million inhabitants.
   The Mayas, the Totonacs and the Mexicas were deeply religious people, totally subservient to the will of their gods and the sovereignty of their priest-kings. These people waged a ritualistic war on each other which was based on magic as much as military strategy and in which the desired outcome, decided in advance by the mysterious agreements of celestial powers, was not the conquest of land or the amassing of riches but the triumph of the Gods, who received in sacrifice the heart and the blood of the vanquished. Disturbed by the mythical return of the ancestors and of the divine feathered serpent, Quetzalcoatl-Kukulcan, the Indians were blinded, unable to see the actual intentions of those whom they had termed the *Teules*, the Gods. And when the Indians understood that the Spaniards, whom they considered as demi-gods, were involved in a massive slaughter of Mexican Indians, from which none of them would emerge unscathed, it was too late. The Spaniards had taken advantage of their hesitation to penetrate deep into the Mexican empire, to provoke dissension, and to conquer lands and take slaves. (Le Clézio, p. 19). See also *Historia Verdadera de la conquista de la Nueva Espana*, written by a member of the Cortès troop, Bernal Diaz del Castillo (1968) and *Historia General de las cosas de la Nueva Espana*, written by Bernadino de Sahagun a few years after the conquest (which took place around 1520) and the destruction of the Aztec and Maya cultures, with the objective

of preserving as far as possible the traces of this civilization which had suffered such an abrupt disappearance. For a thorough analysis of culture collisions in colonial history see Urs Bitterli (1989).
3. A famous Swiss novelist, Charles Ferdinand Ramuz, has often set the relations between communities as a background to his novels. *La Séparation des races*, for instance, is the story of the kidnapping of a young girl from Bern by her Valaisan lover and the consequent mobilization of their respective communities.
4. The literature review carried out by Inkeles and Levinson (1969) is certainly the most exhaustive one (100 pages) available. It might appear somewhat dated, but since national character changes over decades and centuries, their review remains largely up to date.
5. War is assimilated here with commerce and industry because, from a historical perspective, war was a *normal* activity. The idea that war produces the vanquished and the victorious but that they are all losers, is rather a new one. When pursuing colonial wars, commerce and industry were legitimately included in the ultimate goals. The idea of bringing civilization to the barbarians included the extirpation of 'evil' beliefs, magic and sorcery, and their substitution of Christianity.
6. An important figure in these studies of childhood and society is Erik Erikson (1950), who has developed a theory of ego development stages (in the Freudian sense) on the basis of field observations of American Indians, Sioux and Yurok, US Americans, Germans and Russians. It is clearly beyond the reach of this book to sum up, even very briefly, the richness of the empirical and theoretical research on national differences which has been published by anthropologists, sociologists and psychologists. The references at the end of this chapter suggest two reviews of such cross-national research: Inkeles and Levinson (1969) and Segall *et al.* (1990).
7. By 'visual inference' is implied the mental system which enables people to transform retinal perceptions into a 'brain image' (Segall *et al.*, 1990, ch. 4).

References

Bitterli, Urs (1989), *Cultures in Conflict*, Polity Press: Oxford.
Carroll, John B. (1956), *Language, Thought and Reality: Selected writings of Benjamin Lee Whorf*, MIT: Cambridge, MA.
Child, J. and A. Kieser (1977), 'A contrast in British and West German management practices: Are recipes of success culture bound?', paper presented at the *Conference on Cross-Cultural Studies on Organizational Functioning*, Hawaii.
Diaz del Castillo, Bernal (1968), *Historia Verdadera de la conquista de la Neuva Espana*, Espasa-Calpe: Madrid.
Eliade, Mircea (1956), *Forgerons et Alchimistes*, Flammarion : Paris. English translation (1962), *The Forge and the Crucible*, University of Chicago Press: Chicago.
Erikson, Erik (1950), *Childhood and Society*, Norton: New York.
Farr, Robert M. (1988), 'Les Représentations sociales', in Serge Moscovici (ed.), *Psychologie sociale*, PUF Fondamental: Paris.
Goodenough, Ward H. (1971), *Culture, Language and Society*, Modular Publications, 7, Addison-Wesley: Reading, MA.
Hawking, Stephen (1988), *A Brief History of Time*, Guild Publishing: London.
Inkeles, Alex and Daniel J. Levinson (1969), 'National character: The study of modal personality and sociocultural systems', in Gardner Lindzey and Elliot Aronson (eds), *Handbook of Social Psychology*, vol. IV, Addison-Wesley: Reading, MA, pp. 418–506.

Jodelet, Denise (1988), 'Représentations sociales: phénomènes, concept et théorie', in Serge Moscovici (ed.), *Psychologie sociale*, PUF Fondamental: Paris.

Kluckhohn, Florence R. and Frederick L. Strodtbeck (1961), *Variations in Value Orientations*, Greenwood Press: Westport, CT.

Kroeber, Alfred L. and Clyde Kluckhohn (1952), *Culture: A critical review of concepts and definitions*, Anthropological Papers, no. 4, Peabody Museum.

Le Clézio, J.M.G. (1988) *Le Rêve mexicain ou la pensée interrompue*, Gallimard: Paris.

Linton, Ralph (1945), *The Cultural Background of Personality*, Appleton-Century: New York.

Malinowski, Bronislaw (1944), *A Scientific Theory of Culture and Other Essays*, University of North Carolina Press: Chapel Hill, NC.

Miner, Horace (1956), 'Body ritual among the Nacirema', *American Anthropologist*, vol. 58, pp. 503–7.

Montesquieu, Charles de (1748), *The Spirit of Laws*, translated from the French by Thomas Nugent (1792), 6th edn, McKenzie and Moore: Dublin.

Moscovici, Serge (1961), *La Psychanalyse, son Public et son Image*, Presses Universitaires de France: Paris.

Segall, Marshall H., Pierre R. Dasen, John W. Berry and Ype H. Poortinga (1990), *Human Behavior in Global Perspective*, Pergamon: New York.

Tylor, Edward (1913), *Primitive Culture*, Murray: London.

Weeks, William H., Paul B. Pedersen and Richard W. Brislin (1987), *A Manual of Structured Experiences for Cross-cultural Learning*, Intercultural Press: Yarmouth, ME.

2

——— ♦♦♦ ———

Cultural dynamics 1: Time and space

Culture is sometimes regarded as a somewhat vague concept. The Swedish writer Selma Lagerlöf defines culture as 'what remains when that which has been learned is entirely forgotten'.[1] Depicted thus, culture may appear to be rather a 'rubbish-bin' concept. Its main use would be as a 'synthesis variable': an explanation that serves as a last resort, that is, when all other concepts or more precise theories have been successfully validated. It would also serve as an explanatory variable for residuals, when other more interpretive explanations are unsuccessful.

However, the definition quoted above does have the important merit of identifying two basic elements of cultural dynamics (at the level of the individual):

1. It is learned.
2. It is forgotten in the sense that we cease to be conscious of its existence as learned behaviour.

Yet culture remains present throughout our daily individual and collective activities, and is therefore entirely oriented towards our adaptation to reality (both as constraints and opportunities). To this extent it is almost unthinkable that a culture could stand perfectly still, except in the case of those primitive societies that live in quite stable natural and social environments, located in remote places and subject to no exterior interference. At the periphery of a fixed set of basic cultural assumptions, other sources of culture intervene, as a result of which new solutions are used for tackling existing issues or for solving entirely new problems.

This chapter takes as a starting point a model of action based on cultural assumptions (section 2.1). It sets a framework for the explanation of culture-related behaviour which extends throughout this chapter and the next one. Basic cultural assumptions which are explained in this chapter relate to time (section 2.2) and to space (section 2.3). Cultures borrow from each other through time and space and section 2.4 is dedicated to this process of borrowing from other cultures and corresponding changes in the importing society. Section 2.5 directly relates to the previous one in as far as it deals with marketing as imported concepts and practices. This is important for the clarity of the paradigm of international marketing which is conveyed by this book: if the underlying theories of marketing and the dominant normative practices are culture-laden (mostly with European and North American assumptions), then it makes sense to consider culture as giving some fundamental clues for marketing internationally. The last section (2.6) is dedicated to cultural hostility: territoriality is the organizing principle of cultures across space and hostility arises from prejudiced views of others and the fear to have space to share with members of alien cultural groups.

2.1   A model of action based on cultural assumptions

Figure 2.1 presents how basic cultural assumptions in three major areas (time, space and the concept of the self and others) influence interaction models, which, in combination with basic assumptions, shape attitudes towards action. Fundamentals assumptions about time, space and the concept of the self and others are explained in greater detail in this chapter and the first section of the next. *Cultural assumptions are statements about the*

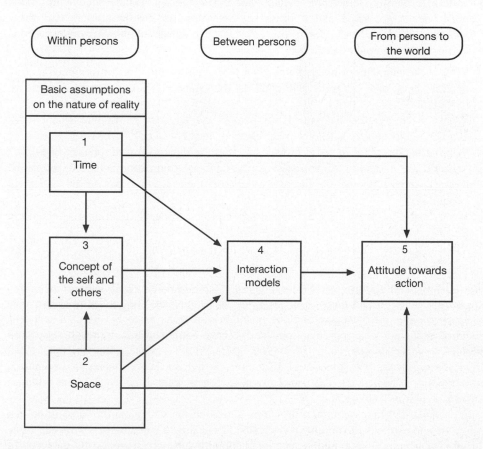

Figure 2.1 A model of cultural dynamics.

basic nature of reality. Some of them are based on the 'value orientations' of the anthropologists Florence Kluckhohn and Frederick Strodtbeck (1961) which are often cited – an indication of their analytical power, at least as far as it is perceived by the social scientists. Kluckhohn and Strodtbeck have tested their value orientation theory across five very distinct cultural communities, each one made up of American citizens living in close proximity to each other in the south-western part of the United States, in similar natural environments:

> Two of the populations are American Indian; one an off-reservation settlement of Navaho Indians . . . the other the Pueblo Indian community of Zuni. The third is a Spanish American village which we have named Atrisco. A Mormon village and a recently established farming village of Texan and Oklahoman homesteaders . . . are the two other communities. (1961, p. 49)

Cultural assumptions are basic responses, expressed in a rather dichotomous manner, to fundamental human problems. They provide the members of a particular cultural community with a basic framework for the evaluation of solutions to these problems, combining a cognitive dimension (*people think it works that way*), an affective dimension (*people like it that way*) and a directive dimension (*people will do it that way*). Kluckhohn and Strodtbeck (1961, pp. 11, 12) have collected these common human problems under six main categories:

1. What is the character of innate human nature (human-nature orientation): good or evil, neutral, or a mix of good and evil? Is this state of human nature mutable or immutable?
2. What is the relation of humans to nature and supernature (nature orientation): subjugation to nature, harmony with nature or mastery over nature?
3. What is the temporal focus of human life (time orientation): past, present or future?
4. What is the modality of human activity (activity orientation): should people be (being), should people do (doing) or should they do in order to be (being in becoming)?
5. What is the modality of the relationship between humans (relational orientation): linearity, collaterality or pure individuality?
6. What is the conception of space? Is it considered predominantly private, public, or a mix of both?

Naturally these modalities are to be found in every society. People *are* and *do*, and there are always children and parents, in the sense that some kind of family nucleus exists everywhere. But different assumptions result in variations as to the kind of response which is dominant in a particular society. We have combined this approach with those adopted by other authors (Hall, 1959, 1966, 1976, 1983; Hofstede, 1980; Triandis, 1983, 1994; Trompenaars, 1993) to depict differences in five successive tables: basic cultural assumptions in Tables 2.1, 2.2 and 3.1, interaction models in Table 3.2, and attitudes towards action in Table 3.5.

Each table highlights common problems across cultures, depicts the most important solutions and explains the dominant contrasts. This leads to a detailed inventory of basic differences in cultural assumptions and interaction models, which are mostly the result of learned behaviour. I have tried to give some country illustrations, without too often citing 'typical' cultures, because it would be at the risk of stereotyping. Except for Hofstede's four dimensions, which are considered mostly in the realm of 'interaction models', are little empirical data mentioned. For those interested in figures, rankings and scores, I have indicated where such information can be found, to the extent that it is available and significant. My objective is not to classify countries or cultures, but rather to provide readers with an understanding of how cultures differ, and to let them combine this with their own knowledge and experience in order to build a self-reliant view of how culture affects our relationships with others and our way of acting.

In doing this, I could not ignore the profound impact of technology on culture. There was the risk that many basic assumptions could be called 'modern' and, their contrast would have been naturally meant as 'traditional'. The real world is fortunately more sophisticated: individualism is globally 'modern', but collectivism is not 'traditional' nor even 'conservative'. Many collectivist nations, especially in Asia, have been brilliant achievers in the past twenty years. 'Modern culture' is predominantly based on western values, those held by philosophers, scientists and politicians in England, France and other European countries, during the period when they experienced industrial revolution and colonized other people, and later by the United States, as the dominant political and cultural actor on the twentieth century world scene. The influence of a cultural assumption being considered as 'modern' is that it is more legitimate, sometimes to the extreme that it is officially considered as the only possible belief. Thus other assumptions tend to be repressed, leading to complex situations where people finally imitate behaviour which does not correspond to the assumptions really prevailing in their culture. Thus, I will try to mention why and how a certain cultural assumption, interaction model or attitude towards action belongs to 'modern' culture.

At this point in the book, some readers may wonder why I am digging into culture, with apparently little interest for managerial issues, including the focus of the book, international marketing. They will find an initial response in Table 3.5, point (c): I come from an ideologist culture where issues are most often addressed first at a very broad level. Later, attempts are made to link culture to action-related issues. My intellectual style is basically French and German: I try to build convincing intellectual frameworks, occasionally at the expense of data. Some readers may consider my statements as sometimes unsupported by data and evidence. I claim to be culturally relative. The second response is: part of the cross-cultural learning experience resides in being confronted with a different mindset. My belief is that developing cultural awareness is possible just by reading something written with a culturally alien mindset. Cultural assumptions are not completely in the realm of *unbewußtsein* (unconsciousness, as deep-seated and inaccessible); in fact, they are rather in the realm of *unterbewußtsein*, that is located at a subconscious level, where interaction and self-questioning can reveal them.

In order to make the link between them, I have tried to mention as often as possible areas of international marketing on which these cultural differences have an impact. In subsequent chapters in the book they are also used as an explanatory framework for consumer behaviour (Chapter 4), market research (Chapter 5), marketing management (Chapters 8 to 11), advertising communication (Chapter 13), buyer–seller interactions and marketing negotiations (Chapters 14 to 16). The last four chapters build on Chapter 12 which is dedicated to language, culture and communication, and explains how language shapes our world-views. Point (e) in Table 3.2 (communication styles) is developed in Chapter 12.

Based on Figure 2.1, our exploration starts with the cultural variability in the concept of time.

2.2   Time: Cross-cultural variability

Most marketing concepts are time-based: product life cycle, sales forecasting or the planning of new product launches to name but a few.[2] Normative time in marketing and management seems indisputable, and its very nature is rarely questioned: it is perceived as linear, continuous and economic. However, time, in a cross-cultural perspective is probably the area where differences are both the largest and the most difficult to catch, because (1) assumptions are very deep-seated and (2) formally we adopt a common model of time. People's relationship with time changes with respect to periods of history and the level of human development, according to the technology available for measuring time, to the emphasis given to natural and social rhythms, and to the prevailing metaphysical views. Each vision of time (*Zeitanschauung*) corresponds to a vision of the real world, its origins and destiny (*Weltanschauung*). Time appears prominently through its social functions in that it allows people to have a common organization of activities and helps to synchronize individual human behaviour. Encyclopaedic approaches to the concept of time (Attali, 1982) show that never has one time pattern eliminated another previous one. Each new time pattern superimposes itself on the one that previously prevailed. As a consequence, individual time perceptions may result from adding or mixing different basic patterns of time. Most of the literature in cultural anthropology considers time perceptions as cultural artefacts. As Gurevitch states (1976, p. 229): 'Time occupies a prominent place in the "model of the world" characterizing a given culture.'

Dimensions of time orientations

Table 2.1 shows time-related cultural assumptions, which correspond to four common problems:

1. To what extent should time be regarded as a tangible commodity (economicity of time)?
2. How should tasks and time be combined (monochronic versus polychronic use of time)?
3. Should lifetime(s) be seen as a single continuous line or as combining multiple cyclical episodes (linearity versus cyclicity of time)?

4. What are the appropriate temporal orientations: towards the past, the present and the future?

As the reader will see, there is some overlap between the prevailing solutions to these four questions. However, I have noted all four basic time assumptions because they need to be considered for having a substantive view of what is a cultural model of time, which is exemplified at the end of this section by the Japanese *Makimono* time.

Table 2.1 *Time-related cultural differences*

Basic problem / cultural orientations	Contrasts across cultures
Is time money? **(a) Economicity of time**	Time is regarded as a scarce resource or, conversely, as plentiful and indefinitely available.
How to schedule tasks **(b) Monochronism versus polychronism**	Only one task is undertaken at any (preset) time, following a schedule ('agenda society'), versus dealing simultaneously with different tasks, actions and/or communications (polychronism) for convenience, pleasure and efficiency.
Is time a continuous line? **(c) Linearity (L) versus cyclicity (C) of time**	Time is seen as linear-separable, cut in slices (L) versus the daily, yearly and seasonal cycles being emphasized (C).
How should we emphasize past, present and future? **(d) Temporal orientations** (i) towards the past	People with high past orientation consider that the past is important, that resources must be spent on teaching history and building museums, referring to oral and written traditions and past works. Their basic assumption is that their roots are implanted in the past and no plant can survive without its roots. Conversely for low past orientation.
(ii) towards the present	People with high present orientation consider that they basically live 'here and now'. Although not always enjoyable, the present must be accepted for what it is: the only *true* reality we live in.
(iii) towards the future	People easily and precisely envisage and plan their future. They are project oriented, prepare for the long-term, appreciate the achievements of science, and so on. For them the future is inevitably 'bigger and better'? Conversely for low future orientation.

Economicity of time

Time may be seen as external to us, and as such be treated like a tangible commodity. The concept of economic time is based on accurate time reckoning, dependent on precise dating and defined duration. It results in people using their time as wisely as possible, scheduling, establishing timetables and deadlines. Measurement of parking meter time by units of 7.5 minutes or sport performance by the hundredth of a second is typical of economic time as precisely measured and bearing direct and explicit financial consequences. Many European countries as well as the United States are emblematic of the 'time-is-money' cultures, where time is an economic good. Since time is a scarce resource, or at least perceived as such, people should try to reach its optimal allocation between competing ways of using it. Norms tend to be very strict regarding time schedules, appointments and the precise setting of dates and durations in a society where time is strongly felt as economic.

Needless to say that attitudes towards money and the money-value of time are inseparable from marketing (Jacoby *et al.*, 1976). A strong economic time assumption has wide-reaching influences on consumer behaviour, because products may save time, as household appliances do, or services may be based on time-values such as bank loans or life insurance policies. Economicity of time also has an impact on buyer–seller interaction, in the waiting process as well as for dealing together.

Monochronic versus polychronic use of time

Hall (1983) has described two extreme behaviours of task scheduling which he calls monochronism (M time) and polychronism (P time). Individuals working under M time do one thing at a time and tend to adhere to preset schedules. When confronted by a dilemma (e.g. a discussion with someone that lasts longer than planned), M-time people will politely stop the conversation, in order to keep to their schedule. In M-time societies, not only the start of a meeting but also its finish will be planned. P-time, on the other hand, stresses the involvement of people who do several things at the same moment, easily modify preset schedules and seldom experience time as 'wasted'. P-time may seem quite hectic to M-time people: 'There is no recognized order as to who is to be served next, no queue or numbers indicating who has been waiting the longest' (Hall, 1983, p. 47). P-time people are more committed to persons than to schedules. When confronted with a conflict such as the one described above, they prefer to go on talking or working after preset hours and break their schedule, if they have one.

The PERT (programme evaluation and review technique) programming method is an example of a typical 'agenda-culture', where M-time is the central assumption. It explicitly aims to reduce a universe of polychronic tasks (they really take place simultaneously, which is part of the problem) to a monochronic solution (the critical path). Management methods, originating in the United States and Europe, favour pure monochronic organization. They clearly push aside polychronic attitudes, which tend to make plans and schedules rather hectic. When it comes to delays and being 'on time', precise monochronic systems give priority to meeting dates and commitments to schedules (Usunier, 1991).

To illustrate sources of tension between people who have internalized different time systems, Hall (1983, pp. 53–4) takes the example of a monochronic woman who has a polychronic hairdresser. The woman, who has a regular appointment at a specific time each week, feels frustrated and angry when she is kept waiting. At the same time, the hairdresser also feels frustrated. He inevitably feels compelled to 'squeeze people in', particularly his friends and acquaintances. The schedule is reserved for impersonal people such as this woman, but since he does not know them personally, keeping to the schedule is not important to him. M or P-time is important for business negotiations, buyer–seller interactions in general, or dealing with a foreign distributor (e.g. scheduling a promotional campaign).

Linearity (L) versus cyclicity (C) of time

It is easy to guess that a strongly economic view of time, when it is combined with monochronism, emphasizes the linearity of time. Time is viewed as being a line with a point at the centre, the present. Each portion of the line can be cut into slices, which are supposed to have a certain money value. Basic religious beliefs play a key role in supporting such a linear view of time: Christianity has a one-shot interpretation of worldly life, and people do not live twice (as in the James Bond film title). People wait until the final judgement for enjoying reincarnation. On the contrary, Asian religions, including Hinduism and Buddhism, assume that, on the death of the body, the soul is born again in another body. The belief in regular reincarnation, until a pure soul is allowed to escape the cycle and go to *nirvana*, changes radically the nature of time in a specific life: it is not all the time I have got, it is simply one of my 'times' across several lives. For most Asians, cyclicity is central in their pattern of time: the *nirvana* is the final release from the cycle of reincarnation attained by extinction of all desires and individual existence, culminating (in Buddhism) in absolute blessedness, or (in Hinduism) in absorption into Brahman. Naturally, patience is on the side of the people believing in cyclical reincarnation of the soul. For the Christians, it is more urgent to achieve, because their souls are given only one worldly life. But, as the New Testament puts it clearly, those who do right, even in the very last moment, will be considered favourably.

Another element which favours a cyclical view of time is the degree of emphasis put on the natural rhythms of years and seasons, the sun and the moon. It largely opposes so-called 'modern' to 'traditional' societies, in as far as modern means technology, mastering nature and, to a certain extent, the loss of nature-related reference points. The Japanese are known for having maintained a strong orientation to nature, even in a highly developed society. Their floral art of *Ikebana* and the emphasis on maintaining a contact with nature, even in highly urban environments, are testimonies to their attachment to the natural rhythms of nature. Even, inside a country, the relationship to nature influences the model of time adopted by urban versus rural people.

Elements of cyclicity are based mostly on metaphysical assumptions or on astronomical observations, but they also include some arbitrary divisions, which are more social than natural. The example of the duration of the week is a good example of the social origins of the reckoning of time cycles. Sorokin and Merton (1937) give the following illustrations of the variability of the week in number of days:

> Our system of weekly division into quantitatively equal periods is a perfect type of conventionally determined time-reckoning The Khasi week almost universally consists of eight days because the markets are usually held every eighth day. A reflection of the fact that the Khasi week had a social, rather than a 'natural', origin is found in the names of the days of the week which are not those of planets (a late and arbitrary development) but of places where the principal markets are held. In a similar fashion the Roman week was marked by *nundinae* which recurred every eighth day and upon which the agriculturists came into the city to sell their produce. The Muysca in Bogota had a three-day week; many East African tribes a four-day week; in Central America, the east Indian Archipelago, old Assyria (and now in Soviet Russia), there is found a five-day week . . . and the Incas had a ten-day week. The constant feature of virtually all these weeks of varying length is that they were always found to have been originally in association with the market.

Elements of cyclicity of time have therefore three main origins: (1) religious assumptions about reincarnation of the soul; (2) natural rhythms of years, seasons and days; and (3) the social division of time periods which is more arbitrary, less natural and 'given', than we assume. Time is naturally both linear and cyclical. I do not argue that one vision of time is 'better' than the other. Generally cultures have definite time patterns which combine both views, as shown later by the example of Japanese *Makimono* time, and by reading A2.4 presenting the Bantu concept of time.

Temporal orientations: past, present, future

The perception of time also tends to be related to temporal orientations *vis-à-vis* the arrow of time. As stated by Kluckhohn and Strodtbeck (1961, pp. 13–15):

> The possible cultural interpretations of temporal focus of human life break easily into the three point range of past, present and future. . . . Spanish-Americans, who have been described as taking the view that man is a victim of natural forces, are also a people who place the present time alternative in first position. . . . Many modern European countries . . . have strong leanings to a past orientation . . . Americans, more strongly than most people of the world, place an emphasis upon the future – a future which is anticipated to be ' bigger and better'.

Being past oriented means that people emphasize the role of the past as explaining where we are now. Europeans are typical of this assumption, as are some Asian people. They will tend to restore old buildings, invest in museums, teach history at school, etc. It does not mean that temporal orientation to the past is only based on cultural assumptions. It also depends on individual psychological traits (Usunier and Valette-Florence, 1994). Furthermore in societies undergoing a rapid process of economic change, past-orientation is often provisionally underplayed.

Present orientation is the most logical assumption, in terms of quality of life at least.

It means that people favour the 'here and now', believing that the past is over and the future is uncertain, theoretical and difficult to imagine. Religion may play an important role in pushing people towards present orientation, if it emphasizes that only God decides about the future. In terms of temporal orientations, the Arabic-Muslim character has been described as fatalistic, rather short-term oriented, and not future oriented (Ferraro, 1990). As stated by Harris and Moran (1987, p. 474):

> Who controls time? A Western belief is that one controls his own time. Arabs believe that their time is controlled, to a certain extent, by an outside force – namely Allah – therefore the Arabs become very fatalistic in their view of time. . . . Most Arabs are not clockwatchers, nor are they planners of time.

Future orientation is naturally related to the view that people can master nature, but also to the view that the future can in some way be predicted or at least significantly influenced. In societies where future orientation is strong, it is backed by the educational system and by an 'imagination of the future' supported by reports on scientific breakthroughs and technological developments.

Combined cultural models of time: The Japanese makimono time

Economic time usually goes with linear time, monochronism and future orientation. It is our 'modern' time, near to R. J. Graham's (1981, p. 335) concept of the 'European-American (Anglo) perception that allows time to have a past, present and future, and to be sliced into discrete units and then allocated for specific tasks.' From this view, time can be saved, spent, wasted or even bought, just like money. Even among the cultures sharing this pattern of time, there may be significant differences. Lane and Kaufman (1992, p. 15) contrast the prevailing patterns in Northern Europe compared with the United States:

> The closed stores on Saturday afternoons and Sundays and short weekday hours are extremely limited by United States standards. Such customs limit the actual clock hours that are available for shopping, reduce weekend employment, etc. The result is a system which encourages recreation and/or social time in the evenings and on weekends, particularly on Sundays. In Europe it is very common to find people taking recreational walks, bike rides, visiting a park or sitting in the cafe. These are not completely foreign to the United States, but seem to exist in Europe on a much grander scale. The use of time in quiet visiting seems to be much greater.

Graham has tried to represent a synthesis of time perception dimensions, not only as a set of different perceptual dimensions, but also as complete temporal systems. He contrasts 'Anglo' time, which he describes as being 'linear-separable', with the 'circular-traditional' time of most Latin-American countries. This perception arises from traditional cultures where action and everyday life were not regulated by the clock, but rather by the natural cycles of the moon, sun and seasons. Graham proposes a third model, 'procedural-traditional', in which the amount of time spent on the activity is irrelevant, since activities are procedure-driven rather than time-driven. This system is typical of the American Indians, and to a large extent it also typifies Bantu time (reading A2.4). Graham's 'procedural-traditional' time is hardly a 'time' in the western sense.

But it is not that simple: some people may share different cultures and move from one time model or another, depending on the other people involved and the particular situation, using different types of 'operating cultures' (Goodenough, 1971). As Hall states (1983, p. 58) 'The Japanese are polychronic when looking and working inward, toward themselves. When dealing with the outside world . . . they shift to the monochronic mode. . . . The French are monochronic intellectually, but polychronic in behaviour.'

A naive view of Japanese temporal orientations would lead one to assume that the Japanese are simply future oriented. In fact, a specialist of Japanese business, Robert Ballon, argues that the Japanese are neither future nor past oriented. For him the Japanese are present oriented and focused on the here and now (in Hayashi, 1988). Hayashi explains the difficult attempt at finding cross-culturally equivalent terms by asserting that: 'Many kinds of Japanese behaviour are extratemporaneous' (p. 2), meaning that *they are not time-based*. Hayashi explains further what he calls the *Makimono* time. In their model of time, the Japanese tend to posit the future as a natural extension of the present. Japanese are basically people working with a cyclical view of time, based on their Buddhist background holding that souls of the dead people transmigrate to newly born human beings, in an eternal ring. As Hayashi states (1988, p. 10) 'In Japanese cultural time, the past flows continuously toward the present and also the present is firmly linked to the future. In philosophical terms, we might say the past and the future exist simultaneously in the present'.

Therefore, the linear-separable model of time, found in western cultures, does not predominate in Japan. The notion of continuity is central in Japanese time, just as the notion of discontinuity is central in western models of time. A Japanese definition would say 'the present is a temporal period that links the region of the past with the world of the future' (Hayashi, 1988, p. 18). The notion of continuity as well as the arrow of the future targeted **to** the present are central in the *Makimono* time pattern (Figure 2.2).

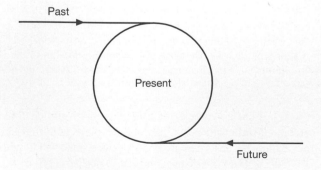

Figure 2.2   Japanese *Makimono* time pattern.
(Source: Hayashi, 1988, p. 9.)

2.3 Space

The key words for space-related cultural assumptions are 'in' and 'out', member and non-member, belonging or not. Here space is meant in its most general sense: the three-dimensional expanse in which all material objects are located. Let us consider that it is mainly occupied by people; more precisely, groups of people and their properties. Spaces can be physical such as a town, a county or a country. Space can also be abstract, that is a grouping of people based on common characteristics such as education, religion or professional associations. Space is the basis for the organizing principle of *territoriality* which we mentioned in the previous chapter. People are by nature territorial: they must define who has ownership and control over certain spaces.

The key problems in space-related cultural assumptions are as follows:

1. Whether people *are* insiders or outsiders.
2. What the rights and obligations are for ingroup members.
3. Whether it is at all possible for outsiders to gain insider status, or a limited part of it.
4. What the group membership conditions are for those willing to 'enter this space'.

Table 2.2 describes contrasts space-related differences across cultures.

Table 2.2 *Space-related cultural differences*

Basic problem / Cultural orientations	Contrasts across cultures
Is emphasis put on what people *do* or on what they *are* (based on *belonging* to family, age, sex, religious or social status groups)? (a) **Personalization versus depersonalization**	Necessity of being personally acquainted with other people if one is to communicate and interact with them efficiently versus ability to communicate easily with unknown persons.
Who is a member of the group and what are the relevant ingroups? (b) **Ingroup orientation**	Belonging to the ingroup (or reference group: family, tribe, clan, club, professional society, nation, etc.) may be a *necessary condition* to be considered as a reliable, *bona fide* partner.
How to gain membership? (c) **Concrete versus abstract territoriality**	What are the group membership conditions: for an individual who belongs to the outgroup, what are the prerequisites for assimilation (if any)?
How to deal with physical space? (d) **Group cultures** with close physical contact versus **individualistic cultures** desiring private space.	Tendency to live near to one another, and to be undisturbed by such intimacy. Conversely, tendency to feel the need for private space around one's body, and to resent intrusion into this space (Hall, 1966).

People being members of a certain space

Strong *being* emphasis is manifested in what people call themselves and others. In many traditional societies, language designates the people by a term meaning 'human being'. Bantu, for instance, means human being. This, more or less, assumes that others are not *real* human beings. Without going so far, the Japanese language gives a good example of a strict divide between 'we' and 'they'. Japanese people call themselves *Nihon-jin* and foreigners *Gai-jin* (those from the outside).

In the 'being' orientation emphasis is put on belonging, that is on characteristics shared by a certain set of people:

1. A set of people sharing family ties, a particular social class, a certain ethnic background, a religion, or a nationality.
2. Age (youngsters versus elders), sex (male versus female), marriage (married versus unmarried people).

What is specific in a strong being orientation is the underlying assumption that what people *are*, naturally, legitimately and forcefully, influences the roles, power and capacities they have in the society. In the next chapter we will see that there is a strong link between a being orientation and the concept of the self and others, which mediates the being orientation and helps translate it into interaction models. A typical causal chain in the being style is: she is a woman, thus belongs to the group of people in charge of reproduction and nurturing roles, thus cannot work. 'Being' does not necessarily refer to purely individual traits, such as personality.

In contrast, the *doing* orientation assumes that what people are *does not* naturally, nor legitimately, influence the roles, power and capacities individuals have in the society. Thus what is important is what people can achieve, given their talents and abilities. Whereas the being orientation results in 'personalization', the doing orientation results in 'depersonalization'. These words should be taken carefully and interpreted cautiously: they will be discussed in more detail in Chapters 12 to 16, which are dedicated to language and communication, personal selling and international business negotiations. 'Personalization' means that assumptions about what a person can *do* (and what can be done with this person) depend fundamentally on what this person *is*. Therefore it is of prime importance to obtain information on what this person is. Since not all is *prima facie* visible, it means that it will be necessary to spend time exploring who this person is.

In contrast, 'depersonalization' means that it is not important to know who a person is, to decide what this person can do (and what can be done with her). Therefore it is not assumed to be necessary to spend a lot of time discovering who the person is (especially if time is strongly economic). 'Depersonalization' means in no way that there is no interest in what people actually *are*, but their belonging to certain space characteristics (class, ethnic, age groups, etc.) is considered rather unimportant compared with purely individual, non-space-related characteristics. In the purest version of the doing assumption, character and personality would be considered as unimportant in what individuals can achieve: tasks are viewed as standard and people as interchangeable, deeds are separated from emotions and *doing* belongs to a world of its own, radically separated from the *being*.

Who is a member of the ingroup?

As explained by Triandis (1983, p. 144):

> In every culture some people are defined as trustworthy, worthy of cooperation or even self-sacrifice for (ingroup), and other people are seen as 'outsiders' (outgroup). The basis of such distinction varies. In most cultures, tribe and family are crucial; in other cultures, nation, religion, language, or political ideology may be important; in still other cases, occupational group may be all-important. Thus the content of ingroups differs from culture to culture. Also, a person, may belong to one, or to many, ingroups.

There is a natural relationship between the being orientation and the emphasis on group belonging, which has to do with natural law and the right of people to occupy a certain territory. The largest possible ingroups are nations. For many older countries, the legitimacy is largely based on having ancestors in the place for a long time. This may translate in nationality being legally based on *jus sanguinis* (law of the blood), people being granted a definite nationality, belonging only if at least one of their parents is a national. Benefits related to nationality are strongly space-related: the right to live, work and enjoy citizenship on a definite territory. On the other hand, certain countries (e.g. the United States and France) base nationality on *jus soli* (law of the soil), that is, being born in the place is enough to obtain citizenship.[3]

This strict opposition delineates two different ways of defining the content of the ingroup (in this case a national group): on the one hand, people emphasize blood and kin; on the other, they do not. But ingroup orientation goes further. It is structured around kin-based loyalties and involves patterns of loyalty and obligation. The family is the basic and smallest ingroup unit, at the other extreme from the nation. Strong ingroup orientation is most often accompanied by a rhetoric based on family relationships, with a dominant father (outside oriented), a protective mother (inside oriented), and sisters and brothers, alternately considered as rivals within the ingroup (because they are competing for parents' love, affection and preference) and allies *vis-à-vis* the outgroup (because they share the same fundamental identity; they *are* of the same kin). The family space is that of the house and the surrounding ground: it is private but not closed to outsiders, who may enter under definite conditions.

Outgroup orientation, in contrast to ingroup orientation, is based on the assumption that there is a fundamental unity of mankind beyond the borders of ingroup spaces, including families, nations and cultures. If the two orientations are roughly opposed, it is not a complete opposition. In certain cultures they coexist, as in the Nordic European cultures which combine a strong sense of national identity (ingroup) with a universal focus manifested in their strong commitment to peace, development of the poorest nations and international organizations (outgroup).

What does membership involve in terms of rights and obligations?

The ingroup bonds involve relationships of loyalty. This loyalty does not extend beyond the borders of the ingroup space. Loyalty is basically about showing allegiance, respecting the values of the ingroup and maintaining a sense of the honour of the group. Loyalty is fundamentally non-reciprocal: people do not expect other ingroup members' loyalty for being loyal themselves. Loyalty is not based on time, except for a sense of eternity: one may wait for fifty years to be rewarded for loyalty or one may never be rewarded; it just does not matter.

Loyalty can be based on kinship or patronage, which is often an extended form of kinship, based on symbolic adoption, that is taking another's child as one's own. The virtue manifested in loyalty is that of maintaining allegiance, even in the face of conflicts with other members of the ingroup or when experiencing unfair treatment from the most powerful members. Strong ingroup orientation increases an insider's loyalty, but decreases the feeling of obligation towards outsiders at the same time. Morality is space-related. It might, for instance, be considered as perfectly virtuous to lie to or steal from people to whom no loyalty is owed. The Mafia is a good illustration of an ingroup oriented society. Morality is based on a set of values favouring strict loyalty, treason being punished by death sentence; the godfather who has ordered it goes to the burial ceremony because he still 'loves' the betrayer. . . . Ingroup orientation partly explains behaviourial relativity. Some national groups have a reputation for their compliant behaviour at home (where rules are strictly enforced) and for looser conduct when being abroad. They not only relax from strong barriers at home, they also consider that, when being out of the ingroup space where bonds and loyalty are strong, they do not need to respect rules (even similar rules as in the ingroup) since outsiders do not deserve loyalty or even interest and respect.

Rights and obligations may be defined according to the ethnic groups, as in Africa where only certain ingroups are allowed to be merchants. Mistrust and disdain against retail activities explain why merchants are most often foreigners (Lebanese in West Africa, Indians in Zaïre), particular local ethnic groups (Dioulas in Ivory Coast) or women (The 'mama Benz' in Benin).

Ingroup versus outgroup orientations have a deep influence on the actual system of ethics and morality in a particular society. Impersonal rules applied by judges to people independently of their belonging is typical of low ingroup orientation. A typical case where such orientations are important is when a family member has committed some crime, the family knows about it, but there is no evidence; what does the family do: denounce one of its members or keep silent?

Outgroup orientation values universal rules, applied to everybody: human rights ethics are a typical feature of outgroup orientation. Objectivity and reciprocity are preferred over loyalty; or stated differently: loyalty is not to the group, not to people, but to the impersonal rules and values that govern the society as a whole; which is largely why the terms above are 'personalization' (people-orientation) versus 'depersonalization' (rule-orientation). However, people with outgroup orientation, precisely because they have a more 'depersonalized' approach, are more sensitive to the problems of other human beings, far from their own space. Their aptitude to behave in a more universal way in no way means that they are less human.

These differences have a major impact on international business negotiations and personal selling: how to make contacts? What information should be looked after if one is to understand connections between the people in front of us? How are decisions made in a particular ingroup? The differences may also extend in the area of consumer behaviour, especially in the area of decision making where ingroup orientation exerts pressures on consumers' attitudes and buying decisions. Any society combines to various degrees ingroup and outgroup orientation and organizes them around specific patterns. For example 'affirmative action, equal opportunity' is a strong outgroup motto, typical of the United States. However, the global rule is still that human beings cannot choose their favourite nationality. Yet it would be the purest form of outgroup orientation.

How can membership be gained?

If people are very territorial, it is important to know how to gain access to them, even as an external partner, a business partner in a joint venture for instance, but as a respected partner (keeping in mind that loyalty and morality are mostly values which are applicable to group members only). If we combine the ingroup/outgroup and the being/doing divides, a simple contrast is as follows:

1. When ingroup and being orientation are strong, membership is mostly gained on the basis of *concrete territoriality*.
2. When outgroup and doing orientation are strong, membership is based on *abstract territoriality*.

If membership is based on concrete territoriality, some necessary characteristics are innate or cannot be acquired for adult people, simply because they are related to birth, socialization and education within the ingroup. In cases where it is impossible to gain membership, one must behave as a friendly and realistic outsider, who can target three possible positions in the long run:

1. A 'tolerated outsider' who is considered as different but useful for practical purposes. This status allows comfortable relationships and, in most cases, is a possible role for developing business. But two aspects have to be kept in mind: (1) such people should not imitate insider status or try to acquire it by too active involvement in the community – 'proactive outsiders' will be reminded, one day or another, of their limited status as a full person; and (2) they should not play insider people again each other to acquire power and influence: in general, conflict in the ingroup should not be used as a Trojan horse because ingroup conflicts are considered as 'home business', not to be shown overtly, and never to be solved at an outsider's advantage.
2. A 'recognized outsider': this status goes nearer to membership, yet is still far from it. Generally the 'recognized outsider' has been living in the culture for a long period of

time, speaks the language fluently and has established strong relational networks. In a conference a few years ago, Robert J. Ballon, a Belgian Jesuit living in Japan for more than thirty years and a specialist of Japanese business (mentioned above concerning the Japanese time patterns), explained how he was always considered as a pure foreigner, despite his profound knowledge of the Japanese society and his very deep involvement with the country. 'Recognized outsiders' often serve the purpose of ambassors, cultural translators or mediators *from* the outside world of foreign groups to the ingroup. They are recognized as useful and friendly people by the insiders, yet would lose their usefulness if they were to become insiders.

3. 'Newly accepted insiders' have gone a step beyond, crossing the cultural group border. They often can do so because they crossed early enough to be considered as still educable persons, suitable for a profound transformation of their being, as in the case of foreigners who arrived as young adults, completed their education and married locally. Such persons will, however, remain somewhat on the fringes, near to the external borders of the cultural community, often considered as adequate ambassadors or mediators from the ingroup **to** the outgroups.

Membership based on doing and *abstract territoriality* corresponds largely to 'modern culture': outgroup orientation is highly valued and ingroup orientation is often, too quickly, equated with narrow-mindedness, provincialism, hostility towards foreigners, and the like. What people have *done* up to now is evidenced by their curriculum vitae (CV). The interview guide for affirmative action compliance programmes considers as discriminatory such enquiries to applicants as age, citizenship, marital status, birthplace, education that is not job-related, language, etc. – pieces of information which in most countries outside the United States are considered as legitimate information for knowing who *is* the applicant. In France CVs, which include this information, are accompanied with a photograph and a handwritten letter accompanying the CV, which is sometimes used for assessing the person's character through graphology. Abstract territoriality is mostly based on professional achievements, evidenced by diplomas, membership in professional societies, being an alumni of an ivy-league university, and so on. The epitome of abstract territoriality is represented by the *golden boys*. For them *insider* trading is a fraud, showing that the use of their natural ingroup advantages is viewed as evil. The space of 'golden boys' is a mix of MBA top schools, market rooms and a 'club of people constantly connected world-wide'. Just try to imagine the difference with a Bengali farmer.

Business school graduates, *Grandes écoles* in France, or those holding a Dr title in Germany belong to these 'modern groups' based on doing and competence rather than being, age, sex and group belonging. It is assumed that access to membership is organized on a non-discriminatory and objective basis and that it is in the best interest of society as a whole because the 'best people' are doing the 'appropriate job'. However, even in a doing framework, relational competence never disappears in favour of pure professional competence, simply because managing relationships is a dark side yet an important part of the doing competences. Paradoxically, when abstract teritoriality is very strong, it largely recreates primitive ingroup behaviour, but based on different criteria. The world of academia, for instance, is very 'outgroupist' for sex, nationality, religion or age, but it is very 'ingroupist' when it comes to doctoral degrees and the journals where people publish.

Group membership assumptions are important for marketing negotiations, when facing a national competitive environment as a foreign firm, for making public relations contacts, for the recruitment and promotion of salespeople, especially in Africa and the Middle East, and for any case involving business ethics. The favouring of one party over another, on the ground of personal relationship, in either political or economic affairs, is dimly viewed – often indeed called corruption – by outgroup oriented people, whereas it remains standard practice for ingroup oriented people.

Pitfalls of excessive ingroup and outgroup orientations

Because extreme positions in space-related assumptions present drawbacks, there is always a combination of both, to varying degrees. Some pitfalls of ingroup orientations are: (1) tribalism – only people of an ingroup based on kin are considered worth interacting with and caring for; (2) localism (we, here): only people belonging to a small geographical unit are considered interesting people; and (3) provincialism – only values and behaviour that are in use in the community are considered appropriate. On the other hand, the pitfalls of excessive outgroup orientation are: (1) unrealistic universalism – the complete cancelling of borders (GATT, General Agreement on Tariffs and Trade, rules are partly based on such open space assumptions) will produce global welfare; if not wrong, this is also far from true; and (2) global village ethnocentrism – if we 'see' what happens everywhere on Earth at any moment a global consciousness will emerge; unfortunately images are global, but their interpretation is not.

Dealing with physical space and other aspects of culture related to space

Territoriality refers also to possessiveness, control and authority over an area of physical space. Individuals need to refer to rules concerning space because they have to defend their space against invasion or misuse by others. The 'language of space' is culturally given and provides the codes concerning social distance – how far should one stand from other people in order to respect their area of private space? A complete approach to relations with space was proposed by Edward T. Hall (1966) in *The Hidden Dimension*. In this book he developed the concept of 'proxemics' – the term he has coined for the interrelated observations and theories of man's use of space as a specialized elaboration of culture. According to Hall, in western cultures, there are three primary zones of space: the intimate zone (0 to 18 inches (0–450 mm)), the personal zone (18 inches to 3 feet (0.45–1 m)), and the social zone (3 to 6 feet (1–2 m)). Touch can occur for westerners in the intimate and personal zones, but sensory involvement and communication is less intense in the social zone. In fact, what differs across cultures in terms of physical space assumptions is the following:

1. What are the size of the three zones? To which extent do they overlap?
2. Who is allowed to enter these zones of physical space?

3. What is considered as adequate sensory exchange within definite interpersonal distances?

The last question is important in marketing terms. It relates to the senses, sight, sound, touch and smells in as far as sensory perception is directly related to interpersonal distance. Americans are, for instance, famous for their suppression of personal odours in public spaces, and this has created a mass market for room deodeorizers, antiperspirants, mouthwashes and deodorizers. Although smell suppression is globally 'modern' (it developed well outside the United States), it is not clear whether it will remain so in the future, with people striving for a more natural expression of themselves. Chapter 8 on product policy gives examples of how our sense of physical space intermingles with sensory codes in a way that is culturally significant for consumers to attribute meaning to product characteristics.

The list in Table 2.2 is not exhaustive: it describes basic space-related cultural assumptions. Although not developed in detail, some other aspects need to be mentioned. The availability of inhabitable physical space and the density population varies greatly across countries, and this has a profound impact on material culture. The high population density in Japan and in many Asian countries has made it essential to make things 'smaller' to fit more in. The assumption would be 'smaller, better'. It is a not minor reason for the talent of Japanese at miniaturizing objects. As shown in Chapter 11, Japanese space at least partly explains the distribution system prevailing in this country. Conversely the availability of space and other resources in North America is a reason for the large size of objects, from cars to servings in restaurants and outside posters. The contrary assumption ('bigger, better') is probably a significant background explanation for the lack of adaptation of US car manufacturers to smaller car sizes after the mid-1970s oil crisis.

Contrasting physical spaces should also be considered carefully in physically heterogeneous countries. A good case is Nepal which combines the Himalaya mountains and subtropical plains near to India in the Tharuwan province. Cultures are different ways to adapt to a certain reality, and Nepali mountain people exhibit, on average, different values and behaviour from people in the lower areas: interpersonal solidarity and work orientation are stronger, because people would not survive otherwise. A last area where significant space-related cultural differences are displayed can be found in urban planning, the ways to organize towns and to relate urban to rural landscape.

2.4 Cultural borrowing and change in societies

It would be wrong to give the impression that cultures are truly different and exclusive in their assumptions. Through time and space, cultures intermingle. Negative events such as wars and colonization convey cultural exchange: the Viennese, and through them all the other Europeans, discovered coffee from the Turks when they besieged Vienna during the sixteenth century. In the process of cultural borrowing the naivety is fascinating with which successful cultural artefacts from other cultures are borrowed without the cultural assumptions underlying these artefacts being understood or even imagined. Yan (1991, pp. 51–2) for instance, quotes the reformer Liang Quichao, who wrote in 1897 on the subject of European countries, considered unlike China as innovative:

> In innovative countries the sovereigns are wise, their mandarins faithful and courageous, their people intelligent and heroic, their politics successful, their business prosperous, their products excellent, etc. Travel in their country brings you such pleasure and joy that you forget to return home. Will you then pose further questions as to the prosperity of these countries?

Isolated cultures, united cultures

Cultures are rarely pure, except in a few areas where people have been almost untouched by foreign influences. An example of such cultural isolation might be Japan which, during the era of Tokugawa shoguns, withdrew from all contact with outside people and cultures. The Tokugawa period lasted for more than two centuries before the Meiji era, which started after 1868 and initiated a period of increased accessibility of foreign influences to Japan. Reischauer, a specialist in Japanese history, explains in his book *Japan: Past and Present* (1946, 1990) that two centuries of complete peace were enforced by the Tokugawa regime with extreme vigour. The Tokugawa shoguns have left their mark on the behaviour of Japanese citizens. In the sixteenth century the Japanese were keen, adventurous and somewhat bellicose. By the nineteenth century they had become docile and humble subjects, awaiting orders from their hierarchical superiors, which they resignedly implemented. Reischauer hypothesizes that the collective regimentation under the Tokugawa shoguns led to an inward-looking people who indulged in conformism, which served as consensus. He further notes that, at the beginning of the nineteenth century, antagonism in Japanese society was almost non-existent: the rules of propriety were strictly observed, and violence was extremely rare. Reischauer argues that when the Japanese were confronted with an unknown situation, they displayed very little ability to adapt, much less than other peoples.[4] The Tokugawa period appears good in many ways, especially as regards the general level of education and the development of the arts. However, it largely interrupted the natural evolution of economic and social change. The Tokugawa shoguns crystallized an outdated political and social order. Only after the beginning of the Meiji era in 1868 did the Japanese begin to interact with the Europeans, who had achieved an enormous breakthrough in the field of scientific knowledge during the previous two centuries. The succession of these two periods, one of great isolation and one of openness towards foreign cultures, probably explains the paradoxical relationship of the Japanese with international trade and international marketing. In one sense they are very ethnocentric, but simultaneously they are quite capable of overcoming their ethnocentrism to become, ultimately, highly successful international marketers.

In many other cases, cultures do mix. Contact may inevitably be bellicose, owing to the conflicting interests of countries and their cultures (religion, language, social and political systems) over borders. The perennial conflicts between the region south of the Mediterranean Sea (mostly Arab and Muslim) and the northern region (mostly Christian) are an example of this pattern of conflict/cooperation. Cultural encounters occur even in wartime. When besieged by the Turks in the fifteenth century, the Viennese were introduced by their opponents to a new, tasty and stimulating beverage: coffee. It is through the Viennese as intermediaries that coffee was introduced into the West. Even during the Crusades (tenth to twelfth centuries), warriors on both sides had quiet moments when, for instance, they enjoyed each other's food. In *The Crusades through Arab Eyes* (1985, pp. 128–9), Amine Maalouf describes how the Templars grew accustomed to understanding and accepting the customs and beliefs of the Muslims. In the following extract, Templars, although themselves Christians, side with a Muslim visiting Jerusalem, the Damascene emir Usamah, in defending Islamic religious practices:

> When I was visiting Jerusalem, I used to go to Al-Aqsa mosque, where my Templar friends were staying. Along one side of the building was a small oratory in which the *Franj* [an Arab word designating the French, or more generally European, Crusaders], had set up a church. The Templars placed this spot at my disposal so that I might say my prayer. One day I entered, said *Allahu Akbar*, and was about to begin my prayer, when a man, a *Franj*, threw himself upon me, and turned to the east, saying, 'Thus do we pray.' The Templars rushed forward and led him away. I then set myself to prayer once more, but this man, seizing upon a moment of inattention, threw himself upon me yet again, turned my face to the east, and repeated once more, 'Thus do we pray.' Once again the Templars intervened, led him away, and apologized to me, saying, 'He is a foreigner. He has just arrived from the land of the *Franj* and he has never seen anyone pray without turning his face to the east.' I answered that I had prayed enough and left, stunned by the behaviour of this demon who had been so enraged at seeing me pray while facing the direction of Mecca.

Cultural borrowing is general . . . and disguised

Culture is identity, but not pure identity: the basic requirement for the introduction of a new cultural item (a product, a lifestyle, a word, a dance, a song) is that it looks (and in fact is) coherent with the culture that adopts it. That is why cultural borrowing is often disguised, by a change of name or by means of 'reinvention', whereby a local inventor/ discoverer is found. It is fascinating to see how many countries seek to claim credit for particular inventions (the Xerox machine, for instance) at the same time.

One may view culture as the accumulation of the best possible solutions to the common problems faced by the members of a particular society. This definition, very Anglo-Saxon in its problem-solving orientation, does have an advantage: it emphasizes the 'shopping' aspect of cultural dynamics. There have always been different kinds of travellers (explorers, warriors, merchants, colonials, etc.) who have brought back foreign innovations to their native country. Usually by accident or sometimes by an almost systematic process (like the Japanese, because they are overly conscious of their insularity and cultural isolation), societies may find good imported solutions. Jeans, as informal trousers for casual wear, have made their way through all cultures. The fabric originally came from France (*de Nîmes* – denim) and the name from Italy – short for Jean Fustian from Genes (Genoa). Afterwards this 'American' invention made its way back to Italy and most of the countries of the world.

Although cultural opportunism is understandable, it is often hidden by the need to maintain cultural identity. Few societies are prepared to accept that a large part of their culture is really foreign: cultural borrowing is therefore somewhat hypocritical. Marketing concepts and theories, mostly US-based, have been imported into a large number of countries. However, in a somewhat linguistically defensive country like France it was considered necessary to create a new word and rename the concept *la mercatique* despite the fact that the original word, 'marketing', contains no letter outside the French alphabet and is more easily pronounced in French.

The word *mercatique*, a neologism, was created in 1973 by the Commission de Terminologie Française, established by the French Ministry of Economics and Finance. Despite this centrally inspired procedure, people in everyday life still use the original word 'marketing'. The argument in favour of *la mercatique* was as follows:

> Not only did mercatique have a clear etymology (from the Latin mercatus the market) but also its definition, by its strictness, allowed for a more profound understanding of the concept and avoided the deviations, misinterpretations and misconceptions that the blurredness of the English expression entailed. These misconceptions were frequent: thus, for Pierre Hazebroucq, secretary of the Académie des Science Commerciales, the word 'marketing' designated 'everything related to influencing markets'; similarly P. Kotler wrote, in *Management Direction* in June 1974, that marketing management was the set of actions which aims at regulating the level, the pace and the nature of demand for one or several products of a company – this dragged up memories of the 1900–50 period, where the supply side was given higher priority, that is demand had to adapt to those products which were actually offered. How, under these conditions, was it possible to get young people interested in commercial action and entrepreneurship?
>
> Whereas, with the French concept of *mercatique* young people passionately fond of trade action discovered an outlet for their enthusiasm; 'manipulative' commercial activities were rejected, as well as activities which were limited exclusively to the act of buying or solely to the act of selling, often with contempt for customers, or at least a definite lack of attention to their needs. (Darbelet and Lauginié, 1988, pp. 133–4)

People who speak the common language have not adopted the word *mercatique*. Other French words created to replace a foreign word or concept have, however, been completely successful. For instance, *ordinateur* has replaced 'computer', which has been borrowed by many other languages from the United States, where computers were invented. Some words and concepts are borrowed easily in their original form when they are obviously related to some well-established stereotype of a particular country: *ersatz* (high reputation of German chemistry), *leitmotiv* (German music), *showbiz* (US dominance), *élégance* (French reputation for style), *kamikaze* or *hara-kiri* (Japanese capacity for self-sacrifice), *mamma* (Italian sense of the motherly role in the family). Sherry and Camargo (1987) show that English language has had a profound influence on Japanese marketing: they report a heavy use of English loanwords in Japanese promotional texts and labels. *Mai* (English 'my'), for instance, is used extensively in compounds such as *mai homu* (my home), because the Japanese equivalent would sound too selfish and stress the private over the collective. Beyond the imported word, it is then the foreign value, individualism, that is imported.

exchanges, trade and merchants (and also thieves). Despite the success and the seemingly general acceptance of the term 'marketing', many examples indicate that there have been some basic misconceptions of it in many countries, especially developing ones (Amine and Cavusgil, 1986). For instance, a survey of Egyptian business people indicates a clear lack of understanding as to what the word marketing really means (El Haddad, 1985). Either managers do not understand what marketing is all about or, if they do, they tend to believe that it has no application to their business. In fact they see marketing as the mere fact of selling, or the promotion of sales. Although 'marketing' has been imported (as a word, and even as a sort of slogan), its former cultural roots and its precise meaning have been forgotten.

In Japan, most of the books on marketing management were borrowed from the United States and then translated directly without much adaptation. Moreover market survey techniques, the underlying concepts and the wording of questions, as well as questionnaire, interview and sampling techniques, were all widely imported. As the Dutchman Van Raaij said (1978, p. 699): 'Consumer research is largely 'made in the U.S.A.' with all the risks that Western American or middle-class biases pervade this type of research in the research questions we address, the concepts and theories we use and the interpretations we give.'

In fact it is more frequently the word than its whole sense and the social practices it involves that has been imported. It is normal to find large gaps between the rhetoric of marketing and the actual selling practices adopted by companies. Marketing did not really replace long-established commercial practices in many countries (Allen, 1971): it superimposed itself on local selling practices and merged with them.

In French companies one often finds a *directeur du marketing* (vice president, marketing, in the United States) and a *directeur commercial* (sales and distribution) at the same time. However, in the United States a vice president, marketing, deals with marketing strategy but also with sales and the sales force. The French *directeur commercial* is actually responsible for a large part of what Americans call 'marketing' as a functional area. The duties of a *directeur commercial* are primarily the supervision of sales, distribution outlets and sales representatives, as well as the management of customer relations. The *directeur du marketing* will most often be responsible for marketing surveys and/or communication. The organizational relationship between the *directeur du marketing* and the *directeur commercial*, whether parallel or hierarchical (the marketing department is usually subordinate to the commercial department) will not encourage them to collaborate. Managers tend to see marketing as somewhat 'intellectual', with little practical orientation, directed towards long-range targets and the strategic consideration of markets, or even as being preoccupied solely with advertising strategy, a rather 'indirect' method of influencing the market.

Marketing: US-based vocabulary, information sources and concepts

The imported nature of marketing concepts and practices is clearly evidenced by the vocabulary, information and reference sources, and the origin of literature on the subject; all demarcate it as an area of knowledge. Marketing vocabulary is now used world-wide:

everybody is familiar with the words 'mailing', 'media planning' and 'merchandising'. Even though efforts have been made in some countries to localize these words, they have generally failed. For instance in France hardly anyone uses the official word *la mercatique* (it sounds ugly). It is legitimate and indeed wise to retain an imported word in its original form until its total integration as a concept has been realized. This evidence of borrowing allows the foreign origin of the concept to be kept in mind and thereby, paradoxically, improves its chances of successful localization. The transplant has all the more chance of being successful because there is a strong fascination for what is made abroad. Although there is a strong attraction for one's own culture, it is essential to accept that there is also success elsewhere. In some ways it is similar to the situation that currently exists with Japan.

Data and information sources (Nielsen panels, for instance) and consultancy businesses (advertising agencies, market consultants) are mostly of American origin, even if they are far from all being American. Last but not least, the *marketing* journals and academic reviews, such as the *Journal of Marketing*, or the *Journal of Marketing Research* and *Advertising Age* came largely from the United States. In Europe (France, Germany, the United Kingdom, Benelux and North European countries) as well as in Canada or Japan, there are many other journals that exist. But research and new advances for practitioners as well as for academicians are made on the basis of imported materials. For instance the percentage of US references in the bibliographies of a British, a German or a French review of marketing are always at least 60 per cent, and often as much as 90 per cent, on specialized topics. As Lazer *et al.* point out about Japan (1985, p. 71), 'what has occurred [in Japan] is the modification and adaptation of selected American constructs, ideas and practices to adjust them to the Japanese culture, that remains intact.' They stress especially the importance of economic non-functionality which 'emphasizes that marketing actions consider individual human factors rather than merely economic efficiency and business profits.'

A progressive integration

A similar situation is also to be found in France, where adaptation to the cultural context has now been broadly achieved. There are now several French textbooks – about ten on marketing management, and at least one or two on each specialized area of marketing. A continuous effort has been made to allow 'marketing' to appear as a '*rationalisation de la démarche commerciale*' ('rationalization of trade and sales practices'). It is seen as confronting the traditional *commercial* style with new concepts that are better suited to international competition (Dayan *et al.*, 1988, p. 14):

> In a [French] company, at the beginning of the industrial revolution . . . selling was not considered to be an honourable activity. The essence of trading – bargaining with the client – is seen as not being codifiable; it is an *art*, based on individual talents, intuitions and experience. Consequently commercial activities do not follow the standards of the company as a whole, which are based on rationality, logic, and organisation. . . . With the advent of *marketing*, brand image activities have been improved, and they have been better integrated to the company as a whole. A full scale *direction de marketing* (marketing department)

attracts significant areas of the human, intellectual, and financial resources of a company: it often has a critical influence on strategic decisions, it uses more and more sophisticated techniques, and it adopts a rational approach, which raises the *direction de marketing* to the level of other functional areas.

In this small passage (from the introduction to a French *marketing* textbook) several elements typify the import process and its limits: the expression 'full scale' (*à part entière*) suggests that there are still many *directions de marketing* which cover only a reduced part of the marketing function; the *power* of marketing within the organization is an important issue *per se*; the dialectic opposition irrationality and art versus logic and rationalization. In French society, only Cartesian logic may give legitimacy and credibility to marketing.

2.6　Cultural hostility

Limits to borrowing clearly appear when it is seen as a threat to cultural coherence. This is especially true of religious practices, social morals and even daily customs. For instance, it is not easy to import polygamy or clitoral excision for babies into cultures where monogamy and child protection are strongly established practices. As previously stated, there must be a minimum level of coherence and homogeneity in cultural assumptions and behaviour in the cultural community if people are to synchronize themselves and live peacefully together.

Racism

Racism is often confused with cultural hostility, whereas in fact it precedes cultural hostility. But cultural hostility does not necessarily imply racism: one may be hostile to people of (some) other cultures, without being a racist. Behind racism there is a theory: that, because of their race (i.e. physiology), some human beings are inferior at various levels (intelligence, creative abilities, moral sense, etc.). The theories of Gobineau and Hitler's *Mein Kampf* are writings which clearly developed and propagated racist views. The following passage on slavery, written by Montesquieu in 1748 (Book XV, ch. 5, p. 242, my emphasis), exemplifies racism:

> Were I to vindicate our right to make slaves of the Negroes, there should be my arguments. The Europeans, having extirpated the Americans, were obliged to make slaves of the Africans, for clearing such vast tracts of land. Sugar would be too dear, if the plants which produce it were cultivated by any other than slaves. These creatures are all over black, and with such a flat nose, that they can scarcely be pitied. *It is hardly to be believed that God who is a wise being, should place a good soul, in such a black ugly body.*

Racist theses and opinions have been progressively abandoned (as scientific theories, at least) over the last two centuries. An issue which is still discussed is that of differing intellectual capacity among people of different races or ethnic groups. It is always measured by IQ tests, which are of western/US origin. Although observed differences across ethnic groups are undisputable, their explanation is debated: some people argue about genetic differences being the explanatory variable, others (Segall *et al.*, 1990) attribute these differences to a series of non-genetic factors. Environmental factors, for instance, such as the absence of a formal education system, on average tend to diminish IQ scores. Such detrimental factors are to be found, significantly, more among groups with low and median IQ scores.

The IQ test itself is biased in as much as it penalizes, by its very construction, those who have been designated from the start as 'culturally inferior'. The IQ test does not take into account many skills and competences that were unknown to the authors of the test. Moreover, recent studies show that the *inter-individual* variability of genetic character-istics is much larger than the *inter-racial* group's variability (Segall *et al.*, 1990, p. 102). In other words, genetic differences among Europeans, or genetic differences among South African Zulus, are *automatically* significantly higher than the genetic differences between the average European and the average Zulu – a strong anti-racist argument.[5]

Cultural hostility

In contrast to racism, cultural hostility does not imply prior prejudices as to who is inferior or superior according to race or culture. Culture is part of one's own patrimony as a person. There is a strong affective dimension, when one feels that one's proper cultural values are threatened. This feeling may result from either of the following:

1. Simple interactions with people whose cultural values are quite different. One does not feel at ease, communication is experienced as burdensome and there is little empathy. A defensive response may then develop, frequently the case of unconscious (and minor) cultural hostility.
2. Collective reactions. Cases are so numerous world-wide that it would need many pages to quote them exhaustively: Transylvanian Hungarians and Romanians, people in ex-Yugoslavia, Armenians of High Karabakh and Azeris of the Azerbaijan enclave in Soviet Armenia; Walloons and Flemings in Belgium; Protestant and Catholic communities in Ulster; etc. *Identity is a matter of culture rather than race.*

It is not only territorial conflicts but also economic competition that may cause cultural hostility. The Japanese are sometimes considered negatively in the United States, which has a large trade imbalance with Japan. In his controversial best-selling book, *The Japan that Can Say No*, Shintaro Ishihara (1991) argues that anti-Japanese racial prejudice is the main cause of 'Japan-bashing' in the United States. Ishihara, a member of the Japanese diet, quotes what he said to politicians in Washington (p. 27):

> I admit that Caucasians created modern civilization, but what bothers me is you seem to think that heritage makes you superior. In the thirteenth century, however, the Mongols under Genghis Khan and his successors overran Russia and Eastern Europe Caucasians

adopted Mongol-style haircuts and shaved eyebrows. . . . Just as Orientals of today are crazy about the clothing and hairstyle of the Beatles, Michael Jackson and Sting, Occidentals of Genghis Khan times copied Mongolian ways.

Cultural hostility, when directed at successful nations, is often a fairly ambiguous feeling, whereby admiration and envy for the other's achievements go along with contempt for many traits of the envied people and obvious unwillingness to understand the root causes of the other's success. This also results in naive copies of selected cultural artefacts as magical ways of becoming stronger – in *Robinson Crusoe* savages were about to eat Man Friday in order to gain his qualities. In the case of immigrants, Mauviel (1991, p. 73, my translation) comments on the frequent confusion between racism and cultural hostility:[6]

> . . . the dominant ideology has been so interiorized that a new, very subtle rhetoric enables us to avoid any direct, frank response to the problems concerning immigrants – the most important issue is not to be accused of 'racism'. And one places under this word the most dissimilar elements, which often have nothing to do with race. in its biological acceptance. . . . The media especially like the meaningless expression 'everyday racism'. As for the phrase 'ethnic group', which has replaced the word 'race', those who use the expression would have a hard time trying to define it.

There are differences across countries: Mauviel shows that the Italians are not so reluctant to speak openly on cultural hostility problems. The Italian press 'lets reality be seen, it does not cover it with an embarrassed veil, it allows the publication of the most diverse opinions'. He describes, for instance, the case of the Nigerian women at Chambave (near Torino) which 'as revealed by the press, demonstrates the irresponsibility of those who vow to have multiracial or multi-ethnic societies' (Box 2.2).

Part 4 further examines the mechanism of cultural hostility, which is sometimes increased by language and communication problems. Intercultural misunderstandings may stem from a lack of competency in the other's language, or from the natural tendency to adopt defensive stereotypes. It often results in a snowballing cultural hostility.

Questions

1. What is the influence of space availability (mostly determined by population density in a definite country or area) on material culture? Give examples.
2. Indicate how the following products and services are 'loaded' with time, in terms of time used in consumption, time-saving device, durability, waiting time, seasonality, time projections in the past and the future, etc. (As an example, Box 5.1 describes the time load in life insurance policies).
   (a) a dish-washing machine
   (b) a haircut

(c) obtaining cash from your bank

(d) spending two-week vacations at *Club Méditerrannée*

(e) fresh orange juice versus dried (powdered) orange juice

3. How would you expect consumer behaviour to vary across cultures for the five products/services above? (Just cite one example per case.)

4. You try to park your car. A sign indicates that parking in this area is limited to fifteen minutes. Another sign indicates 'Long term parking, 300 metres.' What do these explicit signs suggest concerning temporal culture in this country?

5. Define what would be the most important criteria for recruitment in a being oriented society versus a doing-oriented society.

6. In most countries, police and justice positions are subject to condition of nationality (being a national is required for entering the function) whereas in universities and research centres it is opened to applicants regardless of their nationality. Why?

7. Find examples of cultural borrowing (in everyday life, in the Press, in people's behaviour, in work as well as leisure activities, arts, etc.).

8. The scooter was invented just after the Second World War at a Californian airport, by putting a body on a motorcycle; this allowed quick moves on the tarmac. The invention was industrially developed by the Italians in the 1950s and 1960s. In the 1970s, the Japanese began to sell scooters world-wide. What does it suggest in terms of cultural borrowing?

9. Try to elaborate on the following assertion: 'the usual traffic in marketing and business texts generally starts with the American text and is then translated to other languages or sometimes used in the original version'. What are the problems likely to

Box 2 .2   *Nigerian women of Chambave*

Hundreds, if not thousands, of Nigerian women – graduates in chemistry, law and other subjects, nurses, etc. – came to Italy in search of a better life. Most of them end up walking the streets, or are love traders on the *tangenziali*, the freeways round cities, and even on country roads. The most striking example to me, because of its symbolic meaning, is that of the 'train of sin', from Turin to Aosta, which brings thirty to forty Nigerian women every summer evening on the 9.15 p.m. bus to Chambave, which is located between Aosta and San Vincenzo; they are joining their 'shift' on highway 26. These *pendolari del amore* (commuters) have lost the dream that they previously held, namely that of being salespeople for Italian shoes. One should not be astonished that the mayor [of Chambave], surrounded by the local council and the population of the valley, has organized a silent protest march. However, there is clearly a flourishing market, if one just looks at the evidence of the numerous cars with roaring engines that wait for the women. One may guess what the relations are between this village of nine hundred people and the African women, who are no longer prepared to accept being kept out of sight. In these matters, the most shocking hypocrisy is the rule; only conspicuous incidents that attract people's attention, like those at Chambave, help us to become aware of these new forms of shameful exploitation, a direct consequence of the under-development of the countries of the South.

(Source: Maurice Mauviel, 1991 pp. 8l–2. Reproduced with permission.)

be encountered by non-US educators and practitioners when using such materials? On the other hand, what are the advantages of using them?

APPENDIX 2

━━━━━ ◆◆◆ ━━━━━

Teaching materials

A2.1   Cross-cultural scenario: Inshallah

Stefan Phillips, a manager for a large US airline, was transferred to Dhahran, Saudi Arabia, to set up a new office. Although Stefan had had several other extended overseas assignments in Paris and Brussels, he was not well prepared for working in the Arab world. At the end of his first week Stefan came home in a state of near total frustration. As he sat at the dinner table that night he told his wife how exasperating it had been to work with the local employees, who, he claimed, seemed to take no responsibility for anything. Whenever something went wrong they would simply say '*Inshallah*' ('If God wills it'). Coming from a culture which sees no problem as insoluble, Stefan could not understand how the local employees could be so passive about job-related problems. 'If I hear one more *inshallah*,' he told his wife, 'I'll go crazy.'

What might you tell Stefan to help him better understand the cultural realities of Saudi Arabia?

(Source: Gary P. Ferraro, 1990, p. 118. Reproduced with permission.)

A2.2   Cross-cultural interaction: Engineering a decision

M. Legrand is a French engineer who works for a Japanese company in France. One day the general manager, Mr Tanaka, calls him into his office to discuss a new project in the Middle East. He tells M. Legrand that the company is very pleased with his dedicated work and would like him to act as chief engineer for the project. It would mean two to three years away from home, but his family would be able to accompany him and there would be considerable personal financial benefits to the position – and, of course, he would be performing a valuable service to the company. M. Legrand thanks Mr Tanaka for the confidence he has in him but says he will have to discuss it with his wife before deciding. Two days later he returns and tells Mr Tanaka that both he and his wife do not like the thought of leaving France and so he does not want to accept the position. Mr Tanaka says nothing but is somewhat dumbfounded by his decision.

Why is Mr Tanaka so bewildered by M. Legrand's decision?

1. He believes it is foolish for M. Legrand to refuse all the financial benefits that go with the position.
2. He cannot accept that M. Legrand should take any notice of his wife's opinion in the matter.

3. He believes M. Legrand is possibly trying to bluff him into offering greater incentives to accept the offer.
4. He feels it is not appropriate for M. Legrand to place his personal inclinations above those of his role as an employee of the company.

(Source: Brislin, *et al.*, 1986, p. 158. Reproduced with permission.)

A2.3   Cross-cultural interaction: Opening a medical office in Saudi Arabia[7]

Dr. Tom McDivern, a physician from New York City, was offered a two-year assignment to practice medicine in a growing urban center in Saudi Arabia. Many of the residents in the area he was assigned to were recent immigrants from the much smaller outlying rural areas.

Because Western medicine was relatively unknown to many of these people, one of Dr. McDivern's main responsibilities was to introduce himself and his services to those in the community. A meeting at a local school was organized for that specific purpose. Many people turned out. Tom's presentation went well. Some local residents also presented their experiences with Western medicine so others could hear the value of using his service. Some of Tom's office staff were also present to make appointments for those interested in seeing him when his doors opened one week later. The meeting was an obvious success. His opening day was booked solid.

When that day finally arrived, Tom was anxious to greet his first patients. Thirty minutes had passed, however, and neither of his first two patients had arrived. He was beginning to worry about the future of his practice while wondering where his patients were.

What is the major cause of Tom's worries?

1. Although in Tom's mind and by his standards his presentation was a success, people actually only made appointments so as not to hurt his feelings. They really had no intention of using his services as modern medicine is so foreign to their past experiences.
2. Given the time lag between sign up and the actual day of the appointment, people had time to rethink their decision. They had just changed their minds.
3. Units of time differ between Arabs and Americans. Whereas to Tom his patients were very late, the Arab patient could still arrive and be on time.
4. Tom's patients were seeing their own traditional healers from their own culture; after that, they could go on to see this new doctor, Tom.

(Source: Brislin *et al.*, pp. 160–1. Reproduced with permission.)

A2.4   Reading: Language and time patterns: The Bantu case

Cultural and linguistic unity of the Bantu area

The Bantu area spreads along the southern side of a line which starts from Douala, Cameroon, by the Atlantic Ocean, and finishes at the mouth of the Tana river in the Indian Ocean. It divides northern and southern Africa. The Bantu area covers most of the southern cone of this continent.

These wide territories (several million square kilometres) are occupied by Bantu people, with the limited exceptions of some other small ethnic groups. The cultural unity of this people has been established on the basis of common linguistic features. As early as the middle of the nineteenth century, W. Bleek (quoted by Kadima and Lumwanu, 1989) had recognized that Bantu languages shared common lexical elements and many grammatical forms. In taking Bleek's work one stage further, anthropologists, historians and linguists have tried to identify the common social and cultural traits which allow a particular area to be classified as Bantu.

Alexis Kagame (1975), for instance, has studied Bantu linguistic systems, especially their underlying structures. He has collated what he terms 'compared Bantu philosophy'. The convergence of authors when describing the conception of time in Bantu cultures is quite marked.

The unification of time and space

At the heart of the Bantu's intuition of time lies the postulate of a very close relation between time and space. Within this postulate none of these basic dimensions of reality exist without the others. Alexis Kagame reveals this conceptual link.

Ontologically, Bantu culture puts into one of four categories whatever may be conceived or said.

1. The being – of intelligence (man).
2. The being – without intelligence (thing).
3. The being – as localizer (be it place or date).
4. The being – modal (incidentality, or modification of the being).

The major assumption made by Kagame is that translation of Bantu words in metaphysical categories is possible. He therefore translates *ha-ntu* by the being-localizer. This common word expresses the unity of space (place) and time (date). In the Bantu language this term means both the 'there' of locus and the 'now' of time. It is an indivisible localizer, both spatial and temporal.

The localizing prefix *ha-*, which forms *ha-ntu*, and its variants *pa-ntu* and *ka-ntu* are found in the eastern zone of the Bantu territory. Its equivalent in the western zone is *va*, whereas it is *go* in the southeastern part of the Bantu area. The idea of unification between space and time in Bantu languages is shared by Emil Pearson, who has lived in the southeast of Angola since the 1920s. He writes in his book *People of the Aurora* (1977, p. 75):

> In the Ngangela language there is no word, as far as I know, for 'time' as a continuous, flowing passage of events or the lack of same. Time is experiential or objective, that is, it is that which is meaningful to the person or thing which experiences it. *Time and space are cognate incidents of eternity*. The same word is used for both 'time' and 'space' (the latter in the sense of 'distance').
>
> 'Ntunda' can either express meaningful time or meaningful space. For example: 'Ntunda kua i li' – 'There is some distance'; and 'Ntunda i na hiti' – 'Time has passed'. The related verb 'Simbula', means 'delay', the thought being of awaiting 'meaningful time'. To the European the African may seem to be idling away useful time, whereas the latter, according to his philosophy, is awaiting experiential time, the time that is right for accomplishing his objective. 'Time' is locative, something that is virtually concrete, not something abstract. The

locatives 'Ha', 'Ku' and 'Mu' are used for expressing 'time' as well as 'place'. Example: 'Ha Katete' – 'In the beginning' (as to either time or place); 'Ku lutue' can mean either 'in front' or 'in the future'. 'Mu nima' can mean 'behind' as to place, or 'after' as to time.

Bantu time experience

Two significant points sharply contrast the way Bantus experience time with the western way of experiencing it within a technological environment. First, Bantus have no theoretical substantive to designate time as an entity *per se*, which can be quantified and measured. Second, for Bantus, the temporal dimension is intrinsic to the event itself. It is not an abstraction as in most Occidental developed cultures. To these cultures it appears as a content which flows regularly from the past to the future, through the present; a flow in which everything moves at the same speed, being 'in time'. For Bantu peoples time has no real value, no meaning, without the occurrence of an event which will serve as a 'marker'. The intuition of time only becomes effective when an action or an event happens: warriors' expedition, arrival of the train, rainfall, starvation on the increase. Time then becomes individualized. It is drawn out of anonymity. It is not anybody's time which would be abstractedly defined. It is concrete time concerning people I know. Instead of considering time as a straight railway track, where events may happen successively, it will only be spoken of as 'the time of this . . .' or 'the time of that . . .', or time which is favourable for this and that. That is why, on many occasions, there is no point in giving dates, that is to refer oneself to ideal time coordinates. History is not a series of dates, but a link between various events. Everything possesses its own internal time. Each event occurs at its own time.

(Source: Usunier and Napoleon-Biguma (1991), pp. 95–114. Reproduced with the kind permission of the publisher and the co-author.)

A2.5   Exercise: World picture test

Objective

To clarify participants' understanding of countries and cultures of the world through their knowledge of geography.

- ◆ *Participants*: Three or more persons. Facilitator.
- ◆ *Materials*: Paper and pens.
- ◆ *Setting*: No special requirements.
- ◆ *Time*: At least thirty minutes to one hour.

Procedure

1. Each participant is given a sheet of paper and a pen and asked to:
   (a) draw a map of the world as best they can within a five minute time period
   (b) name as many of the countries as they can
   (c) checkmark any country they have visited for a week or longer

    (d) exchange papers with other members of the group and discuss what differences are evidenced in what the other person put into their drawing and/or left out of the drawing.

2. Discuss the following points:

    (a) Does a person's awareness of the shape of a country reveal that person's awareness of the shape of the culture?

    (b) When a person leaves out a country, what does this mean?

    (c) When a person leaves out a continent, what does this mean?

    (d) What country did the person place in the centre of the map and what does that mean?

    (e) When a person draws a country out of place in relation to other countries, what does this mean?

    (f) Were they better acquainted with countries they had visited?

    (g) When the person objects violently to doing the drawing, what does that mean?

    (h) How well did persons draw home countries of other group members?

    (i) What do the persons plan to do as a result of what they learned in this exercise?

(Source: Weeks *et al.*, 1987, pp. 107–8. Reproduced with the kind permission of the publisher.)

Notes

1. This aphorism (my translation) is attributed to the Swedish writer Selma Lagerlöf by Karl Petit (1960, p. 100). Selma Lagerlöf is the author of, among other works, *Gösta Berling* (1957), Editions Je sers: Paris, a unique account of the Swedish soul.

2. The concept of time, and therefore of time-related behaviour, has been studied in numerous fields (Jacoby *et al.*, 1976; Feldman and Hornik, 1981). Contributions are to be found in such diverse disciplines as psychology, economics, sociology, theology, linguistics, mathematics, physics, literature and anthropology.

3. In the real world nationality laws are much more complicated and, in many cases, combine the two basic inspirations, kin and soil, as relevant criteria for being awarded nationality.

4. Reischauer's book is now published under the title *Japan: The story of a nation*. The text has been updated since it was first published as *Japan: Past and present*, and the ideas about the consequences of the Tokugawa period on Japanese behaviour are no longer to be found in the new version, perhaps because they were resented by Japanese readers. Even distant historical events and periods may still be controversial nowadays, when different interpretations are at stake.

5. See ch. 5 of Segall *et al.* (1990, pp. 93–112), which asks 'Are there racial differences in cognition?' and which offers an in-depth review of the empirical studies of the difference in intellectual performance across ethnic groups.

6. Mauviel remarks that numerous studies have been dedicated to immigrant populations as such, but little research is concerned with the relations between the native lower-class population and the immigrant communities (this is true of France, and probably many other countries). This explains why we know little about cultural hostility, which has been more or less taboo as a research topic, probably because of the fear that unveiling somewhat negative attitudes could encourage their expression. This taboo is especially strong in countries with a significant

colonial history (the United Kingdom, France, the Netherlands), which explains a certain feeling of guilt.
7. The rationales behind the alternative explanations for A2.1, A2.2 and A2.3 can be found in section A3.3.

References

Allen, David E. (1971), 'Anthropological insights into consumer behaviour', *European Journal of Marketing*, vol. 5, no. 3, pp. 45–57.

Amine, Lyn S. and S. Tamer Cavusgil (1986), 'Demand estimation in a developing country environment: difficulties, techniques and examples', *Journal of the Market Research Society*, vol. 28, no. 5, pp. 43–65.

Attali, Jacques (1982), *Histoires du Temps*, Librairie Arthème Fayard: Paris.

Brislin, Richard W., Kenneth Cushner, Craig Cherrie and Mahealani Yong (1986), *Intercultural Interactions: A practical guide*, Sage: Newbury Park, CA.

Darbelet, Michel and Jean-Marcel Lauginié (1988), *Economie d'Entreprise*, vol. I, Editions Foucher: Paris.

Dayan, Armand, Jérôme Bon, Alain Cadix, Renaud de Maricourt, Christian Michon and Alain Ollivier (1988), *Marketing*, Collection PUF Fondamental, Presses Universitaires de France: Paris.

El Haddad, Awad B. (1985), 'An analysis of the current status of marketing in the Middle East', in Erdener Kaynak (ed.), *International Business in the Middle East*, de Gruyter: New York, pp. 177–97.

Feldman, Lawrence P. and Jacob Hornik (1981), 'The use of time: an integrated conceptual model', *Journal of Consumer Research*, vol. 7, March, pp. 407–19.

Ferraro, Gary P. (1990), *The Cultural Dimension of International Business*, Prentice Hall: Englewood Cliffs, NJ.

Goodenough, Ward H. (1971), *Culture, Language and Society*, Modular Publications, no. 7, Addison-Wesley, Reading, MA.

Graham, Robert J. (1981), 'The role of perception of time in consumer research', *Journal of Consumer Research*, vol. 7, March, pp. 335–42.

Gurevitch, A.J. (1976), 'Time as a problem of cultural history', in L. Gardner *et al.* (eds), *Cultures and Time: At the crossroads of cultures*, Unesco Press: Paris.

Hall, Edward T. (1959), *The Silent Language*, Doubleday: New York.

Hall, Edward T. (1966), *The Hidden Dimension*, Doubleday: New York.

Hall, Edward T. (1976), *Beyond Culture*, Anchor Press/Doubleday: Garden City, NY.

Hall, Edward T. (1983), *The Dance of Life*, Anchor Press / Doubleday: New York.

Harris, Philip R, and Robert T. Moran (1987), *Managing Cultural Differences*, 2nd edn, Gulf Publishing Company: Houston, Tx.

Hayashi, Shuji (1988), *Culture and Management in Japan*, Tokyo: University of Tokyo Press.

Hofstede, Geert (1980), *Culture's Consequences: International differences in work-related values*, Sage: Beverly Hills, CA.

Ishihara, Shintaro (1991), *The Japan that Can Say No*, Simon & Schuster: New York.

Jacoby, Jacob, George J. Szybillo and Carol K. Berning (1976), 'Time and consumer behavior: an interdisciplinary overview', *Journal of Consumer Research*, vol. 2, pp. 320–39.

Kadima, K. and F. Lumwanu (1989), 'Aires linguistiques à l'intérieur du monde Bantu: Aspects généraux et innovations, dialectologie et classifications', in Théophile Obenga (ed.), *Les Peuples Bantu, migrations, expansion et identité culturelle*, Editions L'Harmattan: Paris, pp. 63–75.

Kagame, Alexis (1975), 'Aperception empirique du temps et conception de l'histoire dans la pensée Bantu', In *Les cultures et le temps*, Payot/Unesco: Paris, pp. 103–33.

Kluckhohn, Florence R. and Frederick L. Strodtbeck (1961), *Variations in Value Orientations*, Greenwood Press: Westport, CT.

Kotler, Philip (1994), *Marketing Management*, 8th edn, Prentice Hall: Englewood Cliffs. N.J.

Lane, Paul M. and Carol Felker Kaufman (1992), 'The United States chases time; Europeans pursue life: A cross-cultural comparison of perceived time', *Proceedings of the first Conference on the Cultural Dimension of International Marketing*, Odense, pp. 1–18.

Lazer, William, Shoji Murata and Hiroshi Kosaka (1985), 'Japanese marketing: Towards a better understanding', *Journal of Marketing*, vol. 49 (Spring), pp. 69–81.

Maalouf, Amine (1985), *The Crusades through Arab Eyes*, Schocken Books: New York.

Mauviel, Maurice (1991), 'La Grande Misère de l'antiracisme français', *Intercultures*, no. 12, January, pp. 69–82.

Montesquieu, Charles de (1748), *The Spirit of Laws*, translated from the French by Thomas Nugent (1792), 6th edn, McKenzie and Moore: Dublin.

Pearson, Emil (1977), *People of the Aurora*, Beta Books: San Diego.

Petit, Karl (1960), *Dictionnaire de citations*, Marabout: Verviers, Belgium.

Reischauer, Edwin O. (1946), *Japan: Past and present*, Alfred A. Knopf: New York.

Reischauer, Edwin O. (1990), *Japan: The story of a nation*, 4th edn, McGraw-Hill: New York.

Segall, Marshall H., Pierre R. Dasen, John W. Berry and Ype H. Poortinga (1990), *Human Behavior in Global Perspective*, Pergamon: New York.

Sherry, John F. Jr and Eduardo G. Camargo (1987), ' "May your life be marvellous:" English language labelling and the semiotics of Japanese promotion', *Journal of Consumer Research*, vol. 14 (September), pp. 174–88.

Sorokin, Piritim and Robert Merton (1937) 'Social time: A methodological and functional analysis', *American Journal of Sociology*, vol. 42, pp. 615–29.

Triandis, Harry C. (1983), 'Dimensions of cultural variation as parameters of organizational theories', *International Studies of Management and Organization*, vol. XII, no. 4, pp. 139–69.

Triandis, Harry C. (1994), *Culture and Social Behavior*, McGraw-Hill: New York.

Trompenaars, Fons (1993), *Riding the Waves of Culture*, Nicholas Brealey: London.

Usunier, J.-C. (1991), 'Business time perceptions and national cultures: A comparative survey', *Management International Review*, vol. 31, no. 3, pp. 197–217.

Usunier, J.-C. and Constantin Napoleon-Biguma (1991), 'Gestion culturelle du temps: le cas bantu', in Frank Gauthey and Dominique Xardel (eds), *Management interculturel: Modes et modèles*, Economica: Paris.

Usunier, J.-C. and P. Valette-Florence (1994), 'Perceptual time patterns ("Time styles"): A psychometric scale,' *Time and Society*, vol. 3, no. 2, pp. 219–41.

Van Raaij, W.F. (1978), 'Cross-cultural methodology as a case of construct validity,' in M. K. Hunt (ed.), *Advances in Consumer Research*, Association for Consumer Research: Ann Arbor, vol. 5, pp. 693–701.

Walsh, Len (1969), *Read Japanese Today*, Charles E. Tuttle: Rutland, VT, and Tokyo.

Weeks, William H., Paul B. Pedersen and Richard W. Brislin (1987), *A Manual of Structured Experiences for Cross-cultural Learning*, Intercultural Press: Yarmouth, ME.

Yan, Chen (1991), 'L'Europe vue par l'empire du milieu', *Intercultures*, no 12, January, pp. 45–56.

3

♦♦♦

Cultural dynamics 2: Interactions, mindsets and behaviours

Let us start with this short excerpt from Adam Smith in the *Wealth of Nations*, where he comments about the 'Education of youth' (1776, 1976, p. 286):

> 'If the teacher happens to be a man of sense, it must be an unpleasant thing to him to be conscious, while he is lecturing his students, that he is either speaking or reading nonsense, or what is very little better than nonsense. It must too be unpleasant to him to observe that the greater part of his students desert his lectures; or perhaps attend upon them with plain enough marks of neglect, contempt, and derision. If he is obliged, therefore, to give a certain number of lectures, these motives alone, without any other interest, might dispose him to take some pains to give tolerably good ones.'

This text seems to be marked by common sense and its conclusion appears indisputable. However, my objective is that, after reading this chapter, you may cite some reasons, based on culture, why such a teacher as the one imagined by Adam Smith may perfectly survive, although many students have left his class. There are few domains where cultural relativity is as strong as in education and teaching.

This chapter complements the previous one. Figure 2.1 showed that, among the basic cultural assumptions, some were related to cultural models of time, others to space, which in turn influence the dominant profile in terms of concept of the self and others. The first section in this chapter is dedicated to concepts of the self and others. They are central to the explanation of how people interact (section 3.2) and thus, finally, which attitudes people develop towards action (sections 3.3 to 3.6; 3.3 on why and how to act; 3.4 about relating thinking to action; 3.5 on wishes and feelings as they relate to action, and 3.6 on coping with rules). Once again, it is all organized around common problems, explained in the three tables (3.1 to 3.3) which relate to Figure 2.1. The last section in the chapter (3.7) discusses how basic cultural assumptions translate into everyday behaviour, especially in the work environment.

3.1   Concept of the self and others

The concept of the self and others does not relate directly to how a society is organized. It deals with how the organization of a society is internalized by people and reflected in the view that they hold of themselves in comparison with others. It is largely about people within a society having responded positively and unconsciously to membership conditions, and thus being largely unaware of those conditions that were necessary for becoming an 'appropriate' member of the society. In fact, men and women, children and older people have basic assumptions about the why and how of their presence in this society, and these assumptions differ across societies.

The concept of the self is a kind of modal view of what people *are* in the society and therefore what they are allowed to *do*. Basic assumptions are related to the main sociodemographic categories (age, sex, social class), but also to idealized conducts in particular roles (the perfect man, businessman, child, etc.). The ideal patterns are shown by books, films, possibly TV series, or any other kind of cultural artefacts that conveys

Table 3.1 *Concepts of the self and others*

Basic problem / cultural orientations	Contrasts across cultures
How should we treat unknown people? (a) Is human nature basically good or bad?	Unknown people are considered favourably and shown confidence or, conversely, they are treated with suspicion when met for the first time.
Appraising others (b) When appraising others, emphasis placed on: (i) age (ii) sex (iii) social class	Who are the persons to be considered trustworthy and reliable, with whom it is possible to do business? (i) Older (younger) people are seen more favourably (ii) Trustworthiness is based on sex or not (iii) Social class play a significant role (or not) in concepts of the self and others
Appraising oneself (c) Emphasis placed on the self-concept perceived as culturally appropriate: (i) self-esteem: low/high (ii) perceived potency: low/high (iii) level of activity: low/high	To give the correct appearance one should behave: – Shyly and modestly v. extrovert or even arrogant – Power should be shown v. hidden – Busy people are the good ones v. unoccupied/idle people are well considered
Relating the individual to the group (d) Individualism versus collectivism	The individual is seen as the basic resource and therefore individual-related values are strongly emphasized (personal freedom, human rights, equality between men and women); versus the group is seen as the basic resource and therefore group values favoured (loyalty, sense of belonging, sense of personal sacrifice for the community, etc.).

subliminal normative messages. Only watching movie films, we have an abundance of identification possibilities from Eliott Ness in *The Untouchables*, to Clyde Barrow in *Bonnie and Clyde*, or to the Sioux–white squaw in *Dances with Wolves*, etc. Doing this, we constantly collect messages on how to behave. We find heroes to be desirable models. Naturally most people have a certain degree of realism and they do know in fact that they are not their heroes. The concept of the self has major implications in the area of consumer behavior (Belk, 1988): our possessions are a major contributor to and reflector of our identities; by ascribing meaning to what we buy and consume, our possessions become the means by which we strive to assert, complete, or attain our 'ideal' self (Wong and Ahuvia, 1995).

Table 3.1 presents major categories in the area of concepts of the self and others.

Human nature: good or bad?

A basic assumption about *innate* human nature is whether it is good, evil or neutral, that is, subject to both good and negative influences. This combines further with the view that this basic nature may or may not be changeable. Indicative of these hidden assumptions (people are largely unaware of it), are attitudes at first contact. A friendly and open-minded attitude towards people whom one does not know is a good indicator of the assumption that innate human nature is good. When visiting the United States, Europeans are often amazed by how well they are received by people with whom they have never been in contact before. Although this cannot be explained solely by human nature assumptions, it is clear that there is a strong positive belief in the American mentality towards new people: they are viewed as basically good and able to improve themselves by education and commitment (human nature is also seen as changeable). One may interpret this as having a functional side in relatively new countries: Western movie films describe, on average, 'bad' Indians and 'good' European settlers. The assumptions of human nature orientation are fairly straightforward: 'civilized' = good; 'uncivilized' (indians, gamblers, desperados) = bad.

In contrast, the Latin Europeans and South Americans do not start from similar premises, which makes them more difficult at first contact. The novels of the Colombian writer Gabriel Garcia Marquez are typical of a view where human nature is basically bad. Novels reflect a view of what is basically human nature for a definite people. But the complete assumptions about human nature are of a dialectic nature (they include the inverse proposition and prepare a totality); they would read more as:

♦ Human nature is basically good, but . . .
♦ Human nature is basically bad, but . . .
♦ Human nature lies somewhere between good and bad, and . . .

The two sides of each basic assumption coexist in most religions, which strive at improving individuals, especially through the social morals that they develop. We need to have some reference points to evaluate others. They are largely culture-based.

The dynamics of friendship are necessarily related to human nature assumptions. If assumed good, then friendship proceeds quickly, but is not necessarily very profound:

social classes are important for consumer behaviour, people expressing their class differences, real or fantasized, by consumption.

Social stratification is based on somewhat different criteria across cultures. Castes are a special kind of social stratification, which, in the case of India consists in four major hereditary classes: the *Brahman, Kshatriya, Vaisya* and *Sudra*, into which the Hindu society is divided. Social classes, and social stratification in general, exist consistently across cultures, thus probably the success of Marxism for quite a long period of time. But the degree of emphasis on social stratification varies across societies, thus, perhaps, the differential success of Marxist and communist regimes across countries. In countries where emphasis is strong, people in higher classes, appraise themselves as *being substantially different* from others, in lower classes. This can go as far as speaking the language differently (or even a different language), prohibiting inter-class marriages, distinguishing oneself by specific tastes and lifestyles. Bista (1990, p. 79) describes the Hindu caste system in the following terms:

> . . . one has to engage in activities that are appropriate to one's caste. Those whose fate is to be workers continue to work, but this work does not necessarily lead to any form of result or reward. The caste principle admonishes that actions have to be without desire, i.e. without a goal. There is a purpose to action, but it is a purpose known only to a supernatural agency. Individual aspirations are inconsequential and behaviour is submissive to a controlling force that is unknown. Learned Hindus emphasize that the material world is *maya*, an illusion, and claim that this is not worth taking seriously.

Appraising oneself

People hold a certain view of themselves, and prefer spontaneously to choose the one which will be perceived as culturally appropriate by others in the ingroup. Triandis (1983) distinguishes three main areas of cultural contrasts. The first is self-esteem which can be low or high according to whether a person thinks of himself or herself as good or not too good. Low self-esteem results in showing a modest and effaced behaviour, whereas higher self-esteem results in showing more assertiveness and self-assurance. Asians, on average, are clearly on the low self-esteem side, compared with Westerners. The reader must be cautious when interpreting these sentences: this is only a standard assumption dictated by culture; it does not mean that Asians deserve less esteem but rather that they assume that they deserve less.

The second contrast in self-concept is perceived potency, that is, to what extent people view themselves as powerful and able to accomplish almost any task or to exercise power. The French proverb *'Impossible n'est pas français'* is a typical high-perceived-potency saying. Where the appropriate level of personal activity is seen as high, people will boast about their being 'workaholics', work on weekends, and generally be satisfied with overwork. When on the contrary the appropriate image of the self is based on a low level of activity, as in the Hindu case quoted above, few hours spent in office, low involvement in work-related issues, having time available for pure inactivity will be standard attributes of a normal self-concept.

Individualism and collectivism: A first note

These are mentioned in Figure 2.1, in the box 'concept of the self and others', because my belief is that they are deeply ingrained in our view of what are the 'borders' of our self. Individualists have a more clear-cut view of where 'oneself' stops ('I, me, mine' as John Lennon's song says) and where 'others' start, whereas collectivist persons have much more fuzzy borders between their self and the near others. The common problem, across all societies, is how persons and the groups they belong to should be coordinated properly for smooth and efficient functioning.

The 'rice argument' is frequently advanced for explaining the differences between individualism and collectivism. Rice culture needs the coordinated flooding of rice fields which promotes dependence among the group members and requires common action. Conversely, the basic staples in the West would be based on 'individualist' cereals (wheat, barley, oats, etc.), where the farmer's achievements depend mostly on his or her own individual efforts.

Individualism is based on the principle of asserting one's independence and individuality. All societies have individuals and groups, but *individualism* stresses the smallest unit as being that where the solution lies. Individualist assumptions are the following:

1. It is at the level of individuals that initiative, effort and achievements can best be developed, because people are separated and *different* (divisibility).
2. Individual achievements can be added to each other without loss (the sum equals the parts: additive model).
3. Therefore, society has to maximize individual freedom, emphasize achieving individuals, value persons (freedom orientation).

These assumptions are not necessarily 'true'. One may subscribe to them because of intellectual conviction, especially for 1, or for getting personal leeway, as is the consequence of assumption 3. They are 'true' to the extent that they are largely a self-fulfilling prophecy. The obvious problems arises from assumption 2: collective action is, generally, not the direct result of simply adding individual deeds. The process is more complex, and this brings grist to the collectivist mill, which displays the following assumptions:

4. It is at group level, and not at the individual level, that initiative, effort and achievements can best be developed, because people are not really separate from each other; they belong to a *common* reality (organic view).
5. Collective achievements are fundamentally different in nature from individual achievements, and the combination of parts (if such a computation is even possible) is much greater than the parts themselves (multiplicative model).
6. Therefore, society has to maximize group coherence, social harmony, even at the expense of individual freedom, and if need be, by downsizing individual achievements (concord orientation).

Collectivism is associated to 'traditional culture' whereas individualism is a strong component of 'modern culture', especially in the area of consumption, a splendid domain for enjoying individual freedom and expressing difference from others. Belk (1985), for instance, notes that, since the Middle Ages, the awareness of self has become less shared and more individualistic, this being evidenced by the growing popularity of self-oriented objects such as mirrors, self-portraits, chairs (rather than benches), etc.

Modern individualism takes its roots in sixteenth and seventeeth century England, based on English philosophers (Moore, Bacon, Hume, Locke) and operationalized by the 'habeas corpus', the first legal edict forbidding the Sovereign to jail somebody without lawful reason. This was furthered by the French *Déclaration des droits de l'homme et du citoyen*, in 1789. The French were only followers of the English, but they have been good exporters of the concept of human rights, even though neither the English nor the French practised them all the time, especially in their colonies. The United Nations Universal Declaration of Human Rights is in the same vein: it favours an individual-based view of what is a 'good' society. The individualist view of human rights is typical of Amnesty International, which has hot debates with some Asian governments, who maintain, rightly, that they hold a different view of what human rights are.

The individualist/collectivist divide is a strong but not a simple difference. In individualist societies, people still belong to groups, live in community and conceive of themselves as integrated to a larger whole. In collectivist societies, people still feel a need to express their personal identity, and strive often for individual success and self-actualization. Thus, what differs fundamentally is the initial assumptions.

The 'modern' aspect of individualist assumptions is now heavily challenged by the rise of collectivist nations, in Asia and in South America, and their achievements in international trade and their high rate of economic growth at home. The debate between individualism and collectivism is not yet finished: they are a little bit like water and oil, not really mixable, apparently mixed when one shakes strongly, but separating afterwards.

3.2   Interaction models

Individualism and collectivism refer to concepts of the self and others (as assumptions located *within* persons) as well as to a model of interaction *between* people. Table 3.2 lists a series of other aspects of what is considered as culturally appropriate interaction models in particular societies. Most of these interaction categories are based on Hofstede (1980a, 1980b). Although Hofstede developed these concepts in relation to organizational issues and through data collection at the corporate level, they are largely transferrable to the society as a whole. A large number of publications are devoted to the impact of cultural differences on management and organization (that is, *within* companies). The impact of national cultures has been assessed on various issues such as structure, hierarchical relationships, management of expatriate personel and variation in motivation patterns across cultures (see, for instance, Hofstede, 1980b; Laurent, 1983; Adler, 1991). These issues are clearly outside the principal remit of this book, which is to consider the interaction of companies with their environment, that is, markets, customers, distribution channels or various influential groups (consumer movements, regulatory authorities, etc.). Nevertheless a summary of the advances made in cultural differences and organization studies is worthwhile for two reasons at least. First, Hofstede's four dimensions of national cultures, although they have been measured for management and organization practices, also make sense for marketing and sales. Second, many issues in this book are on the fringes of marketing management and organizational issues: sales force stimulation, business negotiation or the global marketing strategies and for consumer behaviour issues, in particular decision making. The stability of these dimensions across replications has been shown (Sondergaard, 1994), and they have now been used extensively in cross-cultural studies in international marketing.

National cultures and the relativity of managerial practices

The cover story of an issue of *Fortune* magazine accurately features the difficult question of the transposability of management styles: it shows an American with slanting eyes eating (or, more probably, trying to eat) a hamburger with chopsticks. Geert Hofstede

Table 3.2   *Interaction models*

Cultural orientations	Contrasts across cultures
Equality or inequality in interpersonal interactions (a) Power Distance (PD)	Hierarchy is strong, power is centralized at the top (high PD); power is more equally distributed and superior and subordinates have a sense of equality as human beings (low PD)
Interacting *with* others or *for* others (b) Masculinity versus Femininity	Assertiveness and personal achievement are favoured (masc.) versus caring for others, adopting nurturing roles and emphasizing quality of life (fem.)
Dealing with uncertainty (c) Uncertainty avoidance (UA)	Tendency to avoid risks (high UA), to prefer stable situations, uncertainty-reducing rules and risk-free procedures, which are seen as a necessity for efficiency. Or, conversely, a risk-prone attitude (low UA) where people as individuals are seen as the engine of change, which is perceived as a requirement for efficiency
Relying on oneself or on others (d) Self-reliance versus dependence	Do people rely on their own forces, find motivation and control within themselves (self-reliance) or do they need to find outside support, motivation and control from their environment (dependence)?
Developing appropriate communication with others (e) Communication styles	See Chapter 12 on 'Language, Culture and Communication'

was one of the first researchers to question the adaptability of US management theories and practices to other cultural contexts. Empirical studies for Hofstede's work were undertaken between 1967 and 1973 within a large multinational company, in 66 of its national subsidiaries. The database contains more than 116,000 questionnaires: all categories of personnel were interviewed, from ordinary workers to general managers. Out of 150 questions, 60 deal with the values and beliefs of the respondents on issues related to motivation, hierarchy, leadership, well-being in the organization, etc. The questionnaire was administered in two successive stages (1967–69 and 1971–73) so as to verify validity by replication. Versions of the questionnaire were drafted in twenty different languages. Not all subsidiaries are included in the final analysis; depending on the data under review, 40–55 countries are finally comparable. The results drawn from these data were further validated by a systematic comparison with the results of thirteen other studies (Hofstede, 1980b, 1983).

Interviewees all belonged to the same multinational corporation, IBM, which has a very strong corporate culture shared by its employees. Consequently there was no variance on this dimension across the sample. Each national sample allowed for a similar representation of age groups, sex and categories of personnel, thereby avoiding a potential source of variance across national subsidiaries' results. Finally the only source of variance was the difference in national cultures and mentalities. Hofstede, by means of factor analysis of the respondents' scores, was able to derive four main conceptual dimensions on which national cultures exhibit significant differences. One of these four dimensions is *individualism/collectivism*, which we have already mentioned in the previous section. In collectivist countries there is a close-knit social structure, where people neatly distinguish between members of the ingroup and members of the outgroup. They expect their group to care for them in exchange for unwavering loyalty. In individualistic societies, social fabric is much looser: people are basically supposed to care for themselves and their immediate family. Exchange takes place on the base of reciprocity: if an individual gives something to another, some sort of return is expected within a reasonable time lag. The three others are explained below. They correspond to the first three cells in Table 3.2.

Power distance

This measures to what extent a society and its individual members tolerate an unequal distribution of power in organizations and in society as a whole (see Box 3.1). It is shown as much by the behavioural values of superiors who display their power and exercise it, as by the behavioural values of subordinates who wait for their superiors to show their status and power, and are uncomfortable if they do not personally experience it. In low power distance societies, members of the organization tend to feel equal, close to each other in their daily work relationships: when the real hierarchical distance is high, power may be delegated. In high power distance societies, superiors and subordinates feel separated from each other; it is not easy to meet and talk with higher ranking people, and the real power tends to be very much concentrated at the top. At society level, power distance translates as shown in Box 3.1.

Box 3.1 *More equal than others*

In a peaceful revolution – the last revolution in Swedish history – the nobles of Sweden in 1809 deposed King Gustav IV whom they considered incompetent, and surprisingly invited Jean Baptiste Bernadotte, a French general who served under their enemy Napoleon, to become King of Sweden. Bernadotte accepted and he became King Charles XIV; his descendants occupy the Swedish throne to this day. When the new King was installed he addressed the Swedish parliament in their language. His broken Swedish amused the Swedes and they roared with laughter. The Frenchman who had become King was so upset that he never tried to speak Swedish again. In this incident Bernadotte was a victim of culture shock: never in his French upbringing and military career had he experienced subordinates who laughed at the mistakes of their superior. Historians tell us he had more problems adapting to the egalitarian Swedish and Norwegian mentality (he later became King of Norway as well) and to his subordinates' constitutional rights. He was a good learner, however (except for language), and he ruled the country as a highly respected constitutional monarch until 1844.

One of the aspects in which Sweden differs from France is the way its society handles *inequality*. There is inequality in any society. Even in the most simple hunter-gatherer band, some people are bigger, stronger or smarter than others.The next thing is that some people have more power than others: they are more able to determine the behaviour of others than vice-versa. Some people are given more status and respect than others.

(Source: Hofstede, 1991. Reproduced with the publisher's permission.)

Masculinity/femininity

Individualism should not be equated with selfishness. When responding to the common problem: 'do we interact *with* others or *for* others?', responses are made on the basis of dominant value systems, which would roughly correspond to male/assertive versus female/nurturing roles. A society is masculine when dominant values favour assertiveness, earning money, showing off possessions and caring little for others. Conversely, feminine societies favour nurturing roles, interdependence between people and caring *for* others (who are seen as worth caring for, because they are temporarily weak). This dimension has been so-called because, on average, men tended to score high on one extreme and women on the other, whatever the society.

In typically feminine societies, such as the northern European countries, the welfare system is highly developed, education is largely free and easily accessible, and there is openness to admit that people may have problems: patience and helpfulness are shown to those who are in trouble; both boys and girls learn to be modest and to have sympathy for the underdog. In typically masculine societies, whether individualist like the United States or collectivist like Japan, weaker people find, on average, less support from the society at large; people learn to admire the strong, as Rambo in the United States. The common problem behind the masculinity/femininity divide could perhaps be phrased differently from what I have written above: should we help people (at the risk of their being weakened by a lack of personal effort) or shouldn't we help people (at the risk for them of being even worse)? Obviously, the response is not easy.

Uncertainty avoidance

A common problem faced by people in any society is how to deal with uncertainty. There are basically two ways: the first is based on the assumption that people have to deal with uncertainty, because it is in the very nature of the situations we face. The future is by definition unknown, but risks can be evaluated, and people and institutions can manage them. The other extreme is marked by risk aversion, which results in the assumption that uncertainty is bad and everything in society must be made so as to reduce uncertainty.

The dimension of uncertainty avoidance measures the extent to which people in a society tend to feel threatened by uncertain, ambiguous, risky or undefined situations. Where uncertainty avoidance is high, organizations promote stable careers, produce rules and procedures, etc. 'Nevertheless societies in which uncertainty avoidance is strong are also characterized by a higher level of anxiety and aggressiveness that creates, among other things, a strong inner urge to work hard' (Hofstede, 1980a). Hofstede outlines that 'uncertainty avoidance should not be confused with risk avoidance . . . even more than reducing risk, uncertainty avoidance leads to a reduction of *ambiguity*' (1991, p. 116).

The cultural relativity of management theories

Table 3.3 shows the value of these dimensions for fifty-three countries/regions. Figure 3.1 presents a diagrammatic map of countries when individualism and power distance are combined. Hofstede's main tenet concerns the *cultural relativity of management theories*. These theories are rooted in the cultural context where they were developed, therefore any simple direct transposition is difficult. For motivation, Hofstede shows the linkage which exists between US-based motivation theories and American culture. For instance, Abraham Maslow's 'hierarchy of needs' and McClelland's theory of the achievement motive are directly related to two dimensions of US culture: its strong masculinity and its individualism. People are seen as being motivated in an overtly conscious manner by the expectancy of some kind of results from their acts: they are basically motivated by extrinsic reasons and rewards. In contrast, Freudian theory, which has not been greatly applied by US management theorists, represents the individual as being pushed by internal forces, often unconsciously, the id and the super-ego interacting with the ego. According to Hofstede, Austria, where Freud was born and where he drafted his theories, scores significantly higher than the United States on uncertainty avoidance and lower on individualism. This may explain why motivation is more related to internalized social values. 'Freud's superego acts naturally as an inner uncertainty-absorbing device, an internalized boss' (Hofstede, 1980a).

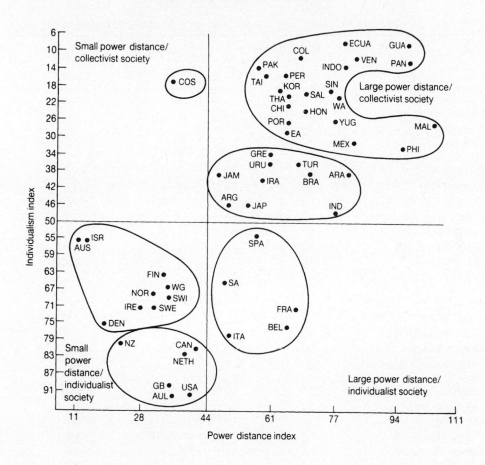

Figure 3.1 Map of fifty-three countries ranked on power distance and individualism indices. (Source: Hofstede, 1980b.)

Interaction clashes

As shown in Chapter 14, these differences have to be taken into account when designing sales force stimulation systems across national subsidiaries which have different cultural contexts. In masculine, individualistic countries, where there is also lower uncertainty avoidance, extrinsic rewards should be preferred (bonuses, gifts, holidays, monetary incentives). In societies which are more feminine, and/or more collectivist, and/or with higher uncertainty avoidance, intrinsic rewards should be chosen because they fit with profound inner values.

Hofstede also takes the example of the direct transposition of the American MBO (Management By Objectives) in France, where it became the DPPO (*Direction Partici-pative Par Objectifs*). MBO stems from a society where:

Table 3.3   *Values of Hofstede's cultural dimensions for 53 countries or regions*

Country/region	Power distance	Uncertainty avoidance	Individualism	Masculinity
Arabic countries (ARA)[a]	80	68	38	53
Argentina (ARG)	49	86	46	56
Australia (AUL)	36	51	90	61
Austria (AUS)	11	70	55	79
Belgium (BEL)	65	94	75	54
Brazil (BRA)	69	76	38	49
Canada (CAN)	39	48	80	52
Chile (CHI)	63	86	23	28
Colombia (COL)	67	80	13	64
Costa Rica (COS)	35	86	15	21
Denmark (DEN)	18	23	74	16
East African region (EA)[b]	64	52	27	41
Ecuador (ECUA)	78	67	8	63
Finland (FIN)	33	59	63	26
France (FRA)	68	86	71	43
Great Britain (GB)	35	35	89	66
Greece (GRE)	60	112	35	57
Guatemala (GUA)	96	101	6	37
Hong Kong (HON)	68	29	25	57
India (IND)	77	40	48	56
Indonesia (INDO)	78	48	14	46
Iran (IRA)	58	59	41	43
Ireland (IRE)	28	35	70	68
Israel (ISR)	13	81	54	47
Italy (ITA)	50	75	76	70
Jamaica (JAM)	45	13	39	68
Japan (JAP)	54	92	46	95
Malaysia (MAL)	104	36	26	50
Mexico (MEX)	81	82	30	69
Netherlands (NETH)	38	53	80	14
New Zealand (NZ)	22	49	79	58
Norway (NOR)	31	50	69	8
Pakistan (PAK)	55	70	14	50
Panama (PAN)	95	86	11	44
Peru (PER)	64	87	16	42
Philippines (PHI)	94	44	32	64
Portugal (POR)	63	104	27	31
Salvador (SAL)	66	94	19	40
Singapore (SIN)	74	8	20	48
South Africa (SA)	49	49	65	63
South Korea (KOR)	60	85	18	39

Table 3.3 *Continued*

Country/region	Dimensions			
	Power distance	Uncertainty avoidance	Individualism	Masculinity
Spain (SPA)	57	86	51	42
Sweden (SWE)	31	29	71	5
Switzerland (SWI)	34	58	68	70
Taiwan (TAI)	58	69	17	45
Thailand (THA)	64	64	20	34
Turkey (TUR)	66	85	37	45
United States (USA)	40	46	91	62
Uruguay (URU)	61	100	36	38
Venezuela (VEN)	81	76	12	73
West African region (WA)[c]	77	54	20	46
West Germany (WG)	35	65	67	66
Yugoslavia (former) (YUG)	76	88	27	21
Overall mean	57	65	43	49
Standard deviation	22	24	25	18

[a] Saudi Arabia, Egypt, United Arab Emirates, Iraq, Kuwait, Lebanon and Libya.
[b] Ethiopia, Kenya, Tanzania and Zambia.
[c] Ghana, Nigeria and Sierra Leone.

1. Subordinates are independent and feel sufficiently at ease with their bosses to negotiate meaningfully with them (low power distance).
2. Subordinates as well as superiors are willing to take risks (low uncertainty avoidance). The outcome is considered important by superiors and subordinates (high level of masculinity).

DPPO enjoyed brief success at the end of the 1960s but had become a flop by the mid-1970s. Indeed in the French cultural context DPPO created anxiety, in a country where hierarchy is traditionally strong (high power distance) and where that structure protects people against uncertainty. MBO assumes a depersonalized authority (role authority) whereas, according to Hofstede, from their childhood French people are used to high power distance and strongly personalized authority. Despite efforts to introduce Anglo-Saxon management methods, French bosses do not easily decentralize management and delegate authority.

In a study at Insead, reported by Hofstede, O. J. Stevens asked students of various nationalities to write their own diagnosis of and solution to a small case study about a conflict between the sales department and the product development department. The French saw the problem basically as one that the hierarchy should solve, a solution being sought from the chairperson. The Germans blamed the absence of formal rules and written procedures. The English saw the problem as resulting basically from a lack of interpersonal communication. Stevens concluded that 'the implicit model of the organization for most French was a pyramid (both centralized and formal); for German a well-oiled machine (formalized, but not centralized); and for most British a village market (neither formalized, nor centralized)' (Hofstede, 1980a, p. 60).

Organization types may be more adapted to some cultures than to others. In a matrix organization, for instance, there is a double hierarchical linkage (with a product division at the European level and a subsidiary general manager at the country level): this is not very well accepted by either the French or the Germans. For the French, it violates the principle of unity of commandment; for the Germans, it thwarts their need for organizational clarity and will not be deemed acceptable unless individual roles inside the organization are unambiguously defined.

Self-reliance versus dependence

Being self-reliant versus showing dependence has naturally to do with self-concept assumptions. For example, valuing elders in the community will tend to decrease the legitimacy of self-reliance among younger age groups. Similarly for sex: traditional sex roles promote dependence among women. Even social classes may have an influence in as much as an implied family model reigns over cross-class relationships, people in higher social classes behaving patronizingly towards those in lower classes. In industrial relations, for instance, the 'paternalist' orientation of factory owners towards their workers typifies the role of the boss as a father and the employees as 'children'.

Self-reliant people rely on their own forces, find motivation and control within themselves, whereas dependence implies that they need to find outside support, motivation and control from their environment. As summarized in Table 3.4, low power distance and uncertainty avoidance, combined with high individualism and masculinity will be related to more self-reliance (the US case; the best applicants for total contrasts being generally Latin countries like Chile, Portugal or Brazil, see Table 3.3). The typical Westerner is on average more self-reliant than the average Easterner. And the typical northern European is more self-reliant than the typical Latin European.

Two assumptions are central in developing self-reliance or dependence among individuals: (1) the locus-of control – whether a person considers that events are contingent upon his or her own behaviour or it is under the control of powerful, unpredictable and complex external forces; and (2) the implicit family role that is underlying typical interaction patterns.

The first basic issue in self-reliance versus dependence is whether people consider they are controlled from an external or an internal locus of control (Rotter, 1966). People with

Table 3.4

Hofstede's dimension	Influence on self-reliance/dependence
Individualism	Increases self-reliance
Power distance	Promotes dependence
Masculinity	Increases self-reliance
Uncertainty avoidance	Promotes dependence

internal locus-of-control will show more self-reliance, because they believe in their ability to manage their own world and to control it by themselves. The locus-of-control concept was not developed by Rotter in a cross-cultural perspective, but rather at an individual level. However, it applies fairly well as a contrasting dimension across cultures.

The second issue in dependence versus self-reliance is the kind of family role that a particular culture favours: in Latin societies, for instance, the parent/child relationship remains a very strong underlying model for interaction and even in situations which are normally assumed as being between equals, some people may unconsciously and spontaneously develop parental attitudes. In case of conflict the superior will easily develop an attitude of 'critical' parent (in the terms of Eric Berne's transactional analysis (Berne 1961, 1964)[1]), leaving little options for their counterparts, apart from behaving as a 'complying child' ('obeying'), or on the contrary, a 'rebel child', or finally exiting. Parent/adult underlying models of interactions clearly place many relationships in the realm of dependence: functional relationships will be based on a filial dependence, whereas dysfunctional relationship will be played in the conflict mode. For people who come from societies where self-reliance is standard behaviour, it is often extremely irritating not to be treated as an adult, equal in rights and obligations, but, symbolically, as a child. France is a good case in point: many aspects of the French culture favour dependence, with the major exception of a strong individualist orientation. This results in a pattern of varying dependence, where people constantly play a game of dispute and reconciliation in teamwork, where true self-reliance can only be fostered by creative activity and/or working independently.

3.3　Culture-based attitudes towards action

Action is about changing the world, even in a minuscule way. Large categories of actions do not involve any problem: they are repetitive and programmed; they are daily or seasonal routines. Non-routine tasks require a more complex course of action, because they involve problematic features:

1. They must be based on a clear sense of purpose (why act?).
2. They involve the future, largely unpredictable, that is risk taking.
3. They need input from the past (taking lessons from previous experience).
4. They imply to articulate collective and individual interests.
5. They need to 'relate the hand to the brain, the heart and the mouth'.

Expressed metaphorically, this last feature means that action (hand), in a cross-cultural perspective, can hardly be separated from how people think (brain), how they relate their wishes and desires to actions (located somewhere between brain, heart and mouth . . .), and how they mix feelings with deeds (located clearly in the heart, for most cultures). Table 3.5 details the main contrasts across cultures in terms of attitudes towards action.

Most marketing and managerial action displays the problematic features given above. They are non-routine tasks, especially in an international context. Individuals and

Table 3.5   *Attitudes towards action*

Basic problem / cultural orientations	Contrasts across cultures
Why to act? (a) Degree of fatalism: mastery of nature versus subjugation to nature; existence and degree of legitimacy of a Promethean (proactive) view of human life.	People believe that it is possible to cope with any problem or any situation and that, to mankind, nothing is impossible; evil is when one does nothing ('master of destiny'); versus the belief that there are many situations where people cannot do anything; destiny binds us and we should not try to find alternatives (fatalistic orientation); evil is when one does not accept one's own destiny (subjugation').
What is action? (b) 'speech' versus 'deed' orientation	Contrast between culture which value speech as action versus those which separate them/contrast between a clear sequencing of action versus a fuzzy view of action.
How to relate thinking to action (1) (c) Ideologism versus pragmatism	Ideologism: thinking patterns, communication (style of speech) and actions should always be set within the context of broad ideological principles (religious, political, social, legal, etc.); versus pragmatism: precise issues must be addressed; a practical attitude is favoured: orientation towards problem solving and concrete results.
How to relate thinking to action (2) (d) Intellectual styles	Differences in assigning a dominant role to theory, data, speech, modesty and virtue in assessing truthful propositions that need to be put into action.
How to relate wishes and desires to action (e) 'Wishful thinking' orientation (WT)	WT tends to emphasize enthusiasm, imagination of the future and the capacity of desires to *shape* reality; non-WT cultures emphasize the principle of reality: desires and wishes have to be checked objectively against the constraints of the real world.
How to relate feelings to action (f) Affective (A) versus neutral (N) cultures	People in N cultures separate feelings from actions, do not mix friendship with business; in A cultures, mixing both is seen as inevitable and positive.
How to deal with rules (g) Obeying practical rules versus coping with ideal rules	Rules can be made for being respected, discussed and implemented rather strictly or there is a discrepancy between ideal rules and what people can actually do, leading them to rule exploring and rule bypassing behaviour.

organizations have naturally a lot of leeway in making and implementing decisions, but most interpretive clues are given by their cultural background.

Basic cultural assumptions, and their combinations, have an influence on the way we cognitively evaluate real-world situations and the issues that face us. Some examples will demonstrate that we do know how to construct our reality but only within our native cultural community.

Why act?

Not everyone is preoccupied with doing, acting, being efficient and achieving tangible results which can be appraised by others. From an existential point of view this preoccupation with 'doing' is not really justified: in the long term we will all be dead, as Keynes said. Moreover, assuming that we do all care about efficiency, there are many different ways of achieving it. Montesquieu (1792, pp. 228–9) illustrates the spontaneous irritation of people who are 'doing' oriented towards those who are more 'being' oriented when, in *The Spirit of Laws*, he comments on what he calls *indolent nations*:

> The Indians believe that repose and non-existence are the foundations of all things, and the end in which they terminate. Hence they consider entire inaction as the most perfect of all states, and the object of their desires. To the supreme Being they give the title of immoveable. The inhabitants of Siam [Thailand] believe that their utmost happiness consists in not being obliged to animate a machine or to give motion to a body.

Not only are the Indians and Siamese (the Thai people) more 'being' oriented, they also have a quite different view of the relationship with nature from Westerners (subjugation to nature rather than mastery over nature). As noted previously, their religions include belief in reincarnation: on the death of the body, the soul transmigrates or is born again in another body, as outlined above. Life therefore is not seen as 'one shot', but more as a cyclical phenomenon. This puts less pressure on people to be 'doing' orientated but also means more inducement to *be* blameless and virtuous since that will influence the status of further reincarnations; inaction is one of the surest ways to lead a blameless life.

The idea that we have a soul plays a substantial role in the sense of purpose that feeds our actions. It is only in the recent, 'modern' times that people have envisioned as a quite legitimate world-view that we are only made of material substance, whose molecules are recycled through flames or decay at the end, according to burial customs. As the Swiss psychologist, Carl G. Jung explains, it is a fairly new idea in world cultures:

> Under the influence of scientific materialism became all that was not to be seen with eyes and touched with hands dubious, and even more, questionable, because suspected of metaphysics. Was only considered as 'scientific', and thus as altogether admissible, either what was recognized as material or what was derived from sensory perceptible causes. (1931, 1990, p. 9, author's translation)

Both ideas (having a soul or not) have their merits and it is obviously difficult to find supportive evidence for either one. Thus, it is more interesting to investigate the consequences for action of the assumption that we have a soul. The idea of a soul generally coexists with that of God. *Metempsychosis* (the migration of the soul from one body to another) is a very strong belief which arises as a response to an important common human problem: what is the relation between the physical world and the metaphysical world? Believers (people raised in the cultures where this belief is prevalent) are more patient, seemingly less 'doing' oriented, simply because achieving position in lives to come is more important than what is achieved in one's present life. Without discussing metempsychosis, let us look at some fundamental monotheist assumptions:

1. God as supernatural force, both protective and threatening.
2. God being almighty and therefore easy to offend.
3. God asking human beings to accept their destiny as it comes to them.
4. God also asking them to do as much as they can to act rightly and justly.

Fatalism is a belief that directly influences action, not necessarily in terms of acting less, but rather in terms of acting *differently*. It clearly posits the locus-of-control outside, in the metaphysical environment. It also provides convenient explanations for unpredictable events, which allow people to restart action quickly after catastrophes (earthquakes, fires, car incidents). Fatalism makes mourning easier and facilitates the acceptance of strongly negative personal events, a bankruptcy for instance.

Where Christianism fundamentally differs from Islam is on assumption 3. The Christian creed more strictly separates the worldly from the heavenly worlds ('Give to Caesar what belongs to Caesar and to God what belongs to Him'). Furthermore, there is a less personal and direct relation to God as in Islam, since, at least in Catholicism, it is largely mediated by the Church. This frees the tendencies towards mastery over nature, since God gives leeway to mankind concerning worldly enterprises. To a large extent, the punishment in the Promethean myth is forgotten about. In Christian religions, the way is cleared for pro-active attitudes.

What is action?

Another important distinction to be made is whether a culture tends to classify words, speeches and, more generally, acts of communication, in the 'deeds' category. In many cultures there are popular sayings which effectively condemn speech on the basis that it is not real action ('do, not talk'). In the real world, life is more complicated: communications are a category of act, and their potential influence on others is beyond doubt. But whether communication (in what particular form?) is considered as significantly related to action, differs across cultures.

Let us take the example of poetry, which in Islam is highly esteemed. One can be fascinated by poetry, by the beauty of words and songs (and the fact of being fascinated can lead to being acted on), as this commentary on the life of the Prophet illustrates:

> Thus, Mohammed was sitting in the great courtyard of the Caaba, surrounded by the faithful, foreigners and Qureichits. The melodious music of the verses of the Koran was playing while the Prophet was gazing at the audience; the sparkle in His eyes and the beauty of the

songs held the people spellbound. The people kept on repeating: 'If You are a prophet, perform a miracle for us, so that we may believe in You.' And the messenger of God invariably answered: 'O Arab People, is not the miracle powerful enough, that your everyday language has been chosen for the Book, in which a single verse makes us forget about all your poems and all your songs?' It is said that, on hearing this response, non-believers committed themselves to convene all the poets of Arabia, so that they might create at least one verse, a few words, the beauty of which would match that of the Koran. The poets arrived at Caaba and began to perspire under the torrid sun. They toiled, they spared themselves no anguish in seeking to perform what had been requested of them. But as soon as they began to recite their works, even the fiercest opponents to the Prophet themselves were compelled to admit that none of their words could rival the verses of the Koran. Poetic spirit is so greatly esteemed among Arabs that many of those who were in the Caaba at that moment knelt down and were converted to Islam. The unrivalled beauty of the language had convinced them of its heavenly origin. (Mohammed Essad Bey, 1934, pp. 98–9, author's translation)

The word 'poetry' comes from the Greek word *poio*, a verb meaning to 'make', to 'produce', to 'build'. Such an etymology, which is at first sight surprising, sheds some light on the opposing value judgements of the usefulness of poetry, which are made according to different basic cultural assumptions. On the one hand it may be seen as rather distanced from action in the real world, on the other as a direct source of inspiration for action. Indeed if a 'classical' model of action is assumed, i.e. one that is culturally European/western-based, the following sequence occurs:

1. Analysis of the problem and the issues at stake.
2. Gathering of relevant information.
3. Listing and evaluating possible solutions.
4. Selecting the 'best' decision.
5. Implementation: that is, mainly articulating individual and collective action since the implementation process is generally scattered among numerous diverse agents, whereas the decision itself tends to be more individualized, or at least taken by a limited number of people.
6. Appraisal of the outcome, control of the difference between target and actual outcomes, and possibly feedback to a previous step in the sequence.

This sequence may be easily criticized for being culturally non-universal: Japanese people have no word for decision-making (Lazer *et al.*, 1985), and action/decision/control processes are viewed mainly as implementation issues. This is why they first insist on consulting each one of a large group of people at various levels in the organization, who will comment on how to do something (not necessarily on why). But even if we were to accept that this sequence is true, it would still involve a great deal of cultural relativity.

3.4   How to relate thinking to action

The categories considered here are the following:

1. How should issues be addressed: broadly, with the premiss that *the parts always*

represent the whole, or narrowly, considering that *focus is the key to relevance* when acting?
2. What are the proofs that a certain course of action, based on previous reflection, is the right one: (a) data; (b) theory; (c) personal conviction; (d) virtue because it is morally correct to think and do so.

Ideologists versus pragmatists

If future partners do not share common 'mental schemes', it could be difficult for them to solve problems together. Buyers and sellers, for instance, should share some joint views of the world, especially on the following questions:

1. What is the relevant information for acting?
2. How should this information be sought, evaluated and fed into the decision-making process?

An important distinction in the field of cross-cultural psychology opposes ideologism to pragmatism (Glenn, 1981; Triandis, 1983). As indicated by Triandis (1983, p. 148):

> Ideologism versus pragmatism, which corresponds to Glenn's universalism versus particularism, refers to the extent to which the information extracted from the environment is transmitted within a broad framework, such as a religion or a political ideology, or a relatively narrow framework. This dimension refers to a way of thinking.

Ideologists will use a wide body of ideas which provide them with a formal and coherent description of the world: Marxism or liberalism for instance. Every event is supposed to carry meaning when it is seen through this ideologist framework. On the other hand, the pragmatist attitude first considers the extreme diversity of real world situations, and then derives its principles inductively. Reality will be seen as a series of rather independent and concrete problems to be solved ('issues'). These issues will make complete sense when related to practical, precise and even down-to-earth decisions. Typically, ideologists will *take* decisions (*prendre des décisions*), that is pick a solution from a range of possible decisions (which are located outside the person who decides). Conversely, pragmatists will *make* decisions, that is both decide and implement: decisions will be enacted, not selected.

Triandis hypothesizes that complex traditional societies will tend to be ideologist ones, whereas pluralistic societies or cultures experiencing rapid social change will tend to be pragmatist. This distinction may also be traced back to the difference between the legal systems of *common law* (mainly English and American) and the legal system of *code law* (mainly French and German). Whereas the first one favours legal precedents set by the courts and past rulings (cases) the latter favours laws and general texts. They are intended to build an all-inclusive system of written rules of law (code). Codes aim to formulate general principles so as to embody the entire set of particular cases.

The ideologist orientation, which is to be found mostly in southern and eastern Europe, leads the negotiators to try to set principles before any detailed discussion on specific clauses of the contract. Ideologists have a tendency to prefer and promote globalized negotiations in which all the issues are gathered in a 'package deal'. The pragmatist attitude corresponds more to northern Europe and the United States. It entails defining limited scope problems, then solving them one after the other. Pragmatists concentrate their thinking on factual aspects (deeds, not words; evidence, not opinions; figures, not value judgements). They are willing to reach real-world decisions, even if they have to be down-to-earth ones.

Communication may be difficult when partners do not share the same mental scheme. The most unlikely situation for success is an ideologist oriented contractor/supplier who tries to sell to a pragmatist oriented owner/buyer. The ideologist will see the pragmatist as being too interested by trivial details, too practical, too down-to-earth, and incapable of looking at issues from a higher standpoint. Pragmatists will resent ideologists for being too theoretical, lacking practical sense, concerned with issues that are too broad to lead to implementable decisions.

What information is relevant for action? How should it be used?

The dimensions of ideologism and pragmatism are, to varying degrees, combined. It would be a mistake to consider Americans as pure pragmatists with no leaning for ideology. In fact they identify problems clearly and precisely as 'issues'. They collect evidence systematically and their attitude is matter-of-fact. To be 'down to earth' is a positive expression in English, whereas its French equivalent may often be pejorative (*être terre à terre*).[2]

But it is also true that free-market/individual oriented ideology has a strong presence in the United States, enshrined in the Constitution, in anti-trust legislation, in corporate law and so on. However, it is rarely present on a daily basis, when information directly relevant to action is gathered or discussed. Ideology is generally accepted unquestionably. It is therefore somewhat irrelevant to debate practical matters as an ideologist would.

Conversely, one may well be conscious of pragmatic considerations when ideology and ideas are the object of debate. In international business negotiations there is often discussion of principles, which may seem inconsequential owing to the inevitable generality of such discussion. However, it may lead to a substantive outcome later on. The fundamental skill of diplomats (who are, in many respects, culture experts) is to occasion the acceptance and underwriting of basic principles by their counterparts, the effectiveness of which is only apparent at a later date.

Actual (empirical) reality versus potential reality: which should be preferred?

It is a frequent mistake to believe that reality is simple, in the sense that it is directly related to our perceptions and the ways in which we act on it and try to change it. It is what we call 'common sense', that is, shared meaning which makes sense in the cultural community *simply because we share it*, even though it may appear nonsense to people belonging to other cultural communities. The English language is more realistic than the French language here, saying common sense (shared meaning) as opposed to the French *bon sens* ('good sense'), a value judgement which is sometimes wrong. Indeed our relation to the real world is heavily filtered by a series of convergent factors:

1. Our perceptual apparatus is partly culturally formed (see sections 1.4 and 8.4).
2. We implicitly choose to limit the search to certain categories of fact and represent them in a particular way.
3. We admit the truthfulness of these facts according to criteria which are determined in part by our cultural background. When and how they are established as true (meaning that there is a consensus about their being a part of the real world) is also culture-based.[3]
4. Even when these facts have been established as true, there still remain different readings and interpretations of them, depending on culture-based values and social representations.[4]

We may favour either *actual/empirical* reality, that is, the ways in which we experience reality here and now (or the way it is revealed by empirical science), or *potential reality*, that is, the reality we imagine and dream about but which also motivates us to achieve. Potential reality is in a sense the *possible* future of actual reality. Our sense of potential reality relies much more on imagination than on actual perceptions. Since it is beyond the reach of our perceptions and we cannot experience it, we have to envisage potential reality. Potential reality is a rich ground for action, because it directly supports our Promethean desires to exert mastery over nature. It helps us to achieve objects and projects which can make us feel equal to gods ('space conquest' projects, for instance).

Galtung (1981) uses this distinction between actual reality and potential reality in order to contrast what he calls the 'intellectual styles' of four important cultural groups:[5] the 'Gallic' (prototype: the French), the 'Teutonic' (prototype: the Germans), the Saxonic (prototype: the English and the Americans) and the 'Nipponic' intellectual style (prototype: the Japanese). Saxons prefer to look for facts and evidence which result in factual accuracy and abundance. As Galtung states (1981, pp. 827–8) when he describes the intellectual style of Anglo-Americans:

> . . . data unite, theories divide. There are clear, relatively explicit canons for establishing what constitutes a valid fact and what does not; the corresponding canons in connection with theories are more vague. . . . One might now complete the picture of the Saxonic intellectual style by emphasizing its weak point: not very strong on theory formation, and not on paradigm awareness.

Galtung contrasts the Saxonic style with the Teutonic and Gallic styles, which place theoretical arguments at the centre of their intellectual process. Data and facts are there to illustrate what is said rather than to demonstrate it:

> Discrepancy between theory and data would be handled at the expense of data: they may either be seen as atypical or wholly erroneous, or more significantly as not really pertinent to the theory. And here the distinction between empirical and potential reality comes in: to

the Teutonic and Gallic intellectual, potential reality may be not so much the reality to be even more avoided or even more pursued than the empirical one but rather a *more real reality*, free from the noise and impurities of empirical reality. (1981, p. 828)

However, Teutonic and Gallic intellectual styles do differ in the role that is assigned to words and discourse. The Teutonic ideal is that of the ineluctability of true reasoning *Gedankennotwendigkeit*,[6] that is, perfection of concepts and the indisputability of their mental articulation. The Gallic style is less preoccupied with deduction and intellectual construction. It is directed more towards the use of the persuasive strength of words and speeches in an aesthetically perfect way (*élégance*). Words have an inherent power to convince. They may create *potential reality*.

Finally the Nipponic intellectual style, imbued with Hindu, Buddhist and Taoist philosophies, favours a more modest, global and provisional approach. Thinking and knowledge are conceived of as being in a temporary state, open to alteration. The Japanese 'rarely pronounce absolute, categorical statements in daily discourse; they prefer vagueness even about trivial matters . . . because clear statements have a ring of immodesty, of being judgements of reality' (Galtung, 1981, p. 833).

These distinctions are important for any situations where a certain course of action has to be based on favourable arguments, for instance, in assessing the quality of a marketing strategy and when doing market research. After the failure of a marketing campaign, people will tend to emphasize different issues: should they for instance (1) find supporting evidence of what goes wrong, (2) convince sales people to be more enthusiastic about the product, (3) re-think the theory behind the strategy, or (4) improve the virtue of the troops being in charge of implementation?

3.5   Dealing with desires and feelings

Management is based on the principle of reality, and not on the principle of pleasure (in Freudian terms), and therefore there is little interest in looking at people's desires and feelings, which are considered to be in the realm of pure subjectivity, and deserving to be treated as almost non-existent. However, in a cross-cultural perspective, they are important, because people have different ways of relating their actions to their desires and feelings. In this section we are dealing with the two corresponding cells in Table 3.5.

How to relate wishes and desires to action

As noted above, words and deeds may be classified either in two separate categories or combined. They may be set opposite each other on the basis that words are empty or hollow, or joined on the basis of the action of words on others: speech implies influencing and often, consequently, causing someone to act. Most acts of authority are only words. To illustrate some culture-based misadventures in the word/deeds relation, Box 3.2 offers the example of the role of wishful thinking (WT) in the international negotiation of a delivery date.

Box 3.2   *Wishful Thinking*

When selling industrial equipment or turnkey projects on world-wide markets, it is always necessary to stipulate one delivery date or more. The effects of such an announcement may be severe: the buyer may cancel the order because the date is too late. However, this date rarely depends exclusively on the person who sets it. One may spontaneously leave some time between the announced date (an actual reality) and the real delivery date (a potential reality), surmised from the previous performance of the seller's organization. Wishful thinking (WT) is a necessary input in this process: it explains why the initially announced delivery date may be very different from the ultimate one. Wishful thinking is a true 'art of communication' which is preferred more in Latin cultures than in Anglo-Saxon cultures. There is no expression in French for *wishful thinking* (except perhaps *des voeux pieux*), so the English expression is used in French. The negative consequences of WT, such as deceitful behaviour, are much less emphasized in Latin than in Anglo-Saxon cultures. The fact that the phrase 'wishful thinking' is rather pejorative, shows that, normatively, in Anglo-Saxon cultures, it should be avoided, whereas in Latin cultures expressing desires appears more natural. Naturally, in addition to the cultural background there are also some personalities and psychological profiles which are more prone to wishful thinking.[7]

WT consists in first thinking, then saying, how one wants things to be, not how they are. Since nobody knows exactly how things will be in the future, a non-WT oriented person will try to say how he or she thinks quite realistically they will be, not as he or she wants them to be. WT deals with the future: when a culture is weakly future oriented, its use is easier. People do not worry about periods which they do not clearly envisage. If a culture clearly divides words from deeds (do what you say, say what you do), the use of WT is inhibited. When, on the other hand, speech is considered as a prominent modality of action, WT may possibly become a necessity (to galvanize people, while at the same time evoking an improbable future). WT is closely related to present orientation: it is a convenient way to escape from the constraints of longer-term realities by focusing on the here and now. It dodges problems to be solved, and hides divergences and possible conflicts. But this is only in the short term.

A seller with a strong WT communication has the tendency to tell a client spontaneously that the delivery date requested is entirely feasible. The seller also manoeuvres verbally around past realities which may not be wholly reassuring: a six-week delay in the last shipment, for instance. The buyer may also have a WT communication framework, and is in fact 'buying' friendly relations rather than hard data, preferring to be 'happy now'. On the other hand, if the buyer is not WT-prone, the seller is judged negatively and the order is not placed, unless there is some compelling rational argument such as a shortage of this type of supply, particularly high quality or exclusive technology.

(Source: adapted from Usunier, 1989, pp. 89–90.)

Of course, every culture has a mixed use of actual/empirical reality and potential reality. But cultures differ in the places granted to each of these, and in the degree of distrust of potential reality. Obviously potential reality is more dangerous to deal with: it is easier to speak about it than to act on it. Facts are not 'stubborn' if they are remote and vague. An important issue for cultural action styles is the problematical link between what one says and what one does. WT is important in any action that deals with the future and potential reality: in bidding situations, management of delivery delays, announcement of prices, and attitudes towards new projects, or an advertising campaign where arguments unknowingly based on wishful thinking may 'explains why' the audience should be convinced by the message.

Affective versus neutral cultures

This contrast is tightly related to the being/doing divide in basic cultural assumptions and to dependence in the interaction models. If people are strictly doing oriented they tend to disregard, on average, what directly expresses the being. Feelings and affectivity are seen as being in the purely personal and private, individual, domain. Anglo cultures, for instance, tend to suppress feelings and to view their direct expression as alien and even inappropriate for effective interaction to take place. Trompenaars phrases it as follows (1993, p. 63): 'Members of culture which are affectively neutral do not telegraph their feelings but keep them carefully controlled and subdued. . . . Neutral cultures are not necessarily cold or unfeeling, nor are they emotionally constipated or repressed.' To a question asking them if they would express their feelings openly, if they felt upset about something at work, the highest score of neutrality was for the Japanese (83 per cent), followed by (West) Germany (75 per cent), the United Kingdom (71 per cent). The Dutch appear somewhat in the middle (55 per cent), while US people are expressing their emotions more easily than the British with only 40 per cent in favour of neutrality. Finally Italy and France are clearly on the side of affective cultures with only 29 per cent and 34 per cent agreeing that they would not express their feelings openly.

In fact the practical problem which all cultures have to face is not an easy one: over-suppression of emotions and feelings may result in flawed interaction, that is poor results in terms of action. People may discover lately that personal antipathy is a major obstacle for further interaction. On the other hand, giving people a free hand to express all that they feel is somewhat dangerous, because feelings may be superficial, short-sighted and uselessly offend the other party. The feelings/action issue is important for the choice of partners, for improving communication and reducing misunderstandings in marketing negotiations, when managing sales personnel, establishing relationship with foreign distribution channels, or preparing locally adequate advertising creation.

Every culture has certain codes and rituals that allow for a compromise between the two extreme positions. What varies is the starting assumption:

1. Expressing emotions is legitimate and useful for action (affective cultures).
2. Expressing emotions needs to be separated from action (neutral cultures).

It needs, however, to be nuanced, by bringing two additional caveats:

1. As emphasized by Trompenaars, in neutral cultures people have no less emotions than in affective cultures, perhaps the contrary is true. Since feelings and emotions are contained, they may pile up and result in hidden negative feelings.
2. A lot is based in pure personality traits and individual interaction; culture, in this area, should not be overestimated. Much is universal rather than culture-specific in the area of feelings and emotions.

Chapter 12 on language, culture and communication explores the issue of affectivity versus neutrality in more detail.

3.6   Coping with rules

Rules and basic assumptions

A rule is an authoritative regulation or direction concerning method or procedure. Rules are formalized norms which generally comprise a scale of sanctions according to the gravity of the breach. Rules can be made for being respected, discussed and implemented rather explicitly, or there may be a discrepancy between ideal rules and what people can actually do, leading them to rule exploring and rule by passing behaviour. Some typical indicators of rule-related behaviour deal with speed limits, traffic lights, queueing at the bank or bus stations, how income statements are filled in, and so on. A naive interpretation of rules would be that they are made for being respected. The real function of rules is more complex. In writing, they are fairly standard across cultures. But, the first precaution is to read rules in the light of basic assumptions and interaction models (Tables 3.6 and 3.7):

1. A positive view of human nature orientation (HNO) leads to designing rules where sanctions are small and often a positive reinforcement, a reward for respecting the rule, will be preferred over a penalty. People are viewed as trustable for respecting the rules and getting benefits out of them (HNO good), whereas high sanctions and severe enforcement are the case for cultures with HNO bad assumption. In Table 3.6 four ideal types of rules, and behaviour in relation to the rule, are presented, based on the type of HNO and the level of power distance. In this table, the HNO assumption must be understood in a somewhat comparative way between the ruler and the ruled: 'good' means that the ruled views oneself as 'better' than or equal to the ruler; 'bad' means that the ruled view themselves as 'as bad' or 'even worse' than their rulers.
2. The level of power distance in a particular society has an influence (a) on the design

Table 3.6   *Types of rules and behaviour according to HNO and power distance*

HNO power distance	Low	High
Good	**Pragmatic rules** (responsible compliance)	**Challengeable rules** (exploring behaviour)
Bad	**Mechanical rules** (automatic compliance)	**Oppressive rules** (bypassing behaviour)

of rules and (b) on their implementation. Low power distance results in general in people being associated in some way to the design of rules, and in their being applied with a sense of fairness and equity to everybody, included those with larger power in the society (remember, as Hofstede makes the points: power is inequally distributed even in low power distance societies). On the contrary, high power distance results in people being applied rules, in the design of which they were not involved. Furthermore, rules apply in priority to those with less power, the most powerful being seen as somewhat beyond the reach of rules that apply only to 'ordinary people'.

3. As noted in the previous chapter on space-related assumptions, strong ingroup orientation leads often to the syndrome of 'here-only-applicable' rules (that is, in the native community, not outside).

4. The inner drive for respecting the rule: guilt (*inner feeling* of responsibility for committing an offense) versus shame (a painful *emotion, directed to the outside*, resulting from an awareness of having done something dishonourable as a group member).

Types of rules and rule-related behaviour

Anglo-rules, including those of northern European countries, are basically 'pragmatic' rules: people generally comply with the rule out of a sense of responsibility built on positive motivation; rules are understood as helping the society to work smoother and better and everyone is supposed to benefit from their being respected. In this picture, people are globally at ease with their rules, even if they may break them sometimes (nobody is perfect in any society).

'Challengeable rules' corresponds to the case in Italy or France: power distance is fairly high and ordinary people view themselves as having a better human nature than those at the top. It is not evil to investigate to what extent rules can be trespassed. Most often rules come directly from the top, without their 'instructions for use'. Rule exploring means looking for the margins of interpretation. The only way to explore a new rule is to breach it discreetly from the start in order to know whether it is intended to be seriously applied or whether it is one more void text that nobody will respect.

'Mechanical rules' would be the German or Swiss case; they are made democratically because power distance is low, but there is distrust in people. Sanctions are explicit and implemented fairly literally: as in the well-oiled machine model of Stevens (the German model of organization as described by Hofstede; see section 3.2), respect towards rules has a fairly mechanical and automatic side: they are applied literally.

The last stereotypical case is to be found in many developing and Third World countries with high power distance and negative assumptions as to the nature of human beings, powerful or not. Rules are often very strict, formal and somewhat irrealistic. Chapter 10 develops the example of foreign exchange control systems, which lead to bypassing the rule by over- or under-invoicing. Oppressive rules oblige long-term ruled people to bypass the law and induce rulers into corrupt behaviour (they can implement unimplementable rules with some lenience in exchange for a bribe). Oppressive rules lead to a strange atmosphere, where there is a high discrepancy between what people say

Box 3.3   *Brazilian traffic lights*

When I travel to Brazil, I stay in Rio de Janeiro with friends who work for the Brazilian census bureau (IBGE). There, I have learnt that the rules for traffic lights are not really the same as elsewhere. It is not as simple as 'red = stop', 'green = go'. Sometimes cars just do not stop when it is red for them. There seems to be no rule. Investigating more carefully, I gradually discovered that the rule is largely situation-specific. In the case of heavy traffic, it tends to be well respected on average, which shows a certain common sense on the part of Cariocas. In case of lighter and smoother traffic, it depends mostly on the relative size of streets (not to mention the driver's personality and propensity to take risks). Those coming from a smaller street must take care before they benefit from their green light: people on the larger street may cross the red lights after slowing down a little bit, but without stopping. Thus, out of rush-hours, traffic lights are semi-optional for those driving on major avenues. The last case comes at night: one should never stop at red lights even when lawfully required. One night as we were coming back from an IBGE party at Jacarepagua (a nice suburb of Rio), Roberto explained to me, while he was driving continuously across the town to Flamengo without apparently noticing traffic lights, that a year ago he had been assaulted by a man who had threatened to shoot him through the sideglass of his car. Naturally, he had given all his money and was fortunate enough to go back home unhurt. The night rule is therefore: never stop at a traffic light, better slow down to catch the green and if necessary cross at red.

they will do and what they actually do, a sort of systematic social schizophrenia (for instance the policeman changes money in the forbidden parallel exchange market). The idea of possible discrepancies between ideal patterns and actual behaviour was expressed by Linton (1945, pp. 52–4):

> All cultures include a certain number of what may be called ideal patterns. . . . They represent the consensus of opinion on the part of the society's members as to how should people behave in particular situations . . . comparison of narratives usually reveals the presence of a real culture pattern with a recognizable mode of variation . . . it [the ideal pattern] represents a desideratum, a value, which has always been more honoured in the breach than in the observance.

Box 3.3 shows how rules more complex than those officially displayed result partly from opportunistic behaviour, and partly from their being difficult to respect. In any country, looking at basic rules in social life (traffic, queueing, taxation) and how they are actually implemented, gives quickly a fairly good idea of local patterns in dealing with rules.

Universal versus local rules

Table 3.7 contrasts universal rules with local rules: the first ones are assumed to be applicable even beyond the borders of cultures and countries. An example lies in US laws

Table 3.7   *Universal versus local rules*

	Type of rule	
	Universal rules	Local rules
Ingroup orientation	Weak	Strong
Inner compliance dynamic	Guilt	Shame

being applicable extraterrritorially, such as anti-trust rules or the anti-corrupt legislation, FCPA, examined in Chapter 14. The legal concept of extraterritoriality is typical of outgroup orientation, and the US legal extraterritoriality is often resented by other sovereign states as an intrusion into their home affairs. On the other hand, strong ingroup orientation as mentioned above leads to the feeling that rules are only local, they apply to the people here, on their territory and not outside.

In the case of people favouring universal rules, the inner compliance dynamic is based on guilt, that is, self-reproach caused by an inner feeling that one is responsible for a wrong or offence. The moral punishment is to a large extent interiorized within the psyche as in the Freudian concept of *schuld* (in German: debt, fault, culpability). Conversely, the inner compliance dynamics for ingroup oriented people is based on shame and is more outer-directed: it has to do with losing face, being threatened in its honour, that is risking rejection by the other group members. Local rules are territory-bound and deal with the breach of loyalty to the ingroup.

Adopting a more open view of how people attribute meaning to rules makes sense for a large array of international marketing issues. As far as consumer behaviour is concerned, waiting rules, attitudes towards queuing, consumer theft in stores, the attention paid by consumers to instructions for use (of pharmaceuticals, food), the attitude towards filling in market research questionnaires, giving truthful information and, more generally, any ethical issue that involves social responsibility of manufacturers, service providers or consumers has to be examined with a view to its cross-cultural relativity.

3.7   Cultural assumptions and actual behaviour

As outlined in the first chapter, all societies face common problems: although there is a dominant solution, the other alternatives are always present, and they combine in a dialectic way. Let us take the example of how individual and collective actions are to be combined. Japanese people are often depicted as collectivist, in contrast to the Americans who are deemed more individualistic. There is undoubtedly an element of truth in this distinction, but it is necessary to outline its limits. For the word 'individual', let us substitute three words which encompass most of its various facets: *human being, person* and *individual*; and for 'collectivity' let us substitute the words *group, community* and *society*. Who is more humane, more personal and more sensitive in interpersonal relations, more attentive and understanding than the average Japanese person? Who cares more about the community than the average American, whose objective is to 'socialize in the community'? In the United States the word 'community' is used extensively. Indeed

Americans and Japanese share a common problem (as defined by Kluckhohn and Strodtbeck 1961): that of combining individual actions and collective undertakings.

This problem may be solved only by a process which is essentially dialectic. In any society there exists a dominant cultural assumption about what the *first* (but not the *sole*) priority should be: either the individual is the most important (as in the United States); or else the group is the basic survival unit to which the individual must be subordinate (as in Japan). Then comes the reverse cultural assumption, which dialectically complements the basic assumption: that the community is where people integrate to build a common society, and their reciprocal links should be strictly and explicitly codified (United States); or (Japan) that the utmost level of sensitivity must be developed in interpersonal relations so that the working of the group is kept as smooth as possible.

The basic cultural assumptions described in the previous sections are in fact deep-rooted beliefs which generate basic values. Indirectly they guide our daily behaviour, but they may also clash with it. By their very nature they are subconscious, as is the process by which they shape our interaction with others and our conduct. There is some leeway for other sources of influence: for instance, we use social representations to make decisions. We are influenced by other values and other standards of demeanour, such as work rules, company codes of conduct, lifestyles or friendship patterns which work closer to the surface than basic cultural assumptions. These standards of demeanour help people to manage adjustments in the short term; they change over much shorter periods of time (ten or twenty years) than basic cultural assumptions (probably formed over centuries). This leads to two questions:

1. To what extent do less profound levels of culture, e.g. corporate culture or educational culture, influence people?
2. To what extent do people, more or less consciously, feel a contradiction between these different sources of prescriptive behaviour?

Taking their views from Schein's (1981) culture model, Derr and Laurent (1989) present what they call the 'levels of culture triangle' (see Figure 3.2). Basic assumptions are at the bottom of the triangle: values and behavioural norms which derive from the society in its present state. At the top of the triangle are behavioural standards, which are prescribed in a much more direct and explicit way, which Derr and Laurent call 'artefacts': for instance, company procedures, business ethics codes and generally all those standards that unashamedly seek to shape employees' behaviour (inside the company). Whereas cultural assumptions are based on national culture, 'artefacts', values and norms are based on organizational culture.

Multinational companies (MNCs) offer their employees the most fruitful opportunities for intercultural exchange. One might believe that, despite differences in national culture, the values shared by executives in MNCs do converge, as they spend years working with different people. In order to grasp differences in cognitive styles, Laurent (1983) asked managers of different nationalities to indicate their agreement or disagreement with the following statement (item 24 of Laurent's questionnaire on management styles): 'It is important for a manager to have at hand precise answers to most of the questions that his subordinates may raise about their work.'

Figure 3.3 reproduces the results (the percentage of respondents replying in the

Figure 3.2 Basic cultural assumptions and actual behaviour.
(Source: Laurent, 1989. Reproduced with permission.)

affirmative) for various national groups. Obviously Swedes do not need omniscient managers (10 per cent). Among Westerners at the other extreme, the Italians (66 per cent) and the French (53 per cent) believe that managers should have precise answers to most of their subordinates' questions. It seems that most Anglo-Saxon and northern European people tend to see managers as problem-solvers, whereas Latin and Asian people see them more as *experts*.

These differences were observed in people working in their home country. Laurent (1989) asked the same question of executives who had been working for a long time in MNCs where teams had been built up from a large number of different nationalities. One would expect to observe a decrease in the differences between national groups of managers. Surprisingly, the situation is exactly the opposite. Laurent has observed in MNCs an increase of differences across national groups. This suggests that, behind superficial agreements, people's basic cultural assumptions are reinforced. When a corporate culture tries to shape a manager's (or more generally an employee's) daily behaviour, it succeeds from the outside (because people are concerned about their job and career). But it only scratches the surface of people and does not significantly affect the two bottom levels of Figure 3.2. Moreover, since values are forced upon them, not only do they fail to impinge on basic cultural assumptions, but they even reinforce them.

Questions

1. Are there cultural roots to personal modesty?
2. Which examples would you suggest to exemplify American individualism?
3. In many countries, there is an institution called 'parliamentary democracy'. On which basic cultural values is it based, in your opinion? Is there a relationship between the development of marketing and parliamentary democracy?

5. What kinds of sales argument (seduction, force, blackmail, etc.) would be used?
6. Does selling exist at all? Is selling meaningful? Why?

The Samoans

The Samoans are a tall, light-brown-skinned Polynesian people living on a small group of islands, part of which belong to the United States. Their way of life is formal and stately. Chiefs and orators, village princes and village princesses, patterned groups of young and old, combined together to plant and reap, fish and build, feast and dance, in a world where no one is hurried, where food is plentiful, nature is generous, and life is harmonious and unintense. They have been Christian for over a hundred years, and have fitted the tenet of Christianity into their own traditions, wearing beautifully starched cottons on Sunday, but still barefoot, and proud of their own way of life.

The Manus of the Admiralty Islands

The Manus people are a small, energetic tribe of fishermen and traders who build their houses on piles in the salt lagoons, near to their fishing-grounds. Tall, brown-skinned, lean and active, with nothing but their wits, their skill, and an ethics which says that the ghost of the dead will penalize the unindustrious, they have built a high standard of living which they maintain by continuous hard work. Puritan to the core, committed to effort and work, disallowing love and the pleasures of the senses, they take quickly to the ways of the Western world, to machinery, to money.

The Mountain Arapesh

The Mountain Arapesh are a mild, undernourished people who live in the steep, unproductive Torricelli Mountains of New Guinea, poor themselves, and always struggling to save enough to buy music and dance-steps and new fashions from the trading peoples of the sea-coast, and to buy off the sorcerers among the fiercer people of the interior plains. Responsive and co-operative, they have developed a society in which, while there is never enough to eat, each man spends most of his time helping his neighbour, and committed to his neighbour's purposes. The greatest interest of both men and women is in growing things – children, pigs, coconut-trees – and their greatest fear that each generation will reach maturity shorter in stature than their forebears, until finally there will be no people under the palm-trees.

The cannibal Mundugumor of the Yuat River

These robust, restive people live on the banks of a swiftly flowing river, but with no river lore. They trade with and prey upon the miserable, underfed bush-peoples who live on poorer land, devote their time to quarrelling and head-hunting, and have developed a form of social organization in which every man's hand is against every other man. The women are as assertive and vigorous as the men; they detest bearing and rearing children, and provide most of the food, leaving the men free to plot and fight.

The lake-dwelling Tchambuli

The Tchambuli people, who number only six hundred in all, have built their houses along the edge of one of the loveliest of New Guinea lakes, which gleams like polished ebony, with a back-drop of the distant hills behind which the Arapesh live. In the lake are purple lotus and great pink and white water lilies, white osprey and blue heron. Here the Tchambuli women, brisk, unadorned, managing and industrious, fish and go to market; the men, decorative and adorned, carve and paint and practise dance-steps, their head-hunting tradition replaced by the simpler practice of buying victims to validate their manhood.

The Iatmul head-hunters of the Great Sepik River

On the big, slow-moving river into which the Yuat River drains, for which the mountains where the Arapesh live is one watershed, to which the Tchambuli lake is connected by canals, are the swagger villages of the Iatmul people, head-hunters, carvers, orators, tall and fiercely, brittlely masculine, where women serve as spectators to the endless theatricality of the men's behaviour. Rich in sago swamps that provide them with a steady food-supply, well fed on fish that the steady industry of the women provides, they have built magnificent ceremonial houses, and beautifully carved war-canoes, and accumulate in their big villages the art-styles, the dance-steps, the myths, of all the lesser peoples about them, outstanding among their neighbours, and vulnerable in the intensity of their pride.

The Balinese

The Balinese, who can be numbered in hundreds of thousands, not in a few thousands like the Samoans or a few hundreds like the New Guinea peoples, are not a primitive people, but a people whose culture is linked through Asia with our own historical past. Light, graceful, wavy-haired, with bodies every segment of which moves separately in the dance, they have a highly complex and ordered way of life that in its guilds and Hindu rituals, its written records and temple organizations, its markets and its arts, is reminiscent of the Middle Ages in Europe. Crowded on a tiny island with a beautiful, highly diversified, changing landscape, they have turned all life into an art. The air is filled with music day and night, and the people, whose relations to each other are light, without enduring warmth, are tireless in rehearsal for a play where those disallowed feelings will be given graceful stylized expression.

(Source: Margaret Mead, 1948, 'The seven South Sea peoples', pp. 52–5. Reproduced with permission.)

A3.3 Rationales for section A2.1 (cross-cultural scenario) and sections A2.2 and A2.3 (cross-cultural interactions)

A2.1 Scenario: Inshallah

This scenario can best be understood by first appreciating the very different views in U.S. culture and Saudi culture concerning 'locus of control.' In the United States it is believed that ultimately people are responsible for their own destiny. If something goes wrong, it is believed, it is frequently possible for the individual to *do* something (that is, to change certain behavior) to bring about the desired outcome. In Saudi Arabia, and indeed throughout the Arab world, people are taught from an early age that all things are subject to the direct will of Allah. All plans for the future (including, of course, business plans) are viewed with a sense of inevitability and will be realized only if God wills it. This is not to say that people in the Arab world would not work hard to help bring about the desired results. Rather, they believe that despite the effort, the desired ends will not happen unless God is willing. Perhaps Stefan would have been less frustrated if he had translated *inshallah* to mean 'if possible' or 'God willing' rather than as a knee-jerk response used to absolve oneself of all responsibility for one's actions.

(Ferraro, 1990, p. 162. Reproduced with permission.)

A2.2 Interaction: Engineering a decision

1. There is little evidence for this in the story. While the financial benefits are relevant, to Mr. Tanaka they are probably a minor consideration in the situation. Please choose another response.
2. It is quite probable that coming from a male-dominant Japanese society he does think it odd that M. Legrand should mention his wife's opinion. However, the decision not to go to the Middle East also appears to be M. Legrand's personal inclination so this does not fully account for Mr. Tanaka's bewilderment. There is another explanation. Please choose again.
3. It is unlikely that Mr. Tanaka would consider this. There are factors far removed from personal gain dominating his concern. Please choose again.
4. This is the most likely explanation. In Japanese and many other collectivist societies a person is defined much more as a collection of roles (parent, employee, servant, official) than by his or her individual identity. As such, fulfilling these roles to the best of one's ability is regarded as more important than one's personal inclinations. Thus Mr. Tanaka would see that M. Legrand's responsibility as a company employee would be to accept the position whether or not he is personally happy about the idea. M. Legrand's refusal is thus bewildering and makes him think that his belief in M. Legrand's dedication has been completely misplaced. M. Legrand however comes from a culture where individual freedoms are highly valued and so exercises his right to refuse the offer with little compunction. The cultural conflict thus resides in different strengths of values applied to the roles occupied by a person in the culture.

(Source: Brislin, *et al.*, 1986, pp. 177–8. Reproduced with permission.)

A2.3 Interaction: Opening a medical office in Saudi Arabia

1. It is unlikely that people would sign up solely to satisfy a newcomer's feeling. There is a better explanation. Please select again.
2. If there is a considerable time lag between when a person makes a decision and the action upon it, it is possible that they may change their mind. However, there is no indication in the incident to support this. Please select another response.
3. Units of time reference differ markedly between Arab and American cultures. To an American, the major unit of time is five minutes. Fifteen minutes is a significant period of time. To an urban Arab, the unit of time that corresponds to our five-minute block is fifteen. Thus, when the Arab is thirty minutes late (by the clock), he is not even ten minutes late by his standards. This is the best answer. Tom's patients may still arrive.
4. While the patients may be seeing their own traditional healers, they would not necessarily do so in the strict sequence suggested by this alternative. There is a more precise explanation. Please choose again.

(Source: Brislin, *et al.*, 1986, p. 179. Reproduced with permission.)

Notes

1. Berne's theory is based on a view of the self as composed of three stratas: the Parent, the Adult and the Child. Transactions between human beings can take place at the same level or across levels of the self, for instance, when a person sends a message based on his Parent to the Child of another person. What I suggest here is simply that some cultures may favour Adult–Adult transactions in interpersonal relationship whereas others tend to promote Parent–Child transactions especially in hierarchical situations.
2. This means implicitly: compared to Latins, such as myself. We are generally much less cautious in taking such steps, if indeed we ever stop to identify them clearly. Even the style of this book reveals that I come from an ideologist-oriented society (French). The expressions 'matter-of-fact'; and 'down to earth', which are both positive in English, may be translated by *être terre à terre*. The French language also has two expressions, but one is pejorative and the other is positive – *avoir les pieds sur terre* (*Harrap's Concise French–English Dictionary*, 1984, Harrap: London, p. 369).
3. Those who wish to enlarge their world-view by freeing themselves, at least partially, from the mental programmes brought to them by culture, risk being misunderstood. This is in fact a legitimate reaction on the part of other members of the group. By trying to escape a single cultural programming, such people exhibit a definite lack of humility in setting themselves apart from the community. Furthermore any homogeneous human group feels fairly threatened when members of the group overstep the threshold of non-conformism. They may finally be understood (because the message is useful as an instrument of change that is needed in the society), or live alone, or be beheaded (e.g. Thomas Moore).
4. Clifford Geertz in *Local Knowledge* (1983) quotes a long passage from a Danish traveller and trader, L. V. Helms, who when travelling in India accurately reports the ritual of the cremation of a dead man and his three (living) widows. Helms describes very carefully the background to the incident, which takes place around 1850. He is horrified by the ritual, amazed by the absence of reaction of the crowd attending the event and stunned by the lack of fear of the three women

who throw themselves alive into the flames. Geertz emphasizes the relations of culture to moral imagination: what is seen as mere barbary by one culture is experienced as wholly normal by another. Another more recent example of cross-cultural differences in the interpretation of facts is given by the totally diverging views during the Gulf War about Saddam Hussein (whose biography and acts are well known): bloodthirsty dictator for some, hero of the Arab world for others. When Saddam Hussein fired Scud missiles at Saudi Arabia and Israel, interpretations of this simple act were also totally diverging. For an interpretation of the Gulf War reportage as advertising for weapons, see Ottosen (1992).

5. The article by Johan Galtung which we quote deals with the intellectual style of academicians. Since it describes 'intellectual styles' in general (not only the style of the intellectuals), this framework is used as 'ideal types'. Johan Galtung, a Norwegian, is a renowned scholar in peace research. His numerous articles and books are an important source of reflection on national culture and the conflicts between cultural communities.

6. The concept of *Gedankennotwendikeit* is typical of German thinking patterns, where abstraction is taken to its limits. It is not by chance that German philosophers have a world-wide reach. The German language is probably the richest in the world for abstract words. It favours pure conceptual thinking. The construction of *Gedankennotwendigkeit* is itself proof (sorry: an illustration . . .) of this: *denken* means 'to think', *Gedanken* are 'thoughts'; *Not* means 'necessity', *wenden* is 'to turn', *-keit* is a suffix which abstracts the whole as 'the state of being . . .'. As a result of this rebus, *Gedankennotwendigkeit* is something like '*the state of being turned into necessary (unavoidable, pure) thoughts*' (*Langenscheidt German–English Dictionary*, 1970, used for the translation of component words, Basic Books: New York).

7. To use a (very elementary) Freudian distinction: the denial of WT responds to the anal principle of tightening oneself up and controlling one's behaviour, when strongly integrating reality as a constraint; conversely, the use of WT denotes an oral behaviour, favourable words (*paroles*), which describe the reality in a much more pleasant way than it actually is, provide wishful thinkers (and above all, wishful *speakers*) with a pleasure of mouth. This oral denial thwarts the frustrations of reality, like the little child that sucks its thumb, when something has made it unhappy.

References

Adler, Nancy, J. (1991), *International Dimensions of Organizational Behavior*, 2nd edn, PWS-Kent: Belmont, CA.

Adler, Nancy J., Nigel Campbell and André Laurent (1989), 'In search of appropriate methodology: from outside the People's Republic of China looking in', *Journal of International Business Studies*, vol. XX, no. 1, p. 69.

Belk, Russel W. (1985), 'Cultural and historical differences in concepts of self and their effects on attitudes toward having and giving', *Proceedings of the 12th Annual Conference of the Association for Consumer Research*, ACR: Provo, Utah, pp. 754–60.

Belk, Russel W. (1988), 'Possessions and the extended self', *Journal of Consumer Research*, vol. 15, pp. 139–68.

Berne, Eric (1961), *Transactional Analysis in Psychotherapy*, Grove Press: New York.

Berne, Eric (1964), *Games People Play*, Grove Press: New York.

Bista, Dor Bahadur (1990), *Fatalism and Development*, Orient Longman: Calcutta.

Brislin, Richard W., Kenneth Cushner, Craig Cherrie and Mahealani Yong (1986), *Intercultural Interactions: A practical guide*, Sage: Newbury Park, CA.

Derr, C. B. and A. Laurent (1989), 'The internal and external career: A theoretical and cross-cultural perspective', in M. B. Arthur, D. T. Hall and B. S. Lawrence (eds), *Handbook of Career Theory*, Cambridge University Press: Cambridge.

Essad Bey, Mohammed (1934), *Mahomet*, Payot: Paris.

Ferraro, Gary P. (1990), *The Cultural Dimension of International Business*, Prentice Hall: Englewood Cliffs, NJ.

Frese-Weghöft, Gisela (1989), *Ein Leben in der Unsichbarkeit*, Rowohlt: Hamburg.

Galtung, Johan (1981), 'Structure, culture and intellectual style: An essay comparing Saxonic, Teutonic, Gallic and Nipponic approaches', *Social Science Information*, vol. 20, no. 6, pp. 817–56.

Geertz, Clifford (1983), *Local Knowledge*, Basic Books: New York.

Glenn, E. (1981), *Man and Mankind: Conflict and communication between cultures*, Ablex: Horwood, N.J.

Hofstede, Geert (1980a), *Culture's Consequences: International differences in work-related values*, Sage: Beverly Hills, CA.

Hofstede, Geert (1980b), 'Motivation, leadership and organization: Do American theories apply abroad?', *Organizational Dynamics*, Summer, pp. 42–63.

Hofstede, Geert (1983), 'National cultures in four dimensions: A research-based theory of cultural differences among nations', *International Studies of Management and Organization*, vol. XII, nos. 1–2, pp. 46–74.

Hofstede, Geert (1991), *Cultures and Organizations: Software of the mind*, McGraw-Hill: Maidenhead.

Jung, Carl Gustav (1931), 'Das Grundproblem des gegenwärtigen Psychologie' in *Wirklichkeit der Seele*, DTV: Munich, 1990.

Kluckhohn, Florence R. and Frederick L. Strodtbeck (1961), *Variations in Value Orientations*, Greenwood Press: Westport, CT.

Laurent, André (1983), 'The cultural diversity of Western conceptions of management', *International Studies of Management and Organization*, vol. XII, nos. 1–2, pp. 75–96.

Laurent, André (1989), presentation to the European Foundation for Management Development Seminar 'Cultural shock', *EFMD Annual Conference* in March, Marseille.

Lazer, William, Shoji Murata and Hiroshi Kosaka (1985), 'Japanese marketing: Towards a better understanding', *Journal of Marketing*, vol. 49 (Spring), pp. 69–81.

Linton, Ralph (1945), *The cultural background of personality*, Appleton-Century: NY.

Mead, Margaret (1948), *Male and Female*, William Morrow: New York.

Montesquieu, Charles de (1748), *The Spirit of Laws*, translated from the French by Thomas Nugent (1792), 6th edn, McKenzie and Moore: Dublin.

Ottosen, Rune (1992) 'The media and the Gulf War reporting: Advertising for the arms industry?', *Bulletin of Peace Proposals*, vol. 23, no. 1, pp. 77–83.

Rotter, J. B. (1966), 'Generalized expectancies for internal versus external control of reinforcement', *Psychological Monographs*, vol. 80, no. 609.

Schein, Edgar H. (1981), 'Does Japanese management style have a message for American managers?', *Sloan Management Review* (Fall).

Smith, Adam (1776), *The Wealth of Nations*, University of Chicago Press edition: Chicago, IL, 1976.

Sondergaard, Michael (1994), 'Hofstede's Consequences: A study of reviews, citations and replications,' *Organization Studies*, 15 (3), pp. 447–56.

Triandis, Harry C. (1983), 'Dimensions of cultural variation as parameters of organizational theories', *International Studies of Management and Organization*, vol. XII, no. 4, pp. 139–69.

Trompenaars, Fons (1993), *Riding the Waves of Culture*, Nicholas Brealey: London.

Usunier, Jean-Claude (1989), 'Interculturel: La parole et l'action', *Harvard-L'Expansion*, no. 52 (Spring), pp. 84–92.

Weeks, William H., Paul B. Pedersen and Richard W. Brislin (1987), *A Manual of Structured Experiences for Cross-cultural Learning*, Intercultural Press: Yarmouth, ME.

Wong, Nancy and Aaron Ahuvia (1995), 'From tofu to caviar: Conspicuous consumption, materialism and self-concepts in east-Asian and Western cultures', *Proceedings of the Second Conference on the Cultural Dimension of International Marketing*, Odense, pp. 68–89.

4

◆◆◆

Cross-cultural consumer behaviour

'*Sehen Sie Mercedes mit anderen Augen. Die neue E-Klasse ist da*' says a 1995 Daimler-Benz poster for their new E-Class car ('Look at Mercedes with other eyes. The new E-Class arrives'). That is what this chapter is all about: looking with other eyes. It deals basically with the influence of culture on consumer behaviour. Looking with the 'same eyes' means that theories, underlying models, concepts and views of what consumers are, what their motives are, and how they behave are assumed to be universal. One may 'add glasses to the same eyes' so that what was previously invisible comes to light. But what Mercedes asks its potential consumers to do may be necessary: changing the eyes in order to have a different perspective. Table 4.1 sums up four perspectives, starting from the view that both consumers (the object) and underlying consumer behaviour theories (the eyes) can be either universal or specific.

Table 4.1 should not be interpreted with the view that a particular cell corresponds to a better perspective than another. However, they display strong contrasts. The first perspective, in its purest form, is now rarely found except in the text on globalization of markets by Levitt (1983) and more generally when consumers are viewed as truly global. It may make sense for particular classes of consumers, such as business people travelling world-wide and their families ('the global nomads'). The global perspective has been widely used and in some cases has led to the design of successful marketing strategies. Kotler's *Marketing Management* is now in its eighth edition (1994): it is a world-wide success which started in the beginning from position 1 and has steadily shifted to position 2. It has been translated into many languages and to various national contexts. For

Table 4.1 *Consumer behaviour in a cross-cultural perspective*

Consumers	CB theories	
	Universal	Specific
Universal	(1) Global perspective	(3) Ethnic consumption perspective
Specific	(2) 'Imported' perspective	(4) Cultural meaning perspective

107

basic personal protection) is not satisfied according to the same criteria in different
cultures. Thus one of the basic axioms of Maslow's theory – that needs must be satisfied
at a definite level in order for the needs higher up in the hierarchy to appear – is not true
from a cross-cultural point of view. In many Third World countries one may deprive
oneself of food so as to be able to buy a refrigerator, thereby replacing the satisfaction of
a physical need of safety with the satisfaction of a need of social status and self-esteem
(Belk, 1988). All the area of conspicuous consumption which is fairly well documented
is in direct contradiction to the hierarchy of needs. As noted by Solomon (1994, p. 426),
the term 'conspicuous consumption' was coined by Veblen who was initially inspired by
anthropological studies of the Kwakiutl Indians:

> These Indians had a ceremony called a *potlach* where the host showed off his wealth and
> gave extravagant presents to their guests. The more one gave away, the better one looked to
> the others. Sometimes, the host would use an even more radical strategy to flaunt his wealth.
> He would publicly destroy some of his property to demonstrate how much he had. This ritual
> was also used as a social weapon: Since guests were expected to reciprocate, a poorer rival
> could be humiliated by inviting him to a lavish potlach. The need to give away, even though
> he could not afford it, would essentially force the hapless guest into bankruptcy.

What this example suggests is that consumer motivations are rooted in the dynamics of
social life. Slightly caricatured, Maslow's picture of motivation describes an individual,
starting from the belly and extending to the brain: although relevant, it cannot provide a
universal view cross-culturally. Mendenhall *et al.* (1995) show that the general findings
of studies that have investigated the cross-cultural transposability of Maslow's hierarchy
of needs offer mixed support: seven studies support it strongly, three partially and it is
refuted by ten research studies. The general message about Maslow's hierarchy is that:
(1) the needs themselves are fairly consistent across cultures; (2) their rank ordering
varies across cultures; and (3) the degree of emphasis on specific needs and the link
between satisfaction at different need levels is also culture-bound.

Individualism and collectivism

Most of the available marketing literature depicts individual consumers who make their
own decisions. Although industrial marketing literature deals with organizational purchase and buying centres, and the effects of family decisions on consumer behaviour
have been meticulously studied, the individualistic conception remains very much at the
heart of the mental picture of marketing. The family is seen as an interacting group of
individuals, all influencing each other. An *organic* conception of the family as a single
decision-making unit is not easily grasped. Moreover research methods themselves are
not totally unbiased: are the people questioned representative and can they be considered
as reflecting family behaviour? Who should be questioned and in what circumstances?
    However, various authors within the field of cross-cultural marketing have pointed out
the role of the group as an organic entity, as opposed to a casual collection of individuals
who share information and some common interests and constraints, living together within

the family cell. This is especially true in Asia (Kushner, 1982; Laurent, 1982; Redding, 1982; Yau, 1988; Yang, 1989). Redding (1982, pp. 104, 112–113), for instance, emphasizes that:

> In most Asian cultures there is a particular grouping to which a person belongs, which involves him in patterns of obligation and behaviour of a special kind. . . . It would, for instance, be naive to suppose that the buying power of a teenage market in a Western country would be equivalent to one in, say, Hong Kong or Singapore. The discretion over the use of income is heavily influenced, in the case of the Chinese teenager, by the expected contribution to the family. The tradition of deference to parental wishes also affects buying patterns in clothing, leisure expenditure, etc., especially as it is normal to live at home until marriage.

In addition, a Chinese individual must always take into account all the members of his family when he takes a purchase decision, compared with an interactive decision-making process undertaken by the husband or wife in the West where important household expenditure is concerned. Yau (1988, p. 49) describes the Chinese relational orientation in the following way: 'Chinese have to observe and act according to the norms prescribed for each instance of interpersonal relations. Thus the king must be kingly, the minister ministerly, the husband husbandly, the wife wifely, brothers brotherly, and friends friendly'. In the East the model of the 'extended family' has survived apparently westernized ways of life (Laurent, 1982); it has a powerful influence on many purchase decisions. Even Chinese people, who may sometimes appear quite individualistic-oriented when outside their national context, remain strongly bound by their family ties. Yang (1989) describes the influence of what he calls 'familism' on their behaviour as individuals, as family members and as consumers (Box 4.1).

Institutions, social conventions, habits, and customs

Institutions, such as the state, the Church and trade unions also have an influence on the marketing environment. In distribution, the French Catholic hierarchy has generally been opposed to Sunday trading (Dubois, 1987). In Germany, the trade unions strongly oppose an extension of store opening hours: stores close at 6:30 p.m. each working day, at 2 p.m. on Saturdays and are closed on Sundays; this is legally compulsory and no store can open out of these authorized times without being severely fined. The result is that German consumers are obliged to shop on Saturday mornings, and to be quick when purchasing. Mail order is a good shopping substitute when stores are opened only a few hours a week, given that many consumers are kept at office by salaried work. As a result, mail order sales are highly developed in Germany, with giant enterprises in the industry such as Neckermann, Bertelsmann and Quelle.

On the other hand, some products are in a sense institution-dependent, whatever their mode of distribution or consumption: examples would be marriage-related goods such as

Box 4.1   *The role of familism in Chinese consumer behaviour*

The single most essential concept to characterize Chinese culture is undoubtedly familism (Ballah, 1970; Yang, 1972). Confucius himself defined five fundamental human relations, three of which relate to family relations: parent and child, husband and wife, and brother and sister. All five of them had roughly equal weight in terms of importance. Later, some of his influential disciples, however, made filial piety the most important among the five (Hsieh, 1967). In any event, a Chinese individual's relationship with family members is a permanent one, which is never grown out of. The Chinese definition of family is often very broad, including various lineages and generations. The single most influential group on an individual's behaviour is his family members, usually extended family members. The influences of family members on an individual's behaviour are extremely extensive; often they extend to areas definitely considered private by Western standards. In contrast to their relationships with their families, Chinese people's relationships with secondary groups beyond the family are usually ill-defined and sometimes non-existent.

The consequences of this emphasis on familism and filial piety are many. First, a Chinese individual's behaviour often cannot be considered as an act reflecting his own preferences or will. It is often the result of a consensus or compromise of himself and his family members, or a take-over by his family's, most often his parents', preferences or wills. Second, social harmony is highly valued in a society whose basic social unit is the extended family (Chien, 1979). To maintain stable and peaceful coexistence is more important than anything else when there are a lot of people who are interdependent and interconnected with each other, constantly involved at any given time and place. Third, an individual's relationships with core family members are not only strong and spontaneous but also collective. The bonds are so natural that they are also very casual. They usually do not need deliberate cultivation by way of saying 'I love you' all the time or showering each other with gifts (Hsu, 1971). Finally an individual's relationship with other non-family members are usually formalized but peripheral. The affection of strangers are not deliberately sought after but can be naturally developed. Strangers are also likely to become a part of the 'extended' family and to be treated accordingly but not until trust has been established between them and a Chinese individual (Fei, 1948). In other words, the Chinese intergroup relationships are often limited to two types; i.e., family (inside) and non-family (outside). Other group memberships are not usually sought and therefore not easily established.

(Source: Yang, 1989. Reproduced with the kind permission of the publisher.)

a wedding dress or the products featured on wedding lists, or many kinds of traditional gifts which are offered for specific occasions.

Of all the cultural conventions that structure daily life in the consumption domain, the most important is probably eating habits. As emphasized by Wilk (1995, p. 372): 'Food is both substance and symbol; providing both physical nourishment and a key form of communication that carries many kinds of meanings.' Actual variations, in addition to the social interpretation of eating habits, exist on the following points:

1. The number of meals consumed each day.
2. The standard duration of a meal, and the position of meals in the daily schedule.
3. The composition of each meal. The portions may differ in size, comprising various

kinds of food (local ingredients or cooking style); the nutritional content may be composed so that the eater can cope with long or short time periods without further calorific input during the day.

4. What are the beverages accompanying the meal (water, coffee, tea, wine, beer, and so on) and what is their 'status': refresher, energizer, coolant, relaxer, etc.; see Box 4.2)?
5. The social function: either as a communal meal where people entertain themselves by eating and chatting together, or simply as a means of feeding oneself, without any symbolic, personal or collective connotation. A meal may be considered merely as 'fuel' or as a daily 'social event'.
6. Is the food ready-made or is it prepared from basic ingredients? Are there servants to help prepare the meal? What is the cultural meaning of the meal being prepared by the housewife or by her husband, and for definite persons in particular situations?

The list of cultural variation in eating habits is endless, because nothing is more essential, more universal (food is vital) and at the same time more accurately defined by culture than eating habits. Eating habits should be considered as the whole process of purchasing food and beverages, cooking, tasting, and even commenting. In many countries, commercials advertising ready-made foods (canned or dried soups, for instance) faced resistance in the traditional role of the housewife, who was supposed to prepare meals from natural ingredients for her family. As a result, advertisers were obliged to include a degree of preparation by the housewife in the copy strategy.

Box 4.2   Café au lait *and 'slow food'*

In France, many people start the day with a simple *café au lait*, a coffee with milk (a real poison according to doctors . . .); in Germany, the United Kingdom and the United States, people start with a larger breakfast, but eat less than the French at noon. My American students have always been astonished by the two hour break for lunch: they always tended to consider it as a 'loss of time', without seeing that this was part of the socializing process in and out of the family, depending on whether the meal is at home or outside. The regularity of meal hours is another difference which may have far-reaching consequences. Americans are more ready than other people to eat at 'non-standard' hours. For McDonald's and other fast-food restaurants this is a big opportunity in terms of activity scheduling. People do not rush at very specific hours as they do in some European countries, where it is quite difficult to maintain the 'fast' aspect, since personnel has to face high peak demand, especially at noon. Then, the restaurants become 'slow food', with up to twenty minutes to be served. But European people do not mind that much: what they want from the McDonald's is not quickness; on the contrary they like to stay longer than the restaurant itself would like them to stay. What they look for is probably cheap and pleasant food, with a modern American image.

4.2   The influence of culture on selected aspects of consumer behaviour

Table 4.2 presents selected aspects of consumer behaviour which can be influenced by cultural differences. It is not to be considered as exhaustive. Some of these issues are developed at greater length later in this chapter and in other chapters.

Loyalty

Consumers can be loyal, that is, they repeat their purchases on a regular basis, buying the same brand. Loyal consumers prefer to be sure of what they buy. However, by doing this they reduce their opportunity to find other, and perhaps better, choices which would provide them with more value for their money. Other classes of consumers try new brands, shift from one brand to another when a new one is promoted, take advantage of temporary price rebates: they are basically disloyal consumers.

Disloyalty is the natural counterpart of *loyalty* (to a brand, a product, a store, etc.): what is culturally meaningful is to observe which one of these two opposite attitudes is considered as the legitimate, fundamental behaviour. In the United States *brand loyalty* is very carefully surveyed and explanatory variables (demographics or lifestyles or situational variables) are researched. Standard behaviour is implicitly assumed to be that of disloyalty, although there are large classes of loyal consumers. A consumer supposedly shifts from one brand to another (brand switching), because it is standard behaviour to test several competing products successively, thereby fostering price competition, or to respond spontaneously to the stimuli of advertising and sales promotion. Equally, it is assumed that consumers are not especially rewarded by their practice of buying the same brand and/or shopping in the same store (they can be 'brand loyal' and/or 'store loyal'). The fact that consumers may enjoy the same stable environment, of which their favourite products would form a basic constituent, is somewhat underestimated. Stated in a different way, it is assumed that consumers enjoy change more than stability. Of course, in the United States, there are large groups of loyal consumers: habits and stability are a reality for many Americans. But the number of these groups is, in all probability, less than in some other countries where brand loyalty is normal behaviour.

Loyalty is a key concept in collectivist cultures, which spreads from people to product, in as much as they are extensions of the self. Chiou (1995) argues that consumers in collectivist (Asian) societies tend to be more loyal on average, because (1) they tend to rely more on information found in their reference group – often by word-of-mouth communication – rather than on information diffused by the media; and (2) they tend to follow the group consensus until there is significant evidence showing that the new product is better. Where consumers are more fundamentally loyal, often less brand-conscious, and less used to rational price/quality cross-brand or cross-product comparisons, it may be assumed that marketing strategies have to be different from those in countries where consumers frequently shift from one brand to another. In the former case it may be necessary to build a loyal consumer base from scratch, whereas in the latter case it may be more effective to persuade disloyal consumers to switch from other

Table 4.2 *The possible impact of cultural differences on selected aspects of consumer behaviour*

Aspect of consumer behaviour	Impact of cultural differences: values involved/issues to be addressed
Perception	Perception of shapes, colours varies across cultures. See section 8.4.
Motivation	Motivation to own, to buy, to spend, to consume, to show, to share, to give.
Learning and memory	Level of literacy/Memory as it is shaped by the education system (see below section 4.3)/Familiarity with product classes shaped by education.
Age	Do people know their age?/Respective valuation of younger and older people in the society (section 3.1)/Influence processes across age groups for buying decisions/How is purchasing power distributed across generations?
Self-concept	See Table 3.1.
Group influence	Individualism/collectivism. To what extent are individuals influenced in their attitudes and buying behaviour by their group? How does consumer behaviour reflect the need to self-actualize individual identity or to manifest group belonging?
Social class	Are social classes locally important? Is social class demonstrated through consumption? What type of products or services do social status-minded consumers buy? Are there exclusive shops (see Table 3.1)?
Sex roles	The sexual division of labour; who makes the decisions? Shopping behaviour; who shops: he or she or both of them?
Attitudes change	Resistance in general to change in consumer behaviour (possibly related to high level of uncertainty avoidance, past orientation, fatalism) and resistance to change in particular areas when change could clash with local values and behaviour (eg. resistance to *fast-food* restaurants in France).
Decision-making	Family models (nuclear family versus extended family). Children's influence and decision-making. Compulsive buying.
Purchase	Loyalty/Purchasing environment, especially legal marketing environment/Influence of salespersons on clients (section 14.1 and 14.2).
Post-purchase	Perceptions of product quality (see section 10.3). Consumer complaining behaviour/Dissatisfaction/ Consumerism.

established brands, and then to try to turn the newly developed consumer base into a loyal one.

Consumer's involvement

The involvement of the consumer in product purchase or consumption varies across cultures. Yang (1989) depicts the Chinese consumer as being in a low-involvement situation when products are used for private consumption: they are likely to adopt a rather simple cognitive stance, favouring the physical functions of the product and being mostly concerned with price and quality. There is a high level of purchasing involvement when the Chinese consumer buys products for their social symbolic value. Since people greatly value social harmony and the smoothness of relationships within the extended family, the social significance of a product is highly important: it may express status, gratitude, approval or disapproval.

Perceived risk

This is an important variable in consumer behaviour, and differs according to its breakdown into various components: physical risk, financial risk, social risk, etc. (Van Raaij, 1978). Whereas people in certain cultures may be more susceptible to physical risk (because the mortality rate is low, death is feared and avoided), others may be more sensitive to social risk (because a purchase may risk the loss of face in other people's eyes). Let us take an example: when buying a car, in a country where road safety is not a high priority, the perceived physical risk is low; where mileage is non-relevant, because gas is so cheap, there is a low perceived financial risk; but where an engine breakdown is a disaster, because of little or no available maintenance, there is a high perceived reliability risk. The perceived risk is quite different from that experienced by the average purchaser of a car in a western European country.

Consumer cognitive styles

The cognitive style assumed by the classical models of consumer behaviour (Howard and Sheth, 1969; Engel *et al.*, 1986) is that of an individual reviewing opportunities, evaluating alternatives, rationally searching for information, relying on opinion leaders and word-of-mouth communication, who is influenced by the social environment and situational factors. This person is additionally swayed by the stimuli of marketing strategies (particularly advertising and sales promotion), tries to choose the best alternative, progressively forms the intention to purchase, and finally (perhaps) actually buys the product. These models have a rather linear, analytical and abstract style. Many authors claim that Asian consumers tend to have a quite different cognitive style: the Chinese as well as the Japanese have a more synthetic, concrete and contextual orientation in their thought patterns (Lazer *et al.*, 1985, Yau, 1988; Yang, 1989). Sections 3.4 and 5.6 show how intellectual approaches vary across cultural groupings to such an extent that the diversity of cognitive styles cannot be ignored.

Legal marketing environment

To a large extent marketing regulations reflect views on whether consumers are predominantly considered as self-reliant (it is assumed that consumers are informed and responsible people) or dependent individuals who find themselves at a disadvantage in relation to the marketer. If assumed dependent, they need to be protected against abuses. If considered self-reliant, they still need to be protected if they have not reached self-reliant age (children) or against what is considered as hurting public morality.

1. Many Latin countries consider that private interest cannot exploit the taste of the public for gambling, and, as a result, lotteries are state monopolies; promotional campaigns that take the form of competitions are considered to be immoral, whereas they are permitted by Anglo-Saxon countries. Certain countries forbid promotional gifts or strictly limit their value, whereas other countries authorize them without any restriction. A possible reason for these diverging regulatory attitudes derives from the differences in response to the following question: are people capable of a rational economic evaluation of the value of the gift, capable of relating it to the full price they pay? Finally, are they considered able to come to a sound buying decision, even though they may have been unduly influenced? Section 11.4 examines the cultural relativity of regulatory approaches and consumer responses vis-à-vis sales promotion.

2. Moral approbation or condemnation for certain practices often leads to public debate which in turn influences the regulator when introducing legislation. For example there are different levels of acceptance of the use of nudes in television or magazine advertising, which lead to moral controversies in the public domain when foreign advertisements, introduced by the means of imported magazines or satellite broadcast, are perceived as shocking by the local audience. Another example is offered by the attitudes of regulators towards advertising targeted to a children's audience. Children are easy to influence, and it is sometimes argued that excessive needs creation, which parents cannot always satisfy, may destabilize family relationships. The following topic is also often debated: how should children be hired and compensated for taking part in a television commercial? Some European countries have such stringent regulations that many of the local commercials, targeting children as consumers, are produced in the United Kingdom, where regulation is more flexible.

3. Agreement with the morality of certain kinds of representation, in advertising in particular: the role of women, representations of 'ideal' people which leads to a desire to identify oneself with those depictions. Chapter 13 presents the cultural relativity of attitudes towards advertising in general, advertising copy and the type of media used.

4.3 Investigating the cross-cultural transposability of consumer behaviour concepts

Any element of consumer behaviour can be seen (inspected, filtered) through cross-cultural lenses. For example 'word-of-mouth communication' seems a fairly robust concept: in any culture, people discuss informally and exchange information on their consumption experiences. Where little relevant information is available, movie films for instance, new products, or when consumers have reduced familiarity with a complex product, people tend to seek informations from acquaintances. However, it may be hypothesized that word-of-mouth communication will be stronger in collectivist and ingroup oriented societies, where outside information provided by an impersonal marketer will be seen as less reliable than opinions from relative and acquaintances.

The best solution for investigating cross-cultural transposability is always to start from the 'common problem' in Kluckhohn and Strodtbeck's terms. For instance: why and how can a consumer express dissatisfaction with a product or a service? The basic concept found in the consumer behaviour literature is not based on all solutions to the common problem but on the dominant normative solution in a definite culture, generally Western and more precisely US. Other alternatives must always be looked for, especially the alternative that the problem may be *without* solution.

The example of consumer dissatisfaction

Attitudes towards consumerism vary across national contexts and the importance given to the consumer movement varies according to certain basic premises:

1. Is it legitimate that consumers should make their dissatisfaction known? This is not the case in societies where very long periods favourable to supply (when, during decades, the local supply has been systematically lower than the demand) have implanted the contrary idca. Shopping in eastern Europe illustrates the extent to which a customer complaint can seem an absurd step to take.
2. Is it legitimate for consumerists to force a producer, whose product quality is dubious, to close down? In other words, may consumers cause job losses and take away the livelihood of workers who are not ultimately responsible for the situation?

I pose these questions not out of a desire to adopt any particular position but merely to demonstrate that it is not inherently obvious that the defence of the consumer has a wholly positive social value. Thus expressing dissatisfaction frankly and openly may be considered as partially illegitimate.

Constructs such as consumer dissatisfaction have been used for assessing cross-cultural differences in consumer attitudes. Richins and Verhage (1985) have studied differences between US and Dutch consumers relating to their dissatisfaction and complaining behaviour, for which they had their questionnaire reviewed by a panel of Dutch experts and made some minor changes to the wording of the questions. They look for conceptual equivalence of the dissatisfaction concept: does it have the same meaning, socially and individually, for the US and the Dutch people to be 'dissatisfied with a product or a service'? Richins and Verhage find 29 per cent of the variance to be attributable to national differences, the most salient ones being as follows:

> Dutch consumers perceive more inconvenience and unpleasantness in making complaint than do American consumers. . . . Dutch consumers were less likely than Americans to feel a social responsibility to make complaints. . . . Seemingly contradicting this finding, however, Dutch consumers are more likely than Americans to feel bothered if they don't make a complaint when they believe they should, a sort of guilt. Perhaps this seeming contradiction indicates that Dutch respondents tend to feel a personal rather than social obligation to make complaints. (1985, p. 203)

The word 'construct' relates to a concept which has several underlying dimensions.

and may be measured quantitatively by identifying these various dimensions. The construct 'consumer dissatisfaction and complaint behaviour' (Richins, 1983) identifies five domains of attitude towards complaining:

1. Beliefs about the effect experienced when one complains.
2. Perceptions of the objective cost or trouble involved in making a complaint.
3. Perception of retailer responsiveness to consumer complaints.
4. The extent to which consumer complaints are expected to benefit society at large.
5. The perceived social appropriateness of making consumer complaints.

Investigating cross-cultural transposability may be done by inquiring whether each of these subdimensions makes sense in a particular national/cultural context. Exercise A4.2 proposes to go further in the investigation by using a consumer complaint scale developed by Singh (1988).

Cavusgil and Kaynak (1984) propose an interesting enlargement of the consumer dissatisfaction concept to the case of developing countries. They distinguish between micro-level sources (e.g. excessive prices, misleading advertising, lack of performance) and macro-level sources of consumer dissatisfaction (e.g. low income, inflation) with the possibility of interaction between the two levels. They state: 'In general micro-level sources appear to lead, over time, to a diffuse, latent discontent with the state of the marketplace; that is to a macro-level dissatisfaction. Unsatisfactory experiences with specific products and services seem to be reflected in a disillusionment with all institutions in the society' (1984, p. 118). Moreover the complaining behaviour does not have the same meaning at all if buyer and seller know each other personally, either as acquaintances or relatives: 'Personal relationships with vendors often prove advantageous. Usually food shoppers get to know how far they can trust a food retailer, and can negotiate prices and other terms' (Cavusgil and Kaynak, 1984, p. 122).

Looking with other eyes: Questioning about consumer behaviour

'Looking with other eyes' implies to decentre oneself. To explain this, I will use a personal example as a consumer which is recounted in Box 4.3

If we try to apply the perspectives in Table 4.1, the universal approach in this case gives few tracks for understanding. The 'imported' perspective gives many more insights. The first is that in European countries automatic cars are associated with high social status. Large and expensive cars come more often with automatic drive than medium or small cars. Another argument is the driving licence requirements: people are allowed to learn and pass the licence exam only with a manual gear-box car. In most European countries, there is only one exception: handicapped persons are allowed to use automatic cars to obtain their licence. In the UK, future drivers can take their test in an automatic without being disabled, but they get a restricted licence that only allows them to drive automatic cars. Learning plays a key role in the resistance to change of Europeans: having been educated on manual cars, they tend to stick to them. Another argument that the imported perspective would probably bring to light is that many Europeans still believe that automatic gear-box cars are reputed for high petrol consumption (or poor gas imagery to denote value in 'Scotch' tape, since the Scottish stereotype of supposed frugality is viewed favourably in the US (Solomon, 1994).

The assimilation model

It may be wrong to equate consumers from a definite ethnic group to a specific market segment which seeks specific products or service benefits. For instance Yankelovitch *et al.* (1982) found Hispanics to be more American than other Americans on a number of characteristics. Assimilation takes place when the relative influence of the culture of origin diminishes while immigrants hold faster to the values and behaviours of the country of residence. Assimilation is evidenced in the following areas: consumption patterns, employment, marriage with people originating from the host culture, participation in the political process as a candidate, acquaintances outside the ethnic community. The process of assimilation is a lengthy one, which may require several generations to be fully accomplished.

In the assimilation process two mechanisms are at work (Wallendorf and Reilly, 1983). The first is based on structural constraints: if people drive on the other side of the road, the individual will be obliged to adapt; compliance is compulsory, not voluntary. The second is based on the newcomer's willingness to adjust to the new culture behaviour and rules; it fits with a certain enthusiasm with what the new culture brings in terms of increased freedom and improved material status. This motivational component depicts the positive side of assimilation. But the negative side, structural constraints, may provoke a false adjustment. As Calantone *et al.* explain it (1985, p. 208):

> ... lack of availability may force some immigrants to make changes in the foods they purchase. Thus, behavioural change may occur without a concomitant change in values or beliefs. In making empirical comparisons, therefore, it is crucial to include only those behavioural patterns that reflect free choices by immigrants and to exclude adaptation to structural constraints.

Ethnicity as identity

When assimilation has fully taken place, that is, probably for third or fourth generation people, they may share much more with the society at large than with their subcultural group. However, there is a resurgence of ethnicity; as Bouchet (1995) remarks, ethnicity has much to do with the evolution of identity in general rather than with the origin of one's historical identity. Bell (1975, p. 171) explains the salience of ethnicity as a quest for identity:

> ethnicity in this context, is best understood *not* as a primordial phenomenon in which deeply held identities have to reemerge, but as a strategic choice by individuals who, in other circumstances, would choose other group memberships as a mean of gaining some power and privilege. In short, it is the *salience* not the *persona* that has to be the axial line for explanation. And because salience may be the decisive variable, the attachment to ethnicity may flush or fade very quickly depending on political and economic circumstances.

Thus ethnic consumption should be considered as a complex and unstable reality, at which marketers need to look with a quite open mind. It gives birth to strange mixtures such as the Chino-Latino cuisine, a fusion of Asian and Cuban cuisine to be found in New York, which has its roots in the Chinese immigration in Cuba in the early 1900s (Straus, 1992). When dealing with ethnic consumption, the following points have to be constantly kept in mind:

1. Translation or spelling mistakes or inadequate wordings may be resented as offending the group's honour. For instance, a *burrito* was mistakenly called in Spanish a *burrada*, which means 'big mistake' (Solomon, 1994). This results in minority group people having a sense of being rejected because their language is not used properly, or at least not understood, that is *not respected*.
2. In ethnic behaviour the phantasm of membership, that is the claim for being 'different', is central and may be pushed to its extreme. Smaller ingroups will be perceived as the best platforms for identification. Hispanics will therefore break further down into Mexicans, Puerto-Ricans, Cubans, etc.
3. The level of acculturation, that is the degree to which people have learned the ways of the host culture, and their age have an influence of ethnic consumption: older people and less acculturated people tend to display a stronger attitude as an ethnic consumer.
4. Identification needs are 'reversible', creating ambiguous and even contradictory demands. Most people belonging to ethnic communities strive for both integration into the society at large and the maintenance of their specific cultural roots. In some areas of consumption, for instance housing and furnishing, they may express their belonging to the larger national ingroup and in another area, food for instance, they may maintain a strong ethnic behaviour.

4.5　Marketing as an exchange of meanings

As suggested by McCracken (1991, p. 5), 'We may see consumer goods as the vehicles of cultural meanings ... consumers themselves as more or less sophisticated choosers and users of these cultural meanings.' But doing this, we have to look with other eyes. Marketing may be seen primarily as a process of exchange, where communication, broadly defined, is central. As Richard Bagozzi (1975, p. 35) states:

> In order to satisfy human needs, people and organizations are compelled to engage in social and economic exchanges with other people and organizations. This is true for primitive as well as highly developed societies. Social actors obtain satisfaction of their needs by complying with, or influencing, the behaviour of other actors. They do this by communicating and controlling the media of exchange, which in turn, comprise the links between one individual and another. Significantly, marketing exchanges harbour meanings for individuals that go beyond the mere use of media for obtaining results in interactions.

Consumers buy meanings and marketers communicate meanings through products and advertisements. Many of these meanings are culture-based: they are intersubjectively shared by a social group (D'Andrade, 1987). Intersubjective sharing of meanings means that each person in the group knows that everyone else knows the cognitive schema. Therefore in the process of exchange through buyer–seller relations, marketing communications or product consumption, interpretations are made spontaneously, as if they were obvious facts of the world, and a great deal of information in the process of marketing as exchange and communication need not be made explicit.

Culture may be considered as a sort of *meta-language* which is central in the marketing process when viewed as exchange and communication, as noted by Bagozzi. It works as a kind of *game rule*, implicitly indicating how people will interact in an exchange relationship, their constraints and their leeway in behaviour and decisions. The attitudinal differences toward market research between American and Japanese people (section 5.6) is a good example of this: what is the 'right' way (legitimate, appropriate) to communicate with the market? What is the market (actual buyers versus potential consumers)? In each case the objective is seemingly the same: to collect relevant information and market data, in order to decide on marketing strategies.

Two examples will help us illustrate the differences in marketing meta-communication: first the role of emotions in Japanese marketing, and second, the emphasis on the symbolic relationship between person and object in the Italian style of marketing.

The role of emotions in Japanese marketing

There is a wide range of books on Japanese marketing, which are unfortunately written only in Japanese *Kanji* and *Hiragana*, thereby limiting access for non-Japanese (*Gai-jin*) readers. But the Japanese provide details in English in the review of the largest Japanese advertising agency, *Dentsu Japan Marketing/Advertising*. Koichi Tanouchi, a professor of marketing at Hitotsubashi University, depicts the Japanese style of marketing as being fundamentally based on emotions and sensitivity. He first insists, as many authors do, that Japan is oriented towards rice production and is not a nation of hunters and gatherers. This means more collective organization and interpersonal sensitivity: the cultivation of rice needs the flooding of paddy fields, which cannot be decided by an isolated landowner; paddy fields have to be flooded simultaneously. This involves a strong collective solidarity, serious planning and individual tenaciousness. Tanouchi states that, in his opinion, 'masculine' values are less developed in Japan than 'feminine' values, which he illustrates by the example of marital relationships in household and personal spending (1983, p. 78):

> In Japan, the husband is supposed to hand all his income over to his wife. If he doesn't, he is criticized by people around him. If she complains about this to his boss in his business company, the boss is very likely to take the wife's side, and advise him to give all his salary to his wife and add that that is the best way to keep peace at home and that everyone else is doing so. The wife has the right to decide how much money her husband can have for daily lunch and coffee. Regularly, about once in a half year, Japanese newspapers carry a research report about the average amount of the money the average husbands get from their wives. Wives decide about their husbands' lunch money watching these figures.

Tanouchi and other authors (Lazer *et al.*, 1985) argue that sensitivity and emotions permeate most aspects of Japanese marketing. It is evidenced by the high level of sensitivity and response to *actual* consumer needs and by the search for social harmony between producers and distributors (see section 11.1 on the *Keiretsu* distribution). It is also prominent in Japanese sales force compensation arrangements, where collective reward systems are often used. They foster cooperation, avoid threatening individual competition, and promote social harmony in the sales team (section 14.3).

The role of the symbolic link between object and person through the medium of design in Italian marketing

It can be said that a specific Italian marketing style is emerging. This style is characterized by heavy emphasis (and corresponding financial commitment) devoted to product appearance and design. The article sold is intended to act as a link between the producer-seller and the consumer-purchaser: both appreciate the aesthetic qualities of the object. The Italians concentrate on the style and functionality of the object, and its integration in the environment. With such premisses, the symbolism of the object and its fit with the meaning attributed by consumers being considered as points of focus, an increasing importance should be given to qualitative studies. Baudrillard (1968) and his 'system of objects', which was fairly successful in France, ultimately achieved real success in Italy, where he is guru of marketing semiology (Box 4.4).

Dino Buzzati (1967), the author of *The Desert of the Tartars*, has written a short story entitled 'Suicide in the Park' which illustrates quite clearly the fusion between the person and the object through the medium of the imagination, leading to a passionate

---

Box 4.4   *The functional form of the cigarette lighter*

The stylised fluidity of the 'functional forms' testifies to the connotation of mental dynamics, the semblance of a lost relationship, in an attempt to reconstruct a purpose through the accumulation of signs. For example, a lighter in the shape of a pebble was successfully launched by advertising some years ago. The oblong, elliptic and asymmetrical form is 'highly functional', not because it provides a better light than another lighter, but because it fits exactly into the palm of the hand. 'The seas have polished it into the shape of the hand': it is an accomplished form. Its function is not to give a light, but to be easy to handle. Its form is, so to speak, predetermined by Nature (the sea) to be handled by man. This new purpose is the sole rhetoric of the lighter. The connotations are here twofold: as an industrial object, the cigarette lighter is supposed to recall one of the qualities of the handicraft object, the shape of which furthers the gesture and the body of man. Moreover the allusion to the sea brings us to the myth of Nature, itself cultured by man, which follows all his desires: the sea plays the cultural role of a polisher; it is the sublime handicraft of nature. As the stone rolled by the sea, furthered by the hand producing light, the cigarette lighter becomes a wonderful flint, a whole prehistoric and artisanate purpose comes into play in the very practical essence of an industrial object.

(Source: excerpt from: Jean Baudrillard, 1968, p. 82–3. Reproduced with permission. Author's translation.)

relationship. The narrator tells the story of one of his friends, Stefano, who became mad about a very nice sports car, which he could not buy. The life of his wife Faustina was literally poisoned by the obsessive passion of Stefano for this car. One day, Stefano appeared driving a long, blue, brand new sports car. The narrator admired the car and asked what Faustina thought of the buy. Stefano, embarrassed, then explained that she had gone; he was vague about the reasons. A few years passed. The narrator asked for news from Faustina each time he saw Stefano, who replied that she was gone forever. A few years later, Stefano, asked by the narrator about this car, said that it had been a good car but it was used now and had to be repaired constantly and no mechanic was able to service the foreign-made engine. At the end of the short story, the narrator reads a strange report in the newspaper about a blue car which started without a driver, ran through various streets and avenues, and finally threw itself against the ruins of the old Sforza palace. The old blue sports car caught fire and was completely burnt. He rushes to Stefano's house and finds him upset. Stefano admits: 'It was Faustina' and he explains how, as absurd as it may seem, some nine years ago, when they were making love one night, she began to cry and to shiver, to swell and had just enough time to go out in the street.

It is of course unrealistic to claim that the Italians are alone in having an awareness of the symbolic meaning of possessions for consumers. But they incorporate it at a very high level and make it an essential element of their marketing communication.

4.6   Conclusion

The other side of the poster, mentioned at the start of this chapter, says '*Bei Mercedes bleibt alles anders*' (with Mercedes everything remains different). Looking at *different* consumer behaviour with *different* eyes is the attitude to be recommended in international marketing, whenever we know that a lot is *similar*. It provides a method of inquiry which favours the discovery of significant differences in consumer behaviour across cultures and offers insights into the way consumers invest meaning into their buys.

Questions

1. Is there a 'modern' lifestyle, common to many cultures around the world? How could it be described? What could be its principal *raisons d'être*?
2. What would you expect to be the link of *consumer loyalty* with the following cultural variables; argue why, in your opinion, consumers having a certain cultural trait would be more, or conversely less, loyal:
   (a) strong future orientation;
   (b) strong ingroup orientation;
   (c) high individualism;
   (d) high uncertainty avoidance.
3. Discuss how strong emphasis on group belonging in a particular culture may influence buying decisions.
4. Discuss possible cross-cultural variability in the concept of 'status-seeking consumers'.

5. Why can 'word-of-mouth communication' among people be considered as a fairly robust consumer behaviour concept cross-culturally?

6. What is *ethnic consumption*?

Teaching materials

A4.1   Exercise: 'Dichter's consumption motives'

Discuss the cross-cultural variability of the major motives for consumption as identified by Ernest Dichter (some 30 years ago!) in Table 4.3. Choose five associations between motives and associated products for your discussion.

A4.2   Exercise: Investigating the cross-cultural transposability of a consumer complaint scale

You will find below a scale of consumer complaint behaviour (CCB) which has been developed by Singh (1988). US respondents were asked to express their degree of agreement or disagreement on a six-point Likert scale on the items listed below (possible behavioural responses to dissatisfaction with a consumption experience). Factor analysis allowed three dimensions to be distinguished for CCB.

1. Voice CCB:
   (a) Forget about the incident and do nothing.
   (b) Definitely complain to the store manager on your next trip.
   (c) Go back or call the repair shop immediately and ask them to take care of your problem.
2. Private CCB:
   (a) Decide not to use that repair shop again.
   (b) Speak to your friends and relatives about your bad experience.
   (c) Convince your friends and relatives not to use that repair shop.
3. Third party CCB:
   (a) Complain to a consumer agency and ask them to make the repair shop take care of your problem.
   (b) Write a letter to the local newspaper about your bad experience.
   (c) Report to the consumer agency so that they can warn other consumers.
   (d) Take some legal action against the repair shop/manufacturer.

You are asked to investigate the cross-cultural transposability of such a scale. Since you cannot do it with a full psychometric design, you have to investigate mostly into the meaning, situations, institutions, and behaviours depicted by the items.

Table 4.3

Motive	Associated products
Power–masculinity–virility	Power: sugary products and large breakfasts, bowling, electric trains, pistols, power tools Masculinity–virility: coffee, red meat, heavy shoes, toy guns; buying fur coats for women, shaving with a razor
Security	Ice-cream, full drawer of neatly ironed shirts, real plaster walls, home baking, hospital care
Eroticism	Sweets, gloves, a man lighting a woman's cigarette
Moral purity–cleanliness	White bread, cotton fabric, harsh household cleaning chemicals, bathing, oatmeal
Social acceptance	Companionship: ice-cream (fun to share), coffee Love and affection: toys, sugar and honey Acceptance: soap, beauty products
Individuality	Gourmet foods, foreign cars, cigarette holders, vodka, perfume, fountain pens
Status	Scotch, ulcers, heart attacks, indigestion, carpets
Femininity	Cakes and cookies, dolls, silk, tea, household curios
Reward	Cigarettes, candy, alcohol, ice cream, cookies
Mastery over environment	Kitchen appliances, boats, sporting goods, cigarette lighters
Disalienation (a desire to feel connectedness to things)	Home decorating, skiing, morning radio broadcasts
Magic–Mystery	Soups (have healing powers), paints (change the mood of a room), carbonated drinks (magical effervescent property), vodka (romantic history), unwrapping of gifts

Source: Solomon, 1994, p. 98.

A4.3 Case: Eliot Greeting Card Company (1)

The Eliot Company was established by Gregory Eliot in the early 1950s in St Louis, Missouri. Although the company only had about 4 per cent of the US greeting card market, it had been profitable since its beginnings, and had shown modest growth in a market environment dominated by Hallmark Company (which maintained over 40 per cent of the market), American Greetings (about 30 per cent market share), and several smaller companies that had market shares of 5 to 15 per cent. Eliot had been successful largely by carving itself a niche, marketing lines of specialty cards for which the other firms seemed to have little interest.

Recently, however, the greeting card market had been experiencing a period of (at least temporary) flat sales. This was seen to be the result of both the relatively weak economy and a dramatic increase in telephone advertising, urging consumers to 'reach out and touch someone' at the expense of sending greeting cards. This has led to rather intense marketing efforts by the larger greeting card companies to gain percentage points of the relatively sluggish market. It was becoming obvious that the competition was turning its attention to the specialty lines that Eliot had been able to use to its advantage for so long (see Exhibit 1).

Exhibit 1 'Greetings, One and All!' Cardmakers Gear Up for Mother's Day, and Every Day

Just in case anyone forgot, the greeting card industry is busy reminding people that Sunday is Mother's Day. Of course, everyone will want to pick up cards for Mom, wife, and Grandma. But what about sisters and favorite aunts? Sure. There are Mother's Day cards for them too, and a host of greetings for a mother-in-law. How about someone expecting a baby in July? No problem. Any number of companies make Mother's Day cards for mothers-to-be. And why should Pop feel left out and have to wait until June for his special day? Hallmark puts out a card that says 'You're a terrific parent, too, Dad!' Why in fact should Mother's Day be restricted to parents? It is not. A card by Recycled Paper Products of Chicago has this touching message: 'Although you're not my mother, your little motherlies mean a lot to me. Happy Motherish Day.'

No business is better than greeting cards at finding imaginative ways to package and promote an old product. The leading companies, Hallmark of Kansas City and American Greetings of Cleveland, have roots that go back almost to the turn of the century, but they strive to be as innovative as fledgling Silicon Valley computer firms. The cardmakers are experimenting with different styles, coming up with novel reasons for people to buy their wares and using new technology that enables cards to play tunes or talk. Hallmark offers 1,200 varieties of cards for Mother's Day, the year's fourth biggest card day (after Christmas, Valentine's Day, and Easter), while American Greetings boasts of 1,300. The products range from a traditional card with a picture of flowers and syrupy poetry for $1 or less to a $7 electronic version that plays the tune of 'You Are the Sunshine of My Life.'

Hallmark holds about 42 percent of the $3.2 billion-a-year greeting card business, followed by American Greetings' 30 percent. The two leaders are now being challenged by Cincinnati-based Gibson Greetings, which has captured an estimated 10 per cent share, up from 5 percent in 1978. Gibson scored a coup in February by striking a deal with Walt Disney Productions for the rights to use Mickey Mouse and his friends, who had previously been featured on Hallmark cards. Gibson had also signed up Garfield the Cat and the Sesame Street characters, but Hallmark's line of Peanuts cards is still one of the industry's most successful. American Greetings got a boost last year by reaching an agreement with Sears to be the exclusive cardseller in all its department stores. That more than matched a similar arrangement that Hallmark has with J. C. Penney.

As the top three cardmakers battle among themselves, they also keep an eye on about 300 smaller manufacturers, which are often daring and inventive. Says Hallmark Chairman Donald Hall, 'Industries that aren't competitive get stagnant after a while. Ours is very competitive, and the fever of creativity is at a high point.' One sign of the industry's brainstorming is the burgeoning number of occasions for which greetings are available. Card buyers can now congratulate a friend on getting a driver license, buying a new car, or completing a successful diet. Customers can use cards to announce a divorce, propose a tryst, or console a pal whose pet dog has died. Carrying that marketing strategy to an extreme, California Dreamers, a Chicago company, has put out an all-purpose generic greeting card. The message: 'Whatever.'

The card manufacturers have been alert to changes in the American family. Says Richard Connor, executive vice-president of American Greetings, 'The divorce rate has brought about new families, single fathers, and working mothers. These new relationships open up new avenues for card sending.' One of Hallmark's Mother's Day cards shows Mom at her office. Both American Greetings and Hallmark have cards with messages to 'Mom and Her Husband' or 'Dad and His Wife.'

Paper Moon Graphics, a small, fast-growing Los Angeles firm has won over customers with a combination of quirky humor and striking visual images. One of its cards shows a bride perched on the shoulders of her groom, who is standing precariously on a high wire. Inside, it says, 'So Far . . . So Good. Happy Anniversary!' Maine Line of Rockport, Maine, has found a profitable niche by specializing in cards that appeal to women. A sample message: 'A woman in the White House would feel right at home . . . She already knows how to clean up the mess men have made.' Maine Line even has a few cards that could be used by homosexuals. One says, 'Hip hip hooray, I'm glad you're gay.'

The industry leaders have responded to the competition by introducing their own yuppie-style cards. Hallmark has a new line called Modern Woman, with messages that might often seem risqué for the venerable 75-year-old firm. Example: 'You're such a totally together man. You're sensitive, kind, understanding and a good listener . . . Nice buns, too! Happy Birthday.'

One of the newest frontiers in the industry is talking cards. The voice comes from a minute speaker connected to a microchip, where the message is stored. One card by American Greetings has the words 'Open this birthday card fast' printed on the outside. When the card is opened, a relieved voice says, 'Thanks, it was really getting stuffy in here. Happy Birthday!' Priced as high as $10, the electronic cards are still a novelty item. But since the cost of microchips is coming down, the industry hopes that tuneful and talking cards may eventually become a mainstay of Mother's Day, and every other conceivable occasion.

(Source: 'Greetings, One and All,' *Time*, May 13, 1985, p. 54.)

———— ♦ ♦ ♦ ————

For the first time in its history, Eliot Greeting was faced with a decline in its modest share, each point of which was worth several millions of dollars in sales. At a brainstorming session by the firm's board of directors, President Tom Eliot suggested that one possible solution to the problem would be to develop an export market for its products to avoid the high costs of head-to-head competition for US customers. He reasoned that it would be easier for the company to design and make cards for English-speaking consumers in countries like the United Kingdom and Australia than to continue to slug it out with the market leaders at home.

Bill Yates, vice president of Sales, had an alternative suggestion. He had recently returned from a vacation in the US Southwest where he had become aware of the large number of Hispanic Americans, who were, according to his sales representatives, beginning to improve their traditionally low economic status. Yates's idea was to create and market a line of greeting cards for this largely Spanish-speaking group of Americans for whom greeting card sending was at a relatively low level, compared with the general population. He argued that, rather than expanding its efforts to approach to foreign customers, the firm would be better able to take advantage of its existing production and distribution system to develop this relatively untapped market at home. An argument developed between Tom Eliot and Bill Yates as to which avenue would be the best source of growth for Eliot Greeting Card Company. Tom had recently seen an article in the local paper (see Exhibit 2) describing his competitor's moves in the US Hispanic market. He certainly did not want another slugfest with competition. Bill argued that the potential of the US Hispanic market was large enough for all greeting cards firms and that they would either have to develop skills now or later in marketing cards to this significant segment in the US market. They agreed to postpone a decision until they could get more information on each option.

Exhibit 2 'Greeting Card Firms Expand Hispanic Line'

Two major U.S. greeting card companies are expanding their lines of Spanish language cards and gift items in response to growing demand from the Hispanic market.

Hallmark Cards, Inc., and American Greetings Corp. have announced plans to publish more greeting cards written in standard, dialect-free Spanish incorporating new designs that eschew old-fashioned stereotypes in favor of popular characters such as Strawberry Shortcake.

Old views knocked

The U.S. Census Bureau says that Hispanics comprised 6.4 percent of the total population in 1980 and increased in number by 61 percent during the 1970s.

The U.S. Hispanic Chamber of Commerce, which meets in San Antonio later this week has reported that the nation's 20 million Hispanics now have purchasing power worth $70 billion – a figure the chamber expects to more than double by the year 2000.

Recent marketing studies have knocked down some old views about Hispanic consumers and provided new data on buyers seeking high-quality goods and services.

Hallmark Cards, the industry leader with $1.5 billion in annual sales, expects to double its Spanish language line of everyday and seasonal cards by next May, said Nancy Matheny, manager of marketing and communications.

American Greetings has launched a new line of Spanish language cards, posters, and calendars featuring popular characters such as Ziggy and Strawberry Shortcake, and the 'classical romantic' expressions of its 'Soft Touch' series.

The 95 new designs, now available in San Antonio stores, will expand the company's current line of approximately 300 everyday and seasonal greeting cards, invitations, and gift tags in Spanish, said product manager Ross Bennett.

American Greetings, the largest publicly held greeting card publisher with $1 billion in annual sales, based its latest expansion on the results of focus group interviews with Hispanic women in Los Angeles and New York City, Bennett said.

Women predominate in both the Hispanic and Anglo card market, accounting for 90 percent of all card buyers and 85 percent of all dollars spent on greeting cards, Bennett said from his Cleveland office.

Bennett said the Hispanic women interviewed told American Greetings:

♦ Spanish language greeting cards are difficult to find, even in mostly Hispanic neighborhoods in large cities.
♦ Cards in Spanish are sent most frequently to older relatives and friends, especially those who still speak mostly Spanish, and to those living in Mexico, Puerto Rico, Cuba, and other foreign countries. Cards in English usually are preferred for young relatives, such as brothers and sisters, and for children, co-workers, and non-Hispanic friends. Exceptions to these general rules are religious observances, such as baptisms, weddings, name days, and fifteenth birthday days, when Spanish-language greetings are preferred.
♦ The industry's offerings in Spanish had been inferior to their English language counterparts. Among the criticisms: limited variety of designs, poor quality of photographs and paper, and overuse of loud, garish colors.

Bennett said the U.S. Hispanic population's growing affluence during the past ten years has created a need for Spanish cards of improved quality and variety. The old stereotypes of sombreros and burros do not work anymore, he added.

But simply translating an English language sentiment into Spanish and slapping on a new cover will not sell more cards to Hispanic customers, industry leaders say.

Both Hallmark and American Greetings employ linguistic consultants and bilingual editors to develop pithy verses in traditional, or Castillian, Spanish.

'We don't regurgitate English words or sentiments straight into Spanish,' Matheny said from Hallmark's Kansas City, Missouri, headquarters. Cultural and linguistic idiosyncrasies are incorporated in the company's line of Spanish cards, which was begun in 1982 with 100 designs.

Matheny predicted the firm will produce 500 to 600 everyday and seasonal designs in Spanish by May 1985. Hallmark and its Ambassador subsidiary publish cards and other items 20 languages for sales in 100 countries, with 11 million cards produced daily.

Differences blur

Bennett pointed out that Spanish greeting cards should be written in a standard grammatically correct version of the language that does not reflect any regional dialect, just as English cards are written.

American Greetings' research showed that card senders preferred to write their own personal message on the card to incorporate any regionally distinct dialect, he said.

A recent survey of the U.S. Hispanic market by Yankelovich, Skelly & White, Inc., revealed a 'blurring of differences' among Spanish-speaking nationalities, leading the researchers to propose that all Hispanics be considered as one population segment for marketing purposes. 'Localized patterns of speech, slang, etc., are felt to be a lessening barrier between Hispanics of different national origins,' the report states.

Rousana Cards, a Hillside, N.J., company specializing in greeting cards aimed at Hispanics, blacks, and other ethnic groups, has been publishing cards in Spanish since 1947.

Rousana President Ira F. Rubin said although his firm's cards generally use vernacular Spanish, some idioms also are included. He cited one example: *yerno*, the standard Spanish word for son-in-law, becomes the feminine *yerna*, daughter-in-law, only in a Puerto Rico dialect. Rubin's company publishes cards for *yernas* and markets them in appropriate neighborhoods. 'We feel very bullish regarding greeting cards in Spanish,' Rubin said. 'People have told us that as Latins become more Anglicized, we would lose our market, but that just doesn't happen.'

(Source: 'Greeting Card Firms Expand Hispanic Line', *Express News* (San Antonio, Texas), September 18, 1984.)

———— ♦♦♦ ————

English-speaking export markets

The English-speaking export market was a potentially large one. Its major components were the United Kingdom (England, Scotland, Wales and Northern Ireland), Canada, Australia and New Zealand. These four countries comprised a total population of 96.2 million, broken down as follows:

United Kingdom	55,226,400
Canada	24,343,200
Australia	13,548,500
New Zealand	3,125,100
	96,243,200

In addition, the Republic of South Africa had a population speaking English as a first language of nearly 1 million. Several other former British colonies, such as Kenya, Hong Kong and Singapore, had English-speaking minorities, but the major English-speaking countries offered a greater immediate potential. All four of the English-speaking nations were economically developed. Canada had been classified by most experts as belonging to the small group of affluent nations even though it had been experiencing serious economic problems in the mid-1980s. The other three countries were clearly in the category of developed nations, having predominantly middle-class populations with considerable disposable income.

Culturally, the four nations share a common heritage with the United States, but each culture has evolved somewhat differently over the years. Although they all speak the English language, they exhibit varying degrees of difference in word usage. Since the Eliot Company's product is written communication, it would be dangerous for its management to assume that identically worded messages would have an identical meaning in each country. Much of the charm and appeal of greeting cards comes from subtle plays on words, and such messages might not be perceived in the same way in the other countries. Canada would present the least difficulty in this matter. Because Canada shares a long border with the United States and Canadians are exposed to large amounts of American media (television and magazines), word usage is very similar in the two nations – similar enough that identical messages would usually be successful. However, in the United Kingdom, where a 'closet' is a 'cupboard' and 'to schmooze' is 'to chat', the danger of miscommunication is very real. This is equally true of Australia and New Zealand. Eliot would have to test all messages with local experts and, in many instances, work out entirely different messages for each country.

A second major cultural difference between the United States and these other English-speaking countries may lie in the use and perception of greeting cards. Historically, in English-speaking cultures, a personally written note or letter has been considered the polite and proper method of communicating with a friend. Standardized, pre-printed messages, such as are found on greeting cards, were considered to be less polite, less caring substitutes. Greeting cards may have complete acceptance in the United States, but before the Eliot Company decides to launch its products in any of these other countries, it must learn how their residents perceive greeting cards today.

The US Hispanic market

Some preliminary demographic data were gathered to support the feasibility of Yates's proposal to sell Spanish language cards to the Hispanic market in the United States. The 1980 census estimated conservatively that Hispanics numbered nearly 15 million in the United States and that their growth rate was much higher than that of the population at large. It was speculated both because of immigration and high fertility rates that by the year 2000, Hispanics would surpass blacks in numbers in the United States and hence become the largest minority group. Yates was placed in charge of conducting secondary research into the idea and he hired the consulting firm of Lorca and Associates, specialists in the US Hispanic market. Yates requested that the firm provide recommendations concerning general customer behaviour of the Hispanic population so that decisions could be made about what the company would need to do to design and market greeting cards to the Spanish-speaking market in the United States.

The consultant's report

Jose Lorca, president of the consulting firm, presented Bill Yates with a review of the literature pertaining to the consumer behaviour characteristics of US Hispanics. He took some pains to point out that empirical data about this subpopulation were very meagre and that much of the information came from articles in trade periodicals. These sources reflect experience by firms who have been interested in the Hispanic market, but do not report much of the hard data which would normally be expected to support conclusions made about Hispanics. He expressed a desire for more extensive consumer research to verify the speculations used to characterize the

Hispanic market. With this caution in mind, Lorca reported his interpretations. He extracted seven themes from these studies which to him summarized the traits attributed to Hispanic consumers:

1. A preference for locally owned, Spanish-speaking businesses as well as a preference for Spanish ethnic products.
2. A high degree of brand loyalty and susceptibility to brand influences.
3. A tendency for purchases to be influenced by pride in Hispanic heritage.
4. A high degree of price consciousness and careful shopping characteristics.
5. A high degree of influence from 'family' in making purchase decisions.
6. Preference for Spanish language media, especially radio and television.
7. A tendency to become 'acculturated' with rising affluence.

Thus, Eliot Greeting was confronted with the prospect of developing the use of greeting cards among a relatively provincial and traditional group of potential customers who appeared to be heavily dependent upon their cultural background for purchase decisions. Moreover, as these individuals become more economically secure, they become more like typical American consumers.

Lorca pointed out several other problems with developing the Hispanic market. First, it could not be said that the consumers in the overall Hispanic market were homogeneous. In addition to the acculturation characteristic (Hispanics were not alike at different economic levels), US Hispanics represent a number of different ethnic subgroups, depending on their national origins. These include Mexican Americans (59 per cent), Puerto Ricans (15 per cent), and Cubans (6 per cent) as well as Hispanics with origins in other Central and South American countries and Europe (20 per cent). These groups differ widely in cultural traits, especially in the particular dialects of Spanish spoken. He also noted that nearly all these people speak a kind of Spanish that is considerably different from the classical Castillian Spanish typically taught in Spanish courses offered at US high schools and universities. This fact seemed particularly important to the creation of Spanish verses for greeting cards, especially in light of the uniquely personal nature of messages used.

Questions

1. Isolate the probable impact of culture on Hispanic preferences and purchasing pattern for greeting cards. Investigate the symbolic meaning of sending a greetings card. (To whom, on which occasions, in which language?)
2. What issues will have to be addressed prior to the development of the English-speaking export market?
3. What are the benefits of each strategy: Hispanic market in the United States versus English-speaking export market?

(Source: Adapted from a case prepared by Joel Saegaert, University of Texas at San Antonio, in Cundiff and Hilger, 1988, pp. 156–63. Reproduced with permission.)

References

Bagozzi, Richard P. (1975), 'Marketing as exchange', *Journal of Marketing*, vol. 39, no. 4, pp. 32–9.

Ballah, R. N. (1970), *Tokugawa Religion*, Bencon Press: Boston.

Baudrillard, Jean (1968), *Le Système des objets*, Gallimard: Paris.

Belk, Russell W. (1988), 'Third World consumer culture', in E. Kumçu and A. Fuat Firat (eds), *Research in Marketing*, supplement 4, JAI Press: Greenwich, Connecticut.

Bell, D. (1975), 'Ethnicity and social change', in N. Glazer and D. P. Moynihan (eds), *Ethnicity, Theory and Experience*, Harvard University Press: Cambridge, MA.

Bouchet, Dominique (1995), 'Marketing and the redefinition of ethnicity,' in Janeen Arnold Costa and Gary J. Bamossy (eds), *Marketing in a Multicultural World*, Sage: Thousand Oaks, CA, pp. 68–105.

Buzzati, Dino (1967), *Le K*, Robert Laffont: Paris.

Calantone, R., M. Morris and J. Johar (1985), 'A cross-cultural benefit segmentation analysis to evaluate the traditional assimilation model', *International Journal of Research in Marketing*, vol. 2, pp. 207–17.

Cavusgil, S. Tamer and Erdener Kaynak (1984), 'Critical issues in the cross-cultural measurement of consumer dissatisfaction: Developed versus LDC practices' in Erdener, Kaynak and Ronald Savitt (eds), *Comparative Marketing Systems*, Praeger: New York, pp. 114–30.

Chien, M. (1979), *Chinese National Character and Chinese Culture: A historical perspective*, The Chinese University of Hong-Kong Press: Shatin, Hong Kong (in Chinese).

Chiou, Jyh-Shen (1995), 'The process of social influences on new product adoption and retention in individualistic versus collectivistic cultural contexts', *Proceedings of the Second Conference on the Cultural Dimension of International Marketing*, Odense, pp. 107–27.

Cunciff, Edward and Marye Tharp Hilger, *Marketing in the International Environment*, 2nd edn, Prentice Hall: Englewood Cliffs, N.J.

D'Andrade, Roy G. (1987), 'A folk model of the mind', in Dorothy Quinn and Naomi Holland (eds), *Cultural Models in Language and Thought*, Cambridge University Press: Cambridge, pp. 112–48.

Dubois, Bernard (1987), 'Culture et marketing', *Recherche et Applications en Marketing*, vol. 2, no. 3, pp. 37–64.

Engel, James F., Roger D. Blackwell and Paul W. Miniard (1986), *Consumer Behavior*, 5th ed., Holt, Rhinehart & Winston: New York.

Fei, X. T. (1948), *Rural China*, Guancha She: Shanghai (in Chinese).

Gans, Herbert (1962), *The Urban Villagers*, The Free Press: New York.

Hirschmann, Elisabeth C. (1985), 'Primitive aspects of consumption in modern American Society,' *Journal of Consumer Research*, vol. 12 (September), pp. 142–54.

Howard, J. and J. N. Sheth (1969), *The Theory of Buyer Behaviour*, John Wiley: New York.

Hsieh, Y. W. (1967), Filial piety and Chinese society, in C. A. Moore (ed), *The Chinese Mind*, University of Hawaii Press: Honolulu, pp. 167–87.

Hsu, F. L. K. (1971), Philosophical homeostasis and jen: conceptual tools for advancing psychological anthropology, *American Anthropologist*, vol. 73, pp. 23–44.

Karsaklian, Eliane (1995), 'Mesure de la mémorisation des messages publicitaires par les enfants: l'Influence du système scolaire', Unpublished doctoral thesis, July, HEC: Jouy-en-Josas.

Kotler, Philip (1994), *Marketing Management*, 8th edn, Prentice Hall: Englewood Cliffs, NJ.

Kushner, J. M. (1982), 'Market research in a non-Western context: the Asian example', *Journal of the Market Research Society*, vol. 24, no. 2, pp. 116–22.

Laurent, Clint R. (1982), 'An investigation of the family life cycle in a modern Asian society', *Journal of the Market Research Society*, vol. 24, no. 2, pp. 140–50.

Lazer, William, Shoji Murata and Hiroshi Kosaka (1985), 'Japanese marketing: Towards a better understanding', *Journal of Marketing*, vol. 49 (Spring), pp. 69–81.

Levitt, Theodore (1983), 'The globalization of markets', *Harvard Business Review*, vol. 61 (May–June), pp. 92–102.

Maslow, Abraham H. (1954), *Motivation and Personality*, Harper & Row: New York.

McCracken, Grant (1991), 'Culture and consumer behaviour: An anthropological perspective', *Journal of the Market Research Society*, vol. 32, no. 1, pp. 3–11.

Mendenhall, Mark, Betty Jane Punnett and David Ricks (1995), *Global Management*, Blackwell: Cambridge, Mass.

Redding, S. G.(1982). 'Cultural effects on the marketing process in Southeast Asia', *Journal of the Market Research Society*, vol. 24, no. 2, pp. 98–114.

Richins, M. (1983), 'Negative word-of-mouth by dissatisfied consumers: A pilot study', *Journal of Marketing*, vol. 47 (Winter), pp. 68–78.

Richins, M. and B. Verhage (1985), 'Cross-cultural differences in consumer attitudes and their implications for complaint management', *International Journal of Research in Marketing*, vol 2, pp. 197–205.

Singh, Jagdip (1988), 'Consumer complaint intentions and behavior: definitions and taxonomical issues', *Journal of Marketing*, vol. 52 (January), pp. 93–107.

Solomon, Michael R. (1994), *Consumer Behavior*, 2nd edn, Allyn and Bacon: Needham Heights.

Straus, Karen (1992), 'Go hog wild with Chino-Latino pork dishes', *Restaurants and Institutions*, vol. 102, no. 19, pp. 43–57.

Tanouchi, Koichi (1983), 'Japanese-style Marketing Based on Sensitivity', *Dentsu Japan Marketing/Advertising*, vol. 23 (July), pp. 77–81.

Van Raaij, W.F. (1978), 'Cross-cultural methodology as a case of construct validity' in M. K. Hunt (ed.), *Advances in Consumer Research*, Association for Consumer Research: Ann Arbor, vol. 5, pp. 693–701.

Wallendorf, Melanie and Michael D. Reilly (1983), Ethnic Migration, Assimilation and Consumption', *Journal of Consumer Research*, 10 (December), pp. 292–302.

Wilk, Richard (1995), 'Real Belizean food: Building local identity in the transnational Caribbean', *Proceedings of the Second Conference on the Cultural Dimension of International Marketing*, Odense, pp. 372–91.

Yang, Chung-Fang (1989), 'Une conception du comportement du consommateur chinois', *Recherche et Applications en Marketing*, vol. IV, no.1, pp. 17–36.

Yang, M. C. (1972), 'Familism and Chinese national character', in Y. Y. Lee and K. S. Yang (eds), *Symposium on the Character of the Chinese*, Institute of Ethnology, Academia Sinica (in Chinese), pp. 127–74.

Yankelovitch, Skelly and White (1982), *Spanish USA: A study of the Hispanic market in the U.S.*, for Spanish Television Networks.

Yau, Oliver H. M. (1988), 'Chinese cultural values: Their dimensions and marketing implications', *European Journal of Marketing*, vol. 22, no. 5, pp. 44–57.

5

— ♦♦♦ —

Cross-cultural market research

A French syrup maker ordered a survey of the Swedish market to a large international market research company: syrup, a solution of sugar dissolved in water and flavoured with fruit juice was improperly translated as *blandsaft*, a Swedish term for concentrated fruit juice, a local substitute of syrup with much less sugar. When results came, they were of no use, because it was a local product rather than the product category at large that had been surveyed. Some brief introductory examples will serve to explain the topic of this chapter, that is, the problems which are met when undertaking market research across national/cultural environments and their solutions. Typical research questions may be similar to the following:

1. How should one undertake a market survey for instant coffee in a traditionally tea-drinking country (i.e. the United Kingdom or Japan); what information and data must be sought? How should the data be collected?
2. Which information-gathering technique should one use for personal care products in a country where, for instance, potential respondents resent interviews as an intrusion into their privacy?
3. Where the starting point is a questionnaire that was originally designed for a specific country/culture, how should it be translated and adapted to the cultural specificity of other countries in which it is to be administered?

This chapter aims to provide the reader with some basic insights, drawn mostly from cross-cultural methodology in the social sciences, on how to solve these problems. The simultaneous launch of new products on several different national markets is becoming more and more frequent, therefore research of these markets has to be undertaken simultaneously. Cultural differences are the main characteristic when contrasting national contexts, as non-tariff barriers are eased. Taking once more instant coffee as an example, there is a marked difference in the research perspective according to which research questions are addressed:

1. How does one recover the market share lost by instant coffee to ground coffee in a traditionally coffee-drinking country? This requires the investigation of consumption

patterns in certain social and family situations, when people are drinking specific coffee-based beverages.

2. How does one increase the market share for instant coffee (out of the total hot beverages market) in a traditionally tea-drinking country?

The formulation of research objectives when developed through differing cultural contexts cannot be the same as the formulation for domestic market research: an understanding of the cross-cultural environment is a basic requirement of research objective formulation. Given the multinationalization of business, establishing the quality of research instruments, the consistency of behavioural/attitudinal constructs, and the equivalence of samples are of paramount concern to the marketer. This chapter presents the main limits to equivalence across national/cultural contexts when one undertakes cross-cultural market research, and in particular the issue of conceptual and functional equivalence (section 5.1), translation problems (section 5.2), measure equivalence related to different units being used cross-culturally (section 5.3), the comparability of samples and sampling procedures (section 5.4), and the equivalence problems in data collection procedures resulting from interviewers' and respondents' attitudes towards surveys (section 5.5). The last section (5.6) goes further in discussing whether international market research should use a different approach from traditional positivistic market research techniques.

5.1 Equivalence in cross-cultural research

If the type of data sought and the research procedures implemented are considered to be of general application, the main difference between domestic and cross-cultural market research lies in the likely difficulties in establishing equivalence at the various stages of the research process.[1] It is not self-evident, as the Japanese style of market research shows in section 5.6, that research procedures and the type of data sought are completely independent of the cultural context of the researcher. But this chapter first emphasizes dependence on the researched context:

1. The complexity of the research design is greatly increased when working in an international, multicultural and multilinguistic environment (Douglas and Craig, 1983), not to mention the difficulties in establishing comparability and equivalence of data.
2. Even larger problems may arise when differences in sociocultural or psychographic variables imply different attitudes and behaviour when using particular types of product.

For instance, Plummer (1977) compared the attitudes of women from the United States, Canada, Europe and several Commonwealth countries regarding housework, child care and the use of deodorants, and demonstrated a wide range of results due to cultural differences. He showed, for example, that the US housewife does not consider house cleaning as important as her Italian counterpart. The benefits expected from cleaning products are more functional for Americans and more symbolic for the Italians, since Italian housewives regard their role in a more traditional way. Therefore the list of benefits shown on cards to potential interviewees should be changed according to each country (see the hair shampoo exercise in section A5.2).

Research approaches: emic versus etic

This classic distinction in cross-cultural research was originated by Sapir (1929) and further developed by Pike (1966). The emic approach holds that attitudinal or behavioural phenomena are expressed in a unique way in each culture. Taken to its extreme, this approach states that no comparisons are possible. The etic approach, on the other hand, is primarily concerned with identifying universals. The difference arises from linguistics where phon*etic* is universal and depicts universal sounds which are common to several languages, and phon*emic* stresses unique sound patterns in languages.

In general, market research measurement instruments adapted to each national culture (the emic approach) offer more reliability and provide data with greater internal validity than tests applicable to several cultures (the etic approach, or 'culture-free tests'). But it is at the expense of cross-national comparability and external validity: results are not transposable to other cultural contexts. This is why we will look now at establishing cross-national equivalence, which is inspired by the etic rather than the emic perspective. In terms of Table 4.1 the issue would be very much at the centre of the four cells; it lies somewhere in between looking with the same eye at an object which is supposed to be different and changing to a slightly different eye in order to have a better look.

Wind and Douglas (1982) propose a hybrid approach which they define in the following way:

> The proposed approach develops country, culture or sub-culture specific concepts and measures. These are compared, combined or modified, and wherever possible common 'pan-cultural' concepts, which do not have a specific cultural bias, and which reflect the idiosyncratic characteristics of each country, culture or sub-culture are identified. Country-specific measures of the 'pan-cultural' and country idiosyncratic concepts are developed and compared. To the extent possible they are combined and country-specific measures are administered, generating the secondary data for the comparison.

Levels of cross-cultural equivalence

Management must provide guidelines for data collection. Consequently the systematic collection of data is vital, either domestic or international. It is important to follow a precise plan which outlines the various steps of the research process (Green *et al.*, 1988), starting with a clear and concise statement of the research problem. The relevant literature comprises several studies which explore the issue of cross-cultural equivalence (Green and Langeard, 1979; Leung, 1989; Poortinga, 1989; Van Herk and Verhallen, 1995). In one of the most exhaustive reviews of equivalence levels, Douglas and Craig (1984) identify thirteen areas where non-equivalence, causing non-comparability, may arise in comparative consumer research. The various levels of cross-cultural equivalence

Table 5.1 *Categories of cross-cultural equivalence*

A. Conceptual equivalence	**B. Functional equivalence**
C. Translation equivalence	**D. Measure equivalence**
• Lexical equivalence	• Perceptual equivalence
• Idiomatic equivalence	• Metric equivalence
• Grammatical-syntactical equivalence	• Calibration equivalence
• Experiential equivalence	• Temporal equivalence
E. Sample equivalence	**F. Data collection equivalence**
• Sampling unit equivalence	• Respondents' cooperation equivalence
• Frame equivalence	• Data collection context equivalence
• Sample selection equivalence	• Response style equivalence

(Source: partly from Douglas and Craig, 1984, p. 95)

displayed in Table 5.1 are explained in the text of the chapter, with six main categories and sixteen subcategories that are further discussed in this text.

Conceptual equivalence

A basic issue in cross-cultural research is the determination of whether the concepts used have similar meaning across the social units studied. Problems of *conceptual equivalence* are more frequent when testing the influence of certain constructs on consumer behaviour; for example, when a uniform cognitive theory is used in several countries (Green and White, 1976). For instance, the hypothesis of the cognitive theory that people do not willingly behave contradictorily may hold true in the United States while not being applicable to some other countries (conceptual equivalence).

The following statement from the anthropologist Clifford Geertz (1983, p. 59) gives a slight feeling of how difficult it may be to reach true conceptual equivalence between cultures:

> The Western conception of a person as a bounded, unique, more or less integrated, motivational and cognitive universe, a dynamic center of awareness, emotions, judgement and action, organized in a distinctive whole . . . is, however incorrigible it may seem, a rather peculiar idea, within the context of world's cultures.

Such basic concepts as beauty, youth, friendliness, wealth, well-being, sex appeal and so on are often used in market research questionnaires where motivation for buying many products is related to self-image, interaction with other people in a particular society and social values. They are seemingly universal. However, it is always advisable to question the conceptual equivalence of all these basic words when designing a cross-cultural questionnaire survey.

Many examples in previous chapters illustrate the practical difficulties in dealing with the conceptual equivalence of constructs used in a survey. When looking at the underlying dimensions across countries, one often realizes that they are not equivalently weighted or articulated in the total construct. For instance, in the construct 'waiting in line' (to be served), the dimension of 'losing one's time' may be emphasized in a time-conscious culture whereas it may be almost non-existent in one that is not economically time-minded. When 'waiting in line', the dimension of 'guilt for pushing in' is more developed in guilt oriented societies. Often the conceptual equivalence of several basic interrelated constructs has to be questioned, in as much as they relate to consumer behaviour idiosyncrasies for the specific type of product or service surveyed. Box 5.1 shows some construct equivalence problems in the case of life insurance policies.

Many popular marketing constructs have been used in cross-cultural research settings (perceived risk, brand loyalty, Rokeach value survey, lifestyles, etc.). Generally speaking, conceptual equivalence is an obstacle to the direct use of constructs which have been uniquely designed for the US culture. The perceived risk construct, for instance, may differ in its components across cultures. It may be broken down into several subdimensions: social risk, physical risk, financial risk (Van Raaij, 1978). The emphasis placed on these subdimensions may vary across cultures: when buying cars, for example, people in some cultures may give more value to social risk (because their purchase and use of car is mostly status oriented) whereas in other cultures people may be more concerned with physical safety (because death in accidents is greatly feared).

Therefore it is necessary to investigate, far more frequently than is actually done, the construct validity in each culture where a cross-cultural consumer behaviour study is undertaken. This should be done by following recognized procedures to assess the validity of the underlying constructs at the conceptual level and reliability at the empirical/measurement instrument level (Grunert *et al.*, 1993).[2]

Similar products and activities performing different functions: Functional equivalence

If similar activities perform different functions in different societies, their measures cannot be used for the purpose of comparison (Frijda and Jahoda, 1966). Concepts frequently used in market surveys, such as preparing a meal, are not necessarily functionally equivalent across countries. When asked: 'what dishes do you cook, or prepare with tomato juice?', Italians and Danes will not think of the same. A similar product may perform different functions (Green and White, 1976): for example, a bicycle in one country may be considered a transportation vehicle (in the Netherlands for instance) while in other countries it may be only a leisure item. Stanton *et al.* (1982) illustrate this functional equivalence problem by taking the example of hot milk-based chocolate drinks. Whereas in the United States and the United Kingdom they are considered an evening drink, best before going to sleep, in much of Latin America a 'Chocolate Caliente' is a morning drink. Functional equivalence is reached neither in the consumption time period nor in the purpose for use (waking/energizer versus sleep/relaxer).

A watch may be used as wrist jewellery or an instrument for handling time and daily schedules. The same holds true for a fountain pen. In some countries its function may be as a simple general-purpose writing instrument; in others it may be regarded mostly as an instrument for signing documents. Elsewhere it may be considered purely non-functional

Box 5.1 *A multinational survey on life insurance: Conceptual equivalence problems in Islamic countries*

In Islam it is considered evil to talk about death. Nevertheless Muslim people do not fear death. On the contrary, they are probably much less frightened by the prospect of death than most people in Western/Christian countries. But the notion of destiny is of the utmost importance: humans may not decide about their own death, nor are they entitled to control the process of it. One is not allowed to challenge the course of destiny, and therefore one should not speculate on one's own life and death. A verse of the Koran says approximately this: ' Behave each day as if your life will be very long, and for your after life, behave as if you will die tomorrow.' In Saudi Arabia, life insurance is forbidden. But some high-risk industries, such as oil production, bypass this prohibition by insuring their local employees through foreign life-insurance companies, with policies located abroad.

In the Islamic world people do not like to invest and bet on the long term. Effort must be rewarded quickly if it is to be maintained. The concept of a financial product such as life insurance needs a long-term orientation and a strong individual capacity to imagine the future. Projection towards the future is a culture-related trait (see section 2.2 and Chapter 12). In Islam, you may certainly imagine how you will be tomorrow, but not at a particular place or moment. The future tense exists, but it is surely not as accurate or meticulous as that of the American or European languages. Moreover, protection of the family and solidarity within the extended family are highly valued and work effectively. If a man dies, his brother will care for his wife and children.

The concept of life insurance is related to culture in at least the following four aspects: protection of the family and/or the individual; future orientation; betting on one's own life and death; the degree of solidarity in the family and extended family group. In Islamic countries it is important not to offend interviewees at first contact. It is better to rely on in-depth non-directive interviews and focus groups carried out principally by briefed local researchers who have a thorough personal knowledge of Islam and the local culture (the Islamic world spreads from black Africa to China). Some research questions will have to be addressed in order to prepare an adequate marketing strategy. Which is the appropriate mix, for the design of the life insurance policies offered to potential consumers, in terms of death benefit (amount of money to be paid when a person under a life insurance policy dies) and annuities (a series of payments made at regular intervals on the basis of the premiums previously paid)? Which term(s) should be proposed for people before they receive the benefits of their life insurance policy? How should the beneficiaries be designated? How to communicate this offer to potential consumers through advertisement: which brand name to adopt and which themes and advertising style should be favoured in the advertising campaign?

since it needs time and care to refill it, and often leaks over one's fingers. Many other examples could be given, such as wine (everyday beverage accompanying meals versus beverage for special occasions), beer (summer refresher versus all-year standard 'non-water' beverage) and perfumes (covering bodily odours versus adding a nice smell after a shower).

The simple word 'coffee' covers a whole range of beverages which are enjoyed in very different social settings (at home, at the workplace, during leisure time, in the morning, or at particular times during the day), in quite different forms (in terms of quantity, concentration, with or without milk, cold or hot), prepared from different forms of coffee base (beans, ground beans, instant). The function of the Brazilian *cafezinho*, very small cups of coffee, rather strong and drunk every hour in informal exchanges with colleagues, cannot be compared with that of the US *coffee* which is very light and drunk mostly at home and in restaurants. One of the best ways to investigate functional equivalence is to examine the social settings in which a product is consumed.

5.2 Translation equivalence

For many reasons which are outlined principally in Chapter 12 on language, culture and communication, translation techniques, even sophisticated ones, might prove incapable of achieving full comparability of data. Let us first make a small review of translation equivalence problems.

Categories of translation equivalence

Translation equivalence may be divided into the following subcategories: lexical equivalence, idiomatic equivalence, grammatical-syntactical equivalence and experiential equivalence (Sechrest *et al.*, 1972). Lexical equivalence is that which is provided by dictionaries: for instance, one may discover that the English adjective 'warm' translates into the French '*chaud*'. The problem of idiomatic equivalence comes when you try to translate a sentence such as 'it's warm': French has two expressions for it, either '*il fait chaud*' (literally, 'it makes warm' meaning 'it's warm (today)') or '*c'est chaud*' (meaning 'it (this object) is warm'). An idiom is a linguistic usage that is natural to native speakers. Idioms are most often non-equivalent: the present progressive (i.e. I am *doing*) has no equivalent in French, except '*je suis en train de . . .*' which is highly colloquial, not to be used in correct French written language.

Grammatical-syntactical equivalence deals with how in a language words are ordered, sentences are constructed and meaning is expressed. English generally proceeds in an active way, starting with the subject followed by the verb and then the complement, avoiding abstractions as well as convoluted sentences. Many languages, including German and French start by explaining the circumstances in relative clauses, before they proceed into the action. This gives complex sentences (as you may find in this book!) starting with relative clauses based on when, where, even though, although, and so on. The Japanese language has a quite different ordering of words compared with Western

Box 5.2 *'Reproductive health'*

Cultural discrepancies are not only evidenced in factual themes, they also manifest themselves in translation difficulties: the concept of 'reproductive health' was translated into German as *'Gesundheit der Fortpflanzung'* (health of propagation). The Arabic translators invented the formula: 'spouses take a break from each other after childbirth', the Russian translators worded this in despair as 'The whole family goes on holiday' and the Chinese translators elevated themselves to the almost brilliant formula 'a holiday at the farm'. This shows that the new word-monsters, elegantly coined by the Americans, are almost non-translatable world-wide; on the other hand, they infuse international conferences with a lot of humour.

(Source: Bohnet, 1994.)

languages: verbs are always at the end of the sentence: *'Gurunoburu no daigaku no sensei desu'* means: 'Grenoble of (the) university of professor (I) am', that is, 'I am a professor at the university of Grenoble'.

Experiential equivalence is about what words and sentences mean for people in their everyday experience. Coming back to *'chaud'* it translates into two English words 'warm' and 'hot': the French do not experience 'warmth' with two concepts as the English, the Germans and many others do. Similarly the special experience of coldness in the word 'chilly' cannot be adequately rendered in French. Translated terms must refer to real items and real experiences, which are familiar in the source as well as the target cultures. An expression such as 'dishwashing machine' may face experiential equivalence problems when people, even if they know what it is, have never actually seen this type of household appliance nor experienced it.

Another example of experiential non-equivalence is given by the Japanese numbering system which reflects a special experience of counting, where the numbers cannot be fully abstracted from the object being counted. Most often the Japanese add a particle indicating which objects are counted. *Nin* for instance is used to count human beings: *yo-nin* is four (persons). *Hiki* is used for counting animals, except birds for which *wa* is used (meaning 'feather'), *satsu* for books, *hon* for round and long objects, *mai* for flat things such as a sheet of paper, textiles, coins, etc., and *hai* for cups and bowls, and liquid containers in general. As a vivid illustration of translation problems, Box 5.2 shows the translation errors in the case of a major concept, 'reproductive health', for the UN World Conference on Population Development, held in Cairo in 1994.

Back-translation and related techniques

The back-translation technique (Campbell and Werner, 1970) is the most widely employed method of reaching translation equivalence (mainly lexical and idiomatic) in cross-cultural research. This procedure helps to identify probable translation errors. One translator translates from the source language into a target language. Then another translator, ignorant of the source-language text, translates the first translator's target language text back into the source language. Then the two source-language versions are compared.

For instance, when translating *un repas d'affaires* ('a business meal' in English) from French to Portuguese in the preparation of a questionnaire for Brazil, it is translated as *jantar de negocios*. When back-translated, it becomes a *dîner d'affaires* ('business dinner'). In Brazilian Portuguese, there is no specific expression for *repas d'affaires*. It is either a 'business lunch' (*almoço de negocios*) or a 'business dinner'. One has to choose which situation to elicit in the Brazilian questionnaire (as would be the case in English): the 'business meal' has to be either at noon or in the evening in the Portuguese version. When back-translating, discrepancies may arise from translation mistakes in either of the two directions or they may derive from real translation equivalence problems which are then uncovered. Then a final target-language questionnaire is discussed and prepared by the researcher (who speaks the source language) and the two translators. In practice, it is advisable to have one translator who is a native speaker of the target language and the other one a native speaker of the source language. It means that they are translating *into* their native language rather than *from* it, which is always more difficult and less reliable.

However, back-translation can also instil a false sense of security in the investigator by demonstrating a spurious lexical equivalence (Deutscher, 1973). Simply knowing that words are equivalent is not enough. It is necessary to know to what extent those literally equivalent words and phrases convey equivalent meanings in the two languages or cultures. Another technique, blind parallel translation (Mayer, 1978), consists of having several translators translate simultaneously and independently, from the source language into the target language. The different versions are then compared and a final version is written.

Combined translation techniques, limits of translation

Parallel and back-translation can be merged, as shown in Figure 5.1. When two languages and cultures present wide variations, such as Korean and French, combining parallel and back-translation provides a higher level of equivalence (Marchetti and Usunier, 1990).

For example (Usunier, 1991), two Koreans translate the same French questionnaire F into two Korean versions, K1 and K2. A third Korean translator, who is unfamiliar with the original French text F, translates K1 and K2 into F1 and F2. A final Korean questionnaire, K3, is then prepared by comparing the two back-translated French versions F1 and F2. English is used to help compare them as it is widely used and more precise than either French or Korean. This example could be refined: the number of parallel translations may be increased, or back-translation processes may be independently performed.

A more sophisticated solution to the problem of translation has been suggested by Campbell and Werner (1970). Research instruments should be developed by collab-

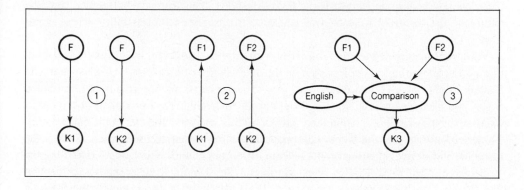

Figure 5.1 Examples of translation techniques.
(Source: Marchetti and Usunier, 1990.)

orators in the two cultures, and items, questions or other survey materials should be generated jointly in the two cultures. After back-translation, or after any initial translation process has been performed, there is an opportunity to change the source-language wording. This technique, called *decentring*, not only changes the target language, as in the previous techniques, but also allows the words in the source language to be changed, if this provides enhanced accuracy. The ultimate words and phrases employed will depend on which common/similar meaning is sought in both languages simultaneously, without regard to whether words and phrases originate in the source or the target languages. In the above example of the business meal, choosing the decentring method would imply changing the words in the source questionnaire to 'business lunch'. In any case, it remains absolutely necessary to pretest the translated research instrument in the target culture until satisfactory levels of reliability on conceptual and measurement equivalences are attained (Sood, 1990).

5.3 Measure equivalence

Variations in the reliability of research instruments

Variation in cross-cultural reliability of underlying instruments has already been assessed, and Davis *et al.* (1981) claim that measurement unreliability is a threat to cross-national comparability. They investigated the problem of measurement reliability in cross-cultural marketing research for three types of consumer behaviour measures (demographics, household decision involvement and psychographics) across five country-markets, utilizing three different reliability assessment methods. Their findings show that it is easier to obtain measurement equivalence between demographic variables than between psychographic variables such as lifestyles. The assessment method and the nature of the construct may be two causes of measurement unreliability across countries.

Variations in knowledge and familiarity with products, concepts or attitudes, evoked in the section above, have a deep impact on the equivalence of measures. Parameswaran and Yaprak (1987) have compared the attitudes of respondents in two countries (the United States and Turkey) towards the people and products from three countries of origin (West Germany, Japan and Italy) using three products (cars, cameras and electronic calculators). They demonstrate that the same scale may have differing reliabilities when used by the same individual in evaluating products from differing cultures. The cars reviewed are the Volkswagen Golf (VW Rabbit, West Germany), the Honda Civic (Japan) and the Fiat 128 (Italy). Cameras considered are Leica (West Germany), Canon (Japan) and Ferrania (Italy). The brands of electronic calculators used are Royal (West Germany), Canon (Japan) and Olivetti (Italy).

> . . . differing levels of awareness, knowledge, familiarity and affect with the peoples, products in general, and specific brands from a chosen country-of-origin may result in differential in the reliability of similar scales when used in multiple national markets. . . . Two alternative courses of action may alleviate this problem. Measures to be used in cross-national market comparisons may be pre-tested in each of the markets of interest until they elicit similar (and high) levels of reliability. . . . Alternatively, one might devise a method to develop confidence interval (akin to statistical spreads based on sample sizes) around the value of the measure based on its reliability. (Parameswaran and Yaprak, 1987, pp. 45–6)

Therefore, comparison of results across countries should be made while simultaneously analyzing and checking for the reliability measures of the rating scales.

Perceptual equivalence

As emphasized in sections 1.4 and 8.4 perception varies across cultures. Colours are perceived differently according to cultures, that is, cultures do not have equivalent sensitivity to the various parts of the colour spectrum, and the corresponding languages do not qualify colours in exactly the same way. The next step (after colour identification) is the symbolic interpretation of colour, which varies widely (Box 8.4).The same is true for smells: the first issue in equivalence is whether people perceive them physically and mentally, related to the training of their olfactory apparatus, the second issue deals with the kind of interpretation they vest in these smells. When researching about packaging, perfumes for washing liquids or other products where perceptive clues are important for product evaluation, it is a key research issue to formulate questions so that interviewees can express their native views on the smell or the colours. Rather than ask them whether they like a lavender smell, it is better to ask them first to recognize the smell, then to comment on what it evokes.

Metric equivalence

The validity of a rating scale in a cross-cultural study is affected by the metric equivalence of the scales and by the homogeneity of meanings. Pras and Angelmar (1978) did a comparison of verbal rating scales (semantic differentials) in French and English. They showed that difficulties can occur in determining lexical equivalents in different languages of verbal descriptions for the scale (see Table 5.2). It is also difficult to ensure that the distances between scale points (adjectives, for instance) are equivalent in the two languages (metric equivalence). In this case the standard deviation for French respondents was significantly smaller than for US respondents, this being due to a greater cultural homogeneity in France.

The method suggested by Pras and Angelmar leads to the rejection of definitional equivalence of concepts with source language measurement instruments: in other words, it is naive to use a differential semantic scale originally written in English, French or any other language and translate it lexically (simply with dictionary-equivalent words) into other languages. Pras and Angelmar favour decentred measurement (Campbell and Werner, 1970), which means constructing reliable and valid scales for all the countries under survey. In this case the original wording of the scale may be changed if it provides better measurement equivalence across countries/cultures.

Sood (1990) studied the metric equivalence of nine scale terms (from 'excellent' to 'very bad') across eight languages (English, Arabic, Chinese, Farsi, French, German, Korean and Spanish). He evidences two facts: (1) some languages have fewer terms to express gradation in evaluation (e.g. Korean), whereas others have a multitude (French); and (2) there are large discrepancies in the 'value' of these adjectives, measured on a 0 to 100 scale: for instance, the Spanish '*muy malo*' was 58 per cent higher than its supposed English equivalent of 'very bad'. Therefore the best solution is not to try and

Table 5.2 *Adjectives which have the same level of meaning in two languages and provide similar distances between the points of the scale.*

Colloquial rating scale				Formal rating scale			
US adjectives			French adjectives	US adjectives			French adjectives
Fantastic	20	20	Extraordinaire	Remarkably good	17	17	Très bon
Delightful	17	17	Superbe	Good	14	14	Bon
Pleasant	14	14	Très correcte	Neutral	10	10	Moyen
Neutral	10	10	Moyen	Reasonably poor	6	6	Faible
Moderately poor	7	7	Assez faible	Extremely poor	3	3	Très mauvais
Bad	4	4	Remarquablement faible				
Horrible	2	2	Terriblement mauvais				

(Source: Pras and Angelmar, 1978, p. 76.)

translate scale terms but rather to start from local wordings based on scales used by local researchers.

Calibration equivalence

To calibrate is to mark the scale of a measuring instrument so that readings can be made in appropriate units. A typical calibration equivalence problem relates to differences in monetary units; especially in high-inflation contexts where daily prices over a year cannot be directly compared with those of a low-inflation country. Naturally, exchange rates and units of weight, distance and volume cause calibration equivalence problems. Calibration equivalence mixes with perceptual equivalence: for instance, how many colour classes are recognized by people from a particular country? This might prove useful for a packaging test or a product test. Western subjects, for example, have more colour classes than African subjects, and some primitive people only have a two-term colour language. The Bantu of South Africa, for example, do not distinguish between blue and green. Consequently they do not discriminate between objects or symbols in these colours (Douglas and Craig, 1984, p. 100).

Calibration equivalence problems arise from different *basic* units being used as well as from *compound units* when they are based on different computation systems (see Box 5.3).

Temporal equivalence

Temporal equivalence is near to calibration equivalence, in terms of calibrating dates and time periods. Information, for instance, ages at different speeds across countries: in a

Box 5.3   *Measuring fuel efficiency across cultures*

Most Europeans use the metric system, an international standard. They count distances in kilometres and liquid volumes in litres (one cubic decimetre). When looking at fuel consumption, they reckon how many litres are necessary for driving a hundred kilometres, at a definite average speed. Fuel consumption is measured in litres/100 km. In the US, 'gas mileage' is based on a reverse concept: given a definite fuel volume, namely a gallon, how many miles can one drive with it? For Europeans trying to understand what miles per gallon mean is somewhat nightmarish. First they have to know which gallon it is: the British or Imperial gallon (4.55 litres) or the US gallon (3.79 litres) and whether it is a statute mile (1.609 kilometre) or a nautical mile. When they understand that it is a US gallon and a statute mile, they still have to make an inverse calculation and try to finish with 100 kilometres in the denominator in order to know whether the car has high petrol consumption or poor gas mileage. Fortunately, gasoline is cheap in the United States.

country where the annual inflation rate is 1 per cent, income and price data are comparable across years; whereas in a Latin American country with 2,000 per cent annual inflation rate, it is necessary to indicate on which exact day the data were collected and what the price indexes and exchange rates were at that exact date. Temporal equivalence also deals with differences in development levels and technological advancement: Certain countries are 'equivalent' to what others were twenty years ago. Assessing time lags may be useful for making analogies: such a market may develop in South Africa now as it did in the United States fifteen or twenty years ago and the product life cycle may be similar even though the two countries are at different points on the curve.

5.4 Comparability of samples

When secondary data – especially published statistical data – are sought, there may be some difficulties in comparing these data across countries:

1. Differences in categories: for instance, for age brackets, income brackets or professions.
2. Difference in base-years, when some countries have no recent data.
3. Unavailable or unreliable data, the data collection procedure by the local census bureau being biased for certain reasons (non-exhaustive census, inadequate sampling procedure).
4. Sampling unit (who should the respondent be?).

Choice of respondents (sampling unit equivalence)

An important criterion is the choice of respondents. Selecting a unit of analysis is a key issue in the conceptualization of comparative research design. The role of respondents in the buying decision process (organizational buying, family buying, information and influence patterns, etc.) may vary across countries. This statement is as relevant for industrial markets as for consumer goods markets. In the United States, for instance, it is not uncommon that children have a strong influence when buying cereals, desserts, toys or other items, whereas in countries that are less child-oriented, children's influence on the buying decision will be much smaller (Douglas and Craig, 1984). The same holds true for the extended-family pattern in South East Asia, which heavily influences individual buying decisions. It is therefore of primary interest to assess, first, the basic equivalent sampling units: for instance, when researching for industrial products, comparing the position, role and responsibility of industrial buyers throughout different countries.

Representativeness and comparability of national/cultural samples

Sampling is a basic step in most market surveys. A complete census, where the whole population of interest is researched, generally proves too costly. Therefore it is advisable to infer the characteristics of the whole population from a limited sample. In this process the following tasks must be carried out:

1. Finding a sampling frame, the basic characteristics of which are known (a telephone directory, an electoral list, etc.).
2. Drawing a sample from this frame, by a method which may be either probabilistic or non-probabilistic.
3. Checking that the selected sample is representative of the population under study.

The main problem in the cross-cultural sampling process is the selection of samples that can be considered comparable across countries. According to Green and White (1976), reaching perfect comparability is very difficult, in fact almost impossible. These limitations should be considered when interpreting research findings. An initial issue to be addressed is the two-level type of sampling:

1. First level: sample of countries or cultures.
2. Second level: samples of individuals within these countries or cultures, i.e. within each national sample.

At the first level, the research question is directly comparative. Hofstede clearly explains that samples of cultures should not be confused with samples of individuals. He draws attention to the risk of abusive stereotyping whereby country characteristics are considered as individual characteristics: 'Mean values are calculated from the scores on each question for the respondents from each country. We do not compare individuals, but we compare what is called central tendencies in the answers from each country' (Hofstede, 1991, p. 253). Samples of countries can be used to compute the average influence of cultural values on certain consumption patterns. For instance, what are the main cultural variables which, in combination with sociodemographic and economic variables, determine the per capita consumption of a particular product or service: motor insurance, telephones, milk powder, etc? Strategic marketing decision-making often needs such research for selecting target national markets and markets with low actual demand but high growth potential, and for deciding where to locate efforts for the future. A cross-cultural/cross-national design may also be useful when one tries to derive an estimated market demand figure in a country where statistical sources are scarce and unreliable. When limited data are available, Amine and Cavusgil (1986) give examples of methods for estimating market potential. They take the case of the Moroccan demand for wallpaper. For instance, it is possible to estimate a regression equation explaining per capita annual wallpaper consumption with explanatory variables such as income per capita, percentage of home ownership, frequency of use of other wall-covering materials, etc. to estimate the parameters it is possible to use a cross-section sample (data for a sample of countries, for the same year), or a pooled cross-section/time series sample, when the countries' data are available for several years. For a country where wallpaper consumption is unknown, it is then possible to compute it with the values of the explanatory variables.

A second issue is the representativeness of each sample in each country or culture (Douglas, 1980). In cross-cultural research it seems a priori relevant to follow a systematic procedure, the same in every country, to achieve reliability and comparability of data. Unfortunately demographic definitions do not correspond exactly from one country to another; age does, of course, as long as people know their birth dates, but occupation, education and socioeconomic status usually do not. If data are presented in categories, say for income or age bracket, these categories will most likely not correspond exactly across countries (category equivalence). Religion and tribal membership will also have to be added to traditional demographics as they are of the utmost importance in some less-developed countries (Goodyear, 1982).

A representative sample?

The researcher then constructs a sample which represents the population of interest. However, a sample split into 50 per cent men and 50 per cent women conveys a different meaning in a country where women's rights are recognized from that in more traditional countries where women's status is lower. As such, the expression 'representative sample' makes little sense if one does not clarify which traits and characteristics this sample actually represents. For instance, shopping behaviour is very different world-wide: in some places men tend to do most of the shopping, in other countries it is mostly women; this also depends on various other factors (income level, type of product, etc.). In this case the samples must represent actual shoppers rather than men and women as they are in the general population of potential shoppers.

In order to define a sampling procedure for cross-cultural research, one must select a method that is based on several national samples, each of them being fully representative of the population of the country which it attempts to represent, and which furthermore provides comparable data across countries. Douglas and Craig (1983) stress the limited availability of an exhaustive sampling framework which corresponds exactly to the characteristics of the population at a global (multi-country) level.

Sampling frames are often biased. A sample drawn from the electoral list in Bolivia may over-represent men since women are not as likely to vote (Stanton *et al.*, 1982). Tuncalp (1988) states that most sampling frames in Saudi Arabia are inadequate: there is no official census of the population, no elections and therefore no voter registration records, and telephone directories tend to be incomplete. Tuncalp suggests further that non-probability sampling is a necessary evil.

Douglas and Craig (1983) also suggest that an empirical method (non-probability sampling procedures) may prove as efficient as probability sampling, when researching cross-culturally. Data can be collected at a reasonable cost, compatible with the objectives of the survey. Therefore the basic criterion for selecting the sampling procedure(s) will remain the comparability of results across countries. Sentell and Philpot (1984) propose a method for evaluating the representativeness of samples taken from imperfectly known parent populations. Their method is based on the comparison of proportions estimated from two independent samples, focusing on situations where the larger sample size is unknown. Their method is implemented by testing two sets of sample statistics of Thai households.

Estimating sample size also appears as a critical step. The use of traditional statistical procedures, such as constructing confidence intervals around sample means, or hypothesis testing, is difficult to implement in as much as they require precise estimates of the variance of the population. This variance estimate is often unavailable in countries which have poor census data. The most frequently used procedure is therefore the selection of sample size, country by country, taking into account their respective peculiarities (Douglas and Craig, 1983).

If research starts from a domestic survey, where the home country representativeness has been emphasized, and is then extended to other countries, it may be difficult to achieve comparability. Although true random sampling is necessary for the successful completion of research projects, studies using non-random samples can also be valuable, if they include all the characteristics of the subjects and environment that could potentially influence the results or their interpretation.

Finally one may conclude that representativeness and comparability of cross-cultural samples can be better achieved by using different samples and sampling techniques which produce equivalent levels of reliability rather than by using the same procedure with all samples. The main problem (before any statistical procedure is implemented) is to secure equivalence in meaning: does it make sense to represent the same populations across various countries? Do the samples actually represent these populations in the same way?

5.5   Data collection equivalence

Where primary data are concerned, discrepancies in response patterns across countries may cause data unreliability and so limit direct comparison. Let us assume that through any of the translation procedures described above we are able to develop equivalent national versions of a common questionnaire for a cross-cultural market research study, and we have consistent and equivalent samples. Response equivalence problems may, however, appear, such as the following:

1. Secrecy/unwillingness to answer (respondents' cooperation equivalence).
2. Response biases (data collection context equivalence).
3. Differences in response style (response style equivalence).

Error measurement sources related to response styles are multiple and may directly create discrepancies between observed measurement and true measurement. Some basic precautions may help to avoid the generation of data with a great deal of measurement error.

Reluctance to answer: respondent's cooperation equivalence
Respondents sometimes feel that the interviewer is intruding into their privacy. They prefer not to answer, or they consciously bias their answers, fearing that their opinion could later be used against them (Stanton *et al.*, 1982). Many countries have strong privacy/intimacy patterns, where the family group is protected from external, impersonal interference. Tuncalp (1988) explains that the very private and reserved nature of Saudi is not conducive to personal interviews. Being independent, Saudis do not want to be

possibly exposed to justifying or explaining their actions when answering a barrage of questions.

Context equivalence of data collection

There is inevitably a social and cultural context of questions; questions are never culture-free. Contextual equivalence relates to elements in the context of the data collection process that have an influence on responses. As Douglas and Craig explain (1984, p. 109): 'In the Scandinavian countries, for example, respondents are considerably more willing to admit overdrinking than in Latin America. In India, sex tends to be a taboo topic.' Any question that deals, directly or indirectly, with social prescription, needs to be worded so that people can elaborate a response without feeling too embarrassed, and responses have to be screened in order to know if the responses reflect actual reality or a view of what is socially desirable. Some well-disposed and open-minded interviewees may be questioned further to deliver their true mind on the question.

Biases resulting from the relationship with the interviewer

Sexual biases between interviewer and respondent are also an important source of the reluctance to grant interviews (Kracmar, 1971). In many traditional countries, house-wives are reluctant to grant interviews to male interviewers. Ethnic bias may also exist between the interviewer and the respondent: a Chinese person may feel uncomfortable when interviewed by a Malay (Kushner, 1982). Much response bias may result from the interviewees not understanding that the process of interviewing them is in order to generate objective data. Informants may perceive the purpose of research as a very long-winded form of selling, especially in developing countries (Goodyear, 1982). The objective and the process of the interview must often be explained at the beginning. When briefing native interviewers (management students) in Mauritania, I was asked the following question: 'What do you want us to tell the interviewee to answer?' It was necessary to explain to the interviewers that interviewing was a distanced and objective process, where interviewees had complete freedom of response. The idea of objective truth, external to personal relations, is unfamiliar to Mauritanians (Box 5.4). Furthermore, among the Mauritanian interviewers, the *Maures* of Arabic descent, clearly explained that they would not interview Black Africans. Fortunately, there were some Black Africans who were potential interviewers for their own ethnic group. Strong ingroup orientation implies that group membership has to be shared between interviewer and interviewee for the process to take place. Maruyama (1990) explains in the same vein that Japanese managers in Indonesia tend to recruit Bataks, because their characteristics resemble those of the Japanese, although they are not necessarily liked by other Indonesians and they may perform poorly as data collectors.

Some respondents, especially in Latin-American countries (Stanton *et al.*, 1982) tend to present a 'courtesy bias' by answering in order to please the interviewer. Respondents tend to tell the interviewer what they think the interviewer would like to hear. This response pattern probably takes place in countries where people tend to have difficulty in answering opinion surveys and market research questionnaires. When they accept, it can be through some kind of personal favourable sentiment towards the interviewer.

Box 5.4 *The weaknesses and strengths of the 'local researcher'*

1. Weaknesses.
   (a) Often of lower intellectual ability and research experience than his or her equivalent in developed countries.
   (b) Often finds it difficult to adopt neutral, objective stance with reference to informants or clients. May want to be didactic in groups and may well prefer to distort findings to reflect a more educated picture of his countrymen than exists in reality. Alternatively, may seek to distance himself from the 'average consumer' by exaggerating their foibles and lack of sophistication. He himself, especially if he is from an educated family, may be out of touch with his countrymen.
   (c) He may be unwilling or unable, even for business reasons, to cross traditional barriers of class, religion or tribe.
   (d) He rarely has the Puritan work ethic and does not always see the value of objective truth. Delays, shortcuts and distortion are likely.
2. Strengths.
   (a) He knows the country and its people. He can usually establish rapport easily and understands what is said. If he knows the Western country he can also interpret the significance of what is said, to explain differences.
   (b) He knows the language. Language can be an enormous barrier, as anyone who has tried to interview through interpreters must recognise.
   (c) He is immune to local ailments and is physically comfortable in the (research) environment. He can cope, through familiarity, with common problems.

(Source: Goodyear, 1982, pp. 90–1. Reproduced with the kind permission of the publisher.)

Response style equivalence

This is the final step (all the rest is equivalent; yet our respondents may offer non-equivalent responses). The three main concerns for response style equivalence are:

1. Yea-saying pattern (and, symmetrically, nay-saying pattern).
2. Item non-response pattern.
3. Extreme response style.

Douglas and Craig (1983) describe this response style as introducing a 'yea-saying' pattern. Response scores tend to be inflated and the mean score of the respondents are biased towards the positive end of the scale. If the 'courtesy bias' is high on average such a bias may be found. Van Herk and Verhallen (1995) evidence such a bias when interviewing Greek and Italian housewives on their cooking behaviour: there is systematic tendency in the Greek sample to give more positive answers in psychographics as well as in product-related questions, than in the Italian sample. The yea-saying bias translates into a higher mean score on almost all questions. Standardizing scores across cultures allows the 'yea-saying' pattern to be eliminated, although it is fairly difficult to differentiate whether people were striving on average to the positive end of the scale or were agreeing strongly with a particular item. Thus the 'yea saying' pattern is diagnosed only when it is consistent across almost all the questions.

Item non-response is an important source of bias in cross-national surveys. Respondents may be unwilling to respond to some questions, such as those relating to income or age. Douglas and Shoemaker (1981), studying non-response of different items in a public opinion survey in eight European countries, found evidence of non-response being higher for income in the United Kingdom and Ireland, whereas the willingness to respond to political questions was highest in Germany and Italy.

Another potential bias may also be introduced by significant differences in extreme response style patterns across countries. The overall response pattern is systematically marked by higher standard deviation. US people tend to respond with more enthusiasm, and therefore present a more extreme response style in answering, than the Japanese (Zax and Takashi, 1967) or Koreans (Chun *et al.*, 1974). This could produce a bias in the standard deviation of data, increasing it artificially in cultures where people tend to over-react to questions, compared to other cultures where people may tend to suppress their opinions, either positive or negative.

5.6 Researching internationally

For some reasons, apart from equivalence issues reviewed previously, international research is different from domestic research: (1) it is more difficult and more costly to implement while the stakes are often smaller than those in the domestic market; and (2) information often needs to be fed more directly into action, thus a 'hands on' approach is recommendable.

The Japanese style of market research

Johansson and Nonaka (1987) show that Japanese firms use market survey techniques that are quite distinct from those used by US companies. Japanese do survey markets, but decide what to do afterwards fairly independently of the survey conclusions. For example, research was presented to Akio Morita, founder and president of the Sony corporation, which suggested that the Walkman would not be bought by consumers: they would not buy a tape recorder that does not record, even a portable one. Following his intuition, though undoubtedly after fairly wide consultation, Akio Morita and Sony took the decision to launch the Walkman, with the success we all know. It is likely that an American boss would not have taken such a decision.

In fact Japanese firms take a direct interest in the realities of the market-place and outlets. They look for information from the actual *buyers* (not the potential consumers), who are interviewed about the products they want, and how the products themselves could be better tailored to consumers' needs. Johansson and Nonaka cite the example of the chief executive officer of Canon-USA. He spent six weeks visiting Canon distribution networks, chatting to sales executives, customers and store managers, in order to find out why Canon cameras were not selling as well as the competition.

This attitude is quite different from the prescriptions of traditional market research, which are as follows:

1. Market research has to be representative, therefore a representative sample must be used.
2. Market research must be scientifically objective. A questionnaire (that is, a systematic but not necessarily *open-ended* information retrieval instrument) should be administered by non-participating researchers (they should not be personally involved in the consequences of the responses given by interviewees).
3. Research has to study the *potential* market, not the actual market (that is, real buyers and real users).
4. As far as possible, the people who undertake market research should not be the same people who ultimately decide on the marketing strategy to be adopted. There is a potential danger that the boss of Canon-USA could be manipulated by customers and distributors, who might take the opportunity to demand lower prices or other benefits by overstating competitors' strengths. There is also the risk that by focusing on the actual market, as yet untargeted market segments could be ignored or neglected.

As Johansson and Nonaka emphasize (1987, p. 16):

> Japanese-style market research relies heavily on two kinds of information: 'soft data' obtained from visits to dealers and other channel members, and 'hard data' about shipments, inventory levels, and retail sales. Japanese managers believe that these data better reflect the behaviour and intentions of flesh-and-blood consumers. Japanese companies want information that is context specific rather than context free – that is, data directly relevant to consumer attitudes about the product, or to the way buyers have used or will use specific products, rather than research results that are too remote from actual consumers to be useful.

Market research as images of reality: atomistic versus organic views

In fact, market surveys are, at best, 'photographs' of the market; they are not the market itself. At the Los Angeles County Museum of Art there is a painting by the Belgian Painter René Magritte, called 'La pipe'. It simply shows a pipe, with a thin trail of smoke going out of it. That is (almost) all. Then there is a short subtitle at the bottom of the painting, saying '*ceci n'est pas une pipe*' (*this is not a pipe*): a very 'down to earth' way of reminding us that *images of the reality* should not be confused with the reality itself. We may create images of the reality, especially through the media (for instance, a war reported on a TV screen) but we may also ignore large chunks of the reality (especially its experiential elements).

On the other hand, we should not underestimate the powerfulness of the process of designing images of the reality, especially for decision-making purposes. Scientific market research provides marketing decision-makers with an image of the actual and/or potential market, consumer behaviour and the competition. Large parts of the reality are beyond our limited perceptual apparatus. Let us take another example: at the Mount Wilson observatory in California, there are photographs of the stars made with a special quality of film, with a shutter exposure of four hours. The stars in the skies are far more numerous than we will ever see with our limited eyes. The same holds true for market research: from panels, or more generally, large and representative samples of consumers, we may derive images of the market, which we will never match simply by talking with anyone who is around.

Our argument is that, across countries, marketing decision-makers do not use exactly the same information for a similar decision process, and that, to a certain extent, culture influences the scope and nature of researched information, and the use of the results in the process of marketing decision-making. Two basic approaches to reality may be set in contrast, as ideal types, the atomistic and the organic approaches (Table 5.3), which we all share, across individuals and cultures. In terms of research traditions the atomistic view would be near to distanced positivistic research; the organic view would be near to humanistic inquiry (Hirschmann, 1986) and action research.[3] First, we can consider ourselves as being outside the real world, as observers, able to depict with a certain degree of preciseness workable images of the real world (atomistic), and then to use them to interact with this external world. Conversely, one may emphasize that we are an integral part of this reality, to which we belong so inextricably that it is not really possible to separate oneself from the reality. We are so deeply immersed in it that it would make no sense. These two approaches are complementary rather than antagonistic. But there can be a dominance in one approach among a group of people, a culture, or an individual, or in an area of knowledge.

The atomistic approach leads us to consider reality as fundamentally divisible into units which display enough independence so that, operationally, we can ignore the interrelation between pieces of reality. In contrast, the organic approach assumes the indivisible nature of reality, its elements (if there are any) being fundamentally interdependent. Reality is global rather than piecemeal. Table 5.3, which builds on Tables 2.1 through 3.5, shows how these approaches are linked to major categories of cultural differences, although the difference between atomism and organism is not as such a cultural difference. The atomistic belief in *divisibility* favours the view that time is divisible, that the basic unit of interpersonal relations is the individual, and that communication can and must be explicit (that is, clearly separated, 'divided' from surrounding issues, topics and preoccupations). Separating emotions from actions, friendship from business, is typically an atomistic attitude towards reality, seen as divisible. Very naturally, the atomistic approach favours data orientation and measurement being the proof of a piece of reality being divisible and (therefore) existent. To

Table 5.3 *Atomistic versus organic approaches*

Approach to reality	Atomistic	Organic
Nature of reality	Divisibility/independence	Global/indivisible/dependent
Time	Linear/divisible	Cyclical/integrative
Communication style	Explicit/low context	Implicit/high context
Interpersonal relations	Individualist/reciprocal	Collectivist/loyal
Intellectual style	Data/measurement oriented	Intellectual modesty
Proof	Validated theory (truth)	Virtue/conviction
Space	Universalist	Localist
Decision-making	Formalized	Weakly structured

illustrate the importance of measurement in the atomistic approach, let us take the case of a company which tries to improve service *within* the company, so that not only front line service providers are concerned with service to customers. Addressing such an issue, a typical atomistic statement will be 'To arrive at a position where excellent service is achieved will be a difficult enterprise. This primarily results from the lack of service measurement knowledge *within* the company.' In fact, scales exist only to measure external service quality, that is, vis-à-vis customers, so that the atomistic solution is to try and develop a measurement instrument, because the reality of within company service cannot be tackled in the absence of measurement instruments. The organistic approach holds the contrary assumption: it is precisely because measurement is difficult that the two issues are considered as unseparate and to be treated as a joint piece of reality. The research approach will be quite different.

On the other hand, a dominance of the organic approach favours collectivism in its strongest sense: people do not consider themselves as being separate from the group to which they belong. Their sense of belonging includes the implicit view that they are not really separable from their group. The communication style is more implicit and contextual, because the sense of the interdependence of pieces of reality is much stronger. In interpersonal relationships, loyalty is characteristic of the organic approach, whereas reciprocity, based on tabulated favours on each side (time, amount and persons being clearly defined), is linked to the atomistic approach. To this list can be added that proof (in the sense of making it work, be accepted, be considered as a necessary piece of reality) is based on validated theory for the atomistic approach, and on arguments favouring conviction and virtue for the organic approach.

With divisible reality, linear time and individual emphasis, the atomistic approach conceives of decision-making as a highly formalized process, followed by implementation, control and feedback. It is a time sequence as we see them in so many managerial textbooks. Conversely, the organic approach emphasizes circularity in time and the integration of time horizons. Preparing, making decisions and implementing them are not seen easily as completely separated pieces of time reality, leading to a fairly unstructured decision-making process. Finally, the organic approach does favour 'localism', local solutions, because solutions are built in the context and there is a difficulty in conceiving universal solutions. Conversely, the data and theory orientation in the atomistic approach favours universalism, because reality, when reduced to figures, shows a fairly high degree of universality.[4]

The case of research on international markets: Doing research with limited data availability and limited resources

More than twenty years ago Keegan (1974) pointed out in a study of multinational scanning by US firms that information searched for international market research is rather different in focus and type from domestic research. His study documented marketing decisions made on the basis of several information sources. In 60 per cent of the instances, survey-based information, often highly subjective, constituted approximately two-thirds of the information package. As explained in the sections above, when researching internationally, the basic conditions of market research are different from those prevailing in the domestic market. Market experience, market share, and availability of people and resources are generally much higher in the domestic environment than in international markets (Grønhaug and Graham, 1987). Cavusgil and Godiwalla (1982) stress the high level of uncertainty in international markets and the limited availability of objective information, both in quantity and quality. It may explain why international marketing decisions are dominated by the influence of subjective and perceptual factors.

The less sophisticated nature of international marketing research is also evidenced by Cavusgil (1984). Officials of seventy companies from Wisconsin and Illinois, involved in international business, were interviewed. Mostly simple survey techniques were used: foreign market research is generally informal, with no standard procedures. Furthermore the frequency of identifying and analyzing foreign markets is much less than once a year. Sophistication increases with the higher degree of involvement in foreign markets, as measured by the percentage of export profits to total company profits. A recent study by Koh (1991) confirms these findings: a large proportion of US exporters, approximately two-thirds of the companies surveyed, do not adopt a formalized marketing plan. But when they do, they tend to focus on issues similar to those researched domestically and to neglect 'strategic issues relating to risks appraisal, environmental issues, cultural considerations . . . which require close contact with the foreign environment' (Koh, 1991, p. 17).

The acceptance of intuition as such in the decision-making process is a key element of those differences. Should we continue with very in-depth research, if the final decision is taken by somebody who may or may not follow the conclusions of the research? Should the researcher and the decision-maker be different people or the same? These questions are raised by the cross-cultural comparison of marketing research practices.

Encouraging feedback from the informant on cultural adequacy

As emphasized by Maruyama (1990), humans are not simple response machines. Maruyama cites 'criticality dissonance', where respondents disguise and transform responses because they fear that information may be misused. As shown above, international market research is full of criticality dissonance. The basic process affecting the truthfulness of responses is 'relevance dissonance': 'the purpose of the questionnaire survey as perceived by the respondent differs from the respondent's own purpose. The questionnaire is perceived as irrelevant and useless. In such a case counterexploitation takes place. The respondent looks for a way to manipulate the survey or interview to produce some benefit' (1990, p. 30).

For these reasons, it seems necessary to design research procedures where feedback from the informant is possible: for instance focus groups, in-depth interviews and open-ended questions (Goodyear, 1982). Unique features of cultural behaviour cause non-equivalence. It is impossible to unveil these levels of non-equivalence if the instrument and methodology prevent them from appearing. A pragmatic solution is to ask inter-viewees their opinion of the relevance of questions, words and concepts used in the questionnaire at the end of the normal interview process (post-test). A pre-test of questionnaires is also necessary.

A questionnaire forced upon interviewees does not elicit information (see the hair shampoo exercise in section A5.2). If emic feedback is to be introduced, both interviewers (especially when they have not personally been involved in writing the questionnaire) and interviewees must be put in a situation where they may comment on the questions themselves and explain what is culturally meaningful in their own context and what is not. Interviewees should be given the opportunity after the normal answering process to elaborate freely on what they think of the questions, the situations described and so on. This orientation is slightly different from the traditional one where interviewed people are simply required to answer, not 'criticize', the questions. Emic feedback allows an improvement in the adequacy of the source culture's constructs and instruments.

Informants should neither be overestimated nor underestimated. They cannot respond to a barrage of questions alien to their knowledge and frame of reference. It means that the content of the research must in some way be kept under strict control and focus on really significant issues; surveys should be parsimonious and not ask too much from your informants. On the other hand, informants need to be carefully listened to because they are those who, as insiders, retain the relevant pieces of information. With interviewers, the same care has to be taken: they must be properly controlled (some – not all – may cheat by surmising responses or even filling in questionnaires themselves) and adequately briefed (professional interviewers may not be found everywhere – see Box 5.4).

5.7 Conclusion

It is dangerous to prepare an international market survey as a pure transposition of domestic research. The nature and scope of researched market information, the ways to collect it, the accuracy of the data as well as the criteria of reliability of the data present cross-cultural variance. This holds true even when they are perceived as normatively quite universal. International market researchers have to unveil their own ethnocentric biases, by giving feedback opportunities to their informants or to local collaborators. From this point on, a systematic search for formal equivalence may appear dangerous. Equivalence of constructs and instruments has to be established first. The final recommendation is to search for the meaning, with six pieces of advice:

1. Scientific methods provide pictures which otherwise would not be available (the '*Mount Wilson*' argument).
2. But images of the reality are not the reality itself ('*La pipe*' argument).
3. Address the relevant questions (only those that can be articulated into decision and action).
4. Respect your informants and consider their competence as insiders as superior to yours as an outsider; but interview only those people who have something to say.
5. Keep a 'hands on' approach to market research.
6. Culture must be examined at each step of the research process: questions, survey methods, interviews and questionnaires, informants.

Questions

1. Define the following terms:
   (a) conceptual equivalence;
   (b) temporal equivalence;
   (c) sexual biases.
2. Discuss the functional equivalence of the following products or consumption experiences. For this, choose countries/culture with which you have familiarity and experience and think in terms of benefits and those which are particularly emphasized in certain cultures:
   (a) a bicycle;
   (b) drinking a beer;
   (c) red wine;
   (d) a watch.
3. What are the obstacles for a sample of consumers to be cross-culturally representative?
4. Discuss how market size can be estimated in a country where there is little or poor statistical data available.
5. List possible benefits for a washing powder or liquid and suggest possible cross-cultural variability in the dominance of certain benefits versus others.
6. Suggest ways to obtain relevant market and consumer behaviour information where potential informants are not used to questionnaires and interviews.
7. How does the individualism/collectivism difference impact the drafting of market research questionnaires?
8. Which constraints does strong ingroup orientation put on the data collection process?

APPENDIX 5

──────── ♦♦♦ ────────

Teaching materials

A5.1 Case: Eliot Greeting Card Company (2)

Based on the same text as in the previous chapter, you are asked the following questions:

1. Assuming that Eliot Greeting Card Company has decided to undertake an in-depth market survey in order to decide whether to develop the Hispanic market, how would you design such a survey?
2. What information is needed?
3. How would you collect it?

A5.2 Exercise: Hair shampoo questionnaire

You will find below a market survey questionnaire, administered by interviewers to women interviewees between the ages of 18 and 30. It was originally designed for the US market.

You are asked to suggest cross-cultural adaptations to this instrument: a similar market survey, as far as the objectives are concerned, will be undertaken in other countries. More precisely, you are asked to do the following:

1. Review the possible problems related to the translation of the questionnaire. Suggest solutions and translate it into. . . .[5]
2. Review the data collection procedure, from the point of view of the interviewer as well as from that of the interviewee.
3. Suggest changes in the questionnaire design and/or wording, and/or modification in survey methods, if:
   (a) the information sought is meaningless in the local context;
   (b) the required information is meaningful but the data collection procedures are inadequate; either they will not enable you to collect the information, or else this information will be biased.

♦ You must do this for each of the following countries: Algeria, Brazil, France, Germany, Thailand.
♦ You should then propose a 'central' version of the questionnaire, that is, a survey instrument which enables you to collect the maximum amount of information, which could be retrieved in a reliable manner, in the largest possible number of countries. This questionnaire would then help the meaningful comparison of countries.

Questionnaire used in hair shampoo study

Time Interview   Started ....
                 Ended ....

Respondent Name ....   Respondent No. ....
Address ....
City ....   State ....
Telephone No ....
Interviewer ....
Name ....
Interview Date ....
Screening Questions (Part S)

Hello, I'm   of the Wharton School, University of Pennsylvania. We're conducting a survey on women's attitudes and opinions about hair care products.
1. On the average, how often do you shampoo your hair at home?

More than twice a week	....
Once or twice a week	....
Once or twice every two weeks	....
Once or twice every three weeks	....
Twice a month	....
Less than twice a month	....

IF LESS THAN TWICE A MONTH, TERMINATE

2. What is your age?

(IF UNDER 18 OR OVER 30 TERMINATE)

PART A

First I'm going to show you a set of 16 cards. Each card contains the name of a benefit that a hair shampoo might provide. (PLACE SET OF WHITE CARDS ON TABLE IN FRONT OF RESPONDENT.) Please take a few moments to look over these benefits. (ALLOW TIME FOR RESPONDENT TO STUDY THE CARDS.)

Now, thinking about various brands of hair shampoo that you have tried or heard about, pick out those benefits that you think are most likely to be found in almost any hair shampoo that one could buy today. (RECORD CARD NUMBERS IN FIRST COLUMN OF RESPONSE FORM A AND TURN SELECTED CARDS FACE DOWN.)

Next, select all of those remaining benefits that you think are available in at least some hair shampoo – but not necessarily all in a single brand – that's currently on the market. (RECORD CARD NUMBERS IN SECOND COLUMN OF RESPONSE FORM A. RECORD REMAINING CARD NUMBERS IN THIRD COLUMN. THEN RETURN ALL CARDS TO TABLE.)

Next, imagine that you could make up an ideal type of shampoo – one that might not be available on today's market. Suppose, however, that you were restricted to only four of the sixteen benefits shown on the cards in front of you. Which four of the sixteen benefits would you most like to have? (RECORD CARD NUMBERS IN FOURTH COLUMN OF RESPONSE FORM A.)

RESPONSE FORM A

(1)	(2)	(3)	(4)
Benefits Most Likely to be Found in Almost Any Hair Shampoo – Card Numbers	Benefits Available in Some Shampoo – Card Numbers	Remaining Benefits – Card Numbers	Four-benefit Ideal Set – Card Numbers

PART B

Now, let's again return to some of the shampoo benefits you have already dealt with. (SELECT WHITE CARD NUMBERS 1 THROUGH 10: PULL OUT CARD 4 AND PLACE IT IN FRONT OF RESPONDENT.)

Suppose a shampoo were on the market that primarily stressed this benefit – 'Produces Hair That Has Body.' If you could get a shampoo that made good on this claim, which one of the remaining nine benefits would you most like to have as well? (RECORD NUMBER IN RESPONSE FORM B.) Which next most? (RECORD.) Please continue until all of the nine benefits have been ranked.

RESPONSE FORM B

(Enter Card Numbers 1 Through 10 Excluding Card #4)

( ) Most Like to Have   ( )
( ) Next Most   ( )
( )   ( )
( )   ( )
( )   ( ) Least Most

PART C

Now, I am going to read to you some short phrases about hair. Listen to each phrase carefully and then tell me what single words first come to your mind when you hear each phrase? (RECORD UP TO THE FIRST THREE 'ASSOCIA-TIVE-TYPE' WORDS THE RESPONDENT SAYS AFTER EACH PHRASE IN RESPONSE FORM C.)

RESPONSE FORM C

(a) Hair that has body

_____ _____ _____

(b) Hair with fullness

_____ _____ _____

(c) Hair that holds a set

_____ _____ _____

(d) Bouncy hair

_____ _____ _____

(e) Hair that's not limp

_____ _____ _____

(f) Manageable hair

_____ _____ _____

(g) Zesty hair

_____ _____ _____

(h) Natural hair

_____ _____ _____

PART D

At this point I would like to ask you a few questions about your hair
1. Does your hair have enough body?
   Yes _____ No _____

2. Do you have any special problems with your hair?
Yes _____ No _____

If yes, what types of problems?

_____

_____

3. How would you describe your hair?
My hair type is:
Dry _____ Normal _____ Oily _____
4. The texture of my hair is:
Fine _____ Normal _____ Coarse _____
5. My hair style (the way I wear my hair) is:
Straight _____
Slightly wavy or curly _____
Very wavy or curly _____
6. The length of my hair is:
Short (to ear lobes)
Medium (ear lobes to shoulder)
Long (below shoulder)
7. How would you describe the thickness of your hair?
Thick _____ Medium _____ Thin _____

PART E
   Now I would like to ask you a few background questions.
1. Are you working (at least twenty hours per week, for compensation)?
Yes _____ No _____
2. Are you married?
Yes _____ No _____
3. What is your level of education?
Some high school _____
Completed high school _____
Some college _____
Completed college _____
4. (HAND RESPONDENT INCOME CARD.) Which letter on this card comes closest to describing your total annual family income before taxes? (CIRCLE APPRO-PRIATE LETTER.)

A. Under $ 9,000	E. $ 30,001 – 45,000
B. $ 9,001 – 15,000	F. $ 45,001 – 60,000
C. $ 15,001 – 20,000	G. Over $ 60,000
D. $ 20,001 – 30,000	

(THANKS VERY MUCH FOR YOUR HELP)

Appendix: Text of the sixteen benefit cards (original text in English + my translation into French)

1. Hair Stays Clean a Long Time
2. Hair Stays Free of Dandruff or Flaking
3. Hair That Looks and Feels Natural
4. Hair That Has Body
5. Manageable Hair That Goes Where You Want It
6. Hair With Sheen or Luster
7. Hair With No Split Ends
8. Hair With Enough Protein
9. Hair That Doesn't Get Oily Fast
10. Hair That's Not Too Dry
11. Hair With Fullness
12. Hair That's Not Frizzy
13. Hair That Holds A Set
14. Hair With Texture
15. Hair That's Easy to Comb When It Dries
16. Hair That Looks Free and Casual

Example of a translation into French. Below are my suggestions.

1. *Des Cheveux qui restent propre longtemps*
2. *Des Cheveux sans pellicules ni noeuds*
3. *Des Cheveux respirant le naturel*
4. *Des Cheveux qui ont du volume*
5. *Des Cheveux souples que l'on peut coiffer à son gré*
6. *Des Cheveux brillants et chatoyants*
7. *Des Cheveux qui ne se cassent pas*
8. *Des Cheveux assez riches en protéines*
9. *Des Cheveux ne devenant pas gras trop vite*
10. *Des Cheveux pas trop secs*
11. *Des Cheveux qui ont de la plénitude*
12. *Des Cheveux qui ne sont pas frisottés*
13. *Des Cheveux tenant la mise en plis*
14. *Des Cheveux ayant une bonne texture*
15. *Des Cheveux faciles à coiffer lorsqu'ils sèchent*
16. *Des Cheveux naturels, en liberté*

(Source: adapted from Green *et al.* 1988. Reproduced with permission.)

A5.3   Exercise: Slogans and colloquial speech

Marketing communications (advertising copy, slogans, promotional offers, text on coupons, etc.) are language-based. The quality of reception of the marketing messages by the target audience is very sensitive to the accuracy of the wording.

Marketing communication is based on everyday – colloquial – speech, often very idiomatic.

The basic purpose of this exercise is fairly simple: it may be implemented with a group composed of people who have different linguistic backgrounds, but yet have a capacity to communicate with each other since some of them speak several languages. It does not imply that total fluency is necessary. Participants should simply take care to translate *into* the language(s) which they speak fluently (not *from*).

The exercise consists of the following:

1. Collecting slogans (and, more generally, short marketing communication texts) from magazines, billboards, posters, television commercials, sponsor announcements or short texts such as those found in greeting cards; translating them into other languages, with the objective of finding the equivalent meaning and local wording. The translation techniques explained in section 5.2 (back-translation, parallel translation and a combination of the two) should be used.
2. Collecting 'identical' slogans (again, generally any short marketing communication text) that are pushing the same international brand in different countries, then analyzing and comparing how similar propositions and concepts are conveyed in the different languages. Bookshops that sell foreign newspapers and magazines will be useful places to find the basic data.

Notes

1. The issue of cross-cultural equivalence has been initially developed in psychology (see Frijda and Jahoda, 1966; Poortinga, 1989) and was later borrowed by international market research.
2. Green *et al.* (1988) give the folowing definitions of validity and reliability of measurement: 'By validity the behavioural scientist means that the data must be unbiased and relevant to the characteristic being measured. . . . By reliability the behavioural scientist means the extent to which scaling results are free from experimental error' (pp. 249 and 253). Validity is then broken down into content, criterion and construct validation: see Green *et al.* (1988, ch. 7, 'Measurement in marketing research'. pp. 240–79.
3. For a clarification of these terms see Easterby-Smith, *et al.* (1993).
4. It is tempting to say that a typical atomistic culture is the United States versus Japan which would be a typical organistic culture. This is possible as a modal characteristic, since the organistic approach also exists in the United States.
5. This is optional. Instructors will define this according to their teaching objectives and to the existing language competencies. Cultural and linguistic contexts may be varied *ad libitum*. This is related to the participants themselves (nationalities, language skills, personal experiences in various countries, etc.) who are one of the main resources as far as cultural and language expertise are concerned. Students may also try to find information on foreign cultural contexts either by using secondary data, or by interviewing natives.

172 *Marketing across cultures*

References

Amine, Lyn S. and S. Tamer Cavusgil (1986), 'Demand estimation in a developing country environment: Difficulties, and examples', *Journal of the Market Research Society*, vol. 28, no. 5, pp. 43–65.

Bohnet, Michael (1994), 'Was Wurde in Kairo wirklick beschlossen?', BMZ, Bonn, October.

Campbell, D. T. and O. Werner (1970), 'Translating, working through interpreters and the problem of decentering', in R. Naroll and R. Cohen (eds), *A Handbook of Method in Cultural Anthropology*, The Natural History Press: New York, pp. 398–420.

Cavusgil, S. Tamer (1984), 'International marketing research: Insights into company practices' in *Research in Marketing*, vol. 7, the JAI Press: Greenwich, CT, pp. 261–88.

Cavusgil, S. Tamer and Yezdi M. Godiwalla (1982), 'Decision-making for international marketing: a comparative review', *Management Decision*, 20(4), 47–54.

Chun, K. T., J. B. Campbell and J. Hao (1974), 'Extreme response style in cross-cultural research: A reminder', *Journal of Cross-Cultural Psychology*, vol. 5, pp. 464–80.

Davis, H. L., S. P. Douglas and A. J. Silk (1981), 'Measure unreliability: A hidden threat to cross-national research?', *American Marketing Association Attitude Research Conference*, March, Carlsbad, CA, pp. 1–40.

Deutscher, I. (1973), 'Asking questions cross culturally: Some problems of linguistic comparability', in Donald P. Warwick and Samuel Osherson (eds), *Comparative Research Methods*, Prentice Hall: Englewood Cliffs, NJ, pp. 163–86.

Douglas, Susan P. (1980), 'Examining the impact of sampling characteristics in multi-country survey research', Proceedings of the 9th Annual Meeting of the European Academy for Advanced Research in Marketing, Edinburgh.

Douglas, Susan P. and C. Samuel Craig (1983), *International Marketing Research*, Prentice Hall: Englewood Cliffs, NJ.

Douglas, Susan P. and C. S. Craig (1984), 'Establishing equivalence in comparative consumer research', in Erdener Kaynak and Ronald Savitt (eds), *Comparative Marketing Systems*, Praeger: New York, pp. 93–113.

Douglas, Susan P. and Robert Shoemaker (1981), 'Item non-response in cross-national surveys', *European Research*, vol. 9 (July), pp. 124–32.

Easterby-Smith, Mark, Richard Thorpe and Andy Lowe (1993), *Management Research: An introduction*, Sage: London.

Frijda, N. and G. Jahoda (1966), 'On the scope and methods of cross-cultural research', *International Journal of Psychology*, vol. 1, no. 2, pp. 109–127.

Geertz, Clifford (1983), *Local Knowledge*, Basic Books: New York.

Goodyear, Mary (1982), 'Qualitative research in developing countries', *Journal of the Market Research Society*, vol. 24, no. 2, pp. 86–96.

Green, Robert T. and Eric Langeard (1979), 'Comments and recommendations on the practice of cross-cultural marketing research', paper presented at the International Marketing Workshop, *E.I.A.S.M.*, Brussels, November, pp. 1–16.

Green, R. T. and P. D. White (1976), 'Methodological considerations in cross-national consumer research', *Journal of International Business Studies*, Fall–Winter, pp. 81–7.

Green, Paul E., Donald S. Tull and Gerald Albaum (1988), *Research for Marketing Decisions*, 5th edn, Prentice Hall: Englewood Cliffs, NJ.

Grønhaug, Kjell and John L. Graham (1987), 'International market research revisited', in S. Tamer Cavusgil (ed.), *Advances in International Marketing*, Greenwich, CT: JAI Press, pp. 121–37.

Grunert, Suzanne C. Klaus G. Grunert and Kai Kristensen (1993), 'Une méthode d'estimation de la validité interculturelle des instruments de mesure: Le cas de la mesure des valeurs des consommateurs par la liste des valeurs LOV', *Recherche et Applications en Marketing*, vol. 8, no. 4, pp. 5–28.

Hirschmann, Elisabeth (1986), 'Humanistic inquiry in marketing research: Philosophy, method and criteria', *Journal of Marketing Research*, vol. 13 (August), pp. 237–49

Hofstede, Geert (1991), *Culture and Organizations: Software of the mind*, McGraw-Hill (UK): Maidenhead.

Johansson, Johny K. and Ikujiro Nonaka (1987), 'Market research: The Japanese way', *Harvard Business Review*, May-June, pp. 16–22.

Keegan, Warren G. (1974), 'Multinational scanning: A study of the information sources utilized by headquarters executives in multinational companies', *Administrative Science Quarterly*, September, pp. 411–21.

Koh, Anthony C. (1991), 'An evaluation of international marketing research planning in United States export firms', *Journal of Global Marketing*, vol. 4, n. 3, pp. 7–25.

Kracmar, J. Z. (1971), *Marketing Research in Developing Countries: A handbook*, Praeger: New York.

Kushner, J. M. (1982), 'Market research in a non-Western context: The Asian example', *Journal of the Market Research Society*, vol. 24, no. 2, pp. 116–22.

Leung, K. (1989), 'Cross-cultural differences: Individual level vs culture-level analysis', *International Journal of Psychology*, vol. 24, pp. 703–19.

Marchetti, R. and J. C. Usunier (1990), 'Les problèmes de l'étude de marché dans un contexte interculturel', *Revue Française du Marketing*, no. 130, 1990/5, pp. 167–84.

Maruyama, Magoroh (1990), 'International meta-marketing: Strategic judo, foreign user habits and interactive invention', *Human Systems Management*, vol. 9, pp. 29–42.

Mayer, C. S. (1978), 'Multinational marketing research: The magnifying glass of methodological problems', *European Research*, March, pp. 77–84.

Parameswaran, R. and A. Yaprak (1987), 'A cross-national comparison of consumer research measures', *Journal of International Business Studies*, Spring, pp. 35–49.

Pike, K. (1966), *Language in Relation To a Unified Theory of the Structure of Human Behavior*, Mouton: The Hague.

Plummer, J. (1977), 'Consumer focus in cross-national research', *Journal of Advertising Research*, vol. 6, Spring, pp. 5–15.

Poortinga, Ype H. (1989), 'Equivalence in cross-cultural data: An overview of basic issues', *International Journal of Psychology*, vol. 24, pp. 737–56.

Pras, B. and R. Angelmar (1978), 'Verbal rating scales for multinational research', *European Research*, March, pp. 62–7.

Sapir, Edward (1929), 'The status of linguistics as a science' *Language*, vol. 5, pp. 207–14.

Sechrest, L., T. Fay and S. M. Zaidi (1972), 'Problems of translation in cross-cultural research', *Journal of Cross-cultural Psychology*, vol. 3, no. 1, pp. 41–56.

Sentell, G. D. and J. W. Philpot (1984), 'A note on evaluating the representativity of samples taken in less developed countries', *International Journal of Research in Marketing*, vol. 1, pp. 81–4.

Sood, James H. (1990), 'Equivalent measurement in international market research: Is it really a problem?', *Journal of International Consumer Marketing*, vol. 2, no. 2, pp. 25–41.

Stanton, J. L., R. Chandran and S. Hernandez (1982), 'Marketing research problems in Latin America', *Journal of the Market Research Society*, vol. 24, no. 2, pp. 124–39.

Tuncalp, S. (1988), 'The marketing research scene in Saudi Arabia', *European Journal of Marketing*, vol. 22, no. 5, pp. 15–22.

Usunier, J. C. (1991), 'Business time perceptions and national cultures: A comparative survey', *Management International Review*, vol. 31, no. 3, pp. 197–217.

Van Herk, Hester and Theo M. Verhallen (1995), 'Equivalence in empirical international research in the food area', *Proceedings of the Second Conference on the Cultural Dimension of International Marketing*, Odense, pp. 392–402.

Van Raaij, W. F. (1978), 'Cross-cultural research methodology as a case of construct validity', in H. K. Hunt (ed.), *Advances in Consumer Research*, vol. 5, Association for Consumer Research, Ann Arbor, pp. 693–701.

Wind, Y. and S. P. Douglas (1982), 'Comparative consumer research: The next frontier', *Management Decision*, vol. 20, no. 4, pp. 24–35.

Zax, M. and S. Takashi (1967), 'Cultural influences on response style: Comparison of Japanese and American college students', *Journal of Social Psychology*, vol. 71, pp. 3–10.

Global marketing or intercultural marketing?

6

Globalization of markets?

'Globalization' is a simple word which has achieved great success. 'Globalization of markets' (Levitt, 1983) is an expression which relates first to demand: tastes, preferences and price-mindedness are becoming increasingly universal. Second, it relates to the supply side: products and services tend to become more standardized and competition within industries reaches a world-wide scale. Third, it relates to the way firms, mainly MNCs, try to design their marketing policies and control systems appropriately, so as to remain winners in the global competition of global products for global consumers.

Globalizing means homogenizing on a world-wide scale. The implicit assumption behind the globalization process is that all the elements will globalize simultaneously.

There seems to be a lot of propaganda (not in a disparaging sense) involved. As Ghoshal points out (1987, p. 425): ' ''Manage globally'' appears to be the latest battlecry in the world of international business.' A central assumption of globalization is that the mostly artificial trade barriers (non-tariff, regulations, industrial standards, etc.) have kept many markets at the multidomestic stage. If these barriers are removed, which is the aim of trade liberalization, 'insiders' who hold a large market share just in their home market may only be protected from new entrants by natural culture-related entry barriers.

From an international marketing point of view, which favours looking at consumers and marketing policies across countries, the idea of globalization has been strongly challenged. It has even been renamed 'the myth of globalisation' (Wind, 1986). Little empirical evidence has been found for the world-wide homogenization of tastes and the preferences of a 'world consumer', for standardized, low-priced, quality goods. Those interested in the influence of culture on consumer behaviour and the implementation of marketing policies (Dubois, 1987) have found arguments in favour of cultural resistance to the globalization process. Natural entry barriers related to culture seem to remain important in particular industries (food, beverages, advertising, printing and publishing, to name but a few).

The purpose of this chapter is to show that there are neither reasons nor evidence that

This chapter is largely drawn from Jean-Claude Usunier (1991), pp. 57–78. Reproduced with the kind permission of the publisher.

The results . . . indicated that life style influences are significant in explaining consumption behaviour, but the effect is not very strong. The data suggest that national and cultural influences continue to determine the consumption patterns across the four countries examined. But it must be emphasized that the inclusion of national identity as an independent variable in the analysis does not eliminate the effect of modern life style . . . but it is not strong enough to influence consumption behaviour at this time. (Eshghi and Sheth, 1985, p. 144)

Zaichkowsky and Sood (1988) have looked at consumer involvement in fifteen countries (Argentina, Barbados, Canada, the United States, Finland, Yugoslavia, Sweden, China, Austria, Colombia, Australia, Chile, England, Mexico, France) with eight 'potentially global' products/services (air travel, beer, jeans, eating at a restaurant, hair shampoo, going to the cinema, soft drinks and stereo sets). The same questionnaire, back-translated in each language, was administered to groups of approximately fifty students for each country.

The independent variables were the fifteen countries, whereas the dependent variables were, first, a PII (personal involvement inventory), intended to measure the respondent involvement level with the goods and services, and, second, the frequency of use of each product or service over a suitable time frame (self-reported).

Results indicate that the greatest variation in use due to country effect was to be found in restaurants (22 per cent), air travel (31 per cent) and hair shampoo (45 per cent). The greatest variation in involvement levels due to country effect (i.e. as a variance source) was found in soft drinks (20 per cent) and going to the cinema (12 per cent). Stereo set product use is weakly influenced by country effect (10 per cent) and involvement level is not related to country (1 per cent). It is difficult to draw simple conclusions about globalization as a whole from Zaichkowsky and Sood's findings. They nevertheless show clearly that the level of consumer globalization is fairly different according to which product/service category is considered.

Huszagh *et al.* (1986) have approached the consumption globalization process empirically by addressing three questions:

1. Which foreign markets are similar?
2. Which products exhibit potential for a global strategy by exhibiting similar acceptance rates?
3. Are there fundamental product characteristics which can explain acceptance rates?

They first clustered twenty-one countries, choosing sixteen variables such as urbanization, consumer price index, life expectancy and average working week. A subcluster of five countries (Belgium, the Netherlands, France, the United Kingdom and West Germany) was finally selected as a 'more homogeneous grouping in order to develop a more favourable empirical setting for a global marketing approach' (p. 35).

Penetration/consumption rates for twenty-seven products were collected for the five countries, and a coefficient of variation was computed for each product's penetration rate across countries. The divergence in acceptance rates (coefficients of variation) was then plotted against three product perception scales: durable/non-durable, household/personal and sensory/functional.

A rather counterintuitive result is drawn from this experimental design:

In summary, the three plots indicate that the more nondurable/sensory/personal a product is, the more consistent the acceptance rate. ... However the relationships are not clearly defined. ... Nevertheless, to some extent, these patterns do support Levitt's promise that 'high touch' products are the most amenable to global marketing. (Huszagh *et al.*, 1986, p. 41)

Woods *et al.* (1985) have investigated differences in consumer purpose for purchasing in what they term 'three global markets', i.e. the United States, Canada and South Korea. The consumer purposes considered are maintenance (basic necessities, convenience), enjoyment, enhancement (satisfied self-image, improves appearance) and defence (protects health, avoids offending). Convenience samples of female shoppers in shopping centres in the United States and Canada and female workers at the workplace in Korea were chosen. Respondents were asked to indicate, for sixteen products, one or more purposes out of fourteen associated with the four major purposes indicated above.

There seems to be a larger use of products for maintenance purposes in Korea than in the United States or in Quebec, whereas US consumers are more hedonistically oriented. Both the Korean and the Québecois female consumers are more defence-oriented.

Different patterns of use of products for enhancement purposes appear across the three national groups.

Woods *et al.* (1985, p. 168) conclude:

Taken as a whole, the findings reported here indicate that the age of universal marketing is not yet upon us. The findings do reveal that Koreans, who are members of a developing economy, are thinking about products in some of the same terms as are those in the United States and Quebec. Yet important differences are found in the reasons why they purchase products familiar to all three cultures. Women in Quebec also differ from those in the United States in the reasons they purchase products. Thus, aside from the economic difference and differences in purchasing power, cultural and psychological differences are pervasive enough to call for differences in marketing strategies.

Some arguments against the existence of a global consumer

It will not be so easy to globalize consumers' motivations. Account managers working large international advertising agencies face the complex task of managing a brand's images across several countries; they accumulate in-depth experience of consumers' response to global product offers. Harold Clark (1987) of J. Walter Thompson argues, with many practical cases at hand, the following:

1. Consumers are not 'global' themselves (national and cultural variance remains quite significant).
2. Consumers do not generally buy 'global' brands or products. They do not really care whether the brand is or is not available elsewhere in the world.
3. Since what consumers value is personal and individual, they will naturally let their individuality affect the values they place on the brands they buy. They contribute actively in this way to the *persona* of the brand in their own situation. (Clark, 1987, p. 35).

These last two arguments are very important ones. Consumers always 'construct' the identity of brands, even for 'global products' and they do so on a local culture and identity base. 'Global brands' might well be portfolios of local marketing assets, federated under a common, lexically identical name (see Box 6.1).

From this review of literature we may conclude that the globalization process is pushed on consumers rather than pulled by them, and therefore one of the main obstacles to globalization (cultural differences) tends to be neglected, despite the fact that it remains significant. These natural entry barriers related to culture are influential both in consumer behaviour and in the marketing environment where strategies are implemented. This explains many of the failures of over-globalizing marketing strategies. Many indicators of existing cultural differences do not seem to be about to vanish in the near future, for example languages, eating habits, political institutions, cultural conflicts between communities in politically homogeneous countries, etc.

Evidence is at least inconclusive about globalization of consumption patterns. The issue of finding convincing proofs of this process is a difficult one. A research agenda for testing consumer globalization would include such issues as the pace and process of it, the market segments involved and the geographically significant cultural areas (Jain, 1989). There are severe methodological problems involved in such a research design. Some of these are listed under the following:

1. Which aspect of consumer behaviour is studied – buying behaviour, shopping behaviour, lifestyle, values, psychometrics and underlying attitudes, influence processes (in the family, word-of-mouth communication), and so on?
2. The use of culturally unique research concepts squeezes differences, even when the toughest cross-cultural precautions have been taken. The concepts and theories of marketing are mostly US-culture based. Their complete ability to capture consumer behaviour aspects which are absolutely specific to other cultures is questionable.
3. The assimilation (often implicit) between 'national' and 'cultural' variables (country = culture) conceals the complex processes behind world-wide cultural homogenization. This relates to the problems of
   (a) clustering cultures;

Box 6.1   *'European' beers*

Typical of the diversity of the European brewing industry is how different brands in their segments are viewed from country to country. Brands, which do not have their origin in a country, which are 'foreign', are invariably viewed as premium segment products. A good example of this is BSN's Kronenbourg 1664, which is sold in France as an ordinary segment beer, but is viewed in almost all other (European) markets as a premium product. As an Italian brewer puts it: 'Foreign brands command a premium price for their image of higher quality.' However, potential hazards exist for brewers in pursuing this policy: 'In Great Britain, (Belgian) Stella Artois is a premium beer, one of the most expensive beers you can get there, and people buy it because it is expensive. It is marketed and promoted that way. The British are travelling people, so now when they come to Belgium, they discover that Stella Artois is a cheap beer. So they ask themselves if it is justified to pay so much for it in Great Britain' (French brewing manager).

(Source: Murray Steele, 1991, p. 58. Reproduced with permission.)

(b) treating subcultural variables within countries (Hispanics in the United States, for instance); and

(c) questioning the relevance of geographic borders as a proxy variable for cultural borders (if any).

4. Which is the relevant sample of relevant countries and relevant products that may help prove a trend towards globalization of consumption patterns?

5. Most of the studies are synchronic in design, because globalization has only recently been studied. In fact they should be diachronic, and the pace of the homogenization process should be examined by using at least two time periods. The best would be an annual survey, which could be regularly monitored in order to check whether the process is really *en route* on the consumer's side.

The most disputable and debatable aspect of globalization is the implicit assumption that we are all converging towards a 'modern lifestyle'; this controversial claim implies that the 'American way of life' would have universal appeal. The true globalization of consumption patterns will occur when the 'globalization route' ceases to be one way. Let us imagine an improbable example: some US consumers of pasteurized *foie gras* (made in the United States by French producers) ask the FDA (US Food and Drug Administration) to remove its regulation prohibiting the import of traditionally prepared French *foie gras*. FDA inspectors visit French *foie gras* laboratories and refuse most of them the right to export to the United States since hygiene standards are not met (too much antiseptic would kill the taste). If US consumers really want to become global, they will have to be able to import genuine, not pasteurized, French *foie gras*, which contains some innocent bacteria but also has real taste and consistency.

Will consumers resist the globalization process?

Another implicit assumption behind consumption-patterns globalization literature is that consumers are pleased with it (low-price, good-quality products) and therefore do not resist the process. They might, nonetheless, be self-contradicting individuals – for instance, buying P & G's Pampers for their baby, and at the same time complaining about the Americanization of society. They might resist at several levels: as citizens voting for protectionist governments, or as consumer lobbyists supporting public action (against fast food, for instance). Therefore they could lobby in order to recreate some kind of artificial entry barriers which had previously been removed.

Global marketing can be presented as a very powerful tool to promote economic development (Cundiff and Hilger, 1982). It would enhance the needs and desires of badly treated consumers who live in sellers' economies. Marketing would then favour the creation of local industries to produce consumer goods and meet their demands.

However, Belk (1988) describes a Third World consumer culture and emphasizes the hedonistic attraction for conspicuous consumption, even when basic utilitarian needs have not been met:

> One 'solution' under such circumstances is to sacrifice consumption expenditure in other areas . . . in order to afford payments on such luxury items as refrigerators, televisions, and

automobiles. . . . A reduction in food consumption in order to afford a refrigerator is more than a little ironic. (Belk, 1988, p. 118)

Thus a growing body of literature, relating to marketing and economic development emphasizes a marketing system which 'must design deliver, and legitimate products and services that increase the material welfare of the population by promoting equity, justice and self reliance without causing injury to tradition' (Dholakia *et al.*, 1988, pp. 141–2). This means clearly resisting some of the uglier consequences of globalization, such as the Nestlé infant formula problem in developing countries.

There is increasing interest in marketing literature concerning 'culture' as a variable. This has long been disfavoured compared to psychological and psychosociological explanations, where the implicit model was that of a universal individual (fully in line with the globalization assumptions). This is the objective of the cognitive anthropology approach (Roth and Moorman, 1988), which tries to understand and explain the patterns in cognitive views of cultural phenomena, and to help discover why members of various cultures appear to respond to market-place phenomena differently. This view clearly recognizes the importance of cultural group members' knowledge and beliefs in consumption patterns.

The culture of consumption is encouraging individuals to interpret their needs exclusively as needs for commodities and people may well have a need to consume culture, which is more tailored and localized (Sherry, 1987); this means consuming both local cultural products and those products whose consumption process is part of the genuine local culture. Sherry (1987, p. 189) states:

> . . . the guiding rule of such a marketing strategy, as in any ethically invasive procedure, is *primum non nocere*: first do not harm. In the rush to globalization, the preservation of local culture has been considered primarily as an opportunity cost. If cultural integrity is epiphenomenal to business practice, splendid; if not, social disorganization is frequently the cost of progress.

There are, of course, two different (but complementary) issues here:

1. Knowing whether there are intellectual, ethical and practical reasons for protecting local cultures and consumers from the globalization of consumption patterns.
2. Identifying whether resistance mechanisms to globalization actually occur at the individual and/or social level.

This echoes Clark's (1987) arguments about false 'global' consumers, buying false 'global' products, with their own culture-bound motivations and purposes. It suggests that most of the resistance will be hidden from global marketers. One example will serve to illustrate this point: McDonald's in France, where there is great cultural resistance against fast food and hamburgers, especially as a matter of national pride. But McDonald's has achieved great success with a limited number of successful 'luxury' (high end of the market) fast-food stores located in the centre of major towns in France. Nevertheless an anti-fast-food consumer association has been established to resist the fast-food movement, and nutrition specialists have clearly shown that traditional French meals (of diverse foods, lasting one hour) is much better for digestion and prevents cancer of the digestive tract. McDonald's is quite popular with the young generation, and today's children will be tomorrow's adults and parents. At the same time, McDonald's is trying to establish some outlets at motorway crossings in the suburbs. But these outlets do not offer breakfast service: how would French people react to 'Eggs McMuffin'?

If a definitive lead of globalized consumption patterns over local ones is predicted in the very long term, the process of mixing both types of consumption patterns, localized and globalized, will be complex. It would be worthwhile to survey some of these processes, at a micro-level and over a long period of time, in order to capture the real globalization process at work.

6.2 Is there a globalization of competition?

Evidence from macroeconomic data

There is little doubt about the globalization of competition. Market areas do not depend mainly on consumer's preferences. Their reach is influenced much more by trade barriers whether tariff or non-tariff (that is, artificial entry barriers), and also, positively, by opportunities of economies of scale and experience effects (that is, natural entry barriers unrelated to culture). Clear evidence from macroeconomic figures shows that competition is globalizing, both at a world-wide level and at a regional level.

Over the past forty years, international trade has expanded steadily and significantly quicker than the sum of the gross national product (GNP) of the nations involved in international trade. On a common 100 basis in 1970, the index volume of world exports was 180 in 1984 against only 154 for total world output. Even more significantly, the index of total world exports of manufactured goods was 238 in 1984 and only 171 for the total world output of manufacturing industries (GATT, 1986). From 1984 to 1994, the annual rate of increase for world trade has been 5.8 per cent against 2.7 per cent for world production (*Focus*, 1995). This points to a long-term trend: the increase of production scales. Industrial productivity goes along with the freeing of international markets and the growth of international trade. Thus in a simple regression equation, the average world-wide industrial productivity is a very good explanatory variable of the ratio of world exports to world total output over a long period (1955–76) (Usunier, 1980).

This rule also holds true in very recent times (Ludlow, 1990): in the six years from 1983 to 1988 (inclusive) trade growth exceeded the increase in world output, generally by two or three percentage points in annual growth rate. Economic linkage between countries and therefore competition between companies continued to grow. A comparable evolution may be observed, at an even greater pace, at the regional level. Distances are less important and the move to world-wide globalization has its roots at regional level. In Europe the growth of intra-regional international trade has been much faster than the overall world trade growth during the 1960s and 1970s (Usunier, 1980). But also intra-West-Pacific trade has grown significantly more (32 per cent p.a.) from 1980 to 1988, compared to 14 per cent p.a. for the intra-western-European trade and 16 per cent p.a. for the intra-North-American trade, for the same period (Ludlow, 1990).

In recent years, from 1992 to 1994, Asia has been doing much better than Europe as an exporting region: 10.6 per cent average annual rate of increase of its exports in value (19.4 per cent for China), against 3.4 per cent for the European Union (*Focus*, 1995). This shows a relative slow-down of the globalization of competition in Europe during the 1980s and 1990s and, as a consequence, a deterioration of its competitive position world-wide. This could change with the implementation of the European Union (EU) 1992 programme and the progressive removal of physical borders due to start on 1 January 1993 (see Box 6.2). However, in 1996, border controls still exist between some countries of the European Union.

Globalization of competition: evidence from business and industries

Many companies have been compelled to globalize their business, for example Black & Decker because of fierce competition with the Japanese power-tool maker Makita. Reasons for this are stated by *Fortune* magazine, reporting the strategic move of Black & Decker towards globalization: 'Makita is Black & Decker's first competitor with a global strategy. It doesn't care that Germans prefer high powered, heavy-duty drills, and that Yanks want everything lighter. Make a good drill at a low price, the company reasons, and it will sell from Baden-Baden to Brooklyn' (Saporito, 1984, p. 24).

This trend towards globalization of competition has been clearly noted, almost advertised, in business journals ('Your new global market: how to win the world war for profits and sales', cover page of *Fortune*, 14 March 1988). In most of these articles,

Box 6.2   *Europe 1992 agenda: Globalizing competition*

From the Treaty of Rome to the Single European Act, the main European treaties have always had one main focus: to increase the size of fragmented national European markets. Custom duties have been abolished between the six founding member-states in July 1968. But the pace of integration has slowed down with the entry of new members.

Increased world-wide competition, especially coming from the Japanese and south-east Asian nations, resulted in an enhancement of awareness about the necessity to really build a large internal market (EC's White Paper, completing the internal market, 1985).

The logic which lies behind the 1992 agenda, which is an appendix of EC's 1985 White Paper, is clearly presented by the authors of the survey on the cost of non-Europe (Cecchini, 1988, p. xx, our italics):

For business and government, *the two main actors*, the road to market integration will be paved with tough adjustments, and the need for new strategies. For business, removing protective barriers creates a permanent opportunity, but signals a *definitive end to national soft options* . . . profits which derive from cashing in on monopoly or protected positions will tend to be squeezed. The situation will be one of *constant competitive renewal*.

(Source: Usunier, 1991, p. 73. Reproduced with the kind permission of the publisher.)

which generally relate to competition dynamics in a specific industry, the vocabulary is often borrowed from the military: war, battlecries, strategic weapons, etc.

Naturally this is not seen so clearly in company brochures, where companies promote an image of themselves as dedicated more to customer service and to product/service integrity. Sumitomo Trading Company (Sumitomo Corporation, 1988) emphasizes that:

> the survival of the Sumitomo name for almost four centuries is testimony to the soundness of [our] business philosophy. . . . That is why we have the confidence to call ourselves Global Market Makers. Being global implies the worldwide, long term perspective from which we build relationships and undertake business.

Michael Porter (1986) has clearly analyzed the change in patterns of international competition. At the industry level, where competitive advantage is won or lost, there is a shift from multidomestic industries to global ones. Porter does not consider a consumer-led globalization but a strategic move of companies trying to integrate activities on a world-wide basis, to gain competitive advantage over their competitors at various levels of the value chain. Nevertheless this process remains conditional on the maintenance of the freeing of trade barriers, e.g. discussions in the GATT framework between nation-states. Companies, even large MNCs, are not parties to the GATT multilateral trade talks. De Bettignies (1989) shows that the globalization of the Japanese economy is posing some real threats to both the United States and Europe. Therefore free trade can be maintained and expanded (to services, for instance) only if a certain equilibrium of the balance of trade of nation-states permits the maintenance of the low trade-barriers environment which favours globalization at the industry level. The establishment of the WTO (World Trade Organization) at the beginning of 1995, appears in this respect as an organizing framework for international competition, building on the rules of the GATT treaty, rather than a major breakthrough of free trade world-wide. It will provide increased competition in the area of services, by relaxing national barriers in a number of service industries (telecommunications, insurance, banking, etc.). It will also provide more homogeneous rules concerning industrial property (patents and trademarks), thereby making it easier for brands to reach global coverage.

6.3 Are international marketing strategies becoming global?

Competition is becoming global, artificial entry barriers tend to disappear. But global markets remain more apparent than real when one looks at consumption patterns (Sheth, 1986). So how can products and marketing strategies be globalized under the fierce pressure of the globalization of competition and also under the constraint of consumers who tend to resist, at least partly, the globalization movement? With respect to this question, two major issues have to be considered:

1. The standardization of marketing programmes: what should be the degree of similarity in marketing strategies from one country to another?
2. Organizational issues: what is required to implement a standardized marketing strategy successfully?

Standardization of international marketing programmes

Before the classic article of Buzzell (1968), 'Can you standardize multinational marketing?', natural entry barriers related to culture were seen as very high, commanding
adaptation to national markets and offsetting the potential advantages of scale economies.
Buzzell clearly showed that with the decrease of purely artificial trade barriers, large
international companies could create natural entry barriers unrelated to culture through
economies of scale. Since then there have been numerous texts which have sought to
advise business people how to make the best choices between standardization and
adaptation of marketing policies to foreign markets (for instance: Hout *et al.*, 1982;
Hamel and Prahalad, 1985; Quelch and Hoff, 1986; Ghoshal, 1987). This literature
advocates either 'hard' or 'soft' globalization:

1. 'Hard globalizers' see globalization as a new 'paradigm' for international marketing
   (Hampton and Buske, 1987). 'Consumers in increasing numbers demonstrate that they
   are willing to sacrifice specific preferences in product features, function and design for
   a globally standardized product that carries a lower price' (p. 263). According to
   Hampton and Buske there is a shift to the global marketing paradigm since the process
   of adapting products to national wants and needs contradicts their global convergence.
2. 'Soft' partisans of globalization see it as a necessary trend, but constrained by the
   environment. The physical conditions of a country as well as the laws relating to
   product standards, sales promotion, taxes or other aspects may affect standardization
   of marketing programmes, especially in developing countries (Hill and Still,
   1984a).

In both cases, what consumers actually want in various national markets is not really
considered: differences are either denied or treated as an external constraint. This
constraint should be taken into account only when ignoring critical differences in
consumer behaviour and marketing environment could lead to market failures (Ricks,
1983). However, many examples show that it is rarely the whole of the marketing
strategy which is globalized: many global brands have marketing strategies which are
significantly tailored to local markets. As stated by Van Mesdag (1987, p. 73):

> Some products that were deliberately developed to sell in global markets are margarine
> (though the originators of the product curiously never adopted a global brand strategy for it),
> IDV's Bailey's Irish Cream liqueur, Ferrero's Tic Tac candy, and Rocher chocolates. Some
> global brands have global strategies. Others – Coca-Cola, Kellogg's corn-flakes, Heineken
> beer, and McDonald's hamburgers – have not. In the food and drink arena brands that
> succeed in using the global marketing approach are few and far between. The reasons are the
> low international convertibility of food and drink products . . . and the increasing difficulty
> of finding brand names for international use.

Behind the globalization debate there is a quite practical issue in terms of the everyday
life of companies: the traditional dilemma between production flexibility and marketing's
tendency to customize products to diversified needs. Factory managers prefer to be
inflexible, for low-cost purposes, whereas marketing managers favour as much tailoring
to customers' needs as possible.

Developments in factory automation nowadays allow product customization without major cost implications (Wind, 1986). New strategies have been found to serve diversified needs, to customize products and at the same time to maintain low costs owing to economies of scale and experience effects. Modular conception of products permits shared economies of scale at the components level, whereas lagged differentiation maintains a high scale of production as long as possible in the production process and organizes cheap final customization either in the factory or in the distribution network (Stobaugh and Telesio, 1983; Deher, 1986; see Box 6.3). So why maintain such a strong 'paradigm for action' emphasis on globalization if consumption patterns are not

Box 6.3   *Increasing standardization of intermediary components*

In the same way as the modular design of products, the greatest possible use of standardized components in the production process enables the manufacturer to postpone final product differentiation. This involves the sharing of identical components for diverse end-consumer products: for example the same plug will fit various different appliances. These standardized components are therefore modules, which are designed to be suitable for a wide variety of possible usages. This approach allows a significant reduction in the numbers of components.

The following examples clearly illustrate the advantages of this lagged differentiation.

The crystal glassworks at Saint-Louis only have a limited number of basic moulds, which they use to produce all their glassware. The many possible finishes (size, engraving, decoration, etc.) are applied at the end of the line to plain glasses. These unfinished glasses of different sizes and shapes are mass produced.

The same basic cream cheese Tartare is packaged in different ways, right at the end of the production line: packed in aluminium foil in individual servings, in a plastic tub, canned or wrapped. In other cases, a basic cheese will be flavoured differently (cherry, walnut, port wine, rose or other flower perfumes, etc.). Some packaging is standardized and can be used for different products. For example small plastic containers can be used for melted cheese as well as various types of fresh cheese.

Canson & Montgolfier manufacture papers of different weights on rolls 2.20 metres wide and several hundred metres long. This 'upstream' operation requires large-scale investment and a high level of technology, and has limited flexibility. As far as possible, each type of roll is manufactured in batches (several times a year) and stored before its final processing. Cutting, shaping and finishing is carried out on standard rolls, which are then customized to the required formats and styles of each country. At Petit-Bateau, which manufactures traditional knitwear, the knitting is done on unbleached yarn. Dying is applied to the yarn subsequently. Likewise, standardized patterns permit the creation of a large number of different clothes. At Dim, a lingerie manufacturer, tights are produced undyed. The dye, which is subcontracted, is applied at the last possible opportunity on untreated standard tights. This allows flexible tailoring to the different shades sought by consumers. Irons by SEB-Calor are all manufactured on the same moulding, which gives rise to 100 different models, according to function, colour, casing, voltage and brand name. Christofle's Arab cafetières, designed exclusively for the Middle East, are manufactured with the same stamping moulds as other cafetières.

undeveloped country; (3) the type of product: consumer or industrial goods; and (4) the control exerted over the subsidiary, wholly owned or joint venture.

Picard *et al.* (1989) replicated a 1973 survey by Hansen and Boddewyn (1976) of the level of standardization of European marketing policies of US multinational companies operating in Europe (fifty usable answers in 1973, seventy-one in 1983). This diachronic approach reveals mixed evolution: in consumer durables there was a decrease across the board in the degree of standardization of marketing policies, apart from product policy. In consumer non-durables, with the exception of branding, the percentage of respondents with standardized marketing policies in all EU countries was much higher in 1983 than 1973. Surprisingly, they note a significant trend away from standardization of products for industrial goods. This trend towards adaptation to national context is also true for other elements of the marketing mix (advertising, branding, after-sales service).

Hill and Still (1984a) examined the international marketing policies of nineteen MNCs that sell to LDC (less-developed countries) markets. Out of 2,200 products sold by the subsidiaries in the sample, 1,200 had originated in either the United States or the United Kingdom. Their findings show that 'nearly seven changes (product adaptation) out of ten (69.4 per cent) are marketing oriented . . . for most products, the process of managing product adaptation is critical' (p. 94). They also found that greater product adaptation was required from MNCs in rural areas than in urban areas in the LDCs (Hill and Still, 1984b).

In many cases, standardization is often done incrementally by transferring existing products at headquarters' level or in important subsidiaries: Hill and James (1991) show that there remains a considerable degree of power at subsidiary level concerning product and promotion transfer in consumer goods multinationals. In most cases market needs are assessed by the subsidiary itself which then uses the world-wide product portfolio as a resource base. In developing countries, subsidiaries initiate product transfer in 85 per cent of the cases, while in developed markets they do it in only 63 per cent of the cases. This suggests that world or regional headquarters exert more authoritative pressure for standardization across developed markets, especially in Europe. In the transfer process some adaptation is made to local requirements (see Chapter 8 on this issue): the degree of adaptation varies according to marketing mix elements. Ozsomer *et al.* (1991), have investigated the degree of marketing standardization for thirty-three multinationals operating in Turkey: products characteristics, brand name, positioning and packaging are the least adapted elements; price, promotion and distribution are more tailored to the local environment. Furthermore, they show that the degree of standardization is larger in wholly-owned subsidiaries than in joint ventures.

6.4   Conclusion

Globalization is a process which occurs mostly at the competition level. Artificial entry barriers, related to duties and standards, are now being progressively replaced by natural entry barriers related to scale and experience. For international marketing, culture-related experience is all the more important since the natural entry barriers related to consumer-behaviour and marketing environments will diminish very progressively and only in the long term. Language-related differences for instance will remain. Therefore, global marketing strategies must be implemented cautiously, especially in culture-bound industries: local knowledge has to be generated, either by research, by organizational learning, by hiring 'cultural' insiders or by acquiring local companies which have culture-specific business experience.

Globalization belongs to the realm of organizational discourse rather than to actual international marketing. Rather than a 'hard' global marketing strategy it is possible, as Chapter 7 emphasizes, to adopt an intercultural marketing strategy which basically follows the same goals but is more respectful of local culture and attempts to serve purely national as well as transnational market segments.

Questions

1. List some arguments and evidence which tend to show that globalization of consumption and lifestyles is underway. Outline limitations and discuss counterarguments.
2. Select a multinational company annual report and find evidence of globalization (global decisions, global products, globalization of competition, consumption patterns, management procedures, etc.).
3. Why is globalization taking place more clearly on the supply side than on the demand side?
4. To what extent are 'modern culture' and individualism primary inputs in the process of globalization of consumer preferences and lifestyles?
5. For the following industries/products discuss to what extent: (a) a world consumer exists; (b) the product or services offered are themselves global (similar world-wide); and (c) the industry itself can be considered as global:
   ◆ Airlines
   ◆ Tobacco
   ◆ Meat-based foods
   ◆ Sheets and pillows
   ◆ Pharmaceuticals

APPENDIX 6

Teaching materials

A6.1   Case: Parker Pen

Parker Pen Company

Parker Pen Company, the manufacturer of writing instruments based in Janesville, Wisconsin, is one of the world's best known companies in its field. It sold its products in 154 countries and considered itself number one in 'quality writing instruments', a market that consists of pens selling for $3 or more.

In early 1984, the company launched a global marketing campaign in which everything was to have 'one look, one voice,' and with all planning to take place at headquarters. Everything connected with the selling effort was to be standardized. This was a grand experiment of a widely debated concept. A number of international companies were eager to learn from Parker's experiences.

Results became evident quickly. In February 1985, the globalization experiment was ended, and most of the masterminds of the strategy either left the company or were fired. In January 1986, the writing division of Parker Pen was sold for $100 million to a group of Parker's international managers and a London venture-capital company. The US division was given a year to fix its operation or close.

Globalization

Globalization is a business initiative based on the conviction that the world is becoming more homogeneous and that distinctions between national markets are not only fading but, for some products, they will eventually disappear. Some products, such as Coca-Cola and Levi's, have already proven the existence of universal appeal. Coke's 'one sight, one sound, one sell' approach is a legend in the world of global marketers. Other companies have some products that can be 'world products,' and some that cannot and should not be. For example, if cultural and competitive differences are less important than their similarities, a single advertising approach can exploit these similarities to stimulate sales everywhere, and at far lower cost than if campaigns were developed for each individual market.

Compared to the multidomestic approach, globalization differs in these three basic ways:

1. The global approach looks for similarities between markets. The multidomestic approach ignores similarities.
2. The global approach actively seeks homogeneity in products, image, marketing, and advertising message. The multidomestic approach produces unnecessary differences from market to market.
3. The global approach asks, 'Should this product or process be for world consumption? The multidomestic approach, relying solely on local autonomy, never asks the question.

Globalization requires many internal modifications as well. Changes in philosophy concerning local autonomy, concern for local operating results rather than corporate performance, local strategies designed for local – rather than global – competitors are all delicate issues to be solved. By design, globalization calls for centralized decision making; therefore, the 'not invented here' syndrome becomes a problem. This can be solved by involving those having to implement the globalization strategy at every possible stage as well as keeping lines of communication open.

Globalization at Parker Pen Company

In January 1982, James R. Peterson became the president and CEO of Parker Pen. At that time, the company was struggling, and global marketing was one of the key measures to be used to revive the company. While at R.J. Reynolds, Peterson had been impressed with the industry's success with globalization. He wanted for Parker Pen nothing less than the writing-instrument equivalent of the Marlboro man.

For most of the 1960s and 1970s, a weak dollar had lulled Parker Pen into a false sense of security. About 80 percent of the company's sales were abroad, which meant that when local-currency profits were translated into dollars, big profits were recorded.

The market was changing, however. The Japanese had started marketing inexpensive disposable pens with considerable success through mass marketers. Brands such as Paper Mate, Bic, Pilot and Pentel each had greater sales, causing Parker's overall market share to plummet to 6 percent. Parker Pen, meanwhile, stayed with its previous strategy and continued marketing its top-of-the-line pens through department stores and stationery stores. Even in this segment Parker Pen's market share was eroding because of the efforts of A.T. Cross Company and Montblanc of West Germany.

Subsidiaries enjoyed a high degree of autonomy in marketing operations, which resulted in broad and diverse product lines and 40 different advertising agencies handling the Parker Pen account worldwide.

When the dollar's value skyrocketed in the 1980s, Parker's profits plunged and the loss of market share became painfully evident.

Peterson moved quickly upon his arrival. He trimmed the payroll, chopped the product line to 100 (from 500), consolidated manufacturing operations, and ordered an overhaul of the main plant to make it a state-of-the-art facility. Ogilvy & Mather was hired to take sole control of Parker Pen advertising worldwide. (Among the many agencies terminated was Lowe Howard-Spink in London, which had produced some of the best advertising for Parker Pen's most profitable subsidiary.)

A decision was also made to go aggressively after the low end of the market. The company would sell an upscale line called Premier, mainly as a positioning device. The biggest profits were to come from a rollerball pen called Vector, selling for $2.98. Plans were drawn to sell an even cheaper pen called Itala – a disposable pen never thought possible at Parker.

Three new managers, to be known as Group Marketing, were brought in. All three had extensive marketing experience, most of it in international markets. Richard Swart, who became marketing vice president for writing instruments, had handled 3M's image advertising worldwide and taught company managers the ins and outs of marketing planning. Jack Marks became head of writing instruments advertising. At Gillette he had orchestrated the worldwide marketing of Silkience hair-care products. Carlos Del Nero, brought in to be Parker's manager of global-marketing planning, had broad international experience at Fisher-Price. The concept of marketing by centralized direction was approved.

The idea of selling pens the same way everywhere did not sit well with many Parker subsidiaries and distributors. Pens were indeed the same, but markets, they believed, were different: France and Italy fancied expensive fountain pens; Scandinavia was a ballpoint market. In some markets, Parker could assume an above-the-fray stance; in others it had to get into the trenches and compete on price. Nonetheless, headquarters communicated to them all:

> Advertising for Parker Pens (no matter model or mode) will be based on a common creative strategy and positioning. The worldwide advertising theme, 'Make Your Mark with Parker', has been adopted. It will utilize similar graphic

layout and photography. It will utilize an agreed-upon typeface. It will utilize the approved Parker logo/design. It will be adapted from centrally supplied materials.

Swart insisted that the directives were to be used only as 'starting points,' and that they allowed for ample local flexibility. The subsidiaries perceived them differently. The U.K. subsidiary, especially, fought the scheme all the way. Ogilvy & Mather London strongly opposed the 'one world, one brand, one advertisement' dictum. Conflict arose, with Swart allegedly shouting at one of the meetings: 'Yours is not to reason why; yours is to implement.' Local flexibility in advertising was out of the question.

The London-created 'Make Your Mark' campaign was launched in October 1984. Except for language, it was essentially the same: long copy, horizontal layout, illustrations in precisely the same place, the Parker logo at the bottom, and the tag line or local equivalent in the lower right-hand corner. Swart once went to the extreme of suggesting that Parker ads avoid long copy and use just one big picture.

Problems arose on the manufacturing side. The new $15 million plant broke down repeatedly. Costs soared and the factory turned out defective products in unacceptable numbers. In addition, the new marketing approach started causing problems as well. Although Parker never abandoned its high-end position in foreign markets, its concentration on low-price, mass-distribution products in the United States caused dilution of its image and ultimately losses of $22 million in 1985. Conflict was evident internally and the board of directors began to turn against the concept of globalization.

In January 1985, Peterson resigned. Del Nero left the company in April. Swart was fired in May, Marks in June.

(Source: this case was prepared for discussion purposes, and not to exemplify correct or incorrect decision-making, in Czinkota and Ronkainen, 1990, pp. 778–82. Reproduced with permission.)

Questions

1. What marketing miscalculations were made by the advocates of the globalization effort at Parker Pen? (You should think in terms of product policy, target segments and competitive forces.)
2. Was the globalization strategy sound for writing instruments? If yes, what was wrong in the implementation? If not, why not?
3. Should the merits of global marketing be judged by what happened at Parker Pen Company?

A6.2   Case: Lakewood Forest Products

Since the 1970s the United States has had a merchandise trade deficit with the rest of the world. Up to 1982, this deficit mattered little because it was relatively small. As of 1983, however, the trade deficit increased rapidly and became, because of its size and future implications, an issue of major national concern. Suddenly, trade moved to the forefront of national debate. Concurrently, a debate ensued on the issue of the international competitiveness of US firms. The onerous question here was whether US firms could and would achieve sufficient improvements in areas such as productivity, quality and price to remain long-term successful international marketing players.

The US–Japanese trade relation took on particular significance, because it was between those two countries that the largest bilateral trade deficit existed. In spite of trade negotiations, market-opening measures, trade legislation and other governmental efforts, it was clear that the impetus for a reversal of the deficit through more US exports to Japan had to come from the private sector. Therefore, the activities of any US firm that appeared successful in penetrating the Japanese market were widely hailed. One company whose effort to market in Japan aroused particular interest was Lakewood Forest Products, in Hibbing, Minnesota.

Company background

In 1988, Ian J. Ward was an export merchant in difficulty. Throughout the 1970s and 1980s his company, Ward Bedas Canadian Ltd, had successfully sold Canadian lumber and salmon to countries in the Persian Gulf. Over time, the company had opened four offices worldwide. However, when the Iran–Iraq war erupted most of Ward's long-term trading relationships disappeared within a matter of months. In addition, the international lumber market began to collapse. As a result, Ward Bedas Canadian Ltd went into a survivalist mode and sent employees all over the world to look for new markets and business opportunities. Late that year, the company received an interesting order. A firm in Korea urgently needed to purchase lumber for the production of chopsticks.

Learning about the chopstick market

In discussing the wood deal with the Koreans, Ward learned that in order to produce good chopsticks more than 60 per cent of the wood fiber would be wasted. Given the high transportation cost involved, the large degree of wasted materials, and his need for new business, Ward decided to explore the Korean and Japanese chopstick industry in more detail. He quickly determined that chopstick making in the Far East is a fragmented industry, working with old technology and suffering from a lack of natural resources. In Asia, chopsticks are produced in very small quantities, often by family organizations. Even the largest of the 450 chopstick factories in Japan turns out only 5 million chopsticks a month. This compares to an overall market size of 130 million pairs of disposable chopsticks a day. In addition, chopsticks represent a growing market. With increased wealth in Asia, people eat out more often and therefore have a greater demand for disposable chopsticks. The fear of communicable diseases has greatly reduced the utilization of reusable chopsticks. Renewable plastic chopsticks have been attacked by many groups as too new fangled and as causing future ecological problems.

From his research, Ward concluded that a competitive niche existed in the world chopstick market. He believed that, if he could use low-cost raw materials and ensure that the labour cost component would remain small, he could successfully compete in the world market.

The founding of Lakewood Forest Products

In exploring opportunities afforded by the newly identified international marketing niche for chopsticks, Ward set four criteria for plant location:

1. Access to raw materials.
2. Proximity of other wood product users who could make use of the 60 per cent waste for their production purposes.
3. Proximity to a port that would facilitate shipment to the Far East.
4. Availability of labour.

In addition, Ward was aware of the importance of product quality. Because people use chopsticks on a daily basis and are accustomed to products that are visually inspected one by one, he would have to live up to high quality expectations in order to compete successfully. Chopsticks could not be bowed or misshapen, have blemishes in the wood or splinter.

In order to implement his plan, Ward needed financing. Private lenders were sceptical and slow to provide funds. This scepticism resulted from the unusual direction of Ward's proposal. Far Eastern companies have generally held the cost advantage in a variety of industries, especially those as labour-intensive as chopstick manufacturing. US companies rarely have an advantage in producing low-cost items. Further, only a very small domestic market exists for chopsticks.

However, Ward found that the state of Minnesota was willing to participate in his new venture. Since the decline of the mining industry, regional unemployment had been rising rapidly in the state. In 1988, unemployment in Minnesota's Iron Range peaked at 22 per cent. Therefore, state and local officials were anxious to attract new industries that would be independent of mining activities. They were excited about Ward's plans, which called for the creation of over 100 new jobs within a year.

Hibbing, Minnesota, turned out to be an ideal location for Ward's project. The area had an abundance of supply of aspen wood, which, because it grows in clay soil, tends to be unmarred. In addition, Hibbing boasted an excellent labour pool, and both the city and the state were willing to make loans totalling $500,000. Further, the Iron Range Resources Rehabilitation Board was willing to sell $3.4 million in industrial revenue bonds for the project. Together with jobs and training wage subsidies, enterprise zone credits and tax increment financing benefits, the initial public support of the project added up to about 30 per cent of its start-up costs. The potential benefit of the new venture to the region was quite clear. When

Lakewood Forest Products advertised its first 30 jobs, more than 3,000 people showed up to apply.

The production and sale of chopsticks

Ward insisted that in order to penetrate the international market properly, he would need to keep his labour cost low. As a result, he decided to automate as much of the production as possible. However, no equipment was readily available to produce chopsticks, because no one had automated the process before.

After much searching, Ward identified a European equipment manufacturer who produced machinery for making popsicle sticks. He purchased equipment from this Danish firm in order to carry out the sorting and finishing processes better. However, because aspen wood was quite different from the wood the machine was designed for, as was the final product, substantial design adjustments had to be made. Sophisticated equipment was also purchased to strip the bark from the wood and peel it into long thin sheets. Finally, a computer vision system was acquired to detect defects in the chopsticks. The system rejected over 20 per cent of the production, and yet some of the chopsticks that passed inspection were splintering. However, Ward firmly believed that further fine-tuning of the equipment and training of the new work force would gradually take care of the problem.

Given this fully automated process, Lakewood Forest Products was able to develop capacity for up to 7 million chopsticks a day. With unit manufacturing cost of $0.03 and an anticipated unit selling price of $0.057, Ward expected to earn a pretax profit of $4.7 million in 1993.

Owing to intense marketing efforts in Japan and the fact that Japanese customers were struggling to obtain sufficient supplies of disposable chopsticks, Ward was able to presell the first five years of production quite quickly. By late 1992, Lakewood Forest Products was ready to enter the international market. With an ample supply of raw materials and an almost totally automated plant, Lakewood was positioned as the world's largest and least labour-intensive manufacturer of chopsticks. The first shipment of six containers with a load of 12 million pairs of chopsticks to Japan was made in October 1992.

(Source: adapted from Michael R. Czinkota, in Czinkota and Ronkainen, 1990, pp. 472–5. Reproduced with permission.)

Questions

1. Why haven't Japanese firms thought of automating the chopstick production process?
2. What are the important variables for the international marketing success of chopsticks?
3. Rank, in order, the variables in Question 2 according to the priority you believe they have for foreign customers, especially Japanese and Korean consumers.

4. How long will Lakewood Forest Products be able to maintain its competitive advantage?

References

Bartlett, Christopher (1983), 'Procter & Gamble Europe: Vizir Launch', *Harvard Business School Case* 9–384–139.
Belk, Russel W. (1988), 'Third World consumer culture', in E. Kumçu and A. Fuat Firat (eds), *Marketing and Development: Toward broader dimensions*, JAI Press: Greenwich, CT, pp. 103–27.
Buzzell, Robert D. (1968), 'Can you standardize multinational marketing ?', *Harvard Business Review*, November-December, pp. 102–13.
Carroll, John B. (1956), *Language, Thought and Reality: Selected writings of Benjamin Lee Whorf*, MIT Press: Cambridge, MA.
Cecchini, Paolo (1988), *The European Challenge 1992*, Wildwood House: Aldershot.
Clark, Harold F., Jr (1987), 'Consumer and corporate values: Yet another view on global marketing', *International Journal of Advertising*, vol. 6, pp. 29–42.
Cundiff, Edward W. and Marye Tharp Hilger (1982), 'The consumption function: Marketing's role in economic development', *Management Decision*, vol. 20, no. 4, pp. 36–45.
Czinkota, Michael R. and Illka A. Ronkainen (1990), *International Marketing*, 2nd edn, Dryden Press: Hinsdale, IL.
De Bettignies, Henri (1989), 'The globalization of the Japanese economy: Implications for Europe and the United States', *IBEAR*, University of Southern California, 1989/5.
Deher, Odile (1986), 'Quelques facteurs de succès pour la politique de produits de l'entreprise exportatrice: Les liens entre marketing et production', *Recherche et applications en marketing*, vol. 1, no. 3, pp. 55–74.
Dholakia, Ruby Roy, Mohammed Sharif and Labdhi Bhandari (1988), 'Consumption in the Third World: Challenges for marketing and economic development', in E. Kumçu and A. Fuat Firat (eds), *Marketing and Development: Toward broader dimensions*, JAI Press: Greenwich, CT, pp. 129–47.
Douglas, Susan P. and Christine D. Urban (1977), 'Life-style analysis to profile women in international markets', *Journal of Marketing*, vol. 41 (July) no. 3, pp. 46–54.
Dubois, Bernard (1987), 'Culture et marketing', *Recherche et Applications en Marketing*, Vol. 2(3) pp. 37–64.
Eshghi, Abdolezra and Jagdish N. Sheth (1985), 'The globalization of consumption patterns: An empirical investigation', in Erdener Kaynak (ed.), *Global Perspectives in Marketing*, Praeger: New York, pp. 133–48.
Focus (1995), Information bulletin of the World Trade Organization, March–April, no. 2, pp. 4–11.
GATT (1986), *Le Commerce International en 1985–1986*, GATT: Geneva.
Ghoshal, Sumantra (1987), 'Global strategy: An organizing framework', *Strategic Management Journal*, vol. 8, pp. 425–40.
Hamel, Gary and C. K. Prahalad (1985), 'Do you really have a global strategy?' *Harvard Business Review*, vol. 63, July–August, pp. 139–48.
Hampton, Gerald M. and Erwin Buske (1987), 'The global marketing perspective', in S. Tamer Cavusgil (ed.), *Advances in International Marketing*, JAI Press: Greenwich, CT, vol. 2, pp. 259–77.

Hansen, D. M. and J. J. Boddewyn (1976), *American Marketing in the European Common Market, 1963–1973*, Marketing Science Institute: Cambridge, MA, report no. 76–107.

Hill, John S. and William L. James (1991), 'Product and promotion transfers in consumer goods multinationals', *International Marketing Review*, vol. 8, no 4, pp. 6–17.

Hill, John S. and Richard R. Still (1984a), 'Adapting products to L.D.C. tastes', *Harvard Business Review*, March–April, pp. 92–101.

Hill, John S. and Richard R. Still (1984b), 'Effects of urbanization on multinational product planning: Markets in L.D.C.s', *Columbia Journal of World Business*, vol. 19 (Summer), pp. 62–67.

Hout, Thomas, Michael E. Porter and Eileen Rudden (1982), 'How global companies win out,' *Harvard Business Review*, vol. 60, September–October, pp. 98–105.

Huszagh, Sandra M., Richard J. Fox and Ellen Day, (1986), 'Global marketing: An empirical investigation', *Columbia Journal of World Business*, vol. XX, no. 4, pp. 31–43.

Jain, Subhash C. (1989), 'Standardization of international marketing strategy: Some research hypotheses', *Journal of Marketing*, vol. 53, January, pp. 70–9.

Kashani, Kamran (1989), 'Beware the pitfalls of global marketing', *Harvard Business Review*, September–October, pp. 91–8.

Levitt, Theodore (1983), 'The globalization of markets', *Harvard Business Review*, vol. 61 (May–June), pp. 92–102.

Li, Tiger (1990), 'Black and Decker's turnaround strategy', in Hans B. Thorelli and S. Tamer Cavusgil (eds)., *International Marketing Strategy*, Pergamon Press: Oxford, pp. 495–8.

Ludlow, Peter W. (1990), 'Global challenges of the 1990s: Future of the international trading system', *Economic Impact*, 1990/1, pp. 4–10.

McCornell, J. D. (1971), 'The economics of behavioral factors in the multinational corporation', in Fred E. Allvine (ed.), *Combined Proceedings of the American Marketing Association*, p. 260.

Ozsomer, Aysegul, Muzzafer Bodur and S. Tamer Cavusgil (1991), 'Marketing standardisation by multinationals in an emerging market,' *European Journal of Marketing*, vol. 25, no. 12, pp. 50–64.

Peterson, Blyth, Cato Associates Inc. and Cheskin Masten (1985), 'Survey on global brands and global marketing', Empirical Report, New York.

Picard, Jacques, Jean Jacques Boddewyn and Robin Soehl (1989), 'U.S. marketing policies in the European Economic Community: A longitudinal study, 1973–1983', in Reijo Luostarinen (ed.), *Dynamics of International Business*, Proceedings of the 15th Annual Conference of the EIBA, Helsinki, vol. 1, pp. 551–79.

Porter, Michael E. (1986), 'Changing patterns of international competition', *California Management Review*, vol XXVIII, no. 2, pp. 9–39.

Quelch, John A. and Edward J. Hoff (1986), 'Customizing global marketing', *Harvard Business Review*, vol. 64, May–June, pp. 59–68.

Ricks, David A. (1983), *Big Business Blunders: Mistakes in multinational marketing*: Dow Jones-Irwin: Homewood, IL.

Rosen, Barry-Nathan, Jean J. Boddewyn and Ernst A. Louis (1987), 'US brands abroad: An empirical study of global branding', *International Marketing Review*, vol. 6, no. 1, pp. 7–19.

Roth, M. S. and C. Moorman (1988), 'The cultural content of cognition and the cognitive content of culture: Implications for consumer research', in M. J. Houston (ed.), *Advances in Consumer Research*, Association For Consumer Research: Provo, UT, vol. 15, pp. 403–10.

Saporito, Bill (1984), 'Black & Decker's gamble on globalization', *Fortune*, 14 May, pp. 24–32.

Sherry, John F. (1987), 'Cultural propriety in a global marketplace', in A. Fuat Firat, Nikhilesh Dholakhia and Richard P. Bagozzi (eds), *Philosophical and Radical Thought in Marketing*, Lexington Books: Lexington, MA.

Sheth, Jagdish N. (1986), 'Global markets or global competition?', *Journal of Consumer Marketing*, vol. 3 (Spring), pp. 9–11.

Steele, Murray (1991), 'European brewing industry', in Roland Calori and Peter Lawrence (eds), *The Business of Europe*, Sage: London.

Stobaugh, Robert and Piero Telesio (1983), 'Assortir la politique de fabrication á la stratégie des produits', *Harvard-L'Expansion*, Summer, pp. 77–85.

Sumitomo Corporation (1988), *Global Market Makers*, Sumitomo Shoji Kaisha: Tokyo.

Usunier, Jean-Claude (1980), 'Les Lois de déformation des réseaux du commerce international', unpublished doctoral thesis, University of Paris II.

Usunier, Jean-Claude (1991), 'The "European consumer": Globalizer or globalized?', in Alan Rugman and Alain Verbeke (eds), *Research in Global Strategic Management*, vol. 2, JAI Press: Greenwich, CT, pp. 57–78.

Van Mesdag, Martin (1987), 'Winging it in foreign markets', *Harvard Business Review*, vol. 65, no. 1 (January–February), pp. 71–4.

Wind, Yoram (1986), 'The myth of globalization', *Journal of Consumer Marketing*, vol. 3 (Spring), pp. 23–6.

Woods, Walter A., Emmanuel J. Chéron and Dong Han Kim (1985), 'Strategic implications of differences in consumer purposes in three global markets', in Erdener Kaynak (ed.), *Global Perspectives in Marketing*, Praeger: New York, pp. 155–70.

Zaichkowsky, Judith L. and James H. Sood (1988), 'A global look at consumer involvement and use of products', *International Marketing Review*, vol. 6, no. 1, pp. 20–33.

7

♦♦♦

Intercultural marketing: The regional dimension

As argued in the previous chapter, globalization is a process that occurs at the competition level. Regional agreements world-wide and the GATT framework allow for artificial entry barriers, mostly tariff and non-tariff, to be progressively replaced by natural entry barriers related to scale and experience. As far as consumer behaviour and marketing environments are concerned, natural entry barriers related to culture will diminish very progressively and only in the long term: there are still many very different marketing 'villages', not a global one. In this chapter the following ideas are defended:

1. Strategic management has to be 'global', whereas marketing management largely needs to be tailored to local contexts.
2. An intercultural orientation to international marketing best serves a global strategic view.

The strategic dilemma is achieving both low cost and differentiation in the minds of consumers *vis-à-vis* the competitors. Although they may at times conflict, because differentiation may result in cost increases, there are possible compromises. Differentiation is naturally a key tenet of this book. However, I do not overlook the necessity of cost efficiency in three major areas: production, transport and marketing. In order to minimize both costs and unnecessary differentiation, and simultaneously maximize relevant differentiation, clustering customers in groups sharing common characteristics is essential. Culture is naturally one of the main 'entries' to clustering, but not the only one; sociodemographic characteristics are also extremely significant in an international perspective.

The first section concentrates on cost arguments and shows that global strategies are fully significant from a pure cost perspective. The second section elaborates on the intercultural marketing approach. The last three sections give clues for the clustering of countries, by explaining what is regional integration and comparing across regions of the world (section 7.3), then developing in more depth the case of the European Union (section 7.4) and the cases of eastern European and ex-USSR countries, and Asian Pacific Rim countries (section 7.5).

7.1   Cost arguments and global strategies

Multidomestic and global markets

This distinction, shown by Michael Porter, has been widely applied since the beginning of the 1980s. At the industry level, there is a shift from multidomestic competition patterns to global ones. According to Porter, competition becomes global when 'a firm's competitive position is significantly affected by its position in other countries and vice-versa' (1986, p. 18). When an industry is multidomestic, separate strategies are pursued in different national markets, and the competitive scene remains basically a domestic one. There are some fundamental reasons for industries to remain multidomestic:

1. Wide differences in consumer needs and attitudes across markets.
2. Legal barriers resulting from domestic regulations (which have long been the case of banking and insurance).
3. Non-tariff barriers which artificially maintain competition between purely national competitors (food and drug health regulations, for instance).

Accordingly, the basic preoccupation of a global strategy is (very briefly defined) the configuration and coordination of activities, including marketing, across national markets.

Trends towards global (competitive) markets

The trends towards global markets differ fairly widely depending on the industry. The causes are multiple:

1. The influence of national regulations and non-tariff barriers varies to a large degree across product categories.
2. The potential for experience effects also varies across product categories: for example, there is less potential for cost reduction due to volume increase in the case of cheeses compared to microchips.
3. International 'transportability', in other words, to what extent do transportation costs impinge on the degree and patterns of globalization of an industry? Exporting may be the dominant pattern for easily transportable products, such as semiconductors. Direct foreign investment may be the prevailing one for industries whose products are expensive to transport long distance (e.g. cement).
4. The degree of culture bonding to a product: the trend towards globalization in the cheese industry is slower (although clearly existent) than the trend towards globalization in the microchip industry.

Experience effects

The potential for experience effects differs widely across product categories. The Boston Consulting Group has isolated one of the main reasons for this through research into the success of various companies, Japanese included, in global markets. Experience effects provide companies with the ability to reduce unit costs dramatically through an increase in product quantity. The experience effects determine the relationship of unit cost to cumulated production volume according to the following formula:

$$C_n = C_1 n^{-\lambda}$$

where C_n is the cost of the nth unit; C_1 is the cost of the first unit; n is the cumulated number of units produced; and λ is the elasticity of the unit cost with respect to the cumulated production volume.

The form of the function reflects a constant elasticity. Let us call k the effect of elasticity. When production is doubled, the cost (and therefore, to a certain extent, the price) will decrease by $1-k = 1-2^{-\lambda}$ per cent each time the experience doubles. If, for example, k equals 70 per cent, the cost will decrease by 30 per cent on a doubling of the cumulated production ($1 - 70\% = 30\%$). Experience effects theory has been supported by empirical verification (Day and Montgomery, 1983). Experience effects have been estimated for such diverse products and services as long-distance telephone calls in the United States, bottle tops in West Germany, refrigerators in Great Britain and Japanese motorcycles.

The source of experience effects is fourfold:

1. The effects of *learning by doing*. The more times one carries out a task or manufactures a component or a product, the more efficiently it is done or, alternatively, the less time is taken to do so.
2. *Scale effects*. By increasing the scale of production, the average cost can be reduced. Many industrial products require a large amount of research and development for product design, yet only a small quantity of raw materials for their manufacture (e.g. pocket calculators).
3. *Technological advances*. The increase in cumulated production offers a dual possibility of technological improvements. On one hand, production equipment may be refined; on the other hand, the product itself can be simplified and rendered cheaper to produce. These product simplifications usually result from a decrease in the number of parts, and not from a reduction in the number of functions and the degree of sophistication which would adversely affect the consumer.
4. *Economies of scope*: component parts may be shared by different products. For instance, the same basic diesel engine may be used for a forklift elevator, a small truck, a van, a car, or as an on-board motor for a boat, at the expense of slight final adaptations. The increase in the production scale of shared components (or shared overhead costs, or any kind of shared common inputs) results in economies of scope.

Not every product has the same potential for experience effects. The potential is clearly smaller for cheese or books than for hi-fi systems or microcomputers. An examination of Japanese successes in world markets demonstrates that the Japanese have concentrated on goods that have very high experience effects, such as motorcycles, motor cars, photocopiers, video equipment, hi-fi systems, television sets, outboard motors, musical instruments and cameras. Right from the start, Japanese companies opted for global markets, even though their domestic market for such products was itself very substantial. Competitors have struggled to resist the competitive pressure of Japanese companies. The motorcycle industry is typical of the lack of experience effects amongst European manufacturers. In an attempt to compete with the Japanese (Honda, Yamaha, Suzuki, Kawazaki), Motobécane, a French manufacturer, launched a 125cc motorcycle twenty years ago. This model had a two-stroke engine that operated on a mixture of petrol and oil, since Motobécane was unable to make a four-stroke engine, like Honda, or an 'oil lube' (a device for mixing oil and petrol automatically), like Yamaha, Suzuki or Kawazaki. This motorcycle emitted a thick cloud of white smoke through its exhaust. The range of models offered has remained very limited, as with other French motor-cycles. The 350cc Motobécane, which could have enjoyed a lucrative market by supplying the French police, was not fast or reliable enough. Both the 125cc and the 350cc were complete flops. Motobécane remained a company operating mainly in the French domestic market and as a result the company was undersized. The lack of experience effects in the company was a barrier to technological improvements. Motobé-cane is now renamed MBK and is a subsidiary of Yamaha.

International transportability

The unit weight, that is, dollar price per kilogram or per pound, differs widely across category of goods, and therefore across the industries that manufacture them. Cement or basic ordinary steel products range from 50 cents per kilogram to several dollars per kilogram, whereas cars range from 10 dollars per kilogram (for example, a small family car at the bottom end of the market) to 60 or 70 dollars per kilogram for luxury cars at the top end of the market (large Mercedes, BMWs or Jaguars). A portable computer may reach a price of 750 dollars per kilogram (or even more), not to mention its component chips which may climb to several thousand dollars per kilogram.

In the international transportation system, shipping charges do not follow a simple tariff, which would be directly proportional to weight. They are calculated on the basis of a mix of criteria, depending on the nature of goods to be shipped and on the shipping line. Shipping lines are also subject to economies of scale. Transportation cost factors are influenced by the forces of competition between transportation companies, and also by the method of transportation (ship, aeroplane, truck or train). The mix of criteria includes weight, volume, dimensions, ease of loading and unloading, perishability, packaging and speed of delivery. However, weight, volume and perishability are clearly the most detrimental factors to international transportation.

Some markets will remain almost exclusively multidomestic, because goods and services cannot be transported – hairdressing services, for instance. Although transport-ability may have a negative influence on the cross-border transactions of goods and services, it does not hamper the globalization of an industry where cross-border investments are possible. In the cement industry, markets are regionally segmented within countries because of the high cost of transportation in proportion to basic unit price. The cement industry still competes on a global basis through foreign direct investment and the sale and licensing of technology.

Transportability concerns also consumers, who may be more 'transportable' than the products or services which are offered to them. Ski resorts are a good example: ski slopes, buildings and equipment are not transportable, nor is snow. But potential skiers may be transported at low cost on charter flights, from countries without mountains, snow or ski resorts (but with some purchasing power). Thus we may observe in the international ski-resort industry a twofold pattern of globalization. On the one hand, some world-famous ski resorts, such as Val d'Isère in France, Kitzbühel in Austria and Zermatt in Switzerland, enjoy a global market. People arrive from many parts of the world, often on package holidays sold by tour operators or travel agencies. On the other hand, there remains in most ski-oriented countries a large number of purely local ski resorts ('ski villages') which compete on a more domestic basis. This part of the industry is multidomestic. Between these two segments, one globalized, one multidomestic, there are in fact many intermediate ski resorts which compete on a regionally globalized basis. This is the case with most medium-size ski resorts in the European Alps: in Austria, France, Germany, Italy, Switzerland and some eastern European countries, which compete for European skiers.

The disconnection between sourcing and marketing

The countries where sourcing and marketing take place may be highly disconnected in industries which compete on a global basis. The sites of most cost-efficient production are often export-processing zones in newly industrialized countries. Consumer markets may be located in very remote places. The same brand may be 'made in' various countries which generate different country-of-origin images (see section 9.2). Consumers, who use country of origin as an information cue for comparing brands, are now becoming more and more aware of the actual disconnection between sourcing and marketing.

A world view versus a local view

A 'global strategy' clearly implies a world view of competition and competitive advantage, not simply a belief that consumers and markets are themselves global. The issue of global strategies has been extensively documented in the strategic management literature; it is clearly outside the scope of this book, which emphasizes the cultural dimensions of international marketing, to discuss in full detail the specific issues related to global strategies.

In cultural terms, the ethnocentrism of the managing team of any company is shown by the way in which it treats the domestic/national market on one hand and 'foreign' markets on the other. This issue is not purely academic; it permeates the ways in which a company organizes its international activities and the nationalities of its top executives as well as other more practical considerations such as the choice of the language(s) to be spoken between subsidiaries and head office.

Once the company has achieved a certain level of development in foreign markets, the 'export' view and the 'international development' view can no longer co-exist effectively. They are dependent on four different perspectives: ethnocentrism, polycentrism, regiocentrism and geocentrism (Wind *et al.*, 1973), two of these (ethno- and geocentrism) being somewhat irreconcilable.

In terms of set theory, the domestic market is perceived as disjointed from foreign markets, whereas in the geocentric view, the domestic market is seen as belonging to the world market in the same way as any other domestic market. Ethnocentric companies view international operations as secondary to their domestic operations. A company that considers its national base as a top priority will impose its own language on its foreign subsidiaries. It will supply the domestic market first when production capacity is overstretched. It will never invite a non-national onto the board of directors unless this person shares the company's native language and culture. Conversely the firm that considers its national base as just one of many, a geocentric company, will make the opposite choices. This is in line with the distinction made by Wind *et al.* (1973) in the EPRG model (ethnocentric, polycentric, regiocentric, geocentric) of behaviour of international companies. Polycentrism results from the recognition of differences that occur in overseas markets. Each country is accepted as one of many ethnocentric places which may have their own marketing policies and programmes. Regiocentrism reflects the change of a company towards a more open understanding or world marketing, where regional marketing strategies are designed.

When companies distance themselves from an ethnocentric attitude by virtue of their management style and corporate culture, they develop genuinely offensive and defensive marketing strategies in foreign markets. Such a strategy manifests itself in flexible reallocation of resources from one market to another. For instance, a company will relocate into market Y, where it holds a solid position, as a reaction to one large competitor launching a price offensive in country X. This type of situation is conceivable in strongly oligopolistic markets where several (five to ten) large multinationals control the world market, as happens in the food industry or the liquefied gases industry.

Nevertheless it seems that stiff competition gives way to forms of cooperation between large companies from developed countries. The theory developed by Kenichi Ohmae, head of the Tokyo office of McKinsey Consultants, in his book *Triad Power: The coming shape of global competition* (1985), emphasizes the need for companies who want to survive international competition to have a solid base in each of the three major industrialized regions' market areas: North America, Japan and Europe. Ohmae further suggests that in each of these regions, companies should establish links of international division of labour with neighbouring developing countries. Companies in Latin-American countries are natural subcontractors for North American companies. South East Asian countries subcontract for Japanese firms. The same cooperation pattern should occur between African countries and European companies. To ensure this necessary tripolar presence (called the 'triad'), Ohmae advocates that alliances should be built between companies belonging to one of the developed market areas. Most of these companies, even large ones, cannot individually afford to make the necessary investment that would ensure a full presence in the three regions of the triad.

Prioritized market(s) often remain undiscussed. To avoid this kind of 'collective unconsciousness', companies must reflect on how prioritized markets relate to corporate culture, to the search for market and business opportunities and to the decision-making process. Some European companies still supply their domestic market as a priority, on the basis that this market is the 'home base'. This attitude has two dangerous consequences:

1. It leads to a bias in product design. The modest sales records of certain European cars, mainly French and Italian, in the North American, principally the US, market is, at least partly, attributable to local French and Italian motor regulations which bias the design of cars, and make them inappropriate for use in America. In France, the speed restrictions on motorways and a high-cost road tax that is largely progressive with the size of the engine, has discouraged the production of large cars and sports cars. The same holds true in Italy, where the high cost of petrol has encouraged the production of small cars, too small in fact for US consumers. This has dissuaded car manufacturers in those countries from building high-speed luxury saloons, a gap in the market which was mostly filled by the Germans and the Swedes, before the Japanese came with their Lexus and Acuras.
2. Home-base-oriented companies often suffer the unfortunate reputation abroad of unreliability with respect to delivery dates. This is due to a 'marginal' conception of foreign markets, which are considered as a provisional outlet when the home market is depressed. It leads to a consistent preference for supplying a domestic customer in preference to a foreign customer. Even though such foreign customers may have ordered earlier, they will be forced to wait and will only receive delivery after domestic customers have been satisfied. A genuine respect for delivery dates should have led to a different outcome.

   As soon as domestic demand increases, such prioritization of national markets implies that production capacity will cease to be used for supplying foreign customers. As a consequence, there is a general risk that attempts to set up stable business relationships with customers and intermediaries in foreign markets will be hampered. Typically, foreign agents will only be visited when business at home is slack, and will be let down (as will foreign customers) as soon as the home market situation improves. This attitude fails to satisfy the essential precondition for effective international development.

The world market share concept: Global size and the diagnosis of economic market share

Computing a world market share helps to prevent a company from being ethnocentric when defining its position *vis-à-vis* the competition. Competition is seen from the outset as being global. Box 7.1 illustrates the dangers of overemphasizing domestic market share.

A diagnosis of a particular company's situation within world markets requires the following evaluations (even though estimates may be only approximate):

1. What is the size of the world market (volume, units, sales figure)?
2. What is the company's production size?
3. What is the company's share of the world market?
4. What is the minimum world market share necessary to remain competitive, considering potential experience effects?

The world market for forklift trucks was roughly 200,000 units per year. Fenwick held only 2 per cent of this market. 'Competitive' market share could be estimated to have been 10 per cent, or 20,000 trucks a year. Fenwick was therefore well below required global size. In view of this, it should have reduced its range to either diesel or electric forklifts and to a limited range of sizes so that the production could have been much greater on the more specialized world market.

There is no precise rule for estimating the 'competitive' world market share. This figure depends on the optimum size of production, which in turn depend on the potential for experience effects for a specific product or service. They are, though, much stronger under the following conditions:

1. When the product/service is mass produced.
2. When the product/service involves a production process with large initial fixed costs (in R & D, and/or in production facilities investment, and/or in initial marketing costs).
3. When the added value of the product/service is high, when the whole production cycle is considered.
4. When the product/service is in a fairly open international market; any producer may sell throughout the world without suffering prohibitive transport costs, customs barrier, statutory restrictions or market barriers (e.g. differences in taste).

Limitations on international size arise in various areas; for example cement (very high transport costs compared to its price), pharmaceuticals (statutory restrictions), foodstuffs (taste differences), etc. As far as services are concerned, the potential for experience effect is much smaller, since in many cases services must be performed in a direct relationship with the consumer, are often intangible and therefore cannot be held in stock. In addition their market area is often fairly localized and they are subject to local customs

Box 7.1 *Fenwick, a synonym for forklift*

Fenwick, the leading company for forklift trucks in France, is also a word used in everyday speech as a synonym for forklift trucks. A few years ago the company controlled 40–50 per cent of the French market and nearly went bankrupt because it lacked international size. This company only produced 4,000 forklift trucks per year, whereas its western competitor, Toyota, produced 35,000 and its main East European competitor, Balkankar (a Bulgarian company, 70,000). This had a negative effect on Fenwick's unit costs. Fenwick should have adapted its marketing strategy, by reducing the depth of its product range, thereby increasing production size within a narrower product range. Toyota was in a position to offer a very wide product range (diesel or electric, with varying loading capacities, etc.). Fenwick, on the other hand, should have restricted its range albeit at the consequent risk of losing customers who expect to find a single supplier capable of dealing with all their requirements.

and ways of life, such as the type of food and service found in a restaurant or the kind of treat offered by hotels.

The easiest empirical solution for the evaluation of 'competitive' market share is to examine the size of competitors, and to determine the size of those competitors who operate most effectively.

Global markets as learning opportunities

Global markets work as a set of coherent opportunities, through markets being at different product life-cycle (PLC) stages and through experience cumulated across national markets. According to product life-cycle theory (Vernon, 1966), national markets at different development stages offer different kinds of opportunities. If, for instance, the market for wallpaper is saturated in developed economies, it may be opening up in newly industrialized countries. PLC theory clearly indicates the way in which sourcing and marketing activities should be disconnected. PLC theory, in conjunction with the world market share concept, assists in the identification of what to supply and from where, and in which countries to market.

Global markets are also full of learning opportunities; the internationalization process has been presented mostly as a learning and experiencing process (Johanson and Vahlne, 1977). Since the cultural variable is fundamental to this learning process, some markets may be used almost purely as learning opportunities. When Procter & Gamble attacked the Japanese market for baby nappies (diapers) it initially achieved great success. Its market share subsequently dropped sharply against the main Japanese competitor Kao. P & G did its best to survive in the face of harsh competition from Kao and other Japanese producers, to satisfy the exigent Japanese consumers and to make its way through the Japanese *Keiretsu* distribution system (see Chapter 11). P & G's experience in Japan has made it aware of the competitive threat of the Japanese producers. P & G realized that it would face harsh competition if Japanese producers were to decide to

Box 7.2   *Stimorol and Hollywood*

A Danish chewing-gum company, Dandy A/S, which produces Stimorol, encountered difficulties in selling its products in France. Dandy was particularly successful at producing chewing gum dragé. Hollywood France (owned by the US company General Foods/Kraft) was less successful in the production of this type of product, but had better access to the major distribution outlets (hypermarkets). In fact, only large companies are able to have their products referenced, that is, registered as products accepted for sale by the channel. Referencing requires the payment of large 'entry fees' to the hypermarkets, which are only semi-legitimate. Dandy of Denmark and Hollywood ended up forging a cross-competence alliance whereby Dandy produces Hollywood dragé products and markets Hollywood products through Dandy's international sales organization, and Hollywood markets Dandy's Stimorol brand in France and produces the Dandy stick products.

(Source: excerpt from Hollensen, 1991, p. 736)

expand in world markets. This has already helped P & G resist the internationalization of Kao which, up to now, never succeeded in becoming a global competitor to P & G.

Global markets may also be seen as partnership opportunities: with the local consumers, with the distributors and (why not?) with competitors (Box 7.2).

7.2   Intercultural marketing: An implementation framework for a global business strategy

As argued above, marketing cannot be global *per se*. Marketing is localizing as much as globalizing. It aims to customize product and marketing strategies to customer needs to diversified distribution channels and to local media and communication styles, within the framework of a global strategy. Intercultural marketing tries to balance cross-national differences, in so far as they require mandatory adaptation, and cross-national commonalities which should be exploited in the building of size and experience effects.

The highest common cultural denominator (HCCD)

When issues related to cultural difference are addressed for designing international marketing strategies, they should refer to precise products or product categories. The relationship of dairy products to Japanese culture is manifestly much weaker than it is to most European cultures. Conversely, in the case of hi-fi systems or televisions it is much stronger. Furthermore, the closer one comes to elements of the *physical* environment which influence the local material culture (climate, density of population, housing, flora and fauna, etc.), the more the HCCD tends to lower. The absence of visible cattle rearing on most Japanese islands, except Hokkaido, distances Japanese people from dairy products to an exceptional degree, particularly when compared to the Netherlands or France, where cows can be seen grazing on any trip to the countryside. Japanese people find cheese, the most sophisticated dairy product, quite a strange kind of food and only a very few of them like it.

Cultural consumption (music, literature, cinema, etc.) is inherently more strongly suffused with cultural particularism. Music and literature in their industrial form, i.e. the book and the record, are two products where global marketing has been employed. Success has sometimes been remarkable, but instances remain limited. The amazing success of Harlequin romance novels and Michael Jackson records, for example, has several characteristics which make them genuine exceptions. Their success is based on cross-culturally equivalent factors of profound attraction. These factors have sometimes bypassed the filter of national cultures. The romantic and melodramatic adventures of Harlequin heroes found a lonely female public eager for tenderness in the majority of urban centres. Likewise the meanings conveyed by the music of Michael Jackson extend far beyond US culture even though it evokes images of the American way of life and is thereby at the forefront of modern music. The character of Michael Jackson touches deep layers of individual character (sexual ambiguity) in his admirers. This process is largely individually based and partly independent of culture.

Cultural products which build on fairly universal feelings and ways of being are the ones to which standardized marketing policy can be applied. For the remainder of cultural products the situation is quite different. There is a wide gulf between marketing techniques which tend towards standardization and the cultural dimension which tends to curb internationalization. In the case of the record industry, and more particularly for the collections of popular music, marketing techniques have generally evolved in the same direction over the past ten years in every industrialized nation. This evolution is characterized by an increased importance in large-scale distribution or specialized chains, an equivalent price level for everyone in relation to average household expenditure, promotion channels and relatively identical advertising with the predominant role taken by traditional media (press, radio, television) and a global standardization of product presentation.

The inherent cultural dimension of the popular song has, however, curbed internationalization and therefore the intercultural marketing of certain kinds of music. American country music has failed, up to now, in its attempt to achieve major success in Europe. Its only real international development occurred in Australia despite achieving critical success in the United Kingdom (Usunier and Sissmann, 1986). A reason for this is the absence of a significant segment of the European population which can identify itself with the images evoked by the music of the American West, the symbol of a tradition of pioneers. The Australian bush, on the other hand, similar in many respects to the American Midwest, has given birth to an Australian musical tradition whose roots are in country music. This facilitated the marketing of American products in Australia and vice versa.

Cultural identification

Intercultural marketing is greatly facilitated when the conditions for product identification are already present in the market to be conquered. Consumers buy the meaning that they find in products for the purpose of cultural identification. This identification can be traced to factors of change in a society. Identification may also result from the desire for assimilation to a particular type of civilization, as in the case of ethnic consumption reviewed in Chapter 4. The first alternative is illustrated by the attempt made by record companies to commercialize classical music on a large scale in the forms of collections. Market surveys have shown that in the West the acquisition of classical records combined with a superficial knowledge of the most famous pieces promotes a personal image of stability and respectability for people between the ages of 25 and 40. These aspirations are further reinforced by a desire for personal achievement in professional life and successful integration into social life.

As a result, certain record companies have launched mass-market collections of classical music, the marketing strategy for which has been a strict implementation of the rules of global marketing: same product, same packaging, same price and same type of communication. The marketing concept behind these collections has, however, been less successful when classical music has ceased to be a major element in the acquisition of respectability for this specific segment of the population. This has occurred particularly in developing countries where the average level of education among the middle class lags somewhat in comparison to western countries. Such has been the case in Latin America.

International marketing can take advantage of the desire for assimilation into a different society

McDonald's Big Mac and Coca-Cola are the sources of meanings that provide their buyers with the possibility of cultural adaptation to a desired way of life. Rock music represents a more tolerant and leisurely way of life for many young Europeans and Asians. Identification with these symbols is one of the necessary conditions for being *trendy*. The international marketing of rock music achieves even greater success where certain values (e.g. individualism, strong desire for equality) are already present in the market segment to be conquered, in this case young people between the ages of 10 and 25.

The process of cultural identification functions in two ways: that of *identity* (the reproduction of national culture as it used to be, the desire to be 'at home'), and that of *exoticism* (the desire to escape from one's own culture, to experience different values and ways of life). These two ways are intermingled in a quite ambiguous fashion in the process of cultural identification. This ambivalence prohibits any simplistic approach to such a process of cultural identification. For marketing implementation, however, it is often necessary to cluster countries or consumers who share certain meaningful cultural characteristics. Such clusters form *cultural affinity zones and cultural affinity classes*.

Cultural affinity zones

Attempts to market records on a global level have led to the pinpointing of cultural affinity zones in which the same marketing strategy with the same type of products can be successfully implemented. In Europe, for example, two of these zones are quite separate (Figure 7.1) – Scandinavia and the Mediterranean countries. A third zone encompasses Central European countries and Great Britain which serve as a bridge between northern and southern Europe, while retaining their own distinct personality. Despite the traditional isolation of the United Kingdom, there are less differences between the United Kingdom and Denmark or Sweden than Italy or Spain. Accordingly a song that is successful in the United Kingdom is more likely to repeat this success in the Netherlands or Denmark than in southern Europe. The long-established differences between Saxon and Latin cultures are reinforced by the religious divide between Protestants and Catholics. Cultural affinity zones display similar characteristics for easily identifiable criteria such as language, religion, family life patterns, work relations and consumption patterns. Intercultural marketing can effectively begin by choosing one of the main countries from a cultural affinity zone. This 'lead country' will subsequently be used as a base for market entry into other countries throughout the zone. A hierarchy of cultural affinity zones can be established. The marketing teams can interact with each

Figure 7.1 A hypothetical map of the zones of cultural affinities in Europe.
(Source: Usunier and Sissmann, 1986, p. 85. Reproduced with permission.)

other across zones, especially in countries which lie at the border of two zones. As an example, Figure 7.1 offers a *hypothetical map* of the zones of cultural affinities for Western Europe.

The operational mapping of these zones is based on criteria at the interface of culture and marketing. They must also have a strong relationship to the category of products studied: for example, opening hours in distribution outlets, attitude towards prices (strong or weak inflation, orientation towards bargaining), attitude towards innovation, etc. (Box 7.3).

Cultural affinity classes

A further step in the intercultural marketing approach is to concentrate not only on nationality-based cultural criteria. One should also take account of consumer attitude, preferences and lifestyles that are *linked to age, class and ethnic- or profession-based cultures*. This does not, however, exclude other possible criteria for segmentation. Cultural affinity zones correspond to a large extent to national cultural groups. Cultural affinity classes exist in terms of age brackets or, more generally, across sociodemographic categories, for example people between the ages of 15 and 20 in Japan, Europe and the United States. People within a cultural affinity class share common values, behaviour and interests, and tend to present common traits as a consumer segment.

Which cultural affinity classes demonstrate the highest variance in terms of cultural affinity zones? Are consumption behaviour, values and lifestyles among the 15-to-20-year-olds more homogeneous across Europe than among the 30-to-40-year-olds? Cultural affinity classes, in as far as they create a sense of belonging to a common group across different countries, are probably an ideal means of defining an international target for standardized products. Furthermore the development of new media such as satellite television channels will help the international launch of products targeted at the same cultural affinity classes across different countries. Accordingly, market research should survey consumer segments, each one corresponding to a box in a matrix which displays countries in columns and cultural affinity classes in rows.

If similar behaviour is observed by market researchers across the different boxes of the matrix with regard to key consumer behaviour figures (e.g. consumption of soft drinks, organization of personal time, time spent listening to the radio or watching television, etc.), the emergence of a common consumption culture can be detected for several countries. If, on the other hand, different cultural affinity classes at the national level adopt similar behaviour at the international level, marketing communication will have to be modified to facilitate the process of diffusion from one country to another. If a drink (white wine, for example) that is popular among 25-to-30-year-olds in one country is also popular among 50-to-60-year-olds in another country, this is an indication of a weak affinity of national cultures.

Box 7.3   *Launching a new record*

When launching a compilation album internationally, a simultaneous promotion of the same record with a strong product image is possible throughout Europe. There is a simultaneous launch in every country. But success is certain when a new product is launched initially in lead countries and only subsequently commercialized in the other countries of the zones. Success in Latin countries during the summer, when waves of migrant holiday-makers come from all over Europe, will have a greater chance of spreading into Nordic countries once the holiday-makers return home and go into record shops to buy the songs they have heard on holiday. Equally, a band may be so successful in a single country such as Germany that its music spreads into neighbouring countries. It spreads particularly rapidly in the border regions because of media overlap. In many places radio and television broadcasts are received on both sides of the border. Belgium, which is located between three other countries, Germany, France and Holland, receives up to sixteen television channels. The Brussels agglomeration is an audience for the French media, and the Flemish area for Dutch and German media. The launch of a new product through cultural affinity zones can take from eighteen months to two years. This is a relatively long period of time, since the normal life span of a song is generally in the order of three months.

(Source: Usunier and Sissmann, 1986, p. 86. Reproduced with permission)

7.3   Regional cultural traits and international marketing

Regional integration is now underway, based mostly on trade agreements. The basic assumptions, interaction models and attitudes described in Chapters 2 and 3 are located at too deep a level to be taken into account in negotiation between nation states. Therefore, convergence is basically economic (as in the case of the North American Free Trade Agreement, NAFTA), more rarely political (as in the case of the EU, and this with obvious pains). Cultural convergence is a more difficult process: it surely happens but in the very long run and with people being unaware of it. If we are to design cultural affinity zones, the issue is then to determine key elements in a regional environment, that is both similarities (which unite it against the rest of the world) and differences (which account for the intraregional diversity that needs to be taken into account). Let us start this section with an assessment of how traditional international trade doctrine has laid the foundations for a denial of culture. Paradoxically, culture becomes all the more important now that the *laissez-faire* doctrine has been successful in the long run.

Free-trade doctrine and the denial of culture

One of the seminal texts on international trade is the seventh chapter of David Ricardo's *On the Principles of Political Economy and Taxation*, which deals with foreign trade. This text dates back to the early nineteenth century. It basically explains why countries (and their traders) may derive benefits from developing international trade and trading their products internationally, instead of simply producing and trading within their own domestic market. Ricardo considers the case of two countries, England and Portugal, and two types of goods, wine and sheets. This law, which is called law of comparative or relative advantage, conveys a very powerful message: a country which would be at a competitive disadvantage for both products, would still benefit from participating in international trade. By trading internationally this country finds a better exchange ratio between the two goods than that which is provided by its domestic market. By concentrating efforts and resources on the product, where they have a relative advantage, then by exporting this product and importing the other one, the countries increase their national welfare (probably) and certainly the global welfare. Many implicit assumptions are not clearly elicited in Ricardo's text, which is both visionary and confused: (1) gains from trading internationally must offset transportation, custom duties and trading costs; (2) there are constant returns to scale; (3) products are identical or, at least perceived as such, both by the consumers and the merchants; (4) information must be easily available and efficient enough, so that merchants in the two countries may be aware of the potential gains deriving from international trade; and (5) no other financial or governmental restriction or market barrier limits international trade for these products.

    The implicit assumption that products and consumers' tastes, habits and preferences are perfectly identical in the two countries (and accordingly by logical extension throughout all the countries in the world) is a strong one. However, England was producing almost no wine. Moreover it is doubtful that the British wine had the same physical characteristics, the same alcoholic content or the same taste as the Portuguese wine. Additionally the preferences of the English and the Portuguese were probably distinct enough to enable them to recognize clearly which ones were 'their' sheets. They certainly had different fabrics and embroideries, and natives of the two countries would have been fully aware of the origin of the sheets on which they were sleeping. Furthermore in English pubs it is beer that is mostly drunk, whereas *vinho verde* or *porto* are the favourite drinks of the Portuguese, while listening to *fado*.

All these 'wine and sleep' considerations have probably appeared as rather anecdotal and naive. The cultural variable – mainly related to national culture – has been somewhat neglected in international trade, whether on theoretical grounds or for practical purposes. In international trade theory, which is almost purely economics-based, it has been ignored from the very start. Classical economists and their successors did not like national culture which has an aura of inertia and resistance to change attached to it. Their theories favour commonalities, not differences. They are based on utility maximization, not on identity building.

Ricardo's theory was contemporaneous with a major decision in Britain's economic policy: the *Corn Laws*. Ricardo demonstrated that England should reduce its custom duties, and therefore open up its domestic market to foreign agricultural commodities – especially those from the Colonies which were more cost competitive – and specialize in certain manufactured goods that it should export world-wide. Nevertheless the rationale behind this type of decision appears rather simplistic when real people are facing its real-world consequences: rapid deruralization, lack of self-sufficiency in food supplies for the country as a whole, changes in the landscape, emergence of new urban social stratas and so on.

From this initial assumption on, it was apparently axiomatic that the defence of cultural identity was inextricably linked to protectionist attitudes in international trade. This is illustrated in France by the *Lois Méline* (end of XIXth century), introduced out of a desire to protect French food supplies and French farmers, even though this meant higher costs for the consumer. This was also true in Germany where the writings of Friedrich List promoted a nationalistic approach to economic growth. In practice it is difficult to make a sharp distinction between the protection of national/cultural interest (their own identity being largely enhanced by what people consume) and the interest of some industries, which may deprive the consumer of some bargains, or even deprive him or her of the opportunity to buy definite products, on the basis of questionable arguments.

Hence there is a natural tendency to ignore the cultural variable or to consider it as an anecdotal and residual explanatory variable, defending local and narrow interests rather than promoting global welfare. This tendency of international trade theory has been largely adopted/inherited by international business and international marketing, where culture remains a subsidiary explanation, with a weak explanatory power. This is exactly how partisans of the globalization of markets see the cultural variable: a reminder of the past, a vestige in a world where we all tend to adopt a sort of 'modern' lifestyle.

The GATT treaty does not take into account the cultural variable. Its fundamental articles are based on quite opposite premisses. Article 1 sets the concept of 'general most favoured nation treatment', stating that, with respect to customs duties and similar charges, 'any advantage, favour, privilege or immunity granted by any contracting party to any product originating in or destined for any other country shall be accorded immediately and unconditionally to the like product originating in or destined for the territories of all other contracting parties' (GATT, 1986, p. 2). This is clearly a multilateral view, based on strong outgroup orientation, whereby the whole world is seen to be open to international trade and not covered by a dense network of bilateral trade agreements that would replace free markets by administered trade. However, it was necessary to make an exception for those countries which, by virtue of their geographical proximity, had a natural interest in establishing closer links, basically by setting to zero customs duties between them, instead of simply reducing progressively the average level of duties, as achieved in the multilateral GATT framework.

The GATT and regional integration

The GATT treaties represent clearly the view of liberal/individualist/utilitarian England and Anglo world. In the long periods, its achievements have been considerable. It has now been succeeded by the WTO (World Trade Organization) whose first meeting took place in January 1995 (WTO–*Focus*, 1995). The GATT was a treaty with permanent staff, but not a fully-fledged international organization. The WTO is now a full international organization with about 130 members. It has taken the pragmatic stance of GATT, and the basic treaty has been kept for the largest part, including the philosophy of self-enforceable rules. There have been many bilateral trade agreements, but the GATT has kept them under control.

Article XXIV of the GATT treaty allows various forms of regional integration provided that the purpose 'should be to facilitate trade between the constituent territories and not to raise barriers to the trade of other contracting parties' (GATT, 1986, p. 41). There are various forms of regional integration, the simplest being that of a free-trade area, where countries have abolished custom duties between members but maintain their own external tariffs and custom procedures *vis-à-vis* third countries. A much stronger form is the customs union, which adds to the former situation, a common external tariff and customs procedures. The EU (previously the European Community) has been a customs union since its inception, whereas the NAFTA is a free trade area (as its name states it clearly). NAFTA has a limited scope, although it has been claimed to be a major evolution for regional trade on the whole of the American continent (there are talks about its extension to some South American countries). As shown in Table 7.1, Americans are fundamentally different from the Mexicans and the Canadians. Furthermore, the size of the US market makes it a region as such. The strongest form of regional integration is the economic union, whereby member countries of a customs union commit themselves to coordinate and even integrate their economic policy. The EU has been an economic union since the Maastricht Treaty came into force, in January 1994, with the prospect of a single currency for 1999. In the GATT arena, now the WTO, no individual EU country is represented. Since the treaty of Rome in 1958, the EU itself has negotiated GATT agreements, after a discussion between member-states has taken place, for preparing a common position.

Table 7.1   *Contrasts across large regional areas*

	European Union (EU)	Eastern Europe (EE)	ASEAN[a]	NAFTA
Type of regional agreement	Customs & economic union	Absence of any real agreement after Comecon[b]	Informal group of nations	Free-trade area
Linguistic diversity	Very large (12 different official languages)	Medium (all Slavic languages except Hungary and Romania)	Medium	Bi-polar (English + Spanish/French), with a predominance of English
Legal style	Legal statutory	'Weak legality'	informal/relational	legal-contractual
Political system	Bureaucratic democracy	Chaotic transition democracy	Authoritarian pluralism	Liberal democracy
Time orientations	Past orientation + linear time	Present time orientation	Cyclical/integrated/ arrowed time	Economic time dominant
Individualism/ collectivism	Individualist	Collectivist individualism	Collectivist	Individualist except in Mexico
Power distance	Low: northern EU High: southern EU	High	High	Low except in Mexico
Masculinity/ femininity	Predominantly feminine	–	Neutral	Masculine
Uncertainty avoidance	High: Roman Germanic nations Low: UK and Nordic countries	High	Weak	Weak
Dominant type of organization (Hofstede, 1991)	A mix of pyramids, machines, markets => No cross-national organizational consensus	'Egyptian Pyramids' (ruins of a centrally planned system, now privately exploited)	'Families'	Markets

[a] ASEAN, Association of South East Asian Nations.
[b] Comecon, economic association of communist countries.

Comparing across regional areas

There is obviously convergence in regional areas of the world; as argued above it is economic rather than cultural. But the process is complex: whereas non-tariff barriers are progressively relaxed, market barriers – based on cultural differences rather than legal dispositions – remain. Table 7.1 gives an idea of significant differences across regional areas. In the two following sections, some features of the EU, eastern European (including ex-USSR) countries and Asian Pacific Rim countries are discussed.

7.4 European Union: Diversity and similarity

The institutional basis of the European Union

The EU is based on the Treaty of Rome, inspired by the principles discussed below. The six original member countries, Belgium, France, Italy, Germany, Luxemburg and the Netherlands, belonged to the Roman-Germanic legal tradition (also called tradition of *code law* or *civil law*). There are four basic principles in the Treaty of Rome: free movement of goods, free movement of capital, free movement of persons and free movement of services. Understandably, such broad statements needed to be clarified, as has been done by issuing 22,000 regulations in about 35 years! Furthermore the European Court of Justice issued about 4,000 rulings that have, to a certain extent, clarified the implementation of rules in precise cases. For countries such as the United Kingdom and Denmark, which entered in 1973, it was never easy to accept this strong legislation orientation. They are low power distance societies, who favour more pragmatic and near-to-the-people ways of solving problems.

The state interventionism tradition has historically been strong everywhere in Europe: even in Northern Europe and Britain, although it is even larger in Latin Europe (see Lessem and Neubauer, 1994). This tradition is challenged by a general trend towards the disinvolvement of the state and public authorities in money-losing businesses which do not necessarily fall under its obvious competence. EU policies have a very wide impact on companies, just to name a few: industrial standards policy, taxation policy, antitrust policy (Articles 85, 86), monitoring of public subsidies to industry, R & D policy, EU legislation on public procurement (EC Committee of the American Chamber of Commerce in Belgium, 1994).

But contrary to what is often said, the EU is not a big bureaucracy; it has a staff of some 20,000. It is rather a small bureaucracy which has incomplete control over the enormous amount of money of the European budget ($\approx$ Ecus 500 billion). Given the number of European civil servants really in charge of policy (about 5,000), each has to control an average amount of Ecus 100 million (about $140 million) which partly explains the lack of control on European fund uses. The decision system works on the basis of weighted votes per country (ten for large countries and two to five for smaller countries) and qualified majority in the council of ministers. In terms of the differences explained in section 3.4, concerning code law versus common law, the legal approach in the EU is completely based on code law. The Roman Germanic legal tradition was fully shared by the original six members, but not by all of the member states which joined later on. Box 7.4 evidences such divergences in the case of the European company statute, a sensitive issue for companies.

Box 7.4   *Twenty-five years discussion and still no agreement*

In fact, company laws in Europe differ widely in their inspiration. Briefly stated, there are three main traditions: German, British and French/Latin. Let us start with the German tradition, that of AG (*Aktien Gesellschaft*). It leaves little room for the shareholders to define their own 'company contract'. The rules are quite strict. A way of characterizing concerning German company law could be '*Alles was nicht erlaubt ist, ist streng verboten*' (all what is not explicitly permitted is strictly forbidden). As a result, in discussing the SE (*Societas Europea*) with the EU Commission, the Germans always ask for a list ('*Eine Liste*') of what is permitted, for instance to define the scope of the decisions of the general assembly of shareholders. By contrast French company law provides for any decision which is not explicitly given to a particular organ in the company to be taken by the general assembly. The German model of public limited company is that of an *institution* (the parties adhere to a system which is entirely fixed) rather than of a *contract* (where the parties have a wide range of 'blank lines' and 'free paragraphs' in the company statute, which allows them to design 'their' company statute as a contract). In the legislations of EU countries with the exception of Germany, parties are allowed to envisage any arrangement which is not explicitly imposed or forbidden by the legal framework.

The Anglo-Saxon system is much more liberal than the German system. Shareholders are supposed to design their future relations within the company on a fairly contractual basis. Contrary to German law which tries as much as possible to protect third parties, workers and minority shareholders by a compulsory and detailed legal company statute, the UK legal tradition solves these problems in different ways. Workers are seen as being tied to the company by work contracts, which they have negotiated in the general framework of labour laws. It is not the function of company statutes to regulate employee/employer relationships. As concerns third parties, especially suppliers and customers, they are protected through contract law governing bonds, bills of exchange, claims and debentures, securities, etc.

The liberal orientation of the British goes so far as to propose that the German dualist system may be offered to SEs registered in the United Kingdom, even if it does not exist for British public limited companies.

An example of EU policy: The free movement of goods

Among the numerous EU policies one deserves special attention, because it is aimed at the free movement of goods. There were many obstacles at the beginning of the 1980s on the road to a real 'common market', especially fiscal barriers, related to different indirect tax rates, and technical barriers due to different industrial standards in the EU. This made the elimination of physical borders problematic (Cecchini, 1988). Fragmented national markets resulted in smaller production sizes and cost inefficiencies at the European level,

Box 7.5   Concrete, Yoghurts and sewage plates: The shock of cultures . . . and climates

> The conditions of use of concrete vary according to climate. The Greeks have no interest in concrete specifications concerning frost except in a few mountain villages. The Finns need concrete which can endure −40 degrees Celsius, but they are not preoccupied with the number of frost–defrost cycles. The French will prefer a concrete which can resist at least twenty frost–defrost cycles. That is why the classes for each use cannot be seen as quality classes.
>
> Similarly, there is no common European definition of what is a yoghurt. Latin countries require that they are produced with living micro-organisms, whereas the Anglo-Saxons favour their sterilisation. This lack of harmonisation is a hindrance for the producers' European marketing strategies.
>
> The Germans wanted to impose a minimal weight for sewage plates. Pont-à-Mousson, a French producer uses ductile cast-iron instead of grey cast-iron for the Germans, with the results that French sewage plates weigh 50 to 60 kilos (so that they can be manoeuvred by a sewerage worker) instead of 100 to 120 kilos for the German (so that they are very steady on the roads). Different industrial traditions exist, corresponding to different functional benefits looked for by each country. The French company succeeded to have the minimal weight not mentioned in the European standard. It saved a billion dollar European business.

(Source: Esposito, 1994.)

especially in comparison with the United States and Japan. The EC White Paper of 1985 set a complete programme of 300 European directives to be adopted by 1992. Many of them dealt with common industrial standards at European level, for which specific standardization bodies were established in order to coordinate standards setting (Comité Européen de Normalisation (CEN), Comité Européen de Normalisation Electro-technique (CENELEC) and European Telecommunications Standards Institute (ETSI)). The whole process was based on several possible means: (1) approximation of regulations (for instance, EU countries design a common legislation Europe-wide for car exhausts); (2) mutual recognition (member states recognize another member state's legislation on a bilateral and reciprocal basis); and (3) the 'home country rule', based on the *Cassis de Dijon* ruling of the European Court of Justice: products which had been manufactured according to the standards and regulations of a particular member state could not be barred from entering any other EU national market, unless the local regulation did not meet the minimal compulsory EU standards. Although a lot has been achieved in the area of common standards, there still remain discrepancies owing to climate and industrial traditions (see Box 7.5).

European consumer?

More than thirty years ago Fournis (1962) remarked that there cannot be such an individual as a 'European consumer' since customs and traditions tend to persist. European countries, and cultures, are deeply rooted in the past. Furthermore a long history of wars and conflicts has maintained strong feelings of national identity. Diverging economic performance between northern and southern Europe have fed sharp income per capita differences, which, added to behaviour differences between European consumers, have been found to be discouraging for globalization (Boddewyn, 1981). Naturally European cultures share some common cultural values: the majority of them, to do with major events of life (birth, marriage, death), share a set of values which differentiate them from the oriental cultures. Patterns of emotions showing for instance differ widely between European and Asians; and where Orientals tend to privilege group harmony, Europeans tend to favour self-esteem and respect of individuals (Valette-Florence, 1991).

Nevertheless this apparent cultural homogeneity of Europe, when compared to Asia, ceases to be so clear when we look at cultural variance inside Europe. Stoetzel (1983) which observed public opinion polls in Europe throughout years ('Eurobarometer'), shows that there are more 'European cultures' than a 'European culture' as such. Family relation patterns, religion, everyday life organization between meals, social, family and business life tend to be rather heterogeneous. There are huge differences in the pattern of household expenditures across EU countries. For instance in 1982, UK households spent 14.7 per cent of their budget on food, West Germany 14.6 per cent, Portugal 37 per cent and Greece 35.6 per cent. The average EU figure at the same time was 20.5 per cent. Italian people consumed 152 kg per year of vegetables, the French 108 kg, and the Germans only 81. French people consume 20.9 kg per year of cheese against 4.7 for the Spanish and 6.3 for the British (source: OECD, 1985). Examples could be multiplied.

Marketing strategies for culture-bound products still need a lot of tailoring to each national market, or to groups of countries, even after 1992. Beer, for instance, is subject to differences in national tastes, in terms of being more or less bitter, foamy, bubbly, sugary, alcoholized, and other taste attributes. Even companies like Heineken who is the leader for beer in Europe continue to tailor their products and marketing policies (distribution systems for beer also widely differ in Europe). Whitelock (1987) shows that standard sizes for pillow-cases differ in the various European national markets: 60×75 cm in Great Britain, 65×65 cm in France, 60×70 cm in the Netherlands and 80×80 cm in West Germany. He interviewed textile companies which all agreed on the necessity to adapt sizes, even after the Single Market has been completed, which is not fully the case in 1996. Nivea Skin care cream, produced by the German multinational company Beiersdorff (BDF) has a leading edge in each national market in Europe. Nevertheless its consistency has to be changed and its formula has to be adapted whether it is sold in northern or in southern Europe (Mourier and Burgaud 1989), and the Single Market programme has not changed this.

Is cultural convergence possible without a common language?

As emphasized by Wolfe (1991, pp. 53–4):

> The most fundamental point of all is that there will eventually be a Euro-market, and there may be one day Euro-retailers, but there will be no European-consumers in the foreseeable future! … It is very easy for English business-people to see English as the language of

Europe. . . . But a pack printed only in English would be understood by at most 2 out of 5 consumers in the EC, and in other languages by even fewer.

An implicit, but extremely strong and time-resisting assumption, of the treaties building the European Union is the respect of national languages, cultures and identities. However, it is phrased in Article 128 section 1 of the Maastricht Treaty in terms which compromise between members cultures and the common European culture to be promoted: 'The Community shall contribute to the flowering of the cultures of the Member States, while respecting their national and regional diversity, and at the same time bringing the common cultural heritage to the fore' (Council of the European Communities, 1992, p. 48). A fundamental element of culture is language, as will be shown in Chapter 12. Language has a strong influence on our world-views and partly shapes our individual and collective behaviour. Even if this assumption in its strongest version (called the Whorfian hypothesis) has been challenged by linguists, it remains a useful metaphor to illustrate its influence on behaviours. Europeans are committed to

Box 7.6   *French fears about English as the common European language*

There is great pride in France about the French language. It is recognized as one of the two official languages of the United Nations, on a par-basis with English. French people have a rather defensive attitude against English, and French authorities have regularly issued during the last fifteen years official decrees prohibiting the use of English words, especially business words, in French texts (Usunier, 1990).

French fears are very typical of resistance to globalization, since it is believed that through consumption patterns the whole French society and culture could be 'Americanized'. The French are fascinated by the American Way of Life as an exotic item. But many French, including politicians, would be horrified to have it 'at home'. If the fears are, perhaps, legitimate, the defensive measures are certainly inadequate. The example of northern European countries shows that it is quite feasible to have a double-language culture. One part is the local one; it corresponds to ways of life, consumption patterns, which are not to be globalized. The other part is in English; it corresponds to international lifestyle and globalized consumption patterns. Television channels in English such as MTV, Sky Channel and Super Channel can be seen in many northern European countries, although not in France, where the development of cable television has been strongly limited. A few years ago the number of householders with cable television in France was half that of Ireland, a country with fifteen times less population, and a much lower per capita purchasing power.

Most people believe that satellite TV in Europe, and other new communication technologies, will contribute to standardize the profile of the European consumer. But it will be achieved in much better conditions if there is a common language to build a common European culture, sustaining new European consumption patterns.

their language as a social and cultural asset. In most European countries there is much stronger emphasis than in the United States on grammatical appropriateness, and correct pronunciation is often a social prerequisite to a number of posts.

The original six countries had four different languages. Since 1986 the twelve had ten languages, and since January 1995 with Finland, Sweden and Austria joining, the fifteen EU member states have twelve different official languages. One of them, Gaelic, the original language of Ireland, is almost no longer in use in its very home country. This 'Babel Tower' situation makes communication difficult and an army of more than 3,000 full-time translators are employed in EU staffs. The issue of a common language for Europe has never been addressed, at least publicly. It is a taboo, even an absolute taboo. In the European Single Act of 1987, Article 34 states that: 'This act (is) drawn up in a single original in the Danish, Dutch, English, French, German, Greek, Irish, Italian, Portuguese and Spanish languages, the texts in each of these languages being equally authentic . . . ' (European Communities, 1987, p. 574). One of the main proponents of the tabooing of the common European language issue is France (see Box 7.6), but the Germans are also very eager to have their language practised, since there are now almost 90 million German speakers owing to the reunification with East Germany and the coming of Austria.

However, it is clear that resistance to change will not suffice to barr English from being the common language, not a first language, but as the standard second language. It is already true in business all over Europe. Even in the publishing business where linguistic differences between countries were traditionally viewed as powerful barriers to inter-nationalization, English is more and more considered as the standard language, especially for scientific and technical publications. Sinatra and Dubini (1991, p. 99) quote an English publisher saying 'All is published in English. In general publishing, anything significant is published in English, regardless of the mother language of the author. Higher level academic journals, they will all be in English.' A Dutch publisher gives a slightly different view: 'I don't think language will be a problem in the near future. I do not adhere to the idea of a common language for all countries of the community, but I think that soon all European citizens will be able to read three or four different languages. People will be citizens of Europe in the next century.'

A good example of how English will spread over the whole community is given by the new ECTS, European Credit Transfer System, sponsored by the EU Commission and designed for facilitating cross-border higher education. The ECTS information package that each university must prepare has to be written in two languages (without mentioning which ones!). Naturally all the universities involved choose their own national language plus English.

7.5 Regional integration and cultural convergence world-wide

Eastern Europe and ex-USSR: Was communism a culture?

Communism meant collective property of production means. In most countries, except Poland, a large part of agriculture was state-owned and managed. The same was true for foreign trade that was the monopoly of sectoral agencies. Administered trade was the rule in the Comecon where both production and trade were centrally organized. Ikarus busses were made in Hungary for the whole of eastern Europe as well as Balkancar forklifts by the Bulgarians. As emphasized by Naor (1986) in the case of Romania, distribution was made to be as cost-efficient as possible, that is, direct distribution from producer to retailers was advocated to the greatest extent possible. But distribution was very poor and parallel, informal distribution often replaced state-run retail outlets where people had to wait to find the few products available. Although the concept of marketing has long been known in countries such as Hungary and Poland, there was an absence of real marketing infrastructures, such as market research consultant, panels, advertising agencies, etc. Communism, although a political system rather than a full culture, has left its mark after forty to seventy years. Consumers have been used to facing systematic undersupply moderated by queues rather than prices. In Bulgaria, for instance, people had to wait several years to obtain a car which they finally paid for at a price so low that it could not be compared with a market price elsewhere. Managers had to take into account political and ideological rather than management criteria, if taking initiative.

Recently, since 1989, marketing infrastructures have been increasing with the de-communization of eastern European countries (Domanski, 1992), the same being true to a lesser extent for Russia (Holden, 1995). Such a process is, however, a lengthy one. A fundamental condition for the development of markets and marketing is the change in ownership structure. In 1992, 83 per cent of the Polish production assets were still state or cooperative property (Dietl, 1992). Privatization programmes have therefore been a major challenge for the governments, with major problems related to their implementation such as valuing companies, establishing a stock exchange, creating notaries and specialized intermediaries for real estate. One of the trickiest problems was to find local shareholders in countries where capitalism had long been associated with exploitation. Private ownership presupposes rules and institutions such as contract law, bankruptcy law, or courts for settling business disputes. The absence of such 'infrastructure' created massive opportunism, such as in the case of ex-Soviet Asian republics (Box 7.7).

The eastern European countries comprise two groups; the northern part has built an alliance called Visegrad group (Hungary, Czech Republic, Slovakia and Poland). The group of southern Balkan states has been traditionally less developed and highly parcelled. National identity has priority over cooperation in an area where ethnic and religious diversity has always been quite strong. The Bulgarians, for instance, have poor relations with all their neighbours except the Serbs. Eastern Europe, and more generally ex-communist countries, are experiencing quick changes. They started from a situation where people had no idea of what a contract, a price and delivery times were, and their countrics arc slowly moving towards market economy. Holden (1995, pp. 36–7), for instance, comments about the two Russian marketing textbooks:

> The one text 'Contemporary Marketing' by Khrutskogo (1991), which stresses the importance of modern marketing knowledge to Russia, introduces marketing in ideological terms, citing both Marx and Engels. The second book, 'Marketing – The Success Formula' by Zayavlov and Demidov (1991) focuses on marketing squarely in terms of 'how to operate effectively in foreign markets'. The differing orientations of these books shed useful light on the Russian approach to marketing knowledge. The Khrutskogo book emphasises a

Box 7.7   *Cotton story*

> In April 1994, a commodity trader discusses about the purchase of raw cotton in the ex-Soviet Asia (mainly Uzbekistan, Turkmenistan and Tadjikistan): 'For two years, the market for raw cotton has been tense, mainly for the three following reasons: (1) climatic hazards in certain producing regions which thus became net importers instead of net exporters, especially China; (2) reduction of cultivated zones in Uzbekistan; (3) to this, you must add that salespeople break their word in ex-Soviet Asia. Last year, the Uzbeks have sold their crops twice or thrice; this year, they seem to be a little more serious; but the worst is to be experienced in Turkmenistan. Last year, I signed several contracts for 20,000 tonnes, one of them for 4,000 tonnes, with an official export licence, a ministerial approval and a shipment certificate; I have never received anything!'
>
> This appears all the more striking when one takes into account that in world-wide cotton trading this is a well-established custom where the professional who does not respect a contract not only must pay damages but also is blacklisted by the whole trading community.

(Source: M. O. Ancel, commodity trader at Louis Dreyfus & Co., Paris, 1994.)

preference for presenting marketing knowledge in relatively intellectual terms, using discredited, yet still very familiar concepts for explaining the market. His approach reveals a Russian penchant for searching for laws that govern social and economic behaviour. The contribution of Zayavlov and Demidov reinforces the conviction that marketing knowledge is held by many Russians to be mainly applicable to foreign business interactions and not so much to home-market activities.

Free-market economy tends to be confused with mere business opportunities, as illustrated by Box 7.7. The absence of rules, which is stronger in ex-USSR than in eastern European countries, further helps the development of corrupt behaviour in business. However, this is only a transitory situation. A big comparative advantage of ex-communist countries is their good level of general education. Even if people in ex-communist countries progressively build marketing infrastructures (Quelch *et al.*, 1991), an international marketer there still has to live a very adventurous life. Anecdotally western European businesspeople coming with their own cars are told to take the wipers with them each time they park their car so that the wipers will not be stolen. If they have to take a taxi, some precautions must be taken as evidenced by Box 7.8.

The East Asian touch

The achievements in the ASEAN countries and in far East Asia have been remarkable over the last fifteen to twenty years. High rates of economic growth have been combined with increasing shares in world trade. The Chinese GNP grows 13 per cent per annum and it exports almost 30 per cent each year. However, in the mid 1960s, there was extensive pessimism about the future of Asia, considered as overpopulated and unable to achieve proper development: a book published in 1972 on the basis of end-of-1960s data by Gunnar Myrdal, a Nobel Prize winner, was entitled '*The Asian dilemma, an enquiry into the poverty of nations*'. This pessimistic view has been largely denied by facts.

Asian commonalities, in contrast to 'Westerners', were viewed as a drawback, non-inducive to business initiative, such as the lack of individualism. Hofstede (1980) established a correlation between individualism and GNP per capita which seemed to suggest that individualism was a precondition for high levels of economic development. Now the perspective has been totally reversed. The issue is now for the West to understand why their collectivist values help many Asian nations to achieve much better than individualist European countries which have lower rates of economic growth and higher unemployment rates over the same period of time.

The Confucian values have been said to be an essential driving force behind such dynamism (see Box 7.9). Some have argued that, at the society level, they are backed by a system of *authoritarian pluralism* (Pohl, 1995) quite different from the liberal democracies in the West. Drug trafficking, for instance, is heavily sanctioned in countries such as Singapore, Malaysia or Thailand. A Dutch prime minister who recently travelled to one of these countries to plead in favour of one of his countrymen sentenced to death for drug trafficking, experienced that rules were applied with much less leniency than in the United States or in Europe: he did not obtain mercy for the condemned.

The components of authoritarian pluralism are as follows:

1. A negation of individualism: group belonging and consequent obligations are more important than individual human rights; persons try to be in unison rather than in discordance with the society.
2. Family, as already emphasized in Chapter 4, is the basic building block. Divorce rates are much smaller than in the West; family is a social insurance which efficiently replaces the costly impersonal welfare systems of western countries.

Box 7.8   *Taking a taxi in Moscow*

A Belgian engineer, with no particular knowledge of 1994 Russia, was due to go to a construction site in Siberia for the German contractor he worked for. When arriving in Russia, he was transferred in Moscow from the international to the national airport by a chauffeur of the German company. After working on the site in Siberia, a much more quiet area than Moscow, he decided to come back home on his own, earlier than initially planned, because the job had been done quicker. When in Moscow, he took a taxi to the local offices of the German company. Taking the first available car, he negotiated the drive for $50. At first, all seemed to be normal, but after a while, the taxi stopped in a fairly remote, deserted and unfriendly area. The driver then explained that he needed an additional $50 to continue to transport him. He paid without discussion and reached the company offices with no problem. He was lucky: it could have been much worse . . . .

(Source: M. O. Ancel, commodity trader at Louis Dreyfus & Co., Paris, 1994.)

3. Education is highly valued and people are ready for financial sacrifices and efforts to get it.
4. Thrift, modesty and renouncement are the rule *until* somebody can show through conspicuous consumption that he or she has really deserved personal enjoyment (Asia is the dominant market for French XO cognac at $80 per bottle).
5. Strong work orientation is facilitated by the collective ambience of effort.
6. 'National teamwork' orientation: trade unions, businesses and the government strive more in the same direction than in the West, although conflicts of interests also exist.
7. The Asian form of *contrat social*: the role of the State is mostly to provide *law and order*, as in Singapore. Citizens follow the rules in as far as the State is *fair and human*.
8. The State is a company and the citizens its shareholders.
9. An orientation towards a 'morally clean environment': unbridled representation of sex and crime are not tolerated while attacks towards other beliefs are inexorably pursued, since most of the societies combine several religions.
10. The Press is free, but not a 'fourth power'. Asian states believe in the necessity of a free press as a condition of good governance. But the Press has not absolute right and must blend with the national consensus.

However *Asian diversity* remains very strong, at least in terms of perceived inter-Asian

Box 7.9   *The fifth dimension: Confucian dynamism*

A new dimension has been added to Hofstede's four dimensions described in Chapter 3. Michael Bond, a researcher based in Hong Kong, has designed a questionnaire called CVS, Chinese Value Survey, which has been administered in twenty-three countries. It is based on basic values as seen by native Chinese social scientists. A new dimension was discovered through the CVS. Bond coined the term 'Confucian dynamism' to emphasize the importance of Confucius practical ethics, based on the following principles:

1. The stability of society is based on unequal relationships, expressing mutual and complementary obligations as for father–son, older brother–younger brother, ruler–subject.
2. The family is the prototype of all social organizations; individuality has to be repressed if it threatens harmony, but everybody's face must be maintained by preserving others' dignity.
3. 'Virtuous behaviour' towards others consists of not treating others as one would not like to be treated oneself.
4. Virtue with regard to one's tasks in life consists of trying to acquire skills and education, working hard, not spending more than necessary, being patient and persevering.

(Source: adapted from Hofstede and Bond, 1988, and Hofstede, 1991, p. 165.)

differences. The Chinese perceive themselves as totally different from the Japanese, the Vietnamese or the Koreans. The Chinese Diaspora is present in several countries with extended economic power and sometimes difficult relationship with native populations. The consensus is at society level: some strong conflicts between ingroups, for instance between Chinese and Malays in Malaysia, although still very present, have been overcome in favour of cooperation.

Three 'regions' (western Europe, eastern Europe and ex-USSR, and East Asia) have now been examined, and we will complete the picture by discussing intra-national, not international, regional differences.

What is the relevant geographical segmentation: national versus regional differences?

Sovereign states (colloquially: countries) have very dissimilar sizes: China (9,600,000 km^2) is more than 232 times larger than Switzerland (49,293 km^2) even though both countries are significant international players on the world scene. Geographical location has a relation to culture: for instance, on average, islands tend to develop more homogeneity than continental countries. A special case is that of mega-countries especially the United States, Canada, Brazil, China and India: their inner diversity is fairly large. Even smaller countries such as the United Kingdom, Spain, Italy, Sweden and France exhibit a strong North–South paradigm (reversed in the Southern Hemisphere). Tiny Switzerland also displays significant inner diversity especially between the French- and German-speaking communities. Therefore, national differences are not the only source of variance in consumer behaviour across different geographical locations.

Any geographical division may be taken as a base for segmenting marketing variables, for instance psychographics, and looking at their generality across different geographic locations (Lesser and Hughes, 1986). The case of the United States is one of the best documented. As emphasized by Garreau (1981), who describes the 'nine nations of North America', regional differences in large countries with multi-ethnic and multicultural backgrounds can explain differences in consumer behaviour. Kahle (1986) shows that geographical segmentation is a basis for finding differences in values, whereas Gentry *et al.* (1987) show that geographical subcultures in the United States vary culturally. In administering a questionnaire in four regions of the United States – west (Washington), north central (Wisconsin), southwest (Oklahoma) and northeast (Massachusetts) – Gentry *et al.* (1987, p. 415) show that 'geographic regions vary in terms of innovativeness and perceived risk. Further differences exist across regions in terms of cultural adherence, religious commitment, and fate-orientation. . . . Residents in those areas with more adherence to traditional values are less likely to try new products.'

But regional differences within countries, even if perceived more clearly by nationals than by foreigners, are most often much smaller than international differences. For instance, Saegaert *et al.* (1978) do not find significant differences in 'fad food' use among Anglo- and Mexican Americans. Similarly, Calantone *et al.* (1985) find English Quebecois women to be more similar to French Quebecois women than to Ontario English women (all of these people being Canadians) in the benefits they seek from a brassière.

Their findings support the idea of the assimilation model, where the cultural values of the immigrants tend to merge with those of the locally dominant cultural group. This supports geography as an operational basis for marketing segmentation.

7.6 Conclusion: Similarities and differences

When building clusters of countries ('cultural affinity zones') that can be approached with a regionally standardized marketing strategy, basic cultural variables have to be taken into account such as language, institutions, membership in a regional integration, and basic cultural traits as described in Chapters 2 and 3. However, some socio-demographic characteristics such as age or income also provide a sound basis for transnational marketing strategies in terms of 'cultural affinity classes'. Thus international marketing segments must be defined in order to allow for the best possible compromise between national/cultural and personal/demographic characteristics.

Questions

1. Describe how experience effects induce firms to standardize products. Give examples.
2. Discuss the relative importance for segmentation of sociodemographic variables, such as age, sex, income, habitat, etc., in comparison with cultural variables based either on nationality or values.
3. How can a company make compromises between world-wide product standardization and customization to local markets?
4. What are zones of cultural affinity?
5. What are the common values shared by people in the European Union? Conversely what may be the differences?
6. To what extent does 'Confucian dynamism' explain the economics of South East Asian countries?
7. Based on the case of eastern European, and more generally ex-communist, countries, explain what is a 'transition culture'?
8. What are the values shared by US, Mexican and Canadian societies? Conversely, on which aspects do they differ?
9. Discuss the limitations of the following statement: 'In the future there will be three major trading blocks: North America, western Europe and East Asia'.

——————— ◆◆◆ ———————

Teaching materials

A7.1   Exercise: Clustering African countries

Relying on basic criteria (for example: language, religion, political system, purchasing power per capita) define on a political map of Africa the main zones of cultural affinity and their overlaps. Maps may be compared across students in class in order to find a common division of the African continent in cultural affinity zones.

A7.2   Case: IKEA

IKEA in the world

IKEA, the world's largest home furnishings retail chain, was founded in Sweden in 1943 as a mail-order company and opened its first showroom ten years later. From its headquarters in Almhult, IKEA has since expanded to world-wide sales of $2.6 billion from 83 outlets in 20 countries (see Table 7.2). In fact, the second store that IKEA built was in Oslo, Norway. Today, IKEA operates large warehouse showrooms in Sweden, Norway, Denmark, Holland, France, Belgium, West Germany, Switzerland, Austria, Canada, the United States, Saudi Arabia, and the United Kingdom. It has smaller stores in Kuwait, Australia, Hong Kong, Singapore, the Canary Islands, and Iceland. A store near Budapest was expected to open by 1990, with others to follow in Poland and Yugoslavia. Even the Soviet Union is not considered out of bounds.

The international expansion of IKEA has progressed in three phases, all of them continuing at the present time: Scandinavian expansion, begun in 1963, West European expansion, begun in 1973; and North American expansion, begun in 1974. Of

Table 7.2   *IKEA's international expansion*

Year	Outlets	Countries	Coworkers	Catalog circulation	Turnover in Swedish crowns
1954	1	1	15	285,000	3,000,000
1964	2	2	250	1,200,000	79,000,000
1974	10	5	1,500	13,000,000	616,000,000
1984	66	17	8,300	45,000,000	6,770,000,000
1988	75 (83[a])	19 (20[b])	13,400[b]	50,535,000[c]	14,500,000,000[d]

Source: *IKEA Facts 88/89*
[a] Stores/countries being opened by the end of 1990.
[b] 13,400 coworkers are equivalent to 10,700 full-time workers.
[c] 14 languages, 27 editions.
[d] Corresponding to net sales of the IKEA group of companies.

Figure 7.2   IKEA world-wide sales expressed as percentages of turnover.

the individual markets, West Germany is the largest, accounting for 30 per cent of company sales. The phases of expansion are detectable in the world-wide sales shares depicted in Figure 7.2. 'We want to bring the IKEA concept to as many people as possible,' IKEA officials have said.

The IKEA concept

Ingvar Kamprad, the founder, formulated as IKEA's mission to 'offer a wide variety of home furnishings of good design and function at prices so low that the majority of people can afford to buy them.' The principal target market of IKEA, which is similar across countries and regions in which IKEA has a presence, is composed of people who are young, highly educated, liberal in their cultural values, white-collar workers, and especially concerned with status symbols.

IKEA follows a standardized product strategy with an identical assortment around the world. Today, IKEA carries an assortment of 12,000 different home furnishings that range from plants to pots, sofas to soup spoons, and wine glasses to wallpaper. The smaller items are carried to complement the bigger ones. IKEA does not have its own manufacturing facilities but designs all of its furniture. The network of subcontracted manufacturers numbers nearly 1,500 in 50 different countries. IKEA shoppers have to become 'prosumers' – half producers, half consumers – because most products must be assembled.

Manufacturers are responsible for shipping the components to large warehouses, for example, to the central one in Almhult. These warehouses then supply the various stores which are in effect mini warehouses. The final distribution is the customer's responsibility. IKEA does cooperate with car-rental companies to offer vans and small trucks at reasonable rates for customers needing delivery service.

Although IKEA has concentrated on company-owned, larger scale outlets, franchising has been used in areas in which the market is relatively small or where uncertainty may exist as to the response to the IKEA concept. IKEA uses mail order in Europe and Canada but has resisted expansion into it in the United States, mainly because of capacity constraints.

IKEA offers prices that are 30 to 50 per cent lower than fully assembled competing products. This is a result of large-quantity purchasing, low-cost logistics, store location in suburban areas, and the do-it-yourself approach to marketing. IKEA's prices do vary from market to market, largely because of fluctuations in exchange rates and differences in taxation regimes, but price positioning is kept as standardized as possible.

IKEA's promotion is centered on the catalog. The IKEA catalog is printed in 14 languages and has a world-wide circulation of over 50 million copies (see Table 7.2). The catalogs are uniform in layout except for minor regional differences. The company's advertising goal is to generate word-of-mouth publicity through innovative approaches.

Local store managers have substantial leeway in promotional decision making (for example, in choosing an advertising agency) but have to adhere to certain guidelines to ensure a universal image.

The IKEA concept is summarized in Table 7.3.

IKEA in the competitive environment

IKEA's strategic positioning is unique. As Figure 7.3 illustrates, few furniture retailers anywhere have engaged in long-term planning or achieved scale economies in production. European furniture retailers, especially those in Sweden, Switzerland, West Germany, and Austria, are much smaller than IKEA. Even when companies have joined forces as buying groups, their heterogeneous operations have made it difficult for them to achieve the same degree of coordination and concentration as IKEA. Because customers are usually content to wait for the delivery of furniture, retailers have not been forced to take purchasing risks.

The value-added dimension differentiates IKEA from its competition. IKEA offers no customer assistance but creates opportunities for consumers to choose transport, and assemble units of furniture. The best summary of the competitive situation was provided by a manager at another firm: 'We can't do what IKEA does, and IKEA doesn't want to do what we do.'

Table 7.3   *The IKEA concept*

Target market:	'Young people of all ages'
Product:	IKEA offers the same products world-wide. The countries of origin of these products are: Scandinavia (52 per cent), western Europe (21 per cent), eastern Europe (20 per cent), and others (7 per cent). Most items have to be assembled by the customer. The furniture design is modern and light. Textiles and pastels.
Distribution:	IKEA has built its own distribution network. Outlets are outside the city limits of major metropolitan areas. Products are not delivered, but IKEA cooperates with car rental companies that offer small trucks. IKEA offers mail order in Europe and Canada.
Pricing:	The IKEA concept is based on low price. The firm tries to keep its price image constant.
Promotion:	IKEA's promotional efforts are mainly through its catalogs. IKEA has developed a prototype communications model that must be followed by all stores. Its advertising is attention-getting and provocative. Media choices vary by market.

Figure 7.3   Competition in furniture retailing. (Source: Martenson, 1987.)

IKEA in the United States

After careful study and assessment of its Canadian experience, IKEA decided to enter the U.S. market in 1985 by establishing outlets on the East Coast. IKEA's three stores (Philadelphia, Woodbridge near Washington, D.C., and Baltimore) generated $93 million in 1988. The overwhelming level of success in 1987 led the company to invest in a warehousing facility near Philadelphia that receives goods from Sweden. Plans call for 60 additional stores over the next 25 years with only gradual expansion to the West Coast.

(Source: Ronkainen, 1990, pp. 203–7. Reproduced with permission.)

Questions

1. Which features of the 'young people of all ages' are universal and can be exploited by a global/regional marketing strategy? How would you analyze them in terms of cultural affinity classes?
2. What accounts for IKEA's success with a standardized product and marketing strategy in a business which is usually described as having some of the strongest cultural influences (styles of furniture, household items and, more generally, lifestyles at home are culture-bound)? Consider, for instance, that an American buying IKEA beds will also have to buy IKEA sheets because the beds are in European sizes.
3. Is IKEA destined to succeed everywhere it cares to establish itself? What are the possible limitations of the IKEA concept?

A7.3   Exercise: *Dangerous Enchantment*

You will first read the short extract from *Dangerous Enchantment*, the evocative title of the novel by Anne Mather (1966). Harlequin books are a world-wide success. They are translated into fifteen languages and read in many countries. Therefore they can be considered as a truly 'global' cultural product. This short extract has been chosen for its capacity to illustrate the style of Harlequin books.

The next day Julie had collected herself. She was glad in a way that she had seen the woman with Manuel. At least it brought it home to her more strongly than any words could have done the completely amoral attitude he possessed.

Marilyn had seen the television as well, however, and said: 'I say, Julie, did you see that Manuel Cortez is back in England?'

Julie managed a casual shrug. 'So what?'

'Darling, really!' Marilyn gave her an old-fashioned look. 'Surely you aren't as indifferent as all that! I know you refused a date with him, but I'm sure that was more because of Paul Bannister than anything else.'

Julie tossed her head. 'I really can't see what all the fuss is about. Paul would make four of him!'

'You must be joking!' Marilyn giggled. 'Get you! I didn't know Paul was becoming such a dish all of a sudden. Why? What's changed him?'

Julie refrained from replying. She had no desire to get involved in an argument about Paul when it meant her stating things that in actual fact were not true. It was no use pretending about Paul's attractions; he was handsome, yes, and tall, yes, and young; but there was nothing particularly exciting about him and Julie could never understand girls who thought men's looks were enough. She had known many men, and in her small experience personality mattered far more than mere good looks.

However, during her lunch break she did borrow a newspaper from Miss Fatherstone in the hope that there might be more particulars about the woman with Manuel, but there was not. There was a picture of him at the airport, and a small article, and that was all.

When they left the building that evening it was snowing, and an icy wind was blowing, chilling them to the bone. Julie, wrapped in a loose dark blue mohair coat, hugged her handbag to her as she started along towards the main thoroughfare accompanied by Donna and Marilyn. She wore knee-length white boots, but between the place where her boots ended and the place where her skirt began she felt frozen, and she wondered whether for the winter at least she should go back to normal-length skirts.

Her hair was blowing about her face, for she was wearing no hat, and she walked straight into the man who stood purposely in her way.

'I'm sorry . . .' she began hastily, a smile lightening her face, and then: 'You!'

Manuel smiled, and her heart leapt treacherously into her throat. She had let go of Donna's arm in her confusion, but both Marilyn and Donna were staring open-mouthed. Manuel took Julie's arm, and said smoothly: 'You will excuse me, ladies,' in a mocking tone, and drew Julie across the pavement to the familiar green Ferrari.

'No, wait!' began Julie, but it was no use. Manuel had the car door open and was propelling her inside, his hard fingers biting cruelly into her arm.

'Don't argue,' he said, for all the world as though it was a natural occurrence that he should meet her from work.

Julie did not want to create a scene in the street, so she climbed into the luxurious warmth of the car and sliding across out of the driver's seat, she allowed him to slide in beside her. He slammed the door, flicked the ignition, and the car moved silently forward, purring like a sated panther.

She stole a glance at him as they turned into the main thoroughfare, and saw, with a sense of inevitability, that far from changing he was much more attractive than she remembered. He turned for a moment to look at her as they stopped at some traffic lights, and said: 'How have you been?'

Julie contemplated her fingernails. 'Fine. And you?'

He shrugged, and did not reply, and she felt like hitting him. How dared he sit there knowing that she must have seen him with that girl yesterday! She looked out of the car window, suddenly realizing that she was allowing him to drive her heaven knows where, and she was making no comment.

'Where are you taking me?' she asked in a tight little voice.

'Home,' he said lazily. 'Where do you think? I thought I would save you the journey on such a ghastly night. Tell me, how do you stand this climate? It's terrible. Me, I like the sun, and the sea, and warm water to swim in.'

'Don't we all?' remarked Julie dryly. This will do.' They had reached the end of Faulkner Road. Manuel shook his head. 'What number?'

'Forty-seven. But please, I'd rather you didn't drive along there. It would only cause speculation, and if you should be recognized. . . .' Her voice trailed away.

'That's hardly likely tonight,' remarked Manuel coolly, and drove smoothly to her gate where he halted the car.

'Thank you, señor.' Julie gave a slight bow of her head, and made to get out, but Manuel stopped her, his fingers biting into her arm.

'Aren't you pleased to see me?' he asked mockingly.

Julie looked at him fully. 'No, not really.'

'Why?'

'Surely that's obvious. We have nothing to say to one another.'

'No?'

'No.' Julie brushed back her hair as it fell in waves over her eyes. It glistened with tiny drops of melted snow and she was unaware of how lovely she was looking.

Manuel shrugged, and lay back in his seat. 'Go, then.'

Julie felt furious. It always ended this way, with herself feeling the guilty one. Well, he wasn't going to get away with it! She swung round on him.

'Don't imagine for one moment that I've been brought home believing your little tales,' she cried angrily. 'I know perfectly well that the reason you have brought me home is because you could hardly take me to the apartment when you already have one female in residence!'

Manuel stared at her, a dull flush just visible in the muted light of the car rising up his cheeks.

(Mather, 1966, pp. 89–92. Reproduced with permission.)

Questions

1. Identify the main sociodemographic characteristics of the target audience of such books.

2. Identify from the text (situation, character and the relations between them) how, and to what extent, this text moves people in such a way as to touch feelings and emotions that are widely shared in the world population.
3. Define the target audience of Harlequin books, in terms of cultural affinity class(es).

References

Boddewyn, J. J. (1981), 'Comparative marketing: The first twenty-five years', *Journal of International Business Studies*, vol. 12 (Spring–Summer), pp. 61–79.
Calantone, R., M. Morris and J. Johar (1985), 'A cross-cultural benefit segmentation analysis to evaluate the traditional assimilation model', *International Journal of Research in Marketing*, vol. 2, pp. 207–17.
Cecchini, Paolo (1988), *The European Challenge 1992*, Wildwood House: Aldershot.
Council of the European Communities (1992), *Treaty on European Union*, Luxemburg: Office for Official Publications.
Day, G. S. and D. B. Montgomery (1983), 'Diagnosing the experience curve', *Journal of Marketing*, Spring, pp. 44–58.
Dietl, Jerzy (1992), 'Determinants of private business activities in Poland', *Journal of Business Research*, vol. 24, pp. 27–35.
Domansky, Tomasz (1992), 'Development of small private companies and their marketing activities', *Journal of Business Research*, vol. 24, pp. 57–65.
EC Committee of the American Chamber of Commerce in Belgium (1994), *Business Guide to EC Initiatives*, Brussels, Winter/Spring.
Esposito, Odile (1994), 'Concurrence: L'Arme des Normes', *L'Usine Nouvelle*, 25 August.
European Communities (1987), *Treaties Establishing the European Commmunities*, Office for Official Publications of the European Communities: Luxemburg.
Fournis, Y. (1962), 'The markets of Europe or the European market?' *Business Horizons*, vol. 5 (Winter), pp. 77–83.
Garreau, J. (1981), *The Nine Nations of North America*, Houghton Mifflin: Boston, MA.
GATT (1986), *Text of the General Agreement on Tariffs and Trade*, GATT: Geneva.
Gentry, J. W., P. Tansujah, L. Lee Manzer and J. John (1987), 'Do geographic subcultures vary culturally?', in Michael J. Houston (ed.), *Advances in Consumer Research*, vol. 15, Association for Consumer Research: Provo, UT.
Hofstede, Geert (1980), *Culture's Consequences: International differences in work-related values*, Sage: Beverly Hills, CA.
Hofstede, Geert (1991), *Culture and Organizations: Software of the mind*, McGraw Hill: Maidenhead, Berkshire.
Hofstede, Geert and Michael Harris Bond (1988), 'The Confucius connection: from cultural roots to economic growth', *Organizational Dynamics*, vol. 16, no. 4, pp. 4–21.
Holden, Nigel (1995), 'A diachronic view of Russian misconceptions of marketing', *Proceedings of the Second Conference on the Cultural Dimension of International Marketing*, Odense, May 27–31, pp. 30–52.
Hollensen, Svend (1991), 'Shift of market servicing organization in international markets: A Danish case study', in Harald Vestergaard (ed.), *An Enlarged Europe in the Global Economy*, proceedings of the 17th Annual Conference of the European International Business Association, Copenhagen Business School: Copenhagen, 736 pp.

Johanson, J. and J. E. Vahlne (1977), 'The internationalisation process of the firm: A model of knowledge development and increased market commitments,' *Journal of International Business Studies*, vol. 8, no. 1, pp. 23–32.

Kahle, L. R. (1986), 'The nine nations of North America and the value basis of geographic segmentation', *Journal of Marketing*, vol. 50 (April), pp. 37–47.

Khrutskogo, V. E. (ed.) (1991), *Sovremennyi Marketing*, Financy i Statistika: Moscow.

Lessem, Ronnie and Fred Neubauer (1994), *European Management Systems*, Maidenhead: McGraw-Hill.

Lesser, J. A. and M. A. Hughes (1986), 'The generalizability of psychographic market segments across geographic locations', *Journal of Marketing*, vol. 50 (January), pp. 18–27.

Martenson, Rita (1987), 'Is standardization of marketing feasible in culture-bound industries? A European case study', *International Marketing Review*, Vol. 4 (Autumn), p. 14.

Mather, Anne (1966), *Dangerous Enchantment*, Harlequin: London.

Mourier, Pascal and Didier Burgaud (1989), *Euromarketing*, Les Editions d'Organisation: Paris.

Myrdal, Gunnar (1972), *The Asian Dilemma, An Enquiry into the Poverty of Nations*, Pantheon Books.

Naor, Jacob (1986), 'Towards a socialist marketing concept – The case of Romania', *Journal of Marketing*, vol. 50 (January), pp. 28–39.

Ohmae, Kenichi (1985), *Triad Power: The coming shape of global competition*, Free Press: New York.

Pohl, Manfred (1995), 'Südostasien: Autoritärer Pluralismus und witschaftliche Dynamik', *Entwicklung und Zusammenarbeit*, vol. 36 (2), pp. 40–3.

Porter, Michael E. (1986), 'Changing patterns of international competition', *California Management Review*, vol XXVIII, no. 2, pp. 9–39.

Quelch, John A., Erich Joachimsthaler and Jose Luis Nueno (1991), 'After the wall: marketing guidelines for eastern Europe', *Sloan Management Review*, 82 (Winter), pp. 82–93.

Ricardo, David (1817), *On the Principles of Political Economy and Taxation*, chapter XXII, 'Bounties on Exportation and Prohibitions on Importation', in *The Works and Correspondence of David Ricardo*, edited by Piero Sraffa, Cambridge University Press, Cambridge, 1951.

Ronkainen, Illka A. (1990), in Michael R. Czinkota and Illka A. Ronkainen, *International Marketing*, 2nd edn, Dryden Press: Hinsdale, IL, pp. 203–7.

Saegaert, J., E. Young and M. Wayne-Saegaert (1978), 'Fad food consumption among Anglo and Mexican consumers: An example of research in consumer behavior and home economics', in H. Keith Hunt (ed.), *Advances in Consumer Research*, proceedings of the 8th Annual Conference, Association for Consumer Research, Ann Arbor, Michigan, USA, pp. 730–33.

Sinatra, Alexandro and Paola Dubini (1991), 'Book publishing', in Roland Calori and Peter Lawrence (eds), *The Business of Europe*, Sage: London, pp. 94–115.

Stoetzel, J. (1983), *Les Valeurs du temps présent: une enquête européenne*, PUF: Paris.

Usunier, Jean-Claude (1990), 'Some contextual aspects of the French international business education system: A pessimistic view', *European Management Journal*, vol. 8, no. 3, pp. 388–393.

Usunier, J.-C. and P. Sissmann (1986), 'L'interculturel au service du marketing', *Harvard-L'Expansion*, no. 40 (Spring), pp. 80–92.

Valette-Florence, Pierre (1991), 'Understanding the European consumer: myths and realities', in Spyros G. Makridakis (ed.), *Single Market Europe: Opportunities and challenges for business*, Jossey Bass: San Francisco, pp. 236–53.

Vernon, Raymond P. (1966), 'International investment and international trade in the product life cycle', *Quarterly Journal of Economics*, vol. LXXX, no. 2, pp. 191–207.

Whitelock, J. M. (1987), 'Global marketing and the case for international product standardization', *European Journal of Marketing*, vol. 21, no. 9, pp. 32–44.

Wind, Yoram, Susan P. Douglas and Howard V. Perlmutter (1973), 'Guidelines for developing international marketing strategies', *Journal of Marketing*, vol. 37 (April), pp. 14–23.

Wolfe, Alan (1991), 'The single European market: National or Euro-brands', *International Journal of Advertising*, 10, pp. 49–58.

WTO-Focus (1995), Information bulletin of the World Trade Organization, January–February, no. 1, pp. 4–5.

Zayavlov, P. S. and V. E. Demidov, (1991), *Formula Uspekha – Marketing*, Mezhdunarodniye Otnosheniya: Moscow.

8

♦ ♦ ♦

Adaptation or standardization of product policy: A model for choice

A central issue in international marketing strategy is the decision whether to adapt products for foreign markets after the consumer, the national markets and their particular characteristics have been surveyed, or to standardize products, which is a simplified strategy based on experience effects and cost reduction. For instance, part of the United Kingdom's loss of dominant position in the Arabian Gulf countries to the Japanese during the 1960s was due to a lack of product adaptation. In contrast to the British, the Japanese were reported by local consumers to have adapted their products to the needs of local markets, after careful research into demographic, economic, sociocultural, political-legal and physical environments (Tuncalp, 1990).

This chapter and the following one (which is devoted to the product's brand name and national image) propose a decision-making framework for the adaptation/standardization of various product attributes: physical characteristics, design, form, colour, functions, packaging, brand name and 'made-in' label. An assessment will be made of the adaptation and international standardization of different levels of product attributes: physical attributes, service attributes and symbolic attributes. The product conveys symbolic meanings through its colour, shape, country of origin, brand name and so on.

The first section of the chapter sets out a systematic model for the choice between adaptation and standardization of product policy. It can be applied successively to each existing national market as well as to markets where a company intends to set up new business. The second section is devoted to the physical attributes of the product. The third section deals with the standardization/adaptation of service attributes. The fourth section relates to symbolic attributes.

The etymology of the word 'symbol' comes from Ancient Greece, where the symbol was originally an object cut into two. The two halves were retained by the host and the guest and later passed on to their children. When these two halves were reunited, this enabled recognition of the owners and served as proof of the bond of hospitality previously created. The symbol therefore replaces, represents and denotes some other entity by means of a conventional relationship or a suggestion, the evidence of which has usually been lost. The meanings that symbols diffuse are, of course, culture-based. They are interpreted differently across countries.

Other important symbolic attributes are the brand name and the national images linked to the product and its country of manufacture. The conversion of a national brand into an international one, and the linguistic problems that may occur, are dealt with in Chapter 9. The issue of global brands, either world-wide or at the regional level, is also considered in Chapter 9.

8.1   A framework for the choice between adaptation and standardization based on product attributes

One may provocatively state that the public are not buying the product itself, but the benefits they hope to derive from the product. A product can be defined as a set of attributes which provide the purchaser/user with actual benefits. There are three layers of attributes:

1. The physical attributes (size, weight, colour, etc.). Standardization of these attributes affords the greatest potential for cost benefits since economies of scale are made principally at the manufacturing stage.
2. Service attributes (maintenance, after-sales service, spare parts availability, etc.). These attributes are fairly difficult to standardize, as circumstances for service delivery differ widely from one country to another. It should further be emphasized that most services are performed in direct relation to *local* customers. Service attributes are more dependent on culture.
3. Symbolic attributes are often the interpretive element of the physical attributes. A

Table 8.1   *Factors influencing adaptation or standardization of product attributes*

Product attributes	Arguments in favour of adaptation	Arguments in favour of standardization
Physical attributes	**1** Cost-reducing adaptations Local standards, hygiene and safety regulations, consumer behaviour, marketing and physical environments	**2** Experience effects Economies of scale International standards International product use
Service attributes	**3** Limited savings related to scale Local peculiarities in service, maintenance and distribution	**4** Significant learning effects 'Mobile' clientele
Symbolic attributes	**5** Unfavourable image of imported products, company, nationality or brand name Inadequate meaning conveyed by colour, shape, etc.	**6** Favourable image of imported products, company, nationality or brand Exotic or ethnic appeal Demands for 'universals'

colour is simultaneously a chemical formula for a painting or a coat, and also the symbolic meaning conveyed by the material. Symbolic attributes affect the choice between adaptation and standardization in a fairly ambiguous manner. Consumers have confused attitudes: a liking for domestic goods based on nationalism will co-exist with a penchant and even fascination for foreign cultures and their goods. Therefore, when adapting or standardizing symbolic attributes, the requirements for nationalist, identity symbols will intermingle with those for symbols of exoticism.

Table 8.1 proposes a systematic description of the arguments in favour of adaptation on the one hand and standardization on the other. Distinctions can be made according to the different levels of attributes: physical, service and symbolic. Some arguments in favour of either adaptation or standardization originate from within the company which can benefit from changing its way of operating. Other arguments are related to external constraints imposed by the environment, consumer behaviour and regulations: they imply company adaptation to demand, either by adapting or standardizing its offer. The numbering of the cells in Table 8.1 is used further in the text.

8.2   The physical attributes

As seen in Chapter 7, the experience effects, and accordingly the cost reductions related to cumulated production, clearly weigh in favour of standardization (cell 2). However one should investigate the opportunity of supplying an adapted product, corresponding to the local demand, in which the adaptation would lead to a sufficient reduction in costs to compensate for the loss in cumulated volume (cell 1). This situation is rare: the success of Japanese pick-up trucks in developing countries is to a certain extent a suitable illustration of this situation. Through adaptation involving product simplification in suspension, engine and gear-box, the Japanese have achieved a low cost level. Historically, there are some examples of 'simplified' cars or 'simplified' computers designed for developing countries' environment. For instance, Ford and General Motors developed a 'bare bones' model T-type of vehicle to sell in developing countries, both of which were failures. Similarly, a computer specially designed for developing countries was developed in the 1980s by Jean-Jacques Servan-Schreiber with French governmental funding. It was a total failure. In these cases, the advantages resulting from 'simplifications' are not at all offset by a decrease in economies of scale (increased unit costs), the losses in product functionality, or the resentment of local consumers for being offered simplified products and thus being treated as unsophisticated consumers.

Compulsory adaptation

Compulsory adaptation for the physical attributes is often related to national regulations and standards. Thus (cell 1):

1. The industrial standards for the electricity supply, for example the voltage, the frequency of the alternating current (50 v. 60 Hz), the shape of plugs, etc. Certain countries use standards which seem to operate as non-tariff trade barriers. Germany is

known for its use of an exhaustive system of over 30,000 industrial standards (DIN) which are determined by standard-setting committees. On the boards of these committees German manufacturers are strongly represented. Nevertheless DIN standards are far from being intended as non-tariff barriers; for instance, German bicycles use drum brakes on the rear wheels which are operated by pedalling backwards, whereas British and French bicycles use brake pads. The German standard, which may at first sight appear safer, is in fact dangerous for other European cyclists because of the risk of skidding on corners by spurious back-pedalling.

2. Safety standards: in the motor industry for example, in relation to lighting, brake systems and vehicle safety. A few years ago Peugeot had to use more than 500 national versions of its 505 range, corresponding to the different engine types and equipment available, adapted for various countries targeted for export. This obviously had an adverse effect on costs. In addition to increased production costs, there was an inflation in required documentation and country-specific spare parts. Control of the marketing management of the 505 around the world was adversely affected.

3. Hygiene regulations: the food processing, chemicals and pharmaceutical industries must carry out adaptations in accordance with hygiene legislation. The producers of *foie gras* which is exported to the United States have to obtain an FDA (Food and Drug Administration) hygiene certification. For this they have to allow the FDA to inspect their laboratories for bacteria as well as their methods of production. FDA inspectors often require *foie gras* to be pasteurized and the laboratories disinfected with an antiseptic detergent. This inevitably affects the taste and conflicts with the traditional image of a home-made quality product. Many of the French *foie gras* producers have decided to install laboratories in the US where the product is prepared according to US hygiene standards.

A huge variety of regulations influences the need for adaptation (marking, labelling locally permitted standard sizes, sales promotion laws, etc.). In many countries, public or mutual bodies offer to assist companies by examining the problems of conforming to the technical aspects of foreign standards, right from the very conception of the product. A good number of companies, through a wholly understandable ethnocentrism, fail to consider the problem of adaptation of products for foreign markets. Newcomers to the export business often consider the problem only from the perspective of adaptation to technical standards and are only concerned with obligatory adaptation; at first they tend not to consider the loss of standardization.

In fact, obligatory adaptations are often minor in comparison to the required adaptations to differences in consumer behaviour and national marketing environment. Three main issues should be considered:

1. Consumption patterns: consumer tastes, frequency of consumption, the amount consumed per helping, etc. The required size of a cereal box and the ability of the packaging to preserve the product will not necessarily be the same for a country in which the average consumer eats 50 grams of cereal daily for breakfast and for a different country where the quantity of consumption is higher but the frequency lower. Even products which are supposed to be the epitome of international standardization are subject to customization to local tastes (see Box 8.1).

2. Climate and the physical environment in general are important, and sometimes neglected, factors behind further obligatory adaptation (cell 1). Motor vehicles must be specifically designed to withstand the harsh Scandinavian winters or the warmth and humidity of the Ivory Coast. The possible range of physical environments where the product will be used must be taken into account: for example, the quality of road surfaces and the existence of tracks suitable for vehicles. The diversity of physical environments is often the source of later shocks and the cause of unexpected failure (Box 8.2). One should take into account in advance the range of elements that constitute potential demands for adaptation. This is not always such an obvious step to take. Ethnocentrism is often the rule in product design. In the case of a sheet-glass factory, the high temperature in the workshops proved to be intolerable for Saudi workers when the factory was set up in Saudi Arabia on the basis of European parameters (Tiano, 1981).

3. Adapting products to local product usage. A number of variables have to be considered for buyers to use the product properly such as: level of literacy, technical knowledge and ability to use written information (such as ingredients list or instructions for use). This is the cause for Nestlé's problems in the Third World with its infant formula: the addition of improper water and the absence of boiling, caused the final product consumed to be dangerous for babies, even though the powder which went out of Nestlé's factories was perfect. Consumers, on average, tend to underread instructions for use and to enter too quickly into a first trial, especially for consumer durables, before they have learnt the basics on how to operate it. The Germans make special adaptations designed for misuse by consumers; for instance, when the knob of a dish washing machine is turned anti-clockwise, whereas it should be used only clockwise, or when it is switched on when the water tap is off (an unfortunate

---

Box 8.1   *'Pizza relativity'*

There is, in the real world, a lot of 'pizza relativity'. During in-depth interviews at Hewlett-Packard in France, some American expatriates told me that they had travelled to Geneva, Switzerland, 100 miles (160 km) from the site where they were located, in order to have a meal at Pizza Hut. Although in Grenoble there are a large number of 'authentic' pizzerias (the town has a very large Italian presence), some Hewlett-Packard American expatriates preferred the taste, crustiness, toppings and cooking style of the American pizza. In September 1990, I was attending a congress in Milan and discovered that the Italian pizza (at least at the restaurant where I ate it) was not at all like those I am used to eating in Grenoble (made by cooks of Italian origin): the crust was much thicker and there was less topping. My last memory is of the oily Brazilian pizzas (which I tried only twice). Conclusion: pizzas, like 'Chinese' food. are largely localized, often because of the lack of genuine ingredients, but also because taste is localized. Local views of what is 'genuine' are mostly based on phantasms about the true' pizza or the 'genuine' Peking duck.

Box 8.2 *Adaptations to the physical environment*

A European drinks manufacturer decided to widen the range of one of its product lines with a giant-size version, with the purpose of its active promotion in several markets, the United States in particular. After completion of production facilities, the new model was launched. The company then realized to its horror that it had forgotten one small detail: the giant-size bottle was a couple of inches too tall for the shelves in the vast majority of the American stores. You can imagine the result: the sales promotion activities that were planned had to be cancelled, there was discontent among the distributors and the sales force lost a great deal of motivation while a new mould was hastily manufactured.*

Quaker Oats has an established share of the Cameroon market: it has been carefully adapted in line with consumption habits. It is easily made into the gruel that the Cameroons call *paf* or *pap*. It is usually eaten with maize or tapioca. In addition, Quaker uses metallic packaging which is perfectly suited to the preservation of the product in the Cameroon climate. The shelf life of the box is about ten years, even in a tropical country. Cameroon itself is not a wholly typical tropical country since in Douala, for instance, there is an annual rainfall of 7 metres. The metallic box ensures the product's preservation despite the humidity. It does, however, rust, and even though the product itself is not affected, certain retailers refuse to repurchase Quaker Oats because of their previous stock having rusted.**

(Sources: *adapted from Giordan, 1988, p. 110; **adapted from Camphuis, 1984. Reproduced with permission.)

circumstance after some minutes!). In Germany, where the sense of uncertainty avoidance is quite strong (section 3.2), a product is called *idiotensicher* ('idiot safe') when all possible product design adaptations have been made to avoid negative consequences of any imaginable misuse. The adaptation to possible misuses is related to the issue of product liability, where quite different legal solutions are found from one country to another. Windshield sun protectors made in Spain do not need special mention, warning the user not to drive with the protector installed, because it is supposed that Spanish drivers are not fools. For export especially to the United States, they need such explicit warning sentences: in case of incident, the manufacturer's responsibility could be legally engaged.

Requirements for international standardization

Yet national requirements sometimes lean towards international standardization (cell 2). This may occur in four situations:

1. Although technical standards largely originate in individual countries there are industries where international standards tend to develop. They can even become the

dominant national standard. Thus in the field of oil drilling, the API (American Petroleum Institute) standards are in force world-wide. Every oil company, whether American or not, must follow the API standards. Oil-drilling equipment manufacturers are also obliged to standardize their products in accordance with these standards. However, the number of industries with world-wide standards remains limited. The adoption of foreign/international standards can even prove to be problematic for selling in the country of origin. For instance, a European iron and steel company obtained certification from ASME (American Society of Mechanical Engineers) for the very thick steel plate used in nuclear and petrochemical plants. In this small industry, they had a quite substantial world market share. ASME certification was recognized world-wide since most nuclear plants use licensed American technology. When they subsequently came to sell their heavy steel plates for plants intended for German and French electricity utilities, US standards were not considered acceptable and they were forced to adopt German and French standards.

2. Some products achieve 'international usage': aircraft suitcases (Samsonite from Belgium, and Delsey from France), portable computers, duty-free articles, etc.

3. Innovative products often experience an international diffusion process (Rogers, 1983). Large R & D expenses are initially incurred for many innovative products, and such products are not greatly affected by culture (VCR, laser disc). The pace of the diffusion of innovations is largely enhanced by the strength of the groups of 'early adopters'. Presumably, these groups correspond to people who have a high level of exposure to international travel and new products in the countries where they are first launched. By word-of-mouth communication, they transfer knowledge of the product to their non-travelling compatriots. These international travellers eventually introduce such products into their native country. They facilitate positive reactions from other consumers without exposure to these new products, in the first phases of the adoption process: awareness, interest, evaluation, testing. More generally, international travel accelerates the process of diffusion of standardized innovations.

4. The final point in cell 2 encompasses the basis of Levitt's assertions about the globalization of markets (1983). According to Levitt, certain aspects of ways of life would tend towards uniformity: differences in cultural preferences, national taste, standards and institutional business environment are remnants of the past. Some inheritances die off slowly, others flourish and spread out as the general preferences of the largest number. Levitt argues that the so-called ethnic markets are a good example: Chinese food, country music, pizzas and jazz now tend to be found world-wide. Although Levitt claims that he is not advocating systematic disregard for local or national differences, he probably overestimates the reality of this common sharing of world product. Whatever value judgements are made on the all-inclusive (that is, across countries, consumer segments and product categories) tendency towards homogenization of world cultures, this issue must be raised for each company, on the basis of careful research on its product, consumers and markets.

The trend towards international standards

There is a definite trend towards common standardization world-wide, especially with ISO (International Organization for Standardization) standards; some of them are now widely applied such as the standards on quality, the ISO 9000 family. European technical standardization participates to this movement. It is based on the EC Treaty, especially Article 30, which prohibits quantitative restrictions on imports from other member states and measures having equivalent effects (that is, mainly protectionist standardization). As explained in the previous chapter, the 'Cassis de Dijon' ruling has firmly established the 'home country rule', according to which a product should not be barred from import into an EU country when it conforms to the standards of the EU country in which it is produced. EU countries, in conjunction with the six EFTA (European Free Trade Association) countries, are engaged in a European standardization process, through three Brussels-based organizations: CEN, CENELEC and ETSI. This largely stems from the 1985 EC White Paper, which identified technical barriers as one of the main obstacles to the achievement of a single market in Europe.

Product standards are in fact a very complex strategic issue (much more so than depicted here), since they have a definite influence on the competitive strategy of the firm (Gabel, 1989). In high-technology industries, for instance computers, consumer electronics or telecommunications, the issue of compatibility of standards over time (multi-vintage compatibility) and across competitors is a very important one. There are examples where promoting a standard and licensing it to the competitors (the VHS of Matsushita) proved a better strategy than keeping a monopoly on one's own standard (the Betamax VCR of Sony). Other examples show that it was more efficient to keep the technology under total control, as Xerox did for its proprietary electrostatic photocopying technology for many years before the patent expired.

8.3 The service attributes

These may include the following (the list is not exhaustive):

1. Repair and maintenance, after-sales service.
2. Installation.
3. Instruction manuals.
4. Other related services (demonstrations, technical assistance).
5. Waiting time, delivery dates (and respect for them).
6. Guarantees.
7. Spare parts availability.
8. Return of goods, whether defective or not.

Adaptation of service owing to local conditions

The extent of service attributes differs according to the type of good to be serviced. Service attributes are essential for industrial equipment and many consumer durables.

Although it might not seem so, they also have a significant role to play in the field of consumer non-durables. Service requirements differ widely from country to country (cell 3) because they are related to environmental factors such as the following:

1. The level of technical expertise.
2. The level of labour costs, which is decisive in the balance between durability and repairability. Africans are experts at repairing and even revamping totally worn-out cars. Anywhere else, these cars would be scrapped.
3. The level of literacy (this may render instruction manuals useless).
4. Climatic differences: certain climates increase the difficulty of performing maintenance operations because of temperature, air hygrometry, etc.
5. The remoteness of locations which can render services difficult and costly to perform (e.g. servicing a gas turbine in the middle of the Amazonian forest).
6. Different ways of performing a seemingly identical service (see Box 8.3).

Actual services in developing countries are traditional ones and are of a limited technical ability, at least when viewed from technologically developed countries. In shortage societies, recycling is essential: African shoemakers, for instance, are experts at making shoe soles from used tyres; technical expertise and craftsmanship are not absent

Box 8.3   *Who's afraid of injections?*

What is more standard in appearance than a syringe and an injection? There are, however, significant differences in the methods used to avoid causing pain to the patient. For intra-muscular syringes, there are two different ways of administering an injection. They correspond to two basic service attributes (correct injection of the substance, avoidance of pain), but are performed in two different ways:

1. Only the needle itself is stuck in, then the body of the syringe (the cylinder containing the substance and the plunger driving it) is fixed into the base of the needle, in accordance with a technique known as *luerslip* (this method is used in America). The first question asked by an American nurse is: does it unscrew? (Service attribute.)
2. French, Italian and Spanish doctors and nurses prefer (and are used to) using the fully assembled syringe. The American method would probably involve the risk of 'slashing' their patient when connecting the two parts of the syringe once the needle has been implanted (an operation they are not used to doing). The service attribute required of the syringe is therefore based on its lightness and being in one piece, which is provided by a bolt system (*luerlock*). The first question asked by a French, Italian or Spanish nurse is: does it hold tight?

Further service attributes relate to who is legally permitted and professionally qualified to administer an injection and where it is possible to buy syringes. In Italy – in contrast to other European countries – syringes are on general sale, even in corner shops. They are available in blister packaging at the supermarket. Traditionally, many housewives actually give injections to members of their family.

(Source: excerpt from a discussion with Beckton Dickinson, world leader in single-use medical items – consumables.)

in developing countries; they are expressed differently, given the prevailing economic conditions. In many African countries for instance, a lot of maintenance is done by small mechanical workshops, which succeed in repairing cars over long periods of time; if not orthodox, their repair methods work. Service instructions by car manufacturers naturally need some adaptation: it will be better to show mechanics how to do a job than to deliver them a free 800-page book on maintenance operations. Services are generally performed by delegation to distribution channels. The shortage of available and/or adequate channels and the small size of the distribution outlets are obstacles to services, particularly in developing countries.

Even across developed countries, differences in the service offered by distribution channels are much greater than one might expect. Daily and weekly shop opening hours vary widely between northern and southern Europe. This may range from less than 60 hours per week total opening time in northern Europe to more than 100 hours per week in southern Europe. This affects the attitude towards distribution services; for example, where weekly store opening hours are limited, people tend to turn to mail-order; they can look at the catalogue at home with no hurry, and pay without wasting their shopping time waiting at the cashier's desk. Where the husband and wife are at work during shop opening hours, an elderly parent with different service requirements may have to do the shopping for them.

Culture and the waiting experience

An important aspect of service is waiting for being served (for obtaining maintenance, spare parts, receiving cash in a bank or being served in a restaurant). In waiting, people have to deal with time, rules and power. The cultural assumptions concerning time are central in the waiting experience: it may be experienced as a waste of time, a painful moment with negative emotions when people have a strong economic time pattern (see section 2.2). Waiting is organized in queues to varying degrees and the rules concerning the waiting process are more or less respected according to culture (see section 3.6). Another important aspect of waiting is power: where power distance is strong, it seems almost legitimate to let the least powerful wait, whereas jumping the queue is standard behaviour for the most powerful. In fact, rather than jumped, the waiting line is bypassed: important consumers have a direct access to the service. On the contrary, in the United States, where low power distance and strong economic time prevail, waiting lines are well organized and everybody is treated fairly, following the principle of 'first come, first served'. Box 8.4 (p. 254) presents the Japanese attitude towards waiting in restaurants.

Waiting time can be reduced or increased according to the level of service personnel available; it can therefore be adapted according to the locally prevailing assumptions about time. In Europe, where time is, on average, slightly less economic than in North America, the fast food outlets are not so quick as they are in America (where the formula was invented). People are not so preoccupied with the waiting time: in the US Pizza Hut gives a free pizza to customers having waited more than ten minutes; in most European countries this does not need to be transferred, because people do not resent waiting and even may value waiting time in a restaurant as a sign of careful preparation.

Another service attribute is the type of waiting rule and the degree to which the waiting lines are organized. In many countries, waiting is not organized at all and the principle 'first come, first served' finds no translation. Since people are used to unorganized waiting they know that they will have to fight against those who jump the queue, by shouting, threatening them or jumping themselves the queue. For instance, the contrast is striking between French and Swiss ski resorts, especially at peak time: whereas in France the absence of waiting corridors results in messy crowds, in Switzerland the waiting process remains fairly peaceful and organized even if the waiting time is slightly longer. It comes as no surprise that for American tourists travelling to Europe the service quality image of French ski resorts appears significantly lower than that of the Swiss and Austrian ski resorts, particularly as concerns honesty and friendliness (Ofir and Lehmann, 1986).

Cultural assumptions and the service encounter

The service encounter implies a person-to-person relationship, in maintenance as well as in restaurant or other services. To this extent, the prevailing cultural norms will apply in service encounters as they apply in any social interaction. Even though a lot is shared, especially from a normative point of view (availability, courtesy, willingness to give information), social codes concerning adequate service vary according to culture. Edward Hall (1976, pp. 58–9), for instance, explains how, staying in a hotel in downtown Tokyo, he was completely mystified by a problem with his room:

> I had been a guest for about ten days and was returning to my room in the middle of an afternoon. . . . Entering the room I immediately sensed that something was wrong. Out of place. Different. I was in the wrong room. Someone's else things were distributed around the head of the bed and the table. . . . I checked my key again. Yes, it really was mine. . . . At the desk, I was told by the clerk, as he sucked in his breath in deference (and embarrassment?) that indeed they had moved me. My particular room had been reserved in advance by somebody else. I was given the key to my new room and discovered that all my personal effects were distributed around the new room almost as though I had done it myself.

Later Hall will discover that, in contrast to the United States where being moved that way is almost an insult, in Japan it was tangible evidence that, after some days, he was treated as a family member, somebody belonging to the group of familiar clients, who can be treated in a relaxed and unceremonial way.

There are many situations where 'good' service is not self-evident. A case in point is when people sleep on an airplane when a meal is served. Kamamoto (1984) explains that, for the Japanese the steward must wake up the sleeping persons so that they do not miss the meal, whereas Westerners prefer not to be disturbed in their sleep. Naturally, the best solution, which applies whatever the culture considered, would be for the steward to wait and serve the sleeping person as soon as she awakes; but it is rarely possible because of schedule constraints. An important cultural aspect of the service encounter is the doing/being divide. Hall (1976, p. 109), contrasting the French and the Americans, phrases it in the following way: 'The French as a rule are much more involved [than the Americans]

Table 8.2   *Cultural dimensions and automated service*

Dimensions	Being	Doing
Affectivity	1 Strong preference for personnel in contact	3 Like the machine but would like the personnel also
Neutrality	2 Do not like the machine but do not like people either	4 Strongest preference for purely automated service

with their employees and with their customers and clients as well. They do not feel they can serve them adequately unless they know them well.' I do not agree with Hall's first sentence: to many foreigners, service quality in France (as in other Latin countries) appears poor in comparison with the United States. Many American visitors perceive the commitment of French service providers towards their clients as quite small. The real key is in Hall's second sentence: 'unless they know them well.' In societies where doing is strongly emphasized, as in the United States, waiters or other service providers, are task-centred rather than person or relationship-centred. It is no real problem for them to serve *unknown* people. To many French or Latin eyes, North American service appears exactly contrary to Hall's judgement, more friendly, more attentive and dedicated than in European countries, especially in southern Europe. Stereotypically stated, in a being-oriented society, the situation in service encounters is dichotomic: dedication and friendliness towards known customers, absence of real commitment towards customers when they *are unknown.*

Another interesting question is whether customers prefer automated service, which is widely expanding (automatic teller machines, ticket machines, etc.) or to be served by real, flesh-and-blood people. There is no research available on this issue. But one can hypothesize that the being orientation implies a preference for personnel in contact whereas the doing orientation gives a favourable attitude towards automated service, which is purely task oriented. The dimension of affectivity versus neutrality (see section 3.5) an important aspect of Trompenaars' relational orientation (Trompenaars, 1993), can be combined with the doing–being divide, for describing possible preferences as in Table 8.2: affectivity will create a preference for personnel in contact, because human relationships in the service encounter are preferred over service automation. Naturally, all this is based on cultural ideal-types; other factors, such age or level of education, have a strong influence on individual acceptance of automated service; older people and less educated persons have difficulties with dealing with automated service devices which they consider user unfriendly.

Factors in favour of service standardization

The decision to adapt services to diversified international requirements implies little cost in terms of economies of scale (cell 3), since increasing returns to scale are far easier to reach for the physical attributes than for the service attributes of a product. On the other hand, there can be substantial learning effects with service attributes. For example, various management procedures such as the stocking of spare parts or hotel laundering may be standardized.

In certain cases (cell 3) the adaptation of service attributes will lead to cost savings because locally supplied services will be far less comprehensive than in the country of origin. This is feasible either when local service requirements are less demanding or when the product has been expressly constructed to be almost maintenance-free. In this case it will also be designed to stand up to 'untrained' users. Physical attributes will then interact with service attributes within the product as a whole.

Box 8.4   *Sabisu (Japanese concept of service)*

Misako Kamamoto, chief conductor of the Japan Travel bureau recounts her experience guiding Japanese tourists overseas:

'When I take a group of Japanese tourists to a restaurant in Europe for the first time, I make a point to advise them in advance as follows: "Quite apart from the problem of whether the food suits the Japanese palate, you must be resigned to the fact that it takes a good deal of time to have a meal in a European restaurant." . . . some members of the party are bound to start complaining despite the warning that I have given them. "Why are European restaurants so slow in serving us? Please ask them to speed up the service." Some get so impatient that they stand up and leave, saying, "I don't want to wait for dessert or coffee. I can't stand a restaurant which gives such bad service." In a European restaurant, the essence of good service is to give the guests plenty of time to enjoy conversation together with the meal. So it makes sense that dishes are served with long intervals in between.

Japanese tourists who go shopping in Paris invariably return full of complaints because they were not treated like "gods" as in Japan. "The sales clerks take the attitude that they are doing you a favor by 'allowing you to buy'. They are so curt. What do they think customers are anyway? The sales clerks have absolutely no interest in doing business. When I asked a clerk to show me something of a different color or different size, she acted annoyed and said brusquely, 'We have none.' She didn't even try to search."

In a Japanese bank, the clerk counts the notes by himself and puts them all together in a tray for the client, . . . few Japanese take the trouble of counting the notes on the spot. . . The Japanese usually consider that it is impolite to distrust anyone and believe that the other party will most naturally live up to the trust placed in him. In restaurants and hotels, Westerners do not make payment until they have thoroughly examined the bill, item by item and make sure that the sum total is correct. In contrast the Japanese have always believed that restaurant and hotel bills are correct. Therefore, even when they are overseas, they assume the same and make payment without examining the bill. This habit sometimes becomes a trouble.

When they travel by train in Europe, the Japanese are struck by the quietness of the stations which are so unlike the noisy Japanese stations. There is no bell or loudspeaker signaling the departure of a train. Their first reaction is, "It's so nice and quiet." But this soon gives way to anxiety. "Why is it that there is no bell notifying us of the departure? It would be a lot of trouble if we missed the train," some say. . . . Whereas European railways give priority to silence and their rule is to have travelers enjoy a quiet journey, Japanese railways seem to think that their mission is to provide passengers with all kinds of information via blaring loudspeakers.'

(Kamamoto, 1984, pp. 26–7. Reproduced with kind permission.)

However, service standardization (cell 4) will be required when the clientele is internationally 'mobile'. Customers move with their service requirements. The global success of truck manufacturers from northern Europe (DAF, Volvo, Scania, Mercedes) is due in part to their ability to offer a standardized service in a range of countries and on sites along the routes that are most commonly taken by international lorry drivers. For instance, an engine or a gearbox can be completely overhauled within a specified period of time at any location on the route. The same holds true for McDonald's restaurants where service is to a large extent standardized world-wide: customers know what they will find in term of services, bad surprises are avoided, when they enter a McDonald's in Tampere, Finland, Osaka, Japan or Montauban, France.

8.4 The symbolic attributes

The symbol can be defined linguistically as the sign that operates a relationship which is non-causal (as opposed to the *indicator*) and non-analogous (as opposed to the *icon*). The *Collins Dictionary and Thesaurus* (1987, p. 1018) defines the symbol as 'something that represents or stands for something else, usually by convention or association, especially a material object used to represent something abstract.' Any animate or inanimate object may be a basis for building symbolic association. A fox may be a symbol of cunning, whereas an oak may be a symbol of strength. The use of the word 'may be' recognizes the fact that not every culture builds such associations. Either there are no foxes or oaks, or other interpretative meanings are applied. Symbols work as a powerful means of suggestion and evocation. The symbolic aspects of consumption are important to consumers: the social meaning of many products is more important than their functional utility, or at least as important, clothes or perfumes for instance. As emphasized by Solomon (1983, p. 320): 'Symbolic interactionism focuses on the process by which individuals understand their world. It assumes that people interpret the actions of others rather than simply react to them.'

In terms of adaptation/standardization, two different issues shall be addressed:

1. The relationship between symbolic attitudes and national product images, with respect to the product category, the name of the company, the brand name and the country of manufacture (see Chapter 9).
2. Cultural differences sometimes entail divergent symbolic interpretations. Meanings are principally conveyed by the packaging and product presentation. If a symbolic attribute which was ethnocentrically conceived has a very different and highly negative interpretation in the target culture, adaptation is required (cell 5).

The link between symbols and culture

This link comprises seven successive steps. The starting point is a conceptual one: colours, for example, are wavelengths of light reflected by objects; a set of waves of different frequencies produces a colour spectrum. If it is stated that an object is red, this means the following:

1. It soaks up all received light except red.
2. The language has the term called 'red', which designates a certain part of the spectrum that reflects the object (which has no colour as such).
3. Our perceptual apparatus – eyes, retinas, optical nerves, brains – are capable of identifying the wavelengths.
4. Through a learning mechanism, both linguistic and visual, we have learned to recognize this colour as 'red' since early childhood; that is, to qualify it by imitation of all the other people who also designate this colour as 'red'.

Perception results from a culture-based adaptive process (points 2 and 4 above). Numerous experimental studies have shown that certain peoples have a less discriminating perception of colour (their vocabulary and identification is more restricted). They 'mix up' certain 'colours' that other peoples can distinguish. It has also been shown that sensitivity to visual illusions (shapes and length) varies according to culture, particularly as a result of the effects of syncretism. Suggestive visual associations result from our daily environment. Our native physical environment shapes our perceptual universe (see section 1.4). In the case of pictorial perception, Cohen (1995) distinguishes two questions: (1) 'what do people see when they look at this picture?' and (2) 'what does the picture mean?' The second question refers to meaning, interpretation and symbolism, but the first question, which has to be answered first, refers to what people *actually see*. Western pictorial conventions representing three dimensionality on a plane, for instance, are based on arbitrary codes: smaller objects, and higher objects in the picture plane, are meant to be farther away; an overlapped object is supposed to be farther away, and the rules of 'perspective' are applied in the form of convergence of lines. As explained by Cohen (1995, p. 219):

> a picture of an empty bowl in front of a child was supposed to show that the child was hungry and malnourished. The two cues which should have indicated three-dimensionality were overlap and size. But when individuals in the target market were shown the picture, they thought the bowl was an empty washbowl. This was because the bowl was in the foreground and was large in size compared with the child.

In order to move on from the *percept* (i.e. the subjects are able to formulate verbally what has been shown to them) to the *symbolic image*, three steps must be added to the four previously set out. The cultural process intervenes at each of these three final steps:

5. An association has been established between a certain colour, form, smell, shape, etc., and a suggested meaning, as in the two parts of the Greek symbol (see the etymological definition of the symbol given in the introduction). Initially there can be a highly tangible link: for example, the colour brown may be tainted by a negative sense in the connotation of waste, since it may be concretely associated with excrement.
6. This link is ignored; there are two complementary parts but the way they are related has been forgotten: why in most western countries is blue the colour for little boys and pink for little girls (important choices on baby-related markets)?
7. Then there is social overspill through education, advertising, the mass media, literature, magazines – in short, throughout society and indeed even to packaging and

marketing communication in general. The symbol shares the characteristics of a language. It conveys rich and diversified meanings, full of nuances, and its messages are often implicit. It conjures up a set of evocations, suggestions and interpretations which are almost subconscious yet still very real in the minds of consumers. Indeed this set of interpretations is to a large extent specific to each national culture. For example: does orange juice have to be yellow, orange or slightly red, full of pulp or clear, thick or very fluid, in order to evoke different product attributes: the sense of its being a nature-based/non-artificial drink, dietary qualities, an image of refreshment, healthy for children as opposed to intended for adults?

Images diffused by symbolic attributes

Symbols, in their capacity as signs with suggestive power that is non-causal and non-analogous, rely on natural elements: colours, shapes, locations, materials, everyday objects, animals, countryside and elements of nature, famous characters, etc. In certain cultures the lake is a symbol of love, the blue of virginity. Most commonly the 'natural' backgrounds of symbols appear fairly arbitrary, in so far as the original link has often been lost or transformed, as and when the symbol became widely used. The interpretation of symbolic messages conveyed by attributes, such as colour, shape or consistency, may differ significantly between the marketer's culture and the consumer's culture. Williams and Longworth (1989) cite the case of Coral Sea tuna fishery in Australia, where the government has spent money to develop exports to Japan. The fishery has been unable to obtain a high price for its fresh tuna air-freighted to Japan, because the Japanese had a problem with the meat colour. After investigation in the Tsukiji central wholesale market, it appeared that the negative interpretation was related to the meat colour which evidenced a non-Japanese origin; this resulted in the Australian tuna being applied a consistent discount. It is obvious that, in such cases, other markets have to be targeted.

Ethnocentrism is instinctive in all symbolic thought. It is therefore quite inevitable, especially on the consumer culture's side. It may even be useful (to a limited extent) for the marketer, in the case of ethnic product, in order to maintain genuineness. However, the inappropriate (or even just poor) use of backgrounds that diffuse symbolic image which are not adapted to the local consumer is a danger for international marketers. Inappropriate use of symbolic meanings may be based on the best possible intentions from the marketer and result in the worst consequences for users: the skull and crossbones symbol used in most western countries to represent lethal danger (electricity, poison, steam, etc.) represents in many African countries a symbol of potency.

Symbolism of colours, shapes, numbers, etc.

White is the colour of birth and in the West usually celebrates a life's happy event, whereas in China it symbolizes mourning. Conversely black, which symbolizes death in the West (because of darkness and fears that the sun will not return?), is an everyday colour in China.

Hidden behind each symbol lies one or more material supports. Red, for example, is the colour of blood: it can evoke and suggest meanings that differ widely depending on the culture (see Figure 8.1). Every culture has an image of blood, which feeds part of the symbolic content of the colour red (see Box 8.4). Naturally, the colour red can be linked to substances other than blood – certain flowers, for instance. Use of red as the dominant colour on a product or its packaging must therefore be very carefully considered beforehand (cell 5 in Table 8.1).

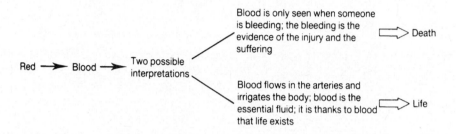

Figure 8.1   An example of diverging symbolic interpretations.

Box 8.5   *Colours, things, numbers and even smells have symbolic meanings . . . often not the ones you think!*

Green, America's favorite color for suggesting freshness and good health is often associated with disease in countries with dense green jungles; it is a favorite color among Arabs but forbidden in portions of Indonesia. In Japan green is a good high-tech color, but Americans would shy away from green electronic equipment. Black is not universal for mourning: in many Asian countries it is white; in Brazil it is purple, yellow in Mexico, and dark red in the Ivory Coast. Americans think of blue as the most masculine color, but red is more manly in the United Kingdom or France. While pink is the most feminine color in America, yellow is more feminine in most of the world. Red suggests good fortune in China but death in Turkey. In America, a candy wrapped in blue or green is probably a mint; in Africa the same candy would be wrapped in red, our color for cinnamon . . . in every culture, things, numbers and even smells have meanings. Lemon scent in the United States suggests freshness; in the Philippines lemon scent is associated with illness. In Japan the number 4 is like our 13; and 7 is unlucky in Ghana, Kenya and Singapore. The owl in India is bad luck, like our black cat. In Japan a fox is associated with witches. In China a green hat is like a dunce cap; specifically it marks a man with an unfaithful wife. The stork symbolizes maternal death in Singapore, not the kind of message you want to send to a new mother.

(Source: from Copeland and Griggs, 1986, p. 63. Reproduced with permission.)

Associating symbols

The following two examples illustrate symbolic associations. Symbols which are diffused by the design of a product or its packaging may be associated with the intrinsic qualities of the product itself.

The Italian company Olivetti produced a typewriter which was such a beautiful object that a New York museum displayed it in its modern art collection. This typewriter proved to be a commercial failure in the United States even though the Americans liked its appearance. Potential purchasers found that its design did not inspire an image of robustness (cell 5). Furthermore, in Anglo-Saxon societies there is often a puritanical attitude that work is an activity required by duty, which is sometimes arduous and should be more painful than enjoyable. This beautiful and enjoyable object was incompatible with such an attitude.

In many cases, symbol associations may work even though, from a rational point of view, individual symbols are somewhat contradictory: consumers' interpretation of symbols association take the form of an impressionistic halo rather than of a detailed content analysis. An example is a German *Weissbier* (a beer brewed with wheat instead of barley), called Oberdorfer. It claims on one side of its label to be brewed according to the Bavarian purity law of year 1516, whereas the other side of the label boasts 'ice-rifing' (sic), 'our new *coole* art to brew beer' (*coole* is a germanification of 'cool', which evokes positive values of quietness and relaxation in many non-English speaking cultures, and 'ice-rifing' probably evokes the belated crop of hop which provides a more bitter taste). Associating (local) tradition and (foreign) modernity is no major problem on average: consumers themselves experience in their daily life the complex mix of modern and traditional, local and foreign, values and behaviours.

A French company exported to West Germany a cheese from the Pyrénées. On the packaging was a shepherd in the midst of his sheep. This picture was directly related to what was shown in the television commercial. In France this image conveyed the idea of natural fabrication and home-made qualities. A consumer test carried out in Germany, after the initial failure of the product, showed that the shepherd was associated by the Germans with dirt. The shepherd was withdrawn and subsequently replaced with a picture of mountain scenery. The product was then able to undergo a successful relaunch. For the Germans, the mountain evokes the image of clean nature. In this example the problem stems from the association of symbolic opposites: country/mountain – dirty/clean – natural/artificial. Clearly in this case the symbolic associations of the French and the Germans are very different.

Colours may also be associated with particular product categories or product attributes. Purple, for instance, is perceived as expensive in the Asian cultures, but inexpensive in the United States. Black is perceived as demonstrating trustworthiness and high quality in China (Jacobs *et al.*, 1991). Colours may also be associated with countries, the products of which are supposed to be the most likely to have this colour dominant on their packaging. By gathering data in four countries (China, South Korea, Japan and the United States), Jacobs *et al.* (1991) show that Asian nations associate red with the United States, but US people do not associate their country with red; purple is associated with France, and the four cultures reviewed associate both France and Italy with the colour green.

Exotic, ethnic and universal appeals

Certain factors weigh in favour of symbolic attributes standardization (cell 6 in Table 8.1): favourable perception of imported products, positive association with the country of origin (perfume with France, fast-food with the United States, etc.) and other factors which are examined in full detail in the next chapter. Many people buy a small slice of American life when they enter a McDonald's restaurant, a touch of French romance when buying a Cacharel perfume, or an instant of German *gemütlichkeit* when drinking a Löwenbräu beer. In these consumptions, ethnic product symbolism is associated with an exotic appeal for the consumer; thus, symbolic attributes must be kept standardized even though the product or its surrounded services are to a certain extent adapted to local markets.

A good example of purely standardized product is the 'Classic Christmas Cake' sold world-wide through mail order by Collin Street Bakery from Corsicana, Texas. The advertisement, sent by mail world-wide, emphasizes that they still bake the 'Deluxe cake true to the Old-World recipe brought to Corsicana, Texas from Wiesbaden, Germany in 1896, by master baker Gus Weidmann'; it boasts the richness of the ingredients ('a full 27% rich pecans') and claims to deliver in 196 countries. Associating symbols of tradition (Old World), genuineness and American richness, they have a full register of images which work world-wide (and claims to do so!). Some brands try also to build on universal symbols: Coca-Cola has always successfully avoided to be associated too strongly with an American image, by creating strong brand association with youth, sports and leisure situations, all universal themes. Packaging consistency is a solution for products who want to diffuse a universal image and build on a highly standardized offer: Coke uses the same red and white logo in each country, and its bottle design is consistent across markets. Similarly, McDonald's never strays from its yellow arches. The symbolic interpretation then shifts from the parts to the whole: rather than interpretations of yellow and arches in particular cultures, it diffuses a message on 'McDo' world-wide.

For designing product attributes which convey appropriate symbolic meanings, the following recommendations can be made:

1. When researching possible standardization, before any product launch, symbols that have a universal or near-to-universal value (as far as they exist) should preferably be chosen.
2. Since there is a very great diversity in the interpretations and associations of symbols, any policy of standardization of the product or its packaging must be systematically preceded by a product and packaging test carried out in each national market with local groups of consumers.

Questions

1. List basic attributes of a perfume at the three levels (physical, service and symbolic). Indicate how the interpretation of symbolic attributes of perfumes may differ cross-culturally.
2. What are basic attributes of Coca-Cola (physical, service and symbolic) in its US

original context? Coca-Cola is adapted according to local tastes and its advertising, although based on core advertising themes and guidelines, is customized for local audiences. Why?

3. Why is service adaptation across market necessary? Outline basic reasons.
4. Telling people in a waiting line how long they still have to wait before being served: what are possible interpretations by consumers of such information?
5. Are there universal, or near to universal, symbols? To what extent can they be used in a marketing strategy? Start from examples.

APPENDIX 8

———— ♦♦♦ ————

Teaching materials

A8.1   Exercise: Interpreting symbolic attributes

For the following products, you are given possible physical attributes; try to imagine how they could be diversely interpreted at a symbolic level, in different cultures (you do not need to relate precisely a definite interpretation to a particular culture, but simply to emphasize probable divergence of interpretation across cultures in general).

* A car/colour black
* Orange juice/thick (with pulp)
* Cheese/with traces of blue (*penicillium glaucum*)
* Beer/foamy
* Orange juice/colour deep orange
* Car/automatic gear box
* Apple juice/vitamins added
* Refrigerator/ice-cube distributor
* Cheese/packed in wooden case
* Car/diesel engine

For further guidance, see Zeithaml (1988) and also Solomon (1994, pp. 67–73).

A8.2   Case: Lestra Design

In May 1990 Mr. Claude Léopold, President of Lestra Design, was wondering what action he should take regarding the Japanese market. For several years, Lestra Design had been trying to enter the Japanese market for duvets and eiderdowns. The Japanese market for these products was certainly the largest in the world, but Lestra Design had faced a number of obstacles that had cooled Claude Léopold's enthusiasm. Then recently, he had met again with Daniel Legrand, a French consultant in Tokyo who had been supervising Lestra Design activities in Japan for the last two years. Daniel Legrand had explained that despite the earlier difficulties experienced by Lestra Design, the company had several alternatives which could enable it to be successful in Japan.

Lestra Design was a subsidiary of Léopold & Fils, a family business established in Amboise, a medium-sized town about 250 kilometers Southwest of Paris (France). Claude Léopold's father had established the parent company in the early 1930s as a feather and down company. At first the company was mainly trading in down and feathers, but Léopold & Fils soon became a major French manufacturer of feather and down-filled cushions, pillows, bolsters and eiderdowns. In 1976, when Claude Léopold took over the business from his father, he decided to establish two new companies: Lestra Design to produce and distribute feather and down duvets; and Lestra Sport to manufacture and distribute feather and down sleeping bags. By using more aggressive sales management and the talents of his wife Josette, a renowned French fashion designer, Lestra Design rapidly became the leading duvet company in France. Josette Leopold's creative ideas for using innovative fabric designs with attractive prints helped Lestra Design and Lestra Sport quickly establish an international reputation for high class, fashionable products. Although in 1990 Léopold & Fils, together with its two subsidiaries (Lestra Sport and Lestra Design), had only 128 employees for revenues of FF72 million (about $10 millions) Claude Léopold believed that the prospect of growth in international markets was extremely promising.

Sales over the past five years had experienced double digit growth, and exports to England, West Germany and other European countries had recently started to boom, representing 20 per cent of Lestra Design sales. A few years earlier, Lestra Design had also placed an order in Japan through Kanematsu-Gosho Ltd., a 'sogo shosha' (large trading company) affiliated with the Bank of Tokyo and traditionally strong in textile. However, the Japanese trading company had not reordered any product from Lestra Design since 1984.

Lestra Design in Japan

In 1983 Georges Mekiès, General Manager, and Claude Léopold, President of Lestra Design, had met with Daniel Legrand, a French consultant established in Tokyo. That same year, Legrand had conducted a market survey for C. Léopold which clearly indicated that a major opportunity for growth existed in Japan. With close to 120 million inhabitants and half of the population using duvets, Japan was clearly the largest market for duvets in the world.

In 1983 and 1984 Claude Léopold had been preoccupied with developing Lestra Design sales in Europe. As a result, he had not taken any immediate action to investigate further the potential of the Japanese market for Lestra Design products. C. Léopold first wanted to provide the French and other European markets with good service before addressing any other market in either the US or Japan. In autumn 1984, during the ISPO exhibition in Frankfurt (West Germany), Claude Léopold and Georges Mekiès were approached by a manager from Ogitani Corporation, a Japanese trading company based in Nagoya. Mr. Hiroshi Nakayama, the representative of Ogitani Corporation, wanted to import and distribute Lestra Design products in Japan. He especially liked the unique designs of Lestra Design's duvets and eiderdowns. He told Messrs. Léopold and Mekiès that the innovative designs as well as the French image with the 'Made in France' label would be the two strongest selling points in Japan.

The trademark issue

In December 1984 Ogitani ordered 200 duvets to be delivered to Nagoya. However, after the goods were shipped, Georges Mekiès did not hear anything from his Japanese distributor. By chance, G. Mekiès discovered on a trip to Japan in April 1985 that Ogitani had registered the two trademarks, Lestra Sport and Lestra Design, under the Ogitani name. Mr. Mekiès decided to call Mr. H. Nakayama and request a meeting in Nagoya to discuss the trademark issue. Mr. Nakayama responded that he was too busy. G. Mekiès then insisted that another executive from the trading company talk with him, but he received only a rebuff.

That same day, a furious Georges Mekiès called Yves Gasquères, the representative of the French Textile Manufacturers Association in Tokyo, for advice. Yves Gasquères who also represented the well-known Lacoste shirts in Japan, explained that Lestra Design was not the only such case. The best advice he could give G. Mekiès was to contact Koichi Sato, a Japanese lawyer specializing in trademark disputes.

Georges Mekiès also saw Daniel Legrand, who confirmed Y. Gasquères' advice. D. Legrand said that, although trademark disputes were rapidly disappearing in Japan, there were still some recent disputes between Western and Japanese firms, especially with several big French fashion houses like Cartier, Chanel, Dior, etc. D. Legrand also mentioned the recent example of Yoplait, a major French yoghurt producer. A few years ago, Yoplait had signed a licensing agreement with a major Japanese food company, to manufacture and distribute yoghurt in Japan. While negotiating the contract, executives at Yoplait discovered that the Yoplait name had been registered by another Japanese food company under various Japanese writing transcriptions. (The Japanese use three different types of transcription together with the occasional use of the Roman alphabet. In addition to Chinese ideograms ('kanji'), 'katakana' is used for the exclusive transcription of foreign words and names. 'Hiragana' is used for all other words not written in 'kanji'.) Although the French company decided to fight the case in court, Yoplait finally decided to use another name ('Yopuleito' using the Katakana transcription) for its products in Japan.

Before going back to France, Georges Mekiès arranged for Daniel Legrand to supervise the trademark dispute with Ogitani. A few weeks later, D. Legrand learned from Mr. Nakayama at Ogitani that the Japanese firm had registered the Lestra Design and Lestra Sport brands under its own name only to prevent other Japanese competitors from doing so. Mr G. Mekiès was not fully convinced, however, about the sincerity of this answer. One month later, he learned from D. Legrand that the legal department of the French Embassy in Tokyo was going to intervene in Lestra Design's favour. Finally, at the end of 1987, D. Legrand informed Léopold & Fils that Ogitani had agreed to give up the two trademarks in exchange for full reimbursement of the registration fees paid by Ogitani to the Tokyo Patent Office.

Looking for a new distributor

During his short stay in Japan, Georges Mekiès was able to size up the many business possibilities offered by the Japanese market. Despite the bad experience with Ogitani, Claude Léopold and Georges Mekiès felt that Lestra Design had a major opportunity for business development in Japan. The Lestra Design trademark was now fully protected by Japanese law. In April 1988 Claude Léopold commissioned D. Legrand to search for and select a new Japanese partner. To shorten the traditional distribution chain and reduce costs, Daniel Legrand decided to use his personal contacts at some of the major Japanese department stores. Department stores such as Mitsukoshi, Takashimaya and Seibu, which sold luxurious products, enjoyed a reputation of considerable prestige in Japan. Moreover, department stores had branches all over Japan, which would enable Lestra Design to cover the whole Japanese market. Most of these department stores were already carrying competitive duvets from West Germany and France, including prestigious brands like Yves Saint Laurent and Pierre Cardin. D. Legrand thought that department stores would be the right outlet for Lestra Design to position its products in the upper segment of the Japanese duvet and eiderdown market. D. Legrand also went to various Japanese companies in the bed and furniture industry as well as to several large trading companies such as Mitsui & Co., Mitsubishi Corporation, and C. Itoh. He also visited Mr. Inagawa, in charge of the Home and Interior Section of Kanematsu-Gosho, which used to import from Léopold & Fils. But Mr. Inagawa said that his company did not intend to import anymore duvets from Lestra Design because its products were too highly priced.

The general reaction from potential Japanese buyers was that Lestra Design's colours (red, green, white) were not appropriate for the Japanese market. However, most of these buyers agreed that, with some modifications to accommodate the Japanese market, the 'Made in France' image was a great asset for selling Lestra Design products in Japan. Duvets and eiderdowns under names like Yves Saint Laurent, Courrèges or Pierre Cardin were being manufactured in Japan under license. They were being sold successfully because Japanese distributors and potential customers tended to view French interior textiles as another fashion product for which France was so famous.

To attract distributors, D. Legrand had advised Léopold & Fils to participate in the yearly Home Fashion Show held in Tokyo. However, C. Léopold and G. Mekiès had not responded to this suggestion. By June 1988, some potential distributors had already been identified, but most of them wanted to license the design and then manufacture in Japan rather than import the final products from France. However, C. Léopold clearly preferred to export directly from France and thus create more jobs for his own employees.

Akira Arai

In July 1988 D. Legrand met with Akira Arai, President of Trans-Ec Co. Ltd., Japan, a firm specializing in importing and exporting down and feathers. A. Arai, 41 years old, had started his own company six years earlier, after working for a large trading company since his graduation from Keio University.

Akira Arai was enthusiastic about French duvets and quilts and the Lestra Design products mainly because of the 'Made in France' label and the prestige attached to French textiles. Like most of the potential distributors D. Legrand had talked to, A. Arai also perceived Lestra Design products as French fashion products similar to the duvets and quilts sold in Japan under prestigious names like Yves Saint Laurent, Cardin or Courrèges. Some French fashion designers almost unknown in France had built a very strong reputation in Japan. Both A. Arai and D. Legrand felt that there was room in Japan for Lestra Design to achieve a strong brand recognition. Akira Arai had had some experience working with other French firms. In the past, he had imported down and feathers from Topiol, a French company which was an indirect competitor of Léopold & Fils. D. Legrand thought that Mr. Arai, who had already heard about Lestra Design, could be a potential partner for the French company. Arai knew the down and feather industry thoroughly, and he had good connections in the complex distribution system of the Japanese duvet industry. A. Arai had also been highly recommended by Mrs. Eiko Gunjima, in charge of fashion items at the Commercial Section of the French Embassy in Tokyo.

Meeting Japanese tastes

In July 1988 Messrs. Legrand and Arai met again in Roppongi, a fashionable district of Tokyo where Mr Arai's office was located. Akira Arai explained that it would be difficult to sell Lestra Design duvets in Japan as they appeared in the current Lestra Design catalogue. In his opinion, Lestra Design would have to adapt its products for the Japanese market. A. Arai proposed that Lestra Design send him a sample that would meet the market requirements (i.e., sizes, colours, fillings, etc.). In particular, he felt that the choice of colours was very important. Although A. Arai liked the innovative motifs and the colours of Lestra Design products, he told D. Legrand that Japanese customers would rarely buy a red, pink or black duvet. Most duvets sold in Japan were in soft colours with many flowers in the design. D. Legrand emphasized that Lestra Design was introducing something really new to the Japanese market, but A. Arai insisted that most Japanese customers would prefer floral motifs on their duvets. Indeed, Daniel Legrand had noticed that almost all the Japanese duvets displayed in Tokyo stores had designs with floral motifs.

Secondly, A. Arai recommended that Lestra Design duvets be smaller than French duvets and should be paving blocked (quilted) to prevent the down from moving too freely inside the duvet. A. Arai noted all these requirements, including all the technical detail needed to manufacture the duvet, so that Lestra Design could meet the Japanese trade expectations. A. Arai's product was quite different from those manufactured by Lestra Design, but D. Legrand was confident that the French company had the flexibility to adapt its products to the Japanese market. A. Arai also requested that Lestra Design deliver the sample within a month. D. Legrand had trouble explaining that Lestra Design, like most French firms, would be closed during the whole month of August for its summer holidays. A. Arai joked about the French taking so much holiday in summer, but he agreed to wait until the beginning of September.

The dust problem

At the beginning of October 1988, D. Legrand went to Arai's office with the sample that he had just received from France. With almost no hesitation, Georges Mekiès had agreed to completely redesign a duvet to meet the Japanese customer's expectations. The fabric was printed with floral motifs, paving blocked and exactly the requested size. Mr. Arai seemed pleased when he first saw the product. Then, as D. Legrand watched, A. Arai picked up the sample, carried it to the window, folded it under his arm and then slapped it vigorously with his hands. Both men were surprised to see a small cloud of white dust come from the duvet. Mr. Arai placed the sample on his desk, shook his head in disappointment and stated, 'This is not a good product. If Lestra Design wants to compete against the big Japanese, German and other French brands, the product must be perfect'.

D. Legrand immediately telexed Mr. Arai's reaction to George Mekiès. In A. Arai's opinion, the problem had to do with washing the duvet. Although Mr. Mekiès was surprised by the result of Mr. Arai's test, he agreed to send a new sample very soon.

Just after New Year's Day D. Legrand arrived at Mr. Arai's office with a new sample. Mr. Naoto Morimoto, in charge of the Bedding and Interior section of Katakura Kogyo, a major textile trading company, had also been invited by Mr. Arai to examine the new sample. In 1988, Katakura Kogyo had profits of US$5.5 million on sales of US$2.8 billion and employed 1,852 people. Naoto Morimoto was an old friend of A. Arai as well as a potential customer for Lestra Design products. After the ritual exchange of business cards between Messrs Legrand and Morimoto, A. Arai proceeded with the same test. Again, some dust came out although less than last time. Messrs. Arai and Morimoto decided to open the duvet and look inside for an explanation to the problem. In their opinion, the feathers had not been washed in the same way as in Japan. Mr. Morimoto suspected that the chemicals used to wash the duvet were very different from those traditionally used in Japan. Moreover, Mr. Arai found that the duvet was filled with both grey and white down. He asked D. Legrand to recommend that Lestra Design use only new white down and no feathers at all, even very small ones. In front of Legrand, Akira Arai also demonstrated the same test with several Japanese and German duvets. No dust came out. As a result, D. Legrand and A. Arai decided to send Mr. Mekiès samples of both a Japanese and a German duvet so that he could test the dust problem himself. With the two samples, Arai attached a note emphasizing that 'to compete successfully in Japan, Lestra Design products must be perfect, especially since the Japanese customer generally believes that textiles and fashion products from France are of high quality.'

At the end of March 1989 a third sample arrived in Tokyo. Mr. Mekiès had phoned D. Legrand beforehand emphasizing that the utmost care had been given to this sample. But again this time, the sample failed Mr. Arai's test. D. Legrand immediately phoned G. Mekiès to inform him of the situation. Mr. Arai was frustrated and, as he listened to Mr. Mekiès' voice on the telephone, it sounded as if Léopold & Fils were about to give up on the Japanese market. Georges Mekiès could not fully understand Mr. Arai's problem because in his whole career at Lestra Design he had never heard any complaint about dust coming out of Lestra Design duvets.

D. Legrand thought that the only way to save the Japanese business would be for Georges Mekiès to visit Tokyo. D. Legrand emphasized again the considerable opportunities offered by the Japanese market and thus convinced Mr. Mekiès and Jacques Papillault, Lestra Design's Technical Director, to board the next flight for Tokyo. Mr. Mekiès said they would only be able to stay 48 hours in order to meet with Mr. Arai.

Mr. Mekiès' trip to Tokyo

A few days later Messrs. Mekiès and Papillault were in Tokyo. Mr. Arai claimed that he was genuinely interested in selling Lestra Design products in Japan, but he explained that in order to compete with existing Japanese duvets, Lestra Design products had to meet the local standards of quality. Messrs. Arai and Morimoto insisted that, since French textile products carried such a high image in Japan, they should be of the finest quality. Mr. Arai also stressed that only new white goose down should be used to fill the duvet. In an aside conversation with Daniel Legrand, Georges Mekiès asked if this requirement came directly from the final customer. D. Legrand replied that it did not seem to be the case. He himself had interviewed Japanese customers in down and duvet shops and had found that the average customer did not know about the different qualities of down nor did customers seem to care whether the down was grey or white. Mr. Mekiès was therefore a bit surprised by Mr. Arai's requirement. In France, as in most European countries, the customer was usually only concerned about price and design. D. Legrand explained that A. Arai meant to use 'new white goose down only' as a major selling point to market Lestra Design duvets as a high quality product to the distributors and retailers. From previous conversations with both wholesalers and retailers, D. Legrand explained that 'new white goose down only' was indeed a reasonable expectation, consistent with the upper positioning of European products in Japan as well as with the high quality associated with French fashion items.

According to the trade, the 'new white goose down only' argument would also justify the premium price charged by the retailers for Lestra Design products. Retail prices for Lestra Design products in Japan were expected to range from ¥60,000 to ¥110,000 (in 1990, $250 to $450) and to be comparable with competitive high quality products imported from West Germany. However, prices varied greatly, from a retail price index of 100 to 300, depending on the quality of the down and feathers and their mixture inside the duvet. In fact, some stores, both in Japan and Europe, allowed customers to choose the filling for their duvets and eiderdowns, a policy which gave the customer a lot of pricing flexibility.

Retail prices for Lestra Design in Japan were more than two times higher than in France. Such a difference could be explained by the typically lengthy distribution system in Japan, which contributed to inflating the price of imported goods. For an ex-factory price index of 100, cost, insurance and freight would add 4 per cent, and duties an additional 6 per cent. Then, Mr. Arai would price the goods so that he could gain a 12 per cent mark-up on his selling price to Mr. Morimoto, who would receive a 10 per cent commission from the smaller wholesalers. In turn, the small wholesalers would put a 20 per cent mark-up on their selling price to the retailers, who would finally sell Lestra Design products at a price which would allow them a 40–60 per cent mark-up. On a retail price basis, Lestra Design products in Japan would be about 30–50 per cent more expensive than most local products of similar quality. Cheap models (either made locally or imported from China) would sell for ¥40,000. On the other hand, Nishikawa, the market leader offered many models in Lestra Design's price range as well as a few prestigious models over ¥1,000,000. In selling competitive products from West Germany in Japan, the German tradition in making duvets was strongly emphasized. Advertising for these products would often carry the German flag, feature the 'Made in Germany' label and include a commercial slogan in German.

The conversation between Messrs. Arai and Mekiès then moved to the dust problem. Mr. Arai explained that, in his view, the problem lay with the composition of the chemical formula used to wash the down. Mr. Arai had already made arrangements to visit a Japanese duvet and eiderdown manufacturer in the afternoon. To get this Japanese company to open their doors, he had simply told the plant manager that a group of French importers was interested in buying the company's products. As a result, the Japanese manufacturer was quite willing to let the French group visit the factory. Georges Mekiès and Daniel Legrand were impressed by the state-of-the-art equipment used by the Japanese firm. Jacques Papillault noticed that the Japanese were using microscopes and some very expensive machines that he had never seen in Europe to determine, for example, the greasiness of the down. Georges Mekiès was also amazed to observe three Japanese employees in white smocks separating down from small feathers with small tweezers. According to Jacques Papillault, not a single Western manufacturer was as meticulous as this Japanese company. During the visit, Georges Mekiès also picked up some useful information about the chemical formula used by the Japanese manufacturer to wash the down and feathers.

The next day, George Mekiès and Jacques Papillault flew back to France fully aware that much remained to be done to crack the Japanese market. Before leaving, G. Mekiès told Mr. Arai that this trip had been extremely useful, and that Léopold & Fils would work hard to make a new sample that would meet the Japanese quality standards. Mr. Arai also promised Georges Mekiès that he would try to get more information about the chemical formula used by the Japanese company they had visited.

New challenges

Two weeks later, Mr. Arai sent Léopold & Fils some additional information on the chemical formula. Georges Mekiès then contacted a large French chemical company that immediately produced an identical formulation for Lestra Design. At the end of April, Mr. Arai told D. Legrand that Lestra Design should hurry with its new samples. Most wholesalers would be placing orders in May for late October delivery to the retail shops. Mr. Arai also indicated that Mr. Morimoto from Katakura Kogyo had already selected some designs and had basically agreed to order 200 duvets at the FOB price of FF. 1,200 each, provided that Lestra Design solved the dust problem.

In late May 1989 three new duvet samples arrived in Japan. Mr. Arai found them much better than the previous ones. However, he still felt that the dust problem was not completely solved. Messrs. Arai and Morimoto decided to have the fabric inspected in the laboratories of the Japanese Textile Association in Osaka. They both explained to Daniel Legrand that the fabric used by Lestra Design did not have the same density of threads per square inch as most Japanese duvet fabrics had. D. Legrand reported this latest development to Georges Mekiès, who was obviously upset by this new complaint from the Japanese. D. Legrand was also worried that the time required to have the fabric inspected would further delay the manufacturing of the 200 duvets that Mr. Morimoto was planning to order. In the meantime, Lestra Design had been obliged to order the fabric with the printed design selected by Mr. Morimoto in order to get exclusivity with its French supplier.

'Gokai' (misunderstandings)

At the end of June 1989 Mr. Takeshi Kuroda, an executive from Katakura Kogyo who was on a business trip in the southern part of France, visited Messrs. Mekiès and Léopold in Amboise. Mr. Mekiès had trouble communicating with the Japanese executive because of Mr. Kuroda's limited ability in English. However, Mr. Mekiès understood from Mr. Kuroda that Lestra Design had the green light to manufacture 200 duvets using the fabric selected by Mr. Morimoto. Mr. Mekiès communicated the good news to D. Legrand who phoned N. Morimoto to thank him for the order. Mr. Morimoto was surprised by D. Legrand's call because he personally had not taken any steps to confirm the order. Mr. Morimoto had first wanted to have the results of the test being conducted in Osaka. Finally, in early July, the report from the Japanese Textile

Association brought bad news for Lestra Design. The Japanese laboratories found that the density of Lestra Design's fabric was far below that of most Japanese duvet fabrics.

The test results confirmed the fears of Messrs. Arai and Morimoto that the fabric problem created a major obstacle for selling Lestra Design duvets in Japan. Although the test could not legally prevent Lestra Design from selling on the Japanese market, A. Arai and N. Morimoto insisted that the French products had to be perfect to be sold in Japan. Thus, Naoto Morimoto told Daniel Legrand that he would not be able to proceed with importing the 200 duvets into Japan. Daniel Legrand tried to counter with the argument that the test was merely a non-tariff barrier for Lestra Design products in Japan. However, N. Morimoto answered that Lestra Design had to meet the market requirements to succeed in Japan.

When Daniel Legrand phoned the Lestra Design office in Amboise, Georges Mekiès was very upset. As far as he knew, the Japanese were the only ones in the world to conduct this kind of investigation, which he believed was a non-tariff barrier to prevent non-Japanese products from entering the Japanese market. Georges Mekiès' exasperation was increased because following Mr. Kuroda's visit, the 200 duvets for Katakura Kogyo had already been manufactured. Because the duvets had been made to fit Japanese specifications, they could only be sold in Japan. Daniel Legrand replied that he would explain the situation to Mr. Morimoto and that he would try to convince him to do something about it. During the following days, D. Legrand tried hard to persuade Naoto Morimoto to accept the order. It seemed to him that Mr. Kuroda was directly responsible for the misunderstanding. But Mr. Morimoto remained inflexible and said that he could not buy products inferior in quality to those sold by Japanese competitors.

During the latter half of 1989 little communication took place between the French and the Japanese. Claude Léopold and Georges Mekiès were upset by the attitude of the Japanese. On the Japanese side, Messrs. Arai and Morimoto said that it was too late to meet with the distributors as most of their orders had already been placed in late July for the winter season. However, Daniel Legrand and Akira Arai had remained loosely in touch. At the end of February 1990 A. Arai said that he was still interested in importing Lestra Design's products. Both Daniel Legrand and Akira Arai were also convinced that, despite all the setbacks, there was still hope for Lestra Design to grasp a share of the huge Japanese market for duvets. Daniel Legrand had learned that Lestra Design's major French competitor had faced similar problems in Japan and had decided to give up the Japanese market. On the other hand, he knew that several German competitors were operating successfully in Japan.

In April 1990, Daniel Legrand took advantage of a business trip to France to visit Messrs. Léopold and Mekiès in Amboise. He was aware that Lestra Design was making a successful start in the US. In fact, Mr. Léopold was just back from an exhibition in New York where a major order had been placed. Daniel Legrand emphasized again the great potential of the Japanese market and the need to take a long-term view of this market. Daniel Legrand recognized that, although Japan was a tough market to crack, persistence would eventually pay off. Claude Léopold said that he had already tried hard and confessed that he was still quite disappointed by the Japanese market. However, at the end of the meeting, Claude Léopold said that he would consider one last try.

The alternatives

In early May 1990 Daniel Legrand again met with Akira Arai and Naoto Morimoto. Mr. Morimoto also mentioned that he would be interested in buying the original designs from Josette Léopold and then have the duvets manufactured in Japan under license. Claude Léopold was not keen on this idea. He knew that Yves Saint Laurent, Lanvin, and Courrèges duvets were manufactured this way in Japan. C. Léopold also knew that Lacoste shirts, although considered a universal product, had been completely adapted to suit the Japanese market. The colours, shape and even the cotton material of Lacoste shirts sold in Japan were different from the Lacoste products sold in the rest of the world. Bernard Lacoste, the son of the famous tennis player and a personal friend of Claude Léopold, ran the Lacoste business around the world. A few months earlier, Mr. Léopold had heard from B. Lacoste himself that in the previous year, the Lacoste company had had trouble with its Japanese licensee. Yves Gasquères, the French consultant in Tokyo who was monitoring Lacoste's operations in Japan, had discovered that the licensee had at one point in time 'forgotten' to pay the full amount of royalties due to Lacoste in France. Claude Léopold was therefore wondering if licensing would be the best solution.

Mr. Arai had also proposed that Lestra Design buy some Japanese fabric and manufacture the duvets in France. He argued that this would definitely solve the dust problem. Moreover, then Lestra Design products could still carry the 'Made in France' label which was so appealing to Japanese customers.

Another alternative recommended to Mr. Mekiès was buying fabric for the duvets from West Germany where textile standards were similar to the ones in Japan. Lestra Design could then print Josette Léopold's designs on the German cloth and still manufacture the duvets in France. Because the Japanese insisted on floral motifs, Lestra Design could even buy fabric with floral prints in West Germany. Mr. Arai had found that many Japanese companies like Nishikawa (the leading duvet manufacturer in Japan) were already buying a lot of German fabric for duvets. However, in order to be granted the design exclusivity, Mr. Mekiès needed to buy a minimum amount of fabric, the equivalent of 300 duvets.

As he was reviewing these different alternatives for Lestra Design, Claude Léopold wondered if he should continue trying to gain a foothold in the Japanese market, or should he simply forget about Japan and focus more on Europe and the United States?

(This case was written by Dominique Turpin, IMD, Lausanne, Switzerland. Reproduced with his kind permission. Some names have been disguised.)

Questions

1. Is the French concept of quality the same as the Japanese concept of quality? If not, how would you relate it to the differences between the French culture and the Japanese culture? If yes, why is quality a culturally universal concept?
2. How would you interpret the attitude of Lestra Design's Japanese partners?
3. What are the difficulties encountered by Lestra Design in the business relationships with its Japanese partners?
4. What reasons could push Lestra Design to continue to try to penetrate the

Japanese market for duvets and eiderdowns? What financial results may be expected, and when?
5. Suggest to Messieurs Léopold and Mekiès a strategic response concerning the Japanese market (go/no go, entry mode, producing locally or not, etc.).

A8.3   Case: Irish Cream O'Darby

Irish Cream is a typically Irish liqueur, prepared from a mix of whisky and cream, with a dash of chocolate. Irish Cream is very popular in Ireland. It conquered the US market in the 1960s and 1970s. Its success abroad has been so great that it is now no longer a negligible portion of total Irish exports.

The most famous brand is Bailey's. It holds a dominating market share, and the brand name tends to be used as a noun. People speak of drinking Bailey's rather than Irish Cream. O'Darby is a challenger to Bailey's, and it competes for the second market share with Carolan's. A fourth brand, Royal Tara, and two small competitors, Waterford Cream and Emmets, share the rest of the market.

O'Darby, whose factory and headquarters are located in Cork, in the southern part of Ireland, was taken over at the beginning of the 1980s by Bacardi Rum, a leading multinational company in the spirits industry. Just a few months after the take-over, Bacardi undertook a large market survey, in the whole of the United States, to investigate how consumers perceived the generic product Irish Cream, and especially the O'Darby brand. It appeared that the green-coloured bottle was largely rejected by potential customers. A new packaging was designed, where brown colour dominated, for the bottle as well as the label. It led to an astonishing growth of sales, not only in the United States, but also in other national markets.

At the beginning of 1991, the director for the marketing of O'Darby hired a young junior marketing executive, Peter Finch, to be in charge of promoting Irish Cream O'Darby in France. Peter Finch, who had just graduated from a continuing education programme for training young export executives, travelled to France to see what could be done to increase sales. The exclusive distributor of Irish Cream O'Darby was the Benedictine Group, a large liquor producer, which sold on the French market through a network of non-exclusive sales agents.

O'Darby was not the first company producing Irish Cream to try to penetrate the French market. In 1982 and 1983, Bailey's had spent a lot of money, especially on advertising, to launch the Irish Cream. The results had been disappointing and sales margins had not been large enough to cover the marketing expenses. Bailey's had not withdrawn, but it had discontinued its costly marketing expenses. Bailey's had concentrated its sales coverage on Paris, the northern part of France, Normandy and Brittany. It appeared that Bailey's was unsuccessful in selling to customers in the southern part of France. When trying to explain this relative failure, sales agents had mainly questioned the price level which according to them, was too high.

During his first stay in France from March to May 1990, Peter Finch had been involved in sales promotion operations, with the help of the Benedictine network.

Shoppers in hypermarkets were asked to taste Irish Cream by giving them miniature bottles of O'Darby. It seemed to be difficult even to induce people to try the liquor.

However, this product was very popular in other developed markets under a variety of uses. For instance, in the United States consumers mixed it with Coca-Cola or orange juice, in cocktails. O'Darby was well placed for use in cocktails, compared to its competitors, because of a special formula that made it easy to mix with other beverages. In many markets, consumers used Irish Cream to coat ice-creams, cakes or strawberries. In Spain, where Irish Cream has achieved a good deal of product knowledge, Spanish consumers tend to call it Bailey's O'Darby.

In September 1991 the situation for Irish Cream O'Darby was as follows:

1. It was sold almost exclusively in very large food stores (hypermarkets); it achieved a low penetration rate as a bar drink; it was rarely to be found in restaurants.
2. The retail price was in the range of 45–50 francs for a bottle of 75 centilitres, compared to Bailey's which was priced in the bracket of 55–60 francs for a bottle of 70 centilitres.
3. The annual sales for 1990 were 24,000 boxes of 12 bottles.
4. Sales coverage was limited to Paris, the northern part of France, Normandy and Brittany. The best-selling area was the *département* of Finistère (Brest, Quimper), which is located in the most western part of France (a *département* is a French territorial unit where there are generally between half a million and one million inhabitants). Finistère is linked by ferries to Ireland. There, per capita consumption of Irish Cream was three times as much as in the Paris region.
5. There was no advertising. Sales promotion was done mostly by means of free sampling, in hypermarkets, disco bars or night clubs ('O'Darby party nights').
6. The promotional budget, which was 300,000 francs in 1989, was more than doubled in 1990 to 700,000 francs.

Questions

1. Discuss and, possibly, criticize the marketing strategy which was adopted by Irish Cream O'Darby in order to enter the French market. In doing this you should, in particular, take care to examine what kind of market research should have been undertaken (a) prior to entering the market, and (b) after results had been achieved, and to question the coherence of the marketing mix. (You are not asked to prepare a marketing strategy as a whole, since the information available in this short case is not sufficient.)
2. Irish Cream O'Darby has to decide on the allocation of its total marketing budget to its various national markets. You are asked to outline the criteria and design of such an allocation method. The problem is allocation between national markets, not between local/regional markets within a particular country.

References

Camphuis, Pierre-Arnold (1984), 'Launching a product on the Cameroon market', Internship Report, Ecol Supérieure de Commerce de Paris.

Cohen, Judy (1995), 'Toward a theoretical understanding of the impact of culture on pictorial perception', *Proceedings of the Second Conference on the Cultural Dimension of International Marketing*, Odense, pp. 213–45.

Copeland, Lennie and Lewis Griggs (1986), *Going International*, Plume Books/New American Library: New York.

Gabel, H. Landis (1989), 'Products standards and competitive strategy: Analysis of the principles, *INSEAD Working Paper*, Fontainebleau.

Giordan, Alain Eric (1988), *Exportez Plus 2*, Editions Economica: Paris.

Hall, Edward T. (1976), *Beyond Culture*, Doubleday: New York.

Jacobs, Laurence W., Charles F. Keown, Reginald Worthley and Ghymn Kyung-Il (1991), 'Cross-cultural colour comparisons: Global marketers beware!', *International Marketing Review*, vol. 8, no. 3, pp. 21–30.

Kamamoto, M. (1984), 'Japanese concept of service', *Dentsu Japan Marketing/Advertising*, January, pp. 26–9.

Levitt, Theodore (1983), 'The globalization of markets', *Harvard Business Review*, vol. 61, no. 3, May–June, pp. 92–102.

Ofir, Chezy and Donald R. Lehmann (1986), 'Measuring images of foreign products', *Columbia Journal of World Business* (Summer), pp. 105–108.

Rogers, E. M. (1983), *Diffusion of Innovations*, 3rd edn, Free Press: New York.

Solomon, Michael R. (1983), 'The role of products as social stimuli: a symbolic interactionism perspective,' *Journal of Consumer Research*, vol. 10 (December), pp. 319–29.

Solomon, Michael R. (1994), *Consumer Behavior*, 2nd edn, Allyn and Bacon: Needham Heights.

Tiano, A. (1981), *Transfert de Technologie Industrielle*, Editions Economica: Paris.

Trompenaars, Fons (1993), *Riding the Waves of Culture*, Nicholas Brealey: London.

Tuncalp, Secil (1990), 'Export marketing strategy to Saudi Arabia: the case of British exporters', *Quarterly Review of Marketing*, vol. 15, no. 2, pp. 13–18.

Williams, Stephen C. and John W. Longworth (1989), 'Factors influencing tuna prices in Japan and implications for the development of the coral sea tuna fishery', *European Journal of Marketing*, vol. 23, no. 4, pp. 5–24.

Zeithaml, Valarie A. (1988), 'Consumer perceptions of price, quality and value: A means–end model and synthesis of evidence', *Journal of Marketing*, vol. 52 (July), pp. 2–22.

Marketing in the intercultural environment

9

$\blacklozenge\blacklozenge\blacklozenge$

Management of images related to nationality and brand name

A name can make substantial contributions to a brand equity, as emphasized by Leclerc *et al.* (1994, p. 263):

> What do Klarbrunn waters, Giorgio di St Angelo design wear and Häagen-Dazs ice cream have in common? All three are successful brands, and all are not what they seem. Klarbrunn is not the clear mountain-spring mineral water from the German Alps that its brand name suggests; it is American water bottled in Wisconsin. Giorgio di St. Angelo design wear is not the latest fashion from Milan but the product of U.S. designer Martin Price. And Häagen Dazs is not Danish or Hungarian ice cream; it is American ice cream made by Pillsbury with headquarters in Minneapolis.

This chapter complements the preceding one directly: it deals with the symbolic attributes that are linked to brands and national images. These issues are particularly significant for a company which does not as yet have an established brand(s) on the international market. It is easy to avoid basic errors in relation to the choice of a brand name when starting from scratch. However, correcting mistakes once brand goodwill has been created can prove a costly and tricky operation. A brand, even one that has a poor impact may be an asset because marketing communication investment has been made. Consumers are often confused by changes in a brand name. Brand name changes, if they are possible, risk wasting time and incurring expenditure.

First, the play of images between the images of the product's country of origin, the company name and/or the brand name of its products is discussed. This complex play of images warrants closer analysis. Once again, when starting without an established brand, there is the potential for intentional diffusion of favourable images, suitable for the product category and the targeted national segments.

The evaluation of product quality by consumers has been documented by a great number of empirical studies. The perception of certain product attributes, according to their national origin, has been experimentally assessed. The second section reviews studies dealing with the country-of-origin paradigm. Consumers in different countries were questioned about their perceptions of their domestic products compared to foreign-made products of various national origins. These studies suggest consistent answers to such questions as the following: Are 'Buy British' or 'Buy American' advertising campaigns successful? Do consumers have strong preferences for their national products? Which countries are best perceived, and on which attributes? Do countries' images change over time?

The third section addresses the issue of the conversion of national brands into international brands. The linguistic obstacles that are met in this conversion are examined. The question of the so-called 'global' brands is also documented since this is becoming a significant issue in international marketing.

9.1   National images diffused by the product's origin and by its brand name

The complexity of national images diffused by the product

The purchasers of Swedish cars, who pay twice as much as for Spanish cars with comparable performance, acquire, at least to a certain extent, the symbolic label 'Made in Sweden' which, for them, suggests reliability and long life, thereby removing any fear of mechanical failure. There exists an important relation between images of products and the symbols diffused by their nationality. Relationships between product and nationality, in consumers' evaluations, were first studied with respect to the 'made in' label (Nagashima, 1970, 1977; Cattin *et al.*, 1982). But the 'made in' label is not the only element that contributes to consumer perception of product nationality (Schieb, 1977; Graby, 1980a).

The following elements can be distinguished (Figure 9.1):

1. The image of imported products in opposition to national products or the image of national versus international products.
2. National images of generic products: yoghurt calls to mind the Balkans, perfume evokes France, a pair of jeans the United States, etc.
3. The national image of the manufacturing company.
4. The image diffused by the brand name.
5. The image of the 'made in' label in the sense of the manufacturing origin legally appended to the product; origin labelling is mandatory in international trade.

Leclerc *et al.* (1994) show that the French pronunciation of a brand name positively affects the perceived hedonism of the product and negatively affects its perceived utility. They further demonstrate that foreign branding changes consumers' perceptions of the product (in this case yoghurt) in an actual product taste test where consumers have direct sensory experience. In many cases, the product category is not clearly associated with only one country: wine is not associated with France only, but also with other European countries (Germany, Italy, Spain, Portugal) and with California, Australia, Argentina and Chile. There are also regional association: furniture in natural pine wood is often associated with Scandinavia as a whole. However, in an experiment looking at customer evaluations of advertisements, Harris *et al.* (1994) showed that the effect of foreign product names on country-of-origins attributions must be checked carefully. Their findings indicate that, contrary to what one might expect, German-named burger restaurants were preferred by US respondents over American ones. Beer, on the other hand, was associated with more than one nationality and a German name beer was not necessarily preferred by consumers.

Japanese consumers associate countries with stereotypes (Nishina, 1990): Germany and France with long history and tradition, Switzerland and Australia with rich nature, California and Brazil with plentiful agricultural products, the United States and Germany with advanced industrial technology, and France with sense of design and high-class products.

Some examples will illustrate the levels on which national images can operate (see Table 9.1). The set of normative recommendations for management of a product's national image includes the following elements:

1. One should diffuse an image which corresponds in each country to what is locally valued (imported or national) in the category of the product concerned. This can lead

Figure 9.1 Several layers of country-, company- and brand-related product image.

Table 9.1   *Some examples of brand names and country-of-origin combined influences on product image.*

Product	National image of the generic product	National image of the manufacturer	Country evoked by the brand name label	Country image diffused by the 'Made in' label
Shalimar (perfume by Guerlain)	French	French	India/Orient	French
Kinder (milk chocolate bars of Ferrero)	Swiss and other countries	Italian (but the manufacturer's name, Ferrero, rarely appears)	German (means 'children' in German)	'Made in' weakly visible – often Italy
National (vacuum cleaner of Matsushita)	Neutral	The manufacturer's name (Matsushita) does not appear	The National brand makes people believe that it is a local production	'Made in' label weakly visible – different national origins
Coca-Cola	International	American	America	Neutral
Kremly (yoghurt by Chambourcy of Nestlé)	Balkan/Bulgarian Slav	Looks French, but is a world-wide brand from the Swiss Nestlé	Kremly (name and graphics) evokes the Kremlin, a Slav image	The 'Made in' label is a local one
Brother (typewriters by Brother)	Neutral	English/American (in fact a Japanese company)	International	The 'Made in' label indicates the origin

to the adoption of a name from the target country, imposed by prevailing nationalistic feelings.

2. If the generic product is generally associated with a specific country of origin, one should not hesitate to change the brand name. For example, a manufacturer of machine tools should not be reluctant to adopt a German name, because of the favourable association of German-sounding names with technical reliability.

3. It is often advisable to reduce the physical size of the 'made in' label if the perception of the country of origin proves negative for local consumers (provided it is permitted, or ignored, by locally prevailing regulations). On the other hand, one should magnify it in the contrary case.

4. The visibility of the company name, the brand name and the 'made in' label should be adjusted depending on their respective ability to convey the desired symbolic meanings.

9.2 Consumer product evaluation according to country of origin

The use of the 'country of origin' attribute

Consumers use the manufacturer's country of origin on a symbolic level. In other words, they use it as an associative link: Germany – robustness, France – luxury, Italy – beauty, etc. The cognitive processes that lead to these evaluations are therefore worth examination. Numerous studies have been devoted the country-of-origin paradigm (Bilkey and Nes, 1982, Samiee, 1994). The simplistic approach which directly assimilates a country image with the image of the product originating from that country is gradually being disregarded. Studies now try to analyze the complex consumer evaluation processes that relate the image of the country of origin to product attributes perception. There follows as accurate a picture as possible of the outcome of this research.

As Bilkey and Nes (1982) point out, the basic objective was to demonstrate that the country-of-origin cue actually influenced consumers' evaluation. Attempting to determine in which direction and why, was only a secondary objective in the first studies (Schooler, 1965, 1971; Reierson, 1966, Schooler and Sunoo, 1969; Etzel and Walker, 1974; Wang and Lamb, 1980). For instance Schooler and Wildt (1968) showed their subjects totally identical products (drinking glasses). Some drinking glasses were supposed to have been 'Made in USA' whereas the others claimed to be 'Made in Japan'. They clearly evidenced an evaluation bias due to the effect of the country of origin. But price discounts may lead the consumer to purchase the 'worst' product – the Japanese one in this case. However, considering the *country of origin* as the only criterion in consumer evaluation of quality leads to an exaggeration in the importance of the 'made in' label.

A set of core standard images

Throughout country-of-origin studies one finds a limited number of certain stereotyped images. These fairly resistant stereotypes are consistent across consumers' nationalities:

the image of robustness of German products, the image of France as associated with luxury goods, the image of Korean products of being cheap. However, shared perceptual elements are restricted and unstable: for instance, the Italians do not have the same image of their products as consumers from other countries, and the Korean image has changed over time.

Generally speaking, many elements of country of origin are not shared by consumers of different national cultures. Often, minimal differences in relationships between countries (similarity of culture and language, past colonial links, etc.) lead to differences in the perception of the same country across other countries (for example, Yaprak, 1978). Krishnakumar (1974) has, for instance, shown that Indian students evaluate British products more positively than do students from Taiwan, a difference attributable to the past colonial links between the United Kingdom and India. Yavas and Alpay (1986) have demonstrated that in two proximate countries, Saudi Arabia and Bahrain, consumers hold the same views of products originating from abroad.

Use by consumers of the image of the country of origin of goods for their evaluation

Country of origin is only one attribute among many that characterize a product. A product possesses intrinsic attributes (size, colour and quality, for example) as well as extrinsic attributes (such as price). Country of origin is therefore only one criterion of evaluation (Erickson *et al.*, 1984). The influence of the country-of-origin evaluation cue is stronger where the consumer is unfamiliar with a product category. In this situation, the country of origin serves as a sort of proxy variable that facilitates evaluation in the absence of other criteria. It also serves to sum up diversified evaluation criteria within a sort of global evaluation (Morello, 1984). In the absence of other information cues, the consumer will use the country of origin to evaluate the product. It seems that knowledge and familiarity with the product category tends to decrease the use of country of origin as an informational cue by consumers: consumer experts base their evaluation on the strength of actual product attributes whereas novices tend to rely more on the country-of-origin cue as such (Maheswaran, 1994).

Various studies have insisted on the mediation of stereotypes concerning the country itself, by means of an association product to country or country to attribute, in the effect of the country of origin on the evaluation of the product. For example, for the Iranians 'The Germans are well-ordered and hard working, the French inventive and DIYers even in business matters, the Japanese copiers . . .' (Bon and Ollivier, 1979, p. 106).

For many reasons, country of origin's influence on consumer evaluation has to be nuanced: (1) it is only one element in the evaluation, associated with other cues (price, store, brand, etc.); (2) it depends on the product category; (3) consumer knowledge and familiarity with the product category has an influence; and (4) customer awareness of country of origin may be quite limited or even non-existent (Samiee, 1994), especially if the country of origin is neither advertised nor labelled.

The mediation of perceived risk

A sound hypothesis which has been proposed by several studies is the mediation of perceived risk to explain the influence of the country of origin on consumer evaluations. Either consumers perceive a lesser risk for national products, which would explain the preference for national products, or they perceive a lesser risk for the products of certain countries with a favourable image (see Box 9.1). Accordingly consumers would tend to prefer certain sources because they perceive a reduced risk in purchasing that country's products (Lumpkin *et al.*, 1985).

Hampton (1977) considered the situation where American goods are manufactured either in the United States or abroad in selected countries. In the sample were some strong perceived risk countries (Algeria, Pakistan, Turkey), some moderate perceived risk countries (Philippines, Hong Kong) and some weak perceived risk countries (Canada, Japan, West Germany). In the questionnaire these origins were combined with a sample of products that offered diverse levels of perceived risk. Overall the results confirmed that consumers perceived less risk for goods manufactured in the United States than for the same foreign-made products, whatever the level of perceived risk of the foreign country of manufacture. In several instances, product–country connections were clearly

Box 9.1   *Confession of a purchaser of Italian products*

When I consider the origins of my purchases I am fascinated by the number of Italian-made goods I have acquired. My Fiat Uno is the seventh Fiat I have bought. One of these Fiats (a 127) saved my life when I was in Paris. I was waiting at a red light when a Mercedes failed to brake and went into the back of me, sending me 30 metres forward. My Fiat had to be scrapped, but I was unharmed. At home, the washing machine and dryer are Zanussi, and the deep-freeze is a Hiberna. When I go trekking, my mountain shoes are from Trezetta. Like many Europeans, I like Barilla pasta and cakes. In fact, I am a price-minded consumer: Italian products are often the cheapest. Being somewhat price-averse (but not stingy), I believe that 'quality' and 'durability' will never match the price advantage. But price is not the only merit of Italian products. Italian products are much more reliable than stereotyped images would sometimes have you believe. Having successfully tried Italian products, my perceived risk is low when buying 'Made in Italy'. Italian goods are probably slightly less solid than German goods, but I very much like their design and function. Even though it is a small car, I like the style of the body and the interior of the Fiat Uno, as well as its sporty engine. If well maintained, the durability of Italian products is excellent. Their price–quality ratio is fairly reasonable in the long run. Paradoxically, Italian products often do not reach their ideal purchasers: many purchasers of Italian products belong to the price-minded segment; they tend not to spend the required time in maintenance. Mercedes buyers, on the other hand, are much more likely to do so. The 'Made in Italy' deserves, in my opinion, better appreciation.

established in consumers' minds, such as the colour television and Japan, the calculator and Hong Kong, or even instant coffee and Brazil, thereby reducing the level of perceived risk of a country as a general place of manufacture. For these specific products, these countries were considered favourable for their manufacture.

In their study of the risk perceived by Americans for clothing purposes – clothes and shoes made abroad versus those made in the United States – Lumpkin *et al.* (1985) confirm that the perceived risk is weaker for a product of national origin. They showed that perceived risk only has a strong influence when consumers are aware of the foreign origin of the clothes. They also detected differences according to the categories of products: certain countries (China, Korea) presented the same perceived risk whatever the product whereas Italy offered a weak perceived risk for shoe purchases and France offered a high perceived risk when buying jeans.

Also using clothing purposes in their experimental setting, Baumgartner and Jolibert (1977) have proved that certain traits of a foreign country may reduce the perceived risk if the consumers (French, in this case) hold the belief that a foreign country, by virtue of its physical, climatic or social environment, is particularly suitable for the manufacture of a particular product: for instance, an English overcoat for the winter. Generally, the overall level of perceived risk for a specific national origin is reduced for its *ethnic* products.

Preference for national products

It has persistently been demonstrated that in most developed countries domestic products generally enjoy a more favourable evaluation than foreign-made products. This has been clearly evidenced for US as well as Japanese consumers (Reierson, 1966; Nagashima, 1970; Gaedeke, 1973; Lillis and Narayana, 1974; Morello, 1984; Heslop *et al.*, 1987). In the case of French consumers, Baumgartner and Jolibert (1977) also showed that there is a strong preference for domestic products. In the case of Finland, Finnish consumers deemed their products to be better in almost every attribute than seven other countries: United Kingdom, France, West Germany, Japan, Sweden, the Soviet Union and the United States (Darling and Kraft, 1977). This preference for nationally made products has been corroborated by several other studies (Bannister and Saunders, 1978, in the case of England; Graby, 1980a and 1980b, in the case of France; Cattin *et al.*, 1982, in the case of France and the United States). Conversely, in the case of developing countries, national products are not preferred to imported goods. Iranian producers, for instance, were shown to prefer imported products (Bon and Ollivier, 1979). In Iran, a product was favourably rated when it had a foreign/imported label. Bon and Ollivier did, however, observe the emergence of a deep-rooted nationalistic feeling in purchasing situations. They noted that there was at the time no 'Buy Iranian' campaign in the style of state-sponsored advertising campaigns for the purchase of national products, such as occur regularly in European countries and the United States, or as are permanently undertaken in India. Despite that, some Iranian buyers had a nationalistic tendency which consisted of buying primarily local products. They perceived imported products as unfair competition to Iranian products and considered the success of foreign-made products a potential brake on the social and economic development of Iran. This attitude, however, did not seem to be very widespread (Bon and Ollivier, 1979, p. 104). In eastern European countries similar images related to nationality and brand name attitudes exist: for instance, the Hungarians generally evaluate foreign products more positively, although their image of domestic products is not particularly unfavourable (Papadopoulos *et al.*, 1990).

Consumer ethnocentrism and patriotism

Different explanations have been proposed to explain this preference for national products, observed mostly in developed countries. Graby (1980b, p. 37) suggests the following explanation for the preference for French-origin purchases by French customers:

> Unemployment appears as a prime argument; however, one should consider that high scores of agreement (on buying French as a way to maintain employment) pertain more to the unemployment problem because of its current prominence, than to a true purchasing motive.

In the same vein, an attempt has been made in the United States to measure 'consumer ethnocentrism'. Customers may consider the purchase of foreign goods to be immoral, since it puts the national economy at risk and leads to job losses (Shimp and Sharma, 1987). Shimp and Sharma studied the level of consumer ethnocentrism in different regions within the United States which were affected to a greater or lesser extent by foreign competition: Detroit, Denver, Los Angeles, North and South Carolina. They observed the consumer ethnocentrism was much stronger where the threat was perceived by individuals whose quality of life was affected by foreign competition, for instance in Detroit where unemployment in the motor industry is adversely affected by Japanese and Korean competition.

A related idea is that of 'consumer patriotism' (Min Han, 1988) which largely influences the outcome of 'Buy American', 'Buy British', 'Achetez français' or even 'Buy Canadian' campaigns (Kaynak and Cavusgil, 1983). Min Han claims that not only do patriotic consumers prefer to buy domestic products on the basis of strictly nationalistic feelings, but they also consider their quality and the service which accompanies them to be better. Min Han shows that for two different products/services, 'consumer patriotism' has contrasting effects: whereas it significantly influences the quality perception for motor cars, it does not affect the quality perception of vehicle maintenance and repair. In the case of television sets and their maintenance, the effect of consumer patriotism is non-existent.

'Buy national' campaigns should therefore be very cautious. The best approach to adopt would be to play clearly on nationalistic feelings as such, and not to attempt to influence consumers in their product evaluation. Consumers will probably remain fairly rational in their product evaluations, therefore an attempt to reinforce the quality perception of locally made products artificially could prove ineffective. The following section addresses this issue.

Are 'Buy national' campaigns effective?

The issue addressed is the assessment of the effectiveness of 'Buy national' advertising campaigns by empirical testing. Ettenson *et al.* (1988) investigated the case of a 'Made in the USA' campaign carried out for American clothing manufacturers. It was forecast that in 1995, 65 per cent of clothing sold in the United States would be cheap imported products. The CWPC (Crafted with Pride in the USA Council) provided a $40 million budget which initially funded a series of television commercials showing American stars boasting the superiority of American clothing. Consumers were subsequently questioned to determine the audience and the effect of the campaign. They proved reluctant to reveal themselves to be unpatriotic. Furthermore, their attitudes towards domestic products failed to correspond with their purchasing behaviour. The results of the campaign were unconvincing: 'retailers who have adopted the "Made in the USA" theme are promoting their merchandise in terms of an attribute that may have relatively little effect on consumers' decision making ... patriotic promotion campaigns should be considered circumspectly by retailers' (Ettenson *et al.*, 1988, p. 96). Johansson and Nebenzahl (1987) confirmed this result by showing that a campaign appealing to people to 'Buy American' had to be based on a normative influence (social norm favouring patriotic behaviour) as opposed to a cognitive influence (trying to convince the consumer that the national product is objectively superior).

Country-of-origin and brand perceptions: The effect of multinational production

As a result of the expansion of multinational firms, companies sell the same products under identical brand names in different countries throughout the world. These products actually have widely differing national origins, not necessarily that of the country of origin of the parent company. Sony products, for example, can be just as easily 'Made in France', 'Made in Germany' or 'Made in Britain' as 'Made in Japan'. In this sense, one must increasingly distinguish between country of origin and country of manufacture (Samiee, 1994). Product design and brand name would originate from the country of origin (Ahmed *et al.*, 1994).

An attempt must therefore be made to distinguish consumer evaluations purely related to the brand (and its country of origin, when it is identifiable) from the particular effect of the country of production (Johansson and Thorelli, 1985). Johansson and Nebenzahl (1986) demonstrated that a change in the place of car production (Chevrolet, Buick, Honda or Mazda) to West Germany is always positively perceived by American consumers. On the other hand, the status and quality images of these makes have suffered when a change has been envisioned in the place of their production to a country where low salaries are paid (Mexico, South Korea or the Philippines). This change clearly resulted in a loss of image in terms of social status and quality–price ratio.

Min Han and Terpstra (1988, p. 244) sought to determine which of the two effects had more influence, and their conclusion was unequivocal: 'the sourcing country has greater effects on consumer evaluations of product quality than does the brand name'. As for

Eroglu and Machleit (1989), they concluded from their empirical study that consumers accord a similar influence to brand and country of manufacture respectively. Ahmed *et al.* (1994), in the case of industrial products, show that country of design is a more important cue in organizational purchase decisions than country of assembly and brand name.

The correlative question deserves consideration: what price reduction do consumers require to 'accept' a less favourable origin, in relation to a specific brand? Johansson and Nebenzahl (1986, p. 120) have succeeded in determining the levels of monetary discounts (dollar values) at which consumers were prepared to purchase products from a 'less favourable' origin. They were, for example, willing to buy a Buick manufactured in the United States for $10,258 rather than pay $7351 for the same car if it were to be made in the Philippines. Jaffé and Nebenzahl (1989) have measured such elasticity of demand in the country of production with Israeli consumers (and Usunier *et al.*, 1993, with French consumers), for three possible countries of production (South Korea, Japan and West Germany) and for three brands (Sanyo, Grundig and Sony). A discount of 30–40 per cent was necessary to sell Japanese or German brand products when they had been manufactured in South Korea. It was shown (Usunier, 1994) that consumers belonging to lower social classes (who are favourite targets for lower-priced goods) did not ask for a larger price discount than higher social status consumers when it was proposed to shift to a less favourable country of manufacture (South Korea). Furthermore consumers from lower social classes evaluate Korea more positively as a country of origin. Thus, it would be wise for the marketing strategy of 'cheap' origin goods in highly developed markets to put emphasis on quality rather than price, especially when modest consumers and lower classes are targeted.

Country image differences across product categories

Various studies have evidenced perceptual linkage between country of origin and product types. Certain products are considered more 'ethnic', more typical of certain countries; consumers tend to associate countries and products: Italy and pizza, Germany and machine tools, Britain and puddings. Gaedeke (1973), for example, found that tinned meat made in Brazil is much more highly regarded than televisions made there, and that video recorders that are 'Made in South Korea' were more highly regarded than shoes from the same country.

Different studies have been devoted to industrial purchasing (White and Cundiff, 1978; Jolibert, 1979; White, 1979; Perrin *et al.*,1981; Cattin *et al.*, 1982). Industrial purchasers were asked about their perception of relevant attributes of the product: price, perceived quality and technological advance. Germany consistently appears to have a substantial lead in product quality and reliability images, and also appears to be the most capable producer of heavy industrial equipment (Jolibert, 1979; Cattin *et al.*, 1982). This favourable image of German industrial products is to be found even in the United States, where American purchasers regard German industrial products as being of higher quality than their own. French and UK industrial products are regarded as being of equivalent quality to US ones, and Italian industrial products as being of inferior quality to American products (White, 1979). A similar favourable image is found now for Japanese industrial products which receive better overall rating from Korean importers than American products (Kraft and Chung, 1992).

Perrin *et al.* (1981) showed in a study of the International Marketing and Purchasing European group that different national markets across Europe are not equally demanding as a whole and furthermore do not emphasize the same requirements. German and Swedish industrial purchasers prove to be more demanding, whereas the Italian and British purchasers are less so. German and Swedish suppliers have the same image of good technical quality and punctual delivery across all European markets. In the case of France, it appears that the unique trait of the achievements of French industrial companies is the exceptional quality of the relationships they construct over time with their French clients: 'actually, in no other country do purchasers accord such an advantage on this point to their national suppliers' (Perrin *et al.*, 1981, p. 102).

Influence of demographic variables on consumer attitudes towards the country of origin

The degree of consumer awareness and sensitivity to the country-of-origin attribute varies depending on the following:

1. The effect of gender: some studies have suggested a more favourable evaluation of foreign products by women than by men (Schooler, 1971; Dornoff *et al.*, 1974; Gopalakrishna *et al.*, 1989). Men are generally more influenced by 'Buy national' campaigns (Ettenson *et al.*, 1988). Nevertheless several other studies have shown that gender is not a discriminating factor (Anderson and Cunningham, 1972; Tongberg, 1972; Graby, 1982).
2. Age groups: generally it would seem that the readiness to purchase foreign products decreases with age (Schooler, 1971; Tongberg, 1972; Dornoff *et al.*, 1974; Graby, 1982). Dogmatism, greater nationalism and stabilized consumption habits are probably the result of ageing, and explain the reluctance to buy foreign goods. However, inconclusive results have been reached by other researchers showing that age has no influence (Johansson *et al.*, 1985; Morganosky and Lazarde, 1987; Usunier, 1994).
3. 'Social classes': generally a more favourable evaluation of foreign products is made by consumers when they have a higher level of education (Anderson and Cunningham, 1972; Dornoff *et al.*, 1974; Wang, 1978) or a higher income level (Wang, 1978), or when they have travelled abroad and are therefore more familiar with the products of these foreign countries (Graby, 1982).

Country image and product image

Country images may become divorced from the image of their products. Imagine, for instance, the case of a country under a bloody dictatorship that nevertheless produces some excellent goods which are exported to democratic countries. The following issue therefore deserves investigation: does the image of a country (in political, economic, cultural and social terms), independently of the perceived quality of its products, have an influence on the willingness of foreign consumers to purchase that country's products? In other words, will consumers remain willing to purchase products originating from a country under a dictatorship or one which acts in contravention of certain internationally recognized rules, even if these products fit their needs? Or alternatively, does the overall level of industrial development influence the evaluations of a particular country of origin and of its products by foreign consumers?

Wang and Lamb (1983) asked ninety-four people, US nationals, about their readiness to purchase products from different countries (thirty-six in all). They also asked them to identify the political, cultural and economic environment of each country. In this way they were able to demonstrate that variables of the sociopolitical image of a country partially explained consumers' readiness to purchase products that come from there. The American consumers were more prepared to buy products coming from politically democratic countries such as those in Europe, Australia or New Zealand. Martin and Eroglu (1993) have developed the construct country image by showing that it can be divided into three subdimensions: (1) political; (2) economic; and (3) technological dimension.

This is in line with Crawford and Lamb's (1981) results: they sought to determine whether purchasers of industrial products were prepared to purchase foreign products and what their preferred sources were in terms of nationality. According to them, 'willingness to buy foreign products is influenced not only by the individual country, but also by the existing levels of economic development and political freedom' (Crawford and Lamb, 1981, pp. 30–1). A study undertaken for industrial goods from eight South American countries (Crawford, 1985) showed that American industrial purchasers preferred national sources on the basis of their political freedom and stability: at the top they put Mexico and then Brazil, and at the bottom El Salvador and Cuba. The degree of industrial development (not only based on objective data, but also perceived by partially un-informed consumers) has an influence on the image of the products. Khanna (1986) demonstrates that among the products of four countries from Asia (India, Japan, Taiwan and South Korea), evaluated by the consumers of the same four countries, the Indian products had the poorest image in terms of quality, creativity, design and technological level. Nevertheless it remains clear that vendors located in less favourable foreign environments may be cheap and reliable suppliers, in so far as they are carefully evaluated and given a fair opportunity to perform. That is the cost of their *learning* should be shared with their customer, and afterwards both will benefit.

How does the image of products from certain countries change over time?

Another important issue in country-of-origin images is whether there are changes in these images over time and, if there are, at what rate they occur. The response to this question seems to be yes, and the rate seems to be fairly rapid (Schieb, 1977). This is particularly true for products originating from Japan and the new industrial countries of Asia, such as Korea and Taiwan (Jaffé and Nebenzahl, 1989). Dornoff *et al.* (1974) observed a change in American consumer perception of imports from Asian countries over a few years towards a more favourable attitude.

By replicating a 1967 study eight years later, Nagashima (1970, 1977) showed that Japanese businessmen's perceptions of their own products had become more favourable and that their image of the Japanese 'made in' label had significantly improved over the previous years. The Japanese stopped seeing their products modestly as simply 'cheap' and 'unreliable'. Kraft and Chung (1992) confirm the dramatic improvement of the image of Japan as a country-of-origin. According to Darling and Kraft (1977), the image that the Finnish consumers held of Japanese products was right in the middle of changing in 1977. At the beginning of the 1970s, Japanese products were seen as being of dubious quality; they were backed by rather restricted guarantees and poor after-sales service. At the end of the 1970s they were seen by Finnish consumers as having improved significantly as far as quality was concerned. 'Thus penetration into the Finnish market with an exceptional effort to win over the confidence of the consumer by extensive guarantees based on a local network of approved retailers, could prove to be a real success' (Darling and Kraft, 1977, p. 528).

There was also a very clear improvement in the acceptance of South Korean products in the United States in the space of just over two years. Khera (1986) has demonstrated this by comparing the results of a May 1982 study (Khera *et al.*, 1983) with those of a November 1984 replication (Khera *et al.*, 1985). Whereas in the first study only a third of consumers declared themselves satisfied with Korean products, in the second they numbered almost two-thirds (65.3 per cent). The perception of the general level of Korea's industrial development (specifically in comparison with Taiwan and Brazil) improved similarly.

Issues related to the measurement of country-of-origin images

Many studies (though not all) have used samples of students to represent the overall population of consumers–evaluators, who were interviewed on products of different origins. It has often been claimed that using student samples may lead to major limitations in the external validity of these studies. Students are not definitely representative of the whole range of consumers. Furthermore the measurement instruments, such as questionnaires, psychometric scales, and the chosen categories of products or mentioned brands create problems of cross-cultural equivalence (Bamossy and Papadopoulos, 1987; Parameswaran and Yaprak, 1987). Cross-cultural equivalence issues for measurement of country-of-origin effects are subject to the same solutions as detailed in Chapter 5.

Jaffé and Nebenzahl (1984) tested the validity and the accuracy of alternative questionnaire formats with the same respondents. They tested two formats of questionnaire (Q1 and Q2), which basically contained the same retrieved information but which were presented in two different ways: scales in Q1 were listed according to attribute and in Q2 according to country. The scores were significantly different which tends to suggest that images of country of origin are therefore not completely comparable across studies, depending on the way in which the questionnaires are presented. In a similar vein, Min Han *et al.* (1994) show that the survey mode, whether personal interview, telephone survey or self-administered questionnaire, influences the ratings of country of origin. Personal interviews may be susceptible to demand artefacts (the subject distorts his answer in the direction intended to fulfil the researcher's expectations), and self-administered questionnaire to haloing biases (the lack of involvement results in all responses being based on a common stereotype). Social desirability biases (the subject responds like the 'average man' would) may be more likely to occur when interviewing by telephone.

Combined effect of the image of the country of origin and evaluations as to the 'true' attributes of the product

Country of origin should not be considered as the only criterion consumers use when evaluating foreign products (Yaprak, 1987). It is often combined with other product attributes in the minds of the consumers. Some research has attempted to measure the relative impact of country-of-origin attribute, with respect to intrinsic attributes such as quality, or extrinsic attributes such as price. Accordingly, two studies dealt with the relative effect of price and perceived quality in interaction with the country of manufacture (Peterson and Jolibert, 1976; White and Cundiff, 1978), without being able in either of these two cases to find truly meaningful links. There was no significant influence of the country of manufacture on the perceived quality.

Thorelli *et al.* (1989), by studying the interaction between store image, level of guarantee and country of origin, concluded that the effect of the country of origin on the perceived quality and the general attitude of the consumer is significantly less when the product is sold in an exclusive store with effective guarantees. This seems to concur with Reierson's conclusions (1967) that the image of a product of a specific national origin can be improved (with respect to its previous image) by association with a prestigious distributor, in this case Neiman-Marcus. For the US market Morganosky and Lazarde (1987) have investigated the link between store image and the national origin of the products they offer (imported versus 'Made in the USA'). It appears that the quality rating of department stores and fashion boutiques was slightly enhanced by their association with American-made clothing, whereas it was negatively affected when their image was associated with that of foreign-made clothing. The quality image of discount stores was significantly improved when associated with American-made clothing, but not significantly hurt by association with foreign-made garments.

Erickson *et al.* (1984) and Johansson *et al.* (1985) began to introduce more complex consumer evaluation models, using the country of manufacture as an informative cue. They introduced other choice attributes and examined whether the true effects of the country-of-origin attribute were operating on attitudes or beliefs. Consumer beliefs are located at a much deeper level in consumer minds than attitudes, and are far more remote from actual buying behaviour. According to Erickson *et al.* (1984), the country-of-origin effect has an influence on the formation of beliefs, but not directly on the attitudes towards the product (cars, in this case). The country-of-origin cue contributed just as much as the 'true' attributes themselves (objective ones such as price or gas mileage) to the formation of beliefs. Beliefs in turn have an influence on attitudes.

How the country of manufacture behaves on a cognitive level: as a halo effect or as (summary) global evaluation effect

Johansson *et al.* (1985) hypothesize that the country-of-origin cue works as a 'halo effect' when it influences consumer beliefs and attitudes. Johansson (1989) suggests two different interpretations of the cognitive effect of the country of origin:

1. It would be used by consumers in order to simplify the decision-making process. Consumers use this choice attribute as a summary criterion, which provides them with a 'ready-made' global evaluation. It will ease their choice, particularly when time is limited.
2. Consumers use the country of origin as a salient choice attribute when they have feelings towards and knowledge of a particular country.

According to Johansson, increased familiarity with product category reinforces the use of the country of origin as a choice attribute, contrary to what had been previously claimed.

Min Han (1990) has tested the 'halo effect' which affects consumers' beliefs and, only indirectly, their evaluations against the 'summary effect', where the country-of-origin cue directly influences consumers under the form of a global evaluation. By testing these two different models on two products (television sets and cars), he has shown that the 'halo effect' is used more when consumers are unfamiliar with the product category, whereas the 'summary effect' is used once they have achieved familiarity.

Conclusion

Taken together, the results of these studies suggest some major guidelines which should be followed when trying to construct a 'national image' strategy for a country's products:

1. Consumers from developed countries have a general preference for their national products, but campaigns in favour of buying national goods do not reinforce this preference as such.
2. Consumers do not use the country of origin as an isolated choice attribute but within the overall purchasing context (product category, perceived risk, knowledge of the brand, knowledge of and beliefs about the manufacturing country, etc.). Furthermore, country of origin is used as an evaluation criterion in conjunction with actual attributes. Attempts to dissociate the image from the reality are therefore unlikely to be successful. There is no advantage to be gained from selling poor-quality products in combination with a good 'made in' label. Such choices could be very deceptive for consumers.
3. Images change fairly quickly over time. This is probably not the result of effective

'Buy national' advertising campaigns, because they had a poor impact on product image as such. Country-of-origin images change over time because products of a particular national origin are of better quality, the industrial expertise of local producers has improved and the guarantees offered to consumers are more extensive.

9.3   National, international and global brands

The majority of brands were originally conceived on a national level. Even among American brands, only a very limited number (Rosen *et al.*, 1989) have achieved international recognition. Most national brands are related to a specific linguistic context. Their evocative power is dependent on the language of the country and markets where they were originally launched. In Europe, easily 99 per cent of all brands are still national, if not purely local, in their appeal (Wilsher, 1992).

However, certain brands were launched right from the start for their capacity to convey meaning internationally. The oil refining and distribution brand name Elf was created at the time of the merger of the petroleum groups ERAP and SNPA. Another example is that of Toyota: this name was chosen at the beginning of the 1960s by the Japanese car manufacturer which previously had a completely different name. The name was unsuitable for foreign markets and the company deemed that in the future, with increasing export sales, it would be necessary to have a name suitable for international markets. Toyota, with its three syllables, which can be pronounced in any language, was the name finally selected.

National brand names are sometimes inappropriate when they are used directly as international brand names . . .

Often, companies that start export and international businesses use their existing brand names which have particular sounds, spelling and pronunciation. The brand name should not have an unfortunate meaning in a different linguistic/cultural context. However, the reflex of questioning the translinguistic ability of a brand name is a long way from being instinctive. There is no shortage of examples: the German hair spray Caby-Net launched on the French market (*cabinet* is a toilet in French); the Japanese guns Miroku, whose name has several meanings including 'look at your arse' in French, although ultimately the name was not changed. The examples of certain American cars in South American markets are also famous. The Chevrolet (Chevy) Nova (the intended meaning was 'new') translates into Spanish as 'does not work', which gave a poor image of the car's reliability. The American Motors Matador meant 'killer' in Spanish, in as far as it relates to the man who kills the bull in traditional Spanish *corridas*. The type of research that must be carried out is straightforward: it is necessary to interview a group of consumers from the target country about the perceptual effects of the intended names.

Often the brand name of products is the name of the company which manufactures them. This is a result of the history of the company. Consequently, there is no question as to whether this brand name is a good one in the minds of consumers. Since the brand name is historically related to the founders of the company, symbolically it would be difficult to change it. Such companies as Procter & Gamble, a name which is difficult to pronounce in many languages, have followed a twofold brand strategy:

1. Product brand names, such as Ivory, Camay, Pampers, Vizir and Tide, have been promoted almost independently from the Procter & Gamble company name (look at the respective sizes of the names on the packaging).
2. The Procter & Gamble name has been colloquially simplified so that it can be more easily memorized and verbalized, either to simply Procter or to P & G.

An example of lack of adaptation is offered by the leading French company for iron and steel and heavy mechanical equipment during the 1970s and 1980s, Creusot-Loire. It branded and sold its products under the company's name in many countries in the world, including the United States. Unfortunately this name was difficult to pronounce for American customers:

1. The hard 'CR' sound hardly exists in English.
2. 'EU' is a typically French diphthong, unpronounceable for Americans.
3. 'S' must be pronounced 'Z' because it is located between two vowels (French rule!).
4. 'O' is a very open sound.
5. 'T' is, here, a mute consonant and must therefore be ignored in pronunciation.
6. 'OI': once again a typically French diphthong (unknown in English).
7. 'R' is a hard 'r', almost unused in English.
8. 'E' is, at the end of the word, a mute vowel, and therefore must be ignored in pronunciation.

Naturally such a brand name is difficult to memorize for most customers in many countries. Moreover, such difficult brand names can be a serious obstacle to clear communication between buyer and seller; they may create confusion when discussing business on the phone. It is therefore necessary to be prepared to carry out the necessary modification.

Examples of changes of inappropriate brand names are suggested by Giordan (1988, p. 198): Kellogg's renamed its *Frosted Flakes* to *Sucrilhos* for Brazil, as well as its *Cocoa Krispies* to *Crokinhos*; similarly Kellogg's had to change its *Bran Buds* brand name in Sweden, so that Swedish people did not read that they were to be served 'grilled farmer' in their breakfast bowls.

Linguistic aspects of the brands' connotations

Table 9.2 shows various linguistic devices which can be used in creating brand names. Whether by accident or design, advertisers and marketers strive to give some punch and evocative capacity to their brand names. Of course this is done, as much as possible, in line with the symbolic connotations that they intend to communicate to product attributes.

There are four main categories of linguistic devices: phonetic devices (sound,

Table 9.2 *Linguistic characteristics, definitions and/or examples.*

Characteristics	Definitions and/or examples
I Phonetic devices	
1. Alliteration	Consonant repetition (**Co**ca-**C**ola, **Co**coon)
2. Assonance	Vowel repetition (K**a**l K**a**n, V**i**z**i**r, **O**m**o**)
3. Consonance	Consonant repetition with intervening vowel changes (**W**eigh**t** **Wa**tchers, Tic Tac)
4. Masculine rhyme	Rhyme with end of syllable stress (Max Pax)
5. Feminine rhyme	Unaccented syllable followed by accented syllable (**Amer**ican **Air**lines)
6. Weak/imperfect/slant rhyme	Vowels differ or consonants similar, not identical (Bl**ack** & D**eck**er)
7. Onomatopoeia	Use of syllable phonetics to resemble the object itself (Wisk, Cif, Wizzard)
8. Clipping	Product names attenuated (*Chevy* for a Chevrolet, *Deuche* for a Citroen Deux Chevaux, *Rabbit* for a Volkswagen)
9. Blending	Morphemic combination, usually with elision (Aspergum, Duracell)
10. Initial plosives[a]	/b/, /c-hard/, /d/, /g-hard/, /k/, /q/, /t/, (Bic, Dash, Pliz, Pim's)
II Orthographic devices	
1. Unusual or incorrect spellings	Kool-Aid, Decap'Four
2. Abbreviations	7-Up for Seven-Up
3. Acronyms	Amoco, Amro, DB, Cofinoga, Lu, BSN
III Morphological devices	
1. Affixation	Jell-O, Tipp-Ex
2. Compounding	Janitor-in-a-Drum, Vache-qui-rit
IV Semantic devices	
1. Metaphor	Representing something as if it were something else (Arrid); simile was included with metaphor when a name described a likeness and not an equality (Aqua-Fresh, Longeurs et Pointes, Head and Shoulders, Tendres Promesses)
2. Metonymy	Application of one object or quality for another (Midas, Ajax, Uncle Ben's, Bounty)
3. Synecdoche	Substitution of a part for the whole (Red Lobster)
4. Personification/pathetic fallacy	Humanizing the nonhuman or ascription of human emotions to the inanimate (Betty Crocker, Clio, Kinder)
5. Oxymoron	Conjunction of opposite (Easy-Off, Crème de peinture)
6. Paranomasia	Pun and word plays (Hawaiian Punch, Raid – insecticide, Fédor – orange juice)
7. Semantic appositeness	Fit of name with object (Bufferin, Nutella)

Source: adapted from Vandenbergh *et al.*, 1987. Reproduced with the kind permission of the publisher.
[a] An initial is said to be plosive if, to produce this sound, one needs first to stop the flow of air completely, then audibly release the air previously compressed.

perceived by the ears), orthographic devices (funny writing, perceived by the eyes), morphological devices (adding morphemes to brand name root) and semantic devices (the figure produces meaning, perceived through culture-based interpretations).

Linguistic devices in Table 9.2 help reflection on the following:

1. That which constitutes the pure linguistic capacity of a brand, independently of the established goodwill (brand recognition may be high for linguistically unadapted but long-standing brand names).
2. Are these advantages transposable into other linguistic contexts? The alliteration of Coca-Cola is, but the composition of the words Janitor-in-a-Drum or even the juxtaposition of opposites (Easy-Off) are not. This is because Coca-Cola does not require a basic comprehension of the words that make up the brand name. Required understanding of complex linguistic figures makes brand names difficult to translate and, more generally, to transpose. As a rule, the linguistic devices in categories I and II are more 'translinguistic'. A good number of the devices in category IV are not at all, especially 1, 4, 5, 6 and 7.

It is not only the purely linguistic content of a brand name that has an influence on its verbal, auditive and intellectual meaning. The brand name is usually associated with a copyright design: the graphic composition of the logo conveys meaning as much as the letters of the brand name. Accordingly Cabat (1989, p. 344) emphasizes that the IBM trademark is inseparable from its graphics in its evocative ability to communicate with the consumer:

> The letters of the IBM logo are actually obtained by the superimposition of characters known as 'Mecanes' and of a 'blind' (alternate slats of coloured bands). The blind is in this case the informative image of the letters IBM, their morphological determinant. ... It thereby becomes the sign of computer language, binary-based. The 'Mecanes' are typesetting characters whose square serif evokes industrial production and rooting in the mechanical world.

The imagery of the IBM brand-logo is translinguistic, and therefore offers a truly international ability to convey meaning. The link between brand and drawing is an intimate one. How, for instance, is the Coca-Cola brand name stored in consumers' minds? As eight letters, as the traditional design of the Coca-Cola words, or as a combination of both? Trademark legislation around the world varies a great deal according to the coverage: in France trademarks can only be composed of alphabetic letters and their design must be separately registered under the design and pattern laws if they are to be effectively protected; in the United States a trademark may be bereft of any linguistic content and can be registered solely under the trademark laws; there is no systematic need, in the United States and many other countries, for the additional registration of a trademark's design.

Transposition of a national brand name to an international level

As advocated by Onkvisit and Shaw (1989), standardized international branding offers more market efficiency, by reducing advertising and inventory costs and providing convenient identification for people travelling internationally. However, the diversity of national regulations and the rarity of brands with similar spellings in some national markets sometimes make it difficult to register a standardized brand across a large number of countries.

Czinkota and Ronkainen (1990) have distinguished different possibilities for the transposition of a brand name originally created for a specific national context:

1. *Translation*, pure and simple.
2. *Transliteration* attempts to reconstitute in the target language the connotative meaning that exists in the source language (i.e. the language of the country where the brand originates). In this way the American hair care product *Silkience* (Gillette) is sold under the same brand name in Germany, under the brand name *Soyance* in France and under the brand name *Sientel* in Italy.
3. *Transparency*: a brand like Sony, for example, is suitable everywhere without translation problems occurring. The name Sony arose from a real 'shooting down' of the company name by the brand name of its products (Yoshimori, 1989). The original name of the firm (Tokyo Tsuhin Kogyo – Tokyo Industrial Telecommunication Company) was changed to Sony as soon as its products' brand name proved to be successful.

Functions of the brand according to national contexts

Lambin (1989) distinguishes the following functions of the trade name for the consumer:

1. *Identity function*: the brand name guides consumers when making their choice.
2. *Practicality*: the brand name works as a summary of information; it permits the retention of information about the characteristics of the products by the association of a trade name with them.
3. *Guarantee*: as the 'signature of the manufacturer'.
4. *Personalization*: the brand name allows consumers to express their individuality and originality through their purchases.
5. *Entertainment function*: the brand allows the exercise of free individual choice, and therefore permits consumers to satisfy their needs for freshness, arousal, surprise, etc.

For the producer, the brand fulfils two essential functions: the positioning within the competitive scene and the *capitalization* of image and advertising expenditure over the long term.

These functions are very diversely valued across different countries, to the extent that some functions of the brand can be almost non-existent in certain national contexts. Accordingly, Contensou (1989) notes that in France there is a certain social mistrust of brands, especially by public authorities: they supposedly increase prices, constituting entry barriers against possible competitors and thereby limiting competition. Furthermore, being set up on the basis of large cumulated advertising expenditure, it is claimed that they increase the price of the product to the detriment of the consumer.

Contensou shows that in fact these fears are groundless and further emphasizes that (1989, p. 246) 'inflationary tendencies have no connection to brand development and the multiplication of products sold under brand names'. Kapferer (1989), taking the same defensive attitude towards brand names, has shown that they support the actual intentions of the manufacturers, their achievements in favour of consumers and that without effective attempts to foster product quality, brand images cannot be sustained. In contrast to France, Japan seems to be a country where the brand is very highly valued. Yoshimori (1989, pp. 277–8) explains this:

> In feudal Japan, the brand was not distinct from the name of the ancestral house itself. This name had great importance, to the extent that everything was done to protect its good image, and above all to perpetuate it. Anyone who tarnished that reputation even through mere carelessness was obliged to rectify the damage through dying ... [Yoshimori then gives examples of Japanese executives who have recently committed suicide because they believed that through their actions or negligence they had tarnished the reputation of their company] ... a trading company, or any such firm, was not merely an economic entity; it also constituted a religious community which transcended the physical life of the family that controlled it. Ancestors occupied an almost divine place: it was therefore believed that the preservation and advancement of *kamei*, the name of the ancestral house, was an almost religious obligation since it (*kamei*) was the concrete translation of the presence of ancestors.

The brand in Japan is a real figurehead of competitive struggle. Abbeglen and Stalk (1986) show how, during the 1950s, the Honda brand name destroyed the Tohatsu brand (which today is completely unknown). They also describe in great deal the episodes of the Homeric quarrel between Honda and Yamaha at the start of the 1980s, which ended with a victory for Honda.

In the United States, as in Japan, brands are central to competition. Brand marketing occupies a stable position in the strategies of US companies, but also one which is constantly changing, as are market shares. The vigour of the brand can only be built on 'tidal waves' of sales promotion and advertising as well as on consistent endeavours towards improvement of product quality. Dupuy and Thoenig (1989) compared brand status in the United States, France and Japan. They noted that brands in France have a much weaker status compared to the strong status in Japan and the even stronger status in the United States.

By 'weak status' they mean that brands are the stakes of an unstable and conflicting appropriation process by economic agents. Large-scale retailers in France (hypermarket) have created their own distributors' brands over the last twenty years (*produits libres*). Distributors' brands do not need any product-related advertising expenditure and tend to compete with manufacturers' brands. Therefore brand competition between distributors and manufacturers constitutes a major stake at the retail level.

Differences in national distribution systems explain to a large extent the degree of brand-related competition. In Japan, the *Keiretsu* distribution (see section 11.1) enables the producer to control the distribution channel and therefore to direct the brand name principally towards the relationship with the consumer. In France, where large-scale distribution is involved in conflicts with producers, the channels develop their own brands. This leads to an inflation of distributors' brands which must therefore struggle to become established.

What is an international brand?

International brands share some common characteristics:

1. Long-term orientation: the main objective of the brand is gradually to establish brand goodwill through consumer brand awareness and recognition. When products share very similar attributes and performance, a well-known brand may have the edge by virtue of its reputation and the consumer loyalty it has created. Accordingly, Procter & Gamble has retained brands for more than a century: Ivory soap, for example, is more than 100 years old. Camay soap is claimed to be nearly 70 years old (the brand name that is, not the formula of the product which has been regularly updated).
2. International brands are therefore usually names whose public recognition has been based on *considerable cumulative advertising expenditure*. They are often supported by the history of prestigious companies (for cars, Mercedes, Jaguar, Ferrari, Cadillac, etc.). This brand goodwill was not 'built in a day'. These world-famous brands are obviously exceptions since, cognitively, there can only be a limited number of brands known by consumers in several countries throughout the world simultaneously (a few dozen, perhaps one or two hundred at most).
3. Many of these international brands (Shalofsky, 1987) have a *basic credibility which is based on a national image*. Accordingly, Coca-Cola is a typical American drink; Marlboro cigarettes is in fact an American brand because of the Marlboro cowboy. Chanel No. 5 is based on the image of French *luxe* and *haute couture*, conveyed by the character of Gabrielle Chanel (Coco). Buitoni is understood as Italian pasta and Johnny Walker is a synonym for whisky from Scotland. Furthermore, as Clark (1987) argues, in each country, consumers 'repaint' the supposed international brand image with their own local images.

Brands and national images: A game of complex meanings

It is therefore advisable to be cautious before saying that a brand is universal. Even Coca-Cola is not known by this name in China since the original name would have a negative connotation. Low-calorie sugar-free Coke is called Diet Coke in the United States as well as in many other countries, but in some countries it is called Coca Light because the word *diète* conjures up the image of a strict diet of bread and water. Table 9.1 shows for various brands the level of national images on which they rely, in combination with the product's origin and the manufacturer's name (also a brand). A name like Brother, for instance, offers a fairly good combination of interpretive meanings:

1. There is no need to evoke any national image which would be related to the national image of the generic product. Brother manufactures typewriters, which are items with no 'ethnic' relation to a specific country.

2. The Brother name diffuses an English/international image which partially hides the Japanese origin of the manufacturer. This may help when targeting nationalistic anti-Japanese consumers.
3. The concept of brotherhood is a good one to support the image of reliability, faithfulness and loyalty of an object with which people may work closely (typing on the keyboard).

Global brands: a blurred concept

Although some people try to defend the concept (Peebles, 1989), global brands are a blurred concept and probably even a deceptive one. As emphasized in Chapter 6, global brands could only be portfolios of basically localized marketing assets (consumer franchise and goodwill based on images which are in fact heterogeneous). Therefore, global brands may be seen as the simple collection of local brands, federated under a *lexically equivalent single name*. It is not even certain that this name, when pronounced, produces equivalent sounds and is heard in the same way. The way in which it is said and heard can be critical for television advertising, for example.

The management of global brands is a complex one. In his overview of the topic, Peebles (1989, p. 76) notes the idea of Marcio Moreira, New Products Director for McCann Erickson Worldwide, according to whom an advertiser should not pursue a global strategy to save money. The global brand, like the global campaign, requires a large amount of creative time and investment. A brand is a *sensitive asset of symbols*, suggested and maintained by diversified marketing communications: sponsoring, advertising, communication, public relations, communication through the product itself or even the style of outlets. This mix of marketing communications must be carefully managed, so that the public never feels betrayed in those beliefs that have been invested in the brand.

Alain Etchegoyen (1990, p. 55, my emphasis) describes in the following way the brand image of Louis Vuitton:

> There is no mythology without gods or demi-gods. That is why one must not expect gods to collapse into the melting pot of the market. Some products have to keep at a distance so that other products appear to come from *somewhere else. The brand can only remain influential at the expense of maintaining a sacred fire.* The imaginary Eden of carefully tended (brand) images will not withstand the boorish hell of bar codes (products).

Furthermore, the complexity of trademark law must be considered on an international level. Although there are several international conventions, copyright and trademark regulations are still essentially based on national decrees. The 'Paris Union', an agreement which has been revised several times (the last in 1967 in Stockholm), provides that after a preliminary registration within a country of the Union, the beneficiaries have six months available for full registration. During this period they have priority (de Chantérac, 1989). But the full registrations are usually done by country, in accordance with locally prevailing regulations.

The World Industrial Property Organization (WIPO), located in Geneva, centralizes the registration formalities for the more than twenty countries that have signed the Madrid Agreement. This does not constitute neglect of the principle of registration, but a simplification of the procedure across a limited number of countries. As for the EC draft convention on European, community-wide trademarks, this draft directive has been gathering moss since 1964. It was finally adopted in 1989 and has been implemented since 1993, thus giving the member-states of the EU a common framework for commercial trademarks (Maronick, 1988). The directive, aiming at harmonizing existing national legislation on trademarks, has been completed by the regulation on the European Trademark which has been adopted by the Council of the European Union on 20 December 1993; implementation has started on 15 March 1994. It allows to register a trademark with a unique procedure and guarantees the rights over the whole territory of the Union. The European office for trademarks is located in Alicante (Spain). The single application procedure will make it easier to register the community trademark but not reduce the costs of filing the trademark or searching for existing similar trademarks in the various EU countries.

In short, the costs and the legal complexity of managing a global brand remain extremely high. When starting from scratch, the creation of an international brand is an undertaking that should be considered as a long-term target. In this respect Yoshimori (1989, p. 279) quotes the reply of Sony's chairman, Akio Morita, in 1955 to an American client who was requesting Sony to subcontract. Morita refused to manufacture 100,000 transistor radios in original equipment manufacturing and, allegedly, said:

> Fifty years ago your brand name was probably as unknown as ours is today ... Today I decide the first stage for the next fifty years of my company. In fifty years I can promise that our name [Sony] will be just as famous as your company's is today.

Questions

1. Discuss the international transferability of the following assemblages (product, company, country of manufacture, brand name):

Generic product	Company name	Brand name	Made in
Pizza	*Dr Oetker*	*Pizza Rustica*	Germany
Computer chip	*Intel*	*Pentium*	United States
Drilling tool	*Bosch*	*Fuchsschwanz*	Spain
Car	*Daewoo*	*Daewoo/Nexia*	South Korea
Tomato sauce	*Mars*	*Dolmio*	The Netherlands
Insecticide	*Bayer*	*Baygon*	Germany

2. A very large German food company, Dr Oetker, still sells its products in France under the name *Ancel* (the brand name of a French company taken over many years ago). Why?
3. Discuss to what extent 'Buy national' advertising campaigns are efficient. What can they achieve? What can they not?

4. Discuss the relationship between a country's image (through its people, its history, its political and social situation, etc.) and the image of products known to be made in this country.
5. Discuss the possible international extension of the following company and/or brand names:

  ◆ *Müller* (German yoghurts)
  ◆ *Barilla* (Italian pastas and cookies)
  ◆ *Procter & Gamble*
  ◆ *Teysseire* (French syrups)
  ◆ *Kuoni* (a Swiss tour operator)
  ◆ *Schimmelpenninck* (Dutch cigars and cigarillos)
  ◆ *Ishikawajima Harima Heavy Industries* (a Japanese industrial equipment company)
  ◆ *Roi des Montagnes* (French dried mushrooms)
  ◆ *Hewlett-Packard*
  ◆ *Douwe-Egberts* (a large Dutch food and tobacco company)
  ◆ *Club Méditerrannée* (a French tour operator)

APPENDIX 9

——— ◆◆◆ ———

Teaching materials

A9.1   Case: Soshi Sumsin Ltd

Sammy Soshi's first assignment for his new job with Soshi Sumshin Ltd. was to recommend a new name for the firm's line of electronic products. Sammy had completed his MBA at Emory University in May 1990 and had returned to Seoul, Korea, to work in his father's firm. Soshi Sumsin manufactured a line of electronic products, which included VCRs, stereos, and televisions. The senior Mr Soshi got involved in electronics manufacturing when he agreed in 1980 to manufacture television components for an American manufacturer. Eventually, he was producing a full line of television sets, as well as VCRs and stereo equipment for three American firms. In addition, since 1987, he had been marketing his own line of products in the Korean market under the Sumsin brand name.

Mr Soshi felt that his firm was now ready, both in terms of manufacturing know-how and capital, to enter international markets under his own brand name. The American market was chosen as the first target because of its size and buying power, and an introduction date of April 1991 had been tentatively set. Having little familiarity with the American market, Mr Soshi was relying heavily on his son, Sammy, to help with marketing decisions.

The first problem to which Sammy addressed himself was the selection of a brand name for the line. His father had planned to use the Sumsin name in the American market. Sammy pointed out that a failure to give careful consideration to the effect of a brand name in a different culture could cause major marketing difficulties later. He cited the experience of Tatung as a case in point. Tatung was a Taiwanese maker of televisions, fans, and computer terminals. When the company entered the American market it did not even consider changing its brand name. The Tatung company had favourable connotation in Chinese and was known in the company's oriental markets. However, in the United States, the name was not only meaningless, but it was difficult to know how to pronounce.

Because of these difficulties, Tatung's American advertising agency finally decided to emphasize the strangeness of the name, and it launched a campaign based on a play on words which might help customers to pronounce Tatung. Each ad carried the query, 'Cat Got Your Tatung?' Sammy believed that a lot of effort that should have been placed on the product itself had been expended to overcome a bad trade name.

Sammy cited a second example of problems resulting from a poorly chosen brand name. Another Taiwanese company, Kunnan Lo, introduced its own brand of tennis rackets in the American market in 1982. Recognizing that their own name would present problems in the American market, they decided to select an American name. Ultimately, they decided on the name Kennedy; it was quite similar to their company name, and it was certainly familiar in the United States. However, after initial promotional efforts, it quickly became apparent that Kennedy was not a neutral name. Many tennis players were Republicans, and for them the Kennedy name had negative connotations. As a result, the name was changed to Kennex, a neutral, artificial word that was still similar to the company name. However, Kennex also quickly proved to be unsatisfactory, because of some confusion with the name Kleenex. To eliminate this confusion, the name was finally changed to Pro-Kennex, which provided both a tennis tie-in and retention of a root similar to Kunnan Lo. The waste of resources in the series of name changes would have been better avoided.

Determined to avoid the mistakes of these other companies entering the American market, Sammy Soshi carefully evaluated the alternatives available to his company. The first was his father's preference – to use a company family name. However, Sumsin was somewhat difficult for English-speaking people to pronounce and seemed meaningless and foreign. Soshi was equally unfamiliar and meaningless, but he was also afraid that Americans would confuse it with the Japanese raw fish, sushi.

A second alternative was to acquire ownership of an existing American brand name, preferably one with market recognition. After considerable research, he chose the name Monarch. The Monarch company had started manufacturing radios in Chicago in 1932 and Monarch radios had been nationally known in the 1940s. The company was badly hurt by television in the 1950s, which reduced the size of the radio market appreciably. The company was finally wiped out by the invasion of inexpensive transistor radios from Asia in the 1960s. The company filed for bankruptcy in 1972. Sammy found that he could buy the rights to the Monarch name for $50,000. The name was tied in with electronics products in the public's mind, but he wondered how many people still remembered or recognized the Monarch name. He also wondered whether this recognition might be more negative than positive because of the company's failure in the market.

A third alternative would be to select a new name and build market recognition through promotion. Such a name would need to be politically and socially neutral in the American market and ultimately in other foreign markets. It should be easy to pronounce and remember and have neutral meaning or favourable meaning to the public. The possibilities might be considered.

The first was Proteus, the name of an ancient Greek sea god. This name would be easy to pronounce in most European languages, but was almost too neutral to help sell the product. The other alternative was Blue Streak, again, an easy name in English, but not necessarily in other European languages. Sammy felt that the favourable connotation of speed and progress might provide a boost for the products to which it was applied.

(Source: adapted from Cundiff and Hilger, 1988, pp. 440–2. Reproduced with permission.)

Questions

1. Evaluate the alternative names being considered by Sammy Soshi. Which name would you recommend?
2. Whatever new name is chosen, should Soshi Sumsin adopt the same name in the Korean market?
3. What are the advantages of selecting different brand names, as appropriate, in each foreign market?
4. Enumerate the characteristics that should be possessed by a good international brand name.

A9.2   Case: Derivados de Leche SA

Derivados de Leche SA, founded in 1968, was the first firm to market yoghurt in Mexico. It distributed yoghurt under the brand name Delsa only in Mexico City, primarily in a limited number of upper-income areas. The company was family owned, and the capital was all local. For the first five years, Delsa was sold in food stores, particularly in the newly developing supermarkets, without any advertising or other promotion. Yoghurt was a new, unfamiliar food product in the Mexican market, but Delsa depended primarily on word of mouth to provide product recognition.

During the next four years, the structure of the yoghurt market changed dramatically with the entrance of three large multinational firms. In 1973, a number of laws regulating foreign investment in Mexico were modified under a single new 'regulation of foreign investment' law. According to this law foreign investors were welcome in Mexico on a joint labour basis so long as the foreign ownership share did not exceed 49 per cent. Labor-intensive industries that helped to decentralize population were particularly welcome. All three of the multinationals entering the yoghurt market operated on this joint venture basis.

The first new brand, Chambourcy, was introduced by a joint venture subsidiary of Nestlé which had operated in Mexico since 1935. This company, Industrias Alimentacias Club SA, was a major Mexican food producer with 7,000 employees. Chambourcy was launched with a strong promotional campaign and wide distribution. The following year, in 1974, a subsidiary of the French food firm, BSN-Gervais, launched their Danone yoghurt in the Mexican market. Danone was also heavily supported with promotion. Finally, in 1976, a third multinational entered the market. Productos de Leche SA, was 51 per cent owned by Mexican capital and 49 per cent by the Borden Company of the United States; it entered the Mexican market with two brands of yoghurt, Darel and Bonafina.

By 1982, the management of Derivados de Leche SA was becoming concerned about its future position on the yoghurt market. All three of the multinational competitors were aggressive marketers and promoters and were strong financially. Although the foreign ownership was a minority (49 per cent), management was dominated in each case by the minority ownership, so that management was competent and professional. In the short term, Delsa benefited from the primary demand creation activities of the multinationals. In 1979, Delsa sales almost doubled to 800 tons, and by 1982, it was 1,900 tons. But Delsa's market share had dropped from over 95 per cent in 1973 (there were some other very small Mexican-owned competitors) to only 21 per cent in 1982.

The three multinationals divided 77.5 per cent of the market among them. If the trend continued, it was feared that Delsa's share of the market might drop so low that it would provide very little product recognition. And it was possible that ultimately sales volume would stabilize and perhaps even decline.

By 1983, Delsa management was faced with the grim reality of competition from financially strong and aggressive, professionally managed multinationals. Delsa managers felt that pricing could not be blamed for this loss in market share; in 1982, the sales price of Delsa was slightly below that of its competitors. A major handicap for Delsa was its failure to promote recognition of its brand name. Although Delsa had been pulled along in the market by the initial marketing efforts which were designed to create a primary demand for yoghurt, marketing efforts of the competitors were now focused almost entirely on selective brand-name promotion. Delsa management had concentrated its efforts on getting the product in retail outlets and maintaining good relationships with dealers; no effort had been made to create consumer recognition and franchise through advertising and other promotion. Management was made up of the family members who owned the company; they brought little professional training to the job.

Owner-managers of small and medium-sized firms in Mexico tended to run their businesses for quick, short-term profit rather than long-term development. New capital investment was needed to enlarge production capacity, and serious consideration needed to be given to investing in a promotional campaign to build and maintain Delsa brand recognition.

Delsa was considering applying for a government-subsidized loan to double its production capacity from 2,000 tons per year to 4,000 tons. These loans were available only to 100 per cent Mexican-owned manufacturers, but were limited to financing of manufacturing facilities. Delsa's marketing manager wanted to emphasize the local Mexican ownership of Delsa and to increase the firm's advertising budget from $20,000 to about $100,000. He also wanted to redesign the package so as to include some statement that indicated the brand was of pure Mexican origin. Delsa's owners wanted to put pressure on the Mexican government to limit the food processing industry to 100 per cent Mexican-owned firms. It was not known what the possibilities were to get such legislation passed.

(Source: adapted from Cundiff and Hilger, 1988, pp. 335–6. Reproduced with permission.)

Questions

1. What are Delsa's strengths and weaknesses in competing with multinationals?
2. What is the impact of 'country of origin' on demand for yoghurt?
3. What recommendations can you make to strengthen Delsa's market position?

References

Abegglen, James C. and George Stalk Jr (1986), 'The Japanese corporation as competitor', *California Management Review*, vol. XXVIII, no. 3, pp. 9–27.

Ahmed, Sadrudin A., Alain d'Astous and Mostafa El Adraoui (1994), 'Country-of-origin effects on purchasing managers' product perceptions,' *Industrial Marketing Management*, vol. 23, no. 4, pp. 323–32.

Anderson, W. T. and William H. Cunningham (1972), 'Gauging foreign product promotion', *Journal of Advertising Research*, vol. 12, no. 1, pp. 29–34.

Bamossy, G. J. and N. G. Papadopoulos (1987), 'An assessment of reliability for product evaluations scales used in country-of-origin research', in Kenneth D. Bahn and M. Joseph Sirgy (eds), *World Marketing Congress*, Academy of Marketing Science: Blacksburg, VA.

Bannister, J. P. and J. A. Saunders (1978), 'UK consumers' attitudes toward imports: the measurement of national stereotype image', *European Journal of Marketing*, vol. 12, no. 8, pp. 562–70.

Baumgartner, Gary and Alain Jolibert (1977), 'The perception of foreign products in France', *Advances in Consumer Research*, vol. 16, pp. 103–5.

Bilkey, Warren J. and Erik Nes (1982), 'Country-of-origin effects on product evaluations', *Journal of International Business Studies*, Spring/Summer, pp. 89–99.

Bon, Jérôme, and Alain Ollivier (1979), 'L'Influence de l'origine d'un produit sur son image à l'étranger', *Revue Française du Marketing*, 1979/2, Cahier 77, pp. 101–14.

Cabat, Odilon, (1989), 'Archéologie de la marque moderne', in Jean-Noel Kapferer and Jean-Claude Thoenig, (eds), *La Marque*, MacGraw-Hill: Paris, pp. 307–53.

Cattin, Philippe, Alain Jolibert and Colleen Lohnes (1982), 'A cross-cultural study of "made-in" concepts', *Journal of International Business Studies*, Winter, pp. 131–41.

Clark, Harold F. Jr (1987), 'Consumer and corporate values: Yet another view on global marketing', *International Journal of Advertising*, vol. 6, pp. 29–42.

Contensou, François (1989), 'La Marque, l'efficience économique et la formation des prix', in Jean-Noel Kapferer and Jean-Claude Thoenig (eds), *La Marque*, MacGraw-Hill: Paris, pp. 231–73.

Crawford, John C. (1985), 'Attitudes toward Latin American products', in Erdener Kaynak (ed.), *Global Perspectives in Marketing*, Praeger: New York, pp. 149–54.

Crawford John C. and C. W. Lamb Jr (1981), 'Source preferences for imported products', *Journal of Purchasing and Materials Management*, Winter, pp. 28–33.

Cundiff, Edward W. and Marye Tharp Hilger (1988), *Marketing in the International Environment*, 2nd edn, Prentice Hall: Englewood Cliffs, NJ.

Czinkota, Michael R. and Illka A. Ronkainen (1990), *International Marketing*, 2nd edn, Dryden Press: Hinsdale, IL.

Darling, John B. and F. Kraft (1977), 'A competitive profile of products and associated marketing practices of selected European and non-European countries', *European Journal of Marketing*, vol 11, no. 7, pp. 519–37.

De Chantérac, Véronique (1989), 'La Marque à travers le droit', in Jean-Noel Kapferer and Jean-Claude Thoenig, (eds), *La Marque*, MacGraw-Hill: Paris, pp. 45–90.

Dornoff, Ronald J., Clint B. Tankersley and Gregory P. White (1974), 'Consumers' perceptions of imports', *Akron Business and Economic Review*, vol. 5 (Summer), pp. 26–9.

Dupuy, François and Jean-Claude Thoenig (1989), 'La Marque et l'échange', in Jean-Noel Kapferer and Jean-Claude Thoenig, (eds), *La Marque*, MacGraw-Hill: Paris, pp. 159–89.

Erickson, Gary M., Johny K. Johansson and Paul Chao (1984), 'Images variables in multi-attribute product evaluations: Country of origin effects', *Journal of Consumer Research*, vol. 11, (September), pp. 694–9.

Eroglu, S. A., and K. A. Machleit (1989), 'Effects of individual and product specific variables on utilizing country of origin as a product quality cue', *International Marketing Review*, vol. 6, no. 6, pp. 27–41.

Etchegoyen, Alain (1990), *Les Entreprises ont-elles une âme?* Editions François Bourin: Paris.

Ettenson, R., J. Wagner and G. Gaeth (1988), 'Evaluating the effect of country-of-origin and the 'Made in the USA' campaign: A conjoint approach', *Journal of Retailing*, vol. 64, no. 1, pp. 85–100.

Etzel, Michael J. and Bruce J. Walker (1974), 'Advertising strategy for foreign products', *Journal of Advertising Research*, vol. 14 (June), pp. 41–4.

Gaedeke, Ralph (1973), 'Consumer attitudes towards products 'made in' developing countries', *Journal of Retailing*, vol. 49 (Summer), pp. 13–24.

Giordan, Alain Eric (1988), *Exporter plus 2*, Economica: Paris.

Gopalakrishna, P., B. L. Garland and J. C. Crawford (1989), 'Consumer satisfaction with foreign and domestic products: A cross-cultural comparison', Proceedings of the Annual Conference of the American Marketing Association.

Graby, Françoise (1980a), 'Consumérisme et produits étrangers' *Coopération-Distribution-Consommation*, no. 5, pp. 17–23.

Graby, Françoise (1980b), 'Le consommateur français et les produits étrangers' *Coopération-Distribution-Consommation*, no. 5, pp. 31–40.

Graby, Françoise (1982), 'Les consommateurs et les produits étrangers: application au marché français', proceedings of the 7th seminar on research in marketing, IAE: Aix en Provence, Lalonde des Maures.

Hampton, Gerald M. (1977), 'Perceived risk in buying products made abroad by American firms', *Baylor Business Studies*, October, pp. 53–64.

Harris, Richard Jackson, Bettina Garner-Earl, Sara J. Sprick and Collette Carroll (1994), 'Effects of foreign product names and country-of-origin attributions on advertisement evaluations', *Psychology and Marketing*, vol. 11, no. 2 (March/April), pp. 129–44.

Heslop, L., N. Papadopoulos, G. Avlonitis, G. Bamossy, J. Beracs, F. Bliemel, F. Graby, G. Hampton and P. Malliaris (1987), in Leeflang and Rice (eds), 'A cross-national study of consumer views about domestic versus imported products', proceedings, European Marketing Academy Conference, Toronto.

Jaffé, Eugene D. and Israel D. Nebenzahl (1984), 'Alternative questionnaire formats for country image studies', *Journal of Marketing Research*, vol. 21, pp. 463–71.

Jaffé, Eugene D. and Israel D. Nebenzahl (1989), 'Global promotion of country image: the case of the 1988 Korean Olympic Games', in Reijo Luostarinen (ed.), *Dynamics of International Business*, vol. 1, proceedings of the XVth Annual Conference of the European International Business Asssociation, Helsinki, Finland, pp. 358–85.

Johansson, Johny K. (1989), 'Determinants and effects of the use of 'made in' labels', *International Marketing Review*, vol. 6, no. 1, pp. 47–58.

Johansson, Johny K. and Israel D. Nebenzahl (1986), 'Multinational production: Effect on brand value', *Journal of International Business Studies*, vol. 17, no. 3, pp. 101–26.

Johansson, Johny K. and Israel D. Nebenzahl (1987), 'Country-of-origin, social norms and behavioral intentions', in S. Tamer Cavusgil (ed.), *Advances in International Marketing*, vol 2, JAI Press: Greenwich, CT, pp. 65–79.

Johansson, Johny K. and Hans B. Thorelli (1985), 'International product positioning', *Journal of International Business Studies*, vol. 16 (Fall), pp. 57–75.

Johansson, Johny K., Susan P. Douglas and Ikujiro Nonaka (1985), 'Assessing the impact of country of origin on product evaluations: A new methodological perspective', *Journal of Marketing Research*, vol. XXII (November), pp. 388–96.

Jolibert, Alain (1979), 'Quand les directeurs d'approvisionnement français et américains évaluent l'image des produits fabriqués dans cinq pays industriels', *Revue Française de Gestion*, January–February, pp. 94–101.

Kapferer, Jean-Noel (1989), 'La face cachée des marques', in Jean-Noel Kapferer and Jean-Claude Thoenig (eds), *La Marque*, McGraw-Hill: Paris, pp. 9–44.

Kaynak, Erdener and S. Tamer Cavusgil (1983), 'Consumer attitudes towards products of foreign origin: Do they vary across product classes?', *International Journal of Advertising*, vol. 2 (April–June), pp. 147–57.

Khanna, Sri Ram (1986), 'Asian companies and the country stereotype paradox: An empirical study', *Columbia Journal of World Business* (Summer), pp. 29–38.

Khera, Inder (1986), 'A broadening base of US consumer acceptance of Korean products', in Kenneth D. Bahn and M. Joseph Sirgy (eds), *World Marketing Congress*, Academy of Marketing Science, Blacksburg, VA, pp. 136–41.

Khera, I., B. Anderson and C. Y. Kim (1983), 'Made in India versus Hong-Kong/Korea/Taïwan', *Foreign Trade Review*, January–March, pp. 362–81.

Khera, Inder, David Karns and C. Y. Kim (1985), 'U.S. consumers' perceptions of Korean products and brands', Pan-Pacific Conference II, Seoul, Korea, 12–18 May.

Kraft, Frederick B. and Kae H. Chung (1992), 'Korean importer perceptions of US and Japanese industrial goods', *International Marketing Review*, vol. 9, no. 2, pp. 59–73.

Krisnakumar, Parameswar (1974), 'An exploratory study of the influence of country of origin on the product images of persons from selected countries', PhD Dissertation, University of Florida.

Lambin, Jean-Jacques (1989), 'La marque et le comportement de choix de l'acheteur', in Jean-Noel Kapferer and Jean-Claude Thoenig (eds), *La Marque*, McGraw-Hill: Paris, pp. 125–58.

Leclerc, France, Bernd H. Schmitt and Laurette Dubé (1994), 'Foreign branding and its effects on product perceptions and attitudes,' *Journal of Marketing Research*, vol. XXXI, no. 2 (May), pp. 263–70.

Lillis, Charles M. and Chem L. Narayana (1974), 'Analysis of "made in" product images: An exploratory study', *Journal of International Business Studies* (Spring), pp. 119–27.

Lumpkin, J. R, J. C Crawford and G. Kim (1985), 'Perceived risk as a factor in buying foreign clothes', *International Journal of Advertising*, vol. 4, pp. 157–71.

Maheswaran, Durairaj (1994), 'Country of origin as a stereotype: effects of consumer expertise and attribute strength on product evaluations', *Journal of Consumer Research*, vol. 21 (September), pp. 354–65.

Maronick, Thomas J. (1988), 'European patent laws: Implications for international marketing', *International Marketing Review*, vol. 5, no. 2, pp. 31–40.

Martin, Ingrid M. and Sevgin Eroglu (1993), 'Measuring a multi-dimensional construct: Country image', *Journal of Business Research*, 28, pp. 191–210.

Min Han, C. (1988), 'The role of consumer patriotism in the choice of domestic versus foreign products', *Journal of Advertising Research*, June–July, pp. 25–32.

Min Han, C. (1990), 'Country image: Halo or summary construct?', *Journal of Marketing Research*, vol. XXVI (May), pp. 222–9.

Min Han, C., and Vern Terpstra (1988), 'Country of origin effects for uni-national and bi-national products,' *Journal of International Business Studies*, vol 19, no. 2 (summer), pp. 235–55.

Min Han, C., Byoung-Woo Lee and Kong-Kyun Ro (1994), 'The choice of a survey mode in country image studies', *Journal of Business Research*, vol. 29, no. 2, pp. 151–62.

Morello, G. (1984), 'The made-in issue: A comparative research on the image of domestic and foreign products', *European Research*, vol. 5, no. 21, pp. 68–74.

Morganosky, Michelle A. and Michelle M. Lazarde (1987), 'Foreign made apparel: Influences on consumers' perceptions of brand and store quality', *International Journal of Advertising*, vol. 6, pp. 339–46.

Nagashima, Akira (1970), 'A comparison of Japanese and U.S. attitudes towards foreign products', *Journal of Marketing*, vol. 34 (January), pp. 68–74.

Nagashima, Akira (1977), 'A comparative "made in" product image survey among Japanese businessmen', *Journal of Marketing* (July), pp. 95–100.

Nishina, Sadafumi (1990), 'Japanese consumers: Introducing foreign products/brands into the Japanese market', *Journal of Advertising Research*, vol. 30, no. 2, pp. 35–45.

Onkvisit, Sak and John J. Shaw (1989), 'The international dimension of branding: strategic considerations and decisions', *International Marketing Review*, vol. 6, no. 2, pp. 22–34.

Papadopoulos, Nicolas, Louise A. Heslop and Jozsef Beracs (1990), 'National stereotypes and product evaluations in a socialist country', *International Marketing Review*, vol. 7, no. 1, pp. 32–47.

Parameswaran, Ravi and Attila Yaprak (1987), 'A cross-national investigation of consumers research measures', *Journal of International Business Studies*, Winter, pp. 35–49.

Peebles, Dean M. (1989), 'Don't write off global advertising: A commentary', *International Marketing Review*, vol. 6, no. 1, pp. 73–8.

Perrin, Michel, Claude Marcel, Robert Salles and Jean-Paul Valla (1981), 'L'image des biens industriels français en Europe', *Revue Française de Gestion*, January–February, pp. 97–107.

Peterson, Robert A. and Alain Jolibert (1976), 'A cross-national investigation of price and brand as determinants of perceived product quality', *Journal of Applied Psychology*, vol. 61, pp. 533–6.

Reierson, Curtis (1966), 'Are foreign products seen as national stereotypes?', *Journal of Retailing*, Fall, pp. 33–40.

Reierson, Curtis (1967), 'Attitude changes toward foreign products', *Journal of Marketing Research*, November, pp. 385–7.

Rosen, Barry Nathan, Jean J. Boddewyn and Ernst A. Louis (1989), 'US brands abroad: an empirical study of global branding', *International Marketing Review*, vol. 6, no. 1, pp. 7–19.

Samiee, Saeed (1994), 'Customer evaluation of products in a global market', *Journal of International Business Studies*, vol. 25, no. 3, pp. 579–604.

Schieb, Pierre-Alain (1977), 'Le consommateur face à la multinationalité des marques et des produits', *Revue Française de Gestion*, vol. 11 (September–October), pp. 59–62.

Schooler, Robert D. (1965), 'Product bias in the Central American common market', *Journal of Marketing Research*, vol. 2, November, pp. 394–7.

Schooler, Robert D. (1971), 'Bias phenomena attendant to the marketing of foreign goods in the US', *Journal of International Business Studies*, Spring, pp. 71–80.

Schooler, Robert D. and D. H. Sunoo (1969), 'Consumer perceptions of international products: Regional versus national labeling', *Social Science Quarterly*, vol. 49, no. 4, pp. 886–90.

Schooler, Robert D. and A. R. Wildt (1968), 'Elasticity of product bias', *Journal of Marketing Research*, vol. 5, February, pp. 78–81.

Shalofsky, Ivor (1987), 'Research for global brands', *European Research*, May, pp. 88–93.

Shimp, T. A. and S. Sharma (1987), 'Consumer ethnocentrism: construction and validation of the CETSCALE', *Journal of Marketing Research*, vol. 26, August, pp. 280–9.

Thorelli, Hans B., Jee-Su Lim and Jong Suk (1989), 'Relative importance of origin, warranty and retail store image on product evaluations', *International Marketing Review*, vol. 6, no. 1, pp. 35–46.

Tongberg, R. C. (1972), 'An empirical study of relationships between dogmatism and consumer attitudes toward foreign products', PhD dissertation, Pennsylvania State University.

Usunier, Jean-Claude (1994), 'Social status and country-of-origin preferences,' *Journal of Marketing Management*, vol. 10, pp. 765–83.

Usunier, Jean-Claude, Israel D. Nebenzahl and Eugene D. Jaffé (1993), 'Pays d'origine et stratégie de prix', *Revue Française du Marketing*, 1993/1, no. 141, pp. 35–47.

Vandenbergh, Bruce, Keith Adler, and Lauren Oliver (1988), 'Linguistic distinction among top brand names', *Journal of Advertising Research*, vol. 27, no. 4, pp. 39–44.

Wang, Chih-Kang (1978), 'The effect of foreign economic, political and cultural environment on consumers' willingness to buy foreign products', PhD dissertation, Texas A & M University.

Wang, Chih-Kang and Charles W. Lamb Jr (1980), 'Foreign environmental factors influencing American consumers' predispositions toward European products', *Journal of the Academy of Marketing Science*, vol. 8 (Fall), pp. 345–56.

Wang, Chih-Kang and Charles W. Lamb Jr (1983), 'The impact of selected environmental forces upon consumers' willlingness to buy foreign products', *Journal of the Academy of Marketing Science*, vol. 11 (Winter), pp. 71–84.

White, Phillip D. (1979), 'Attitudes of U.S. purchasing managers toward industrial products manufactured in selected Western European nations', *Journal of International Business Studies*, Spring/Summer, pp. 81–90.

White, Phillip D. and Edward W. Cundiff (1978), 'Assessing the quality of industrial products', *Journal of Marketing*, January, pp. 80–6.

Wilsher, Peter (1992), 'Diverse and perverse', *Management Today*, July, pp. 32–5.

Yaprak, Attila (1978), 'Formulating a multinational strategy: A deductive cross-national consumer behavior model', PhD dissertation, Georgia State University, College of Business Administration.

Yaprak, Attila (1987), 'The country of origin paradigm in cross-national consumer behavior: the state of the art', in Kenneth D. Bahn and M. Joseph Sirgy (eds), *World Marketing Congress*, Academy of Marketing Science: Blacksburg, VA, pp. 142–5.

Yavas, Ugur and Guvenc Alpay (1986), 'Does an exporting nation enjoy the same cross-national image?', *International Journal of Advertising*, vol. 5, pp. 109–19.

Yoshimori, Masaru (1989), 'Concepts et stratégies de marques au Japon', in Jean-Noel Kapferer and Jean-Claude Thoenig (eds), *La Marque*, MacGraw-Hill: Paris, pp. 275–304.

10

◆◆◆

The critical role of price in relational exchange

Price is, at first sight, anything but 'cultural'. That must be conceded. In fact it resembles an intrinsically objective element of exchange. It is usually a figure, a number, a unit – at least in appearance. It is therefore assumed that price determination is, in general, an issue reserved for rational economic factors. At this point in the book you are probably asking yourself what further evidence I have for insisting that everything is marked by culture. I have three remarks on this issue: (a) I am not denying (as I am myself an economist) that price is above all an objective element of exchange; (b) I am therefore insisting on human and subjective aspects of relational exchange where price is examined from a sociological and interactive point of view; (c) all authors, by definition, are the promoters of the ideas they choose to defend.

Price is a significant element of communication between buyer and seller, a short-term and/or long-term bond between them, and, for customers, a means of evaluating products in terms of social representations (Prus, 1989a) strongly akin to culture. Price is a decisive element in the social interaction between buyer and seller. It endorses their agreement. It shapes their immediate relationship and the long term.

In this chapter, the strictly economic aspects of price in international marketing are not considered: for instance, the relationship between price and costs in international marketing or the law of one price which states that, in the absence of transport, transaction-related costs and price discrimination, trade takes place in only one market and only one price prevails. I do not consider either the incidence of exchange rate variance on price strategies in international marketing. It is the subjective rather than objective side of prices which is examined in this chapter; price is viewed as a signal conveying meaning (section 10.1).

Bargaining is examined in section 10.2: a form of relationship between buyer and seller which is classical, primitive and normal, particularly in the absence of compulsory price labelling. In modern mass markets, the influence of customer on prices fixed by anonymous sellers usually takes the form of a 'take it or leave it' bargain. This dichotomous attitude (choice/no choice) is contrary to the purpose of bargaining and relational exchange, where price is always supposed to be a 'friendly price', even a 'friend's price'. Each party wants to make a good deal: *human relations are practically inseparable from economic transactions.* In contrast to bargaining described in section 10.2, the third section of this chapter deals with the use of price in those situations where it is clearly marked and hence known by the customers so that they are in a position to appraise the price–quality ratio.

In the last three sections, company attitudes in pricing decisions in international markets are considered. This is a somewhat anthropomorphic approach since a company and its markets are considered as interacting parties to exchange. Companies are led to distort and manipulate prices between domestic markets, either to increase consumer 'brand loyalty' in certain markets through offensive strategic pricing, or to avoid parallel imports which undermine their local distribution system (10.4). Price can also be used as a tactical weapon *vis-à-vis* competitors in particular national markets (section 10.5). Finally, price can be manipulated either because of a severe inflationary context or by over- or under-invoicing in order to make deals that otherwise would not be concluded (section 10.6).

10.1   Price as a signal conveying meaning

In many cases, prices are fairly objective, especially in most consumer goods and consumer durables markets, where goods are sold to households in mass distribution

Table 10.1   *Price-based signals*

Meaning conveyed by price in	By . . .	Section
Buyer–seller interactions	Bargaining rituals, price offers and relationship development	10.2
Consumer behaviour	Differences in consumer price-mindedness across cultures	10.3
Product evaluation	To what extent is quality inferred from price?	10.3
(Tough) competition	Signalling willingness to compete by dumping prices	10.4
Target market(s)	Showing commitment to customers in a target market by attractive prices	10.4
Distributors (grey markets)	Signalling willingness to avoid parallel imports from opportunistic distributors who disturb international price policy and risk damaging brand image	10.4
(Peaceful) competition	Signalling willingness to enter 'peacefully' in a cartellized market	10.5
Price increase policy	Meaning conveyed by price in high-inflation contexts	10.6
Relationship to suppliers	Overcoming the barriers for the supplier to receive the real price by using over- or under-invoicing	10.6

outlets with extensive possibilities of price comparison across stores. Then the meaning conveyed by the price centres mostly on the value of the good and the money transfer which will be necessary for it to be acquired. Prices start to be a more central object in the relationship between buyer and seller, or the company and its customers, distributors or competitors, when: (1) price is not displayed; (2) it is not necessarily the seller who will announce the first price; (3) there is no clear market reference for what would be a 'fair price'; (4) a particular price is understood by both the seller and the buyer as taking place within a series of transactions, past, present and future; (5) prices for particular transactions are not necessarily meant to cover even marginal cost (manipulative prices); (6) prices may be distorted by inflation and governmental price regulation; and (7) the total price is a combination of direct and indirect prices (e.g. a product's price but also prices for its maintenance, spare parts, updates, etc.). Price is less strictly 'economic' and more 'relational' in a variety of situations which correspond to one or more of the seven conditions presented above, namely industrial goods, high inflation contexts, etc. As shown in Table 10.1, price can convey meaning and be an object of interaction between the various participants of the market situation (manufacturers, distributors, consumers, competitors).

10.2   Bargaining

*The limits of price as an element of social relation:
bargaining versus no bargaining*

The importance of bargaining is often underestimated because we have become accustomed to being informed about prices because, as a rule, they are displayed. If we do not find them satisfactory we will not buy the product. In many countries today, people no longer bargain; at least in appearance. Bargaining is either legally prohibited or strictly controlled in most developed countries. Most sales of consumer products take place within oligopolistic distribution channels which offer merchandise for sale from producers who are themselves organized in oligopolies. In direct relations with customers, prices are unilaterally set by vendors and are therefore non-negotiable. This price is either taken or left. Bargaining at the checkout in a supermarket is unheard of and, to be blunt, rather boorish. (This is without any consideration of the various epithets that could be applied from impatient customers behind in the queue.)

Yet, once the price of a product attains a substantial level, people return to bargaining because of one of its irreplaceable functions: splitting a surplus between buyer and seller. In many markets exchange still takes place through bargaining, either legally or from necessity: for example, consumer durables and equipment for firms and households such as new cars, furniture, second-hand cars, property and industrial machinery.

In most developing countries, on the other hand, bargaining is still the rule, even for items of low value and products of little vital interest. A weak purchasing power considerably increases the importance of bargaining. In certain African markets, where sugar is sold by lump and carrots by slice (seen at the Nouakchott market in Mauritania in 1988), bargaining becomes essential for survival. Moreover, people are not pressed for time: the dividends from bargaining in relation to its cost are fundamentally different between developing and industrialized nations. Finally, bargaining has a fun dimension as well as a human one. The fun dimension exists because, in some ways, it is similar to a role play. The human dimension exists because the friendly/unfriendly aspects of commerce and bargaining are contemplated with more seriousness in developing countries than in industrialized ones where commercial intercourse has been largely 'de-personalized' (at least for consumer goods – much less so for equipment and industrial goods).

This is in fact one of the major reasons that bargaining is either legally prohibited or socially restricted in developing countries. As stated by Allen (1971, p. 49):

> ... it has conventionally been supposed that bargaining is socially disadvantageous, on the grounds that it breeds hostility, rivalry and distrust. ... While it is true that there is always an element of suspicion as to the real value of the commodity (and subsequently of the price), this suspicion never turns into an open conflict if the bargainers intend to conclude the sale. Any bargainer, whether seller or buyer, is careful not to offend his partner, for fear of putting an end to the transaction. Thus, though initiated by suspicion, bargaining tends rather to eliminate it, instituting instead an atmosphere of common interest and trust, which often leads to a lasting client relationship. In this way it cements community relations, rather than subverts them.

Ritual aspects of bargaining

Brand marketing is, by definition, unconducive to bargaining. Self-service and other non-personalized services do not allow people living in modern societies with advanced distribution systems to experience the rituals involved in bargaining. These rituals are a challenge in themselves. They are independent of the price negotiation, yet at the same time complementary. People who bargain more are no less rational; they are rational in a different way.

A Lebanese anthropologist (Khuri, 1968) describes the rituals involved in bargaining in the Middle East by emphasizing that such intercourse always begins with standard signs of respect, affection, common interest and trust. Words pertaining to parental relations are used in such circumstances to evoke affection and create an impression of friendliness and fraternity. As soon as a potential buyer shows interest in an item and requests information on the product, the seller replies vaguely:

> Between us there is no difference; we share the same interest, price is not what pleases me, what pleases me is to find out what pleases you; pay as much as you want; brothers do no disagree on price; for you it is free; it is a gift.

Nothing in this speech should be taken literally. No single potential customer would consider it as such. The opening incantation is a way of expressing a social bond of mutual interest and trust through allusions to a probable family tie in a metaphorical sense. The potential customer then insists that a price be indicated. The vendor hesitates and, perhaps, proposes a price after having presented and lauded the merits of his product at great length. In fact, a potential customer must never pretend to doubt the qualities of the proposed item, because that could make him seem ignorant and, as such, more vulnerable. The discussion continues, each party maintaining its price (a maximum price for the seller and a minimum price for the customer) below or above which no transaction can take place. The potential buyer suggests a price, but is not necessarily willing to pay it. After an agreement has been reached, the transaction then takes place, i.e. the buyer decides to purchase the item for cash. The bargaining operation could have been primarily just to seek information on the price. This is one instance where the bargaining activity is partly, but only partly, disconnected from the sales activity. It could be disconcerting for people who are used to displayed prices and who, as a result, *do not envisage entering into any sort of pleasant economic intercourse* merely to obtain information.

The relationship between bargaining and price display is obvious. Wherever the law forces the vendor to display prices clearly, bargaining practices will diminish. It is understandable that people who do not bargain every day, and who have thereby lost the habit of personalized commercial relations (if indeed they ever had it), should be rather embarrassed in these situations of implicit communication, where affection and economics, friendship and self-interest are seemingly intermingled. The novice bargainer also risks provoking the seller's hostility if the seller gets the impression (or wishes to give the impression) of being 'taken for a ride' by the buyer. In fact, what remains of bargaining in Western societies is disguised behind 'rational' arguments such as quantity discounts, stock liquidation operations and auctions on deleted items, etc. Moreover, bargaining could smear the image of the distribution channel as well as that of the goods it sells. Prus (1989b, p. 146) quotes certain remarks made by Canadian vendors:

> We're flexible, where if they're getting a larger order and they suggest it, we'll give a little. . . . Some customers feel that they have to have a discount to buy it. (Sales manageress, luggage)
>
> You can dicker in furniture, appliances, carpeting, something like that, here. But not on the smaller things, like clothing, giftware, shoes. (Department store salesman)
>
> Normally I try not to dicker. I am quite firm on the prices. I've found that dickering can be rather awkward. It is awkward for the merchant and the customer. And it is especially awkward if other people are around. If you can stay away from dickering, you can also avoid an image as someone who will go down. I have been known to dicker, but it is something I try to avoid. (Women's clothing)

Declaring prices

Cavusgil (1990, p. 505) notes that international pricing is not a topic that lends itself to easy generalization and the setting of export prices must first address the unique nature of the individual firm or buyer with whom one is dealing; he takes the example of the Middle East where 'Regal Ware, a producer of kitchen appliances and cookware, uses a higher list price in such markets to leave a margin of discretion.' Indeed, proposing a price is a tug-of-war exercise. Who will give way, the seller or the customer? Who should be the first to make concessions, by virtue of the position of strength that is internalized within a particular society? At least, four items play a major role in answering these questions:

1. The initial power situation of each party.
2. The degree of urgency for either the buyer or the seller to close the deal.
3. The importance of the negotiation margin from the start: whatever price is initially suggested, it must leave room for further discussion. It could be in the vendor's interest to exaggerate the first price in order to leave the customer some room for manoeuvre: when the vendor is dealing with a buyer whose performance is subject to confirmation by superiors, that buyer is supposed to obtain a discount. The buyer's job is to reduce the price: ironically, in such a case, the vendor would be doing the favour by opening the negotiations with an exaggerated price (see Box 10.1).
4. The kind of social process by which buyer and seller progressively adjust their price; for instance, in the case of competitive bidding situations, based on a tender offer, an excessively high price would eliminate that vendor from the short list of pre-selected candidates.

Box 10.1   *Price levels and the buyer/seller relationship*

Scenario 1: The seller wishes to offer a fair price from the start, close to the final price, expecting that it will win the customer's loyalty. This should convince the buyer of the vendor's honesty, openness and genuine desire to do business. It so happens that the customer shares these (European and American) values and decides to cooperate. An agreement is quickly reached, and each party is satisfied.

Scenario 2: The same vendor suggests the same price, close to the final price, as a sign of goodwill towards the buyer. The buyer who comes from a different culture (say India or Pakistan) is embarrassed: rather than a low price, his boss expects him to obtain the greatest possible discount from the seller. His role centres on the price rebate rather than on the price level. The announced price, close to the final price, leaves almost no room for rebate negotiation. With no grounds to negotiate, buyer and seller will separate, dissatisfied.

Scenario 3: The vendor announces a much higher initial price. Doing this, he leaves room for negotiation right from the start so as to allow the buyer to demonstrate skill in a mutually beneficial bargaining exercise and to enable the two parties to increase the long-term value of their social relationship. The ultimate agreed price is very close to that of Scenario 1. The buyer being interested mostly in rebate and the seller in price level, both can achieve better satisfaction than in Scenario 1.

10.3 Price and consumer evaluations

Culture-based appraisal of quality and price

It is common knowledge that consumers use price as a surrogate indicator of quality, especially when other criteria are absent. Subjectivity plays a major role in such instances (Zeithaml, 1988) for various reasons:

1. It is very difficult to measure quality objectively. There is no generally accepted method of measuring the objective quality of a product (much less so a service).
2. Even more difficult to measure is the perceived quality of a product. This concept of quality is subjective but not irrational, in the sense that it is based on an evaluation of intrinsic product attributes (e.g. taste, physical characteristics) and extrinsic product attributes (e.g. advertisement, brand, price).
3. Perceived quality combines with other evaluation criteria (perceived monetary and non-monetary prices) to form a perceived value which shapes and determines the consumer's decision to buy or not to buy.

Perceived monetary price means that consumers may not recall the exact price, but may have framed in their minds a simplified, general impression ('it is expensive' or 'it is not so expensive after all'). This price impression should be sufficiently close to consumer expectations if they are to buy (Jacoby and Olson, 1977). With regard to perceived non-monetary price, consumer reactions could be better understood in terms of Becker's (1965) conclusions that an objective price is not the only sacrifice accepted by consumers when they buy a product. Other 'sacrifices', such as the time spent in shopping, cooking and sitting at table, should be included in the consented price (perceived non-monetary price) before enjoying any satisfaction from the product.

Some elements of Becker's model, which has firm roots in American society and culture, are not cross-culturally equivalent: what is a costly 'sacrifice' in one country may be true enjoyment in another. Consumers do not build these subjective evaluations (of quality, monetary and non-monetary price) through irrational individual idiosyncrasies but through unconscious submission, in their everyday lives, to social representations dictated by their cultural upbringing. To cite a few examples of common aphorisms (the reverse of each aphorism is also defensible):

1. 'It is important to measure time, time is money' (see section 2.2): therefore, perceived non-monetary price will be higher in general for economic-time minded consumers.
2. 'Home-made food is the best': this maxim could, for instance, influence the perceived quality of frozen foods, even though there is no reason why the objective qualities (taste, dietary, conservation) should not be better.
3. 'Where there's pleasure, time doesn't count.'

Certain representations directly influence the perceived non-monetary price of a product, particularly the desirability/non-desirability or the convenience/inconvenience of an activity forming a part of the perceived non-monetary price. To put this in a simpler way the price of a nail, for example, is not easily separable from the non-monetary price involved in driving it in (i.e. the risk of hitting one's finger in the process). Non-monetary price is related to time costs, search costs and the psychic costs: these costs all enter into the consumer's perception of the sacrifice involved in the consumption experience in exchange for the satisfaction which is derived. Non-monetary price varies a great deal across cultures: a trip to buy a product, or the preparation of meals, may be perceived as enjoyable in certain cultures (no sacrifice; low non-monetary price) and as an inevitable and tedious task in other cultures. For instance, the rapid expansion of the 'do-it-yourself' market in France, in comparison to other neighbouring countries, is related to a marked preference for doing small jobs oneself instead of hiring the services of a tradesman. This behaviour can be traced to a social representation in a high-power distance society where being served is negatively valued: the French concept of *égalité* tends to assimilate service with servitude and humiliation. The French fiscal system has long corroborated this representation by offering tax rebates to people engaging in DIY, while restricting the opportunity of hiring domestics to the very upper classes.

Relationships between objective quality and price, and choice strategies

The weakness of the price–quality relationship has been examined in many studies (mostly objective quality, as in Curry and Riesz, 1988). Objective measures of the price–quality relation have been proposed: in his comparative study of the relations between objective tests of product evaluations and their price, carried out by consumer magazines (mainly consumer reports), Sproles (1977) found a positive correlation for 51 per cent of the 135 products retained in the study; in other words a high price objectively corresponded to higher quality. However, for 35 per cent of the products he found no correlation and for 14 per cent a negative correlation (lower quality products were priced higher). Similarly, Riesz (1978) found a positive rank correlation of only 26 per cent between price and objective quality among 685 categories of product. All subsequent studies exploring the same issue have reached similar conclusions (Zeithaml, 1988): there exists a positive but weak correlation between objective price and objective quality. This in a way, is reassuring; a negative correlation would have been decidedly disturbing. Indeed it is not possible to state with any certainty that, for example, the Miele washing machine, three times more expensive than the Zanussi, lasts three times longer and is a considerably better performer in washing linen. When consumption experience is immediate, which is often the case for consumer good, quality can be assessed quasi-instantly and the price is not a significant cue for inferring quality. Sjolander (1992), for instance, shows that when evaluating the quality of the same ice-cream, Polish and Swedish consumers do not differ in their evaluations: whether high, medium or low priced, they rate its quality at the same level.

Consumers experience difficulties in establishing a clear price–quality relationship when the consumption experience takes place over a long period of time, such as for household appliances and consumer durables in general. This can be explained by the presence of a subjective, perceptual evaluation of total price (monetary as well as non-monetary price); consumers need a better understanding of the costs involved in using the product to guide them in a rational decision process. Often, in the absence of the information based on actual product use, they are forced to resort to simplified formulae to guide their choice.

Tellis and Gaeth (1990) depict three basic choice strategies when the consumer has a better knowledge of price than quality, information on the latter tending to be sparser and more difficult to assess:

1. *Best value*: people, from a rational standpoint, choose the brand with the least overall cost in terms of price and expected quality (utility maximizing).
2. *Price seeking*: price is used as a proxy for the unknown quality (inference); the consumer chooses the highest-price brand.
3. *Price aversion*: people choose the lowest-price brand, in order to minimize immediate costs (risk aversion).

The significance of these three models varies according to the situation of the consumers – the amount of information they have, their capacity to establish price–quality relations and experience; Tellis and Gaeth show such relations for the United States. But we could also expect different attitudes in making a strategic choice, according to the consumer's national culture.

Cultural dimensions of price–quality evaluation and consumer choice strategies

That consumers are rational and attempt to evaluate, as objectively as they can, price–quality relations is a generally accepted idea. Yet this idea of the best price–quality relationship could be contested in various ways, for example by the introduction of the concept of minimum levels of quality and maximum levels of price, below or above which consumers will eliminate a product from their list of products to consider.

1. North European consumers: one may be surprised at the level of prices in northern European shops but also by the robustness and durability of products. A possible explanation is that these countries are Lutheran: this religion favours a certain austerity (in terms of material well-being) as a general way of life. Goods should be expensive in order to limit their consumption (see Box 10.2). On the other hand, people prefer lasting goods, in line with an austere, thrifty and utilitarian outlook in life. As a result, to furnish homes, for instance, they prefer sturdy, long-lasting furniture. This means looking for the best price–quality relation where the minimal level of quality is relatively high, thus eliminating a range of possibilities (even where the price is low enough to enhance the price–quality relationship). IKEA's strategy corresponds to this type of choice (see the case study at the end of Chapter 7).
2. South European consumers: purchasing power in southern Europe is somewhat lower compared to the north European average. People stay outdoors for longer because the climate is warmer; social life often takes place outdoors and is much less materially austere, hence the more pronounced taste for seasonal fashions and for appearance and show. In addition, the Catholic doctrine is rather ambiguous about money, and has

little to say about the price–quality ratio. Moreover, the Catholic Church has never been preoccupied, either explicitly or implicitly, with the price and quality of material possessions. The Catholic religion is not a 'lover of money' and could therefore be said to support spending implicitly. Like all idealistic systems with a worldly dimension, the Catholic doctrine manages to sustain the paradox of being anti-money but not anti-expenditure. This is the complete opposite of the Protestant paradox of thrift which considers expenditure as a catalyst for poor morality while still favouring the accumulation of wealth. The difference exists in where the shame lies: for the Catholic, spending is not really shameful, but money is, and the religion rejects money while accepting its pleasures. For the Protestant, (excessive) spending is shameful.

Max Weber (1958, p. 31) emphasizes the relative goodheartedness of the Catholic Church, 'punishing the heretic, but being lenient with the sinner', in contrast to the Reform Church which imposes stricter rules and regulation. Catholic influence lacks the austerity and rigour of Protestants. In a way, it accords free will to material choice, as in the famous 'Give unto Caesar what belongs to Caesar.' Consequently, the Latin (Catholic) consumer is more diverse, particularly in relation to displaying social class. Social classes are more distinct and buying has the function of reinforcing one's social image. With marked differences in buying power, one would expect diversified choice strategies among consumers:

1. Snobbish consumers who, by definition, buy the most expensive foods (the Veblen effect of preferring high prices).
2. Consumers who are more concerned by price and who would automatically buy the least expensive items (price-averse consumers).

Box 10.2   *The Puritan paradox*

I fear, wherever riches have increased, the essence of religion has decreased in the same proportion. Therefore I do not see how it is possible, in the nature of things, for any revival of true religion to continue long. For religion must necessarily produce both industry and frugality, and these cannot but produce riches. But as riches increase, so will pride, anger, and love of the world in all its branches. How then is it possible that Methodism, that is, a religion of the heart, though it flourishes now as a green bay tree, should continue in this state? For the Methodists in every place grow diligent and frugal; consequently they increase in goods. Hence they proportionately increase in pride, in anger, in the desire of the flesh, the desire of the eyes, and the pride of life. So, although the form of religion remains, the spirit is swiftly vanishing away. Is there no way to prevent this – this continual decay of pure religion? *We ought not to prevent people from being diligent and frugal; we must exhort all Christians to gain all they can, and to save all they can; that is, in effect, to grow rich.*

(Source: citation of the Methodist minister John Wesley at the end of the eighteenth century, a few years before the beginning of the Industrial Revolution in England. Quoted by Max Weber, 1958, last sentence italicized by Max Weber.)

3. Consumers who use price–quality relations, in line with the Latin temperament which includes a propensity for intellectual logic and rationality.

10.4   International price tactics

Price manipulation

Vendors may interact with the customers in the markets by using price with diversified objectives. Pricing may serve three kinds of interrelated objectives focusing on (1) profits; (2) sales; and (3) market interactions. Profits is the most classical objective, either by trying to achieve maximum company profits or to reach a target level of profits. The second category centres on the increase of unit volume of sales, sales figure or cash flows. The third category focuses on interaction with other market actors (customers, distributors, competitors, regulatory authorities) in order to:

1. Set a price parity with competitors.
2. Promote the image of the company and/or its products and/or brands.
3. Achieve greater market stability.
4. Develop new markets.
5. Maintain customer loyalty.
6. Eliminate competitors.

Price is a tactical variable in marketing and, quite often, a policy variable against competitors. Prices can be manipulated and distorted between (domestic) markets as long as customer or distributor arbitrage can be avoided. In fact, consumers cannot always arbitrate because of transaction costs, complexities of international trade operations for private people, customs regulations and technical standards; but agents are often tempted to do it for them. Agents can reduce the transaction costs and rapidly gain experience in such practice. For example, certain agents may specialize in re-importing into a country products sold at lower prices in a neighbouring market. Price is both a tactical tool, in local markets, and a strategic tool in front of global competition: price tactics on domestic markets must take their place within a global strategy of cost domination (based on the search for economies of scale and experience effects; see Chapter 7) or differentiation (obtained by designing a product offer differentiated from competitors or tailored to local markets; see Chapter 8). Keegan (1984, pp. 359–60) describes three possible positions for international strategic pricing:

1. The extension/ethnocentric position: a single global price based on the factory price of the goods, the customer being charged for insurance, freight and customs costs.
2. The polycentric adaptation position: local subsidiaries fix their own prices according to local market conditions.
3. The intermediate geocentric inventive position: the subsidiary takes into account local competition and seeks to maximize the firm's total income through international coordination of tactical pricing.

There follows an examination of some of these cases of tactical use of price in international markets.

Signalling willingness to compete: Domestic markets, export markets and dumping

Who gets the lowest prices? This question requires consideration when a company operates on different national markets, in which the opportunity exists to increase profits through price discrimination. It naturally presupposes that buyers or distributors do not have the possibility of arbitrage, buying where cheapest, either for themselves or for resale at a higher price in another national market. Other reasons for price discrimination across national markets may also be found among the eleven pricing objectives cited above.

A basic issue in international pricing is the price discrimination between the domestic market and the foreign markets. It depends on the situation of the domestic market *vis-à-vis* the export market on the company's cost curve. Basic micro-economic theory teaches that for a firm to maximize its profit, it must sell its products at a price greater than or equal to marginal cost (expenses incurred in the production of the last unit, that is, the direct cost of additional production). In practice, people refer more to the cost price (cost price based on total costs) and may discard it in favour of direct costing (variable costs directly engaged in production) in industries where overheads are high (aerospace, aircraft, chemicals, steel, etc.)

When a completely new model of aircraft is launched on to the market with initial fixed expenses of $5 billion, or a new model of car with overhead costs of $1 billion, is the domestic market or export market supposed to 'pay' for the depreciation of these sunk costs? This is a substantive question. Nevertheless it calls for a number of subjective considerations. Should the domestic market (or other exclusive markets) pay for their loyalty or, on the contrary, should they benefit from price cuts as compensation and encouragement for their loyalty? If British, French and Italian potential car purchasers were aware of the surcharge they pay (between 10 and 15 per cent) in comparison to, say, Belgian purchasers, perhaps they would show less loyalty.

Figure 10.1 addresses the problem of where to situate the domestic and export markets respectively on the horizontal axis of the cost curve. Since sales (whether domestic or export) usually take place simultaneously, the problem is one of subjective (but stable) conceptualization of the base of the cost curve as corresponding to exported quantities. It is this concept that leads directly to the practice of dumping. Dumping is prohibited by Article VI of the General Agreement on Tariffs and Trade (GATT) where it prejudices the production of one of the contracting parties. It allows certain countries to impose anti-dumping taxes on dumping prices. The United States regularly exercises this clause, especially on European and Japanese steel exports. Dumping is based on the following assumptions:

1. The role of the domestic market (or other exclusive markets) is to contribute to the recovery of sunk costs. These markets should therefore be situated on the ascending part of the cost curve in relation to the *x*-axis (quantities).
2. In placing the home market on this zone, the remaining zone where marginal costs decrease would be reserved for foreign markets where competition is supposed to be more open or where more attractive prices are offered. It should, however, be remembered that one company's home market is its competitors' foreign market.

Figure 10.1 Dumping and the relationship between unit costs and cumulated production.

3. Dumping assumes that foreign markets are considered as rubbish bins. This is true
   except in the situation where the aim is to assume the role of a predator, momentarily
   flooding the market with the deliberate intention of raising prices after a sizeable
   market share has been secured.

Showing commitment in a a target market: Gaining market share through pricing

Slashing prices in the short term may appear an attractive strategy for obtaining new
clients, building customer loyalty and finally increasing market share. This could even
result in the consumer being trapped if prices are subsequently raised and if competitors,
who have lost market share, are not prepared to engage in a price war to regain their
previous share. Competitors will therefore accept the new status quo and products will be
priced high.

   Slashing prices is a price tactic when viewed from the perspective of a single market.
Across markets, however, it is the implementation of a global strategy. The Japanese are
unsurpassed in the art of initially penetrating a market through price rebates in order to
obtain a sizeable share in it. Johansson and Nonaka (1990, p. 592) describe the pricing
strategies of Japanese firms as follows:

> The general theme was one of seeing the entry into a market as a long-term 'investment' and
> market penetration was accordingly a much more important pricing objective than quick
> profit taking with a skimming approach. Several of the firms employed a version of the
> 'experience curve pricing strategy' where a relatively low price was expected to lead to large
> volume and future cost savings. It became rather clear that individual markets were not seen

as 'profit centers' but rather as pieces in one large global puzzle. By generating sufficient funds at home and in selected country markets where the share positions were strong, the lower returns emanating from a low price penetration strategy in newer markets could be sustained over a relatively long period.

Thus, in many African countries, Japanese car manufacturers entered the market twenty years ago offering cheap, reliable, air-conditioned cars (in comparison to the European cars available). Since their objective was not to eliminate competitors, the Japanese left room for European cars after having acquired the lion's share of the market. They did this by raising prices. The benefits of this were threefold: they calmed hard-pressed rivals, raised their profit margins and finally avoided the risk that their relatively low pricing would lead to a lasting unfavourable image of their products.

Avoiding parallel imports: combating grey markets and opportunistic distributors

Grey market occurs when 'an exporter knowingly or unknowing sells to an unauthorized agent who competes directly with the sole agent appointed by the exporter within the same territory' (Palia and Keown, 1991, p. 47). Grey markets are based on parallel imports that hamper the effectiveness of a marketing strategy across various national markets. For instance, if a company sells at a discount to a distributor in a Central American country because the local consumers cannot afford European or US price levels, there is a risk that the goods will be shipped back from this country to the United States and sold there through unofficial channels (Weigand, 1991). Fragmented national markets are geographically proximate, not only in Europe but also in West Africa, Latin America or South East Asia. Once different price levels are set between two neighbouring countries, consumers, and probably distributors, seek supplies from the cheapest sources, making the manufacturer compete with its own products. If the price differential is large enough to offset transaction costs, unauthorized intermediaries may compete with sole agents or exclusive dealers on national markets where a specific marketing strategy has been defined (see case A10.2).

Many companies that manufacture home appliances and consumer durables struggle to control the ultimate destinations of their products. For instance, Belgian, Dutch or French agents in cities close to the German border sometimes buy from German wholesalers instead of their domestic distributor, who may sell at a higher price. When price policies implement country-specific prices, they should consider all opportunities for consumer and/or distributor arbitrage. As emphasized by Weigand (1991, p. 53), consumer arbitrage is often effected through holiday travelling: 'An English tourist taking a holiday in Miami bought a place setting of bone china made in Britain. She didn't pay Britain's substantial value added tax. Further the dollar was cheaper that day . . .'. Weigand notes that British manufacturers recognize that these personal imports affect their domestic sales. However, they have not found a way to stop them.

The same problem applies to products whose novelty is their major commercial argument. For example, a new music album is marketed in Britain before being put on sale in Italy. In such cases it is difficult to avoid a grey market flourishing, since a segment of well-informed Italian fans receive the news as soon as the album is on the market and will happily pay a premium to be among the first to have the album. The inflated profit margin is pocketed by the 'smart' people who organize the parallel market but who, in doing so, show that they understand the mechanics of urgent demand. Sales by the record company suffer as a result because the company may run out of stock in Britain and, a short time later, may be unable to sell its surplus Italian stock.

The objective of monitoring product price positioning across markets is a difficult issue. Indeed, in certain countries, agents may be forced to sell at prices lawfully dictated by producers. In other countries, however, legislation may consider such practices contrary to effective competition. Resale price maintenance laws prohibit the imposition of prices by the producer on an agent, even though this may be required by marketing strategy. Firms then manoeuvre around these laws through recommended retail price labelling, thus controlling agents' discretionary margin. The agent could, for example, try to sell the product at an offer price (e.g. to promote the agent's store) and conflict with the producer's pricing strategy.

Exclusive distribution agreements in home markets would appear to be a plausible solution to the problems of the grey market. But the implementation of such clauses of exclusivity is somewhat difficult. In the United States, there is some reluctance to limit competition by granting enforceable exclusivity rights to dealers. In the United States parallel importers, competing with authorized dealers of leading brands were accorded an almost complete victory by the K Mart ruling handed down by the US Supreme Court. Large companies with well-known brands such as Cartier and Seiko were struggling against parallel importers, but the Supreme Court judged that they cannot prevent unauthorized importation of products under their brand name, since their right to control the trademark is exhausted by the sale.

European Union legislation also restricts exclusive distribution agreements. EU competition rules (Article 85 of the Treaty of Rome) prohibit any kind of market-sharing agreement by which a company could limit the sales of its distributors exclusively to their domestic market. In order to increase competition across EU countries, Article 85 and several jurisdictional decisions of the European Court of Justice have legitimized parallel imports. A company cannot prevent its 'exclusive' German distributor from selling to Italian customers. even if this company has also appointed an 'exclusive' distributor in Italy. It is therefore difficult to prevent distributors from seeking arbitrage opportunities. Hence grey markets have developed in Europe and other areas, seeking to overcome the many non-tariff barriers whenever price differentials offset the costs of parallel importing.

Possible solutions to the problems of grey markets, i.e. solutions which may counter parallel imports, are as follows:

1. Lower the price in a national market where it is too high and/or inflate it where it is too low, in order to offset not all, but enough, of the price differential, so that there is no more profit in parallel importing. This, however, may be at the expense of the global coherence of the marketing strategy in either one or both countries.
2. Change the product so that the official product is favourably differentiated against the parallel imported product. If changes are only superficial ones, importers and

consumers will not be fooled. If changes are more significant, economies of scale are lost. Other possibilities entail changing minor product attributes: extended warranties can be granted only to authorized dealers, so that parallel importers will offer products with little or no after-sales service and guarantee. A label 'not for export' or 'for domestic sale only' may be attached to the packaging (which also clearly identifies the national origin). This may prevent some dealers from re-exporting. The effectiveness of these labels is very limited, since in most countries it is not legal for a manufacturer to prohibit the export sales of its own products.

3. Educate the dealer (Cavusgil and Sikora, 1988): weaker dealers may be prime targets for gray market attacks and may have, at first, an outburst of anger, because it seems that the manufacturer makes an excess profit at their expense. Explaining why such price differences exist is in the manufacturer's role in as much as explanations are considered credible by the dealer.

3. Terminate the dealer agreement (or threaten to do so) when the dealer buys from unauthorized parallel sources. Weigand cites the case of Apple, which prints the following statement: 'Any Apple dealer or VAR (Value Added Retailer) found to be in violation of the mail-order or transhipping prohibitions will be stripped of its authorized status.'

4. A provisional solution to stop the flow of unauthorized parallel imports is to buy back the grey market goods. This is positively perceived by authorized dealers, who feel actively protected by the brand owner. Generally, this solution is possible only when a permanent solution to parallel imports has been found and is quickly implemented.

Finally it is important to emphasize the risk that consumer perceptions of the product positioning may be adversely affected by discrepancies in price for the same good across markets. For example, a Toyota Celica (1990 model coupe with a 16-valve engine) cost US$17,000 in October 1990 (that is about 85,000 French francs or £8,500). The American market is a competitive one in which indirect taxes are about 10 per cent lower in comparison with the French market. The same car was sold (without options, like a compact-disc player, as in the United States) for 150,000 French francs (approximately £15,000) in France where Japanese cars were limited by agreement to 3 per cent of the market. It is in the interests of the Japanese car manufacturers to position their cars in the luxury bracket by setting higher prices. Taking into consideration the differences in indirect taxation in order to make a fair comparison, the same car was being sold at a 60 per cent premium in France compared to the United States.

For informed consumers (currently a rather rare species), buying in the home market is no longer attractive when they become aware that home-market prices are artificially inflated. Today, it is generally accepted that consumers are poorly informed as to international price differentials, and even when they are informed, they resign themselves to the idea that tariff and non-tariff barriers are set so that customers remain 'prisoners' of their home market prices. In the future both these assumptions may not still hold. Regional integration, either in South America, Europe and South East Asia, is speeding up. Consumers are slowly becoming aware of the price levels for similar goods and services in neighbouring countries. They are also being offered increased opportunities for buying abroad, with no customs duties or clearance formalities.

10.5   Market situations, competition and price agreements

Ideal versus actual competition

One may wonder what is the status of price in the exchange process: is it an objective equilibrium point of a contract between the two parties or is it the instrument of a social relationship, a subjective equilibrium resulting from the social interaction between buyer and seller? In classical economic terms, the social exchange relationship disappears behind Adam Smith's 'invisible hand' of the market. However, it is debatable whether human nature tends more to alliance or to fighting. Both form part of human nature. The 'invisible hand' of the market puts the real behaviour of competitors in a 'black box', as if their innate tendency is to battle it out to bankruptcy. Is it quite normal that firms engage in fierce competition? Is it not more in keeping with human nature to seek agreement, to divide territory between companies and to sign pacts, even though their duration may be limited?

On the world-wide market for household cleaning products four main firms compete severely against each other: Procter & Gamble, Colgate Palmolive, Unilever and Henkel; to this list the Japanese Kao should probably be added. They are competing head to head for market share on some segments, brands and national markets, whereas in other areas and for other brands armistices have been implicitly signed. Competition patterns have therefore to be surveyed case by case. In fact it is easy to appreciate that behind the normative position which we have largely adopted through its incessant repetition – it is essential to be competitive – a more complex reality exists. To varying degrees, competition and alliances between companies will always occur as mixed realities. Even more complex is the code which delineates to newcomers to the competitive scene (a national market) how they should behave towards those who are already established players on that scene. It is frequent that big newcomers face a combined attack of all the firms, domestic and foreign, already present in a national market: they, for instance, lower their prices, spread rumours on the newcomer product or service policies, and its real long-term commitment to local customers. This results in poor competition, which is somewhat detrimental to customers: such a (hidden) agreement exists on the French market for fire safety systems, where a norm stricter than the European standard (EN 54) bars outsiders from entering the market; as a result, prices for fire detectors are twice the price in France than in Britain. For all these arguments, the necessary customization of marketing strategies must be done according to the *actual* rather than the ideal competition patterns.

Market situations and competition avoidance patterns

Competition is not necessarily self-perpetuating. The dynamics of competition may lead to the concentration of supply amongst a limited number of companies and therefore to an actual decrease in the sum total of competing forces. The United States, the archetype of enacted liberalism has been much more realistic in this regard than other countries since they introduced effective institutions at an early stage (for example, anti-trust legislation and the Sherman Act) to oversee the proper functioning of competition, to discourage dominant positions and the establishment of monopolies through mergers and acquisitions.

However as Cateora emphasizes, perhaps to an exaggerated extent (1983, p. 128): 'Except in the United States, 20th century orientation toward competition has been to avoid it whenever possible'. Inevitably one thinks of the large German cartels, Interessen Gemeinschaft Farben for example, which prior to the Second World War brought together the three major chemical companies, Bayer, BASF (Badische Anilin und Soda Fabrik) and Hoechst, that are now at the forefront of the world chemical industry. One also thinks of the Japanese *zaibatsus*, Mitsui, Mitsubishi and Sumitomo, industrial giants, which, under the control of one extended family, encompass activities ranging from banking to car production, and from trading to shipbuilding. The Americans prohibited these *zaibatsus* after their victory over the Japanese in 1945. This has not stopped their continued existence on an informal basis, nor has it prevented competition from progressing extremely effectively within the Japanese market.

Abegglen and Stalk (1986) have demonstrated using the example of the motorcycle industry how competition between companies in Japan is often savage. Honda, which in the 1950s was far behind Tohatsu, has completely overtaken this firm to the extent that in 1964 Tohatsu went bankrupt. After entering the motor car sector during the 1960s, Honda suffered a relative loss of competitiveness in the face of competition from Yamaha which achieved almost the same market share in 1981. At the beginning of the 1980s, Honda decided to attack Yamaha. Whereas Honda introduced eighty-one new models and ceased production of thirty-two (113 changes in product range in all), Yamaha 'only' introduced thirty-four new models and withdrew three (37 changes). This strategy, in combination with a fierce attack on prices and distribution, led to the collapse of Yamaha at the start of 1983. In addition to substantial losses, Yamaha announced redundancies and a restructuring programme as well as a reduction in stocks. Yamaha's chairman, Koike, was forced to acknowledge his failure publicly. This story, along with many similar ones, shows just how cut-throat the competition is in Japan, contrary to popular opinion. It is one of the principal sources of strength of the Japanese when stepping into foreign markets. This fierce domestic competition is also underestimated by foreign companies that want to establish themselves in Japan (see for illustration case A8.2).

The simple truth is, however, that an industrialist's vocation is not to enjoy competition as an end in itself. Competition is imposed by public authorities through the opening of frontiers, and ultimately by competitors themselves. If companies possess the legal and informal means to reduce it, they will do so, as long as the type of agreement is stable and they do not allow themselves to be taken advantage of by the competing firm with which the agreements are made.

A German economist, Von Stackelberg (1940), had the idea of combining supply and demand situations to construct a typology of forms of markets. He distinguishes buyers and sellers according to whether they number one, several or many (see Table 10.2).

Table 10.2 *Basic forms of markets according to Von Stackelberg*

Buyers	Sellers		
	One	Some	Many
One	Bilateral monopoly	Contradicted monopsony	Monopsony
Some	Contradicted monopoly	Bilateral oligopoly	Oligopsony
Many	Monopoly	Oligopoly	Pure competition

Every country has a few monopolies, some markets where pure and perfect competition reigns and a large number of oligopolies (large-scale consumption and durable consumer goods), oligopsonies and bilateral oligopolies (industrial input goods, such as steel, chemicals, rubber, and capital goods). What varies according to culture is the social approval or disapproval – the level of agreement and implicit consensus between local decision-makers as to whether a monopoly, through the restrictions on excessive competition, may be desirable for the community, or constitutes a danger to it. Intruders, coming from abroad, will then be seen either positively (from the point of view of the consumer) or negatively (from the point of view of the firm in competition with the foreign company, since ultimately the consumers are also often employees and thus potentially unemployed).

Indeed the Americans are often shocked by the amount of protection afforded to their flagship national companies by certain European governments. The Airbus-Boeing saga is typical of these conceptual differences that partly derive their roots from culture. The Europeans consider that the money lent by their governments, often viewed as sunk costs, was used wisely in view of the success of the Airbus aircraft, the number of jobs created, the positive effects on the trade balance and the preservation of the civil aeronautic industry in Europe which was previously under threat (a collective view/not purely liberal). However, for the Americans the affair was a costly mess that helped no one: the successful Boeing company was challenged by disloyal competition, the European taxpayer was further burdened and the standard rules governing international trade were distorted. In many respects, this is all true. Nevertheless, if Airbus did not exist, then Boeing would be in a situation of quasi-monopoly (except for McDonnell Douglas, but its share of the market is insignificant compared with that of Boeing). Then, the lack of competition could also be seen as a problem.

10.6   Managing prices in highly regulated environments

In many countries over the last twenty years, the annual rate of inflation has been a double digit one, and sometimes more than 100 per cent per year (which means several per cent a month and, in some extremes cases, several per cent a day). This sets definite constraints on pricing policies since prices cannot be increased every day or every week to adjust for inflation.

The case of high-inflation countries

Price stability, at the overall economic level, is a discipline based not only on macro-economic policies but probably also on definite cultural values. The necessary discipline is based on: (1) future time orientation which provides the monetary authorities with real continuity in their fight against inflation; (2) control of the creation of money and credit; and (3) a belief in free market forces that may keep price increases under control because of active competition (such a belief is, on average, related to individualism and low power distance).

One of the main reasons for inflation being high, and remaining so, is that it profits some of the actors in the economic system: inflation transfers wealth fairly 'smoothly' from some social stratas to others. When comparing countries with high power distance (Table 3.3) with those having high inflation, one may note a fairly high level of correspondence. With some notable exceptions (such as Japan), the higher the power distance in a country, the higher its inflation rate. The typical case for high inflation is a developing country, with a semi-authoritarian government and heavy financial regulation (price controls on most goods, foreign exchange control, strict import controls and high duties). High power distance at the society level is expressed in bureaucratic controls and restricted freedom for businesses unless they have the appropriate connections at the top.

High inflation rates generally result in the local currency being systematically weak against the main stable and convertible, foreign currencies, because of a constant decrease of its nominal purchasing power. In this stereotypical portrait, which can nevertheless be found in a good hundred countries in the world, the local currency is inconvertible. Furthermore the exchange rate is maintained at an artificial parity which has more to do with wishful thinking than with economic reality. This results in a parallel foreign exchange market, illegal but tolerated by the authorities most of the time. In comparison to the official exchange rate, parallel rates are favourable to foreign currency sellers and disfavourable to buyers. In Iran in 1993, after very high inflation in the previous years, the official exchange rate had reached about 1,500 more than the grey market exchange rate, before it was decided to align the official rate. In such situations, foreign exchange controls serve the purpose of enriching the most powerful (because they can buy foreign currencies at the favourable official rate), and restricting the capacity of local exporters to receive a real price (because they are obliged to sell their exports receipts in hard currencies at the official rate which is most often grossly overvalued).

Inflation is supposed to be combated by price control, an expression of the power of regulatory authorities over companies. In a high power distance context, oppressive rules (see section 3.6) are the most frequent. Price increases which are vital for companies to survive can be delayed by the public authorities even though the last months or last week's inflation rate has brought all the industry into the red, costs having soared while sales figures stagnated because of controlled prices. For instance, the Brazilian auto industry is subject to 'staircase' price increases by which Volkswagen, Fiat or Ford are suddenly allowed to increase their price by 50 per cent or more. Currently, the strong orientation of Brazilian public authorities' action favours high inflation, as is the case in many Latin American countries.

There is literally a high-inflation culture that consumers and companies are used to living with. Consumers delay their purchases after price increases, buy excess quantities just before they occur (or because they may occur soon, as price increases are not officially announced). If possible, they stock items bought during favourable periods. As a result, sales are largely shaped by price increases or their announcement; the potential threat of a next price increase is used to motivate customers to buy 'now'. Present orientation is also necessary for customers: they must be always ready to buy at the best possible moment; at the extreme, 'inflation bargains' correspond to buying goods because they are currently cheap, rather than because they are actually needed. Such customer opportunism may be a problem for the consumers themselves, because they tend to be too price-minded and neglect other important criteria in their decision-making process. Furthermore, if they stock perishable items in excess quantities, it may result in spoilt goods. On the other hand, companies do not depend on consumers for defining prices. The key for price policy, which is mostly short term, is to negotiate price increases with public authorities. Pricing depends more on governmental authorization than on customers and competition.

The terms of discussion with price regulatory authorities is highly relational and manipulative, rather than strictly economic. In order to obtain price increases, and the highest possible ones, companies have to argue about losses incurred because of price limitation, which now have to be compensated. Understandably, cost prices declared in negotiation with regulatory authorities will be systematically overestimated and losses in the previous period will be slightly exaggerated in order to get as favourable a new price as possible. A company will argue for a substantial price increase so to have a 'reserve' before the next increase. Naturally all this process fosters inflation rather than slows it. Another way of obtaining the necessary price allowances – to be mentioned, although it is illegal and unethical – is to propose a baksheesh or some favours to the civil servants in charge of price control within the public administration.

Over- and under-invoicing

As explained above, many high-inflation countries have legislation which aims to control prices. The control may be effected either at retail, wholesale or production level, or at several levels simultaneously. Price increases may be curbed or limited, or even frozen. Trade profit margins may be monitored. The rationale for price control is usually a basic mistrust of free-market mechanisms, often augmented by a long-established tradition of state intervention in the economy.

The foreign exchange regulations also influence the practice of over- and under-invoicing. When countries experience balance-of-trade (and, more generally, balance-of-payments) problems, they often use administrative decrees which aim to stop outright the flow of foreign currency out of the country. Local exporters are controlled: they are forced to repatriate their earnings in foreign currencies as soon as possible and to change them for local currency at sometimes derisory exchange rates. Local importers are also under close scrutiny: the absolute necessity of their purchases abroad must be assessed before they are allowed to receive foreign currency for paying their imports. Furthermore, they are often obliged to deposit a guarantee which may be more than the equivalent of their foreign purchase; this sum is deposited at the central bank in the months before payment, with little or even no interest. Where strict foreign exchange controls are enforced, there is no convertibility of the local currency into foreign 'hard' currencies.

A number of reasons clearly induce firms to practise under- or over-invoicing: they would not be willing to do this otherwise.

1. When a country involves a high level of political risk, which is the case with many developing countries, local businesspeople seek to transfer funds to foreign banks as fears of political upheaval increase.
2. Local businesspeople may wish to expatriate money through under-invoicing, simply because they need cash to buy a prohibited (or scarce) product or equipment for their production facilities and particularly for the manufacture of products for export.

Verna (1989) describes various cases of over- and under-invoicing in international trade, relating to differences in currency convertibility. Total convertibility of a currency implies the possibility of its use in all international commercial and financial operations, whatever the object, place or sum concerned. Only a limited number of countries enjoy total convertibility of their currencies. The non-convertibility of local currencies (even more than quantitative restrictions which lead to smuggling) is responsible for over- and under-invoicing (Verna, 1989). Local business people ask their foreign customers to under-invoice, their foreign suppliers to over-invoice, and wait for the extra money to be paid into their bank account abroad. Currency black markets exist only in countries where the national currency is totally inconvertible. As a result, huge discrepancies may be found between the black-market exchange rate and the official (central bank) exchange rate. Exporters, obliged to go through official channels, lose major benefits from their transactions. Either they have to sell foreign currency at the official rate, which is abnormally low, or buy currency for their purchases at parallel rate which, conversely, is abnormally high. Local exporters are therefore tempted to under-invoice; the foreign customer will transfer to a foreign account the extra money in a fully convertible currency. The local exporter should have complete confidence, or a forceful means of pressurizing the foreign customer.

Over-invoicing works in a symmetrical way for imports. When local importers ask for an import licence from their national authorities, the face value should be as high as possible, since the allowance for buying foreign currency will be increased accordingly. They will ask their suppliers to over-invoice and to transfer the extra money into a convertible foreign account to maximize their overall profits. As Verna states (1989, p. 115):

> An import licence will authorize the importer to order goods from a foreign supplier; a specified amount in foreign currency is paid by the local authorities in the name of the importer. In return, the importer should refund the authorities in local currency, at the official rate, and also pay customs duties on arrival of the goods. To obtain such an import licence may be a sort of 'windfall' because it allows the importer to buy foreign goods at a better price than is offered on the free market, mainly through the (favourable) exchange rate differential between the official and black markets . . . import licences can sometimes be transferable. They then become objects of exchange and even the subject of an auction . . .

to the extent that some governments, which have become aware of this trade, sell import licences to the highest bidder.

Questions

1. To what extent does price bargaining involve friendship?
2. What is the relationship between bargaining and 'modern culture'?
3. Discuss the notion of 'economic rationality' from a cultural point of view.
4. How may price levels reflect Protestant versus Catholic values?
5. What are the limitations for a consumer to display obvious price-mindedness when shopping? How do these limitations relate to culture?
6. In certain countries smuggling is fairly legitimate: custom officers are not very concerned with arresting smugglers, consumers buy smuggled products knowingly, and smugglers are known by everyone for what they do. Why and under which circumstances is it so? What are the consequences for marketing of smuggling being accepted as a legitimate activity?
7. Since the start of the Single European Market, UK citizens have been allowed to buy up to one hundred litres of alcoholic beverages (beer, wine and spirits) on the continent and bring them back to Britain. Excise duties on alcohol are much higher in the United Kingdom than in France. UK consumers buy massive quantities of drinks in Calais, France, on the other side of the Channel, twenty miles (33 km) from Dover. French stores have opened special areas for these one-day British travellers who receive special fares from the ferry companies. What are the consequences for the UK brewing industry and for the distribution channels in the United Kingdom? What are possible responses for the UK brewing industry?
8. Is over- or under-invoicing legal? Why is it sometimes inevitable?

APPENDIX 10

Teaching materials

A10.1   Case: Saito Importing Company

Some years ago, Saito Importing Company, located in California in the United States, brought in a shipment of wood carving from Bali in Indonesia. At the time, the official exchange rate was 78 Indonesian rupias per US dollar. The 'black market' rate (as it was viewed by the Indonesian government), or 'free market' rate (as it was viewed by most of the rest of the world), was approximately 1300 Indonesian rupias per US dollar.

The seller requested a letter of credit for one-half the value of the shipment, to be provided by a US bank and confirmed by an Indonesian bank. A request was made that the other half of the money be deposited in an account in a bank in New York.

Obviously, the 'half' that was received in New York had a value of many times that of the 'half' received in Indonesia. The money in the bank account in New York was available for the seller to invest, to purchase goods for shipment to Indonesia or elsewhere, or to use if leaving Indonesia. Money which was held in Indonesia could, at that time, be used for such purposes only with the express approval of the Indonesian government. What the Indonesian exporter did was, of course, illegal under Indonesian law.

Saito Importing Company did not receive the goods until over a year later. Since Bali does not have a port which will accommodate ocean-going vessels, the letter of credit specified that transhipment was allowed. In the process of transhipment, the goods travelled around much of the world and were delayed while waiting for on-going vessels at points of transhipment.

When the wood carvings finally arrived in the US, Saito Importing Company declared the actual price paid for the goods, and indicated to customs why there was a discrepancy between purchase price and the value shown on the documents. The American company did not do anything illegal under US law.

(Source: Saito Duerr, 1989, p. 310. Reproduced with permission.)

Questions

1. Should the US company have refused to agree to make the payments as requested by the Indonesian exporter? What would have been the expected effect on the price the Indonesian exporter demanded?
2. What effects would you expect the unrealistic official exchange rates to have had on Indonesian exports?

A10.2   Case: Riva International

Françoise Gain, the *directrice du markeing* at Riva in Brussels, Belgium, received astonishing results from the consumer panels and distributor panels for September and October 1995. It appeared that sales in Belgium and France of one of its main products, the *crème base* Riva, were 20 per cent lower than the production level in the Belgian factory, which supplied both markets. No signs of excess inventories in the distribution in France or Belgium were noticed by the sales force during visits to the distributors.

Riva Belgium was the subsidiary of Riva Products Corporation, a large US-based multinational, whose main business lines were related to the cosmetics and beauty care industry. The Belgian subsidiary was in charge of both the French and the Belgian markets. In 1991 a scientific breakthrough by the corporate R&D laboratories had led to the development of a new skin care cream. Several patents had been filed and registered to protect the property. In Europe, the industrial use of these patents had been licensed to Riva Belgium, which began producing and selling the new skin care cream in February 1992. Sales increased quickly and the new product was received favourably by Belgian and French consumers, who liked both its efficiency and good price–quality ratio. Following instructions from international headquarters, the output of Riva Belgium was intended exclusively for supplying the Belgian and French markets as well as the markets of French-speaking Africa.

In January 1995 the English subsidiary of Riva, UK Riva Ltd, started producing the same *crème base* product. Hefty investments had been made in the English factory to ensure the best quality and a large production capacity. This product had been launched at the top end of the market for skin care cream. It was priced high and supported by heavy advertising and promotional expenses. After a promising start, deliveries had been falling off since August 1995. Actual deliveries to English distributors steadily diverged from target sales.

Françoise Gain knew about this situation as she had been engaged as an internal consultant in the launching of *crème base* Riva in the United Kingdom. However, what worried her most in November 1995 was the gap between sales to consumers in France and Belgium and ex-works shipments. She informed Jacques Graff, chief executive of Riva Belgium and a member of the international board.

At first he did not seem to be bothered by such a gap, and showed little interest in this 'problem': 'Françoise, you know: panel data, what does it mean really? Our product sells well and that is all that matters! Tell your panel company to reconsider their samples and their data collection procedures, and you will see that everything is in fact normal.'

Françoise Gain nevertheless made the decision to undertake an audit by an external consultant. His findings exactly confirmed those of the panels and brought evidence of no sizeable excess inventory at the distribution level. Furthermore it followed from the auditor's investigations that deviations had to be ascribed mostly to deliveries to two large wholesalers, who ranked among the five largest customers of Riva Belgium.

One month after his talks with Françoise Gain, Graff received a confidential note, issued by the chief executive of UK Riva Ltd. It stated that a member of his sales force had accidentally seen, at an English wholesaler, a carton containing *crème base* Riva with country-of-origin label 'Made in Belgium'. The wholesaler had been evasive if not reluctant to tell the sales representative where it came from. Jacques Graff asked Françoise Gain to come to his room, and handed her the note without comment.

'I am not surprised by this note', answered Françoise. 'On the contrary, it is evidence for my suspicions about parallel imports of our Belgian products to England. I have noticed that our sales which vanished from Belgium and France were precisely equal to the drop in the deliveries of UK Riva Ltd. It is now quite clear that some of our wholesalers export to English distributors and that, before doing this, they did not warn our sales and marketing group. I examined the cost structure of UK Riva production and found that our product made in Belgium could be sold by Belgian wholesalers to English distributors at a profit. Belgian distributors may price it at 15 per cent below the English price list, even though there are transport costs.'

'How is that possible?' asked Graff, amazed.

'The English *crème base* Riva was launched with heavy production and promotion costs,' explained Françoise Gain. 'It is positioned at the high end of the market. Its price is higher than any of the competing products. I told them, before launching it, that this retail price level was too high. But I faced disapproval. The finance department at UK Riva Ltd wanted a quick return on investment, taking into account the large cash outflows at the start. The marketing people, backed by the advertising agency, claimed the opportunity to seize a segment which was at the very top end of the market and which had been, up to then, neglected by competitors. Consequently my opinion was put aside.'

Jacques Graff started to walk back and forth. 'As a chief executive of the Belgian subsidiary, I am delighted. Our plant works at full capacity. But, as a member of the international board, I cannot let the English subsidiary plunge. What can we do?'

'One thing is certain', answered Françoise Gain. 'We cannot prevent our customers, namely independent wholesalers, from exporting to England, if they wish to do so. As for the English distributors, one cannot blame them for seizing a better-priced offer and simultaneously taking advantage of the promotional effort of UK Riva! I know it is more easily said than done, but you should have defined, a long time ago, an international pricing strategy at the international board level.'

'It is never too late to do the right thing! Françoise, please prepare a report on your suggestions to cope with this problem of parallel imports of the *crème base* Riva', said Graff in conclusion.

(Source: adapted from a case written by Alain Ollivier, Ecole Supérieure de Commerce de Paris. Reproduced with the kind permission of the author.)

Questions

1. Why are there problems of parallel imports? Where do they come from?
2. What can be done to stop wholesalers exporting to England?
3. Is it necessary to change the marketing strategy of *crème base* Riva, and especially its price? Where and how?
4. How should one organize for co-ordinating international marketing strategy across national markets? Prepare the suggestions Françoise Gain is supposed to present to Graff and to the international board.

A10.3   Critical incident: Taman SA

At Taman SA, a Spanish company, sales systematically exceed production. Is it a fortunate circumstance due to the know-how and energetic efficiency of the marketing and sales department? Or is it an unfortunate circumstance owing to the lack of production capacity, or to the inability of the production department to plan demand peaks effectively? Nobody knows the exact answer.

To tell the truth, one should excuse both the production department and the sales department. In fact the market for high-technology products, in which Taman has built a strong European share, is growing rapidly, at about 50 per cent p.a. Not only is Taman experiencing difficulties in trying to supply its clients, but its competitors also face the same problems.

Costs, be they direct or total, are somewhat uncertain and fuzzy. In spite of a rather elaborate cost accounting system, accountants may endlessly argue about the real cost price of a given order. Diverse and changing factors tend to blur the calculation of costs, such as the allocation of R&D expenses, the cost of components, shared expenses between different orders, price-volume relation, etc.

The director of marketing and sales and the director of production and operations are constantly in conflict. Conflicts focus on such cases as that of Magnusson AB. Magnusson AB is a new customer from whom Taman has never, up to now, received an order. Following technical tests of Taman products by Magnusson people at their factory, and after a successful certification procedure, Magnusson is ready to place a fairly large order.

The marketing and sales director argues that getting a new client is something you have to pay for. The director of production and operations considers that the largely positive margin that this order brings is smaller than that of other orders. Besides, he fears that it could disturb the production schedule for the coming weeks and consequently that it could result in numerous delivery delays.

Write in thirty lines how you would describe this problem. What ways and means would you suggest to these two directors to solve their conflict and/or to serve their customer base better?

References

Abegglen, James and George Stalk Jr (1986), 'The Japanese corporation as competitor', *California Management Review*, vol. XXVIII, no. 3 (Spring), pp. 9–27.

Allen, David Elliston (1971), 'Anthropological insights into customer behavior', *European Journal of Marketing*, vol. 5, no. 3, pp. 45–57.

Becker, Gary S. (1965), 'A theory of the allocation of time', *Economic Journal*, vol. 75 (September), pp. 493–517.

Cateora, Philip R. (1983), *International Marketing*, 5th edn, Richard D. Irwin: Homewood, IL.

Cavusgil, S. Tamer (1990), 'Unraveling the mystique of export pricing', in Hans B. Thorelli and S. Tamer Cavusgil (eds.), *International Marketing Strategy*, 3rd edn, Pergamon Press: Oxford, pp. 503–21.

Cavusgil, S. Tamer and Ed Sikora (1988), 'How multinationals can counter grey market imports', *Columbia Journal of World Business*, vol. 23, no. 4, Winter, pp. 75–85.

Curry, David J. and Peter C. Riesz (1988), 'Price and price–quality relationships: A longitudinal analysis', *Journal of Marketing*, vol. 52, January, pp. 36–51.

Jacoby, Jacob R. and Jerry C. Olson (1977), 'Consumer response to price: An attitudinal, information processing perspective', in Y. Wind and P. Greenberg (eds), *Moving Ahead with Attitude Research*, American Marketing Association: Chicago, pp. 73–86.

Johansson, Johny K. and Ikujiro Nonaka (1990), 'Japanese export marketing: Structures, strategies, counterstrategies', in Hans B. Thorelli and S. Tamer Cavusgil (eds), *International Marketing Strategy*, 3rd edn, Pergamon Press: Oxford, pp. 585–600.

Keegan, Warren J. (1984), Multinational Marketing Management, Prentice-Hall: Englewood Cliffs, NJ.

Khuri, Fuad I. (1968), 'The etiquette of bargaining in the Middle-East', *American Anthropologist*, vol. 70, pp. 693–706.

Palia, Aspy P. and Charles F. Keown (1991), 'Combating parallel importing: Views of US exporters to the Asia-Pacific region', *International Marketing Review*, vol. 8, no. 1, pp. 47–56.

Prus, Robert C. (1989a), *Pursuing Customers: An ethnography of marketing activities*, Sage Publications: Newbury Park, CA.

Prus, Robert C. (1989b), *Making Sales: Influence as interpersonal accomplishment*, Sage Publications: Newbury Park, CA.

Riesz, P. (1978), 'Price versus quality in the marketplace', *Journal of Retailing*, vol. 54, no. 4, pp. 15–28.

Saito Duerr, Mitsuko (1989), in Gerald Albaum, Jesper Strandshov, Edwin Duerr and Lawrence Dowd, *International Marketing and Export Management*, Addison-Wesley: Reading, MA.

Sjolander, Richard (1992), 'Cross-cultural effects of price on perceived quality', *European Journal of Marketing*, vol. 26, no. 7, pp. 34–44.

Sproles, George B. (1977), 'New evidence on price and quality', *Journal of Consumer Affairs*, vol. 11 (Summer), pp. 63–77.

Tellis, Gerard J. and Gary J. Gaeth (1990), 'Best value, price-seeking, and price aversion: The impact of information and learning on consumer choices', *Journal of Marketing*, vol. 54 (April), pp. 34–45.

Verna, Gérard (1989), 'Fausses facturations et commerce international', *Harvard l'Expansion*, no. 52 (Spring), pp. 110–20.

Von Stackelberg, H. (1940), *Die Grundlagen der Nationalökonomie*, Springer Verlag: Berlin.

Weber, Max (1958), *The Protestant Ethic and the Spirit of Capitalism*, Charles Scribner's Sons: New York.

Weigand, Robert E. (1991), 'Parallel import channels: Options for preserving territorial integrity', *Columbia Journal of World Business*, vol. XXVI, no. 1, pp. 53–60.

Zeithaml, Valarie A. (1988), 'Consumer perceptions of price, quality and value: A means-end model and synthesis of evidence', *Journal of Marketing*, vol. 52 (July), pp. 2–22.

them. Accordingly, they will have the benefit of a wide range of services which, although straightforward, do make life easier for the Japanese consumer:

1. Daily opening times of up to twelve or thirteen hours.
2. Very restricted periods of closure during the year, for both weekly and annual holidays.
3. Availability of free home delivery.
4. Easy acceptance of returned goods, even though the goods may not be defective.
5. Credit accounts with monthly payments for regular customers.

The compensation for the retailer is in higher gross profit margins which are about 30 per cent higher than the European average (Dupuis and de Maricourt, 1989, p. 129).

Description of the system

This strong relationship – service and loyalty, willingness to pay for the retailer's commitment to their customers – is passed on to the entire distribution structure right through the wholesalers and semi-wholesalers to the producers. Shimaguchi (1978) describes the principal characteristics of the relationships within the Japanese system of distribution by distinguishing both the practice of and the philosophy behind the system of vertical control in the distribution system that the Japanese call *Keiretsuka ryutsu*, or *Keiretsus*. This may be approximately translated into English as 'distribution channelling arrangements' or 'integrated marketing networks' (Czinkota and Woronoff, 1991, p. 57). First the practical aspects will be considered; then, after a description of the negative reactions they provoke from the non-Japanese (*Gai-jin*), there follows an attempt to show how Japanese business customs and the social representations behind them render these criticisms largely invalid.

The practical aspects revolve around a system of discounts, which is widespread and extremely complicated. These rebates operate on three levels: to encourage sales promotion (new consumers, support for products that are selling badly, clearing expensive stocks, etc.); as rewards (for the favourable placing of a product in the shop window or on the shop counter, in an attempt to increase sales); and finally as a means of control (limitation of turnover of competing products, reductions in the rate of return of sold goods, payments in cash or within a short period of time, respect for 'recommended' prices, etc.). These rebates are calculated either on a percentage basis or on a flat rate based on different kinds of sales calculations. Rebates are often confidential to encourage retailers to believe that they are receiving more than the others. However, to avoid frustration and jealousy, many producers have encouraged more explicit systems of rebate.

The system of *tegata* is the second aspect of these sales practices. *Tegatas* are deferred payment systems, based on promissory notes which allow the offer of extended credit periods to the operator at the next stage of the channel. The relationship between two successive layers in this vertical distribution network can be described as (financially) 'protected/obliged'. Trade credit is largely and liberally extended throughout the whole distribution system, rather like in Italy and France, but unlike the United States and

Germany where payment times are much shorter. Payment periods range from 60 to 120 days and sometimes to 180 days. Glazer (1968, p. 20) remarks that 'everybody uses them [promissory notes] and some are referred to as "pregnancy" notes, in that they may not become due for nine months and more'. The practice of deferred payments has a snowball effect, where everybody in the network, financially strong or not, is threatened by notes which become uncollectable. Accounts receivable are made heavier by the *tegata* practices. Financial reliance becomes not only an individual, but also a collective issue: if one member fails, it may lead to a chain reaction of bankruptcies.

Japanese distribution's commitment vis-à-vis *service to consumers*

The right to return unsold products is extremely liberal. It inevitably begins with the consumers at the end of the chain. The retailers cannot afford to hold in stock those products that have been returned by customers. This requires a system similar to that prevailing in some European countries in the publishing industry. Without any explicit order from the distributor, the producer will send a *mihakarai-okuri*, which is a delivery based on the producer's estimate of the level of stock held by the intermediary. The wholesalers accept these deliveries, although sometimes grudgingly. They then have to try to sell these extra consignments further on down the line within the network. This presupposes the fairly liberal opportunity accorded to the intermediary or to consumers to return goods even when they may not be defective.

A further aspect of the Japanese method of distribution is centred on the high frequency of deliveries. Shimaguchi (1978) explains this high frequency (retailers and wholesalers are in contact daily) in terms of limited financial resources, powerful competition and a tradition of wide personal contact between those who trade with each other. As a result the wholesalers are obliged to sell to retailers in small quantities and at short and regular intervals. Although wholesalers have a tendency to regard the system as inefficient, they accept it because, on a global level, it achieves an economic compromise between increased delivery costs and decreased inventory costs. It is worth noticing the similarities with the *kanban* system of just-in-time deliveries in the field of industrial procurement and subcontracting. One might expect these quasi-affective relationships between channel members to translate into non-aggressive price negotiations and ultimately non-competitive pricing. Nothing of the kind: the whole distribution system is very much concerned with price levels. Distributors enforce competition, without the need to shift frequently from one supplier to another in order to compel them to keep product prices low. Thus Weigand (1970, p. 24) notes:

> As a consequence of the Japanese commitment toward their employees, Japanese sellers must view prices as a highly flexible marketing instrument. The notion of marginal pricing and the importance of selling at prices that contribute to costs is well understood both by businessmen and by academicians. . . . Prices may be cut at any level in the marketing channel by firms that must have sufficient immediate income to meet their unavoidable costs, but the move ultimately will affect the retailers' cost of goods.

Furthermore, initial price setting in Japan is a key decision. Raising the price afterwards may be as difficult as reducing it. The Japanese place a high symbolic meaning on prices;

344   *Marketing across cultures*

a price reduction may spoil the image of the product, especially when it is intended as a gift (Montgomery, 1991). In fact, Japanese traders in the distribution system fight over price a great deal, in spite of their loyalty to each other; this, in turn, stimulates demand.

'Traders ... try to resolve their disputes flexibly not necessarily based on formal contacts but on their mutual trust and confidence which has been built up by human relationships and a long, stable continuity of transaction' (Kuribayashi, 1991, p. 55). The

Box 11.1   *'Master's' retailers at Dunlop France (a subsidiary of Sumitomo Rubber):* Keiretsu *distribution in France*

> The sports division of Dunlop France (a subsidiary of the Japanese Sumitomo Rubber) manufactures and markets tennis balls. It has developed a system of privileged relationships with its dealers, which is very much like the *keiretsu* system.
>
> The object is to select a limited number of retail shops that procure their articles from Dunlop France. In exchange for certain commitments, retailers receive advantages from Dunlop France. Dunlop aims to improve its brand image and to increase consumer brand awareness. Which retailers may apply for the 'Master's' label? They must be independent retail stores; this excludes large specialized sportshops and hypermarkets. They should have a good reputation with potential buyers and be recognized as experts in tennis equipment; they must also offer product lines for golf and squash. Moreover, they must enjoy total freedom of procurement.
>
> 'Master's' retailers enjoy beneficial trading conditions, as in *Keiretsu* distribution. Dunlop France is committed to informing them of new products before other retail stores, and supplying them with the new products first. Finally, Dunlop France publishes a complete list of the 'Master's' points of sale in the specialized tennis press (*Tennis de France* and *Tennis Magazine*). These benefits naturally imply some obligations for retail stores. Retail stores commit themselves to maintaining a defined level of inventory and products on display, both tennis rackets and tennis balls as well as lines for golf and squash. They also commit themselves to sell at least 70 per cent of their tennis balls annually under the Dunlop brand name.
>
> Moreover the retailer must report to Dunlop France any remarks made by consumers that may lead to improvements in the quality of new products. Ultimately, the retail store manager provides a sponsor (usually a well-known tennis professional) with Dunlop France rackets and balls. Presently about 150 stores bear the 'Master's' label. Dunlop France carefully ensures that the selected stores fulfil their obligations. The outcome, as far as brand awareness and brand image are concerned, proves quite satisfactory, especially for tennis rackets.

(Source: adapted from Zeller, 1989, pp. 33–4. Reproduced with kind permission.)

personal relationship and human association between the members of the system clearly introduce an emotive element. It is further supported by the practice of gifts. Twice a year, in the middle of the year at *ochugen* and at the end of the year at *oseibo*, the companies send out an enormous number of presents (Shimaguchi, 1978) whose cost, importance and nature conform to a complex code. This practice is further reinforced by business lunches and trips with clients, which are intended to win their friendship rather than to discuss directly any business. This would be considered the height of bad manners.

In addition to the practices cited above, producers often give support to the distribution channels in the areas of sales promotion, for example by sending out extra demonstrators and salespeople to supermarkets, or 'kits' for product presentation within the department. There are incentive schemes for retailers whereby they are offered bonuses such as a *kabuki* show, a weekend in Hong Kong or even a week in Hawaii. Although the majority of these practices do exist in other countries to varying degrees (see Box 11.1), sources agree that in Japan they exist in the strongest and most systematic form (Weigand, 1970; Shimaguchi, 1978; Kuribayashi, 1991).

Traditional Gai-jin *criticisms of the Japanese system of distribution*

Numerous converging criticisms of the Japanese distribution networks are made by foreign firms:

1. There are complaints about the distribution system being in collusion with Japanese public authorities trying to protect local business. Cateora, for instance, explains the case of the Coca-Cola company when it introduced Fresca in Japan: 'The Japan Soft Drink Bottlers Association staged an anti-*Coca-Cola* campaign in which they charged unfair marketing practices. Then, when the Coca-Cola company applied to introduce Fresca, the association put so much pressure on various Japanese ministries that the company withdrew the application' (Cateora, 1983, p. 622).
2. The *Keiretsu* distribution creates such a chain of affective relationships operating vertically between producers, wholesalers and retailers, enacted by all the practices cited above, that foreign producers find the systems impenetrable. One of the most heavily criticized aspects is the *itten itchoai* system ('single outlet, single account') which requires retailers to order only from specified wholesalers and prohibits these same wholesalers from selling to other retailers, thus restricting competition to the wholesale stage. In the same way, numerous territorial restrictions (exclusive distribution) are reinforced by the setting up of dealerships for specified areas, which cooperate amongst themselves and increase the producers' ability to impose their marketing strategies (Ishida, 1983).
3. Japanese channels are supposed to be inefficient: long, costly, complex and imposing an ultimate surcharge on the consumer. The main reason for their continued existence, despite their inefficiency, must be the Japanese wish to exclude foreign competition, to protect 'Japan Inc.' For this reason, the Japanese system of distribution has become a major target of criticism from abroad.

4. Japanese distribution systems are apparently one of the main problems encountered by foreign firms seeking to penetrate the Japanese market and are a cause of their failure (Ross, 1983).

Is the Japanese system of distribution impenetrable?

Hidden behind this question are further questions, as follows:

1. What is the philosophy of the *Keiretsu* system in Japanese distribution?
2. Is there really a practical intention (implicit or explicit) to eliminate foreign rivals?
3. Do real-life examples indicate that foreign companies have achieved original and efficient market entry?
4. What are the stages that must be followed to permit successful entry into Japanese channels while respecting the uniqueness of Japanese culture? Czinkota and Woronoff (1991) emphasize that the *Keiretsus*, which also exist in the production system, aim to 'keep it all in the family': subcontracting networks are institutionalized, whereas elsewhere they would be fluid and informal. Shimaguchi (1978) has described the main factors, deeply ingrained in the Japanese mentality, which underlie the *Keiretsu* distribution system.
5. A well-known Japanese psychoanalyst, Doi, wrote a famous book in 1973, entitled *Amae-no-kozo*, that is 'the anatomy of dependence'. Apparently *amae* is a unique feature of Japanese society, which is diffused throughout society, including the distribution channels. *Amae* is 'the indulgent, passive love which surrounds and supports the individual in a group, whether family, neighbourhood, or the world at large. Close dependency and high expectancy of others in a group seems to be the way of life in Japan' (Shimaguchi, 1978, p. 58). Nakane (1973) has also emphasized the role of *amae* in the building and the maintenance of group bonds in Japanese society. It means that relationships between channel members are not depersonalized ones, even when members belong to different companies. Frequent visits of suppliers (producers and/or wholesalers) to retailers are required for maintaining close human relationships in the channels and fostering the quality of the services rendered to the ultimate consumers.
6. A vertical structure is virtually inevitable in view of the Japanese mentality. The notion of social status is central to Japanese culture. In the field of interpersonal relationships there are three distinct levels: the *sempai* are people of advanced years, very respected, addressed by their name and the suffix *san*; younger, less experienced people (the *kohai*) are addressed by their name with the suffix *kun*; colleagues on the same level in the hierarchy (same age, experience and seniority) are the *doryo* and should be addressed without a suffix The determination of social status is extremely important and is one of the major reasons behind the widespread practice of exchanging business cards. Vertical relationships exist between organizations in much the same way as between individuals.
7. The Japanese are fairly long-term oriented and their sense of time (*Makimono* time, see section 2.2) emphasizes continuity, stability and perseverance. According to Inagaki (quoted in Turpin, 1990) Japanese persistence is instilled into Japanese people

by their mothers from early childhood. A survey based on a representative sample of 3,600 Japanese (over 16-years-old) has shown that, among the ten preferred words of the Japanese, *doryoku* (effort) ranks first, *nintai* (persistence) second, and *kanjo* (tenacity) ranks fifth.

8. Japanese business is much more turnover- than profit-oriented. Japanese companies tend, as far as possible, to accept business as soon as the sale price covers direct costs and begins to cover fixed costs. This fact is illustrated by Hanawa (quoted by Shimaguchi, 1978): '*Kami yori usui Kosen* (margins thinner than paper) is a common saying in Japanese business circles. In certain cases, with a complete disregard for producers' price lists, Japanese distributors end up bargaining machines after harsh negotiations at a price lower than list. Why such low margins'? There is a Japanese business philosophy which believes that 'A deal done is better than none'.

9. The Japanese themselves (Yoshino, 1971; Shimaguchi, 1978; Ishida, 1983; Kuribaya-shi, 1991) admit that the *Keiretsu* system is infused with a sense of conservatism, and that it does not lead to innovation. They probably appreciate in the distribution system (a very relational and human sector, everywhere in the world) the warm, sensitive and emotional tradition which permeates marketing and business in Japan.

The question of whether or not *Keiretsu* distribution is intentionally a barrier to the entry of foreign goods on the Japanese market is a difficult one. It seems to be an accusation against the Japanese for what is essentially their way of being. As stated above they are themselves quite critical of their distribution system. According to Ishida (1983, p. 322):

... the formation of distribution keiretsu in oligopolistic markets for highly differentiated products has the following consequences:

1. Elimination or reduction of interbrand and intrabrand price competition.
2. Strengthening of barriers against new entrants to the market.
3. Restriction of dealer independence with a consequent loss of business enthusiasm, innovation, and rationalisation.
4. Preservation and strengthening of oligopolies.

It may be argued that the above aims to accord tokens of goodwill to the American negotiators (in the Americans' relations with their Japanese counterparts, and in the GATT arena in general), greatly irritated by the Japanese distribution channels which Americans clearly do not understand. This does not prevent the Japanese from recognizing the way in which they may be seen by the *Gai-jin*. But they are not really prepared to change that part of the system which is authentically Japanese, and which constitutes the major barrier resented by non-Japanese business people.

Overcoming the barrier of Japanese distribution

Many instances tend to show that the barriers imposed by Japanese distribution channels may be overcome. Ohmae (1985) quotes the case of the US pharmaceutical company Shaklee, which has directly transferred its door-to-door sales system from the United

348   *Marketing across cultures*

Box 11.2   *Rosenthal in Japan*

> Rosenthal, a German company, exports porcelain items, fine glassware and trinkets, which sell quite well on the Japanese market, more as gifts than for the buyer's use. The range of products offered in Japan is somewhat different to that in other countries: emphasis is put more on tea-drinking items, which may be offered as presents, than on dishes. Rosenthal constantly surveys the Japanese market, in order to adapt its product range to Japanese tastes and to find those items which could best be sold in Japan. Over the last twenty years, Rosenthal has established close relations with its Japanese distributors. They are frequently invited to visit Rosenthal's production facilities in Germany. Rosenthal assists them a great deal in the display of its products on the shelves and maintains a full-time team of window dressers in Japan. The main dealers, that is large department stores, are visited at least once a week. Moreover Rosenthal has initiated a special training session for Japanese retailers: each year a group of Japanese retailers is invited to a ten-day session in Germany, with all expenses paid by Rosenthal, in order to learn how to advise customers. Retailers greatly appreciate this support, and they willingly push Rosenthal's products, especially since margins are hefty.

(Source: Dupuis and de Maricourt, 1989, p. 152. Reproduced with kind permission.)

States to Japan. Shaklee had noticed that no legal rule obliged the sale of vitamins and nutritive pills through medical doctors or pharmacists. It was only a habit: no regulation had formally imposed it. The Japanese pharmaceutical companies observed the phenomenal growth of Shaklee sales but were unable to react. They were afraid of damaging relations with their traditional intermediaries, especially wholesalers and retail pharmacists. They were still obliged to rely on them for the sales of their drugs. Another US-based pharmaceutical company, Bristol-Meyers, also implemented such a door-to-door sales programme, with their Japanese joint-venture partner (Cateora, 1983). The product was sold in a box which contained toothpaste, analgesics and other home remedies, and was offered to households on the basis of consignment sale: every six months a salesperson visited the household, replenished the collection and collected the payment for the products that had been used.

Such cases as Rosenthal (see Box 11.2) or ComputerLand (case A11.1) clearly prove that Japanese distribution channels are penetrable by foreign companies. Montgomery (1991) also provides evidence of US companies, such as Williams Sonoma, successfully circumventing the *Keiretsu* distribution system, via catalogue sales and limited retail stores of their own. Moreover, the Japanese distribution system does change, especially under the harsh competitive forces of the Japanese market. As stated by Ohmae (1985), it is not a 'stone statue', nor are there written rules which prohibit its change.

How to deal with the Japanese distribution system

A five-stage approach for the successful introduction of a foreign product into Japanese distribution channels can be recommended (Shimaguchi and Rosenberg, 1979; Montgomery, 1991):

1. Find a Japanese partner; it is a key to securing adaptability to the unique cultural environment. The *sogoshosha* (trading companies) are potential partners, provided that they do not represent a competing Japanese producer or export the products of a Japanese competitor, and are not related to a larger group (*zaibatsu*) which has competing lines of products. An important choice is to decide whether to ally with a company in the same industry or in a non-related industry. Whereas one may tend naturally to the former in order to ensure a smooth start (the two partners share the same business culture), it may prove much more dangerous in the long run. The Japanese local partner may become a competitor on world markets through new products which were originally designed by the joint venture and then transferred to the Japanese partner's main operations (Czinkota and Woronoff, 1991).
2. Find an original positioning on the market, either by offering a significantly higher level of quality or a significant price advantage, or by emphasizing the exoticism of the product as being foreign and imported.
3. Identify alternative opportunities for distribution channels. Philips, for instance, has succeeded in splitting its sales of electric shavers and small household appliances between two different types of channels: large department stores and chains on the one hand, small retailers on the other.
4. Be patient, target for the long term and be prepared to wait for a long pay-back period (five to ten years probably).
5. Be aware that it is necessary to adopt the mentality of Japanese distribution channels. Build a network of personal relationships, develop loyalty, spend time and resources building relationships of trust.

11.2   Criteria for choosing foreign distribution channels

The method for selecting channels abroad that is advocated by Cateora (1983) is entitled the 6-Cs method, and Czinkota and Ronkainen (1990) distinguish 11-Cs as criteria for such a selection. They present a checklist of issues that have to be dealt with in the choice of foreign distribution channels. The 9-Cs criteria, which seemed most significant are as follows:

1. *Consumers and their characteristics*. Some geographical segments in a foreign market may be, for instance, more import-oriented. Channels serving these segments should therefore be preferred. The French beer Kronenbourg, for example, entered the United States and was initially available only in the centre of New York, before reaching the whole metropolis including the suburbs. The reason for this is that people within this area consume large quantities of imported as well as US beer. It was not until five years later that Kronenbourg became available throughout the whole of the United States.
2. *Culture*. This point has already been considered in the example of the Japanese distribution networks. Distribution is the element of the marketing mix which is most deeply rooted in culture: because it is tightly related to everyday life and human relationships (even in large-scale, self-service, apparently depersonalized stores). The

next section describes in more detail the impact of culture on selected aspects of distribution.

3. *Character*. It is important that the image projected by the channel, its sales' methods, shop locations and clientele as well as appearance, should correspond to the image and character that the product is intended to convey. An important reason behind the success of Louis Vuitton-Malletier relates to the large scale of investment in a global network of exclusive retail outlets, located in high profile areas in major cities throughout the world.

4. Necessary *capital* relates to the issue of what financial resources are necessary to start and maintain the channel (fixed capital, working capital, possible initial losses which will need to be financed).

5. *Cost*. This criterion is strongly linked to the previous one, but relates more to trade margins than to overhead costs. It depends largely on the respective positions of strength of producers and distributors. In the United Kingdom, for instance, distribution is in the hands of a very limited number of large chain stores such as Tesco, Sainsbury or Asda. These giants exert pressure on major manufacturers to make them bear part of the cost, in particular those relating to storage; they also request smaller, more frequent deliveries with mixed items. A similar situation exists in France where the powerful hypermarkets impose numerous constraints on the producers which increase their overheads: payments of fixed commissions in return for the right to carry the reference number, layout of the counter displays by the producer's own staff, direct help in sales promotion, etc.

6. *Competition* arises in channels either through competing products being placed side by side on shelves, or through competitors refusing other producers access to the distribution channels. Czinkota and Ronkainen (1990) cite the case of the American manufacturers of caustic soda, which is used in the manufacture of glass, steel and chemical products, who have proved incapable of successful entry into the Japanese market despite their price advantage. The Japanese union of manufacturers of caustic soda formed a cartel which apparently set the level of imports, specified which trading company was to work with which American supplier and bought up the cheap American imports in order to sell them through the intermediary of its members. The success of the operation was twofold since they received the profit in place of the American exporter and still managed to keep control of their market. The American exporters were equally unsuccessful in their attempts to deal directly through small distributors, since the industrial users of the product were concerned about the risk of cutting themselves out from their main source of supply (the Japanese) if they placed orders directly with the American exporters.

7. *Coverage* is another important element. It is important to cover markets that are widely scattered. Furthermore, markets that are very concentrated tend also to concentrate maximum competition, since demand attracts supply. The coverage in terms of product range, sizes and options, must also be considered, especially when channel members look for complementary products, spare parts and so on.

8. *Continuity*. It is vital that the channel in which investment is to be made does not turn out to be unusable for some reason (e.g. bankruptcy or financial difficulties, recapture of market share by more aggressive competition, the introduction of legal prohibitions

on the sale of products through the channel, etc.). Continuity may be hampered by slick competitors. Cateora (1983) cites the example of an American firm which lost roughly half its local sales in South America. Two of its European competitors had unofficially agreed to force the American company out of the market. One of the two, which was selling a wide range of products, forced the distributors to stop representing the even wider range marketed by the American. The other competitor purchased shares in the company that distributed the American company's products.

9. *Control*. The ideal situation is of course where the company creates its own distribution network, which ensures maximum control. It appears that the decision to integrate the company's own distribution abroad should be considered, particularly when the product differentiation is large (i.e. where there are few substitutes) or where the network assets are transaction-specific, such as a product which requires lengthy training for the consumer as well as the seller (Anderson and Coughlan, 1987). The alternative to control by equity is control set up by carefully drafted contract (the written base), or more preferably through long-established trustful relationships with the local distributor (personal verbal base). For example, the Caterpillar company sells world-wide without sales subsidiary companies, by using a system of dealers. Some Caterpillar dealers have been in business for more than half a century.

11.3 The role of distribution as a 'cultural filter'

Culture at the interface between shoppers and the stores

Distribution forms subtle relationships with consumers by means of direct contact. People get into the habits of buying certain products which are backed by fixed services, at clearly defined times, in particular shops. Table 11.1 presents guidelines for enquiring how distribution is affected by the prevailing cultural patterns in a definite country/ culture context. The table refers to specific sections in other chapters where some of the underlying rationales have already been exposed. Naturally culture explains only part of the variance in distribution systems; another part is related to shoppers and their sociodemographic characteristics or to economic conditions.

Shopping behaviour differs in many ways according to culture. The first point is whether the shopping experience is partly experienced as a waste of time in the whole consumption process, which may be the case in countries where time is strongly economic. The differences in opening hours between northern and southern Europe clearly illustrate the influence of culture on the distribution system: in northern Europe, Sunday is sacred and a prevailing feminine orientation strives at protecting store employees' quality of life which would be spoilt by extensive opening hours.

Certain products may be banned from a definite type of outlets because of legal dispositions based on religious or social beliefs. In France, for instance, basic drugs, and more generally non-ethical drugs such as aspirin, can be sold only through pharmacies; in the United States, as in many countries, drugstores sell basic medicines. This corresponds to differing views of whether people can have recourse to self-medication. The French legislator does not trust patients and obliges them to proceed in any case through doctors and pharmacists, whereas the US system is confident in people's common sense for distinguishing what is 'flu and what is a serious illness. Another example is given by the distribution of beer in Turkey, a Muslim country; up to June 1984, beer was considered a non-alcoholic beverage and thus sold in coffee-houses; beer consumption had increased sixfold between 1969 and 1983. Under pressure from religious authorities, the government reclassified beer as an alcoholic beverage (which it is), banned its advertising on radio and television and prohibited its sales in outlets lacking alcohol licences. The prohibition of sales through the channel of coffee-houses resulted in a dramatic drop of beer sales in Turkey (Miller and Demirel, 1988).

Wide differences also exist in the waiting and service conditions at the cashier's desks: in the United States and Japan it is standard practice in supermarkets to help customers pack their purchases; an employee is often specifically in charge of packing; in most of Europe, where mass distribution is oriented towards low price rather than service, customers have to pack their things in a hurry while paying their bill (Turcq and Usunier, 1985).

Theft, either by customers or store employees, is an important phenomenon in distribution that has to deciphered, country by country, in light of cultural differences. Naturally economic constraints (purchasing power per capita) play a certain role but they do not explain all: in France or Italy, theft is more developed than in Greece which has

Table 11.1 *Influence of culture on some aspects of distribution* vis-à-vis *shoppers*

Selected aspects of distribution	Traits which *may* differ according to country/culture
(1) Shopping behaviour	Is time spent shopping experienced as wasted (economic time; section 2.2)
	Is return of goods standard behaviour (complaining behaviour; section 4.3)
	Who is the shopper? (sex roles, age, etc.)
	Degree of loyalty to the shop and the shopkeeper (section 4.2)
(2) Opening hours	Religion-based arguments in favour of restricted store opening hours
	Femininity-based arguments (store personnel should not be exploited)
(3) Product range	Products may be banned because of religious or legal prescriptions
(4) Willingness to service consumers	Human nature is good (friendliness towards shoppers) versus bad (indifference)/negative view of service to others (section 8.3)
(5) Waiting lines	Compliance with rules (see Tables 3.3 on, sections 3.6 and 8.3)
(6) Thefts by consumers or personnel	Ethical behaviour – in-group orientation (see sections 2.3, 3.6 and 14.6)
(7) Self-service vs personnel in contact	See section 8.3

a much smaller per capita income. In some countries, theft is not a problem because it is clearly understood as evil by everybody. The kind of consensus which brings this favourable result is hard to explain, and probably even more harder to replicate. Where the rate of theft to sales reaches several per cent, it is not simply economic conditions, namely poverty, that explain such records. Theft is valued as a sport and is implicitly understood as a legitimate way of social redistribution. Another explanation is the strong ingroup orientation whereby ethical behaviour is limited to the ingroup: in countries where retailers are immigrants belonging to a particular foreign group, thieving from a store that belongs to a foreigner may not be felt as something evil but rather as a way to recover one's own good from this 'outlander'.

The influence of culture on the relationship between channel members

Depending on the country the relationships between domestic producers and distributors may be stronger, more loyal and collaborative, or weaker, more unstable and conflictual. Strongly established links between domestic channels members generally make entry more difficult for foreign firms. France, which largely invented the concept of the hypermarket, benefits from a distribution set-up that is effective, powerful and strongly independent of producers. It is so strong that products bearing the store name compete head to head with the producers' brands, creating a conflictual atmosphere between producers and distributors where loyalty is difficult to maintain. The system is inherently susceptible to penetration by imports: foreign suppliers are perceived as more flexible and a good alternative to domestic producers. At the other extreme Japan is the place where links between producers and distributors are traditionally very strong and positive. Central to this are the *Keiretsus* of distribution, true vertical relationships, mixing business and emotion in typically Japanese fashion, described in section 11.1. These networks are based on a powerful sense of loyalty, with many services being rendered by one party for the other, and therefore are more difficult for foreign companies to penetrate.

Kale and McIntyre (1991) posit a series of hypotheses on channel relationship based on Hofstede's (1980) four cultural dimensions. They first consider the initiation process where firms try to draft the distribution agreement. According to them companies coming from high uncertainty avoidance (UA) societies will be biased in favour of finding partners who have a solid reputation and can offer written performance guarantees; conversely, in the case of weak UA, partners will be sought more informally and more flexibility will be shown in negotiations. Firms in highly individualist and masculine cultures (typically the United States) will tend to choose partners on objective criteria, negotiate the terms of the agreement from an adversarial standpoint, and engage in new relationships as well as divorce from the old ones on the basis of economic criteria. Conversely, partners coming from collectivist and relatively feminine societies (for instance South Korea, Taiwan, Thailand) will be more relationship-centred, expect more harmony in the partnership, and dissolution will be less aggressive and less frequent.

During the implementation process, Kale and McIntyre hypothesize that high power distance (PD) will lead firms to use coercion in their influence attempts, whereas small

PD firms will avoid it, stress face-to-face communication over memos and engage in consultative rather than unilateral decision making. High individualism and masculinity will result in more frequent and manifest conflicts between channel members and lower cooperation. In contrast to these orientations, they cite a senior executive of Coca-Cola in Japan explaining that: 'Once the partnership was in place, it wasn't just the Coca-Cola company selling in Japan; it became a family, a spirit of togetherness, of common purpose.'

O'Grady and Lane (1992), by interviewing chief executive officers of almost 300 companies on both sides, show that Canadian retailers when they enter the US market have to face different values. Americans are significantly more competition oriented (more achievement oriented, more risk taking) and more oriented towards a Protestant work ethic than the Canadians. The Canadian retailers are shown to be less individualistic and masculine and higher in power distance and risk avoidance than the American distributors. These findings are largely consistent with the hypotheses of Kale and McIntyre in distinguishing competitive/confrontational distribution scenes versus collaborative ones: 'The executives frequently commented that Americans were found to be much more competitive than Canadians. Frequently the executives voiced comments typically used to describe battles such as "It was all out war" or "Their arsenal was impressive" ' (1991, p. 8).

In the case of Greek exporters (collectivist/high UA and PD) and their British importers (individualistic/low UA and PD), Katsikeas and Piercy (1991) show that the relationships are fairly stable with a low degree of conflicts and communication problems, except on pricing issues. This is reinforced by the fact that, among the British importers, there are a good number of Greeks or Cypriots, which shows the value of having one's own countrymen as 'beachheads' in the target market.

11.4 Sales promotion: other customs, other manners

Sales promotion techniques as such are fairly universal. It is mostly their use and the conditions of their implementation which vary cross-nationally and depend on cultural variables (see Box 11.3). Sales promotion targets some basic marketing objectives that are cross-culturally valid. It aims to engage the consumer in either of the following: (1) a first trial; (2) a first purchase; (3) an immediate purchase; (4) re-buying; (5) increasing purchase frequency; and (6) entering a point of sale.

Promotional techniques combine the sales proposal with the following:

1. Discounts or rebates of various kinds: coupons, 'in-pack' money-off, reimbursement offers, etc., mostly directed at immediate purchase.
2. Competitions: games, contests, lotteries, sweepstakes, etc.
3. Collection devices of various kinds (stamps and continuity plans), oriented towards increasing purchase frequency and building consumer loyalty.
4. Free samples or some kind of cross-product offer, for the purpose of consumer trial especially.
5. Gifts: 'in-pack' gifts, purchase with purchase, reusable packaging, product bonus, etc.

Box 11.3   *Global transferability of sales promotions*

A case in point was Lego A/S, the Danish toy marketer which undertook American-style consumer promotion in Japan a few years ago. Earlier, the company had measurably improved its penetration of U.S. households by employing 'bonus' packs and gift promotions. Encouraged by that success, it decided to transfer these tactics unaltered to other markets, including Japan, where penetration had stalled. But these lures left Japanese consumers unmoved. Subsequent investigation showed that consumers considered the promotions to be wasteful, expensive, and not very appealing. Similar reactions were recorded in other countries. Lego's marketers thus got their first lesson on the limitations of the global transferability of sales promotions.

(Source: from Kashani, 1989, pp. 92–3. Reproduced with permission.)

Cross-national differences in the use of sales promotion techniques

The first question to be addressed is: who is the target? Sales promotion may also address the store personnel by encouraging them to stock the product or to display it in a favourable position, or to promote the product directly. In some countries, batteries are sold mostly because store personnel put a brand in a more favourable display than others; reasons for this might be the gifts they receive from the batteries' manufacturers, ranging from a camera to vacations abroad. In less-developed countries, where retailers in rural areas lack resources, they may be more appropriate targets for sales promotion than the final consumers who have little choice but to buy what is actually in the only store available. Similarly, where people have servants who shop for food and household supplies, it may be better to target them, who are the actual buyers, rather than the members of the family who employs them (Foxman *et al.*, 1988).

A second question is whether a technique is considered moral or immoral: sales promotion regulations differ cross-nationally according to various assumptions about what is moral or immoral and what is fair or unfair in the relationship between a merchandiser/sales promoter and a customer/shopper. Most developed countries strictly regulate sales promotion in order to prevent abuses (Boddewyn and Leardi, 1989). There is also some fear, as with advertising, that sales promotion costs would result in excessive overpricing of products. Czinkota and Ronkainen (1990) cite the example of AC Nielsen, which tried to introduce money coupons in Chile that had to be sent to the manufacturer for reimbursement. The supermarket union opposed the promotion on the grounds that it would raise costs unnecessarily and recommended its members not to accept the coupons.

The areas where ethical issues are mostly raised are competitions, gifts and cross-product offers. The United Kingdom and the United States are the most favourable countries for sales promotions (Boddewyn and Leardi, 1989). Anglo-Saxon countries are generally more liberal than other countries, especially for competitions: most kinds of lotteries, free draws and sweepstakes are legally permitted. In most Anglo-Saxon countries, private organizations for betting are permitted (bookmakers), whereas in most other countries in the world, betting (horse races, lotteries) is state-controlled, since it is seen as immoral for private individuals to profit from organizing lotteries and betting games. Italy authorizes lotteries and sweepstakes where prizes are not in cash but in kind. Prizes in competitions are often limited to small amounts: the Netherlands limits prizes to 250 guilders, which severely restricts the attractiveness of sales promotion competitions. France allows competitions, but these are carefully controlled so that no purchase is needed to enter the competition. This leads in many countries to precisely drafted regulations where terms such as 'purchase obligation' and 'chance' are strictly defined (see Box 11.4 describing regulation of sales promotion by competition in the canton of Geneva, Switzerland, where Swiss precision leaves little room for ambiguity).

Many national regulations prohibit gifts or limit their value. In France, the value of a promotional gift cannot be higher than 4 per cent of the retail price and must not exceed ten francs (two dollars). The idea behind this prohibition is that consumers should buy products, not gifts. If the value of the gift is too high in comparison to the total price of the item, this could result in the consumers being fooled by the merchandiser. Collectors' items are subject to the same kind of regulatory ceiling as gifts: the value of the collector's item associated with the purchase is often legally limited. Sales promotions encouraging a first trial, such as cross-product offers, purchase with purchase offers, are often controlled by national legislation because when consumers pay for two products at the same time they cannot clearly assess the one for which they actually pay. A description of the rules of the main countries concerning sales promotion (regularly updated) may be found in Boddewyn (1992).

Some sales promotion techniques are fairly resistant cross-culturally, since they appear less questionable: free samples as a way to induce people to try the product; money off the next purchase as a way to induce consumers to repeat their purchase; point-of-purchase materials, product tasting or demonstration as a way to increase consumer knowledge of the product, etc. However, some countries object to sales promotion techniques in general because of the risk of consumers being misled. Whereas some countries believe in the personal responsibility and ability to seek and evaluate information (the United Kingdom, the United States), others have less confidence in the capacities of individual consumers to make free and responsible choices (Latin-European and northern European countries). In Scandinavian countries, the greatest difficulties are met when implementing sales promotion, since every promotion has to be approved by an official body.

Socio-cultural factors influencing the implementation of sales promotion techniques

Table 11.2 presents a series of socio-cultural factors, some of them already mentioned above, which influence the implementation of sales promotion techniques. The level of literacy is obviously an important variable to be considered: promotion is often associated with text and if the target is near to illiterate, people will not respond to a coupon campaign for instance. Level of literacy becomes crucial true when the purpose of the campaign is consumer education. Case A13.2 gives examples of promotional campaigns in Africa, where a promotional film was used in Kenyan villages with the driver operator

Box 11.4 *Sales promotion through competitions in Switzerland (Geneva)*

Competitions for sales promotion are governed by the law on lotteries. The basic principle is fairly simple: *chance cannot be linked with an obligation to purchase.* On this basis there are three situations where a competition is considered lawful:

1. There is no purchase obligation and the right answers are not to be found by chance.
2. There is a purchase obligation and the right answers are not to be found by chance.
3. There is no purchase obligation and the right answers are to be found by chance.

Consequently, it is necessary to define the two expressions 'purchase obligations' and 'chance'

Definition of 'purchase obligation'

1. A label, a cap, or any part of a packaging has to be sent by post.
2. The entry form for the competition is printed on the reverse of a label.
3. The entry form is inside the packaging.
4. There is a participation fee for the competition.
5. The competition is announced in a place where people are attending a paying performance.
6. Where the competition is organized by a newspaper and is publicly advertised and the newspaper or magazine has to be bought in order to cut out the entry form.
7. A piece of information is required which is on the label or packaging, and cannot be found by simply looking at the product on the shelves.
8. If, to obtain such information, people are compelled to enter a sales room where they cannot 'escape' the salesperson, the judge may consider that there is a 'moral constraint' on the purchase.

Definition of 'chance'

1. Random draw.
2. Random draw in the event of tied entries.
3. A question which cannot be answered by skill, science, calculus or knowledge, for instance: time duration of the winner covering the distance of a race; flight time of a plane; number of cigarettes or matches which have to be put end to end in order to cover the distance between two cities; to be the tenth visitor to an exhibition, the twentieth buyer of a product, and so on.

(Source: adapted from Gambiez *et al.*, 1988, pp. 12–13.)

handing free samples of the product to the audience. Visual and oral promotion should be preferred over written materials as soon as literacy rate is low.

Retailer sophistication is required when the promotional techniques need some follow-up, such as for coupon redemption or dealing with stamps, or collectors' devices, that is each time the retailer needs to be an intermediary between the manufacturer and the final consumer in a fairly organized way (stocking coupons, reckoning, ordering premiums, etc.). If prizes are given, they must fit with the target tastes: this is especially important for competitions where the prizes are advertised. Cars, trips, various household equipment goods, or cash can be seen as possible prizes: whenever legally possible, cash is the most universally accepted kind of prize, since it allows further spending freely.

Unethical behaviour of trade *vis-à-vis* the manufacturer is possible in a number of cases: retailers can decide to sell what were supposed to be free-samples or they can pocket price-off offers by increasing prices. Retailer employees can 'swerve' samples, gifts or premiums. Strict control of retailers involved in the promotion is required wherever such opportunistic attitudes are possible.

Promotional techniques can be associated with images of social status. Foxman *et al.* (1988) give the example of Hong Kong where response to coupons is very positive, while use of stamps is popular in Thailand, both of these locally popular techniques being associated with middle-class status. In many countries coupons or price-off offers can be associated with low class status, because the implied price-consciousness mediates an image of low purchasing power. On the other hand, promotional techniques based on a price-reduction cannot be implemented in countries where basic prices are not displayed and bargaining is the rule: the rebate has a sense only in as much as a clear market price is known by the consumer. Once again, in such cases, it is better to target channel members rather than the end user, for instance by offering the retailer a rebate for quantity after a certain period of time, which he or she will be obliged to transfer in advance to customers in order to build volume.

Table 11.2 *Cross-cultural adequacy problems for selected sales promotion techniques*

Technique	Culture-related features which may affect implementation
Coupons	Level of literacy, consumer and retailer sophistication/ low social status implied
Contests and sweepstakes	Legal requirements/prize choice must fit with target market tastes
Price-offs	Absence of price labelling and display/bargaining/trade misuse
Stamps and collections	Future orientation needed/high inflation/level of channel sophistication
Free samples	Interpretation of gratuity/trade misuse/theft of sampled products
Gifts (in, on or near packs)	Legal requirements/theft by channel employees or customers

Some promotional techniques require extended involvement, which is the case of collectors' devices, stamps or self-liquidating premiums, refunds after a series of purchases, etc. Cultures with a present time orientation respond poorly to these techniques which require future orientation because of delayed gratification (Foxman *et al.*, 1988). Similarly high inflation is very detrimental to any sales promotion whose rewards are not near to immediate: the face value of coupons, price-off and other rebates may make little sense after a few weeks, which were necessary for printing, sending to the trade and for consumers to claim the rebates.

The final caveat is that it must be checked that the very purpose of the promotional technique is locally understood (a problem in conceptual equivalence). For instance, in many societies being given a free sample is difficult to interpret. The basic rationale that a producer wants consumers to try a product in order to have them buy it is not self-evident. Gratuity is understood either as a sign of poor quality ('they give it because they cannot sell it') or as a sign of naivety of the manufacturer ('let's take as much as possible'). P & G, which is now quickly expanding in eastern Europe, experienced major problems with free samples in Poland in 1993, where some people disregarded free samples while some others broke mailboxes to steal as many samples as they could. In any case, it must be kept in mind that price reductions are by far the most popular sales promotion techniques (Boddewyn and Leardi, 1989).

Questions

1. A distribution formula is successful in the United States; you are asked to extend it through a franchise system to several countries around the world. How would you devise a policy for those franchisees who want adaptation to the standard recipe for their home market, in the following areas: size of the store, personnel recruitment, servicing, stocking, brands represented, display, store name, etc?
2. What are the ways in which retailing know-how is transferred internationally?
3. Discuss the distinguishing features of the Japanese distribution system.
4. Why do exporting firms tend to have somewhat different distribution channels abroad compared to their domestic market, apart from the peculiarities of the local distribution systems?
5. By law, the typical store in Germany is opened each day, from Monday to Friday, from 9 a.m. to 6.30 p.m. On Saturday, German shops close at 2 p.m., and they all close on Sunday. Once a month there is a special shopping Thursday, and stores open till 8.30 p.m. Conversely, opening hours in the United States are much broader and some supermarkets have 24-hour opening, seven days a week. Stores employees in Germany are highly unionized and unions have traditionally opposed any increase in opening hours.

   To what extent do time-related cultural differences explain the huge difference in store opening hours between Germany and the United States?
6. Discuss how store size can be related to culture.
7. Explain how cultural values can have a negative impact on self-service and automated service in general (that is, without personnel in contact with the shopper/consumer).

8. Based on available statistics, review key differences in the retailing systems in the countries of the European Union.

APPENDIX 11

—————— ◆◆◆ ——————

Teaching materials

A11.1   Case: ComputerLand in Japan

ComputerLand recognized that they would need a Japanese partner in order to enter the Japanese market. Because of government regulations and attitude, it probably would not have been possible to obtain permission to establish a wholly owned subsidiary. Additionally, the complexities of the Japanese market would have made development of franchises there very difficult. (Both McDonald's and Kentucky Fried Chicken entered the market with Japanese partners.)

ComputerLand wanted a partner who had experience in both procurement and distribution of computer products. Though they talked with a number of companies, Kanematsu-Gosho Ltd emerged as the top candidate. Kanematsu-Gosho was a major trading company, had experience in the desired areas, and already had business dealing with IBM.

ComputerLand entered into negotiations with the Japanese company in order to try to develop a joint venture. The discussions, which lasted for nine months, were detailed and difficult. The Chairman of ComputerLand was concerned that if his vice-president went to Japan to negotiate, he would be at a disadvantage trying to operate in the different culture. He therefore insisted that the negotiations be done in the United States by telephone from Japan.

This made it difficult for the Japanese to negotiate. The Japanese decision-making process requires much more consultation and agreement with the company than would normally be necessary in European and American firms. There were long delays and a lot that had to be done through telex correspondence. Among other things, the Japanese government had to be persuaded to allow the American partner to have a 50% ownership rather than the customary (at the time) minority position.

The agreement was finally concluded with ComputerLand contributing knowledge, trademark, and technology and Kanematsu-Gosho contributing cash to start the joint venture, ComputerLand Japan Ltd.

The Vice-President of ComputerLand then went to Japan to head the operation as Vice-President and Resident Director. A number of policy and operational problems had to be solved.

In the United States, franchisees were required to pay cash before merchandise would be shipped to them. An attempt was made to follow this policy in Japan. Retailers in Japan, however, are used to receiving credit from wholesalers – often for 0 to 90 days or even longer. A cash-in-advance policy proved to be impossible in Japan, so the company eventually went to a 10-day-open-credit policy.

In the United States, franchises were given only to individuals, not to corporations or other businesses. This was done so that the stores would be personally managed by the owners. ComputerLand Japan was not able to find a sufficient number of individuals who had or could obtain the necessary cash. Eventually the policy was changed to allow a company to own a minority interest.

As in Europe, store locations and format were also a problem. Within the United States, ComputerLand insisted on a minimum size for a store of 2000 square feet [185 m²], a location with a large amount of traffic going by, and a parking lot in the rear. This was simply not possible in most locations in Japan.

It was also difficult to attract top-quality people as employees to work for a foreign company in Japan. Finally, there were simple problems of coordination between proprietor-owned ComputerLand and large, publicly owned Kanematsu-Gosho.

In spite of these difficulties, ComputerLand Japan was very successful, growing to 50 franchises with annual sales of US$50 million. It was assisted greatly by the fact that, for the first two years of operation, ComputerLand had the exclusive distribution right in Japan for the IBM PC.

Over the years, Kanematsu-Gosho found it increasingly difficult to continue to accept some of ComputerLand's policy. Additionally, they felt that the American partner was simply exercising too much control. When ComputerLand offered to buy them out, Kanematsu-Gosho agreed. The operation then became a wholly owned subsidiary of the United States corporation. Eventually, this subsidiary was sold to one of the franchisees who continues to operate it under a license agreement with ComputerLand.

(Source: written by John T. Sakai, Director, AZCA Inc., former Vice-President of Computer-Land. Reproduced with the kind permission of the author.)

Questions

1. Was it wise for ComputerLand to insist on holding the negotiations in the United States? What were the advantages and disadvantages to each of the parties? Why did Kanematsu-Gosho agree to the location?
2. Analyze the differences between the Japanese and American distribution systems as they appear in this case. Which elements of the 'ComputerLand model' are transferable to Japan?
3. When exporting to another country or setting up a joint venture there, how can you decide which of the local customs and business practices you should accept, and which of your home country practices you should introduce?

A11.2 Case: Aunt Sarah's Fried Chicken

Early in March 1993, Jean Michel, president of Aunt Sarah's Fried Chicken–Europe, was faced with the problem of maintaining quality control among franchisees in Germany. He had received reports that several of the franchisees in Germany were serving potato pancakes instead of French fries. Also, there were reports of inconsistency in the size of the servings of chicken. Aunt Sarah's had built its reputation on its ability to offer a completely standardized product of high quality in every retail outlet.

Aunt Sarah's Fried Chicken was started by Sarah Browning in a little shop in Dallas, Texas, in 1958. The great popularity of her home-style fried chicken led to expansion to other locations in Dallas and in neighbouring cities. Because of limitations of capital expansion to other American markets was accomplished through franchises. By 1977, Aunt Sarah's had 760 franchise outlets in the United States. From the time she opened her second location in Dallas, Ms Browning had found that her most difficult continuing problem was in maintaining consistent standards of quality in all retail outlets. When she launched into franchising, she recognized that this problem of quality control would become even more serious, since the many individual franchisees lacked the same experience and commitment to a standardized product as did members of the Aunt Sarah's organization. Franchisee visitation and quality control were placed under the direction of a separate division headed by Ms Browning's daughter, Cynthia. In 1993, the American market was divided into nine regions, each with its own Sales, Site Selection and Construction, and Operations and Quality Control divisions.

In 1978, an entrepreneur in Paris, France, sought and received the first franchise outside the United States. As requests began to be received for other foreign franchises, it became necessary in 1981 to establish Aunt Sarah's Export Company, a wholly owned subsidiary. Aunt Sarah's chicken fitted into European eating preferences well as a popular foreign novelty item. It soon became evident that the European market was potentially large and should be actively cultivated. In 1983, the European division was set up with Jean Michel, a Belgian advertising executive, as the new director, with the headquarters office in Brussels. Michel was successful in establishing new franchise outlets at the rate of about ten per year. By 1987 there were sixty-one outlets in Europe, more than Michel could personally supervise. Since the Aunt Sarah reputation was just as dependent on high-quality food preparation and absolute consistency in Europe as in the United States, it was necessary to improve the system for maintaining careful supervision over the franchise outlets. Consequently, in 1988, Mr Michel divided the European division into four regions – England, Benelux, Germany and Italy – each headed by a regional manager.

From the start, the regional division managers had difficulty enforcing company operating procedures among the international franchisees. Mr Schmidt was having particular difficulty with the fifteen franchises in Germany. The franchisees had little confidence in Mr Schmidt and resented his attempts to control their activities. Most of the franchisees had been with the firm longer than he had. Each had gone through a company training programme, either in Dallas or in Brussels, and had subsequently operated his business without the help or advice of a German regional manager. During the period of minimal supervision, many had modified their product to fit what they felt were the unique needs of the local market. For example, three franchisees had decided that potato pancakes would be more popular than French fries in their parts of Germany. Two others had modified the carefully developed mixture of spices used in the chicken batter. Although these modifications had been accepted in the local markets where they were made (the franchisees involved had excellent sales performance), these aberrant outlets failed to present the standardized product and atmosphere expected by the Aunt Sarah customer throughout the world. Mr Schmidt was a graduate of the INSEAD graduate programme in business in Fontainebleau, France, in 1985. Before joining Aunt Sarah's in 1992, he worked for a large department store in Bonn. He was bright, well trained and 36 years of age. The typical franchisee in Germany was in his forties and had worked in the restaurant or food business for a minimum of 10 years. These entrepreneurs were reluctant to accept suggestions about how to run their business from Mr Schmidt.

(Source; adapted from Cundiff and Hilger, 1988, pp. 295–7. Reproduced with permission.)

Questions

1. Evaluate Aunt Sarah's policy of standardizing operations and recipes according to the American pattern in different cultures such as Germany and France.
2. How can Jean Michel help Mr Schmidt in his relations with the German franchisees?

References

Anderson, Erin T. and Anne T. Coughlan (1987) 'International market entry and expansion via independent or integrated channels of distribution', *Journal of Marketing*, vol. 51 (January), pp. 71–82.

Boddewyn, J. J. (1992), *Premiums, Gifts and Competitions*, International Advertising Association: New York.

Boddewyn, J. J. and M. Leardi (1989), 'Sales promotion: practices, regulation and self-regulation around the world, *International Journal of Advertising*, vol. 8, no. 4, pp. 363–74.

Cateora, Philip R. (1983), *International Marketing*, 5th edn, Richard D. Irwin: Homewood, IL.

Cundiff, Edward W. and Marye Tharp Hilger (1988), *Marketing in the International Environment*, 2nd edn, Prentice Hall: Englewood Cliffs, NJ.

Czinkota, Michael R. and Illka A. Ronkainen (1990), *International Marketing*, 2nd edn, Dryden Press: Hinsdale, IL.

Czinkota, Michael R. and Jon Woronoff (1991), *Unlocking Japan's Markets*, Probus Publishing: Chicago, IL.

Doi, T. (1973), *The Anatomy of Dependence*, Kodansha: Tokyo.

Dupuis, Marc and Renaud de Maricourt (1989), '*France/Etats-Unis/Japon, trois mondes, trois distributions*', Cahier ESCP no. 89-81, Ecole Supérieure de Commerce de Paris.

Foxman, Ellen R., Patriya S. Tansuhaj and John K. Wong (1988), 'Evaluating cross-national sales promotion approach strategy: an audit approach,' *International Marketing Review*, vol. 5 (Winter) pp. 7–15.

Gambiez, Chantal, Hélène Lelièvre and Véronique Surget (1988), *La Publicité et la promotion de vente en suisse*, Research paper for the International Marketing Seminar, Ecole Supérieure des Affaires, University of Grenoble.

Glazer, Herbert (1968), *The International Business in Japan: The Japanese image*, Sophia University: Tokyo.

Hofstede, Geert (1980), *Culture's Consequences: International differences in work related values*, Sage: Beverly Hills, CA.

Ishida, Hideto (1983), 'Anticompetitive practices in the distribution of goods and services in Japan: The problem of distribution Keiretsu', *Journal of Japanese Studies*, vol. 9, no. 2, pp. 319–334.

Kale, Sudhir H. and Roger P. McIntyre (1991), 'Distribution channel relationships in diverse cultures', *International Marketing Review*, vol. 8, no. 3, pp. 31–45.

Kashani, Kamran (1989), 'Beware the pitfalls of global marketing', *Harvard Business Review*, September–October, pp. 91–8.

Katsikeas, Constantine S. and Nigel F. Piercy (1991), 'The relationship between exporters from a developing country and importers based in a developed country: Conflict considerations', *European Journal of Marketing*, vol. 25, no. 1, pp. 6–25.

Kuribayashi, S. (1991), 'Present situation and future prospects of Japan's distribution system', *Japan and the World Economy*, vol. 3, no. 1, pp. 39–60.

Miller, Fred and A. Hamdi Demirel (1988), 'Efes pilsen in the Turkish beer market: marketing consumer goods in developing countries', *International Marketing Review*, vol. 5 (Spring), pp. 7–19.

Montgomery, David B. (1991), 'Understanding the Japanese as customers, competitors and collaborators', *Japan and the World Economy*, vol. 3, no. 1, pp. 61–91.

Nakane, Chie (1973), *Japanese Society*, University of California Press: Berkeley.

O'Grady, Shawna and Henry W. Lane (1992), 'Culture: an unnoticed barrier to Canadian retail performance in the United States', Academy of International Business Annual Conference, Brussels, November 22.

Ohmae, Kenichi (1985), *La Triade, Emergence d'une stratégie mondiale de l'entreprise*, Flammarion: Paris.

Ross, Randolph (1983), 'Understanding the Japanese distribution system', *European Journal of Marketing*, vol. 17 (Winter), pp. 5–15.

Shimaguchi, Mitsuaki (1978), *Marketing Channels in Japan*, Ann Arbor: Michigan.

Shimaguchi, Mitsuaki and Larry J. Rosenberg (1979), 'Demystifying Japanese distribution', *Columbia Journal of World Business* (Spring), pp. 38–41.

Turcq, Dominique and Jean-Claude Usunier (1985), 'Les Services au Japon: l'efficacité . . . par la non-productivité', *Revue Française de Gestion*, May–June, pp. 12–15.

Turpin, Dominique (1990), *World Competitiveness Report*, IMD/World Economic Forum: Lausanne.

Weigand, Robert E. (1970), 'Aspects of retail pricing in Japan', *MSU Business Topics*, vol. 18 (Winter), pp. 23–30.

Yoshino, Michael Y. (1971), *Marketing in Japan: A Management Guide*, Praeger: New York.

Zeller, Eric (1989), Thèse professionnelle, Masters thesis, Ecole Supérieure de commerce de Paris.

—————— ◆◆◆ ——————

Intercultural marketing communications

12

◆◆◆

Language, culture and communication

Glen Fisher, a distinguished scholar in the field of intercultural relations, has described a conversation with a Latin-American friend about the words used in English and Spanish for business relations. His friend first remarks that in English the word 'business' is positive. It connotes the fact of being 'busy' and emphasizes doing things. Expressions such as 'getting down to business' highlight people who have a responsible concern for their work. Fisher further explains that

> In Spanish the word is 'negocio' . . . The key is the 'ocio' part of the word, which connotes leisure, serenity, time to enjoy and contemplate as the preferred human condition and circumstance. But when harsh reality forces one from one's 'ocio,' when it is negated, then one has to attend to 'negocio.' The subjective meaning is obviously much less positive than in English. (Fisher, 1988, pp. 148–9)

In this chapter, several such examples show how a linguistic/cultural group, through words or language structure, expresses a definite world-view, *'eine Weltanschauung'* as the Germans express it. The anthropologist and linguist Benjamin Lee Whorf went even further, arguing that language shapes our world-views, our behaviour towards others, and our manner of acting. Language is obviously a major – though not the only – component of culture. However, it is underemphasized in international business literature for many converging reasons. First, language seems to be translatable: there are dictionaries and, if need be, professional translators. Unfortunately this ignores the fact that a part of the message which is culturally unique is lost in the translation process (as the Italian proverb says *'traduttore traditore'*, translator betrayer). Secondly, management literature is in general centred on decision-making and strategy formulation rather than the implementation of decisions. Language is important mostly in the implementation phase because implementation is largely based on communicating with others, buyers, employees, colleagues, superiors. The logic of the planning stage can overlook the significance of language and communication, because they are implementation-related. The third argument is that language differences have been systematically underestimated in international business literature because of an understandable bias in American culture: since English is really the *lingua franca* of international business there is no major reason for native speakers of English to learn foreign languages. There is much more motivation for people from Germany, Japan, France and Italy who are citizens of the four countries which, with the United States, make up the five major trading nations in the world, to take the question of language seriously.

In this chapter we will review the main aspects of language and communication having both a direct and an indirect impact on international business operations:

1. Verbal communication styles and their relationship to contextual factors.
2. Non-verbal communication, especially through gestures and eye and body language.
3. The way language shapes and reflects definite world-views.[1]
4. Ways of dealing with language differences in international business.

Awareness is even more necessary than knowledge in relation to the impact of language and communication differences on international business. Given the variety of national and regional languages, one cannot expect to be able to speak and write them all. Even multilingual business people will frequently be faced with language contexts in which they have little or no proficiency. What is needed then is an awareness that large chunks of reality will always be partly hidden from us because we are not native speakers.

12.1   Verbal communication: The role of context

'Verbal' implies words and sentences and, in most of what follows, spoken discourse, not written communication. Written communication is a special case and it is treated in more detail in other sections of this book devoted to international negotiation and contracts. Verbal may be opposed to non-verbal communication, which is often said to occupy a dominant place in actual communication flows. However, language is legitimately seen as having a prominent place in communication, perhaps because it is largely explicit and therefore more easily amenable to consciousness. Thus linguistic differences are perceived as one of the main causes (though not the only one) of intercultural communication misunderstandings. Where differences in the coding/decoding process are ignored by the communicators, they may persist throughout the whole interaction process; instead of disappearing they may become more marked, even when people seem to be better acquainted with each other.

A first distinction in language-based communication is whether or not the messages sent by the speaker are explicit, that is to be taken literally and not necessarily to be set 'in context.' Setting messages 'in context' would imply that what is literally said has to be in some way reinterpreted using various cues taken from the context, particularly the cultural context of the speaker.

The context of language-based communication

The use of the word 'context' and the emphasis that is put on the role of context in communication derive from Edward T. Hall, an American anthropologist. During the 1940s Hall studied the culture and social integration of Hopi and Navajo Indians. He first advised diplomats in the 1960s, and then later on business people in their dealings with other cultures. This naturally led him to an interest in intercultural communication, a field where he has been a major contributor during the last forty years. Hall is the kind of individual who is fascinated by foreign cultures, sometimes showing a certain prejudice in their favour and against his own native culture.[2]

The communication mode that first springs to mind is the verbal mode. Phrases and words in a single language have (more or less) a precise meaning; in any case, we live with the necessary assumption that words and their combinations have a particular meaning, and that the listener gets a clear message from the speaker. This assumption allows us to avoid the time-consuming task of constantly verifying that the message received is the same message that was sent. However, the communication mechanism incorporates many elements:

1. Even in an exchange that is primarily verbal, part of the message is non-verbal: gestures, gesticulations, attitudes, etc. The issue then is to know to what extent non-verbal/implicit messages (which will be discussed in the next section) *mix* with verbal/explicit messages.
2. Communication integrates feedback mechanisms to verify or improve the clarity of messages. In many cultures, the accuracy of the communication process needs to be checked by various means, including repetition, paraphrases, interruption, etc.
3. In most cases, communication is dependent on its context, that is, who says it and where and when it is said. Contextual factors may distort what actually seems to be said literally.

Although Edward Hall does not define context precisely, the following components can reasonably be presumed: location, people involved (age, sex, dress, social standing, etc.), the context of the conversation itself (at the workplace, in a showroom, during a round of labour negotiations, in a sales visit . . .). He contrasts high context (HC) and low context (LC) in the following way: 'a high-context (HC) communication or message is one in which most of the information is either in the physical context or internalized in the person, while very little is in the coded, explicit, transmitted part of the message. A low-context (LC) communication is just the opposite; i.e. the mass of the information is vested in the explicit code' (Hall, 1976).

Context will often influence communication without the participants being aware of it. For example, cultural prejudices may intervene, with such unspoken questions as: does this young speaker deserve trust? The relationship assumed by a particular culture between age and credibility may be positive, negative or neutral, and therefore have an impact on the flow of communication. Another important issue is whether it is necessary to know one's conversation partner relatively well to be able to talk seriously to him or her about business. This relates to the intensity of the personalization, or conversely the depersonalization of the communication process.

Context brings together the sum of interpretation mechanisms that originate within a culture and allow the message to be explained. In his collection *The Snows of Kilimandjaro*, Ernest Hemingway (1976, p. 33) recounts a story, entitled 'A day's wait', where a young boy is told that he has a fever of a hundred and two (in degrees Fahrenheit) – though he does not know it. Since he had previously been staying in

France, he thinks of this in the context of the Celsius temperature scale, asking: 'About how long will it be before I die?' His mother does not know what the matter is with him and explains that people do not die of a fever of a hundred and two. The young boy goes on arguing: 'I know they do. At school in France, the boys told me you can't live with forty-four degrees. I've got a hundred and two.' Finally his mother understands that he has been waiting to die all day and she explains that, like kilometres and miles, what is thirty-seven degrees on one thermometer is ninety-eight on another.

Low-context cultures and explicit communication

As explained above, in certain cultures, communication is based on low context and explicit messages. These messages are almost 'digital' and could be translated into simple computer units (bytes). The Swiss, for instance, have a reputation for talking quite literally, with explicit messages and low context. This implies a great deal of precision in the verbal aspect of communication, implying precision with respect to time commitments and so on. Thus, in Switzerland a speed limit is interpreted as literally just that. The speed limit on motorways is 120 kilometres an hour, and when a driver is caught speeding by the police, a speedometer error of 6 per cent is allowed and then the fine is given in proportion to the speed violation. When arriving late for a doctor's appointment in certain Swiss cantons, a patient has to pay a cash penalty and reschedule the appointment if the doctor is unavailable.[3]

These two examples should be taken for what they are: not illustrative of an unhealthy preoccupation with punctuality, exactness and respect for rules, but as evidence of a tight social order, a highly organized social system that is costly to run but is also greatly beneficial for all. In the case of the health service, a Swiss doctor who has made a preliminary evaluation over the phone with a patient will schedule their time together very precisely. If each party makes an effort to keep the appointment, the result is a genuine saving. The patient will also avoid a long stay in the waiting room, exposed to the germs of the other patients.

Appointments are one example of explicit messages that in low-context cultures must be taken literally. Another would be an arrangement such as: 'I can offer you a price of 140 dollars per package of twelve, to be delivered in cases of 144 within five weeks' (an example of a seller's explicit message to a potential buyer).

The North American cultures (United States and Canada) feature together with the Germanic cultures (Germany, Switzerland and Austria) and the Scandinavians among the cultures with explicit communication and low context.[4]

Contextuality of communication is partly related to whether the language itself expresses ideas and facts more or less explicitly. Japanese, for instance, is on average less precise than English or French. For example, personal pronouns are often not explicitly expressed in Japanese, and the number of tenses is largely reduced (especially in comparison to French). In Japanese, both spoken words (that is sounds) and written words (based on *kanjis*, that is pictograms) often have multiple meanings, so that the listener needs some kind of contextual clarification. Sometimes, Japanese people write the *kanjis* (ideographs) briefly on their hand to make clear what they are saying.

Naturally it would be a mistake to say that certain languages are vague and others precise. The real world is more complex. This has to be strongly nuanced when one looks more carefully at the structure of the language. For instance, German has many verbs that have quite different meanings according to context. It is easy to discover such examples just by consulting a German–English dictionary. For instance, the verb *absetzen* means, according to context, to deposit or deduct a sum, to take off a hat, to dismiss an official, to depose a king, to drop a passenger, to sell goods, to stop or pause, or to take off (a play).[5] The same holds true for the Finnish language, even though the Finns may have a reputation, like many northern Europeans for their explicitness in communication. Finnish has a very special language structure which renders the use of context useful in communication, that of Finno-Ugrian languages, really only shared with Estonia and Hungary. The Finnish language uses sixteen cases which virtually replace all prepositions used in other languages. Even proper nouns can be declined using these cases.

All languages share a common objective, that is, they have a common problem to solve, which is conveying meaning in an appropriate way from people to people. But they achieve it differently, relying to varying degrees on precise words, structured grammar or, in contrast, on contextual indications of how ambiguous meanings should be made precise. English is a precise and fairly context-free language. This holds especially true for 'international English'. The *lingua franca* of international business is context-free, that is both impoverished and made precise.

High-context cultures favour a more diffuse communication style

A notion that helps in the understanding of the differences in context-related communication styles is the distinction between specific and diffuse. In low-context cultures, people tend to focus on specific issues and address their counterpart in a specific role (as a buyer for instance), not really impersonally but with a specific view of what the person in front of them has to do. In high-context cultures, people generally address broader issues and move easily between different conceptions of their counterpart (as a private person, as a buyer, as a potential friend). Diffuse in style should not be equated with 'confused' in communication, but it is clear that to speakers from low-context cultures, communication with people from high-context cultures may at times appear complicated.

Among the high-context cultures, according to Hall, we find the Latin Americans, the Middle Eastern and the Japanese.[6] In Japan, context plays a significant role. One example is the rules of politeness; the manner of speaking perceptibly shifts in register between more than twenty subtly different forms according to the age, sex and social position of the conversation partner, as well as the relative positions of the speakers in the social hierarchy (pupil/teacher, buyer/seller, employee/employer). The word 'no' practically does not exist in the Japanese vocabulary – a '*yes*' in certain circumstances can actually mean 'no'. Keiko Ueda (1974) distinguishes sixteen ways to avoid saying 'no' in Japanese. The range of possible solutions varies from a vague 'no', to a vague and ambiguous 'yes', a mere silence, a counterquestion, a tangential response, exiting (leaving), making an excuse such as sickness or a previous obligation, criticizing or refusing the question itself, saying 'no, but . . .' or 'Yes, but . . .', delaying answers ('We will write you a letter') and making apologies.

No person belonging to cultures of this sort which use implicit messages and high context can communicate without a fairly good understanding of their conversation partner. Impersonal dealings (such as an American businessman who comes for a day to discuss a contract, rapidly gets to the heart of the matter, and uses the limited time available for discussion, insisting on concentrating on crucial matters) will make a person from those cultures ill at ease and impede their conversation.

A misunderstanding between the two communicators may come up over their differences of opinion as to what is truly important. The person from a high-context/ diffuse communication culture will prefer spending some time chatting about life in general with the very purpose of getting to know their negotiating partner. The person from a low-context/specific communication culture, on the other hand, will prefer to get straight down to business with the aim of avoiding wasting time on chatting and proceeding directly to a rational discussion of the project.

Occasionally, some cultures, which fall in the middle range, may shift from an explicit/ specific to an implicit/diffuse communication style and vice versa. The United Kingdom and France are examples of such a tendency. The British practice of 'understatement' values complicity between people at the expense of clarity. French has often been considered as a good language for diplomacy because it can be alternately vague and precise, according to the kinds of words and style chosen. Sometimes French can be written with very precise words, with simple sentences (subject verb complement), but it can also, if need be, be styled in a very vague manner, starting with long dependent clauses describing circumstances and possibilities.

The cultural context of communication styles

Up to now the discussion has been mostly about low- and high-context communication and their relationship to precision in the languages, as well as to the specificity versus the diffuseness of the communication focus. However, verbal communication styles include a series of other elements: tone of voice, frequency and nature of conversational overlap, speed of speech, degree of apparent involvement in what one says, emphasis on talking versus emphasis on listening, digressive and indirect speech styles, etc. These are marked by cultural norms which implicitly define what is 'good' communication ('good' meaning appropriate between members of the cultural community in so far as they share the same code). There are at least three areas where communication style is strongly culture-bound:

1. The style may reflect self-concept. In cultures where the self-concept is strong, one may expect a communication style based on talking and self-assertion; where, on the contrary suppression of the self is valued, a modest, listening communication style is likely in a participant, all other things being equal (especially purely individual personality characteristics).
2. Communication styles reflect a view of what is appropriate interaction. The Latin style

of interruption, for instance, is a lot about showing interest. Latins often find themselves speaking when others have not finished their sentence, and those who have some familiarity with the Anglo-Saxon and the Nordic communication styles may feel sorry about what could seem an overlap or even interruption, although it is really well intentioned and positive. In Latin cultures, interruption and overlap show empathy with the other speaker and shared interest in the topic. Furthermore, Latins are (or they believe they are) able to speak and listen at the same time.

3. Communication styles also reflect the appropriate emphasis put, according to cultural norms, on talking and listening respectively. Japanese top executives often behave like a 'sphinx': they are almost pure listeners. Their role is to hear people. With exceptions, Japanese bosses often display mediocre talents at public speeches and appear as poor tribunes. In contrast with Latin cultures, for instance, where inter-actions may appear to be held between 'two speakers,' the Japanese have often a tendency to display a 'two listeners' communication culture. Silence is in fact valued as a full element of communication. It conveys messages, which, although implicit, may be interpreted through contextual factors. In a novel entitled '*Shiosai*', the Japanese writer Yukio Mishima, features a young fisherman Shinji, who brings back his salary to his mother, a widow with another younger son. Shinji's salary is the family's only resource. Mishima recounts: 'Shinji liked to give his pay envelope to his mother without uttering a word. As a mother, she understood and always behaved as if she did not remember it was pay day. She knew that her son liked to see her looking surprised' (Mishima, 1969, p. 57).

A lot of messages are included in silent communication, and, in general, Europeans and Americans tend to fear them much more than Asians in general. The issue of shared meaning attributed to communication behaviour inside the cultural group is important, whether the values are positive or negative. Silence may be experienced positively, as a moment for listening (especially to what is 'not said'), or negatively as a sign of possible loss of interaction, a time-waster, or even as a sign of possible animosity on the part of the conversation partner. Similarly conversational overlap may be seen as diluting the clarity of exchange, mere impoliteness, a lack of interest in what one says, or as fatuity on the part of the overlapper. Conversely, it may be interpreted as a sign of empathy, a quick feedback saving time, or even a necessary sign for pursuing the exchange.

As we hope to have shown, the rules of achieving 'good' communication are largely cultural. The feeling that the flow of messages is going smoothly between two conversation partners is based on their ability to avoid a 'bad' conversation, where messages would be altered or interrupted. The value judgement on the means that are 'good' or 'bad,' appropriate or inappropriate is largely based on unconscious cultural standards. In a domestic setting, people agree implicitly on the appropriate rules of communication. In an intercultural situation, people have to allow themselves the informal opportunity to discuss and establish the rules of their communication (what is called meta-communication). It is quite clearly a difficult task. Box 12.1 illustrates the substantive difficulties involved in clarifying the rules of communication about what friendship means and involves.

Box 12.1   *The language of friendship*

The American finds his friends next door and among those with whom he works. It has been noted that we take people up quickly and drop them just as quickly. Occasionally a friendship formed during school days will persist, but this is rare. For us (Americans) there are few well-defined rules governing the obligations of friendship. It is difficult to say at which point our friendship gives way to business opportunism or pressure from above. In this we differ from many other people in the world. As a general rule, in foreign countries friendships are not formed as quickly as in the United States, but go much deeper, last longer and involve real obligations. For example, it is important to stress that in the Middle East and Latin America your 'friends' will not let you down. The fact that they personally are feeling the pinch is never an excuse for failing their friends. They are supposed to look out for your interests. Friends and family around the world represent a sort of social insurance that would be difficult to find in the United States. We do not use friends to help us out of disaster as much as we do as a means of getting ahead – or, at least, of getting the job done. The United States systems work by means of a series of closely tabulated favors and obligations carefully doled out where they will do the most good. And the least that we expect in exchange for a favor is gratitude.

The opposite is the case in India, where the friend's role is to 'sense' a person's need and to do something about it. The idea of reciprocity as we know it is unheard of. An American in India will have difficulty if he attempts to follow American friendship patterns. He gains nothing by extending himself in behalf of others, least of all gratitude, because the Indian assumes that what he does he does for the good of his own psyche. He will find it impossible to make friends quickly and is unlikely to allow sufficient time for friendships to ripen. He will also note that as he gets to know people better, they may become more critical of him, a fact that he finds hard to take. What he does not know is that one sign of friendship in India is speaking one's mind.

(Source: Hall, 1960. Reproduced with permission)

12.2   Non-verbal communication

Since a lot of what is exchanged in communication is only implicitly meant and agreed on, not talked about, non-verbal communication is largely used as an additional interpretative framework which allows people to overcome the shortcomings of verbal communication. The rules, rites and usage of non-verbal communication are also culture-bound.

When business people from different cultures communicate, they also exchange elements of non-verbal communication. This constitutes a large part of what Edward Hall calls 'context,' which is used in the decoding of implicit messages. The elements of context can be separated into four levels:

1. The analogical components of verbal messages,[7] such as a way of saying 'yes' that makes it mean no, profuse thank-yous that contain a meaning other than their 'digital' content precisely because of their excess, etc.
2. Non-verbal communication such as gestures, gesticulations, eye contacts, etc.
3. Messages that are often emitted unknowingly by the speakers according to their

personal characteristics of age, size, weight, sex, dress and so on. All of these characteristics are culturally encoded in the culture of the speaker, and decoded by the listener using his or her own cultural programmes.

4. Elements of interpretation dictated by the circumstances of the conversation, including type of place, atmosphere of the meeting, how the space is organized in the office,[8] time, etc.

Although all of these four elements interact, this section focuses on the second aspect of non-verbal communication, while recognizing that status, circumstances and the other aspects of context combine with it in bringing about culture-bound interpretations.

Communication through gestures

Body language is an infinite source of differences and misunderstandings. Condon and Youssef (1975) give the following account. A professor who was of English origin and taught at the University of Cairo was sitting in his chair with his feet in front of him, the soles of his shoes facing towards his Egyptian students. A Muslim considers this to be one of the worst possible insults. A student demonstration followed, and it was taken up by the newspapers who denounced British arrogance and demanded that the professor be sent back to his home country.

Ways of greeting people differ greatly between cultures. While the French make a custom of shaking hands the first time they meet a person each day, the Anglo-Saxon cultures use this custom much less extensively. They are surprised at the excessive (for them) use that the French make of the handshake. In Japan a bow is the appropriate manner of greeting. In certain large department stores there are hostesses whose sole job is to bow to each customer who comes into the store. Anyone who has observed bowing rituals in Japanese rail stations or airports cannot help but be struck by the complexity of these bowing ceremonies, where the number, depth and synchronization are accurately codified. As Ferraro emphasizes: 'In fact it is possible to tell the relative social status of the two communicators by the depth of their bows (the deeper the bow, the lower the status). . . . The person of lower status is supposed to initiate the bow, and the person of higher status determines when the bow is completed' (Ferraro, 1990, p. 73).

A challenge in intercultural communication is to understand what hand gestures mean in a particular culture. As Box 12.2 shows, a simple piece of advice would be to avoid gesturing with the hand for fear of being misunderstood. Yet there are circumstance and places where it may be adequate.

The meaning of head gestures is also a point of great cultural difference. Moving the head back and forth means yes in most western European countries, but it means no in Greece and Bulgaria, and moving the head from left to right is a sign of negation for some and affirmation for others. In many western countries it is considered a gesture of affection to pat a child on the head, but in Malaysia and many Islamic countries the head is considered to be the source of spiritual and intellectual activity and is therefore sacred (Harris and Moran, 1987).

Another area of non-verbal communication where the importance of cultural variations cannot be denied is that of physical contact. Ferraro (1990) offers a complete description of forms of non-verbal communication involving physical contact:[9] various groups kiss (the cheek, lips, hand, foot), take a person by the arm, clasp the shoulders, pinch the cheek, shake hands, tickle, stroke, give a little pat, etc. These gestures, running over into the realm of familiarity and sexual conduct, are subject to extremely varied codes of use. The kiss regarded as normal between Russian men or Arab men who hold hands in the streets may appear shocking to Anglo-Saxons.

Ferraro (1990, pp. 85–6) recounts his own experience while conducting anthropological field research in Kenya:

> After several months of living and working with Kikuyu, I was walking through a village in Kiambu district with a local headman who had become a key informant and a close personal acquaintance. As we walked side by side my friend took my hand in his. Within less than 30 seconds my palm was perspiring all over his. Despite the fact that I knew cognitively that it was a perfectly legitimate Kikuyu gesture of friendship, my own cultural values (that is, that 'real men' don't hold hands) were so ingrained that it was impossible for me not to communicate to my friend that I was very uncomfortable.

The significance of communication codes is complex, and it would be wrong to make quick opposition between peoples who are reserved in their physical contact (including Anglo-Saxons) and those who are more liberal. Nowhere does there exist true freedom from customs. The way in which American and European men and women show their feelings for each other by kissing in public may seem to be the shocking demonstration of something that should be kept private when seen by other peoples. Dancing, which is a large part of social gatherings, may seem indecent to some and perfectly innocent to others.

Box 12.2 *Avoid gesturing with the hand, and yet . . .*

In general, avoid gesturing with the hand. Many people take offence at being beckoned this way, or pointed at, even if only conversationally. In parts of Asia, gestures and even slight movements can make people nervous. If you jab your finger in the air or on a table to make a point, you might find that your movements have been so distracting that you have not made your point at all. Unintentionally, Americans come across as aggressive and pushy. Yet, in other parts of the world, particularly in Latin America or Italy, gesturing is important for self-expression, and the person who does not move a lot while talking comes across as bland or uninteresting. As always, watch what local people do. Or ask. While in England we once asked, 'How do you point out someone without pointing?' Our companion dropped a shoulder, raised his eyebrows and jerked his head to the side, as though tossing it in the direction he meant to point. Clear as day, he pointed without pointing.

(Source: Copeland and Griggs, 1986, p. 111. Reproduced with permission.)

Facial expressions and communication with the eyes

Laughing and smiling, frowning and knitting one's brow express communication. A smile can be a sign of satisfaction, of agreement, of embarrassment . . . or even not a sign at all. Certain cultures consider the spontaneous expression of attitudes and emotions by a facial expression to be normal. The reverse is true in other cultures, particularly in Asia where it is considered desirable not to show emotion; this has given rise to the impression of Asians as unreadable and stoic. According to Morsbach (1982):

> Self control, thought of as highly desirable in Japan, demands that a man of virtue will not show a negative emotion in his face when shocked or upset by sudden bad news; and, if successful, is lauded as *taizen jijaku to shite* (perfectly calm and collected) or *mayu hitotsu ugokasazu ni* (without even moving an eyebrow). . . . The idea of an expression-less face in situations of great anxiety was strongly emphasized in the *bushido* (way of the warrior) which was the guide-line for samurai and the ideal for many others.

Visual contacts (looking someone straight in the eyes, or, conversely, looking away, or lowering the eyes, or turning them away when they meet someone else's eyes, when they will also do the same) are all given different meanings in different cultures. This is proof that the same conduct (innocent as it may be) can be arbitrarily given totally opposite meanings. As Harris and Moran (1987) have remarked, Arabs often look each other straight in the eyes because they believe that the eyes are the windows of the soul and that it is important to know the heart and soul of those one is working with. By contrast, Japanese children are taught in school not to look their teacher in the eyes, but to look at the level of the neck. When they become adults, it is considered a gesture of respect to lower their eyes in front of their superiors. The French have a tendency to look people straight in the eyes; like the Americans and other Europeans, they tend to associate a lack of honesty with someone who looks away, and see it as potentially signalling an unfriendly, defiant, impersonal or inattentive attitude.

Dealing with unknown communication styles, especially non-verbal ones, is not an easy task. Exhaustive knowledge of the wide range of cultural interpretations of physical behaviour, gestures and contact is impossible. Although it is clear that one can avoid major behavioural mistakes, it seems more difficult to develop adequate behaviour oneself without staying long enough in a particular country to have time for learning. Besides, part of the locally 'adequate' behaviour was learned in childhood, through rearing and education practices, and it translates into a physical demeanour which is profoundly ingrained. Once again knowledge appears not to be enough. Awareness begins with the capacity to *unlearn*, that is to discover progressively the cultural relativity of one's own verbal and non-verbal communication behaviour. The *unlearning process* is a key point, a condition, for the learning process to take place.

In everyday adjustment courtesy is a resource not to be ignored. The word courtesy is based on the word 'court' meaning the residence of a king or an emperor. It emphasizes the kind of noble behaviour that enhances self-respect through the respect of others. Most languages have such a word. German, for instance, has the word *höflich* (polite), based on the German word for court, *Hof*. Much is forgiven to foreigners provided that they are not arrogant, and show consideration for their opposite numbers, even in the ignorance of their customs. Modest, though firm, behaviour facilitates the acceptance of cultural mistakes by the other party.

12.3   Language shaping our world-views

As we have seen in previous chapters, with national languages reflecting idiosyncrasies in emotions, language tends to shape our world-views. It contains pre-shaped images of the real world which partly condition our experiences. In this section, we give examples showing that language shapes and reflects different assumptions in terms of time, attitude to action, social hierarchy, and how this is expressed in the colloquial phrases used in marketing communications. That language influences culture (shapes it), and thereby behaviour, is a major causal assumption which can be challenged (in many cases language simply reflects culture). That is why we set the limits of this assumption in the second part of this section.

Language influencing culture

The first proponent of the idea that language has a decisive influence on culture was the linguist Edward Sapir. Language creates categories in our minds, which in their turn directly influence the things we judge to be similar and those that *deserve* to be differentiated. It is our *Weltanschauung* that will be determined: our way of observing, of describing, of interacting and finally the way in which we construct our reality. Sapir (1929, pp. 214) writes:

> The fact of the matter is that the real world is to a large extent unconsciously built up on the language habits of the group. No two languages are ever sufficiently similar as to be considered as representing the same social reality. The worlds in which different societies live are distinct worlds, not merely the same world with different labels attached.

The linguist and anthropologist Benjamin Lee Whorf developed and extended Sapir's hypothesis. The Whorf–Sapir hypothesis contends that the structure of language has a significant influence on perception and categorization. But although the empirical testing of this hypothesis seems to have been fairly thorough,[10] it is not considered valid by many linguists. For example, the gender given to words is not necessarily indicative of a particular cultural meaning (for example the gender of the Earth, the sun and the moon, of vices and virtues, etc.); for most often it seems to reflect an arbitrary choice. It may be the case however that this attribution of gender had a certain meaning at the genesis of the language, but that the meaning has since been lost. Box 12.3 illustrates how languages reflect different patterns of time.

Languages in relation to actions, thoughts and emotions

Another example may be given of the language–culture link by the way – linguistic as well as cultural – an Anglo-American deals with action, especially in business. There is

Box 12.3   *Time patterns revealed by language*

Time representations are conveyed through the medium of language, as a means of communication and therefore collective action. Whorf comments about the Hopi language in the following terms:

> After long and careful study and analysis, the Hopi language is seen to contain no words, grammatical forms, constructions or expressions, that refer directly to what we call 'time', or to past, present, and future, or to motion as kinematic rather than dynamic (i.e. as a continuous translation in space and time rather than as an exhibition of a dynamic effort in a certain process), or that even refer to space in such a way as to exclude that element of extension or existence that we call 'time', and so by implication leave a residue that could be referred to as 'time'. Hence, the Hopi language contains no reference to 'time', either implicit or explicit (Caroll, 1956, pp. 57–8).

Time vocabulary also tells a lot about the linkage between language and cultural representations. For those who have doubts about the existence of differences in cultural representations of time which are revealed, conveyed and reproduced by language, the example of the English/US word 'deadline' is very illustrative. A quick translation in French would give 'échéance [temporelle]' or 'délai de rigueur' (Langenscheidt, 1989) but would not render the intensity of this word. Taken literally, it seems to suggest something like 'beyond this (temporal) line, you will (there is a danger of) die (dying)'. It therefore gives a genuine notion of urgency to what was originally a very abstract notion (a point which has been agreed upon on a line of time). The word deadline is used in French by many businesspeople as such (*un deadline*), even though it is not in the official dictionary, because it conveys a typically Anglo-American sense of urgency that French people do not find in their own language.

Language also reflects (and pre-shapes) how people envision the future. In some African languages (Kamba and Kikuyu), there are three future tenses which express (1) action in two to six months; (2) action that will take place immediately; and (3) action 'in the foreseeable future, after this or that event.' Commenting on the uses of these African tenses, M'biti demonstrates how coherence and sophistication in the accurate use of the near future, are important to people:

> You have these tenses before you: just try to imagine the tense into which you would translate passages of the New Testament concerning the Parousia of Our Lord Jesus Christ, or how you would teach eschatology. . . . If you use tense no. 1, you are speaking about something that will take place in the next two to six months, or in any case within two years at most. If you use no. 2, you are referring to something that will take place in the immediate future, and if it does not take place you are exposed as a liar in people's eyes. Should you use no. 3 you are telling people that the event concerned will definitely take place, but when something else has happened first. In all these tenses, the event must be very near to the present moment: if, however, it lies in the far distant future – beyond the two-year limit – you are neither understood nor taken seriously. (1968, pp. 8–20)

Levine, researching on Brazilian versus US time, highlights the way concepts of punctuality are reflected in the language. He takes the example of the translation from English to Portuguese of a questionnaire containing the verb 'to wait':

Several of our questions were concerned with how long the respondent would *wait* for someone to arrive versus when they *hoped* the person would arrive versus when they actually *expected* the person would come. Unfortunately for us, it turns out that the term *to wait, to hope* and *to expect* are all typically translated as the single verb *esperar* in Portuguese. In many ways our translation difficulties taught us more about Brazilian–Anglo differences in time conception than did the subjects' answers to the questions.' (Levine, 1988, pp. 48–9)

There is a sort of continuum across languages in the accuracy of description of the waiting phenomenon (a fundamental issue in time experience!). French language, which lies somewhere between English and Portuguese in terms of temporal accuracy, uses two words: *attendre* (to wait) and *espérer* (to hope). To expect has no direct equivalent in French and must be translated by a lengthy circumlocution ('*compter sur l'arrivée de . . .*').

a rich vocabulary to be used, which is often difficult to translate into many other languages, if real equivalence of meaning is sought. The words might include, for instance: *problem solving, issue, matter of fact, down to earth, (empirical) evidence, completed, feed-back, to perform, achievement, individual, data, to check, to plan, deadline, cognitive, emotional, successful.* . . . Even such an elementary word as *fact* contains a rather demanding content: in English it must be an *established* piece of reality; its French equivalent, *fait*, is less demanding in terms of unanimously agreed-on reality (*les faits peuvent être discutés*, corresponding to a spirit of the facts being 'challenged' rather than just discussed); in German, a fact may be translated by *Tatsache, Wirklichkeit, Wahrheit*, or *Tat* – it can mean equally a piece of *reality*, a piece of *truth*, or a piece of *action*.

The following short passage caricatures the English way of acting:

This man is achievement and deadline oriented. He first reviews the issues at stake. Then he tries hard to gather data, to verify, measure. As much as possible he will bring hard facts, empirical evidence, not simple opinions. If and when his thoughts and his emotions are conflicting, he will choose to behave as a matter-of-fact and down-to-earth guy. Being individually rewarded, he is therefore eager to perform the task and complete the job. He (almost) always meets his schedule.

When trying to translate this small text into other languages,[11] the difficulties extend far beyond the pure lexical and grammatical ones. They are *cultural translation* difficulties. These problems correspond to what is often called the spirit of a language (in French, *Le génie de la langue*): far from being merely a linking of a chain of words, a language contains a series of stands taken on the nature of our relationship to reality.

Let us compare, for instance, the respective qualities of the three most important western European languages. By 'qualities of languages' we mean that one of these languages may be better at expressing either ideas, facts, or moods, etc. than the others.

A comparison between English, French and German[12] suggests that German is stronger than English in the expression of abstractions.[13] In German, word endings such as *-heit, -keit, -ung, -schaft, -tum* and *-nis*, allow the 'abstractification' of concrete notions. English is not only less able to express pure concepts, it is also less prone to. English is more action- and more outward-oriented, with a view that data-oriented and objective approaches to issues allow a separation between feelings (inner) and actions (directed towards the outside). French expresses inner states more accurately, with an emphasis on emotions rather than pure thoughts, describing the self and others corresponding to a view that any action is related to affectivity. Stereotypically, we could say that English is a language of action, French a language of emotions and German a language of thoughts.

Language as a reflection of status, hierarchy and a vision of appropriate social relationships

The way we address other people is another example of how language shapes/reflects social hierarchy. There is only one word used in English for 'you', even accompanying the first name, and this is most often considered as reflecting a society which has strong assumptions about equality between people. It is said to reflect informality. By contrast, the French often use the formal *vous* for people they do not know very well instead of the informal *tu* which they reserve for family and friends. Thus the French are reputed to be more formal. The Germans use *du* (second person singular) in informal and personal settings and *Sie* (third person plural) in formal address. The Germans, like the Spaniards have three forms of address: while the second person plural (*ihr*) has been lost in practice in German, it remains in Spanish. In fact, a closer look at these forms shows that the English 'you' was not originally a second person singular, which was 'thou' in old English (as in Shakespeare's plays), but the more polite second person plural. That means that the only address kept in English is based on an assumption of full respect and formality and not on the everyday and less formal form of 'thou'. In fact, the assumed informality of English address, advocated by many native English speakers, is difficult to grasp for a Latin. In people being called by their first name and together with 'you', the Latin sees a different kind of formalism rather than true informality. Language reflects quite complex assumption about equality between people. It is true that the French address with *vous* reflects the strong emphasis on hierarchical and status differences in French society. But it can be very diversely nuanced, adding for instance *Monsieur* (formal *vous*) or simply the first name (informal *vous*). It is naturally not simply because they have long used the polite form that the French have a fairly hierarchical society. But the language context contributes to constantly reframing culture-bound assumptions about hierarchy in the society.

Language used in writing advertising messages

A function of language is to convey messages. A common problem for advertisers world-wide is how to use language in order to describe consumer benefits, suggest product

Box 12.4   *Global marketing communications?*

The slogan 'Put a Tiger in your Tank', although often taken as the most perfect example of standardized advertising campaign, is not as standardized as it might seem. It has been argued that it is standardized, because at first reading it looks as if it were fully equivalent across countries. However, studying the advertisements more closely, in some countries the power is located in the tank (northern Europeans: '*Pack den Tiger in den Tank*' in Germany, '*Stop'n Tiger in uw Tank*' in Holland). In other countries, the powerful tiger is located in the engine (in French '*Mettez un Tigre dans votre moteur*', in Italian '*Metti un Tigre Nel Motore*'). The interpretation differs as to where the power source is located. Note, however, that an engine cannot work without fuel and vice versa. Nobody is really right, it is simply the interpretations that differ, the Anglo interpretation (tank) being more passive and the Latin interpretation (engine) more active. In Thailand, and some neighbouring countries the tiger is experienced quite differently from Europe, America or Japan. Until recently the tiger was a danger for the local population, especially in the countryside; therefore its image is that of jungle danger rather than of power. The view expressed by the word 'tiger' is not the same in a country where tiger is experienced as a physical threat and sometimes as a source of terror for the local population as it is in countries where tigers have only been seen in books, films and zoos.

qualities and convince potential buyers. It must be done using words that represent local world-views. That is why international advertising is very 'Whorfian', even if advertisers and their agencies are not conscious of it (see Box 12.4). The language input in marketing communications is much more significant than it may seem at first. It is directly useful in designing copy strategy and indirectly useful, when trying to understand consumer moods or viewers' emotions. For example, life insurance advertising implies the evocation of death, which may be tabooed in certain cultures, or subject to the use of a particular vocabulary and subdued style. Advertising – especially when it comes to targets and strategies – is never as standardized as it appears to be at first sight. In Box 12.4 we illustrate the diverging cultural interpretations of a sign which *prima facie* seems universal (but is not so).

Languages and new international cultures

People have a lot of leeway in using language. This is more clearly expressed in French than in English since two words correspond to 'language': *la langue* (in English, literally, 'tongue' – the same word serving in French to express both the physical organ and what it helps to create) and *le langage*. *La langue* is the language itself and *le langage* is largely how people use *la langue*, and possibly other means, in order to communicate.

The most obvious influence of culture on language is that of a vocabulary with its own particular capacities and limits. Specific examples of this are the new technological vocabularies from computer science, nuclear technology, audiovisual communication, aerospace technology, etc., which are largely borrowed and exchanged between linguistic and national cultures, the benefit being the creation of a nearly universal technical culture. There are also vocabularies which have been enriched because of physical occurrences that demand precise description, as in the huge number of terms for different types of snow that exist in the language of Eskimos and all peoples who live near the Arctic Circle. Another case in point is the rich culinary vocabulary in France, where a preoccupation with good food is an element of society that strongly influences daily life.

However, without taking up a debate on the causality of language and culture, which is scientifically very complex and which also risks turning into a 'chicken and egg' argument, common sense reasoning reveals limitations on the Whorfian hypothesis in relation to those who speak many languages, or those who were raised in diverse linguistic and cultural environments, or the Swiss who share a strong national culture in spite of language differences.[14] Taking a static scenario, that is, one where an individual or a certain group has been educated in a totally homogeneous cultural environment, language can have an influence on world-view and on one's actions when confronted with reality. But the theory is much less valid in a dynamic scenario, that is, one where language changes from generation to generation or where people travel abroad. Then they will encounter opportunities to borrow language and culture. Interaction between language and culture is reciprocal, in particular in light of cultural borrowing.

12.4 Ethnocentrism, stereotypes and misunderstandings in intercultural communication

One may add that the cultural mechanism (living according to one's culture in daily life) is almost an unconscious action. The cost of adopting the cultural demeanour of the environment in which one lives is minimal. Along with the fact that they are eventually rejected, the identification and adoption of the traits of another culture are generally associated with a high cost. This is clearly shown by the difficulties encountered by immigrants in integrating, even those who have immigrated voluntarily.

Ethnocentrism

Owing to the high cost of changing one's culture, most people live without even envisioning such a possibility. This causes what James Lee (1966) calls the SRC (Self Reference Criterion): we all have an automatic and unconscious tendency to refer to our own thought framework, which is mainly tied to our national culture (which in general we did not choose), to interpret situations, evaluate people, communicate, negotiate or decide which attitude to take. This framework is generally modelled by ethnocentrism. The concept of ethnocentrism was first introduced by G. A. Sumner (1906) more than eighty years ago, to distinguish between *ingroups* (those groups with which an individual identifies) and *outgroups* (those regarded as antithetical to the *ingroup*).

Ethnocentrism has been extended by psychologists at the level of the individual, where it relates to the natural tendency of people to refer themselves spontaneously to the symbols, values and ways of thinking of their own ethnic or national group (their ingroup). Ethnocentrism may lead to disinterest and even contempt for the culture of other groups (Levine and Campbell, 1972).

Lee (1966) suggests the following steps in order to try to eliminate the decisional bias related to the SRC when dealing with international operations:

1. Define the problem or the objectives, as would be done according to the customs, behavioural standards and ways of thinking of the decision-maker's country.
2. Similarly, define the problem or the objectives, as would be done according to the customs, behavioural standards, and ways of thinking of the foreign country (where the decision will be implemented).
3. Isolate the influence of the self-reference criterion on the problem, and identify the extent to which it complicates the decision-making problem.
4. Redefine the problem (and often the objectives), without the bias related to the SRC and then find the solutions and make decisions which fit with the cultural context of the foreign market.

In this way one can imagine the following situation. People are standing in line at an amusement park, such as Disneyland, where there are some very popular attractions. In the original context in the United States, discipline with respect to queues is strong: they are usually well organized and there are even tangible precautions for this (yellow line on the ground indicating to people where to stop for queueing, visible corridors for queuing in line, etc.). In the foreign context of France, where there is a developed sense of 'free-for-all' and less of a habit of organized queues combined with a reluctance towards anything that seems too socially structured, the problem will not present itself in the same terms.

Although it constitutes the first practical framework that allows us to attribute all operational value to cultural representation, the SRC also comprises a degree of naivety and insufficiency. It presupposes that it is possible to penetrate easily the mysteries of a culture without being a native. Cultural expertise is a complex reality. Sometimes neither marketing experts from the original country (in total ignorance) nor foreigners (through lack of consciousness of their own culture) are capable of diagnosis in the second and third phases. The effect of the effort of bias removal and the results achieved by the use of the SRC are not immediate.

Stereotypes

As emphasized by Gauthey and Xardel (1990, p. 20), if the French perceive Americans as being tough in business and arrogant, and see the British as insincere, it is for the most part due to stereotypes, which give a distorted view. American arrogance is, in fact, related to a different hierarchy of values: professional relations are centred on the task in hand, the object of discussion, to the exclusion of personal relations with the other party.

Stereotypes, although sometimes representing a simplification which is intellectually useful, none the less have the function of reducing and conserving our differences, which can make them dangerous. Gauthey (1989, p. 63) notes the personal aspect: 'It seems a thousand times easier to stay attached to our own values and to transfer onto the foreigner the responsibility to change his point of view than to decenter ourselves, that is to leave our system of reference and put ourselves in the place of the other.' Characteristic of stereotypes is a cognitive function (wherein they work as a simplified intellectual representation of other people) and also an emotional function (self-defence against a difference that provokes anxiety). Michel Droit, in his book *Chez les Mangeurs d'hommes* ('With the Man eaters'), exposes the stereotype of the sorcerer in primitive societies. He describes the people of Papua New Guinea as seen by civilized observers who are necessarily their ideological enemies (1952, p. 124, author's translation):

> Armed with tamed snakes which they use to execute their victims, with poisons, enchanted prayers and medicinal herbs known only to them, sorcerers, through well-organized propaganda and strong cooperative solidarity, let entire populations live in fear and sometimes in terror of their '*nepou*', that is their evil powers.

The point is not to pretend that Michel Droit's description of the sorcerer is false. His reading partially reveals reality but also ignores how the sorcerer is integrated into the

---

Box 12.5 *Some stereotypes of the French (undeserved?)*

How various nationalities perceive the French:

The Germans: Pretentious and offhand. Fashionable, womanizing, frivolous, fickle, well-mannered, resourceful.

The British: Nationalistic, chauvinistic, intransigent, centralist, dependent on the state, polite but not open-minded, humourless, short-tempered.

The Dutch: Cultured, fond of good living, fidgety, talkative, not very serious, feelings of superiority.

The Spanish: Pretentious, early sleepers, cold and distant, hypocritical, impolite, patronizing, hard working.

The Swedish: In-built superiority complex, scornful, boastful, talkative, immoral, dirty, neo-colonialists, disorganized, cultured. Gastronomy, suffocating hierarchy.

The Finns: Xenophobic, superficial, scornful, chauvinistic, courteous, romantic, enjoying life, patriotic, chaotic.

The Americans: Chauvinistic, well-mannered. Combination of good food and good conversation, Paris. Curious about foreign people, pretentious, talkative, pleasant, intelligent.

The Russians: Talkative, self-satisfied, lazy. Luxury, inequality, culture. Pleasant, intelligent, resourceful.

The North Africans: Fairly racist, a little stingy, reasonably honest. Good education and good food. Selfish.

The Asians: Exhibitionist, indiscreet. Reticent in making friends. Bureaucracy and red tape.

The Black Africans: Racist, honest, lacking respect for elders and betters. At odds with themselves and nature. Not spontaneously hospitable.

(Source: Gruère and Morel, 1991, p. 51. Reproduced with permission.)

Papuan community. Stereotypes are often used to capture the salient traits of a 'foreign' national character. Box 12.5 shows how French people are viewed (at least stereo-typically) by people of other nations.

Self-shock

It is necessary to acknowledge that the problem of cultural representation is more complex than simply 'getting to know the other'. As shown by Zaharna (1989) in a review article on the culture shock experienced by people of different cultures, the problematic representation of the 'other' may evolve into a confrontation (equally problematic) with oneself. Zaharna calls this process 'self-shock'. Experiencing how others actually are may be somewhat destabilizing: identity confusion is a typical feature of culture shock (Oberg, 1960). Self-shock is probably one of the principal causes of stereotyping. Stereotypes often protect 'the self', much more than they really provide information on 'the other'.

When meeting people from other cultures, such as expatriates meeting local executives or international sellers meeting local buyers, the encounter is an intercultural one where the absence of previous knowledge of the other's culture makes for uncertainty. At first, one might think that the basic problem is 'getting to know the other'. But in the intercultural encounter, there is in fact a 'progressive unfolding of the self' which can be attributed to 'a set of intensive and evocative situations in which the individual perceives and experiences other people in a distinctly new manner and, as a consequence, experiences new facets and dimensions of existence' (Adler, 1975, p. 18). In intercultural encounters, the necessary introduction of the 'other' risks disturbing one's personal identity, which is placed in question by the 'mirror effect'.

Within our own cultural context, we have unconsciously built our 'self-image'. We necessarily construct an image of ourselves from the observations that we make, based on the responses of others to our conduct. This is emphasized by Erikson (1950, p. 13): 'Identity is the confidence gathered from the fact that our own ability to maintain interior resemblance and continuity equals the resemblance and continuity of the image and the sense that others have of us.' But the process of the creation and maintenance of personal identity has two characteristics that make it problematic in the intercultural encounter:

1. It happens for the most part outside our consciousness.
2. It requires a good capacity for interpersonal communication.

According to Zaharna 'self-shock', contrary to culture shock which is seen as a reaction to difference between oneself and the other, is a concept that extends to differences with and inside the self. The root of 'self-shock' lies in the intimate workings of the relationship between the ego (that is, personal identity), our behaviour and the 'other' (as the 'other' actually is, and as perceived by us, and also as forcing us to reflect upon ourselves). Self-shock emerges as a deep imbalance between our need to confirm our identity and our ability to do so. In one way, this situation places the individual in a position of 'double-bind' (Bateson, 1971). The self-shock situation increases our need for the reinforcement of our personal identity, while at the same time resulting in a loss of ability to satisfy this need. Thus, one can understand more easily that certain stereotypes or abrupt judgements about foreigners result almost directly from our attempts to defend ourselves by avoiding the painful double constraint of self-shock.

Gauthey (1989, p. 64) cites the case of the general manager of a software company, a subsidiary of a French advertising and communications group, who says: 'I can't stand the English, and when I go to London, I never leave the airport.' This attitude is clearly defensive: in refusing to leave the airport, he stays on neutral international ground, with no risk of being confronted by the image of himself that he will be shown by the English.

International empathy: a naive concept

Here we can catch a glimpse of the immense naivety of those who well-meaningly argue in favour of cultural empathy (being open-minded, sincerely interested in the other, ready to listen, etc.). This communication tactic, although well-meant, may only last for a brief period – the time during which the personal identity of the 'empathizer' has not yet come into play. There are a series of concrete issues at stake, which are operational issues for people involved in intercultural communication:

1. Which personality types and/or personal backgrounds are best suited to intercultural communication?
2. Correlative questions: are we able to communicate better with particular countries and cultures? How can we increase our abilities?
3. A question rarely dealt with is if an adjustment must be made during the intercultural encounter, who should be the one to adapt? Beyond personal capacities, empathy or the position of strength, can the intercultural learning situation be led other than bilaterally? In other words, why learn if the other does not learn too? Why not learn simultaneously, rather than in two parallel learning situations that may never meet?

12.5   How to improve communication effectiveness in international business

A 'reasonable' version of the use of the Whorfian hypothesis

The first consequence of the Whorf–Sapir hypothesis, in so far as one chooses to adhere to it, is that businesspeople from different cultures not only communicate in different ways, but also perceive, categorize and construct their realities differently. This therefore supposes a 'state of alert' in communication, a readiness to accept that words, even those that are translated with no apparent difficulty, offer only an illusion of sharing in the same vision of reality. It is necessary to retain as many foreign words as possible in their original form, in the following ways:

1. By forcing oneself to recognize their unique nature and therefore keeping culturally unique concepts in the native language form to signal their uniqueness.

2. By questioning the interpreters, or even one's foreign business partners, about the inner meaning in the context of a particular culture.
3. By clearly identifying areas of shared meaning.

For instance, in the examination of contract clauses, it is necessary to try to extricate the true meaning of each clause, starting from the perspective that they are never exactly equivalent. This is true even in the case where a dictionary seems to indicate (falsely) that an English term such as 'act of God' is a strict equivalent of a French term (here '*force majeure*').[15]

Linguistic ethnocentrism versus linguistic polycentrism

An unfortunate consequence of the Whorf–Sapir hypothesis is that linguistic ethno-centrism is largely inevitable. One might wonder whether it would be a more realistic approach to have only natives of a language and culture write about cultural topics for their fellow citizens. If we think of anthropology, a discipline with a high record of reporting on other cultures, it seems that the answer would be 'yes'. Famous anthro-pologists generally belonged to the cultures of their publishers and readers, not to the cultures they observed. The same holds true for area specialists. For instance, the two specialists of French culture who are best known are Theodore Zeldin of Harvard University and John Ardagh, a British journalist. Similarly, the most prominent specialist of French contemporary civilization in Germany is a German, Ulrich Wickert. It is often useful to be an outsider in relation to what is observed and culturally and in language terms an insider in reporting what has been observed. This evokes the important issue of *cultural mediation*, which is discussed briefly in this book (pp. 43–44). However paradoxical and provocative it may seem, it is sometimes more important to be understood than to understand, inasmuch as the *understanding* depends on the mind-frame of the observer as well as on the object to be understood. What is said by mere cultural insiders is often difficult to understand unless it has been in some way recalibrated in the linguistic background of the reader, which means more than simply translated.

For international businesspeople to be linguistically non-ethnocentric, does not mean that they have to have a full command of several foreign languages. It is more important, and in fact much easier than learning to read and speak fluently, to catch what is unique in the structure of the foreign language and some of its words. A look at a book of basic grammar and careful attention to specific words are a good start. Very often authors of books on Japanese business customs or management style keep Japanese words as they are originally pronounced when they want to signal a culturally specific meaning.[16] Sometimes words are forged that partly bridge the cultural divide. Boye de Mente cites for instance the Japanese word *nomination* which is made up of the first part of the Japanese word *nomimasu* (to drink) and the last half of 'communication': 'This Japlish word refers to business conversations and socializing that takes place in bars, cabarets, and other drinking establishments, and it is one of the institutionalized ways of "wisdom gathering" in Japan' (de Mente, 1990, p. 261).

Culturally unique life concepts have a major impact on decision-making processes inside companies and especially on the issue of labour–management relationships. They are signalled by words such as *management by objectives* for the Americans, *ringi* for the Japanese, *mitbestimmung* for the Germans, or *concertation* for the French. The same holds for the managing institutions of a company: a German *Aufsichtsrat*, often translated into English as 'supervisory board' should be considered a specific institution, typical of German business culture, with particular consequences in the real life of real businesses (Schneider-Lenné, 1993).

Although linguistic ethnocentrism is largely inevitable, we must strive for linguistic polycentrism, by trying to keep original words, understanding meaningful elements in the grammar (such as gender, tenses and sentence construction), and trying to behave as 'explorers' of the meanings and world-views expressed by different languages.

Taking the true measure of language and communication abilities in international business

In considering English as the *lingua franca* of international business, we have to differentiate two groups: native English-speakers and non-native. Their position is clearly different. For non-native English-speaking businesspeople, learning English and often one or two other languages is a must. For instance, the Swedes, Finns, Danes and Norwegians often speak three or four foreign languages: English, another Nordic language and French, German or Spanish. The situation is very different for native English-speakers. Simon observes 'The United States continues to be the only nation where you can graduate from college without having had one year of a foreign language' (Simon, 1980, p. 2). Although regrettable, this may be explained and understood. The United States is a vast country which is linguistically homogeneous in that nearly everyone shares the common language of English. There is no real need to learn foreign languages, compared with Europe where most large cities are located less than 200 miles (320 km) from a foreign-speaking area. Although the US is now the fourth largest Spanish-speaking country in the world and more than half the population of Miami is of Spanish-speaking origin, this does not necessarily require Americans to learn Spanish but for Hispanics to learn English. Moreover, there may be a lack of symmetry in the efforts for learning certain foreign languages. If an American or a European wants to really learn Japanese, the characters have to be learned, which implies a much larger effort than for the Japanese to learn the Roman alphabet: the *gai-jin* (non-Japanese) has to learn two syllabaries of about 100 characters each (*hiragana* and *katakana*, phonetic symbols) and about 1,850 *kanjis* (ideographic symbols), whereas the Roman alphabet to be learned by the Japanese has only 26 phonetic characters, not a large addition given the skill needed to master Japanese writing. Lastly, Americans fairly easily find English speakers during their travels, and they can count on their foreign business partners having – at least seemingly – a good command of English. Furthermore Americans are tolerant and lenient towards the mistakes of their non-native counterparts: 'international English' sometimes has little to do with real English grammar and words.

Thus these are good reasons why native English-speakers are a little bit lazy about foreign languages. Understandably, therefore, the impact of language differences has been systematically underestimated in international business literature because of a unique bias in Anglo-American culture. Most international business textbooks do not include a single reference in a foreign language. Even a text devoted to the cultural dimension of international business such as Ferraro (1990) does not have a single *truly* foreign reference, that is, from a foreign author in a foreign language (out of about 200 references), although some works by foreign authors are listed when they have been published in English. This may imply a substantial bias, since these authors would not be read in their own linguistic contexts and any foreign authors who have not been translated into English are not even considered. However, there are naturally good and practical reasons for maintaining language homogeneity in sources, namely that the reader would not be able either to find or to read these references, so this should not be considered only as a reflection of linguistic ethnocentrism.

What is unfortunate, however, is that native-English speakers are at a disadvantage, although it may appear to be the exact contrary. The main disadvantage for them is that they cannot grasp the features of the foreign language in terms of world-view and communication style. Furthermore, many native English speakers cannot imagine what it means to express oneself in a language with little proficiency unless they themselves have tried to learn and speak a foreign language. Thus native English speakers have to develop an awareness of their paradoxical competitive disadvantage in terms of language. However, the message to be conveyed cannot be simply and plainly to learn foreign languages. It is a different thing to understand and speak a foreign language as such and to understand the consequences of languages being different. Absolute proficiency in many languages is not needed. International businesspeople do not have to be multilingual by definition; they do, however, need to have an awareness of what language differences imply.

On the other hand, non-native English speakers must not fool their counterparts. Although many foreign businesspeople seem to have a good command of English, they still have the kind of world-view that has been shaped by their native language and culture. Thus proficient non-native English speakers may be somewhat misleading partners for their opposite numbers, looking quite the same, while being fairly different. This may be especially true for northern Europeans. They may seem quite similar, especially to Americans, since their English pronunciation has largely been shaped by television viewing. Nevertheless, they may have in reality a different mindset and also a much better proficiency for oral than for written communication, which may cause problems in discussing the written details of business contracts.

Some guidelines for effective communication in international business

1. Start by assessing as accurately as possible the possible intercultural obstacles that exist, such as language and problems of communication in general. Businesspeople often underestimate or even completely overlook this point, since they often share a technical culture with their conversation partner. They are also deceived by an almost international atmosphere that can be quite misleading. Glen Fisher emphasizes:

   Obviously, the modern intensity of international interaction, especially in business and in technological, communication and educational fields, has produced something of an internationalized 'culture' which reduces the clash of cultural backgrounds and stereotyped images. Happily for us this *modus vivendi* is largely based on Western practices and even on the English language, so many otherwise 'foreign' counterparts are accommodating to the American style of negotiation. (Fisher, 1980, p. 8)

Unfortunately, in the real world, the person who does not feel the need to adapt, especially as far as language is concerned, may be indulging in indolence. The result will be the mistaken impression that one's partner is just like oneself. That is to say that often similarities are illusions, especially when foreigners seemingly share the same 'international culture'. Those who adapt are aware of differences, whereas those who must be adapted to remain unaware.

2. Beware that what is explicitly said is not necessarily what is implicitly meant. Check, verify. Spend time on checking communication accuracy, especially when the stakes are high (orders, delivery dates, contractual involvement in general).

3. Learning the non-verbal communication style of other cultures may prove very difficult. Deep cultural learning in this area is very hard after childhood. It is better to aim for a state of alertness so that one does not decode non-verbal messages erroneously, rather than try to gain full command of different types of non-verbal communication.

4. In many cases interpreters may serve a crucial purpose, that of transposers of meaning. They do not work 'like a dictionary', translating literally. They may translate better from one language to another than in the reverse direction, and this will depend not only on which their native language is, but also on some personal leaning towards one party. It is also necessary to make sure that they are truly loyal to the party which has hired them. It may be advisable to hire several interpreters when the business at stake justifies it.

5. It must be clearly appreciated that there is always a part of the language which cannot be translated. Culture-specific meaning is conveyed by language as it reflects the culture. Always keep in mind the Italian adage, cited above, *traduttore/traditore* (translator/traitor).

6. Develop a 'bomb squad' ability to defuse a conflict based on negative stereotypes. (Subjective) misunderstandings in intercultural communication often snowball and mix with purely interest-based (objective) conflicts, resulting in confrontations that may not be productive. There are sometimes necessary conflicts and even good ones, where confrontation should not be avoided. But in many other cases, cultural misunderstandings may have a purely negative influence on the dealings that follow, possibly even leading to the breaking off of negotiations.

7. Keep in mind that all this depends on advance preparation, and unfortunately cannot be improvised. An effort to help the other intelligently and agreeably to understand one's own culture is a prerequisite, and it may often be 'wine and dine' related. When formal business negotiations or even preliminary business talks start and one side lacks minimal knowledge of the partner's culture, the relations will often turn sour. It will soon be too late to approach basic issues affected by common understandings and cultural differences. Then the only way to negotiate is to discuss on the substantive ground of 'business is business'. In this light, training in intercultural business seems

more like a preliminary investment to improve the effectiveness of business deals than a way of resolving urgent problems. In medical terms, cultural understanding in business appears as the prevention rather than the cure.

Questions

1. Comment on the following sentences: 'it is the subjective meaning of words and expressions that needs to be captured. Time spent exploring why a given utterance does not translate well may be more productive for the one who is actually trying to communicate than concentration on technical excellence' (Fisher, 1988, p. 172).
2. Give examples of low context versus high context communication.
3. Transform the following sentence in low-context and high-context sentences: 'Your price is too high compared with that of the competitors' (buyer).
4. Why can the obvious showing of emotions be considered as dangerous? Why do cultures vary in the degree of emotional restraint?
5. Consider the gender aspect of words in the following languages. In English almost everything is neutral except persons and some animals, and exceptionally an object such as a ship. French has feminine and masculine but no neutral. In German, persons, objects and concepts can be either feminine, masculine or neutral. For instance 'sun', 'earth' and 'moon' are all neutral words in English; in French they are respectively masculine (*le soleil*) and feminine (*la terre, la lune*); in German the same words are feminine (*die Sonne, die Erde*) and masculine (*der Mond*). Elaborate on the possible cultural meanings of attributing gender to words. To what extent can we speak of more or less 'sexualized' languages? (I mean here 'sexualized' and not simply 'gendered'.) Outline the limitations of such an interpretive approach.
6. In Japanese there are no articles either definite or indefinite. *Hon*, for instance, means either 'the book', 'a book', 'the books' or 'books'. What does it imply for the Japanese when they want to express their thoughts?
7. Consider gift-giving practices as an element of communication. What are the main dimensions of gift-giving? (Consider the donor, the receiver, the size and nature of the gift, the circumstances, and its meaning for either side.) How would cultural interpretations differ? Take into account the values involved. (You can base your discussion on elements found in articles about gift-giving.)
8. Can you describe at least one circumstance when you had an ethnocentric attitude? If you find it hard, can you explain why?

APPENDIX 12

———— ◆◆◆ ————

Teaching materials

A12.1   Exercise: Multicultural class

Look at the person seated next to you in class, or anyone with whom you have frequent interaction. Then select somebody originating from a foreign culture. List three examples of non-verbal communication that she or he uses, describe them accurately and decode their meaning. Now ask this person to look at you and do the same. Then work together and compare both interpretations and try to understand why meaning was shared or, possibly, not shared.

(This exercise can be implemented only with a good degree of cultural diversity within the student group.)

A12.2   Exercise: I 'love' cake

Start from the English verb 'to like' and find its equivalents into French, German and Spanish. Do not hesitate to translate them back into English in order to detect differences in meaning. Include in your search some basic etymological grounds (e.g. *gusto* in Spanish is based on the word for 'taste'). What differences in terms of world-views are suggested by the different conceptual dimensions of 'liking' (preference, affective, pleasure, love, enjoyment, eating/ingesting, etc.) and their attributions to people, things or situations? Suggest possible consequences for international marketing and advertising strategies.

A12.3   Exercise: Following directions

Objective

To clarify for participants the formats of their communication and the difficulties and inaccuracies encountered when implementing those formats.

Participants

Any number of dyads, each individual in a given dyad representing a different culture. Facilitator.

Materials

1. One or more index cards for each participant (see Figure 12.1).
2. Answer sheets and pencils for each participant.

Setting

Dyads should be seated around a table. If there are several dyads, each should be seated at a different table.

Time

Variable, depending on participant characteristics, number of cards per participant and processing phase; anywhere from ten minutes to an hour or more.

Procedure

1. Participants are divided into culturally mixed dyads and seated around tables.
2. At each table, one participant sits on one side of the table and is designated as source. The other is seated on the other side and is designated as 'respondent'.
3. Each participant is given an answer sheet and one or more index cards. The index card, as shown in Figure 12.1, contain eight matrices of twenty-five dots each. The cards contain one matrix of twenty-five dots, on which five of the dots are connected by five lines. Each card design is unique.
4. Each source must verbally communicate the design on one of his cards to the respondent seated across from him who must reproduce it on one of the blank matrices on his answer sheet within a recommended time limit of ten to fifteen seconds.
5. Participants alternate being sources and respondents and may change their partners with each new round of activity.
6. Facilitator leads discussion tying in participants' experience with the exercise objective, emphasizing the role cultural difference may play in confounding communication.
7. Suggestions variations of this exercise are:
   (a) Ask participants to draw their own designs and then communicate them to each other.

Figure 12.1 Index card.

(b) Draw and communicate more complex designs (eight dots and eight lines) in the same amount of time.

(c) Communicate designs drawn on irregular matrices.

(d) If several dyads take part in the exercise, make each correct communication worth one point. Besides the element of inter-dyad competition, the success of each dyad member becomes contingent upon the success of the other. Some interesting effective data may be generated for discussion.

(Source: Royal Freuhling, of the University of Hawaii, 1975, in Weeks *et al.*, 1987, pp. 10–13. Reproduced with the kind permission of the publisher.)

A12.4 Case: Supreme Canning

The Supreme Canning Company (the true name of the company is disguised) is an independent United States packer of tomato products (whole peeled tomatoes, chopped tomatoes, katsup, paste, pizza and other sauces, and tomatoes and zucchini). The company is located in the State of California. Although it produces some cans with its own brand label, much of its output is canned for others and their brand names and labels put on the cans. It produces shelf-size cans for eventual sale at retail, gallon-size cans for use by restaurants and industrial users, and 55 gallon drums for use by others for repacking or further processing. Its annual processing capacity is in excess of 100,000 tons of tomatoes (processed during an operating season of approximately three months in length).

During the decade before 1987, the California canning industry had suffered from heavy competition from abroad and inadequate local demand. A somewhat increasing domestic demand for specialty tomato products, especially pizza and other sauces, was not adequate to absorb increasing imports. The high value of the US dollar, through 1985, had made it difficult for United States companies to sell abroad. Excess capacity and the resulting depressed prices had led to bankruptcy for a number of Californian canners. With the decline of the value of the dollar during 1986 and 1987, and the efforts of Japan to reduce its trade barriers and increase imports, it appeared that Supreme Canning Company might be able to get into the Japanese market. An inquiry received from a foodpacker and distributor in Japan indicated interest from that side. The Japanese firm produced and distributed a large number of products, was well known in Japan, and was much larger than the US company.

Since Supreme Canning Company did not have well-known brand names of its own, the company was interested in acting as a large-scale supplier of products made to customer specifications for use by the customer or distribution under the customer's label. Thus, the inquiry from Japan was most welcome.

The Japanese company invited senior executives of the American firm to visit their production facilities and offices in Japan. Both the president and chairman of the board of Supreme Canning Company had a four-day visit with the executives of the company in Japan. The president of the US company, who had some knowledge of Japanese business practice from studies at Stanford University and from his widespread reading, attempted to act as a guide to Japanese business practice. The chairman of the board had little knowledge of Japan, and viewed himself as a decisive man of action. Although there were a few minor misunderstandings, the visit was concluded successfully and the Americans invited the Japanese to visit their plant in California for four days.

The Japanese indicated their interest in the signing of a mutual letter of cooperation.The American chairman of the board was not interested in this, but rather wanted some specific agreements and contracts. As the time for the Japanese visit to the United States drew near, the Japanese indicated that their president would not be able to come. Some senior executives would be able to meet, but they would only be able to spend two days instead of four. The vice-chairman of the board of the California company wrote asking why the Japanese were not going to send their president, and inquiring why they could not spend four days instead of two, 'as we did in Japan.' The letter was frank and direct. The tone was that of a person talking to an equal, but not with any great deal of politeness. The Japanese company decided to cancel the visit, and no further negotiations or serious contacts were made.

Some months later, a local businessman of Japanese extraction asked the president of Supreme Canning Company if some representatives of another (and even larger) Japanese food products producer and distributor could visit the plant. Four Japanese showed up along with the local businessman, who acted as interpreter and go-between. The three middle-aged Japanese produced their *meishi* (business cards) and introduced themselves. Each spoke some English. The older man did not present a card and was not introduced. When the president of the American company asked who he was, the go-between said, 'He's just one of the company's directors.' The visit concluded without discussion of any business possibilities, but this was to be expected in an initial visit from Japanese businessmen.

Supreme's president later found out the family name of the unknown visitor and immediately recognized it as being that of the president of the Japanese company. He assumed that the president of the Japanese company had come but had hidden the fact. He felt that he had been taken advantage of. He telephoned the go-between and told him that he never wanted anyone from that company in his plant again. From a description of the unknown visitor, a consultant to the company realized that the visitor was not the president of the Japanese company. Rather, it was the semi-retired father of the president. The father retained a position on the board of directors and maintained an active interest in company activities, but was not active in day-to-day affairs. Unlike his son who was fluent in English, he spoke only Japanese.

(Source: Saito Duerr, of San Francisco State University, 1989, *International Marketing and Export Management* pp. 85–7. Reproduced with permission.)

Questions

1. Was the chairman of the American company wrong for not having found out in advance about Japanese business practices? Why did he not do so? (Same questions for the Japanese companies and US business practices.)
2. What are the principal cultural mistakes made (a) by the Americans from the Japanese perspective, and (b) by the Japanese from the American perspective?
3. What should the president of the American company do now?

A12.5   Case: Doing business in China: a success in getting paid

In recent years, the People's Republic of China (PRC) has become much more open to trade with the West, and has also made substantial internal economic reforms. Companies in Japan, the Western European countries, the United States and elsewhere have viewed the Chinese market as having enormous potential. With a population of a billion and a growing economy, it has appeared to many to be worthwhile to make a major effort to gain a foothold in the market. Both direct exports and joint ventures have been used.

In spite of the economic reforms, however, the PRC remains a tightly controlled, centrally directed economy. Most commercial enterprises and almost all production facilities are state owned and state run. Only a small number of designated organizations are allowed to engage in international trade, and all of these are state owned.

All contracts for trade must receive several government approvals. Larger contracts receive more approvals than smaller ones. It is not always apparent to the outsider, or perhaps even to some of the Chinese, what specific approvals will be required in particular cases. While letters of credit may be issued to companies exporting to China, these do not provide the same level of assurance that a letter of credit issued by, say, a London bank would. The Chinese bank will simply not release foreign exchange, regardless of the existence of a letter of credit, without the approval of appropriate government agencies. Foreign companies selling to the government may not receive a letter of credit, but may feel that they can rely on the good faith of the government.

A major United States exporter recently called upon the US Embassy in Beijing requesting assistance in solving a problem. About one year earlier they had sold approximately US$8.0 million worth of equipment to the China National Technology Import Company for use by the Chinese Ministry of Petroleum Industries (MOPI). To date, no payment had been received, and the company did not seem to be getting anywhere in its attempts to collect. The commercial attaché at the embassy called the Technology Import and Export Department of the Ministry of Foreign Economic Relation and Trade (MOFERT), the Chinese department which would appear to be in charge of the transaction. MOFERT agreed to a meeting at 10.00 a.m. the next day. After the commercial attaché had briefed MOFERT representatives on the problem, they indicated that they were not in charge of the transaction; it came under the jurisdiction of the Import and Export Department, not the Technology Import and Export Department. Nevertheless they agreed to see what they could do to help. The commercial attaché expressed hope that the problem could be resolved as expeditiously as possible since the payment was already a year overdue.

At 2.00 p.m. the same afternoon, MOFERT officials called and informed the commercial attaché that the problem had been resolved and that payment would be forthcoming. They explained that MOPI had delayed submitting the request for initial contract approval and had sent that along with the request for payment. This had caused a delay. The rules had been changed so that, in addition to the approvals required when a contract is to be signed, an additional set of approvals is required from the same organizations when the goods are delivered. In the case of this contract, two separate sets of approvals were required from each of the following:

1. MOPI;
2. MOFERT;
3. the State Planning Commission;

4. the State Administration for Foreign Exchange Control.

(Source: George Lee, of San Francisco State University and formerly Commercial Attaché, US Embassy, Beijing, PRC. Reproduced with the kind permission of the author.)

Questions

1. Why does the People's Republic of China have a State Administration for Foreign Exchange Control, and so many approvals required for a purchase of goods from overseas?
2. Is the additional difficulty in trying to sell to the People's Republic of China, compared with trying to sell to France or Taiwan, worth the trouble? Why or why not?
3. If you wanted to export to the People's Republic of China, would you go to your own government or embassy in China for assistance? Why or why not?
4. If the United States company had a similar problem in France, is it likely they would have contacted their embassy for assistance? Why or why not?

A12.6   Critical incident: Scandinavian Tools Company

A major Swedish company that specialized in metal tools and factory equipment had created a French subsidiary a few years ago, based in Lyons, France. This plant was at first supplied with inputs (speciality steels, high-speed steels for blades and saws, etc.) from Sweden. It mostly produced and sold for the French markets and for exports to the other southern European markets, namely Italy, Spain and Portugal. The drive and energy for creating this new venture had been brought by a young Swedish executive, Bo Svensson. Svensson had spent part of his curriculum as a student and then as a young engineer in France. Thereafter he had been in a position to convince the top management of this large Swedish multinational company to launch a new subsidiary in France.

Svensson was very enthusiastic about France. He liked the country very much and had learned the language, which he spoke fluently with a slight northern European accent. In the rush of starting the new company everything went smoothly. Svensson, who was chief executive officer of the French venture, knew how to secure customers and make them loyal; he also knew how to deal with the headquarters in Sweden. The market was quickly growing and competition was not particularly harsh. At the beginning, products were made in Sweden and then exported to France, where Svensson and the subsidiary dealt with marketing and distribution.

After a few years demand began to swell, so the parent company in Sweden decided to build a production plant in France. Machines and factory equipment for the new plant came from Sweden, and the factory was quickly operating at normal capacity. Svensson then hired a vice-president for administration, André Ribaud, an ambitious young executive, also in his thirties, with a law background. The two men got on well together, although their backgrounds and personal profiles were quite different. They shared the work and responsibilities: Svensson was in charge of relations with headquarters, marketing and the monitoring of financial performance; as plant manager, Ribaud was in charge of production operations, human resource management, cost accounting, monitoring cost prices and delivery delays.

After a few years it appeared that Svensson felt more and more relaxed in his job. Autonomous in his profitable subsidiary of (at that time) 200 employees located in a place remote from Sweden, he was very free with his timetable. He was also very free with personal expenses, which he was entitled to have reimbursed by the subsidiary: he simply had to sign his own expenses receipts. Svensson did not hesitate to use this facility: he did not make a clear distinction between his own money and the company's money. Svensson gradually got into the habit of abusing company-paid personal expenses. Ribaud was shocked. Svensson even went so far as to have the expenses of his mistress paid by the subsidiary.

Meanwhile Ribaud was still working as efficiently as during the initial years. Growth had been impressive. Starting with a few employees in an office of two rooms in Lyons, the subsidiary had grown to a dynamic medium-sized company with more than 500 people on the payroll; Scandinavian Tools France had bought out two plants from competitors. Following these changes, Ribaud's responsibilities quickly increased. He had involved himself completely and passionately with the company. He knew each member of staff personally and was respected by them.

Over time the relationship between the two men had considerably worsened. Svensson saw that Ribaud was winning more and more influence and power inside the company, and was well known by the customers. He felt jealous of him and tried his best to make Ribaud's life in the company difficult. Ribaud, on the other hand, increasingly resented the excessive expenses and the catty remarks of his boss, for whom he no longer felt any esteem. Svensson was a complex, energetic and whimsical character. His charisma and stamina had enabled him to seduce the French clients as well as the management staff at the headquarters in Sweden. The excellent financial performance of the French subsidiary had been feeding a confidence relationship with his superiors, who were also Swedish compatriots. They had trust in his management talents and therefore they allowed him a large degree of freedom. He had also established friendships with some of the senior directors at the headquarters, especially with the director in charge of public relations. Svensson was well known at headquarters level, and he understood company 'politics' quite well.

After fifteen years of almost steady growth, the market was reaching the stage of maturity. Competitors were aiming at the horizon of 1993, with its concomitant cancelling of borders within the EU, and there were many acquisitions by large European and American competitors. The French subsidiary had lost part of its profitability. The middle management was complaining to Ribaud about Svensson's lack of interest in the subsidiary and his mismanagement. Everybody believed that emergency decisions had to be made before the situation got even worse. But Svensson turned a deaf ear to their complaints and remained unwilling to enter into discussion with either Ribaud or the other executives. The French were also amazed, and somewhat shocked, to see that there was no reaction from head-quarters. It looked as if headquarters had little interest in the destiny of the French subsidiary. People at headquarters still seemed to have confidence in Svensson, who knew how to make them feel secure.

Ribaud did not feel comfortable in this situation. He felt that the financial balance of the subsidiary was threatened and that one factory would probably have to close in the near future. It also seemed to him that the interests of Swedish shareholders were not being adequately taken into account. Relations between Svensson and Ribaud were so damaged that Svensson was convinced that Ribaud was plotting against him. Svensson therefore systematically took a contradictory stance to Ribaud, at the risk of making inappropriate decisions which could possibly lead the subsidiary almost to the brink of bankruptcy.

Each time Ribaud brought up these problems during meetings with people from headquarters, Svensson abruptly interrupted him, shifting from English to Swedish in order to keep him out of the conversation. Under heavy pressure from some of the executives of the subsidiary who were about to resign and leave the company, Ribaud felt obliged to react. He had tried, during visits from members of the Swedish headquarters to give them an idea of the situation in a very allusive manner. But he got the impression that he was not being heard. They had their own image of the chief executive officer which was clearly different.

In desperation, Ribaud decided to send an official note to the top management in Stockholm, in which he told them that he would be obliged to resign if nothing was done to put an end to the present disorder. He tried to write it as objectively as possible in a matter-of-fact style, citing evidence and hard facts. This was not an easy task since objectivity may prove difficult in such circumstances and, moreover, he was denouncing his boss, which is never very pleasant. He called one of the members of the top management in Stockholm whom he knew a little better than the others, explained about the letter and sent him a copy. What answer could he expect?

Notes

1. Depending on your own linguistic background, in reading this chapter you may be wondering how the linguistic mix (original French text, English translation) has influenced the kind of arguments put forward and the way in which they have been expounded. The Whorfian hypothesis, briefly explained in section 12.3, is presented in detail in the writings of Benjamin Whorf, collected after his death by John B. Carroll (1956).
2. A good example is the following assertion in Hall (1966, p. 50): 'In the Northern European tradition most Americans have cut themselves off from a powerful communication channel: olfaction. Our cities lack both olfactory and visual variety. . . . During World War II in France I observed that the aroma of French bread freshly removed from the oven at 4:00 A.M. could bring a speeding jeep to a screaming halt. . . . In the typical French town, one may savor the smell of coffee, spices, vegetables, freshly plucked fowl, clean laundry, and the characteristic odor of outdoor cafés.' Although there is some truth in Hall's words, I am not so sure that France is so odourful and the Americans so cut off from olfactive communication.

3. The example made known to me took place in Geneva, where the penalty was 15 Swiss Francs (about $12).

4. We do not argue that these national cultures share much in common. The concept of low context/explicit messages relates only to communication; in other aspects they may widely differ.

5. Langenscheidt, *German–English Dictionary* (New York: Pocket Books, 1970).

6. Hall posits the American as being more HC (or less LC) than the Swiss, the Germans and the Scandinavians (see *Beyond Culture*, p. 91), and the French and the English as more HC than the Americans but less than the Japanese. A possible tentative ranking on a scale starting with LC and moving across to HC would be: Swiss-Germans, Germans, Scandinavians, Americans, English, French, other southern Europeans, Latin Americans, Middle Easterners, Japanese.

7. Analogical components of verbal messages are those which work by imitation of existing models or regular patterns, but cannot be reduced to binary, digital, information. In first place a 'yes' is a '1' as opposed to a 'no' being a '0' (digital component); secondly, the meaning derived from how this 'yes' is said is the analogical component of the message.

8. In this chapter, we have not paid special attention to the 'language of space'. This includes the codes concerning social distance: how far should one stay from another person in order to respect their area of private space and does such an area even exist? A complete approach to these relations of space was proposed by Hall (1966) in *The Hidden Dimension*, where he developed the concept of 'proxemics' – the grouping of observations and theories dealing with the use of space by human beings, especially as far as private space and social space are concerned. Hall further developed an interesting cross-cultural comparison of proxemics between the Germans, the English, the French, the Japanese and the Arabs.

9. See Ferraro (1990), chapter 4. The teaching of non-verbal communication is, however, very difficult. It is better to aim for a state of alert in order not to decode non-verbal messages erroneously, rather than to try for full mastery of different types of non-verbal communication. Deep cultural learning is very hard to acquire after childhood.

10. The verifications of the Whorf–Sapir hypothesis seem to have been fairly conclusive, in particular those related to the comparative experiments based on Navajo children on the one hand and Anglo-Americans on the other. They both shared all principal socio-cultural characteristics (education, family income, religion, etc.) except language (see the experiments reported by Ferraro, 1990, pp. 54–5).

11. I wrote this short English text myself, therefore it is not a 'valid text' but a caricature or exercise in reflection. Native anglophones will notice the 'Gallic' style with respect to idioms.

12. This is related to English, French and German intellectual styles, which are described in more detail in chapter 3, using the typology of Galtung (1981).

13. What is said here is fairly tentative; there are no definitive proofs, and so there are at best illustrations, and many people may disagree with what I say here. Think of it as proposed rather than imposed.

14. However, in Japan I had a student who was the son of the Turkish embassador to the United Nations. Having been raised in France, Belgium, Italy and Brazil, he was studying for a Master's Degree in International Management at the American Graduate School of International Management in Phoenix, Arizona. Already speaking fluent Turkish, French, English, Italian and Portugese, he was learning Japanese. But he was really unable to pass flexibly from one of these languages to another. When in the middle of a conversation I asked him for the English translation of a French word (I taught in English), he could never do this without a considerable delay. In fact *he thought separately in each one of these languages*, which is fairly consistent with the Whorfian hypothesis.

15. To show a practical progression of an investigation in equivalence/non-equivalence of terms, take two dictionaries and look in each of them at the translations in both directions. The Langenscheidt compact dictionary translates *act of God* as *force majeure*, but it translates *force majeure* as *overpowering circumstances*; Harrap's Concise does not include the expression *act of God* in the English section and translates *force majeure* as 'circumstances outside one's control'. The next step is to consult a lawyer to arrive at the meanings of all these expressions, and find their respective legal consequences. *Force majeure* is used, as such, in English and US contracts.

16. It is naturally impossible to keep Japanese words in their original, spoken and written, form; they need to be transliterated into the Roman alphabet. The system often used is the *Hyojunshiki* (standard system) which is an adaptation of the Hepburn system.

References

Adler, Peter S. (1975), 'The transitional experience: An alternative view of culture shock', *Journal of Humanistic Psychology*, vol. 15, pp. 13–23.

Bateson, Gregory (1971), introduction to *The Natural History of an Interview*, University of Chicago Library Microfilm Collection of Manuscripts in Cultural Anthropology, Series 15, Nos 95–8.

Carroll, John B. (1956), *Language, Thought and Reality:.Selected writings of Benjamin Lee Whorf*, MIT: Cambridge, MA.

Condon, John C. and Fahti Youssef (1975), *Introduction to Intercultural Communication*, Bobbs Merrill: Indianapolis.

Copeland, Lennie and Lewis Grigg (1986), *Going International*, Plume Books/New American Library: New York.

De Mente, Boye (1990), *How to Do Business with the Japanese*, NTC Books: Chicago, Il.

Droit, Michel (1952), *Chez les Mangeurs d'hommes*, La Table Ronde: Paris.

Erikson, Erik (1950), *Childhood and Society*, Norton: New York.

Ferraro, Gary P. (1990), *The Cultural Dimension of International Business*, Prentice Hall: Englewood Cliffs, NJ.

Fisher, Glen (1980), *International Negotiation: A cross-cultural perspective*, Intercultural Press: Yarmouth, ME.

Fisher, Glen (1988), *Mindsets*, Intercultural Press: Yarmouth, ME.

Galtung, Johan (1981), 'Structure, culture and intellectual style: An essay comparing Saxonic, Teutonic, Gallic and Nipponic Approaches', *Social Science Information*, vol. 20, no. 6, pp. 817–56.

Gauthey, Franck (1989), 'Gérer les différences dans l'entreprise internationale', *Intercultures*, no. 6, April, pp. 59–66.

Gauthey, Franck and Dominique Xardel (1990), *Le Management Intercuturel*, PUF, Collection 'Que Sais-Je?': Paris.

Gruère, Jean-Pierre and Pierre Morel (1991), *Cadre français et communications interculturelles*, Eyrolles: Paris.

Hall, Edward T. (1960), 'The silent language in overseas business', *Harvard Business Review*, May–June, pp. 87–96.

Hall, Edward T. (1966), *The Hidden Dimension*, Doubleday: New York.

Hall, Edward T. (1976), *Beyond Culture*, Doubleday: New York.

Harris, Philip R. and Robert T. Moran (1987), *Managing Cultural Differences*, 2nd edn, Gulf Publishing Company: Houston, TX.

Hemingway, Ernest (1976), *The Snows of Kilimandjaro and Other Stories*, Charles Scribner's and Sons: New York.

Langenscheidt (1989), *Compact Dictionary French–English/English–French*, by Kenneth Urwin.

Lee, James A. (1966), 'Cultural analysis in overseas operations', *Harvard Business Review*, March–April, pp. 106–11.

Levine, Robert A. and Donald T. Campbell (1972), *Ethnocentrism: Theories of conflicts, ethnic attitudes, and group behavior*, John Wiley: New York.

Levine, Robert V. (1988), 'The Pace of Life Across Cultures', in Joseph E. McGrath ed., *The Social Psychology of Time*, Sage Publications: Newbury Park, CA, pp. 39–60.

M'biti, John (1968), 'African concept of time', *Africa Theological Journal*, vol. 1, pp. 8–20.

Mishima, Yukio (1954), *Shiosai* (French translation, Paris, Gallimard, 1969).

Morsbach, Helmut (1982), 'Aspects of non-verbal communication in Japan', in Larry Samovar and R.E. Porter (eds), *Intercultural Communication: A reader*, 3rd edn, Wadsworth: Belmont, CA.

Oberg, Kalvero (1960), 'Culture shock: Adjustment to new cultural environments', *Practical Anthropology*, vol. 7, pp. 177–82.

Saito Duerr, Mitsuko (1989), in Gerald Albaum, Jesper Strandskov, Edwin Duerr and Lawrence Dowd, *International Marketing and Export Management*, Addison-Wesley: Reading, MA.

Sapir, Edward (1929), 'The status of linguistics as a science', *Language*, vol. 5, pp. 207–14.

Schneider-Lenné, E. (1993), 'The governance of good business', *Business Strategy Review*, vol. 4, no. 1 (Spring), pp. 75–85.

Simon, Paul (1980), *The Tongue Tied American*, Continuum Press: New York.

Sumner, G. A. (1906), *Folk Ways*, Ginn Custom Publishing: New York.

Ueda, Keiko (1974), 'Sixteen ways to avoid saying "no" in Japan', in J. C Condon and M. Saito (eds), *Intercultural Encounters in Japan*, Simul Press: Tokyo, pp. 185–92.

Weeks, William H., Paul B. Pedersen and Richard W. Brislin (1987), *A Manual of Structured Experiences for Cross-cultural Learning*, Intercultural Press: Yarmouth, ME.

Zaharna, R.S. (1989), 'Self shock: The double-binding challenge of identity', *International Journal of Intercultural Relations*, vol. 13, no. 4, pp. 501–26.

13

◆◆◆

Intercultural marketing communications 1: Advertising

In the mid-1970s, when Polaroid introduced its cameras in Europe, it used the same advertising strategy, including TV commercials and print ads, as in the United States; these campaigns never achieved much impact in either raising awareness of instant photography or pulling customers into the stores. Later on, Polaroid developed very successful European campaigns on the basis of the strategy of one of its smallest subsidiaries, that in Switzerland, a multicultural and central country in Europe. The strategy of Polaroid Switzerland, promoting the functional uses of instant photography as a way to communicate with family and friends, proved to be transferable in European countries (Kashani, 1989). Advertising, being based on language and communication, is the most culture-bound element of the marketing mix.

This chapter could be subtitled 'national cultures, technological advances and the globalization of marketing communications'. Indeed it attempts to show, as Chapters 6 and 7 did, that globalization is not the very simple process that it is often believed to be. The first sections of this chapter describe cultural differences as they pertain to various aspects of advertising: what are the general attitudes *vis-à-vis* advertising (13.1)? How are creative standards affected by local culture (13.2)? How is media selection affected by differences in media availability and style (13.3)?

Since advertising is largely based on language and images, it is influenced by culture. Cross-national differences continue to exist, for the simple reason that we have not yet ceased to have different languages. Moreover language, be it through words or images, is the strongest link between advertisers and their potential audiences in marketing communications.

The management process for marketing communication *per se* does not depend on the particular country where the advertising campaign is launched. It is composed of six steps (Figure 13.1). Logically, these steps should be taken in order, although feedback at any step is possible and often necessary, especially after testing the campaign. The six basic steps are as follows:

1. Isolate the communication problem to be solved: increase brand awareness, change the brand image, increase sales, differentiate from rival brands, take points of market share from the competition, etc.

2. Identify the relevant target population: which consumer segments? What are their sociodemographic characteristics, consumption habits, psychographic characteristics (consumer lifestyles and values), etc.?
3. Define the marketing communication objective in terms of influencing the target population, either at the attitudinal or the behavioural level. Communication objectives may be, for instance, to convince consumers that they like the product (to improve product acceptance), to let people retry (to increase sales by building consumer loyalty), to let people act, or to educate the consumer, etc.
4. Select the advertising themes and a creative strategy: how will the brand name be emphasized? Which copy strategy should be used?
5. Design a media plan: which media to use, how to optimize the best media to reach the target audience, etc.
6. Implement and monitor the advertising campaign: pre- and post-tests of the advertisement effectiveness; research of different aspects (message recall, brand recall, aided brand recognition, actual influence on sales); etc.

The international dimension naturally has an influence on the implementation of each

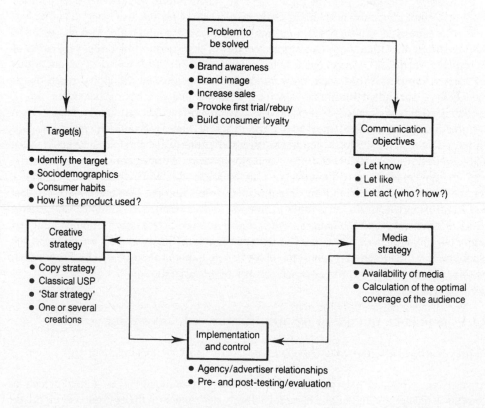

Figure 13.1 Main steps in the management of advertising communication. USP = Unique Selling Proposition.

of these steps, but not an equal influence on each step. Let us take an example: to advertise life insurance in Tunisia, it should be taken into account that the life insurance market is a new one, where consumers have little knowledge of this kind of financial service. For this reason, the message shows a man and a woman watering a tree which grows by leap and bounds. Finally, a large pine tree protects them with its branches, while they sit happily in its shade. Certainly culture will influence the objective: the education of the consumer would be a basic objective in a country where life insurance is almost unknown. But the changes caused by cultural differences are most obvious with respect to the creative strategy (step 4). One should acknowledge and respect the values of Tunisian consumers who belong to an Arab-Muslim culture which is nevertheless strongly linked to two European cultures (Italy and France). The complex mix of Muslim and western culture has to be considered, since values that involve important matters (life and death, protecting one's family, betting on the future) are at stake.

The media plan will also be strongly influenced by local idiosyncrasies: media availability, viewing habits and media regulations still differ a great deal across countries. The topic of how culture influences creative strategy and media planning will be dealt within the first section.

Conversely, the other steps in Figure 13.1 are not strongly affected by local factors: defining a communication problem or a communication objective, or testing the effectiveness of a campaign, calls for a similar approach in each country although the solution may be different. Although the first three sections of this chapter favour customization of advertising, section 13.4 may appear to be in contrast to this. Technological advances that are now in progress world-wide, such as satellite television and the global reach of the media, have an undeniable impact on local attitudes and purchasing behaviour. In all probability, the emergence of world-wide advertising media will partly break down cultural resistance. In fact, they will open different lines of communication between cultures that previously were geographically and culturally separated, such as western and eastern Europe, or southern Europe and North Africa. Furthermore they will open the way to new marketing communications in areas of the world which are culturally fragmented, for ethnic, linguistic or political reasons: Europe, Southeast Asia, Central and Latin America. In this new style of international marketing communication, strictly national segments and audiences will be differentiated from cross-border regional segments and audiences. The choice of the appropriate media as well as the choice of the language in which to advertise will therefore be key factors for success. The final section of this chapter deals with the issue of advertising globalization.

13.1   Influence of culture on attitudes towards advertising

General attitudes towards the role and functions of advertising

Advertising, which is a large part of marketing communications, is a field which is constantly changing. On the one hand it is closely dependent on the cultural and linguistic attitudes of the local target population. On the other hand, in so far as social representations are not fixed, advertising is a privileged method of cultural borrowing; advertising mirrors changing social behaviour. The relative freedom of advertising creation and the need to capture the audience mean that advertising is sometimes challenging and often innovative. It is therefore the ground for societal debates. This is illustrated below by several advertising-related issues, e.g. 'publiphobia' (rejection of advertising), attitudes towards comparative advertising and attitudes towards its informative content.

General attitudes towards publicity and 'publiphobia'

One view that has always existed is that advertising is nothing more than wasted money. This negative view of advertising is vaguely rooted in the ideas of the Saint-Simonist doctrine, in which anything that does not involve the production of material goods is considered to be socially unproductive. (Saint Simon was a nineteenth-century social philosopher who advocated the view that distribution and services in general were economically unproductive activities.) Retail sales and the service industry, including advertising, are considered to be parasitic activities. This view is often reinforced by the (misleading) argument that consumers pay for advertising costs which are included in the price of the product they buy.

This social representation was a part of the Marxist doctrine, and its influence on real socialism often produced disastrous consequences, such as shortages of basic staple items. This was largely caused by the absence of any effective distribution system through which products would have been made available to consumers. The shortage was further reinforced by the absence of a marketing communication system to inform people which goods and services were available to them, when, where and at what price (traditional and useful functions!).

In many European countries, especially in northern Europe and in France, there are still some traces of 'publiphobia'. The advertising profession in France was even forced to launch a huge poster and billboard campaign about fifteen years ago, against those known as 'publiphobes'. In certain countries such as Kuwait, advertisements for pharmaceutical products are strictly controlled or even forbidden. It is often considered immoral to spend too much on advertisements and sales promotions for ethical drugs, assuming that it unduly increases the final price of a drug and thereby reduces the chances of the poorest people to buy essential medical supplies and recover their health. As a consequence, many countries put a ceiling on pharmaceutical advertising, or subject it to a special tax.

At the international level, more attention is now being given to the idea that advertising, though undeniably useful to society, can also have negative results such as the encouragement of conspicuous consumption and the creation of needs that cannot be satisfied, or that advertising may be deceptive. Therefore the economic and social committee of the UN (United Nations) has proposed a resolution that would protect consumers in developing nations. Wills and Ryans (1982) have looked at how consumerists, students, academicians and managers differ in their attitudes towards advertising, across fourteen countries. They show that, across all the countries, the views held by consumerists and managers are quite different: managers often find advertising to be quite factual (75 per cent), providing important information about products or services

(71 per cent), and both entertaining and informative (78 per cent), whereas consumerists rate it at a lower level on these dimensions (61, 48 and 50 per cent respectively). On the other hand, the attitudes of consumerists and managers do not differ significantly on various aspects of advertising: whether the advertisements are humorous, aesthetically pleasing or informative about prices. In all these aspects consumerists have a slightly less positive opinion. More than 50 per cent of the consumerists, on average (across the fourteen countries), tend to have a very negative opinion about the information content of advertising.

Andrews *et al.* (1991) show that there are substantial differences across young people from various countries (the United States, Denmark, Greece, India and New Zealand) in the perception of advertising in general. US students were shown to have more affective responses towards advertising, using statements such as 'stupid', 'entertaining', 'annoying'; they were also the least critical of advertising among the five nations surveyed. The potentially negative effects of advertising, in economic as well as social terms, represented only 22 per cent of US students' statements versus 60 per cent for the Greeks and 51 per cent for the Indians. New Zealand students, belonging to a country where advertising regulation is quite strict, were those with the most negative views of advertisements, emphasizing the fact that they were 'meaningless repetition' or that they 'interrupt good programmes'.

Attitudes towards comparative advertising

Attitudes basically depend on the responses that are given in a particular society to the following questions:

1. What is the social function of comparative advertising?
2. What are the prevailing arguments concerning the legitimacy of comparative advertising?
3. How should competition between brands be facilitated?
4. Does comparative advertising result in fooling the consumer by using disputable information to praise one's own brand and put down others?

Socially dominant responses to these questions directly influence comparative advertising regulations in a given country. In some countries, comparative advertising is held in low esteem. This is the case in France, where it is considered a denigration of competing brands. It is therefore forbidden under Article 1382 of the Civil Code. In order for the advertisement to be considered comparative, there need only be a comparison of two competing products, even if the terms are neither inaccurate, nor tendentious, nor antagonistic. For instance, about twenty years ago Lip, the top French watchmaker, was forced to pay heavy penalties to Timex, the top company in the American watch industry. The main feature of Timex's Kelton brand was its distribution through tobacconists, while Lip was confined to the more traditional channel of watch and jewellery stores. Lip was under attack from Kelton which, through the tobacconists, caused Lip huge sales losses. With the purpose of counter-attacking in order to regain market share Lip began an advertising campaign that showed a broken watch in an ashtray surrounded by a thick cloud of smoke, with a slogan that read: 'The watches sold in tobacconists are like cigarettes: they go up in smoke.'

Belgium, Italy and Germany are some other European countries that forbid comparative advertising (*Comunication et Business*, 1988). It is sometimes argued that some countries forbid comparative advertising as an indirect way of protecting their national products from unfavourable comparisons with imported goods. According to Boddewyn (1984) the French authorities, which were about to legalize comparative advertising, took a step backwards, fearing that Japanese car manufacturers would use comparative advertising to communicate aggressively the advantages of their cars, thereby increasing their share of the French market where competition with other European producers is already active.

However, in the United States comparative advertising is legally permitted. The basic arguments in favour of comparative advertising seem to make sense: it facilitates consumer information, choice and competition between brands. Hence automobile advertising frequently gives performance statistics of competing models, such as fuel consumption, speed and comfort. Opponents of comparative advertising take the argument further and cast doubt on the possibility of using truly objective measures, which would be handled by completely independent testing organizations. As a consequence, comparative advertising would often end up giving either no information at all or partly misleading information to the consumer. Opponents of comparative advertising also implicitly support the idea that it is necessary to moralize business relationships between competitors. The role of marketing communications, by means of advertising, is to praise the virtues of their own product, not to put down (however indirectly) the virtues of competing products.

James and Hensel (1991, p. 55) emphasize the possibility that malicious comparative advertising can derive into negative advertising. They take the example of Kentucky Fried Chicken advertisement which made explicit reference to McDonald's:

The first ad, sponsored by Kentucky Fried Chicken, opens with a red-haired Ronald McDonald surrogate (sans clown outfit) being interrogated by a Senate 'subcommittee' rivalling the likes of that faced by Oliver North. Allegations are raised as to the defendant's lack of expertise and questionable ability to provide quality chicken (McNuggets) to the public. When pressed as to how he expects to be able to sell chicken given this lack of expertise, 'Ronald' responds, 'Toys, lots of toys!', while the man who appears to be his legal counsel buries his head in his hands.

Allowed in the United States, but forbidden in many countries, comparative advertising is in a process of change at the European level. It is already permitted in some European countries, and is the subject of a directive proposed by the European Commission in Brussels. A modification of the 1984 directive on misleading advertising allows comparison under definite constraints. Legislation requires that advertising be based on features of the competing products or services that are material, relevant, verifiable and fairly chosen. Comparisons should be objective and not discredit competitors or their brands.

Attitudes towards the informative content of advertising

The basic function of an advertisement is to communicate a message to an audience. Advertising style in communicating with the audiences of viewers, readers or listeners can be roughly divided into three basic categories:

1. Persuasive.
2. Informative.
3. Oneiric (i.e. dream-oriented).

Thus, when comparing advertising practices in Turkey, Canada and Sweden, Kaynak and Ghauri (1986, p. 127) state:

> In developed countries, such as Canada and Sweden, advertising copy in general contains more writing and technical information, because most consumers have a high level of literacy and education. . . . Comparative shopping practices are limited in Turkey, and the general level of education is not high. Unlike Canada and Sweden, most of the advertising copy used by the Turkish agencies is persuasive in nature rather than informative.

The Turkish word for advertising is *Reklam*: this corresponds to a more traditional vision of advertising, where persuasion and slogans are the key issues.

Stern and Resnik (1991), based on a review of existing evidence, found that the information content (the number of information cues contained in advertisements) varies cross-nationally. In comparing the information content of American and Swedish advertising, by using a systematic analysis of the content of television commercials, Rita Martenson (1987) shows that Swedish ads have less information elements than American ads. She attributes this fact to the atmosphere of intense competition for the attention of television viewers that exists in the United States. The consumers change channels to avoid commercials, use commercial breaks to look at the programmes on other channels, etc. 'This means that [in the US] any commercial that does not have a very clear and simple message will strongly reduce its chances of getting the slightest amount of attention' (Martenson, 1987, p. 141).

Keown *et al.* (1992) compare the information content of advertising across four countries (the United States, Japan, South Korea and the People's Republic of China); their findings support the view that there are definite differences in advertising patterns. The highest level of information cues is found in the United States, followed by Japan and the PRC, while South Korean advertising scores lowest in informative content. In all countries, television and radio advertising is less informative on average than print advertising.

Assuming that consumers are rational information seekers (which is not true in most cultural contexts), advertising content should be related to information sought by consumers in order to improve the relevance of their choices. If for any reason consumers are not 'good' (motivated and educated) information seekers, they will be less sensitive to the information content of an ad. This is the case if they do not directly use advertising information in their brand evaluations in order to reduce perceived risks when purchasing. Hoover *et al.* (1978) compared Mexican consumers with their American neighbours: they found that Mexicans generally displayed a much lower level of perceived risk related to their purchases. Hoover *et al.* argue that the lower level of perceived risk is related to a somewhat fatalistic tradition which exists in Mexican society. Conversely, in the United States a more 'master-of-destiny' orientation implies a greater perceived risk of being disappointed by any purchase. Thus Mexican consumers and, more generally, consumers belonging to fatalistic oriented societies react more easily to persuasive message (the brand name repeated numerous times) and also oneiric messages (a dream which allows one to escape from a daily life which is not always bright).

Relying on the dream oriented part of the advertising audience is typical of the 'Seguela' doctrine. The dream-like dimension that surrounds the product is favoured at any price. Italian and French ads often appear as very dream oriented: viewers and readers are supposedly willing to escape from the real world. The oneiric style of advertisement enhances the fantasy of the consumer and emphasizes the imagination of satisfaction and enjoyment. It does so in a rather holistic way (the product and its benefits tend to be implied rather than actually shown). The oneiric style does not really concentrate on actual buying and consumption experiences. Germans, unlike the French or the Italians, are known to have a taste for highly informative advertising. A young German advertising specialist, Konstantin Jacoby (quoted in *Communication et Business*, 1988, p. 18) criticizes French advertising, and especially the most well-known publicist Jacques Séguéla (co-founder of the RSCG agency, reputed for oneiric, dream-orientated copy strategies):

> Certainly it [French advertising] is better than German advertising, but the French should take care not to sink in art for art's sake or in *séguélomania*. The message of the Citroen advertising campaign is horrible. What is the link between the Great Wall of China and Citroen? Are Citroen cars manufactured there now?

13.2 Culture and the creative part of advertising

Language: The slogan

Language differences are one of the main barriers to effective communication. Advertising uses colloquial language, very subtle yet precise. Although not always apparent, colloquial language is very precise as far as meaning is concerned. Furthermore it is often based on almost slangy wordings, which are particular to local people. One rarely finds vernacular language in 'official' dictionaries. The viewer or the listener understands (and feels at ease) all the more readily when a great deal of work has been required to put the message into colloquial speech. The messages on greeting cards (such as those in case A4.3) show how difficult it is to put into words the delicate messages of daily life – sentiments, sensations, family relations, friendships, love affairs – that are reflected in creative advertising. Translating colloquial speech is especially difficult: there is little literal equivalence; colloquial language uses idiomatic expressions, which change from one language to another.

Marcel Bleustein-Blanchet (quoted in *Reader's Digest*, 1987, p. 42–3), a publicist for more than sixty years, describes changes in the role of slogans in advertising as follows:

> Of course, things have changed in this field as well. The art of the slogan, as with advertising in general, changes in line with the public. Slogans have become simpler and more sophisticated at the same time. They are also less frequently used. Other techniques for increasing consumer brand recognition are taking over. But before the war, when the public was less demanding and less blasé, slogans were the best means of launching a brand. Especially when radio began to advertise. Actually, my pre-war slogans were a sort of *comptines* [little nursery rhymes]. *They were assonantal forms that the ear picked up instinctively.* Ultimately they became choruses and the public joined in. For example, when Berretrot, the announcer in the Vel d'Hiv (Paris cycling stadium), announced a prize during the 'Six Jours cyclistes' saying: 'Un meuble signé Lévitan . . .', ten thousand voices shouted back '. . . est garanti pour longtemps.'

As argued in the previous chapter, the slogan 'Put a tiger in your tank', for instance, is not as standardized as it might seem. It has been argued that it is standardized because at first reading, it looks as if it is fully equivalent across countries, but the interpretation differs as to where the power source is located, engine or tank. Examples of translation and conceptual equivalence problems abound, especially for advertising campaigns in which message standardization has been attempted (for examples see Ricks *et al.*, 1979). A full rewrite is usually needed to transpose slogans from one language to another. This implies a thorough search for words which have the same intended meaning, provided that this can be found in the target language as well as the source language (see section 5.2).

For advertisements that must be easily internationalized, one should avoid at all costs any problems related to language. This is entirely possible if the visual element of the message is emphasized, to the detriment of the textual component. As a consequence, television commercials aimed at a European audience often use a script where the characters speak neither to the audience nor to each other. Then a voice-over message on a sound track can be added to the image track. This avoids the drawbacks associated with dubbing. Most people lip-read unconsciously, at least in part. When watching a dubbed commercial, many people feel uneasy about the lag between lip movements and sounds. Written communication should also be avoided in messages targeted at a multilingual audience. For instance, a commercial or a detergent where a housewife is handed a packet of *Waschpulver* will be identified by British, Italian or French viewers as foreign or German. A few years ago, IBM used the character of Charlie Chaplin and the mode of a silent film in a multinational campaign, the goal of which was to foster corporate image. This allowed the advertisement to be used in any country of the world. The same can be applied to magazine advertisements where the text can be reduced or even virtually deleted. It may sometimes be kept in its original language in advertisements for ethnic products. The text must then be short and must strongly support an ethnic image (French for perfume, English for a large international newspaper, Italian for luxury leather shoes, etc.). The text must be universally understood, although not necessarily in full detail; the message should at least make sense with respect to the 'halo' of meanings around the product proposal.

Roles represented in advertising creation

When depicting characters, advertising must be extremely careful. Whether it is the age, dress or situation of a character which is represented, nothing should be left to chance in advertising messages. An important issue is the representation of women: as consumers, domestic workers, housewives or as professional women, they are an influential consumer group within most societies. Advertising is often accused of condoning traditional societal sex roles, sometimes even acting as a vehicle for outdated ideas. The real situation is much more ambiguous: in most countries advertising acts as an agent of both social change and social maintenance. Advertising creation sometimes acts as an agent of change because social challenge is a method of capturing the attention of the audience, and because social innovators are also opinion leaders for new products and new ways of life. Advertising also reinforces traditional and sometimes old-fashioned social patterns: it is the mirror of society as a whole.

In a comparative study (Australia, Mexico, United States) of the advertising industry's attitude towards sex roles, Mary Gilly (1988) analyzed, for each country, twelve hours of programmes: 275 American, 204 Mexican and 138 Australian commercials were viewed. In neither the United States nor Mexico (as opposed to Australia) were women pictured in professional or executive positions. In these two countries men, more often than women, were shown in roles of authority or expertise with respect to the product, whereas women were more often shown in the role of the consumer. Finally, the only country where there is a difference in the situations in which men and women appear is the United States, where a woman is more likely to be shown at home. One would have expected a more traditional image in Mexico and a more modern image in the United States, with Australia somewhere in between. These results show that our basic intuitions as to which country gives the most 'modern' image of women are not necessarily backed up by facts.

As a consequence, one should study a representative sample of local advertising messages, whether commercials or magazine advertisements. This will give a good idea of the sex roles, age roles, typical everyday situations and social relations in a particular country. It can be achieved in a systematic way by a content analysis of newspaper, magazine and television advertisements, at least several dozen of each type.

Traditional roles that are not present in the source culture may unintentionally appear when they are used in the target culture. A 'spurious' meaning may appear in the target culture which was not intended by the advertiser in the source culture. Douglas and Dubois (1980) give the example of a brandy advertisement which was targeted at the South African Bantu market. It showed a couple seated at a table with a bottle superimposed over them. Many Bantus thought that the woman was carrying the bottle on her head, as many traditional African women do. This created an unintended and confusing contrast between the traditional, local aspect of the characters and situation and the modern, imported aspect of the product. It therefore prevented clear and effective marketing communication.

This, logically, brings us to the following statement: an advertisement should be created in cooperation with a native of the target culture, who would act as a test audience; or, in the case of internationally standardized ads, messages in the various linguistic/cultural contexts should be reviewed by natives of each target culture.

In order to avoid creating spurious associations, the advertising script may go so far as not to present any characters at all. For instance, certain Renault models were shown moving without a driver in French advertisements. This avoided having to choose a specific character, whose age, sex or appearance would influence the product's positioning unfavourably. When the target audience is not clearly defined, or is very large, the choice of characters is a difficult one. The car in the Renault ad drove around the middle of a scale-model scene, with no driver. This may be negatively interpreted in countries where such a situation is associated with a safety problem (runaway car) or a distortion of reality (how can a car drive without a driver?). This may inhibit a positive response to the message.

The influence of mores and religion

As shown in sections 4.5 and 8.4 products convey meanings: it is therefore crucial to choose the appropriate symbolic elements by which cultural meanings may be communicated to the audience. For instance, the influence of mores and religion transforms factual information components (a nude woman washing her hair in her bathroom, for example) into elements of culture-based meaning (it incites people to sexual debauchery). If one concentrates on information rather than meaning, it is difficult to become aware of the influence of mores and religions on advertising messages. This point is illustrated by examples from Saudi Arabia (see Box 13.1).

Many of us have some superstitions, even though we may deny it. Rarely will advertisements show people walking under ladders, unless, for the sake of humour, something happens to them. This is proof of the force of superstition. The social habits of daily life also play a role, particularly those that are related to what is (locally) considered polite, courteous or hospitable. In this way, a well-known brand of tea alienated the Saudi public when it showed a Saudi host using his left hand to serve tea to one of his guests. Moreover, the guest was wearing shoes, which is considered in Saudi Arabia to be the height of rudeness.

Attitudes towards nudity can change from one country to another. French advertising is considered to have more nudity than nearly any other country. It is well accepted in French society, since the meaning conveyed by nudity there is very much related to beauty, excellence and nature. At opposite ends of the spectrum one can cite the example of the advertisements for the Guy Laroche perfume Drakkar Noir in France and Saudi Arabia (Czinkota and Ronkainen, 1990, p. 616). The original French advertisement showed a man's nude forearm, held at the wrist by a woman's hand, with the man's hand holding a bottle of cologne. The Saudi advertisement showed the man's forearm covered by a suit jacket, with only the cuff of the shirt showing, while the woman lightly touched

Box 13.1   *The influence of religion on advertising in Saudi Arabia*

The Saudi legal system is unique in the sense that it identifies law with the personal command of the 'one and only god, the Almighty'. The Islamic laws known as *Sharia* are the master framework to which all legislation, existing and proposed, is referred and with which it must be compatible. The *Sharia* is a comprehensive code governing the duties, morals and behaviour of all Muslims, individually and collectively in all areas of life, including commerce. Sharia is derived from two basic sources, the Quran or Holy Book, and the *Hadith*, based on the life, sayings, and practices of the Prophet Muhammed. . . . At the very minimum, an understanding of fundamental *Sharia* laws as contained in Quranic injunctions is necessary in order to gain insights into advertising regulation and content. . . .

Three sets of Quranic messages have special significance for advertising regulation. First there are strict taboos (*haraam*), such as alcohol, gambling, cheating, idol worship, usury, adultery and 'immodest' exposure. . . . For example alcoholic products are banned. There are no local ads, and foreign print media are only allowed into the country after all advertisements of alcoholic beverages have been censored. Promotions involving games of chance are illegal. . . .

Other dangers for advertisers include messages which may be considered as deceptive by religious standards. According to Islam, fraud may occur if the seller fails to deliver everything promised, and advertisers may need to use factual appeal, based on real rather than perceived product benefits. Statuary should not appear in advertising, since it may be perceived as a symbol of idol worship. Since religious norms require women to be covered, international print ads may have to be modified by superimposing long dresses on models or by shading their legs with black. Advertisers of cosmetics in Saudi Arabia refrain from picturing sensuous females; instead, in typical ads a pleasant-looking woman appears in a robe and headdress, with only her face showing. . . .

A second set of Quranic injunctions governs the duties a Muslim must perform, such as praying five times daily, fasting during the month of Ramadhan, giving *zakaat* (charity) to the poor, and respecting and caring for parents and the disadvantaged. Advertisers have to ensure that they do not hinder the performance of these obligations. For example, during the five prayer times, which last from 10 to 20 minutes, products cannot be promoted on radio or TV, retail shops close, and no commercial or official transactions are permitted. Ads should not depict, even humorously, children being disrespectful to parents and elders, whereas the image of a product could be enhanced by ads that stress parental advice or approval. . . .

A third set of Quranic injunctions remind the faithful of God's bounties and enjoins them to thank Him for such blessings as good health, peace of mind, food, water and children. It is legal and sometimes recommended practice for advertisers to introduce their messages with Quranic words: 'In the Name of Allah, the Most Gracious, the Most Merciful'; 'By the Grace of God'; 'God is Great (Allah-o-Akbar)'; Al-Rabiah and Nasser, a manufacturer of water pumps, uses a Quranic-verse: 'We made from water every living thing.' Such verses may also be used to legitimise operations or to assure that services are in accord with Islamic principles.

(Source: Luqmani *et al.*, 1988, pp. 61–4. Reproduced with permission.)

his hand with one of her fingers. Respect for the existing social conventions in the target society will long remain a prerequisite to the localization of advertising messages. Furthermore, the role of advertising has never been (at least officially) to change a society's mores, but rather to sell a product.

Generally the relationship between men and women, depicted by advertising, are a ticklish problem. For instance, Miller and Demirel (1988) depict advertising for beer on the Turkish market which portrays men and women drinking the beer in social activities at home. Emphasizing a family setting as the consumption situation is a response to the problem that showing men and women together in coffee houses and beer pubs, predominantly male institutions, would violate Turkish customs of courtship and social interaction.

Similarly, a country's degree of orientation towards traditional values has an impact on advertising messages. For instance Japanese magazine advertisements show more respect towards elders than their American counterparts (Mueller, 1987).

Adapting advertising copy: problems of cross-national transferability

Transfer of promotional materials is a practice which is frequent in multinationals (Hill and James, 1991): they are adapted as necessary. When trying to transfer advertising copy cross-culturally there are three main issues:

1. What is transferable in the copy itself.
2. Are there groups of countries within which cross-national transfers are easier?
3. What are the precautions to be taken when transferring copy?

Differences in creative style are noted by many authors. As stated by Lin (1993, pp. 44–5) the Japanese cultural values stress status symbols in advertising, whereas Americans place emphasis on individual determinism:

> Japanese advertisements reveal an indulgence with sensitive crafting of product image and appearance slated within a subtle frame of reference. This contrasts sharply with the American fixation on presenting facts and attributes to showcase product superiority. . . . [In Japan] 'boasting' of product quality and 'bribing' consumers into submission are not in line with the custom of respectful treatment of consumers and respectable projection of company image. These same rationales explain why comparative and testimonial messages are not a desirable form of advertising in Japan.

Even between countries that look culturally very similar, such as the United States and the United Kingdom, there are very significant differences in the style of advertising copy. The first obvious differences is that broadcast television remains more commercialized in the United States than in the United Kingdom. Katz and Lee (1992) looked at differences in US and UK prime-time television advertising: they found that the categories of product advertised differ significantly: personal care, travel and cars are more frequently advertised in the United States, whereas services are more frequently advertised on the UK prime-time. Even within Europe there is no evidence of the content of advertising copies converging; it seems on the contrary that the cultural content, specific to each country, is even increasing over long periods of time (Snyder *et al.*, 1991).

Advertising copy is complex and inevitably tends to reflect the cultural background of those who have created it. For instance, Huang (1993) showed that colour is used differently in US and Taiwanese industrial advertising: yellow, the favourite colour of Chinese, meant to be the colour of royalty, is found more often in Taiwanese ads, whereas brown was preferred in many American ads. Background themes, setting, roles depicted are also important aspects of the copy. By systematically comparing Brazilian and US advertisements for cars over a ten-year period, Tansey *et al.* (1990) showed that Brazilian ads use significantly more urban themes and depict more leisure situations than US ads.

The use of visual components (colours, characters, etc.) varies also across cultures. Cutler *et al.* (1992) have investigated the visual component of print advertising across five countries (the United States, United Kingdom, France, Korea and India) through a detailed content analysis of about 250 advertisements per country. Indian ads use significantly more black and white and show more children than in any other country; Korean ads show price twice to three times more frequently than for other countries, and significantly represent more elderly persons whose wisdom is valued in Far Eastern cultures; French ads are by far the more aesthetic oriented: five times more than either US, Korean or Indian ads, but only twice as much as British ads. US ads appear by far the most comparative, ten times more frequently than France for instance.

An interesting track is to try to cluster countries according to cultural values (Hofstede's ones being the best applicants for operationalization) in order to determine whether there is a possible transferability of part or the whole of advertising creation or even a full campaign. Kale (1991) gives the example of the promotion of tourism in India for the US tourist market. When trying to adapt, both the target (US) and the source (India) cultures have to be considered: they differ mostly on power distance (40 versus 77) and individualism (91 versus 48). Kale insists that the (Indian) message must be targeted to the (US) individual: the message must reflect friendliness and informality, and it must value autonomy, variety and pleasure, all positive values for highly individualistic cultures, such as that of the United States. He further suggests that, since democracies are perceived as small power distance institutions, the message should emphasize that India has a democratic government, which would help bridge the gap of power distance between the source and the target country.

Alden *et al.* (1993) related Hofstede's values to the use of humour in advertising, by comparing two individualist cultures (the United States and Germany) with two collectivist and high power distance cultures (Thailand and South Korea). They first assessed some common dimensions of the use of humour across cultures: incongruent contrasts were used in the four countries in about the same way in television advertising. Culture-specific dimensions were found in the number of central characters depicted (higher in the two collectivist countries) and in the fact that more humorous ads feature unequal status between main characters in the two Asian countries, high on the power distance dimension, than in the two western cultures.

Since Hofstede's dimensions seem to be meaningful, it is interesting to try to cluster countries according to them. Sriram and Gopalakrishna (1991) have combined them with economic and demographic indicators, on the one hand, and media availability indicators (televisions per 1,000, radios per 1,000, advertising spending per capita, etc.). They cluster countries, for advertising strategy, in six groups: Japan is isolated in one group, and most other groups are fairly heterogeneous geographically, except northern Europe and a sort of central Asian area extending from Iran to the Philippines. The two Hofstede dimensions that discriminate significantly between these groups are once again power distance and individualism.

If a transfer has been decided, the following elements have always to be carefully checked for cultural adequacy of the final copy: (1) comparative or not, degree and type of informative content, style; (2) adequacy of basic copy themes with the local mores and customs; (3) execution: background themes, colour, use of words (puns, suggestive words), use of humour, use of symbols, type of characters and roles (age, sex, status), situations and types of relationship depicted; and (4) implementation constraints, such as a lack of media available locally.

13.3   Media world-wide

World-wide differences in advertising expenditure

One cannot help but be struck by the difference in advertising expenses across countries, even though these countries may have comparable levels of economic development. This can be partially attributed to media availability (radio, television, newspapers, magazines, film, billboards). Where some media are non-existent or their availability is limited, expenses are automatically restricted by the lack of space for advertising. In the mid-1990s, the world average per capita advertising expenditure was about US$60. Countries such as Switzerland, Denmark and the United States have the leading edge with figures in the range of US$350–400. Many industrialized nations are clustered around the figure of US$200 per capita p.a.: Japan, the Netherlands, Canada, Australia, Norway, the United Kingdom, Sweden, New Zealand, West Germany, etc.

Obviously advertising expenditure is much less in developing nations. In the poorest African countries, the figures of annual per capita advertising expenditure barely surpass US$1 per capita. The percentage of total GNP spent on advertising is small in developing nations. The figure in Turkey in 1981 was 0.31 per cent, as compared to 1.13 per cent in Sweden and 1.27 per cent in Canada (Kaynak and Ghauri, 1986). Since the population of developing countries is large with respect to their GNP, the per capita expenditure is very low: barely more than US$10 in comparison with US$200 in developed countries.

Cross-cultural differences in media availability and use

The availability of advertising media is influenced by a country's level of economic development and also by its view of what is the appropriate mix between business/ commercial activities, on the one hand, and cultural/recreational activities on the other hand. Tuncalp (1992) gives the example of Saudi Arabia, where traditional values do not permit the showing of films to public gatherings; as a result, the cinema medium does not exist in Saudi Arabia. Ethical debates about which products can be advertised on which medium have an influence on regulations: there is now virtually no media space available for cigarette and alcohol advertising in France.

Advertising is largely based on news and entertainment media. The communication support systems (television stations, transmitters, audiovisual equipment, printing presses, photographic equipment, etc.) are costly, in an area where financial support is not easy to find. Financial support in countries where banks have limited lending capacities is often based on political influence (which may prove unstable). In many countries the Press is even more dependent on politics than on advertisers.

Independent of purely economic factors, the availability of the media is also influenced by two social representations which relate to the relationship between the media and its audience:

1. What will be accepted by the viewer, listener or reader as a ratio between advertising time and entertainment time, such as (for television) talk shows, soap operas, news or informative content in general? What is considered adequate as far as the sequence between advertising and entertainment is concerned – should television movies, for instance, be interrupted by advertising, and how frequently?
2. Is advertising an entertainment in itself? Are people entertained by television commercials as such (i.e. waiting for television commercials, just because they like them)? The broader issue is: does the viewer/listener/reader expect to be compensated (entertained) for paying attention to the advertisement?

Many countries have instituted rules which place limits on television advertising. Sweden has no advertising on its national channels. West Germany limited advertising to twenty minutes per day over three to five time periods. There are now several private TV stations such as Sat 1, Pro 7 or Vox, with no limitation on advertising time, while the limitations on public channels (ARD and ZDF) have been loosened. France controls all its channels, public and private, with regulations (*cahier des charges*) that limit television commercials to about an hour per day. New Zealand has two state-controlled TV stations which forbid advertising on Sunday, and a third station, totally commercial (Andrews *et al.*, 1991).

Conversely, where little or even no advertising regulation exists, there can sometimes be such an invasion by advertising that viewing TV programmes becomes little more than watching advertisements, a frequent reproach addressed by Europeans to American television channels. The general contrast here seems to be between America (the United States, Mexico, Brazil and Canada), with liberal advertising regulations, and most other countries in the world where media availability is strongly limited by regulation, such as Saudi Arabia which bans commercial advertising on radio (Tuncalp, 1992).

In Mexico City for instance, there are no less than 7 radio stations, and there are 775 radio stations for the whole country. On most of these stations there are twenty-four minutes of commercials per hour, and two minutes of news during each break with eleven breaks per hour. This hectic schedule is extremely unpleasant for listeners, who therefore constantly change stations and cannot listen to one station, programme or speaker for any length of time. For this reason many advertisers buy a large quantity of media space for the same time block across several stations (Engels-Levine, 1982).

The question of finding the acceptable advertising dose is an important one. Studies have shown that in the United States an increasing number of consumers consider that television advertising is sometimes stupid and tends to be less intelligent than previously. US television viewers are therefore dissatisfied (Martenson, 1987). The situation is fairly paradoxical: as the media are increasingly available, it becomes more difficult to reach a target audience since viewers' saturation with advertisements can lead, first, to the scrambling of the consumer's ability to listen to advertising and, second, to reactions such as 'zapping' which can render audience monitoring quite difficult. It is surprising that the issue of whether the viewer/listener is entertained by advertising should be so rarely addressed, given its practical importance. 'Zapping' has been fairly widely studied, but most studies have only sought to demonstrate how an advertiser can avoid its unfortunate results. It is taken for granted that the audience has no saturation threshold, or at the very least an extremely high one. This assumption suggests the absolute legitimacy of mass advertising communication within a society that willingly portrays itself as being free-market oriented. In contrast, many European countries started from the opposite assumption, and advertising therefore took a long time to assert itself on television.

This leads to another important question: is it necessary to reward the audience (viewer/reader/listener) for having seen the advertisement? In other words: is entertaining the target *per se* a necessary condition for capturing the attention and interest of the viewer? Consequently, is the additional creative effort at the risk of reducing the marketing effectiveness of the ad? The spectator who is attracted by the creative side of the message may end up forgetting the product that is being presented. Responses to these questions probably differ between the United States and Europe. The aim of this book is not to answer questions as complex as these, but only to emphasize that the answers which are implicitly given to these questions in a specific country directly explain how entertainment and advertising are interrelated, television programmes being 'sliced up', or not, by advertisements.

The emergence of global media

The previous section placed much emphasis upon difference in advertising across countries. These differences do not offset certain similarities and convergences. Diverse media combine into a 'media landscape' which is primarily shaped by the freedom of choice of the media consumer. Some media have achieved almost world-wide recognition and a truly global audience. Among the international advertising media that have achieved the most impressive world-wide reach, is the monthly *Reader's Digest*. It is the world's most widely read magazine, with a circulation of 28.7 million in 15 languages and 169 countries. It was founded in 1920 by DeWitt Wallace and his wife Lila Acheson. The first issue came out in February 1922 (see Box 13.2).

There are now some 'global' newspapers such as the *International Herald Tribune*, the *Wall Street Journal* and the *National Geographic* magazine. Their circulation covers almost the entire world. *Time* magazine publishes 133 different editions, which enables advertisers to reach precise target audiences in a large number of locations throughout the world. Many French magazines such as *L'Express*, *Le Point* and *Elle* and German magazines such as *Der Spiegel* and *Burda Moden* also publish international editions. The advertising clientele of these world-wide publications (or those on the road to globalization) nevertheless remains fairly limited. It consists of 'global' advertisers who are themselves mostly targeting a global clientele, namely a segment of well-off consumers who travel internationally. Industries that use media with global reach are basically airlines, banks and financial services, consumer electronics and telecommunications, cars, tobacco and alcohol, perfumes and luxury products.

As noted earlier, the picture has two facets: along with the preservation of culture-

Box 13.2   *The internationalization of the* Reader's Digest

'Since the formula of the Digest is so effective in the United States, why not attempt to repeat it elsewhere?' thought DeWitt Wallace. But exporting the formula of a magazine requires that the obstacle of language be overcome. The simplest solution was to begin in England, which could serve as a gateway into Europe. Accordingly, the first foreign edition of the *Reader's Digest* appeared in Great Britain in 1937. The second foreign edition, however, did not appear in Europe. In 1940, in the midst of the Second World War, the first issue of *Selecciones del Reader's Digest*, the Spanish-American edition, came out in Cuba. Why Cuba? The long-term objective was to attack the South American market, even if sales had to be made at a loss (as indeed occurred for many years). But for the time being, DeWitt Wallace's objective was more of a missionary one, for he sought to combat the Nazi advance. In 1942, a Portuguese edition in Brazil followed. This edition reached a print run of 300,000 copies. In 1943, there was a return to Europe with the publication of a Swedish edition. The war was not yet over, but DeWitt Wallace was already contemplating market entry into Europe. He offered cut-price subscriptions of the *Digest* to families of young Americans who had been called up. Along with chewing gum and nylon stockings, the *Reader's Digest* was to arouse the interest of young Europeans. After the war, in 1947, *Sélection du Reader's Digest* finally appeared in France under the management of General Thompson. There was an initial print run of 275,397 copies, which almost doubled for the second issue. The global expansion of the *Reader's Digest* did not stop . . . Germany, Italy, Switzerland and Belgium, as well as India, South Africa, Australia and New Zealand, were all in turn to have their edition of the magazine. Today, thirty-nine editions of the *Reader's Digest* are published, including one for schoolchildren, another in large type for those with sight problems and an edition in Braille. It can justifiably claim the distinction inscribed on every cover of being the most widely read magazine in the world.

(Adapted from *Reader's Digest*, 1987, pp. 10–11, and *Reader's Digest* news release 'Products and services', June 1988.)

based differences in consumer behaviour and marketing communication practices, a globalized supply of media is emerging. With regard to advertising media, technological breakthrough in international telecommunications will greatly serve the globalization of advertising. In turn, this will inevitably conflict with some national idiosyncrasies.

13.4   Technological advances and cultural convergence

The influence of television satellites

In the years to come, the television satellites which now reach all over the world will change the availability of media with regional or global coverage, particularly in Europe. The United States is a pioneer in this field – no less than thirty satellites were in service in the United States in 1990 (Mariet, 1990). They serve an impressive number of television stations. This section focuses on Europe, which, until now, has remained nationally fragmented. Television channels were purely national ones, mostly state-owned, with some development of private hertzian channels (traditional transmission by earth stations) and cable channels during recent years. Europe is now slowly following the United States.

Many satellites covering most of Europe are now available for transmission, such as Astra from Luxemburg, TDFl and 2, TVSAT 1 and 2, which are French-German. Television is at the very centre of this technological change, but is not the only beneficiary. Daily newspapers can also become globalized as a result of computerized typesetting in which the core part of a newspaper (headlines and main articles, which are common to any local edition) is sent in the form of numerical (digital) information by telephone to automated printing workshops. The various editions can be 'localized' by adding local articles and advertising to a core text which is the same world-wide.

There are different possibilities for the use of television satellites:

1. The transmission of images that will be used to make up a programme (primarily news and sports). Images transmitted by the satellite will ultimately be re-broadcast in a traditional form, e.g. hertzian ground television.
2. The broadcasting of satellite images to viewers via a cable network. An infrastructure of ground receiving stations is then needed, before the images are sent to viewers through the cable. Ground stations can receive signals of minimal strength, amplify them and redirect them to private homes. The satellite does not need to emit very powerful signals, therefore it can broadcast over a broader range of channels than in the previous case. Thus the channels can be scrambled and paid for with the purchase of a decoder, or received, unscrambled and paid for by subscription to a cable channel or an hourly toll.
3. A broadcast which is directly received by the viewer with a parabolic antenna (dish). In this case the satellite must broadcast much stronger signals so that they can be picked up on the ground. Because of this, the number of channels of a DBS (direct broadcast satellite) will be reduced.

Europeans lagging behind

The problem of satellite and cable network infrastructure is just as complex as the creation of new programmes which can fill the screens of the new television channels. For the European television industry the problem is acute. These stations cannot show only news from international news agencies and cheap talk shows, for the overall purpose of reducing the hourly cost of programmes. Television stations must set up some really entertaining programmes in order to attract viewers, so that they are given a reason to watch the shows and the commercials. The failure of the Europeans to keep up with these advances in the creation and international sales of television programmes is especially evident when compared to America (Sarathy, 1991). It is estimated, for instance, that the sudden changes in the European televisual industry will necessitate over 50,000 hours of new programmes per year. In 1987 the rights to one hour of the *Dallas* series cost US$32,000, compared to US$400,000 for the production of one episode of the series *Chateauvallon* by a European consortium led by the French state-owned station Antenne 2. In 1989, the re-broadcast rights to an American television film cost US$70,000, compared with almost a million dollars for the production of a comparable European film (*Business Week*, 1987, 1989).

We can therefore expect the following three-part evolution in Europe:

1. The advent of media giants in Europe. Those who are likely to take control of large parts of the European televisual industry are Berlusconi from Italy, the German Springer Verlag and Bertelsmann, the French group Hachette, the Luxemburg television company, Jerome Seydoux, the late Robert Maxwell's empire, and the Australian press magnate Rupert Murdoch (who has a strong European base) and the Canadian ITC group. The bulk of these groups are multimedia interests and are equally engaged in the development of the press media covering Europe as a whole.

2. Many European countries have invested in cable systems, which are competing with direct television (DBS). Some countries are already equipped with dense cable networks, such as Ireland, Belgium and Germany, where more than half of all households are linked in. Other countries such as France are lagging behind and attempting to catch up. In general, there is much technology at stake and the standards for telecommunication technologies have not yet all been defined: high-definition television (HDTV), fibre optic networks, electronic transmission standards, etc. This all combines to make the scene rather confused. An effort is now being made at the European level to design new communication technologies in a coordinated way Technological, industrial, media, cultural and legal interests overlap in a realm of complex influences, where national state influence is still strong, as is the tradition in the European media and television industries.

3. Certain European regulations aim to protect the cultural identity of European audiovisual networks. The French, in particular, were somewhat disturbed by the invasion of American programmes, to the detriment of European culture and creation. (Once again, self-contradiction is possible: some people may be both faithful viewers of American television series and opponents of imported television programmes as a whole.) This implies an increasing influence of the English language, which the

French and other Europeans fear could further damage the influence and reach of their own languages. In May 1989, the EU adopted a directive that required at least half of the programmes on European television to be produced in Europe. Nevertheless the text of this directive was fairly vague and allowed loose interpretation by the member countries. The European Commission is also pushing, according to the 1985 EU White Paper on the completion of the internal market by January 1993, for common regulations in the field of advertising across the EU (see Box 13.3).

Enlargement and overlapping of media

The influence of media globalization and potential media overlap on marketing communications is quite significant, encompassing two major aspects:

1. A large increase in the available media space on television; new channels are all private, and must finance their operations either by advertising or by subscription (cable and/or scrambler/decoder).
2. Satellites have large overlap zones. This, combined with the extension of direct satellite television over the next few years, will produce greater overlap zones – not only in Europe – where viewers will be able to receive a large number of channels.

It is questionable whether media overlapping will be a problem in Europe, especially since 1993, when the physical borders between the twelve member states of the EU were progressively abolished. Some people tend to underrate the importance of media overlapping.

Much is made of overlapping media particularly in classroom situations. Yet the impact of imported overlapping media has only a marginal beneficial effect on audiences. Evidence from Ireland, Austria and Switzerland indicates that where advertising comes in from adjacent countries it is largely ignored unless the product is also advertised locally, thus undermining the increased coverage potential. There is a need to harmonize creative presentation where overlaps occur to prevent confusion in the minds of potential customers (Dudley, 1989, pp. 287 and 290).

One has to address the issue of whether media overlapping in Europe may lead to a compulsory standardization of brands and of the creative themes and presentation of advertisements. Sarathy (1991) illustrates this issue by citing Unilever's difficulties creating advertising for its household cleanser which is called Vif in Switzerland, Viss in Germany, Jif in the United Kingdom and Greece and Cif in France. Mourier and Burgaud (1989) suggest that companies that adapt marketing plans to each European market risk being misunderstood by consumers. Indeed in switching channels, consumers would be disturbed if the same product were advertised under different brand names and had diversified packagings, and if different product uses and benefits were emphasized.

However, not all viewers will watch foreign channels, and not all products will be marketed throughout Europe. It seems more likely that there will be a combination of standardized marketing plans for European products that become regionally global, and local marketing plans for national or regional (within countries) target audiences.

Technological, economic and regulatory advances in progress open the door for more specific and segmented marketing

This section is strongly related to Chapter 7, which described the design of intercultural marketing strategies by the cross-over between zones and classes of cultural affinity. The

Box 13.3 *Advertising regulations to globalize as well . . .*[1]

Marlboro Man is headed for a showdown at the Brussels corral. The European Commission is trying to round up a posse to run the Stetson-wearing hero of the cigarette industry's leading brand and the rest of its most potent symbols off the Community's advertising hoardings. It would also curb the use of brand names to market non-tobacco products such as lighters and fashion accessories. If the Commission has its way, the directive on 'advertising of tobacco products in the press and by means of bills and posters' will be approved some time this year to take effect from January 1, 1992. From that date cigarette manufacturers would be expected to comply with standard Single Market rulings on the size and content of health warnings on cigarette packets, the presentation of tobacco products themselves and a ban on indirect advertising. . . .

As in many a Hollywood Western, the lawmakers are up against some powerful vested interests. . . . The market is divided between multinationals and state-owned companies. The multinationals led by the UK's BAT industries, Switzerland's Rothman's International, and US giants Philip Morris and RJ Reynolds, account for almost half the 560 billion cigarettes sold annually in the EC. Advertising is a vital weapon in their fight for market share. . . . State-owned companies, though, have little interest in siding with the multinationals. Public monopolies control the production, distribution and, in some cases, retail sales networks for cigarettes in four EC members: France, Spain, Portugal and Italy. . . . Cigarette advertising in all four countries is either banned (Italy, Portugal), soon to be abolished (France), or severely restricted (Spain). . . . Within the Commission only the UK, Germany and the Netherlands are opposed to the draft proposal, on the grounds that it encourages restrictive practices. Their votes are a blocking minority that present EC officials with a stark choice. Either they can withdraw the proposal and submit a new one supporting a total ban on tobacco advertising . . . or they can aim for a compromise that would meet the timetable and produce a partial ban.

But as the Commission tries to unite its forces it is coming under pressure from other interested parties . . . the sharpest shouting comes from advertising groups. 'For the first time, Community legislation is purporting to restrict indiscriminately the fundamental principle of freedom of speech,' declares European Advertising Tripartite (EAT), a Brussels-based group representing media, advertisers and agencies.

(Source: 'Tobacco warning', *International Management*, February 1991, p. 56)

concept of segmentation is crucial in appreciating the limits of the technological advances now in progress. National, geographic and cultural variables will become a major factor in the process of market segmentation. Until now, domestic markets were considered to be the most likely units to be segmented. We will see the emergence of complex segments where country is not necessarily the segmentable unit *par excellence*. The following examples illustrate this:

1. Pan-European market segments, which account for a homogeneous population across countries – for example, age groups. This is the case when dealing with products for young people. Television stations such as MTV and Sky Channel are well prepared for this. The rock radio image, supported by the emergence of European rock, is carefully cultivated by MTV. As emphasized by Tom Freston, the president of MTV: 'Music crosses borders very easily, and the lingua franca of rock'n'roll is English. Rock is an Anglo-American form.' Freston further indicates what he considers to be the mission of MTV: 'We want to be the global rock and roll village, where we can talk to youth world-wide' (cited by Sarathy, 1991).
2. Ethnicity may also work: pan-European market segments may be fairly effective when cultural and linguistic minorities are targeted. At the national level, these minorities do not reach critical numbers which could justify the creation of specific media, since they are scattered all over the countries of Europe. But minorities may be more significantly served at the European level. Mariet (1990) cites the case of the development of Hispanic television in the United States. There are two principal networks: Univision-SIN, started in 1961, now reaches 5.1 million households, that is, 85 per cent of Spanish-speaking Americans; the other large Hispanic network, Telemundo, covers 77 per cent of these households and is present in 35 states. In 1989, US$305 million were invested in advertising on the Spanish-speaking media. It is predictable that such initiatives will also flourish in Europe, in that they can fulfil the need for television communication of Arabic-speaking North African immigrants, Turks, Armenians or Jews. Erbil (1995) describes the case of ethnic community viewers in Germany: the largest foreign group is the Turks with 1.9 million people and seven channels (one on cable); the Italians are 560,000 with three channels available, the Greeks 350,000 with two channels; the Poles 260,000 with five channels; the Spaniards 135,000 with six channels (four on cable); the Japanese community has 27,000 members and can have access to a Japanese-speaking channel (JSTV) both on cable and by satellite.
3. Segments which are based on classes of cultural affinity (see Chapter 7). In these groupings, consumers share similar buying habits or a common language; segments may be further divided on the basis of traditional criteria such as sociodemographics (age, sex, income, etc.). For example, a relevant segment may consist of beer drinkers in the zone of cultural affinity of Mediterranean Europe, identified by several common sociodemographic characteristics and/or by criteria linked to their consumption habits and psychographics. MTV, TNT-Cartoon and Eurosport are typical media for reaching classes of cultural affinity.
4. Market segments, the base of which will remain mostly a domestic one. As a consequence, they will be only slightly influenced by the regional market global-

ization in Europe. Car maintenance or ethnic food products such as the German *Knödel* would fall into this category.

5. Finally, the possibility of targeting very precise and quite small populations. Regional and local marketing will develop alongside European global marketing. Local radio stations have emerged over the past ten years, but local television channels are almost non-existent in Europe. The marketing strategy of small segments of the service industry could be supported by emerging local media. Local cultural products have been relatively deprived of a true marketing strategy: local cultural products such as sports events, shows, private tutoring, etc., have been confined to direct marketing and door-to-door sales. When marketing at the local level, countries can be broken down instead of being treated as homogeneous segments. For example, a county in the north of France may be grouped with a county in French-speaking Belgium (Walloon) in a common segment for strategic marketing.

In the future there will undoubtedly be more standard brand names across Europe. Advertising and product offers could possibly be quasi-standard throughout Europe – Europe being divided into two principal zones, a Latin cultural-affinity zone and an Anglo-Saxon cultural-affinity zone. Among the industries that are potential candidates for regional marketing globalization in Europe are the following:

1. Services, such as banks and financial services for private clients, European and transcontinental airlines.
2. Products: almost all consumer goods distributed by hypermarkets and mass distribution, as well as many consumer durables such as cars, household appliances, stereo and video systems, and photographic equipment.

13.5 The globalization of advertising

Agencies internationalize

Advertising agencies are nowadays largely internationalized. Saatchi and Saatchi, which ranks as one of the top agencies world-wide, is also one of the strongest proponents of global advertising; it has a total turnover of nearly US$13.5 billion. The largest Europe-based agencies are often smaller than American ones: the French advertising group, Eurocom, has a total turnover of about US$3.3 billion (*Advertising Age*, 1989). The largest American agencies (Young & Rubicam, McCann Erickson, FCB, Ogilvy & Mather, BBDO, J. Walter Thompson, Lintas, Grey, etc.) have built up a network of subsidiaries covering most countries in the world over the last twenty or thirty years.

The largest advertising agency in the world, Dentsu Inc., is Japanese. Japanese agencies are now present in a growing number of countries. The Japanese advertising market is a large one: it remains very attractive to Japanese agencies, which then target South East Asia and Australia in the first stages of their international expansion. Twelve Japanese agencies rank among the fifty largest advertising agencies world-wide (Denstu, Hakuhodo, Dai-lchi Kikaku, Daiko, Tokyu, Asatsu, Yomiko, Asahi, Chuo Senko, Nihon Keizaisha, Orikomi, Nan Nen Sha).

It is not always easy to launch 'triadic' agencies successfully. HDM, which was ranked seventeenth in the world (*Advertising Age*, 1989), appeared to be an attempt at merging European (Havas), Japanese (Dentsu) and American assets (Marsteller, a large subsidiary of Young & Rubicam). It aimed to become a specialist in global marketing communication due to its clearly triadic position. At the beginning of 1991, the European part of HDM (Eurocom-Havas) withdrew from the alliance with Dentsu and Young & Rubicam/ Marsteller, to form a joint venture with the British group WCRS.

Other agencies that are large but nationally based are compelled to follow this route to the internationalization of marketing communications, especially the internationalization of media and audiences. If they do not want to lose their customer base, they have to be able to organize cross-border campaigns for advertisers; but they must also remain knowledgeable experts on local idiosyncrasies in the implementation of marketing communication strategies. National agencies are trying to combine identity and knowledge of their national and cultural milieu on the one hand and the opportunities of the international market on the other. Because of their (sometimes) limited financial resources, they proceed by the acquisition of agencies in neighbouring foreign countries or by building an international network of national agencies through alliances or joint ventures in neighbouring countries.

The French Publicis group, for instance, has become associated with the American group FCB. The first French group for the purchase of media space. SGCMD, is now associated with the English group WCRS, ranking second in Europe and eighth world-wide (*Communication et Business*, 1988). There are many such examples.

Relationships between advertisers and agencies

As a consequence of the internationalization of advertisers, agencies have equally increased their operations in foreign countries. In the case of large multinational corporations with diversified product lines, this can lead to a complex advertiser/agency organization. The various levels (national, regional and world-wide) within both the multinational agency and the multinational advertiser must be in constant contact with each other. The usual communication problems of large international organizations are more than doubled by adding the problem of the relationship between advertiser and advertising agency at each level.

Different approaches may be chosen for the organization of international marketing communication with respect to the agency/advertiser relationship. The Levi Strauss case, at the end of this chapter (section A13.1), offers several possible solutions:

1. Using only one large international advertising agency, which allows for centralization of communication; this can be implemented for each product division separately, or for large brands, or for the purpose of managing the corporate image world-wide.
2. Hiring local agencies that are well acquainted with local constraints with regard to media and consumers.
3. Possible intermediate solutions between these two extremes which attempt to find an effective trade-off between world-wide coordination and local tailoring of advertising campaigns.

Advertising standardization: feasibility and desirability

After a review of arguments pro and contra-advertising standardization world-wide, Onkvisit and Shaw (1987, p. 51) conclude that a more meaningful question is whether it should be used or not, even if it is feasible. Harvey (1993) considers the four following arguments in favour of standardized advertising: (1) consistent image across markets; (2) avoids confusing mobile consumers; (3) may decrease the cost of preparing campaign themes, copies and materials; and (4) firmer control over the planning and execution of campaigns across markets. He gives a complete checklist of factors to be considered in order to assess whether the standardized approach is appropriate which includes product factors, competition, organization variables, media infrastructure, regulations and market/societal variables; some aspects of the advertising process may be standardized while others are not. The danger of this approach is that it does not distinguish desirability of standardization (which has to be assessed first) from its feasibility, stating initially that 'given the strong economic and administrative rationale it is assumed that, if possible, advertisers would prefer to standardize advertising' (Harvey, 1993, p. 58).

Evidence from companies concerning advertising standardization shows a mixed picture. For instance, Ryans and Ratz (1987) exploited thirty-four usable responses from international advertising/marketing managers who were delegates at an international advertising conference. They self-reported on their company's practices, in the framework of a questionnaire survey. Ryans and Ratz's findings indicate relatively high levels of advertising standardization for campaign themes, creative execution and media execution. Only parent company managers were interviewed and their quantitative report (based on levels of agreement or disagreement on a rating scale) may be rather distanced from actual local decisions as advocated by Clark (1987). An interpretive key to their findings is offered by Ryans and Ratz themselves (1987, p. 157):

> It is interesting to observe, however, that the majority of respondents thought that usage situations for their products were very similar worldwide ... [an] explanation is that international advertising managers have adopted the position of the globalists and assume it holds true for their products.

In order to determine the level of standardization, Mueller (1991) analyzed print and television campaigns for American consumer goods and services advertised in the United States and either in Germany or Japan (for which market distance with the United States is larger than for Germany). Between the United States and Germany, the highest level of advertising standardization was exhibited by Mars Candy bars, followed by Marlboro cigarettes; the lowest levels were associated with Camel cigarettes and credit cards. In the case of Japan the level of adaptation was on average much larger, signalling the more important role of market distance compared with product type.

The global campaign concept

One cannot underestimate the serious complexity of managing an international campaign (Clark, 1987), especially in the reality of agency/advertiser relations, which are often difficult to manage even when both agency and advertiser are excellent enterprises. For instance, Procter & Gamble has always been reputed to be a demanding advertiser for its agencies, but also very loyal to them. P & G, like many large companies, has had very stable relationships (sometimes for forty years or more) with a group of agencies; some of them have world-wide responsibility for a product line and/or a major brand (*Advertising Age*, 1987). But the creative work is sometimes a source of conflict between major advertisers and their agencies: their views concerning the strategy to be followed do not always correspond. Most advertisers then try to adopt a democratic style, by discussing opinions, facts, data and drafts of potential advertising campaigns. The final say always comes when campaigns are actually put into practice and their impact on various objectives may be monitored (brand awareness, brand image, sales increase, etc.).

The objective of a global advertising campaign has to be clearly defined: it does not seek to save on creative costs. It aims to promote a global brand name and image. Accordingly, the creative director for McCann Erickson world-wide, Marcio Moreira, emphasizes that an advertiser should not pursue a global advertising strategy as a way of saving money, trying to achieve in only one campaign what may in fact require twelve. The correct implementation of a global campaign requires a great deal of effort and creative time, and ultimately its cost may prove higher than the sum total of individual campaigns (Marcio Moreira, quoted by Hill and Winski, 1987).

Dean M. Peebles (1988), who was for many years the manager of international communications for Goodyear, the world's leading tyre manufacturer, recommends the following steps for the design and implementation of a global advertising campaign:

1. Choose a large advertising agency with subsidiaries all over the world; select in this agency an international account manager, who reports to the advertiser's headquarters.
2. Establish multinational planning meetings between the client and the agency, as well as a multinational creative team.
3. Brand managers and headquarters level should conduct and supervise consumer research and the pre-tests of the draft communication.
4. The resulting draft global campaign should be sufficiently finalized in order to facilitate discussion, but flexible enough to be transposed (rather than translated) into the various cultures and lifestyles of the target audiences.

Figure 13.2 presents a flowchart of headquarters–subsidiary relations for the planning and coordination of world-wide advertising at Goodyear. This flowchart indicates the tasks to be performed and the (tight) time schedule imposed (Peebles and Ryans, 1984, p. 83).

Practical implementation of global advertising campaigns is not an easy task. The organization must be completely interactive, as emphasized by the American expression 'bottom-up, top-down'. Communication between headquarters and subsidiaries should not be a 'sham' dialogue in which decisions already taken at the very top level would have to be accepted by local executives as if they were their own. This issue is all the more complex because interaction problems between various levels within the multinational advertiser (international headquarters, regional headquarters, country subsidiaries) are aggravated by problems of communication, coordination and agreement with the international agency (see the Levi Strauss case, section A13.1).

Global communication is primarily intended to establish the corporate image of a company or foster recognition of one of its major brands across a large number of countries (e.g. McDonald's, Goodyear, Michelin, Nestlé). The next step is to advertise the products themselves, and at this point the creative input of local subsidiaries and regional headquarters, as well as their influence on the advertising strategy, is much more significant. But local campaigns, even if they advertise local products and local brand names, must be carefully coordinated so that they make a positive contribution to the global message. The core values which are conveyed by the company's corporate image should also be recognizable in its brand and product advertising at the local level (e.g.

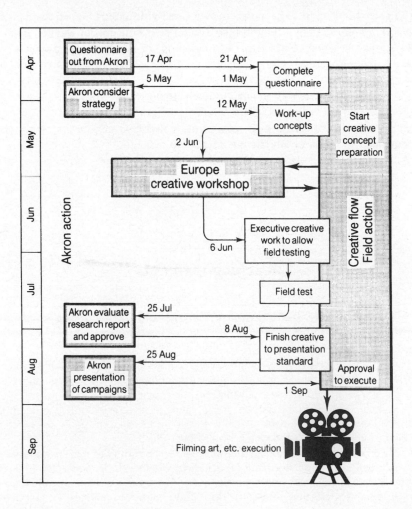

Figure 13.2 Flowchart for the management of multinational advertising campaigns at Goodyear.
(*Source:* Peebles and Ryans, 1984, p. 83. Reproduced with the kind permission of the original publisher, the *Journal of Marketing*.)

high technology, security, robustness, innovativeness, style, social responsibility). Finally, communication with market segments which remain specific to certain countries should be fully delegated to the local level. Not every piece of communication can be globalized. Accordingly, it is preferable to let local businesses develop on their own, even though they have only local coverage, as they may some day be extended to other countries.

Questions

1. The English word 'hair' corresponds to two (totally different) French words: *cheveux* (of head) or *poil* (on body). Interpret the difference in concepts of what is 'hair'. What might be the consequences in terms of marketing for personal care products?
2. Describe the respective cultural adequacy of persuasive, informative and oneiric messages.
3. Why does the acceptance of comparative advertising vary cross-culturally?
4. What are the target audiences of satellite TV in Europe?
5. Give examples of mores which vary cross-culturally and outline their possible consequences in terms of advertising adaptation.
6. What are the real benefits of a global advertising campaign?

APPENDIX 13

—— ♦♦♦ ——

Teaching materials

A13.1 Case: Levi Strauss Company: World-wide advertising strategy or localized campaigns?

The Levi Strauss Company, manufacturer of the famous LEVI'S jeans and other wearing apparel, markets its products in 70 countries. The company owns and operates plants in 25 countries and has licensees, distributors, and joint ventures in others.

The company is now in the process of evaluating its advertising policy to determine whether to apply a worldwide strategy to all advertising or settle on localized campaigns for each country in which it sells its products.

You have been asked to evaluate their present programs and to make recommendations that will assist management in deciding whether it is better (1) to create advertising campaigns locally or regionally but with a good deal of input and influence from headquarters as they presently do, (2) to allow campaigns to be created independently by local advertising companies or (3) to centralize at national headquarters all advertising and develop a consistent worldwide advertising campaign.

You are asked to do the following:

1. Prepare a report listing the pros and cons of each of the three approaches listed.

2. Make a recommendation as to the direction the company should take.
3. Support your recommendation and outline major objectives for whichever approach you recommend.

The following information should be of assistance in completing this assignment.

Company objectives

In a recent Annual Report, the following statement of objectives of Levi Strauss International was made:

In addition to posting record sales, Levi Strauss International continued to advance toward two long-term objectives.

The first is to develop a solid and continuing base of regular jeans business in markets throughout the world, thus proving a foundation for product diversification into women's-fitjeans, youthwear, menswear, and related tops.

The second objective is to attain the greatest possible self-sufficiency in each of the major geographic areas where Levi Strauss International markets: Europe, Canada, Latin America, and Asia/Pacific. This requires the development of raw material resources and manufacturing in areas where the products are marketed thus reducing exposure to long supply lines and shipping products across national borders.

Unlike some competitors, Levi Strauss International does not, in its normal markets, seek 'targets of opportunity,' that is, large one-time shipments to customers it may never serve again. Rather, the goal is to develop sustainable and growing shipment levels to long-term customers.

Organization

Western European group.
The company's European operations began in 1959 with a small export business, and, in 1965, an office was opened in Brussels. The company now has 15 European manufacturing plants and marketing organizations in 12 countries. This group includes all Western Europe served by the Continental and Northern European divisions.

The Continental European Division is headquartered in Brussels and is responsible for operations in Germany, France, Switzerland, the Benelux countries, Spain and Italy. *The Northern European Division* is headquartered in London and is responsible for all marketing and production in the United Kingdom and the Scandinavian nations.

Other international group.
The divisions in this group report directly to the president of Levi Strauss International. They are Canada, Latin America, and Asia/Pacific. *The Canadian Division* consists of two separate operating units: Levi Strauss of Canada and GWG. Levi Strauss and Company is sole owner of GWG which manufactures and markets casual and work garments under the GWG brand.

The Latin American Division traces its origins to 1966 when operations began in Mexico. In the early 1970s, the business was expanded to Argentina, Brazil, and Puerto Rico. In addition to these countries, the division now serves Chile, Venezuela,

Uruguay, Paraguay, Peru, Colombia, and Central America. Plans call for the division to explore new markets in Central America and the Andean Region.

The Asia-Pacific Division had its beginning in the 1940s when jeans reached this market through U.S. military exchanges. In 1965, a sales facility was established in Hong Kong. Markets now served include Australia and Japan, the two largest, as well as, Hong Kong, the Philippines, Singapore/Malaysia, and New Zealand. Business in Indonesia and Thailand is handled through licensees. The markets served by this division present opportunity for growth in jeanswear. However, diversification potential in Asia/Pacific is centered in Japan and Australia.

Other operating units.
One other unit, EXIMCO, not aligned with either Levi Strauss USA or Levi Strauss International, reports directly to the president.

EXIMCO has two major responsibilities; market development and joint ventures in Eastern Europe, the USSR, and the People's Republic of China, and directing offshore contract production for the company's divisions.

Comments

The director of advertising and communications for International shares with you the following thoughts about advertising:

The success of Levi Strauss International's advertising is derived principally from their judging it consistently against three criteria: (1) Is the proposition meaningful to the consumer? (2) Is the message believable? and (3) Is it exclusive to the brand?

A set of core values underlies their advertising wherever it is produced and regardless of strategy: honesty/integrity, consistency/reliability, relevance, social responsibility, credibility, excellence, and style. The question remains whether a centralized advertising campaign can be based on this core of values.

Levi Strauss' marketing plans must include 70 countries and recognize the cultural and political differences affecting advertising appeals. Uniform advertising (i.e., standardized) could ignore local customs and unique product uses, while locally prepared advertising risks uneven creative work, is likely to waste time and money on preparation, and might blur the corporate image.

Consistency in product image is a priority.

International advertising now appears in 25 countries. Levi currently uses seven different agencies outside the United States, although one agency handles 80 percent of the business worldwide. In Latin America, they use four different agencies, and still a different agency in Hong Kong.

Levi is not satisfied with some of the creative work in parts of Latin America. The company wants consistency in Latin American strategy rather than appearing to be a different company in different countries. They are not satisfied with production costs and casting of commercials, and the fact that local agencies are often resistant to outside suggestions to change. They feel there is a kneejerk reaction in Latin America that results in the attitude that everything must be developed locally.

The risks of too closely controlling a campaign result in uninteresting ads compared with decentralizing all marketing which produces uneven creative quality.

Competition

At the same time that Levi is looking at more centralized control of its advertising, another jeans maker is going in the opposite direction. Blue Bell International's Wrangler jeans company has just ended a six-month review of its international advertising and decided against coordinating its advertising more closely in Europe.

The concept of one idea which will work effectively in all markets is attractive to Wrangler. Yet the disadvantages are just as clear; the individual needs of each market cannot be met, resistance from local managers could be an obstacle, and the management of a centralized advertising campaign would require an organizational structure different from their present one.

To add to the confusion, a leading European jean manufacturer, the Spanish textile company Y Confecciones Europeas, makers of 'Louis' jeans, recently centralized its marketing through one single advertising agency. Louis, fourth largest jeans maker after Levi, Lee Cooper, and Wrangler, is intent on developing a worldwide international image for its Louis brand.

Review of current ads

A review of a selection of Levi advertisements from around the world provided the following notes:

> European television commercials for Levi's were super-sexy in appeal, projecting, in the minds of some at headquarters, an objectionable personality for the brand. These commercials were the result of allowing complete autonomy to a sales region.

> Levi's commercials prepared in Latin America projected a far different image than those in Europe. Latin American ads addressed a family oriented, Catholic market. However, the quality of the creative work was far below the standards set by the company.

> Ads for the United Kingdom, emphasizing that Levi's are an American brand, star an all-American hero, the cowboy, in fantasy wild West settings. In Northern Europe, both Scandinavia and the U.K., they are buying a slice of America when they buy Levi's.

> In Japan, where an attitude similar to that in the U.K. prevails, a problem confronted Levi's. Local jeans companies had already established themselves as very American. To overcome this, Levi's positioned themselves against these brands as legendary American jeans with commercials themed 'Heroes Wear Levi's,' featuring clips of cult figures like James Dean. These commercials were very effective and carried Levi's from a 35 percent to a 95 percent awareness level in Japan.

> In Brazil, unlike the United Kingdom, consumers are more strongly influenced by fashion trends emanating from the European Continent rather than from America. Thus, the Brazilian-made commercial filmed in Paris featured young people, cool amidst a wild traffic scene – very French. This commercial was

intended to project the impression that Levi's are the favored brand among young, trend-setting Europeans.

Australian commercials showed that creating brand awareness is important in that market. The lines 'fit looks tight, doesn't feel tight, can feel comfortable all night' and 'a legend doesn't come apart at the seams' highlighted Levi's quality image'. and 'since 1850 Levi jeans have handled everything from bucking bronco . . .' amplified Levi's unique positioning. This campaign resulted in a 99 percent brand awareness among Australians.

(Source: Cateora, 1983, pp. 525–9. Reproduced with permission.)

Questions

1. Based on the various copy strategies described in the case, analyze the possible themes which can be used to support Levi's image.
2. How should one operationalize the set of core values: across the various countries/cultures where Levi advertises its products, how can precise criteria be set which enable one to judge whether a commercial respects the core values?
3. Prepare a comparative table showing the pros and the cons of each of the three approaches listed at the beginning of the case.
4. Make a recommendation as to the choice which should be made by Levi's (one of the three approaches or a combination of them). Please argue your choice.

A13.2   Case: Agencia de Publicidad Aramburu SA (APA)

Mr. Aramburu was worried about the growing complexity of the operations of his advertising agency, from the point of view of both creativity and implementation of the advertising campaigns.

The agency not only created and implemented advertising campaigns for various Spanish products for the Spanish market but also had been creating and implementing since 1975 – at least in part – the advertising campaigns for Semo semolina, manufactured by Invesa, in various East African countries, in Morocco, and in the Middle East; subsequently, since 1983, it had agreed to create advertising campaigns for African or Arab customers to be aired in their respective countries.

On the one hand, it seemed worthwhile to put to use the body of knowledge acquired over the last ten years on how to advertise in Africa and the Middle East. On the other hand, he wondered if these markets really offered any opportunities in the medium term or if the good results obtained so far owed more of having ridden on the crest of a wave of favourable circumstances.

Previous international experience

Agencia de Publicidad Aramburu S.A. (APA), had its origin in 1940 as the advertising department of a food conglomerate (Vascalisa) and gradually developed into Publicom S.A., a wholly owned subsidiary of Vascalisa. In 1985, APA was founded as the result of a management buy-out. The buy-out came about because Vascalisa was an industrial group with only limited interest in advertising activities. Even as a separate entity APA continued to work with Vascalisa during a transitional period, on the basis of fees and other conditions stated in the purchasing contract.

Exporting advertising services

In 1979 Vascalisa set up an export department to sell semolina to countries in Africa and the Middle East. For this purpose, 'Semo' was developed in 1981, a semolina which could be defined as a tropicalized durum formula Semolin. In the same year, the Vascalisa subsidiary Internacional Vasca Export S.A. (Invesa) was created as the company within the group that would manufacture and market Semo. Invesa soon began to open markets in Central and East Africa, especially in the countries that made up the Horn of Africa. Vascalisa decided to rename its export semolina, calling it Semo – which locally sounds something like 'semu' – which sounded better and was easier to pronounce than Semolin. The product itself was tropicalized too to make it more resistant in the environment of extreme climatic conditions, especially considering the length of time that passed between manufacture in Spain and consumption in countries such as Somalia, Tanzania, or Sudan. The product would be retailed in small individual bags, following local usage and to increase rotation, instead of boxes containing several bags, which was the format used to sell Semolin in Spain.

Right from the start, Vascalisa turned to Publicom S.A. for help in designing its marketing strategy in Africa. The product's name, the adaptation of the product's quality to the markets it would enter, its presentation (without box) were all minutely analyzed. From the business point of view, Publicom S.A. treated Vascalisa just like any other company, providing full service within the legal restrictions imposed by each African country. Vascalisa paid Publicom S.A. in Spain, using pesetas for the services provided.

In 1983, both Vascalisa and Publicom S.A. began to feel the need to evolve toward a more aggressive sales strategy; by 1984, this feeling had become a determination to gradually progress from push marketing to pull marketing.

As Mr. Aramburu explained: 'At first, we had to feel our way; it did not seem reasonable to us to invest in expensive advertising campaigns in markets whose possibilities we did not exactly know. Later on, we saw that the sales of Semo were growing, that we had a large potential market, and that it could be profitable to invest money in "pulling" the product from the point of sale. We also understood that any campaign we made had to be aimed at promoting a specific demand, and not just a purely generic demand, as some Italian brands had already been around over there for much longer than us.'

The first task was to decide *how to advertise*. It was obvious that the methods and ideas used in Spain could not be easily exported to the markets in East Africa. There was also the language problem: In Tanzania, for example, the only official language was Swahili, a widely used native language that was written using the Latin alphabet, although English was fairly common at certain levels; there were also several major dialects that were spoken but not written. Swahili is a Bantu language spoken in Tanzania (including Zanzibar) and Kenya, where it is the official language, in Uganda, where it is the official language with English, and in some areas of the Congo River basin. It is the most widely spoken Black African language and has been considerably influenced by Arabic and Persian. Although originally written in Arabic characters, in the nineteenth century Latin characters were introduced. Swahili is widely used as a written language in magazines and newspapers.

In view of the reduced level or even non-existence of television and the low readership levels, especially among women, the media that seemed to be the most suitable was radio; in any case, there were no audience surveys and it also had to be borne in mind that the radio stations were usually run by the respective governments, with very little room for manoeuvre, and centered on news. The same could be said about television in those countries where it existed, to the extent that there were no censuses of the number of television sets.

'Advertising,' commented Mr. Aramburu, 'is just one more cultural phenomenon. Each advertisement must stimulate the consumer's preference toward the brand, and the advertisement's message cannot be dissociated either from the product that sponsors it or from the idiosyncrasies of the potential consumer it is directed toward. We avoided "advertising colonization" as much as possible because of our lack of knowledge concerning the region and because it seemed advisable to us from the point of view of working relationships with the government authorities. Thus, only an observant and open-minded person would realize that in those countries the housewife appearing in TV commercials would have to be a plump and well-fed woman; or that a dish must be tasted almost unavoidably with the fingers.

In those countries where they existed, we reached agreements with local agencies. This was the case in Tanzania, Somalia, Ethiopia, and Kenya. In other countries where there were no established advertising agencies, we had to work directly with the advertising departments of the broadcasting stations.'

Publicom S.A. tried to generate ideas in the meetings held with the staff of the local agencies. Normally, these were young people who had studied in Europe or occasionally an English expatriate who had started up on his own. All their ideas, collected in the field and processed in Bilbao, were expressed in a video, in a radio spot, in a jingle, in an image, that Publicom S.A. then showed in Madrid to a group of contacts from the country concerned – mostly students – to ensure that the message was appropriate.

'In Kenya, in 1987, we ran a campaign consisting of a truck with a film projector that toured through the jungle and when it arrived at a village, showed a promotional film; the driver–operator then handed out free samples of Semo to the audience. In 1988 we launched the multimedia campaign "The Four Pleasures" in Tanzania, a country which has color television. It referred to the four pleasures of cooking: the purchase of the ingredients, the preparation of the dish by the housewife, the offering of the food to the head of the family (the father), without whose approval the meal cannot be served, and the tasting of the dish by him. The commercial was announced by a "kotch-barma" a mythical character, a king's witch doctor, a kind of oracle who – unlike other counselors who may indulge in intriguing – always tells the truth. This character combs his hair with two perpendicular partings so that it is divided into four parts like a harlequin. In the commercial, the witch doctor shows his head with his hair dyed in the four colors of the Semo bags while he recommends its use for cooking to be able to enjoy the four pleasures it provides to the consumer. Before launching the message on the market, we wanted to be sure that the video would not be sacrilegious or scandalous and so we showed it to about a dozen Tanzanians we had contacted in Madrid who could read and write Swahili. This campaign was shown on television in two countries and broadcast on radio in a further five; produced in 14 different dialects, as well as Swahili, French, and English. At the time it was the basic advertising communication in those markets.

'In 1988, we also launched a jingle on the radio in Uganda with such intensity that many thought that it was the national anthem and stood up every time they heard it. In each case, we tried to get maximum advertising benefit from the media available to us and for this we had to know the particular features of each region and the coverage of the various media. Thus, we discovered that in some villages it was the custom for families to get together in large groups to watch television. On other occasions, it was impossible for us to get around the pressure we were subjected to by associated agencies or the media themselves to advertise through certain media, such as newspapers, which seemed ineffective to us.

'We also launched two blind-test commercials: in these, people tasted two different soups, one of which was made with Semo. Everybody delightedly guessed which was Semo after successively dipping their fingers in each and licking them.'

The trips to Africa

In line with his philosophy of adapting the advertising and marketing to the particular idiosyncrasies of each national market, Mr. Aramburu went to Africa for the first time in 1986. The purpose of the trip was to 'smell out' the market on the spot, to find out for himself what it was like. In Dar-es-Salaam, Carlos Aramburu had the opportunity to deal directly with the distributor of Semo, with some of his salesmen, and with retailers.

'One thing that stands out straight away is the vital importance of the point of sale for effectively marketing the product. In the markets of the large capitals, the stalls measure barely one meter square. They may be open-air or lightly covered and are usually attended by a mammy. [Mammy or, perhaps less frequently, mummy is used generically in Africa to refer to women who sell in the market.] These mammies are usually extraordinarily fat women who sit on a box and arrange the consumer products they sell on the ground in front of them. In the countryside, the retail outlets are shacks where no more than a dozen different brands are stacked.

'I have visited a large number of these bazaars and street markets, sticking stickers or offering posters showing the Semo squares, colors, and logo; this aspect of loyalty to an image is vital in those countries where the written transmission of slogans or even of the product's name is virtually useless. This direct contact with the mammies, with the salesmen, with the agents, even with the personnel of the media advertising departments, with the market, and with the country in general has been very useful. We have found out what the market is really like, it's given us idea, it's enabled us to gain the channel's trust. In fact, I don't think that any other manufacturer has made so much effort to get close to the market. The fact is that we are gaining market share and I suppose the other manufacturers are getting pretty worried.'

Diversification of APA's export business and its opening up to local advertisers

Little by little, on the basis of the reputation gained from the marketing of Semo, Publicom S.A. began to make a name for itself in some of the countries in which it operated. The distributors were pleasantly surprised by the success of Publicom S.A.'s campaigns; the personal contacts made during the visits helped to create an atmosphere of rapprochement and trust; the dinners held in the Carvajal family's house, to which the small but warm-hearted Spanish colony in Dar-es-Salaam was invited, were the scene of interminable conversations which gave Carlos Aramburu a clearer idea of life in those countries.

The importers and/or distributors of Semo were usually influential men of In-dopakistani or Lebanese origin who had businesses in several industrial and commercial sectors. Mr. Aramburu spoke of them with a certain air of indecision. 'In my opinion, it is vital to deal directly with people. I think that everyone likes being treated on an equal footing in a natural and respectful manner; I have always tried to establish a climate of polite deference and I think that it has opened a lot of doors for me. In any case, not all Europeans agree with me and there are some who have had undoubted success in the area in spite of – or perhaps thanks to – their rather arrogant and scornful attitude.'

In the spring of 1987, the importer of Semo in Tanzania requested Publicom S.A. to design the advertising campaign for the umbrellas it manufactured and sold, bypassing Counterpoint, which was the local agency that Vascalisa, Publicom S.A., and the importer itself had worked with right from the first day Semo was marketed there. In another two countries, Publicom S.A. was given direct assignments from the respective importers. The importer of Semo in Zanzibar also sold a line of Italian detergents and it placed Publicom S.A. in charge of the advertising campaign for these detergents.

The main problems facing Publicom S.A. at that time were basically two-fold. First, the importers did not have or were simply not used to providing the type of information on the market, the channel, and the markups that was essential to organize a meaningful campaign. 'Over there,' said Mr. Aramburu, whose voice had recovered its forceful tone, 'you've got to be prepared to listen. If you hand the potential client your BID (Basic Information Document – a briefing or questionnaire often used by advertising agencies to gain information on the basic features of its client and the product to be marketed) the chances are he won't be able to fill it in because to do so, certain basic knowledge is required not of marketing but of the market, of what you really want to achieve. Also, in addition to the problem of the lack of a qualified sales manager, you've also got the lack of statistics on media audiences and, worse still, the lack of awareness of advertising techniques.'

There was also the problem of payment because until then Publicom S.A. had always been paid by Vascalisa in Spain, using pesetas. When it started to work directly for local companies, as the product that Publicom S.A. sold to its new companies was an intangible consisting of advertising ideas and action techniques, sometimes it was difficult to justify the origin of the dollars received in fees to the customs authorities at the airport when leaving the country.

Basic features of exporting advertising services to Africa

'In all these countries,' said Mr. Aramburu, 'the normal procedure is to start talking about money. When they decide to invest, it is because they feel it is advisable to do so but normally they don't know how much. It can even occur that they say to you, "I've got so many million shillings. What can I do with them? Maybe I could put posters on buses, or print ads in the newspapers?" They are at that point where a country or company is starting to feel interested in advertising. It happened in Spain 30 years ago and it's happening to them now.

'The advertiser has no information on the market in his own country and neither do we. So somehow we have to complement the "empirical" information available. Mr. Abdullah Bequer, for example, does not know for sure who is buying his products; he knows his customers are natives because he knows the points of sale. But he doesn't know their social class, their age, their background. Neither does he know to what extent his customers are loyal, that is, repeat buyers, or whether his sales are usually only occasional first purchases. You have to work a bit on trial and error to get an idea of the situation. Also, and as a result of the above, major changes may occur in the course of the campaign. For example, if it is seen that the campaign is successful, its budget may be considerably increased.'

In Spain, on the other hand, the process was usually started on the advertiser's initiative, who nearly always had a certain idea of the market situation. The advertiser selected an agency, who proposed his fees and method. Advertiser–agency 'marriages' were frequent, i.e., an advertiser may consistently use the same agency to advertise some or all of its products. After preparing the briefing, the agency was in a position to be able to define the campaign's total cost. After that, it started to develop the creativity, the idea, or concept to communicate and the way to communicate it most effectively. The next steps were media definition, budget distribution, contracting the media chosen, and putting the campaign into action and monitoring it.

In other cases, it was the agency that took the initiative, seeking out a client with whom to reach an initial agreement for the presentation of a tentative campaign based on an overall budget. From that mutual loose commitment, the agency developed the creativity to present it to the advertiser. If the advertiser was satisfied with the agency's ideas, it implemented the ensuing steps of defining the media, distributing the budget, contracting the media, and executing the campaign. On the other hand, if the ideas created by the agency were not to the budding client's liking, it could cancel the contract on the spot.

Carlos Aramburu commented on the differences between the situation in Africa and the normal working methods used in Spain: 'You cannot place all the local agencies under the same heading. For example, in Mogadishu, Vascalisa has its local agency, Oggi, which is very dependable. Oggi contracts the media and bills Vascalisa locally for them. Also, Oggi creates the idea, designs the storyboard, and films the commercial or records the spot and prepares the original graphics. Our function in this case is to closely supervise the operations and ensure that the standards desired by Vascalisa are met.'

In other cases, for example, the United Arab Emirates, APA does the complete creativity and the local agency buys the media, supervises the copy, determines the amount of posters to be printed, and gives information on local culture.

'Finally, in those countries where there are no local agencies, APA resorts to the managers of the advertising media for advice on local culture, review of the copy in the local language, hire actors and speakers.'

Carlos Aramburu's concerns in September 1990

Carlos Aramburu was aware of the prudence required to manage a company recently starting out on its own and with rather limited financial resources. He also liked to define himself as a businessman 'like they used to be,' concerned to get the most out of every peseta spent and unwilling to take on additional expenditure items if it was not clear that they were absolutely necessary.

As part of this line of thought, APA's prime goal was to consolidate a market in Spain. The image its team of professionals had created for themselves over the last 30 years, the successes achieved, and the enormous amount of creativity shown by campaigns as varied as those for a major Japanese photocopier manufacturer ('Japanese through a Tube'), a well-established Bilbao newspaper ('In Writing, Please'), a chain of super-markets covering the entire Basque Country, Navarre, and Rioja ('We Sell Quality') or a cookie manufacturer ('Heaps Better'), among many others, provided a major business asset which had to be capitalized upon.

Furthermore, the team of professionals in APA had been working in the sector for many years, knew everybody in Spain, and were in a position to present themselves as a group experienced in working together, that had been enriched after the purchase of Publicom S.A. with new human and technical resources and was able to offer each advertiser a dual response of creativity and service adapted to each client's particular situation.

However, the general manager of APA did not want to give up the idea of strengthening his markets abroad and he was well aware that a significant part of the agency's billing for creativity – excluding therefore the buying of media – came from Vascalisa and the overseas clients.

Carlos Aramburu realized the enormous prospects that were opening up to him in the East African and Arab countries. The multinational agencies had yet to establish any significant presence in these quasi-virgin territories and Mr. Aramburu was afraid that, if he let time slip by, he would end up losing his lead to them. He had noticed that the sales office of an Italian agency in Mogadishu had been recently relaunched after years of inactivity. In this area, he considered that he had several possible alternatives: establish branches (wholly owned subsidiaries), continue as until now cooperating with the agencies existing in each country on the basis of agreed 'contractual' collaborations, or form associations with the local agencies, buying some of their shares and providing basically technical assistance, such as training personnel in Spain or dealing with certain aspects of the creativity. In any case, it seemed clear that each country would require individual treatment.

APA, both in Spain and in the other nine countries it had worked in, had developed a know-how and an image that it should not let go to waste. They had been four years of work well done by Publicom S.A. and APA in Tanzania, Somalia, Kenya, Uganda or Morocco; four years of traveling, learning, contacting markets, agencies, and media, of winning the company's first clients. To wait two years, which was the least time required to ensure continuity in Spain, for pushing strongly abroad, was not without risk.

Mr. Aramburu did not forget Vascalisa, the temporarily captive customer he had gained with the agency buy-out, which for the time being guaranteed a certain minimum billing for the agency. In any case, the terms were not particularly generous and Mr. Aramburu was considering renegotiating – updating – some of the clauses because, in his opinion, the quality of the service given by APA was improving day by day and in some cases was significantly higher than that given when the contract for the management buy-out of Publicom S.A. was written.

In Mr. Aramburu's opinion, the policy of exporting services could be focused along two approaches: the European companies that exported to Africa and the Middle East and the local companies. APA had already made contacts with some Spanish companies that were looking for markets in those regions.

In addition to these general issues, Mr. Aramburu also pondered on a number of other more specific but no less important problems.

Among these was the question of the profitability of the foreign clients. Most of these were medium-sized companies and – especially in the case of the foreign clients – required traveling. This inevitably meant an increase in the cost of the service, should traveling expenses be charged direct to the clients, or a significant decrease in profitability should APA include such costs as one more item in its income statement. Mr. Aramburu wondered to what extent, in the medium term, these charges could be borne by him or by his customers and, looking at the problem from another viewpoint, what should APA's fees be for it to be worthwhile for him and his clients.

Mr. Aramburu was also aware that, in September 1990, APA had no export manager; there was the feeling in the agency that such a position would unnecessarily burden the overhead and the time for such a person was not yet ripe. As Mr. Aramburu explained: 'There's no doubt that an export manager – or foreign accounts manager as we would call him – would significantly lighten my workload and enable me to give greater attention to the Spanish market. In November, for instance, I should be going to three countries and the way things are, it looks that I won't be able to go. A trip abroad, in addition to totally absorbing your attention for a few days, always leaves a few loose ends to be tied up because when you get back you have to send a leaflet or agenda to the inquisitive government officer who asked for them, send an answer to this or that client, review the conclusions of this or that matter, write a letter of intent, report to the board. But I think that it's best to wait a while because to fill this position would cost money and it's got to be done properly. We would need someone who would fit in with the company's corporate philosophy, who was familiar with the bureaucratic problems existing over there, who knew the methods of payment and the systems of credit, and who could feel at ease in those countries.

'Then there's what I call advertising "colonization" and which we have consistently avoided: we sell creativity not preconceived ideas tailored to the European markets; also, you've got to bear in mind our own limitations, our lack of in-depth knowledge of the reality and idiosyncrasies of each country, of the need to know how to work with people over there.'

The conception of a business strategy: strengths and possibilities

Deep down, what worried Mr. Aramburu most was the doubt he constantly had as to the suitability of the present business strategy. Sometimes, he caught himself muttering, 'The idea of a medium-sized Basque agency going out and running campaigns in Africa is ridiculous! A thousand things could happen to convert it into instant disaster.'

In any case, Carlos Aramburu tried to look at the situation from another viewpoint. He was aware that the agency he owned and managed had not yet had time to attain large volumes but he knew that he had a wide range of possibilities before him and the decision he took – which under no circumstances should endanger the company's continuity – could differentiate the advertising product he offered and speed up the company's growth path. In short, APA seemed to be facing the following strategic options:

1. Stop all exporting of advertising services – giving up also Vascalisa with a billing volume of 23 million pesetas and a margin of 12 million pesetas a year – in view of the risk that in the medium-term, as local agencies appeared in the various

countries, the local advertisers would leave APA, preferring to work with these native agencies. Mr. Aramburu could not quite get out of his mind the niggling sensation that all that had been achieved through Vascalisa was only a fly-by-night affair without any real substance.

2. Continue to let himself be carried along by Vascalisa without actively trying to gain new clients for campaigns outside Spain. This meant continuing to sell 'without pushing,' to carry on 'waiting for them to come'; in any case, even if this option was chosen, it seemed advisable to define the time when such a strategy would no longer be sufficient and the company should launch itself with more determination in the conquest of new markets.

3. Continue to think how to make best use of the know-how acquired but to preferably direct efforts toward Spanish companies with sales activities in those countries. Mr. Aramburu could not wait to find out who was exporting to the countries that APA knew so well; Mr. Aramburu would initiate contacts – first by letter/pamphlet and then by personal visit to each of these exporters – to offer them APA's services, backed by the successes achieved with Vascalisa. This offer could be made in at least two ways:

   - Directly approach the exporting agencies.
   - Approach these companies' advertising agencies. APA could act as a specialist consultant in these countries.

   Or, looking at things from another point of view:

   - Only approach those companies that were already exporting.
   - Try to find out (how? where?) which companies were potential exporters to the countries in the area and approach them.

4. Preferably direct efforts at the native companies in each African country, which to a certain extent was the path followed so far under Vascalisa's wing. In any case, it seemed clear that the BID to be used for these local clients would have to be refocused.

   In addition to these four options related to client segments, at a more general level of the organization there existed the possibility of seeking associations with another larger advertising agency or even with some group that wished to create, develop, or cultivate markets in East Africa. This idea did not particularly appeal to Mr. Aramburu from a 'personal fulfilment' viewpoint but he was sure that any company who bought APA would be buying valuable know-how that would enable it to gain rapid penetration in certain countries. This know-how was an asset that increased the company's value and, in a services company – which is what an advertising agency is par excellence – this meant a great deal. After all, Mr. Aramburu said to himself with a slight smile of self-satisfaction,'I don't know any other agency apart from APA that has in its files, for instance, the prices of market media in Kenya.'

(Source: adapted from a case prepared by Pere Gil, a second-year student at IESE, under the supervision of Francesco Pares, lecturer, and Professor Lluis G. Renart. Copyright 1987 IESE, Barcelona, Spain. Reproduced with kind permission.)

Questions

1. How would you identify APA competencies, especially as far as cultural know-how is concerned?

2. What is the value of this know-how? For which advertisers, in which markets?
3. Which course of action would you recommend? Who should implement it?

A13.3 Case: Nove Ltd

Nove Ltd is a large concern located in Hong Kong which manufactures a line of household appliances in which sales expansion has been very rapid. For certain new articles this increase has been so fast that production capacity could not keep up with demand. For one of the new products – electric (dry) shavers – management foresaw and provided for more than normal commercial expansion. Production capacity for these articles has been enlarged to the extent that even in the face of a rapid sales growth, a sufficient number of dry shavers could be manufactured. In view of the enlarged production facilities, more effective sales efforts became necessary. Total 1994 sales amounted to three million shavers. The 1995 sales target was set at three and one-half million pieces.

In order to put the planning indicated above into effect, a more intensive marketing communication campaign was considered desirable. In countries A, B, and C (countries so designated for purposes of disguise) particularly favorable results were expected from a stepped-up advertising campaign. The approved advertising budget for these countries was therefore separated from the normal sales budget and determined individually. The company's advertising manager felt that for the most effective results, the advertising budget should at least be doubled. In view of the enormous amounts planned for advertising the management suggested a preliminary investigation in the countries concerned to ascertain why dry shavers in general, and the company's own brand, 'Nover,' in particular, were purchased. Nove intended to obtain arguments that might best be used in its advertising and get some tips for sales promotion.

Consumer investigation

Before the investigation, Nover enjoyed a strong market position in the three countries. Otex was its largest competitor while Porde accounted for an insignificant market share.

Shaving habits

From the answers about shaving habits it appeared that in Country A approximately 100% of the men shaved themselves, while in Country C an important number (23%) went to the barber shop for a shave. The portion of men who shaved themselves daily varied from 13% in Country C to 77% in Country A. The majority of dry shavers were found among the men who shaved themselves daily. To stimulate sales it might thus be useful to promote the habit of shaving daily.

Following a request to indicate the advantages of dry shaving, the most frequent reactions were: ease, speed, and absence of skin irritation. All wet shavers were asked why they had not yet switched to dry shaving. Between 40 and 50% replied that dry shavers were too expensive.

Characteristics of the dry shaver

Table 13.1 indicates, in percentages of total dry shavers, replies made to the question: 'Why do you shave electrically?'

How did users obtain their dry shavers?

It appeared from the market research that an important part of the dry shaver owners had received the shaver as a gift – in Country A, 52%; in Country B, 40%; and in Country C, 40%.

The greater part of those receiving gifts (approximately 65%) had expressed the desire for a shaver themselves. Usually the wife or the fiancee (in approximately 60% of the cases) made the gift. It was also important to determine the place of purchase. Most dry shavers (75 to 80%) were bought in radio shops and electrical appliance stores. An entirely different situation, however, appeared to exist in Country A. There, radioshops and electrical appliance stores accounted for only 30% of sales. Most dry shavers in this country were bought in barber shops and department stores.

Choice of brand

In the process of buying, it is important to know what portion of future buyers has gained information in advance about various brands. It appears that more than 50% of the buyers had in fact formed an opinion in advance about the brand to be selected and intended to ask for additional information. Factors which favored the purchase of a certain brand are expressed in Table 13.2 in percentages of the total answers recorded.

Further investigation of brand choice was based on brand distribution among the shavers in use. The brands in use in each country are shown in Table 13.3.

Familiarity with three brands is shown in Table 13.4.

Replies to a question about the best brand generally favoured Otex, rather than Nover.

Results indicated that brand loyalty is very important. In the case of Otex, this loyalty seems to be somewhat stronger than for Nover. In Country C, however, a larger percentage of Nover users seem to be willing to switch brands than among Otex users. Relating the findings about brand switching to the results concerning the best brand (as expressed by wet and dry shavers), it can be concluded that there is a greater

Table 13.1

Arguments	Country A	Country B	Country C
Ease	52	84	80
Speed	38	52	50
Absence of skin irritation	24	52	30
Other arguments	76	64	30
Total	190	252	190

preference for Otex than for Nover by the wet shavers. This last observation could be an important aspect in attacking the potential market. Subsequently the question was raised: 'Which brand are you likely to buy?' Reactions are expressed in Table 13.5 in a percentage of those intending to buy and who at the same time mentioned a brand name.

Table 13.2

Motive	Country A	Country B	Country C
Seen in shop and advertisement	28	22	18
Advice of acquaintances	23	26	20
Price of shaver	13	12	10
Advice from shopkeeper	11	11	10
Other reasons	25	29	42
Total	100	100	100

Table 13.3

Brands in use	Country A	Country B	Country C
Nover	24	64	50
Otex	33	8	30
Porde	1	1	2
Miscellaneous	42	27	18

Table 13.4

Brands known	Country A	Country B	Country C
Nover	67	88	79
Otex	80	33	60
Porde	4	2	15

Table 13.5

Brands	Country A	Country B	Country C
Nover	14	55	44
Otex	57	22	34
Porde	1	1	11

Factors which favor the purchase of a certain brand

Seen in shop and advertisements

It is known that advertising and sales promotion are important influencing factors. The extent to which this has affected dry shavers, however, has not yet been determined. The number of men, both wet and dry shavers, who have noticed advertising for dry shavers, is expressed in percentages of the group in Table 13.6.

It thus seems that dry shavers are more quickly aware of dry shaving advertising than wet shavers. This could be explained by the concentration of shaver owners in the higher-income brackets. This group reads more, and consequently is confronted with more publicity and advertising matter than the lower-income classes. In view of the high percentage of shaver owners remembering publicity, it is probable that shaver owners in general have an active interest in dry shaving publicity. Of the replies to the question, 'Where, or in which media have you noticed dry shaving advertising?,' those favoring Nover were divided among publicity media as set forth in Table 13.7.

Price of shaver

Wet shavers generally regard price as an objection to buying a dry shaver. However, the influence of price in brand selection was not unfavorable for Nover, compared with other brands. In percentages of total Nover shaver owners, price was important in their selection of Nover to 12% in Country A, 17% in Country B, and 12% in Country C. The price of a shaver may be an important deterrent to a great segment of the population. This factor plays an important role in the gift market, where traditionally the cheaper brands are favored.

(Source: Albaum *et al.*, 1989, pp. 350–3. Reproduced with permission.)

Table 13.6

Advertising noticed by	Country A	Country B	Country C
Wet shavers	60	48	28
Dry shavers	67	58	39
Both groups	62	51	30

Table 13.7

Publicity medium	Country A	Country B	Country C
Newspaper	62	67	29
Weekly magazine	44	39	54
Shop	26	39	46
Posters	3	25	8
Movie	–	8	8
Folders, etc.	3	6	3

Question

Explain why Nove Ltd can or cannot standardize its advertising in countries A, B, and C.

A13.4 Critical incident: Excel and the Italian advertising campaign

Excel is a multinational company, based in northern Europe, which produces television sets, video recorders and other consumer electronics. It recently went through a phase of external growth by the take-over of the German and French subsidiaries of a large US-based company which had decided to divest itself of this industry. Within two years this Nordic company has tripled in size. It changed from having a mainly Scandinavian base to a complete European spread, with an 11 per cent share of the European market. The group, built in successive layers, inherited numerous local brands, namely those of the companies taken over. These brands are basically localized marketing assets, with only national coverage and brand recognition. Excel plans to have only one pan-European brand in the long run, with one local brand for each individual country.

European headquarters have been installed in Switzerland, near Lausanne. This location was chosen so that headquarters would be situated in Central Europe but not in a country where Excel already has a plant, as this might imply some sort of 'national preference'. Besides, over the past two years an important reshaping of the industrial base has been undertaken, with massive lay-offs in some plants and industrial investment aimed to increase productivity.

Excel wants to minimize advertising expenses while simultaneously giving its brand a strong, similar image across Europe. In fact it has inherited some very diverse brand names, which were those of the companies recently acquired in their home markets. Excel is therefore willing to design a pan-European advertising campaign. The national subsidiaries were invited either to join this campaign or to design their own campaign. In the latter case, they would have to finance it with their own money. The campaign has been scheduled for autumn 1990.

Because of the World Cup taking place in Italy in June 1990, the Italian subsidiary decided that it could not wait until the autumn, as this type of sports event usually generates increased demand for television sets and video recorders. They managed to go ahead by themselves: they made an advertisement which proved to be a real hit and generated a significant sales increase. A television commercial was created and a poster also. The same advertising theme was used for sales promotion. The advertisement showed a superb television set with a video recorder as an integral part, encircled by a red ribbon which largely hid the screen. The slogan was '*Venite a veder lo; dal vero*' (come and see it; for real).

This campaign was a success soon after it started, and was presented to the subsidiary general managers, who met for a residential seminar in Switzerland with the people at European headquarters in Geneva. Reactions were very positive. They proposed the idea of using the same campaign, themes and creation in other

European markets. At the beginning of March, Mr Makinen, in charge of marketing communications at European headquarters, decided to send a memo to the marketing/advertising managers of each subsidiary. A poster and a video presenting the Italian campaign were also enclosed. This memo was aimed at a concrete offer to the subsidiaries to adopt the themes and creation of this campaign. It asked them for feedback on their opinions. Makinen invited them to study the feasibility of using such a campaign in their home market and to send back their comments quickly, so that a pan-European campaign could possibly be launched in August. The Italian advertising manager, Signor Ragoli, was available if the European headquarters or national subsidiaries wanted any additional information.

'Responses' from the subsidiaries (that is, the answers plus the course of action finally adopted) were as follows. Answers were quite long in coming back, which could be explained by the overload of work experienced by people in the subsidiaries during this period of reorganization. Some countries never answered the proposal. Otherwise reactions were quite positive, except for that of France. The Spanish answer came quickly. The advertising and public relations manager, Senor Gonzales, sent a copy of the letter to his Italian colleague at European headquarters. He wrote that Spain had decided to use the campaign created in Italy, in order to unify Excel marketing communication. The Spanish wanted to use five different television channels for a total of twenty-two slots. They supported this with a press campaign and sales promotion in distribution channels. They needed the original version of the Italian television commercial, with music on one track and speech on another (one image track plus two sound tracks). In Spain the final version of the Excel campaign was launched in May 1990. The image track remained unchanged, but the music had been modified and there were several other minor changes. What seemed, at first sight, to be a straight copy of the Italian concept, finally turned out to be a largely modified version. Nevertheless Spain was the only country where the marketing team made the decision to use the experience of their Italian colleagues.

Sweden and Norway also responded quickly to the memo in similar terms. In neither of these two countries was advertising allowed on national television channels; furthermore, they traded under the Scandinavian brand name Scantel, rather than Excel. The Swedish response explained that the subsidiary did not advertise on television, since TV1 and TV2 did not offer any space; but with the growth of satellite television the Italian proposal might be interesting for the future. The Swedes thought that the Italian campaign was well designed and implemented. The model presented (Excel 7181) was usable with their brand name since they had the same make. The Norwegians' answer had also been very positive. They promised to keep in mind the concepts of the Italian campaign and further indicated that they would recommend its implementation for 1991.

In France the advertising and public relations manager, Monsieur Dubois, initially contacted by telephone, expressed a positive but rather cautious opinion. He said that he had first to discuss the themes and creation with his advertising agency. He called back to make it clear that even if he had any advertising funds left (in fact they were already entirely spent), he considered that the Italian campaign was not appropriate for Ariane (the brand name of the recently acquired French subsidiary). According to him, it did not fit in with the French criteria of what actually makes good advertising. In his opinion Ariane had a fairly traditional image in France, and French consumers would need more serious arguments to change their views. Consequently 'good' advertising for the Ariane brand had to emphasize, first of all, the high-technology image. Ultimately, he thought that the Italian campaign was not sophisticated enough, and that French people prefer more in-depth, sophisticated and detailed campaigns.

How can the failure of the European headquarters in having the Italian campaign adopted by the other European subsidiaries be explained? What is the right way to go about this in the future? What has to be changed?

A13.5   Exercise: Borovets - a Bulgarian ski resort

Compare the two short texts below (each dated the beginning of 1990). Both depict the Bulgarian ski resort Borovets. The first one is an extract from the magazine *Actuel* (no. 122), an article entitled 'Guide des bons plans à l'Est' (A guide to travelling in Eastern countries), p. 69. The other is an extract from the trade brochure of the Bulgarian state tourist corporation, *Balkanturist*, entitled 'Bulgaria welcomes you', p. 10. This short exercise is not meant to serve any other purpose than as a pedagogical exercise; it does not aim to describe any real situation and should not prejudice readers concerning holidays in Bulgaria.

Text 1: A charter flight to Bulgaria

The phenomenon already exists, it never stops swelling. Bulgaria is a hospitable place for exhausted proletarians in quest of cheap snow and sun. For the time being, most of the troop comes from Britain: 75 per cent of the tourists are English, 20 per cent are German, the remaining 5 per cent are Dutch, Swedish or French.

The Bulgarian government rubs its hands. The blaze of freedom which blasts through the East has already brought hordes of capitalist tourists. Bulgaria is in urgent need of foreign currencies. The country hopes to have its holiday resorts working at full capacity. Borovets is the most famous resort: in fact, it is a concrete boil encrusted on the mountains. The eight hotels, of luxurious appearance, offer limited comfort: water shortages, telephones out of order, ghost reception desks, bad-tempered staff and rooms where the cleanliness is somewhat dubious. Infrastructure, equipment and service do not meet minimum requirements.

Bulgarian tourism turns out dissatisfied customers. Like Franco's Spain of the 1970s, it is the same reinforced concrete everywhere. Varna and Burgas on the Black Sea coast look like Benidorm. The sea coast is built up with concrete rabbit hutches which swarm with Bulgarian city-dwellers, Greek spendthrifts or drunk Britons. Apocalypse! The rare night-clubs are inaccessible. Meals in the 300-place restaurants have all the style and allure of gymnasium banquets.

Text 2: Borovets

In Bulgarian, Borovets literally means 'beautiful place'.

Borovets during the winter has pure, ozone-rich air; it has 150 days of snow cover which provides exceptional ski slopes, from 1,300 to 2,500 meters high.

Each year Borovets is host to numerous international ski championships. Ingemar Stenmark, the Mahre brothers, Girardelli and many other famous skiers have spoken highly of this resort which welcomes everyone.

It is a very fashionable ski resort, with its numerous comfortable and cosy hotels, its enticing restaurants and various entertainment facilities for day and night. Borovets is located 50 miles from Sofia, and it has been enjoyed by children and adults since the end of the nineteenth century, when it was only a small holiday centre.

It is no exaggeration to say that Borovets can compete with the Swiss or the French ski resorts.

Now why wait any longer to visit us? We wish only to welcome you.

Questions

1. Why is there such a difference between these two pictures? Do these two articles refer to the same reality?
2. How can one get an idea of the level of service in this resort?
3. How should the state company for Bulgarian tourism (which manages the resort) communicate? What prevents them from doing so?

Notes

1. The directive on tobacco products advertising has not yet been adopted. Some directive projects have been under review for 25 years without reaching a consensus for qualified majority.

References

Advertising Age (1987), 'The house that built ivory', 20 August, pp. 26–7.

Advertising Age (1989), 'Saatchi leads top 11 mega-groups' and 'No 1 Dentsu Hits Lofty $1.2 billion in gross income', 29 March.

Albaum, Gerald, Jesper Strandskov, Edwin Duerr and Lawrence Dowd (1989), *International Marketing and Export Management*, Addison-Wesley: Wokingham.

Alden, Dana L., Wayne D. Hoyer and Chol Lee (1993), 'Identifying global and culture-specific dimensions of humor in advertising: a multinational analysis', *Journal of Marketing*, vol. 57 (April), pp. 64–75.

Andrews, J. Craig, Steven Lysonski and Srinivas Durvasula (1991), 'Understanding cross-cultural student perceptions of advertising in general: implications for advertising educators and practitioners', *Journal of Advertising*, vol. XX, no. 2, pp. 15–28.

Boddewyn, Jean J. (1984), 'The regulation of advertising around the world in the 1980s and beyond', in Gerald M. Hampton and Aart P. Van Gent (eds), *Marketing Aspects of International Business*, Kluwer-Nijhoff Publishing: Boston, MA, pp. 73–83.

Business Week (1987), 'The media barons battle to dominate Europe', 25 May.

Business Week (1989), 'Keeping up with the Murdochs', 20 March.

Cateora, Philip R. (1983), *International Marketing*, 5th edn, Richard D. Irwin: Homewood, IL.

Clark, Harold F. Jr (1987), 'Consumer and corporate values: Yet another view on global marketing', *International Journal of Advertising*, vol. 6, pp. 29–42.

Communication et Business (1988), *Numéro 'Spécial Europe'*, no. 70, 14 March.

Cutler, Bob D., Rajshekhar G. Javalgi and M. Krishna Erramilli (1992), 'The visual component of print advertising: a five-country cross-cultural analysis', *European Journal of Marketing*, vol. 26, no. 4, pp. 7–20.

Czinkota, Michael R. and Illka A. Ronkainen (1990), *International Marketing*, 2nd edn, Dryden Press: Hinsdale, IL.

Douglas, Susan and Bernard Dubois (1980), 'Looking at the cultural environment for international marketing opportunities', in P. Kotler and K. Cox (eds), *Marketing Management and Strategy: A reader*, Prentice Hall: Englewood Cliffs, pp. 388–96.

Dudley, James W. (1989), *1992: Strategies for the Single Market*, Kogan Page: London.

Engels-Levine, Erika (1982), 'Commercial radio in Latin America', *International Advertiser*, January–February.

Erbil, Kurt (1995), 'Ein Stückchen Heimat', *TV Spielfim*, vol. 10, pp. 30–1.

Gilly, Mary (1988) 'Sex roles in advertising: A comparison of television advertisements in Australia, Mexico, and the United States', *Journal of Marketing*, vol. 52, April, pp. 75–85.

Harvey, Michael G. (1993), 'Point of view: A model to determine standardization of the advertising process in international markets', *Journal of Advertising Research*, vol. 33, no. 4, pp. 57–65.

Hill, John S. and William L. James (1991), 'Product and promotion transfers in consumer goods multinationals', *International Marketing Review*, vol. 8, no. 4, pp. 6–17.

Hill, J. S. and J. M. Winski (1987), 'Goodbye, global ads', *Advertising Age*, 16 November.

Hoover, Robert J., Robert T. Green and Joel Saegert, (1978), 'A cross-national study of perceived risk', *Journal of Marketing*, July, pp. 102–8.

Huang, Jen-Hung (1993), 'Color in US and Taiwanese industrial advertising', *Industrial Marketing Management*, vol. 22, pp. 195–8.

James, Karen E. and Paul J. Hensel (1991), 'Negative advertising: the malicious strain of comparative advertising', *Journal of Advertising*, vol. XX, no. 2, pp. 53–67.

Kale, Sudhir H. (1991), 'Culture-specific marketing communications: an analytical approach', *International Marketing Review*, vol. 8, no. 2, pp. 19–30.

Kashani, Kamran (1989), 'Beware the pitfalls of global marketing', *Harvard Business Review*, September–October, pp. 91–8.

Katz, Helen and Weio-Na Lee (1992), 'Oceans apart: an initial exploration of social communication differences in US and UK prime-time television advertising', *International Journal of Advertising*, vol. 11, pp. 69–82.

Kaynak, Erdener and Pervez N. Ghauri (1986), 'A comparative analysis of advertising practices in unlike environments: A study of agency–client relationships', *International Journal of Advertising*, vol. 5, pp. 121–46.

Keown, Charles F., Lawrence W. Jacobs, Richard W. Schmidt and Kyung-Il Ghymn (1992), 'Information content in advertising in the United States, Japan, South Korea, and the People's Republic of China', *International Journal of Advertising*, vol. 11, pp. 257–67.

Lin, Carolyn A. (1993), 'Cultural differences in message strategies: A comparison between American and Japanese TV commercials', *Journal of Advertising Research*, vol. 33, no. 4, pp. 40–8.

Luqmani, Mushtaq, Ugur Yavas and Zahir Quraeshi (1988), 'Advertising in Saudi Arabia: Content and regulation', *International Marketing Review*, vol. 6, no. 1, pp. 59–71.

Mariet, François (1990), *La Télévision Américaine*, Editions Economica: Paris.

Martenson, Rita (1987), 'Advertising strategies and information content in American and Swedish advertising: A comparative content analysis in cross-cultural copy research', *International Journal of Advertising*, vol. 6, pp. 133–44.

Miller, Fred and A. Hamdi Demirel (1988), 'Efes pilsen in the Turkish beer market: marketing consumer goods in developing countries', *International Marketing Review*, vol. 5 (Spring), pp. 7–19.

Mourier, Pascal and Didier Burgaud (1989), *Euromarketing*, Editions d'Organisation: Paris.

Mueller, Barbara (1987), 'Reflections of culture: An analysis of Japanese and American advertising appeals', *Journal of Advertising Research*, vol. 27, no. 3, pp. 51–9.

Mueller, Barbara (1991), 'Multinational advertising: factors influencing the standardised vs. specialised approach', *International Marketing Review*, vol. 8, no. 1, pp. 7–18.

Onkvisit, Sak and John J. Shaw (1987), 'Standardized international advertising: A review and critical evaluation of the theoretical and empirical evidence', *Columbia Journal of World Business*, Fall, pp. 43–55.

Peebles, Dean M. (1988), 'Don't write-off global advertising: A commentary', *International Marketing Review*, vol. 6, no. 1, pp. 73–8.

Peebles, Dean M. and John K. Ryans (1984), *Management of International Advertising*, Allyn and Bacon: Boston, MA.

Reader's Digest (1987), 40th anniversary special edition, *Sélection du Reader's Digest*, Paris.

Ricks, David A., Jeffrey S. Arpan and Marilyn Y. Fu (1979), 'Pitfalls in overseas advertising', *Journal of Advertising Research*, reprinted in S. Watson Dunn and E. S. Lorimer (eds), *International Advertising and Marketing*, Grid: Columbus, OH, pp. 87–93.

Ryans, John K. and David G. Ratz (1987), 'Advertising standardization: A re-examination', *International Journal of Advertising*, vol. 6, pp. 145–58.

Sarathy, Ravi (1991), 'European integration and global strategy in the media and entertainment industry', in Alan M. Rugman and Alain Verbeke (eds), *Global Competition and the European Community*, vol. 2, JAI Press: Greenwich, CT, pp. 125–48.

Snyder, Leslie B., Bartjan Willenborg and James Watt (1991), 'Advertising and cross-cultural convergence in Europe, 1953–1989', *European Journal of Communication*, vol. 6, pp. 441–68.

Sriram, Ven and Pradeep Gopalakrishna (1991), 'Can advertising be standardized among similar countries? A cluster-based analysis', *International Journal of Advertising*, vol. 10, pp. 137–40.

Stern, Bruce W. and Alan J. Resnik (1991), 'Information content in advertising: A replication and extension', *Journal of Advertising Research*, vol. 31, no. 3, pp. 36–46.

Tansey, Richard, Michael R. Hyman and George M. Zinkhan (1990), 'Cultural themes in Brazilian and U.S. auto ads: a cross-cultural comparison, *Journal of Advertising*, vol. 19, no. 2, pp. 30–9.

Tuncalp, Secil (1992), 'The audio-visual media in Saudi Arabia: Problems and prospects', *International Journal of Advertising*, vol. 11, pp. 119–30.

Wills, James R. and John K. Ryans Jr (1982), 'Attitudes toward advertising: A multinational study', *Journal of International Business Studies*, Winter, pp. 121–41.

14

♦ ♦ ♦

Intercultural marketing communications 2: Personal selling and public relations

'Mouth smiles, money smiles better', is a Ghanean saying. Money is always at the very centre of personal selling, as price is discussed as well as 'side price'. Person-to-person relationships are also at stake in this part of marketing communications which is based on personal selling and public relations, which mix rational and non-rational arguments, hard business facts and human relationships. There are four ways of achieving marketing communications: advertising (examined in the previous chapter), sales promotion (section 11.4), personal selling and public relations. Understandably enough, cultural differences (time and space assumptions, interaction models and attitudes towards action, as described in chapters 2 and 3) have a major impact on how relationships start and develop. It is argued in section 14.1 that people who want to take into account cultural differences have to be *relationship*-centred rather than purely *deal*-centred (commerce rather than simply marketing). We then discuss how culture impacts buyer–seller interactions (section 14.2), which, involving personal contact, are more culture-bound. Personal selling issues are afterwards examined in an organizational perspective focusing on how sales forces can be managed in a cross-cultural perspective. The fourth section deals with public relations, which, if not directly contributing to sales, may be of prime concern to defend corporate image in front of various publics. Lastly we examine ethical issues related to selling in the last two sections, first by emphasizing facts about bribery (14.5) and second by suggesting some ways to appreciate the cultural relativity of ethical attitudes (14.6).

14.1 Intercultural commerce

Commerce as implementation of marketing programmes

Commerce is about personal selling and establishing continuity in the relationship with individual customers, organizational buyers and intermediaries. Commerce is defined by the *Collins Dictionary* as follows: '1. the activity embracing all forms of the purchase and sale of goods and services; 2. social relationships; 3. *Arch.* sexual intercourse.' Commerce favours the social interaction between vendor (producer and/or distributor) and consumer. The quality of this social interaction, including marketing strategies which respect cultural integrity, guarantees the effective implementation of global strategies. Commerce is simply non-technocratic marketing.

The four 'P's model (McCarthy, 1964) of the marketing mix (product, price, place and promotion) has been extensively used; as a paradigm it continues to assist greatly in the design of marketing strategies, serving to question their coherence and soundness. But, little by little, it has led to rather ritualized marketing practices where functions and their content are seen as fairly independent. Market research specialists are not product managers, nor are they advertising managers or sales promoters; as we have argued in section 5.6 an atomistic view of reality leads to decisions made by experts, each one having closely tabulated tasks. Whenever an issue does not fall clearly within their explicit responsibility, it will not even be considered. For instance, when questions arise as to consumer complaints management, it is not always clear who should be in charge of it. The correct answer should be that *everybody* is in charge of consumer complaints and great care should be taken to avoid *nobody* being in charge of consumer complaints.

Technocratically oriented market research treats the customer too impersonally, as all abstract units in a sample. Messages coming from consumers are filtered by close-ended questions, which pre-shape what people actually say. A large part of what they *would be willing to say* is in fact often ignored. The four 'P's paradigm of marketing theory has led to practices which are sometimes overly ignorant of company environment (Zeithaml and Zeithaml, 1984). Various segments of the public (consumers, actual buyers, competitors, etc.) are often ignored simply because there is no established communication channel to hear their voice.

Continuity in commercial relationships

A new style of marketing, more consumer and relation oriented, less strategy oriented, recommends 'Hearing the voice of the market' (Barabba and Zaltman, 1991), or *Making Sales* (Prus, 1989). The preoccupation with *marketing continuity* is a directly operative one. There are many reasons why the relationship and the lines of communication between a producer and the ultimate consumer may be broken. Here are some examples:

1. Distribution acts as a filter; consumers complain but there is no specific communication channel with the producer and these complaints are not taken seriously or indeed are simply ignored (see Box 14.1).
2. A product is refused by the distribution, for substantive reasons which nevertheless remain ignored. For instance, packets of biscuits are delivered to stores in cardboard boxes. Store employees experience difficulties in opening these boxes, which are stapled in such a way that employees are injured when they try to open them in order to put the biscuits on the shelves.
3. A class of potential consumers is neglected by marketing communications, since only actual buyers are targeted.

The example of Japanese *Keiretsu*, presented in section 11.1, demonstrates the value of

Box 14.1   *'Tubeless tyres', you said . . .*

A consumer bought a leading European make of tyre for his car. He asked his garage to fit the tyres. In fact they fitted tubeless tyres since they were supposed to be cheaper (as they did not need air chambers). These tyres, however, kept deflating. When complaining for the first time, the consumer was told by the garage to be slightly more careful in inflating the tyres. They had to be reinflated roughly twice a week. The customer contacted his garage again but was merely told that it 'didn't usually happen'. The customer asked if the tyre manufacturer would take back the defective tyres but the garage told him that that was impossible and that in any case the tyres did at least stay inflated for a couple of days.

Finally, after going backwards and forwards several times, the customer had air chambers put into the tyres. The problem immediately ceased. When he spoke to his garage, they informed him that the wheel rims had warped slightly owing to the 30,000 miles (48,000 km) that the car had done. Other cars (the garage mentioned a German make) had rims made out of a thicker steel which was more resistant and therefore did not warp. Such a car could have tubeless tyres fitted successfully, whatever its age. The customer asked the garage to pass on this information to the tyre manufacturer so that it could inform tyre centres which cars were not suitable for tubeless tyres after a certain mileage had been covered. The garage said that this was impossible.

The information was not passed on. Tubeless tyres continue to deflate in a fairly large number of cases. Customers either fit air chambers or buy a different car . . . or they change their make of tyre.

building communication channels which help in the design and implementation of marketing strategies. Where opportunities for the return of products are liberal, distributors may warn producers about products which are defective or with which consumers are simply not happy. When, conversely, producers or retailers reject consumer complaints and therefore the return of products, they will often shift responsibility for the failure on to the consumers. They will, for instance, tell them that they have not read the instructions, or have misused the product, or fixed it incorrectly.

A negotiation and human resource emphasis

A commerce orientation means that not only personnel but also clients should be seen by a company as its human resources. The frontiers of the organization should be less clear-cut. Most companies are very dichotomous, that is, they have their 'inside' and their 'outside'. Insiders are generally people listed on the payroll. It is often claimed in slogans emanating from within the company that consumer are 'kings' (to be found everywhere: *le client est roi, der Kunde ist König*, etc.), but in reality they are treated as pure *outsiders* and there is little personal knowledge of who the consumers actually are. A consumer who wants to meet a manager (just to explain something about the product or the service, with a positive view towards its improvement) will generally not even be received. Very often distribution channels will be used as 'shock-absorbing mattresses'. As distribution channels are in direct contact with customers, if something goes wrong, it is *their* job to deal with it. Splendid isolation of manufacturers is too often the rule of non-commerce oriented organizations, whenever they claim to be marketing oriented. To avoid this bias, consumers must be viewed as one of the key human resources of the company. They are not kings, but suitable people with whom to negotiate reasonable changes to the buyer/ seller relationship. Personal selling is the main tool of commerce: it allows direct relationship and communication with distributors and final customers and must convey messages in both directions, from the manufacturer to the market and vice versa.

Making contacts

Commerce puts equal emphasis on the marketing offer (product, price, delivery dates, etc.) and on the quality of the social relationship between buyer and seller, manufacturer and consumer. That is why making appropriate contacts and developing relationships is an essential part of commerce, this being true for personal selling, public relations as well as marketing negotiations. The issue is at what level of the organization and which people must be contacted to maximize the chances of a successful outcome. When making contacts, in a cross-cultural perspective, people should be aware of the following: (1) status is not shown in the same way according to culture; (2) influential persons are not the same and individual influence is not exerted in the same way; and (3) the decision-making process differs. Box 14.2 illustrates with an African example the first two points.

Credibility is an initial condition of trust-building in relational marketing. According to

Box 14.2:   *The little man in rags and tatters*

> The story takes place in the corridor to the office of the minister of industry of the Popular Republic of Guinea in the beginning of the 1980s. Whether you had an appointment or you came to solicit a meeting, you had to be let in by the door-keeper. Besides, the door was locked and he had the key. This little man looked tired and wore worn out clothes; his appearance led foreign visitors to treat him as negligible and to pay little attention to him. When those visitors were waiting lengthily while seeing others being given quick access to the minister, they often spoke out unrestrainedly their impatience to the old man who seemed to have only limited language proficiency. In fact, the door-keeper spoke perfect French and was the uncle of the minister, what gave him power on his nephew according to the African tradition. It was notorious that the Minister placed high confidence in his uncle's recommendations. Thus some foreign contractors never understood why they did not make the deal although they had been developing winning arguments with the minister himself.

(Source: Gérard Verna, Université Laval, Québec. Reproduced with permission.)

Slatter (1987), the salesperson's job in competitive bidding situations (quite frequent for international sales of equipment, turnkey plants and in the case of public procurement) consists of five main tasks:

1. Establishing the salesperson's personal credibility.
2. Undertaking market research.
3. Influencing design and specifications.
4. Establishing the firm's credibility.
5. Establishing a communication system.

There are clearly two levels where credibility has to be established: personal and organizational. The credibility of a particular person obeys cultural codes. People emit messages about their own credibility which are linked to physical status and/or behavioural attributes (see sections 3.1 and 15.3). The vendor will try to become personally acquainted with key decision-makers in potential target companies. There may be some problems in clearly identifying the key decision-makers, and establishing one's credibility with them. They may resent dealing with 'mere salespeople', especially in countries where sales status is low and power distance is high, because it conflicts with their self-image and their organizational position. Hierarchical relationships *across* organizations are a very sensitive issue; all the more so because they supposedly exist only subjectively. Complex codes of interpersonal relationships govern the establishment of credibility: it is therefore often necessary to use sales assistants or market researchers as 'door-openers', who will quickly be succeeded by higher-ranking sales executives or sales managers (Box 14.3).

Any 'detail' may be of importance in establishing credibility in the absence of more profound informational cues which come only when the relationship is more established. Business cards are important because they provide clear information on business persons: what is their family and first names, how to reach them, what is their status within the company etc. A foreign language card will also reflect sensitivity to the host culture (Freivalds, 1991) and when one is working mostly with a particular culture (e.g. a US business person exporting to Japan), it is advisable to have a card printed in English on the one side with the Japanese transliteration on the other side. Credibility is often based on first impression: accent has been shown to influence the credibility and effectiveness of an international businessperson. Tsalikis *et al.* (1992) have compared the effect of accent type on credibility of business people in a Latin American context: in Guatemala, for instance, Guatemalan Spanish evokes more favourable judgements than the same sales pitch in foreign accented Spanish.

The decision-making process in the buyer's organization is a key issue for making adequate contact. Power distance (PD) plays an important role in the style of organizational decision making: the higher it is, the more centralized it is. In a French context, for instance, with high PD, individualism and uncertainty avoidance, decision-making and budgetary power are located at the top of the organization. Most people cannot make a decision by themselves, including buying a pencil, without referring to the top. Thus, for personal selling, one has to target contacts at the top while keeping friendly contacts with people at intermediate levels because they could resent their lack of power being openly manifested by the seller's attitude and could therefore obstruct. In countries where power

Box 14.3   *The Japanese 'message-boy'*

During research into the key factors surrounding the success of Japanese engineer-
ing companies in world markets, I had the opportunity to interview several
Japanese engineering specialists. One of them had worked for C. Itoh, a large
Japanese trading company, on the sale and project follow-up of an oil refinery in
Algeria. He explained by the use of a diagram (Figure 14.1) the Japanese 'method'
for selling turnkey factories.

He stressed the central role of the *sogoshosha* (GTC: general trading company)
as an *organizer*, a function that includes the responsibilities of information source,
business intermediary and coordinator. An *organizer* is roughly equivalent to a
'sales prospection expert before, during and after the sale of a large and highly
complex item'. One of C. Itoh's small offices in Algiers, specializing in import–
export, principally of textile products, learned of the existence of a new tender for
an oil refinery which was shortly to be published. The Algiers office sent a fairly
detailed telex to Tokyo – step (1) in Figure 14.1 – where the engineering
company(ies) and the manufacturing companies (MFG) who would be in a
position to tender for the project were sought out – step (2).

Even at this early stage, a project team will begin to assemble from among the
different companies involved (3). The trading company contacts the official
bodies: first, the foreign insurance division of the Ministry of International Trade
and Industry (GOV) to determine whether the project has a chance of being
covered for political and commercial risk (4). The Japanese Exim-Bank, the public
export-finance body (BKG), will also be contacted for a preliminary study into
financing options. These bodies will not make any firm commitment, but they will
give a preliminary response: if the project risks not being covered by official
guarantees, or only receiving limited cover, the project team instituted by the
trading company may decide to abandon the tender. While all this is going on, and
even before the bid documents are available, a preliminary team will be sent to the
site to examine the possibilities of water and energy supply, transport facilities, etc.
Already the Japanese are gaining time (5). Once the bid documents are available
to companies (6), the trading company's local representative will go to collect
them personally from the future owner and dispatch the documents to Tokyo after
having summarized the main points in a long and detailed fax or e-mail. The
representative will not hesitate to stay up most of the night to draft this fax or e-
mail. By this stage, the Japanese have already gained fifteen days on their
international competitors (7).

Once the detailed fax or e-mail has been received, a larger team will go to
examine the technical and economic conditions on site. The results of this survey
and the consultation with various engineering partners, heavy equipment manufacturers (MFG) and carriers (TRP), will enable the formulation of a detailed bid,
which very often has to be submitted within a fairly short time span (thirty days)
after the publication of the tender. The bid will not be sent, but handed over by a
young executive, who will be 25 to 30 years old: a 'message-boy' (8). His task is
an important one: thanks to him, there is no risk of the documents being blocked
by customs; he also has the job of 'sizing up' the people being dealt

with and of discerning the people who will really make the final decision. Once more the Japanese have gained time; they are never late in submitting a tender, whereas a number of their foreign competitors submit theirs after the deadline. Although late delivery of a bid is usually accepted (bidding times are fairly short), it does not necessarily reflect favourably on the capacity to meet delivery dates.

Now the negotiation phase begins (9). This will easily last several months and in extreme cases will stretch, with long interruptions, over several years. Much shuttling back and forth between the various levels (10) will allow the finalizing of an offer. If successful, the offer will lead to the signature of the contract for a large-scale project (11), in which the trading company and the engineering company will generally be joint contractors. As a result, the trading company will adopt the role of coordinator between the various companies carrying out the project (12).

According to my Japanese informant, Nobuhiko Suto, now a professor at Tokai University, who had been personally involved in the deal, the 'message-boy' is typical of the Japanese way of doing business. He is even requested to scrutinize the face of the people to whom he submits the offer to determine their reaction to the Japanese bid. In the West, it is difficult to conceive of such care being taken to assess subjective reactions objectively.

Figure 14.1 The role of Japanese general trading companies as 'organizers' in the negotiation and implementation of international turnkey operations: a Japanese view.

distance is small, decision-making is more decentralized, and there are financial thresholds for decisions at each level of the hierarchy, especially when it combines with an individualistic orientation. Then level of contact is roughly proportionate with the financial amount involved by the sales contract.

The Japanese style of reaching decisions by committee can disorientate people of other nationalities who are used to decisions being made by a boss, which thereby concentrate a great deal of power in one person's hands. There are many examples of firms which, after protracted negotiations with Japanese firms, heard nothing more for several months. They assumed that they had lost the deal, but to their surprise they ultimately received an agreement: the process of *ringi* had been at work in the Japanese company – a procedure of written consultation which requires the input of various interested parties, meetings and careful consideration of objections and suggestions. Box 14.3 shows how the Japanese manage the process of preliminary contacts in a situation where both the seller's and the buyer's organization are complex.

14.2   Buyer–seller interactions

Seller's and trade status

In many countries of the world a low status is associated with sales work. Selling is implicitly associated with persuasion techniques and taking money out of people rather than usefully bringing products and services to them. Trade has some negative connotations in Latin countries for instance, where it was traditionally associated with exploitation, especially when buying for resale, leading to the view that distribution, and services in general, were economically unproductive activities. With this view, engineering and production are considered as noble activities in contrast to marketing and sales which are devalued. Such poor status often makes people consider that personal selling requires no formal training, but rather innate communication talents, a certain lack of scruple, and a good deal of opportunism.

The value placed on money is also central in trade status since sellers sell goods and services *against* money. In fact most cultures have a problem with money, which is often implicitly viewed as depriving activities from a higher sense of purpose, making people *bassement intéressés* (meanly self-interested). A range of possible solutions are shown by the different values placed on price bargaining, presented in section 10.2: either explicit reference to price is avoided whenever possible, explicit talks about price come quite late (which may at times be embarrassing), or a supposedly 'favourable' price is ritualistically associated with friendship or common belonging.

Seller status is in fact often related to membership of a particular ingroup, such as the Chinese who have been prominent merchants in many south east nations or the Lebanese in West Africa. The reader will recognize here some of the basic assumptions presented in Table 2.2, especially the being/doing divide. The status of a minority as 'commercial group', reflecting strong being orientation, is ambiguous: members of this minority may have taken this charge because it was somewhat rejected by the majority, while their success and influence as tradespeople is resented. On the other hand, in many countries, it is an absolute necessity for the seller to be personally acquainted to the buyer, common membership in the same ingroup may be required or some personal characteristics of the seller may be difficult to accept for the buyer, such as a European export saleswoman selling to a Saudi buyer.

Power distance also has an influence on the seller's status: in high power distance countries, the seller is often in charge of voicing the producer's conditions to the customer, with very limited leeway for negotiation – especially about price and delivery conditions. Jolibert and Tixier (1988, p. 11), both French, coming from a high power distance society, give a good example of the distinction between sales (understood as a low power/low status situation) and marketing negotiation (considered a high power/high status role):

> During sale the business conditions are fixed by the vendor. The purchaser is not in a position to debate them. ... The job of the vendor therefore consists of convincing the purchaser of the worth of his offers, of the appropriateness of the product offered to meet the needs of the purchaser. ... Negotiation begins when there is a *possible discussion* about the terms of business between the purchaser and the vendor.

In this definition the salesperson role is only to convince; he/she is given no role in representing the customer needs and making them known to his or her company! More paradoxically, in this definition, the purchaser is also in a subordinate situation to the supplying company.

Selling styles: arguments and presence

Let us begin with a question framed in radical terms: what must a salesperson do when asked to sell poor-quality products, or less radically, when the seller perceives the weaknesses of a product through clients' comments? Should the salesperson inform the company, in particular the production department, or merely consider the terms of the business offering as fixed and stick to the role of persuasion? In fact, when preparing arguments, a salesperson has two main concerns: one is for the customers and their needs; the other one is for achieving the sale, for 'closing the deal'. Adcock *et al.* (1993, p. 306) combine it as in Figure 14.2.

If one regards the seller's role as strictly separate from that of the business negotiator, sales staff being supposed obediently to sell products as they are and not to debate the marketing mix, then the role of salespeople is principally that of persuasion, the art of persuasion being subject to highly significant cultural variations. The following questions outline possible ways of differentiating the sales persuasion technique:

1. How far can one take persuasion without becoming insistent, annoying, irritating?
2. Is one persuasive merely by listening, where clients appreciate salespeople to whom they can talk, or by talking?
3. What arguments will be the best and the quickest to persuade the prospective purchaser?

Cateora (1983) proposes some stereotypes of selling styles:

1. In Asian countries, where people mind arrogance and the showing of extreme self-confidence, vendors should make modest, rational, down-to-earth points; they should avoid winning arguments against the buyer, who could suffer from a 'loss of face', and react quite negatively.
2. In Italy, on the contrary, the lack of self-confidence would be perceived as a clear sign of lack of personal credibility and reliability; thus one needs to argue strongly in order to be considered as a serious partner.
3. In Switzerland, you have to speak precisely and your words will be taken quite literally.
4. In the United Kingdom, it is advisable to use the *soft sell* approach (do not be pushy with your prospective buyer). The very favourable position of the 'soft sell' approach in Figure 14.2, excerpt from British authors, gives some support to this.
5. In Germany, you should use the *hard sell* approach (make visits, offer trials, be very visible).
6. When selling to a Mexican buyer, one should emphasize price.
7. In Venezuela, a vendor will have to emphasize the quality of goods.

If a true variety of selling styles related to national culture exists, it is not to be denied that the style of selling depends also on the personality of the salesperson and the type of industry, from the market trader to the executive, selling billion-dollar contracts, from the friend to the distant acquaintance. However, culture dictates assumptions about their role adopted by the majority of sellers. For instance if the view is that a good salesperson should be able to close the deal, then the job is that of short-term persuasion at any price. Conversely, if the seller is viewed as the representative of the client within the company, salespeople should have a long-term outlook, listen to the client, and even be willing to lose an order once in a while. Selling styles also depend on which type of concrete results (winning new customers, reaching a sales target) and/or more subjective achievements

Figure 14.2 Selling orientations.

(getting on well with clients, maintaining a friendly atmosphere in the sales team) are considered as evidence of the seller's efficiency or inefficiency.

Equality in the buyer–seller relationship

Some of the basic conditions of the buyer–seller interaction are partially dictated by culture, especially the relative position of strength of buyer and seller. Numerous empirical studies have been undertaken to determine which role, buyer or seller, holds the *ab initio* position of strength in intracultural marketing negotiations. Graham (1981) suggests that one of the reasons for the American trade deficit with Japan was the difference in the representation of the buyer–seller relationship regarding the position of strength. The Japanese believe that strength lies with the purchaser whom the salesperson must do the utmost to satisfy, whereas the Americans envisage a more egalitarian position, as Graham (1981, p. 9) points out in his examination of which party adapts to the other in the relationship of intercultural business negotiation:

> Anthropologists tell us that power relations usually determine who adopts and adapts behavior in a cross-cultural setting. Japanese executives in an American setting are likely to be the ones to modify their behavior. ... However, if an American seller takes his normative set of bargaining behavior to Japan, then negotiations are apt to end up abruptly. The American seller expects to be treated as an equal and acts accordingly. The Japanese buyer is likely to view this rather brash behavior in a lower status seller as inappropriate and lacking in respect. The Japanese buyer is made to feel uncomfortable, and he politely shuts the door to trade, without explanation. The American seller never makes the first sale, never gets an opportunity to learn the Japanese system.

Table 14.1 gives a summary of the influence of culture on buyer–seller interactions.

Table 14.1   *A summary of the influence of culture on buyer–seller relationships*

Cultural value	Influence on seller and buyer
Inferior status for trade	Poor status for sales/selling is reserved to a minority group
Being/doing	More personal relationship oriented/more impersonal deal oriented
Money	Price bargaining as friendship ritual
Ingroup orientation	Only people from a certain ingroup are considered as adequate for sales roles/transactions have be made preferably across ingroup members
Family orientation	Buyer–seller relationships are viewed as an element of a larger family network
Short-term orientation	Achieving the sale is the paramount goal
Long-term orientation	Keeping the client is the paramount goal
Low/high power distance	Equality/inequality between buyer and seller
Listening versus talking	Soft sell versus hard sell

14.3   Sales force management in a cross-cultural perspective

Several authors in the field of international marketing have stressed the influence of culture differences on the sales force compensation systems (Still, 1981; Hill *et al.*, 1991, Cateora, 1993). The idea that the promotion of sales personnel is made on merit and that decisions are made on an objective basis is very strong in the United States. This is linked with a 'master of destiny' philosophy which underlies much of US management thinking (Cateora, 1993). People are in control of their own destiny and therefore responsible for the effective use of their own resources. In many cultures which have a more fatalistic approach to life, controlling individual performance does not seem to make sense. Uncontrollable higher-order forces largely shape our acts and future. Ali and Schwiercz (1985), for instance, report that Saudi Arabian performance and evaluation control systems work informally, without systematic controls, established criteria or definite procedures.

   The question of the influence of culture on sales force management is not considered exhaustively here. Many of its facets are infused with human resource management and therefore subject to significant cross-cultural variance. For instance, many inquiries considered in the United States as discriminatory when recruiting sales people according to a US 'affirmative action compliance program' (e.g. Chonko *et al.*, 1992, p. 410) would never be considered as discriminatory in most countries of the world. The birthplace of applicants, their marital status, age, citizenship or language competencies are standard, non-discriminatory, inquiries in most cultures where there is still some *being* orientation. The 'affirmative action, equal opportunity' programme lies on extremely strong *doing* and *outgroup* orientations, whereby it is seen as almost evil to describe persons as they *are*.

   In this section the question of what type of sales representative to employ (local versus international sales representatives) or the expatriation of sales and marketing personnel are not considered, nor is the case of the company that sells to international customers with highly qualified and often multilingual 'selling globe trotters' dealing with equipment goods, advanced technology or turnkey projects. The situation described here relates to companies that sell durable or non-durable consumer goods, equipment goods for small businesses or intermediary industrial goods. In each country where they are established, they have a local consumer base and local sales representatives, and therefore the influence of culture on salesforce compensation systems is much stronger. Problems arise when multinational companies try to unify the remuneration systems of local sales staff and when they attempt to apply a standardized incentive system linked to the parent company's culture to local sales representatives.

Incentives for sales representatives

Hofstede's (1991) parameters can be used (section 3.2) as well as Hall's theory of communication (1976) to clarify this issue, which is an organizational one. The organization must encourage its sales reps and/or the sales team to attain specific objectives (turnover target, profit target, promotion of certain products, gaining market

Table 14.2 *Contrast models*

Cultural traits	Model 1	Model 2
Power distance	Low	High
Individualism	High	Low
Uncertainty avoidance	Low	High
Context of communication	Low	High

share at the expense of competitors, etc.). There are therefore several steps which are influenced by cultural differences:

1. Setting objectives.
2. Evaluation, i.e. setting up a system to calculate target-to-actual-sales deviation followed by feedback to the salespeople.
3. Compensating the sales force achievements: designing the incentive system and attempting to standardize it across countries.
4. Implementing the sales force compensation system.

Two incentive systems for monitoring the sales force (models 1 and 2 in Table 14.2) are described below. They are Weberian 'ideal types', not necessarily to be found in their pure form in the real world. The first model is appropriate for a firm belonging to an individualistic society where communication is fairly explicit (weak context, see section 12.1), power distance is small and uncertainty avoidance is weak (e.g. the United States). Model 2 is appropriate for a company originating from a society where communication is implicit (high context), power distance is high and uncertainty avoidance is strong (e.g. Japan). One can hypothesize that the masculinity/femininity cultural dimension also influences the practical implementation of these two models of sales force compensation: assertive (masculine) and nurturing (feminine) feedback to low-performing salespeople and corrective actions are carried out differently.

Attitudes towards the setting of objectives and their use in performance measurement

The first step is the setting of sales objectives. Here, differences in the preciseness and contextuality of communication style across societies (Hall, 1976) affects the setting of objectives. Objectives that are precisely set, quantified and openly negotiated correspond to societies where people communicate fairly explicitly with a weak context. On the other hand, the stronger the tendency to communicate with a high context, the more a system based solely on numbers will seem poor. 'Number crunching' is not a trait of high-context societies: figures are not assumed to depict correctly the complexities of the real world. In high-context societies, numbers are considered as efficient, but oversimplified. Despite that, some kind of quantified objectives are needed, but they are not considered as accurate and do not serve the same purpose. According to the model (1 or 2), objectives may have different roles:

1. A role of *formal and realistic evaluation* (model 1), where the sellers must deserve their salary. In societies where relations have been relatively depersonalized people call be evaluated by figures: the bottom line is related to what an average seller is expected to attain. Target levels of sales are negotiated with the salesperson. Only results are relevant. The deviation from target to actual sales is measured precisely. Corrective actions, sanctions and rewards result from the monitoring of the salesperson's performance carried out by the boss.
2. A role of *internal incentive* (model 2), if the seller cannot easily be dismissed (societies with lifetime employment and strong uncertainty avoidance, emphasizing a high level of job security). The staff turnover is low and closer personal ties exist within a stable personnel. The risk is that sellers may seek security and lack personal initiative and drive. The objective is not openly and truly negotiated, as in model 1, since high power distance clashes with the idea that task objectives should ideally be set by oneself. It is assumed that the boss knows what the sales staff should achieve, not the salespeople themselves. The objective then is not necessarily as realistic as in model 1. The boss may manipulate by setting 'instrumental' objectives: excessively high target levels are set which serve as an ultimate level of attainment. Although everybody 'knows' that a lower performance level will be achieved, this will still be a better performance than if such an ambitious objective had not been set.

Accuracy of goal setting

After setting objectives, deviation from the target must be measured. The accuracy of systems of performance evaluation and incentive calculation is always higher in a situation of explicit communication, corresponding to model 1. This orientation rewards individual merits, even more so when the company emphasizes individual rather than team achievements. In other words, the individual is seen as the very source of the performance (see individualist assumptions detailed in section 3.1). In the case of high-context/implicit communication (model 2), the evaluation phase is not necessarily precisely and formally implemented since the objective may be significantly higher than that which can realistically be attained. In failing to attain the set objectives, sellers will, nonetheless, have employed their very best efforts. If model 1 were applied at this step only, they would be considered as underperforming. However, owing to the implicit system of evaluation, they are not considered so. There is unspoken awareness in the organization that sales objectives are not wholly realistic. No formal and quantified evaluation is implemented. Furthermore, what constitutes a good sales performance is implicitly clear within the company, making it relatively useless to assess performance very precisely.

Individualism/collectivism, uncertainty avoidance and performance measurement

The individualist or collectivist orientation in a society is a meaningful axis of cultural differentiation (Hofstede, 1991). In the United States, where individualism is very strong, the cultural emphasis is put on individual achievements (Kotabe *et al.*, 1992). It implies precise and individualized sales targets, fostering competition within the sales force. Competition between the salespeople, within the sales team, is considered legitimate, even though it may undermine the coherence of collective action when this is needed (exchange of information on customers and accounts, training other salespeople in sales practices, transfer of experience from senior salespeople to junior ones, etc.).

More traditional societies tend not to engage in individual goal setting and variable commission rewarding. Still (1981) argues that, in Thailand, family background largely determines social position, much more than money which confers only limited status. Therefore, fixed salaries, which demonstrate social status, stability and group belonging are more respectable and desirable than a larger income that includes a substantial but variable commission component, which emphasizes individualism and instability. Hill *et al.* (1991, p. 23) emphasize the following:

> Tradition is also an important determinant of Japanese compensation plans. Because their social system is based on hereditary and seniority criteria, salary raises, even for sales forces, are based on longevity with the company. Similarly commission systems are tied to the combined efforts of the entire sales force, fostering the Japanese team ethic and downplaying the economic aspirations of individuals.

Precise measurement of salespeople's performance may even be considered almost evil in some countries. In South East Asia, the ethics of non-confrontation clearly clashes with an objective review of performance. It could bring the subordinate to 'lose face' and would infringe a societal norm (Redding, 1982). Motivation theories, which in fact underlie sales force compensation systems, are culturally bound, because they were developed in the United States by Americans and for Americans (Adler, 1991). They put strong emphasis on individualism and rationalism as bases for human behaviour. According to Hofstede's empirical description of work-related values, collectivist societies such as Japan tend to favour a global stimulation of the sales force as a team. Intrinsic rewards are favoured. Conversely, more individualistic societies such as the United States will favour individual performance variables (individual sales, profits per area, etc.) and extrinsic rewards. As a consequence the marketing information systems needed to run these stimulation methods are rather different. The same retrieved information may serve different functional purposes according to the country. In Germany, very detailed market information will be sought in an attempt to reduce uncertainty in decision-making, since Germans fear uncertainty and try to avoid it (Hofstede, 1991). In the United States, where a high value is put on assertiveness and personal achievement (masculine society, with low uncertainty avoidance) the same detailed information will be used for the precise control of salespeople.

Femininity/masculinity and ways of remedying underperformance

When sellers are clearly underperforming, there are different methods to deal with the problem, particularly from the point of view of the immediate superiors. In a masculine society, the absence of results will be emphasized in a fairly crude manner. In a company where the individual is supposed to be efficient and perform well, unsatisfactory achievements will probably lead first to a clear warning that performance must be improved. Then, if the salesperson fails to come up with arguments relating to factors outside his or her control and if underperformance continues, the employee will be dismissed. This hard-line method does not, on balance, lead to better sales performance than the methods employed by companies based in feminine oriented countries.

In countries that are more femininity-oriented (Sweden, northern European countries, France), values are placed more strongly on quality of life. There is a protective and maternal attitude on the part of the organization towards its members. This does not mean, however, that these societies strive less for efficiency than masculine societies. Sellers who underperform will simply be entitled to more undertanding. Checks are initially made to see if there are any explanations, apart from their abilities as salespeople, which may excuse their weak performance, such as poor definition of a sales area with too small a potential, or particularly strong competition within the sector, etc. When the reasons for their underperformance have been assessed with them (formally or informally), they receive assistance from colleagues and from the organization (especially in the form of additional training). It is only after the organization has done everything within its power to help the salesperson to increase his or her performance that a final decision is taken.

Compensation systems based on cultural values and industry characteristics

Table 14.3 describes some basic sales force compensation systems according not only to the cultural values involved but also to the type of goods sold. Fixed salaries, for instance, will be preferred where uncertainty avoidance is high. Employees who enjoy job security have a preference for a fixed salary, possibly with a limited part of it related to variable commissions. Salespeople accept pure commission payments, with no fixed

Table 14.3   *Basic sales force compensation systems, sectors and the cultural values involved.*

Objectives/type of goods	Compensation plans	Values involved
Long-term sales efforts; equipment goods, turnkey sales	Fixed salary and promotions	Lifetime employment; cooperation within the sales-team; collective performance
Reach precise sales quotas; consumer goods	Pure (or quasi-pure) commission	Own business: no loyalty to the company; individualistic and competitive
Achieve more precise goals (sales of certain products, new territories or segments)	Fixed salary, plus monetary and non-monetary incentives	Mixed values: contract and long-term orientation; loyalty but not unlimited commitment

salary at all, only in model 1. Cultural dimensions combine with the type of industry, which also has a strong influence on the compensation system: sellers are not rewarded in the same way for the sale of nuclear plants, batteries and photocopiers. Large individual sales, requiring lengthy sales efforts and sales force teamwork, tend to be in line with straight salary compensation, as do the cultural values of model 2. Smaller individual sales, requiring individually identifiable sales efforts, tend to correspond with commission payments and the cultural values of model 1.

The rewards can be intrinsic or extrinsic. Intrinsic rewards are related to the satisfaction of inner needs. They are rewards which individuals give to themselves (Anderson and Chambers, 1985). They involve no pecuniary element and have no influence on material life. People may be intrinsically motivated by a job well done, the esteem of their colleagues or even the securing of a contract *per se*.

On the other hand, extrinsic rewards are material and are generally made in cash or in kind. They involve different forms of bonuses and commissions. Extrinsic rewards can be linear (in direct proportion to sales exceeding the objective), progressive or degressive, or can be triggered once a single objective has been attained; the criteria and formulae for calculating variable extrinsic rewards are very varied (Hill *et al.*, 1991; Chonko *et al.*, 1992). Purely extrinsic rewards, such as variable commissions on sales, are motivators which work 'from the outside'. Some rewards are on the fringe of intrinsic and extrinsic rewards: for example, medals or titles (best salesperson for the period). Rewards can be centred on the individual, on the group (e.g. a leisure trip for the whole sales team) or on a mix of both (e.g. awards for the best sales teams). As is frequently the case in Japan, group rewards may take the form of a joint holiday for the sales team which is both an individual and a group reward simultaneously, contributing to the consolidation of the intra-group relationship. Various forms can be considered for rewarding individuals: short breaks or long holidays, presents to the sellers or their relatives, payment by the company of certain personal expenditures, etc.

Models 1 and 2 depict extreme characteristics, but real-world compensation systems combine intrinsic and extrinsic, individual and collective rewards. Rewards such as promotion and salary increases combine recognition (intrinsic) and money (extrinsic). A large range of possibilities for compensation exists which can be used to design a salesforce compensation system adapted to the local culture. Two caveats must be added: (1) model 2 is not the paradise of salespeople in contrast to the extreme pressure to achieve in model 1 – nothing has to be derived from the models in terms of different salespeople's satisfaction across cultures, and/or perception of being treated fairly; and (2) standardization of sales force compensation is possible at the regional level where cultural variance is limited.

Kotabe *et al* (1992) show that the perception of equity in pay, promotion and other employment-related criteria is higher for US salespeople than for either their Japanese or Korean counterparts. US salespeople perceive that they are treated more fairly by their organizations than the Japanese, especially in terms of the pace at which their sales managers require them to perform their tasks and assignments. Japanese employees, traditionally regarded as highly motivated and productive, are also under strong pressure to perform as a way to maintain their place in the group. As for Koreans, Kotabe *et al.* (1992, p. 45) note that

... many Korean employees appear to have little control over their destinies in their organizations because of the seemingly autocratic management style and the use of non-contingent reward-based systems. Management decisions, as they relate to employees, apparently are often predicated on criteria unrelated to an individual's performance. This kind of situation may lead employees to experience inequity.

Programmes aiming at the improvement of sales force productivity can be standardized at the regional level, as shown by the example of Digital equipment corporation, for the 2,500-strong sales force of its seventeen European subsidiaries (Kashani, 1989, p. 94); they must be prepared carefully, with respect for people and their cultures:

... sales managers were at first predictably unenthusiastic about using the system. It was considered an infringement on their authority. What gradually sold them on it was the continuity of attention the program got in the two years after its highly visible launch, through watchful monitoring of progress toward full implementation, coordinating sessions among local sales managers, and periodic messages of reinforcement from top management. ... The coordinating sessions for subsidiary sales managers were particularly helpful, high-lighting the payoffs from use of the system and furnishing a forum for dealing with common problems.

14.4 Public relations across cultures

'Public relations consists of all forms of planned communication, outwards and inwards, between an organization and its publics for the purpose of achieving specific objectives concerning *mutual* understanding' (Jefkins, 1989, p. 217). The 'publics' concerned by public relations (PR) can be internal, such as employees, or external to the firm, such as the general public, customers, suppliers, distributors or the media. Other targets for PR actions are government, for the purpose of lobbying about new or existing legislation, or stockholders and the financial community. The function of public relations in a cross-national, and therefore most often a cross-cultural context, is made difficult especially in terms of *mutual* understanding. The functions of PR are twofold: (1) in normal situations, to create and enhance a favourable corporate image with the various publics concerned, with the view that a foreign firm is easily susceptible to nationalistic criticism; (2) in crisis situations such as boycott, accidents, strikes, product recalls, and so on, to maintain goodwill by responding to criticism, explaining remedial action that is taken to overcome the problem, and anticipating and countering messages that may damage the corporate image.

Cross-cultural differences can been noted in the way companies react to disasters such as airplane crashes, major pollution, etc. They reflect the prevailing sense of responsibility *vis-à-vis* the community but also the companies' sense of secrecy and the view of what is culturally adequate in front of these events: adopting a very low profile and waiting for the tempest to calm down or adopting a high profile, pleading either guilty or unguilty. Swiss pharmaceutical companies, when confronted with major pollution in the Rhine river which were allegedly their fault, have adopted an extremely low profile, with very little communication, reflecting the Swiss penchant for secrecy and dislike for public display. When JAL suffered its worst-ever crash in 1985, with 520 dead, the JAL response was very elaborate, going far beyond what Westerners would expect in such situations, including the dismissal of its president and public apologies to the Japanese people (Pinsdorf, 1991).

PR enters the scene as a very different form of communication: it is not advertising, or salesmanship. PR people, a full-time officer or an outside PR consultant, have nothing to sell. They use publicity as a means which is the securing of editorial space, but also any kind of films, videotapes, slides conveying messages to the publics, as well as the organization of events, meetings, conferences, sponsorship. The Channel Tunnel, for instance, burdened as it has been with financial problems and construction delay, has had to do public relations with the two basic stockholder communities, French and British, and with the international banks that are financing the project. A lot may differ cross-culturally, including the very notion of PR which is rooted in modern corporate culture, and may be unknown in particular cultural contexts.

Cultural variance for selected aspects of the PR process may be the following: (1) the recommendations in making contact are basically the same as in section 14.2, except that the PR officer sells nothing which may make the contact both easier (there is no money involved) and less efficient (PR may be considered as purposeless); (2) managing relationships; (3) disclosing information, especially in the case of private, secret or sensitive information; (4) developing arguments some of which cannot be understood locally; and (5) dealing with nationalistic feelings.

Managing relationships: thinking locally

For people coming from western countries, where outgroup is strong, it is not natural to think in terms of who is a member of which groups: working with the key ethnic groups is, however, a key element for good PR in many foreign contexts. The model of a free press must also be partly abandoned: in many countries its freedom is curtailed by the government, often in much more subtle ways than mere censorship. Also the influence of local competition shall not be underestimated: the lack of antitrust laws in many countries reflects the legitimacy of making market-sharing or price agreements with competitors and the lack of concern with the benefits for consumers of 'fair trade'; consequently, PR officers may be involved in talks with competing firms which would be considered as unethical in the United States because they infringe the antitrust legislation. It is all the more important when the local competitors are technologically inferior to the foreign firm but can play their nationalistic legitimacy against a foreign intruder.

When making arguments, PR officers should avoid (1) disclosing unnecessarily information which is considered by local parties as due to remain secret, the sense of confidentiality being culturally relative; (2) making arguments which are not understood because their basic logic does clash with the host country culture; and (3) conveying messages that are perceived as negative about local people and culture.

Foreign firms have to face nationalism: being foreign makes things slightly worse for a company when it is under attack. When Audi cars faced the problem of sudden acceleration with its 5000 series in the United States, the German company, a subsidiary of the Volkswagen group did not adopt a low profile, convinced as it was of the high quality of its engineering. It took a very negative stance against the sixty minute CBS broadcast that showed problems of sudden acceleration and interviewed drivers, attacking the tests made for this programme. Audi further denied the allegations, attributing sudden acceleration to the negligence of the drivers. Finally Audi took action too late and recalled 25,000 cars in January 1987. The market response was dramatic and sales in the United States dropped from 74,000 in 1985 to 23,000 in 1988 (Czinkota and Ronkainen, 1990).

Ambiguous arguments must be avoided as much as taking too strong a position. If the local employees of a multinational company receive better pay than the average worker in the country, this can be seen as beneficial to these people individually but detrimental to the collectivity as whole, because for instance it lures farmers to the industrial sector, or it causes merchants to raise their prices because of the purchasing power of a small affluent group.

Emphasizing local citizenship is always necessary: it must be done with unambiguous arguments such as IBM which emphasized in the mid-1980s in European countries its importance as a local employer, citing the number of employees in each country and the local R & D efforts. Such a view of local citizenship embodied in a global attitude was expressed by Percy Barnevik, the Swedish-born president and chief executive officer of ABB (the merger of Asea (Sweden) and Brown Boveri (Switzerland)), when he was asked by William Taylor (1991, p. 91), the associate editor of the *Harvard Business Review*, what it means to be a global company:

> ABB is a company with no geographic center, no national ax to grind. We are a federation of national companies with a global coordination center. Are we a Swiss company? Our headquarters is in Zurich, but only 100 professionals work at headquarters and we will not increase that number. Are we a Swedish company? I'm the CEO and I was born and educated in Sweden. But our headquarters is not in Sweden, and only two members of our board of directors are Swedes. Perhaps we are an American company. We report our financial results in U.S. dollars, and English is ABB's official language. We conduct all high-level meetings in English. My point is that ABB is none of those things – and all of those things. We are not homeless. We are a company with many homes.

Facing social responsibility in a culturally alien context: The case of Bhophal

The case of Union Carbide Corporation (UCC), one of America's largest chemical multinationals, with their factory in Bhopal on Sunday, 2 December 1984, is a good case in point for showing what are the problems involved in facing social responsibility, an 'extreme form' of PR. Union Carbide India Limited (UCIL), under pressure from the Indian authorities, had built a new factory in 1978 to produce pesticides in Bhopal, the capital of Madhya Pradesh, a town situated 375 miles (600 km) south of New Delhi. It produced Sevin, a pesticide composed primarily of methyl isocyanate, extremely dangerous for humans and to be carefully kept in liquid form below 25 degrees Celsius. The project was plagued by problems of safety from the outset: in 1978, its year of construction, a huge fire broke out. Five major gas leaks in 1981 and 1983 left one dead, and forty-seven injured. In 1982, a detailed inspection by American experts uncovered ten serious faults in the factory's safety systems. In fact, the factory's alarm system was ringing so often that people living in the vicinity of the factory treated it almost as background noise.

The Indian government imposed restrictions on foreign companies, limiting their direct participation by requiring that they negotiate local partnerships. UCC was able to continue operating in India only by agreeing to the formation of a new company, Union Carbide India Limited (UCIL), in which UCC was reduced to a majority shareholder with 50.09 per cent of the share capital. A further 22 per cent went to the government and the remainder was divided among 23,500 private Indian investors. Bhopal's social and political environment developed rapidly as a result of the factory. Attracted by the availability of work and the water and electricity which were supplied to the site at reduced rates, people poured in to the surrounding area. As a consequence, the population grew from 385,000 in 1971 to 671,000 in 1981. By 1984, it stood at nearly 800,000. From its original position of isolation, the factory was soon totally enveloped by the town's growth. Creaking under the strain of this huge influx of population, the town struggled to accommodate everyone. In the absence of a better alternative, the poorest of the new arrivals congregated in 'Khasi Camp', a shanty town situated between the centre of Bhopal and the factory.

Links between UCIL and the local Indian political establishment were mutually rewarding in many ways. The factory's legal adviser, for instance, was a former local head of Indira Gandhi's Congress Party. The former local Police Chief magically won the contract to guard the factory. One of the nephews of the former State Education Minister was the head of public relations at the factory.

There were also financial difficulties. In 1982, a slump in sales of its products resulted in the factory suffering a dramatic reduction in profitability. UCC, the parent company of UCIL, even considered shutting the plant down completely, but the Indian government refused to countenance such a possibility for fear of frightening away potential foreign investors. To balance the books, UCIL determined to reduce the factory's overheads. They chose to make many of their most qualified personnel redundant. These vacant posts were then either filled by less experienced personnel or simply scrapped. The consequent loss of morale and expertise amongst the workforce adversely affected work at the factory.

News of these unfortunate mishaps was carefully suppressed thanks to the close working relationship between UCIL and the local authorities. The Indian authorities would even extend UCIL's operating licence for a further seven years despite objections from the Press and opposition members in the State Parliament.

The incident took place in the night of 2 December 1984. Water in substantial quantities was mixed by error with methyl isocyanate, causing high pressure, the explosion of the vessel, and massive leaks of lethal gas in the surroundings of the factory. The local population had no idea of what to do in the event of a serious incident at the factory: simply putting a wet cloth on the face would have protected a great many people.

Even the local doctors were completely ignorant about the effects of the product being manufactured on their doorsteps. Warren Anderson, the chief executive officer of UCC, courageously decided to go to India. That proved not to be the good decision: in case of major problems one should not react on the basis of home country behavioural standards (see Box 14.4).

In the case of Bhophal, Union Carbide had in fact little direct and active responsibility: it had been obliged to build a factory that was basically managed by Indians, with almost no say for the foreign partner who became passive. Public relations in such a context were extremely difficult to organize since most hard facts arguments may seem insults to the Indian management, public authorities, doctors or even to the general Indian public. The solution was found in complex litigation: each party argued that the case should be heard in the jurisdiction of the other. Finally, UCC came out with the favourable decision that the final judgments be made in India where relevant jurisprudence was almost non-existent. On 14 February 1989, the Indian Supreme Court rendered its judgment: the American defendants were found liable and ordered to pay a total of US$470 million, US$50 million was to be paid in rupees by UCIL and US$415 million by UCC; the remaining US$5 million had been paid under the previous order of the American Federal Court as first aid to the victims. Many people found that the final award was rather low. For example, if this sum represented only those killed in the incident, it would be roughly equivalent to US$130,000 per victim. If it included those permanently disabled, the amount would represent only US$18,000 per person and if it was intended to compensate every injured person, it would represent an average of US$1,350 per person. It is always recommendable (1) to treat safety problems as key issues from the very start, and (2) at any cost to avoid an all-litigation solution whose complexity is not understood by the general public and is interpreted as a lack of interest for the victims (see litigation issues in section 15.7).

Box 14.4   *Coming to Bhophal: A mistake*

Following the disaster, the State government of Madhya Pradesh carefully drew up an initial list of the human cost of this night of horror. The toll was a heavy one: they estimated that 3,828 people had been killed and 358,712 injured. Of these, 22,955 were left with a permanent disability. A single night of tragedy in Bhopal had claimed 362,540 victims. Ten years on, the government believes that about 6,600 people were killed in the incident. Bhopal pressure groups put the death toll at 16,000 and still rising by a few each week. They claim that up to 600,000 people – more than half the city – suffered damage to their lungs, eyes and immune systems.

On 4 December 1984, Warren Anderson flew to Bhopal with a team of experts to try and discover the cause of the tragedy. His efforts were in vain. Anderson was arrested and imprisoned, then finally expelled. It was not until 20 December that the Indian authorities allowed a Commission of Enquiry to begin its work on site. They arrived to find that the factory had been closed since 6 December and was already being dismantled.

(Source: excerpt from Usunier and Verna, 1994.)

The case of product liability

Product liability is a case in point where public relations are needed. Nestlé, the Swiss food company, one of the largest in the world, faced a boycott because its infant feeding formula had allegedly caused many deaths of babies in the Third World. In 1974, a report by a British journalist and a pamphlet entitled 'Nestlé kills babies' started an accusation process that developed through the mid-1970s. Nestlé withdrew its infant formula advertising and decided to participate in consumer education programmes. The key reasons for Nestlé Third World consumers' problems were cultural: the belief in the magic properties of western products and the pressure to give what is the best, the most modern, as a sign of love for babies. A more down to earth reason was the poor use of the product, mixed with contaminated water. Nestlé should have anticipated the key reasons for misuses of its, otherwise excellent, product: (1) illiteracy – people just cannot read the instructions for use; (2) even when literate, people rarely rely on written material which have an abstract image; and (3) the inability to cope with ambiguous messages (the product is good but can be bad). This is a problem for pharmaceutical companies: most drugs have side effects. However, in many countries it is dangerous to mention them too explicitly since people will not believe in a drug whose manufacturer clearly acknowledges the potentially adverse consequences (most of which can be avoided by proper use!).

14.5 Bribery: Facts

Bribery is associated with selling, obtaining favours, making things work: it is a practice which can be found in almost all cultures. The German call it *Schmiergeld* ('grease money'), the French *pot-de-vin* (literally jug of wine), in the middle East it is a *baksheesh*, in Italy a *Bastarella* (little envelope) and in Mexico a *mordida* (a bite). These practices know few borders and even the Japanese construction industry has been heavily plagued with bribery scandals in recent years. Naturally every country officially prohibits bribery, but laws are locally enforced. Principles are often universal, whereas their enforcement may be a matter of place (see Tables 3.6 and 3.7 on the types of rules).

Facts

Information and data on illegal payments is very sparse and often fragmentary. Such issues are sensitive and companies remain very secretive. Factual data have, however been collected, both through the investigations carried out by financial journalists (Péan, 1988) and academic researchers (Walter, 1989), and more systematically in the United States, as a consequence of prosecutions under the Foreign Corrupt Practices Act 1977 (Gillespie, 1987).

The practice is too widespread to be ignored. It takes various forms:

1. *Small and large gifts*: Beaudeux (1980) reports in the following way the remarks of the director of international operations of a large multinational company: 'It is

common practice for a permanent secretary or a leading (foreign) politician to be offered two weeks at a hotel in Paris, and also lent a limousine for the duration of his stay, which ultimately he will always forget to give back'; likewise the general manager of an engineering company states:

> These stopovers in Europe seem to be trivial affairs, but when you add in all the additional expenses: receptions, restaurants and, above all, pretty hostesses for an evening, you are talking about at least 500 or 600 pounds a day! A Secretary of State has just announced his arrival. We gave a sigh of relief when he told us that he had come with his wife! A Nigerian official left us a bill for 15,000 pounds for a twelve day stay.

2. *Percentages* based on the contract value itself. Here the form of illegal payments result in much larger sums being paid because of the size of the contract (sale of a squadron of fighter planes, or a turnkey plant, etc.). Indeed, in the United States, in the public disclosure of the illegal payments involving American multinationals in the 1970s, sums of up to 70 million dollars were mentioned. The companies involved were, amongst others, Lockheed, United Brands, Gulf Oil. There were many other firms implicated, principally in the mining, aeronautic and engineering sectors. The famous Lockheed scandal destabilized Japan's Prime Minister, Tanaka, Prince Bernhardt in Holland, the Christian-Democrat parties in Germany and Italy, and even President Lopez of the Honduras.

Beaudeux (1980) quotes the official of an American multinational, who considered Venezuela and Mexico as major centres in South America for 'baksheesh'; with percentages tending to settle around the 10 to 15 per cent mark. At the time there also seemed to be widespread corruption in Uruguay and Paraguay since according to the experts, even in deals of around 25 million pounds, a third of the total would be laundered through a nominee company, acting as a figurehead, keeping the money safe before its collection by high-ranking South American civil servants.

3. *Tips*: when civil servants are poorly paid, but hold authority and responsibility (e.g. a police officer, a customs officer, or a tax inspector) it may be 'implicitly understood' that in exchange for carrying out poorly rewarded public duties, such officials may supplement their income. Thus when passing through customs, obtaining a tax form (for a mandatory declaration) may require some greasing payment, which can be assimilated to an implicit salary, in so far as the authorities are perfectly well aware of the existence of such practices. In China in 1993, more than 60,000 cases of civil servant corruption were unveiled, with more than a half million people being under investigation and more than 10,000 already tried before a court (Galtung, 1994).

Methods

Whether illegal payments are made and what sums are involved vary very widely from one country and one industrial sector to another. They will be much more substantial, for example, in the construction industry or in Nigeria than in electronics or in Australia. Also the important caveat must be added that not everyone is corrupt. There is nothing worse than attempting to bribe someone who strongly disapproves of such immoral behaviour. This last point is clearly illustrated by Agpar (1977) who quotes the case of the Managing Director of a large American multinational who offered 500 Saudi Riyals in cash to a Saudi police officer (about US$140) so as to ensure that a decision on a fairly minor offence against labour law would be favourable. In a fury, the officer reported the attempted bribe to his superiors. After spending twenty days in prison, the businessman was sentenced to a fine of 25,000 Riyals and was fortunate to escape a more serious penalty.

This case clearly demonstrates the danger and also the ineffectiveness of the direct method (passing cash from one hand to another). Accordingly, more indirect methods exist instead:

1. Slush funds are set up to effect small payments by cheque, nominally as payment for services rendered. In the 1980s, for instance, Braniff Airlines sold 3,500 plane tickets in South America for a total of US$900,000 without making any record of the transactions in their accounts. This money was used to set up a slush fund that in turn fed a secret bank account. This money was mentioned neither in the parent company accounts, nor in those of the subsidiary. This secret account was used to pay additional commissions to organizers and travel agents in clear breach of the Federal Aviation Act.
2. The transfer of 'brown paper packets' (English expression) is often made by an intermediate consultancy company. These companies often have their head office in Luxemburg or Liechtenstein, or in some other tax haven. The consultancy company is often involved right from the tender stage in the case of a factory or turnkey project. Consider the scenario where one of the key decision-makers for the final selection of the foreign contractor controls a local construction consultancy company. During a reception, this person will whisper to the head of the negotiating team of a large engineering or construction company he is dealing with that it would be advantageous if his consultancy company were to be requested to carry out preliminary technical studies. These studies will in fact be largely fictitious. The fees paid for these studies will correspond to the commission. If these studies are further sub-contracted to a nominee company in Luxemburg, the baksheesh money will be transferred to a 'safe place'.
3. Nominee and local consultancy companies, to whom 'phoney' consulting contracts are given, may be used in different ways. For example an approach may be made to an adviser of the Transport Minister for country X who is well placed to influence the decision on an underground railway project in town Y. It will be suggested that he be made a part-time employee of the Luxemburg-based nominee company. Without having to move at all he will receive a salary each month which, for reasons of discretion and convenience, will be paid into an account in Switzerland. When going skiing with his family, the adviser/consultant will take the money out of his bank account in Geneva, then discreetly spend it in an exclusive ski-resort. Money spent abroad is less compromising than money brought back home.
4. Two other accounting solutions are frequently employed (Daniels *et al.*, 1982): the over-invoicing of certain transactions, expenditure or receipts, and the recording of fictitious transactions. For example, the American Hospital Supply company was

obliged to pay a 10 per cent commission to obtain the contract for the construction of
a hospital in Saudi Arabia. AHS artificially inflated the price of the contract, then
recorded a commission for consultancy fees, even though no service of this type had
been rendered. This allowed the 10 per cent commission to become tax-deductible
expenditure, and made the payment apparently legitimate, whereas in fact it remained
illegal.

14.6   Bribery: Ethical aspects

Bribery is considered by most businesspeople as a key ethical issue in international
marketing. According to Mayo *et al.* (1991), more than one-third of a sample of US
executives ranked bribery as the top ethical concern out of ten possible ethical problems
that may arise in international marketing operations.

   The first ethical position is that of cultural relativism: whether it is right or wrong,
good or bad, depends on one's culture. This is based on the view that rules are applicable
locally in the ingroup territory and thus 'when in Rome, do as Romans do'. The first sub-
section tries to give a view of cultural relativism in the case of Africa where corrupt
money is largely, but not completely, redistributed in society. However, one cannot
ignore the negative consequences of such widespread corrupt practices. Galtung (1994)
and others show the heavy burden placed by corruption on economic development: for
instance, the property of President Mobutu Sese Seko of Zaire is said to be equivalent to
the whole of the external debt of the country. A second position is therefore cultural
universalism, which is based on the view that there are core ethical principles which are
universally applicable, whenever and to whomever, independently of territory and group
membership. The Foreign Corrupt Practices Act of 1977, revised in 1988, is an example
of such universalist approach to ethics *and* rules. The third possible view is a pragmatic
and respectful view of how ethical behaviour can be developed in a cross-cultural
context.

Cultural relativism: The bribe as bonanza

There is often a tendency to oversimplify the issue of international corruption to one of
a face-to-face meeting between two people, a donor and a recipient. In reality the donor
of the baksheesh often faces a group of recipients. The benefit of an illegal payment has
a group aspect. It rarely benefits one single person. As a result bribery is intermingled
with a dense network of social relationships:

1. Bonds of fraternity and complicity between people of the same ethnic background or
   tribe. These people are necessary intermediaries for ensuring that the influences, the
   information search and the handing over of the baksheesh may all be effectively
   implemented.
2. Bonds of everyday cooperation, which call for redistribution of small parts of the
   bribe. The secretary who guesses the existence of the baksheesh, the customs officer
   who intercepts a 'brown paper parcel', etc. However, each should take their part

proportionately to their level of influence and power in the society and should take care not to exaggerate (Box 14.5).

3. Bonds caused by potential retaliation; those who have not requested a baksheesh, but who have a strong suspicion as to its existence, may either inform the authorities or exert a sort of implicit blackmail by demanding their 'cut'. They may even take no action by simply closing their eyes to what is happening. They are guided by their rationality: they can either take the risk of participation in illegal remuneration and benefit personally; exert blackmail and thereby take the risk of offending those in power leading to ultimate punishment; or lastly inform against the bribee and suffer any adverse consequences that may result.

Primitive civilizations of hunting and harvesting that are described by ethnologists can be used as an archetype for the redistribution of a bribe considered as plunder. While the men hunt (symbolically: those who hold power and go 'hunting' for large sums), the women, children and the elderly devote their efforts instead to harvesting (symbolically: those who collaborate on menial levels, but are still aware of what is happening). Ultimately the bribe/plunder is divided up according to fairly precise rules. Redistributing plunder and crops among the members of one's tribe is basic moral behaviour in many countries (see Box 14.6).

Box 14.5 *'Article 15'*

On the banks of the large (Zaire) river just as in the province of Shaba, no one in Zaire is surprised to see a civil servant demanding a 'matabiche' in return for a passport or some other official document. On the contrary, people would be worried if such a request was not made. No Zairian would take offence at having to pay for an official hearing, or to have a letter sent to a department head. Seals and headed note paper are bought and are even sometimes forged. In Zaire, civil servants are 'resourceful people' and know how to supplement their income. The police set up roadblocks when they need money: drivers never have the requisite paper and are therefore obliged to put their hands in their pockets.

At the main post office in 'Kin' (Kinshasa, the capital), letters and parcels may – like anywhere else in the world – be posted in a box, but it is less than certain that they will ever arrive at their destination. The 'citizen' (in Zaire, the 'Supreme Guide' has brought into fashion this revolutionary title) greatly increases the chances of this occurring if he greases the palm of the postman. Likewise, a citizen may make a telephone call to the other end of the planet for the price of a tip. All this comes under 'Article 15' a shameful way of designating the small scale corruption practised by civil servants. This corruption is institutionalised and widespread; it also goes under the name of 'matabiche': bribe, backhander, a 'little something', brown paper packet.

The practice is so ingrained that President Mobutu did not shy away from encouraging it in a speech on the 20th May 1976: 'If you are going to steal, steal a small amount and do it intelligently, in a nice way. If you are going to steal so much that you become rich in a single night, you will be arrested.'

(Source: excerpt from Péan, 1988, pp. 139–40. Reproduced with permission.)

Box 14.6   *A good minister in Senegal*

> For the man in the street, a good minister is a demagogue, someone who is adept at
> by-passing the law and its rulings to keep the voters from his region, his parents and
> his friends happy. If you try to behave like a minister acting objectively by treating
> your cousins, your allies, members of the branch of your party in the same way as all
> other citizens, even political opponents, the people will be totally confused. You will
> not be understood. You are not respecting the rules of the game. You will be the
> object of public contempt. You are not a minister for the purpose of serving the nation
> or carrying out the policies of a government which is in power for the good of all its
> citizens. You are first and foremost a minister for your own good, so that you may take
> advantage of your position, and enable your parents and allies, your friends and the
> members of your party to benefit too. No one will reproach you, everyone will
> understand. Those who are out of office are the only ones who will criticise this
> behaviour although if they were in office themselves they could not be sure of
> resisting the demands of their own tribe, family, or parents-in-law. There is nothing
> wrong in taking advantage of one's position to help out one's relatives; the ideal
> would be to consider all citizens as your own relatives.

(Source: excerpt from Ndao, 1985, pp. 34–5. Reproduced with permission.)

Anti-corrupt action and cultural universalim: The FCPA

The United States has been brave enough to look into the problems of business ethics
posed by illegal payments. In the mid-1970s the Attorney General's enquiry into the
Watergate affair revealed that suspect payments had been made to foreign politicians by
large American companies. In 1977 the FCPA (Foreign Corrupt Practices Act) made it
illegal for companies to influence foreign officials by personal payments or transfers of
money to political groups. This law obliges firms to institute an internal accounting
control. The FCPA's definition of what constitutes bribery is very wide. It does, however,
exclude small payments known as 'backhanders' and tips paid to minor civil servants to
speed up customs clearance or any administrative formalities.

After the introduction of this legislation, over forty articles appeared in the management literature in the United States criticizing the FCPA on the basis that it was
detrimental for American companies abroad (Gillespie, 1987). The following are among
the arguments that derive from this business pragmatism:

1. Kaikati and Label (1980) claimed that the FCPA placed American companies at a
   competitive disadvantage as compared with European or Japanese competitors. In
   France, Switzerland or (West) Germany, although illegal payments paid to nationals
   were illegal and not tax deductible, those paid to foreign officials were.
2. Jacoby *et al.* (1979) pointed out that in response to the FCPA the majority of
   American multinationals substantially reduced or eliminated these practices. Either
   they abandoned certain export businesses, or they turned their former agents into
   separate companies, independent of themselves, who could buy and sell in their own
   right, or sometimes they even abandoned their long-standing competency as a prime

contractor and acted as simple sub-contractor for French, German, Japanese or Korean companies.

3. A further frequent criticism of the FCPA is that it has destabilized political regimes that are friendly to the United States. It is alleged that the leaders of these countries were sometimes forced into making compromising revelations.

Gillespie (1987), studying affairs of corruption in the Middle East for the last ten years, carried out an analysis of about sixty cases of corruption where foreign companies were involved. She concluded that arguments against the FCPA were not strictly borne out by the facts. Some regimes remained stable despite major scandals (e.g. Turkey, Egypt, Saudi Arabia), others fell (in the case of the Shah of Iran) for more deep-rooted reasons. Furthermore, the study made by Gillespie of the changes in the export market share of the United States (in comparison with its major international competitors) showed that US foreign trade with the Middle East had not been adversely affected by the FCPA.

Comparison of ethical attitudes across industrial nations

The ethical attitudes within the major developed countries towards illegal payments are not uniform (Lee, 1981). Up to recently, in France, Germany or Switzerland, bribery was simply seen as a cost of doing business abroad and could be claimed as a corporate tax deduction. The French call it FCE, *frais commerciaux exceptionnels* ('exceptional sales expenses'), and it was not only deductible from corporate income, up to recently, but also eligible for export credit insurance in case the foreign client takes the bribe but does not pay for the contract (Usunier and Verna, 1994). US managers tend to adopt stronger ethical standpoints than their European and Japanese counterparts. Becker and Fritzsche (1987) suggested a scenario which posed a business ethics problem linked to an illegal payment. Three sample groups of businessmen were interviewed, one from the United States (124 respondents), one from West Germany (70 respondents) and one from France (72 respondents). The scenario was as follows:

> The Rollfast Bicycle company has been barred from entering the market in a large Asian country by collusive efforts of the local bicycle manufacturers. Rollfast could expect to net 5 million dollars per year from sales if it could penetrate the market. Last week a business man from the country contacted the management of Rollfast and stated that he could smooth the way for the company to sell in his country for a price of $500,000. If you were responsible, what are the chances that you would pay the price? (Becker and Fritzsche, 1987, p. 89)

While the replies from the French and German managers differed little, those of the Americans indicated that they were, by and large, less prepared to pay the secret payment. While 47 per cent of the American respondents gave as an explanation that this was unethical, illegal and contrary to the corporate code of conduct, 38 per cent of Germans and 55 per cent of the French thought either that 'the competition would force us to accept', or that 'it's simply the price you have to pay for doing business'.

France and West Germany have legislation prohibiting the bribing of public civil servants, but these regulations do not apply extraterritorially. French and German businessmen cannot be prosecuted for bribes effected outside their national territory. Conversely, the FCPA as well as numerous other American regulations (anti-trust, fiscal . . .) does have extraterritorial application. Despite the fact that FCPA increases the probability of disclosure, the corruption scandals in the Middle East have by no means involved only the United States. Gillespie (1987) notes that the affairs of corruption in the Middle East involving European or Asiatic multinationals were revealed either locally or by newspapers in the countries making the payments. In not one of the scandals that she studied (for the period 1970–85; forty-two involving American companies, twenty-nine involving European or Asiatic companies) were Americans imprisoned, whereas Europeans or Asians were put in prison in seven instances.

Pragmatic and respectful ethical behaviour in a cross-cultural context

The first consideration is pragmatic: businesspeople who make illegal payments take (real) personal risks for (potential) organizational benefits, either through company loyalty or personal interest (sales commission or promotion). Doing this, they (1) involve their company in the risk of being implicated in a scandal; and (2) risk themselves being implicated, indicted, imprisoned and ultimately sentenced to a long term of imprisonment. In the case of turnkey sales, the favourite domain for big bribes, it is important to clarify the mandate for negotiation which is given to the project negotiators by the engineering company or consortium of contractors. As one may put it in straightforward terms: 'If you must grease palms do it right.' Unless the negotiators actually bring up the bribery issues directly and openly, the exact extent of their powers and responsibility will be insufficiently clarified. The executives who sell factories or turnkey equipment often 'go into battle' with little prior warning or protection. An illustration of this is given by Beaudeux (1980) who quotes the case of a British business engineer who negotiated a 50 million dollar contract in Algeria.

> I knew that my competitor's offer was about 40 million dollars and I battled for several weeks to convince the purchaser that I was overall the cheapest. So afterwards I was absolutely outraged, as well as scared to death (you know what they do to bribers in Algeria), when I learned on my return that my head office had negotiated over my head, and that the true price was 40 million. The other 10 million was the baksheesh that we had paid to win the order.

The payment of a baksheesh always involves the individual responsibility of the donor, even if his or her company, or the consortium that he or she represents, also risks being drawn into the scandal. As Graham (1983) states: 'From a legal standpoint, the recommendation is clear – avoid questionable deals. The loss of the few "questionable" contracts is not worth the risk of indictment, prosecution, conviction. . . . Moreover, if you are indicted, will your company support you or opt to plead guilty and accept the fine?' A pragmatic view for an individual requires reference to a personal norm, not a corporate one. Useful guidelines for those confronted with this issue are provided by the definition of a 'moral personality' proposed by John Rawls in his *A Theory of Justice*

(1971). A moral personality is characterized by two capacities, namely the capacity to conceive good and the capacity to develop a sense of justice. The first is realized through a rational project for one's life. The second implies a continuing desire to act in a way that one believes is just. Thus for Rawls, a moral personality has chosen his or her own goals; and he or she prefers those conditions which enable him or her to fully express his or her nature of rational, free and equal being. The unity of the person is then manifested by the coherence of his or her project. This unity is based on a higher-order aspiration to follow the principles of rational choice in a way which is suitable with his or her sense of justice. It means that if you are asked to do something which violates your sense of right and wrong, it is better not to do it, even if it means not behaving as a Roman in Rome.

A final remark: Rawls's definition of a 'moral personality' remains a rather western one, in that rationality, individualism and the sense of equality with others are strongly emphasized. In many other cultural contexts, where moral personalities actually exist, these traits would not be emphasized in such a definition.

There is unfortunately no common international legal framework which can circumvent bribery. Moreover, national based legal texts, since they simply prohibit or permit certain acts, do not explain how to behave in the real world. The only universal sources for guiding one's behaviour are for instance the guidelines which stem from United Nations codes and from some analyses which provide the basis for the identification of ethical issues, based on case studies. Ethical conflicts must therefore largely be documented on a moral rather than purely legal basis, keeping in mind that moral judgements are partly universal, partly culturally relative.

Questions

1. Indicate elements of variation in selling styles (including basic views of what is a buyer–seller interaction, the kind of arguments developed and the communication style).
2. Personal selling often plays a more important role in foreign rather than domestic markets. Why?
3. Discuss the limitations to the standardization of a sales force stimulation system.
4. Discuss how a strong emphasis on group belonging in a particular culture may influence the recruitment of salespeople.
5. What is the borderline between a 'gift' and a 'bribe'? Outline possible criteria for defining such a border which allow for some cross-national flexibility.
6. How can bribery be related to space-related cultural assumptions?
7. WTD, a large US multinational chemical company, has been recently attacked in several large Latin American countries where it has plants. The company has been attacked by the local press for alleged pollution and poor safety conditions for employees. Arguments have been made that WTD has much lower standards in these areas than in the US and that the company shows its Yankee and imperialist orientation in such choices. The company executive officers think it is largely wrong: inadequate local legislation and poor respect of safety rules by local employees have

caused problems rather than a deliberate neglect on WTD's part. Advise the firm on a public relations programme.

8. Discuss the cultural relativity of the framework for a manager facing an ethical dilemma, who should ask the following questions:
   - What are the **facts**; what are my alternatives?
   - What parties will be affected?
   - What do **I** owe to each of these parties?
   - What would produce the greatest **benefits** for **all** parties?
   - What **rights** does each party have, and how can these rights best be **respected**?
   - Are all parties treated **fairly** and **justly**?
   - On balance, what is the most **ethical** alternative?
   - How do **I** best **implement** this alternative?

In bold are those words which offer the best route for questioning about the cultural relativity of this framework.

APPENDIX 14

Teaching materials

A14.1   Case: When international buyers and sellers disagree

No matter what line of business you're in, you can't escape sex. That may have been one conclusion drawn by an American exporter of meat products after a dispute with a West German customer over a shipment of pork livers. Here's how the disagreement came about:

The American exporter was contracted to ship '30,000 lbs. of freshly frozen U.S. pork livers, customary merchandisable quality, first rate brands.' As the shipment that was prepared met the exacting standards of the American market, the exporter expected the transaction to be completed without any problem.

But when the livers arrived in West Germany, the purchaser raised an objection: 'We ordered pork livers of customary merchantable quality – what you send us consisted of 40 percent sow livers.

'Who cares about the sex of the pig the liver came from?' the exporter asked.

'We do,' the German replied. 'Here in Germany we don't pass off spongy sow livers as the firmer livers of male pigs. This shipment wasn't merchantable at the price we expected to charge. The only way we were able to dispose of the meat without a total loss was to reduce the price. You owe us a price allowance of $1,000.'

The American refused to reduce the price. The determined resistance may have been partly in reaction to the implied insult to the taste of the American consumer: 'If pork livers, whatever the sex of the animal, are palatable to Americans, they ought to be good enough for anyone,' the American thought.

It looked as if the buyer and seller could never agree on eating habits.

(Source: reproduced with the kind permission of the Dun and Bradstreet Corporation.)

Questions

1. What does 'customary merchandisable quality' mean? Where? In which language and cultural context?
2. Discuss how ethnocentrism and SRC (self-reference criterion) are at work in this case.
3. In this dispute, which country's law would apply, that of the United States or of Germany?
4. If the case were tried in US courts, who do you think would win? And if tried in German courts? Why?
5. Is formal litigation justified in such a case? How can one solve this problem? How can one avoid this type of conflict in the future?

A14.2   Critical incident: Setco of Spain

Planning target sales for the sales force is a universal practice. Nobody questions it. So it was when Mr Gonzales, a Spaniard, was recruited by Setco of Spain, the Spanish subsidiary of a large US multinational company. Soon after his job began, he was assigned a product line, of which he had some experience, in a new sales territory. The sales manager of Setco of Spain did not know precisely the market potential of this new area. Until then, potential customers in this area had never been regularly visited. Moreover few indicators were available in order to estimate the market potential of this new area in a quantified and precise manner.

When he first met the sales manager for Spain, Gonzales was amazed by his friendly tone; dialogue within the sales team and horizontal communication were the rules. Instead of being set an objective, he was invited to give his opinion on the matter. In fact, he could set his quarterly sales target himself, after visiting the area and making some preliminary contacts with prospects. Because of the newness of this area, the sales manager made no comment. Gonzales was confronted with a new freedom: in his previous positions as sales representative, he had never fixed his own sales targets by himself. He had always been given targets by his boss. His reaction was therefore to reduce significantly the objective relative to the sales he was reasonably expecting, in order to retain some leeway. . . .

After four months, actual sales per area were released. Gonzales was surprised to see that he received a detailed report on his sales figures (he was used to this, since it was basic data for computing possible bonuses) but also his target sales, and the difference between actual and target sales. It looked flattering. The individual achievements of the other members of the sales team were mentioned in this memo as well. They did not match that of Gonzales.

At the meeting of the sales force, quarterly sales were examined, as well as the targets for the next quarter and the marketing programme. Gonzales was surprised to see how embarrassing his 'performance' appeared to the other sales representatives. Never had any sales representative at Setco of Spain so largely overshot the mark. He was teased by his colleagues, who made some bittersweet remarks and jokes. He felt bad about it, especially because he had been trying hard. He had used all his skills as a salesman, which were considerable and had been proved in his previous positions.

During the discussions, he acknowledged that his area's market potential had been largely underestimated. His sales target was therefore revised and increased by a large amount. This was done in full agreement with all the members (including him) of the sales team, who democratically discussed targets and achievements together during the quarterly sales meetings.

In the companies for which he had worked before, sales objectives were settled in a somewhat hierarchic way. The objectives were, fortunately, too high to be achieved. Being out of reach, the objectives worked as a sort of line of sight, an ideal level. It worked as a way of forcing lazy people to do more and of motivating the achievers to surpass themselves. Logically enough, actual sales were not carefully monitored, nor were individual achievements calculated by comparisons of target sales and actual sales.

At the end of the third quarter, Gonzales began to think that he had been set too high an objective. He had been working extremely hard for almost six months, pushed by enthusiasm for his new job. Moreover an unusually large order from a company in his sales area had swollen his first quarterly sales. This did not happen during the second and third quarters.

When the quarterly sales meeting took place, Gonzales once again appeared as the 'star' of the meeting: he had a record shortfall. No sales representative at Setco of Spain had ever experienced such a wide negative gap between target and actual sales. His colleagues made fun of him. They were slightly relieved to see him bite the dust. Some days later he received a personal memo from the marketing director, who made it clear that he had to adapt quickly or leave the company.

'You should know that in our company a salesman has to be able to settle his own objectives in a precise, realistic and dynamic way. Targets are the result of negotiations with the sales manager: they are based on market data. Individual sales targets are summed up, at every level in the corporation. They are the basis for the quarterly corporate sales figure forecast. The stocks of our company are registered on the New York Stock Exchange. Operators on the Stock Exchange are extremely sensitive to this kind of data. If every salesman in this company performed like you, our forecasts at the corporate level would be meaningless. Our headquarters simply cannot accept this.'

What should Gonzales do?

A14.3   Case: Houston Oil Supply

Fred Allman, director of marketing and sales for Houston Oil Supply, was faced with the difficult job of penetrating the Mexican oil market. The Mexican market consisted of a single firm, PEMEX, the government-owned oil production and marketing monopoly. Allman had had no previous experience with foreign buyers until last June, when he was approached by a representative of British Petroleum, who was interested in Houston's new service station pump for its Canadian stations. This started him thinking about the enormous potential for sales abroad, and he immediately focused his attention on the rich Mexican market south of the border. Houston Oil Supply had operated in the oil-producing regions of the southwestern United States since 1946. The company was founded by Jake Grashof, an unsuccessful wildcat oil producer, to supply the needs of oil producers in the field. The company prospered over the years, and by 1980 was one of the leading oil well supply firms in the industry. At that time, Grashof, who had surrendered active management of the company to his two sons, was approached by the inventor of a revolutionary new electronic gasoline pump for service stations. Recognizing a potential winner in the market-place, Grashof obtained production and distribution rights to the pump and established a new division to produce and market it. It was at this time that Fred Allman was hired to sell the new product. By 1985, the new pump was being sold in all major markets in the United States, and sales for the division had climbed to US$11 million. Allman was attracted by the Mexican market because of the PEMEX monopoly. Although the Mexican market was large and growing rapidly, it was nowhere near as rich as the American or Canadian markets because of the lower percentage of ownership and usage of automobiles. However, it was still a large user of gasoline pumps, and its unique attraction lay in the fact that the entire market could be reached through a single buyer, PEMEX. Fred Allman had no idea how PEMEX officials made their buying decision, but he was aware that their methods of doing business were very different from those of American buyers from reading newspaper accounts of the US Justice Department action against Gary Bateman and Crawford Enterprises. (See Exhibit 1 for a description of *Bateman/Crawford Enterprises* case.) The parties involved apparently had obtained purchase orders from PEMEX through payoffs to officials of the government-owned company. While such action is not legal, he understood that Mexico's political and business infrastructures have permitted monetary 'subsidies' to influence and/or dictate transactional decision making. Known as the *mordida* or 'bite', public corruption had permeated all socioeconomic levels, becoming a 'way of life' among Mexicans. Since bribes are effected in various forms, no country is immune to their existence. In Mexico, however, payoffs were conducted more openly – a catalyst for prompt, assured action.

Exhibit 1   *U S v. Gary Bateman/Crawford Enterprises*

In October 1982 the US Justice Department brought action against Crawford Enterprise, and Gary Bateman, former marketing vice-president of Crawford Enterprises, for bribery and corruption of two PEMEX officials. PEMEX is a petroleum production and distribution monopoly owned and operated by the Mexican government. The indictments charged that the parties involved had obtained purchase orders from PEMEX through payoffs to official of the Mexican oil monopoly. Late in 1981, Gary Bateman, former marketing vice-president of Crawford Enterprises of Houston, Texas, pleaded guilty to making payoffs totalling US$342,000 in bribes to Guillermo Cervera, administrative secretary to the chief of purchasing at PEMEX. When fired from Crawford Enterprises on 9 February 1979, Bateman opened his own business – Applied Process

Products Overseas, Inc. – with the idea of transaction business with PEMEX. Bateman had offered to pay Cervera 30 per cent of Applied's gross profit in exchange for assistance in obtaining business. Cervera presumably agreed and became 'administrator and handler' of the money, which would be divided with other PEMEX officials. Bateman's company obtained approximately US$5 million in purchase orders from PEMEX until March 1981, when Bateman signed a cooperation agreement with the US government bribery investigation in return for minor offence charges.

However, the US government stated that while marketing vice-president at Crawford Enterprises, Gary Bateman handled company dealings with PEMEX and usually carried large amounts of currency from Houston to Mexico City. This led to further investigation, and in October of 1982, the US Justice Department alleged that a bribery scheme was set up by Crawford Enterprises paying US$10 million in bribes to two former PEMEX officials to secure orders for gas compression equipment totalling US$225 million between June 1977 and March 1979. The US government contended that Crawford Enterprises funnelled cash to a Mexican intermediary company, Grupo Industrial Delta, to be passed on to the PEMEX officials. Crawford Enterprises, Inc., had been accused of representing the additional interests (in submitting bids to PEMEX) of Solar Turbines International, subsidiary of Caterpillar Tractor Co., and Ruston Gas Turbines, Inc., a subsidiary of General Electric England Ltd. Crawford Enterprises has denied any wrongdoing in connection with the allegations.

—————— ♦♦♦ ——————

While corruption had been overemphasized as the cause for Mexico's current state of the economy, the new administration of President de la Madrid, which took office in 1983, was striving for a 'moral renovation' that would include an attempt to reduce waste and political graft. To set an example, the Mexican government formally charged and subsequently dismissed three PEMEX officials for accepting over US$42,000 in bribes from the US firms in the Crawford Enterprises affair. Allman found himself in somewhat of a quandary. The US government had taken a consistent stand against the corruption and bribery of foreign buyers and particularly foreign government officials. And the Justice Department had followed an aggressive course of action against American offenders. Yet it seemed evident that despite current Mexican government opposition, the *mordida* was still a part of the Mexican culture and might be a necessary requirement for getting the attention of PEMEX buyers.

(Source: adapted from Cundiff and Hilger, 1988, pp. 123–5. Adapted from a case prepared by Carol G. Spindola. Reproduced with permission.)

Questions

1. Why are there differences in business practices between the United States and Mexico? What are these differences?
2. Is bribery the same thing as corruption? A bribe is defined as 'money or favour given or promised to a person in a position of trust to influence his judgement or conduct: something that serves to induce or influence.' Corruption is defined as

'the impairment of integrity, virtue or moral principle; morally degenerate and perverted'.
3. How are ethics established and whose ethics prevail in a foreign environment? Must foreigners comply with local customs, or can traditional business practices be challenged? Should marketers behave as 'change agents' in foreign markets?
4. If you were Fred Allman, competing for foreign contracts worth millions of dollar in sales, what would your ethical parameters be? Which actions would you take?

A14.4 Case: G. H. Mulford Pharmaceutical Company

Grace Mulford, president and chief executive officer of G. H. Mulford Pharmaceutical Company, asked Sam Gregory to review the political and legal ramifications of the Latin American market before the company embarked on a proposed major expansion in South and Central America later in 1990. In the past, the company had been strongly oriented toward the American market; it had stumbled into the Latin American market almost by chance. When Grace Mulford became president in mid-1988, she focused efforts on international markets as the most promising area for expansion. One of her first administrative changes was to establish an international division and to hire Sam Gregory to head it. Gregory was particularly familiar with the Latin American market, having worked for Coca-Cola in Brazil. In 1943, George Mulford leased a portion of an abandoned textile mill in Fall River, Massachusetts, to manufacture aspirin. His aspirin, which was introduced under the brandname Blue Seal, was positioned to sell at a price one-third lower than that of Bayer, the industry leader. During the next twenty years, he added antacid tablets to the line and gradually expanded his market throughout northeastern United States.

In 1965, his son Daren joined the firm. Concerned with the company's dependence on two mature products that might at any time become obsolete, Daren persuaded his father to develop a research division and to introduce antibiotics and other prescription drugs. By 1989, Mulford was marketing a line of seventeen drugs. Although Blue Seal aspirin still accounted for 39 per cent of sales, sales of prescription drugs were steadily increasing as a share of company volume. In 1989, Mulford had a 1.7 per cent share of the American pharmaceutical market. In 1975, Bailey and Sons, a Boston export agent, suggested that Mulford could find a market for Blue Seal aspirin in Argentina. The market proved to be profitable, and ultimately Mulford opened a sales office in Montevideo to service both Argentina and Uruguay and a second South American office in São Paulo, serving Brazil.

In 1986 Daren Mulford investigated the possibility of launching the full line of prescription drugs in the Latin American market. He discovered that it would be necessary to learn a lot more about the political and legal hazards in new Latin American markets and to design a new marketing strategy for each market. As a consequence, he delayed further action on this market. Gregory wanted to concentrate his efforts on Latin America, first because Mulford already had a toehold in the area, but, more important because it was potentially rich. In a study by Sogen-Swiss Corporation in 1986, Mexico and Brazil were classified as the eighth and ninth largest pharmaceutical markets in the world with sales of US$580 million and US$550 million, respectively, representing 4.1 per cent of the world market. Since that time, both countries had continued to experience explosive population growth. Although per capita consumption of pharmaceuticals was much lower than in the United States in all of Latin America, the market was still a huge one, and competition was less rigorous. A logical starting point in evaluating the individual Latin American markets was the market potential as measured by population and wealth, but in Gregory's opinion a second factor of major importance was the political climate. Latin America had a reputation for political instability.

The Mulford Company had experienced major problems early in their tenure in Argentina when the military regime was causing problems for all foreign companies and their employees. Mulford's expansion in the Brazilian market had been much more rapid because of a stable government. Despite the stereotype of instability, Latin American governments ranged from very stable, as in Mexico, Venezuela and Brazil to wildly unstable, as in the case of Bolivia, where the government had changed at least fifteen times in fifteen years. Gregory found that methods had been developed to measure political risk in foreign markets, so he could compare the various promising Latin American countries. However, he was not sure that political instability was as dangerous for a firm selling products essential to health as for firms selling luxury products from abroad. In addition, he was not sure what level of risk would be acceptable in relation to potential profits. He did not want to make the mistake made by a number of large international banks, who were so attracted by potential profits from loans to Latin America, that they badly underemphasized the risks of non-payment.

Gregory found that a pharmaceutical firm faced a different legal and ethical environment in Latin America from that in the United States. For example, in the United States, physicians obtain information about drugs from the *Physicians' Desk Reference*, a standard reference book providing information on all ethical drugs. The statements found in this reference book reflect the official attitudes of the FDA and its expert consultants. Each manufacturer must submit statements about its drugs to the US FDA for approval: it is from these statements that the descriptions in the *Physicians' Desk Reference* are drawn and, also, all package inserts, medical journal advertisements, and all other labeling and promotion are drawn. The FDA requires full disclosure of unpleasant, dangerous or potentially lethal side effects. In general, American manufacturers have welcomed these disclosure requirements as both clinically essential and socially desirable, but also as an important protection in product liability litigation.

The situation is very different in South America. Although the extent of government protection of drug consumers varies somewhat from country to country, the level of control is much lower. The standard reference books, commonly called PLM (*para los medicos*) by the doctors, allow much more extensive and unsupported statements about the drugs, and the listings of hazards are curtailed, glossed over, or totally omitted. The same is true of advertising, both to the physicians and to the patients. There is much more use of hyperbole and omission of undesirable facts. The medical reference book for Brazil indicates that the information was provided by each manufacturer based on texts approved by the government's Servicio de Fiscalizacaõ de Medicina e Farmacia, but apparently Brazilian law does not require that the promotional material is subjected to government approval. The situation in Argentina is quite different. The texts of *Therapia Vademecum* were written by the staff from materials contributed by the manufacturers, and the material was not submitted to laboratories for approval.

For the past three years, there had been a running battle between the advertising department in Fall River and the manager of the Montevideo office. The director of advertising wanted the promotional and informational copy prepared for the United States market to be translated into Spanish and Portuguese and used unchanged in the Latin American markets. He believed that such action was not only morally and ethically proper, but that it provided protection from litigation by injured customers. Lopez, in Montevideo, argued that Mulford products could not compete effectively in the local markets unless he was allowed to follow competitors' practices of overstating potential benefits and understating hazards or limitations, all of which was legal under local laws. Grace Mulford asked Gregory to propose a company policy on this matter.

(Source: adapted from Cundiff and Hilger, 1988, pp. 226–8. Reproduced with permission.)

Questions

1. How important is political risk for a foreign manufacturer of ethical drugs (e.g. sold under a physician's prescription)?
2. Product liability: examine the differences which are evidenced by this case between the United States and Latin America.
3. What are the cultural differences between US (and more generally western European people) and Latin Americans which may explain differences in marketing communication practices (advertising claims, information content of instructions for use, and so on)?
4. What should Gregory's recommendation be with respect to advertising claims in the Latin American market? Which style and content should he give to directions for use of the drugs? Which instructions should he give to medical visitors?

A14.5 Critical incident: The Brenzy nouveau has arrived!

Legritte Company was founded just after the Second World War by a skilful engineer, Monsieur Legritte. Aided by the reconstruction boom which was followed by the rapid economic growth of the 1960s, the Legritte Company developed more by improving the quality of its products than by investing money in marketing and sales. The intrinsic quality of the products, namely electrical connections for industrial use, has been the strong point of the business from the very beginning.

The company is located near Lyons (France) and employs about 200 people, with an annual turnover of 80 million francs. Two years ago Legritte was taken over by a US-based multinational company, Brenzy. Monsieur Legritte, drawing near to retirement age and with no qualified successor, sold his property to the Brenzy Corporation, which now owns the full 100 per cent. Brenzy has progressively introduced more up-to-date management methods in this traditional family business. Inventory management, cost accounting and delivery systems have all been changed to fit with Brenzy's procedures.

Sales promotion in France and Europe is based on nicely printed catalogues, technical instructions and directions for use. The price list is degressive according to the size of orders. Products are promoted through small gifts given to the purchasers. Thus the launch of a new pre-insulated line of products, recently certified by Electricité de France (EDF), came with a free gift (electrical pincers) for any order higher than 10,000 francs. This offer was open for six months. In order to receive the gift, the buyer simply had to fill in the gift voucher and enclose it with the order, provided the amount was sufficient.

Brenzy-Legritte was a newcomer to advertising. Being a fairly traditional medium-size industrial company, they had not up to now invested a lot of money in advertisements. When they decided for the first time to advertise their products they did it by promoting their products along with what they called '*le Brenzy nouveau*', with a play on words between Brenzy and Beaujolais, a freshly harvested red wine and a fashionable drink.

An advertisement in a specialist journal showed a bottle of Beaujolais nouveau, with the following slogan above the image: 'The Brenzy nouveau has arrived!' Text in bold characters at the bottom stated: 'You are thirsty and craving a new line of effective products! Brenzy-Legritte is happy to join you in ordering Beaujolais nouveau!' It was indicated that a minimum order of 3,500 francs entitled buyers to receive three free bottles and a minimum order of 5,000 francs entitled them to receive six free bottles. The expiry date for this offer was stipulated. The new line of Brenzy-Legritte products was shown on the label of the bottle of Beaujolais.

EDF, which is a large customer of Brenzy-Legritte, was not very happy about this humorous advertisement. It seems that EDF experienced problems amongst its personnel when the boxes of Beaujolais arrived at its offices. . . .

Brenzy-Legritte is now undergoing drastic changes in its organization. Computers have been linked to the European headquarters in Brussels. Strictly defined management procedures have been imposed by headquarters. Brenzy has issued a professional code of conduct, the implementation of which is compulsory for the French subsidiary as well as for all the other subsidiaries around the world. It is a complete code of business ethics, comprising precise and detailed prescriptions. Below are some extracts.

Suffice it to say that this code of conduct is perceived by most people at Brenzy-Legritte, especially the salespeople, as largely inappropriate to the French context and a mere interference in their business. They prefer to disregard it.

Excerpts from the code of conduct at Brenzy-Legritte

Correct use of company funds

1. Company funds will not be used in order to make payments, or concealed loans, with the purpose of dishonestly influencing a supplier, a client or a civil servant. This prohibition applies not only to direct use of company money, but also to any kind of indirect payments, by the means of consultants/intermediaries, or by reimbursing to employees payments made by them.
2. No payment shall be made, for and in the name of the company or one of its subsidiaries, with the intent or knowledge that part of such a payment will serve other purposes than those described in the documents related to this payment.

Gifts, favours and entertainment

Small gifts of symbolic value, minor favours and modest receptions may be offered at the company's expense only when they meet all of the following conditions:

1. They must be compatible with the rules of the company and current business practices.
2. Their monetary worth must be limited; they must be presented in such a form as not to appear as a bribe or remuneration; they must not give rise to suspicions about the impartiality of the beneficiary.
3. They must be approved by the general manager of the subsidiary or by a vice-president at Brenzy Corporation; they must be compatible with the instructions previously approved by the direct superior, the managing director and a senior vice-president at Brenzy Corporation.

Gifts and entertainment for civil servants

As indicated above, gifts, other than symbolic ones or gifts of a very modest value, whatever their nature, or a sumptuous reception, whatever its motives, are not allowed.

Issues related to these procedures and their violations

1. Any employees who want to ask questions about this code and its implementation shall discuss it with the head of the department. If it entails legal or accounting matters, they shall refer to qualified personnel from the legal services and the accounting department, who shall be consulted.
2. The discovery of a case which is fraudulent, illegal, or violates the rules of the company, shall immediately be reported to the legal counsellor. If such cases are identified, which imply senior executives in the corporation, this case shall be reported to the executive vice-president, for examination by the chairman of the board, the chief executive officer, and the chairman of the audit committee.
3. No derogation to this procedure will be accepted in these matters. There will probably be some 'business opportunities' in the future, when it would be necessary to make questionable payments in order to succeed against a competitor, for one reason or another. The duty of the employee, in this case, is to reject such 'opportunities'.

4. Any infringement to the above-mentioned principles will result in disciplinary sanctions, including dismissal, a suing of the employee and a detailed report to competent regulatory authorities.
5. Moreover disciplinary sanctions will be decided against any executive who initiates or approves such actions, or knows about them, or may have known about them, and did not quickly act to rectify them in accordance with this code. Adequate disciplinary sanctions will also be directed against any executives who neglect their hierarchical responsibilities, by not ensuring that their subordinates have been properly informed about the rules established in this code.

References

Adcock, Dennis, Ray Bradfield, Al Halborg and Caroline Ross (1993), *Marketing, Principles and Practice*, Pitman: London.

Adler, Nancy J. (1991), *International Dimensions of Organizational Behavior*, 2nd edn, PWS-Kent: Boston.

Agpar, M. (1977), 'Succeeding in Saudi Arabia', *Harvard Business Review*, January/February, pp. 14–33.

Ali, Abbas and Paul M. Schwiercz (1985), 'The relationship between managerial decision styles and work satisfaction in Saudi Arabia', in Erdener Kaynak (ed.), *International Business in the Middle East*, De Gruyter: New York, pp. 138–49.

Anderson, Paul F. and Terry M. Chambers (1985), 'A reward/measurement model of organizational buying behavior', *Journal of Marketing*, vol. 49 (Spring), pp. 7–23.

Barabba, Vincent P. and Gerald Zaltman (1991), *Hearing the Voice of the Market*, Harvard Business School Press: Cambridge, MA.

Beaudeux, Pierre (1980), 'L'économie du backchich', *L'Expansion*, 5 December.

Becker, Helmut and David H. Fritzsche (1987), 'A comparison of the ethical behavior of American, French and German managers', *Columbia Journal of World Business*, Winter, pp. 87–95.

Cateora, Philip R. (1983) *International Marketing*, 5th edn, Richard D. Irwin: Homewood, IL.

Cateora, Philip R. (1993), *International Marketing*, 8th edn, Richard D. Irwin: Burr Ridge, IL.

Chonko, Lawrence B., Ben M. Enis and John F. Tanner (1992), *Managing Sales People*, Allyn and Bacon: Boston, MA.

Cundiff, Edward W. and Marye Tharp Hilger (1988), *Marketing in the International Environment*, 2nd edn, Prentice Hall: Englewood Cliffs, NJ.

Czinkota, Michael R. and Illka A. Ronkainen (1990), *International Marketing*, 2nd edn, Dryden Press: Hinsdale, IL.

Daniels, John D., Ernest W. Ogram and Lee H. Radebaugh (1982), *International Business: Environments and Operations*, 3rd edition, Addison–Wesley: Reading, MA.

Freivalds, John (1991), 'Foreign-language business cards', *Agri Marketing*, vol. 29, no. 3, pp. 48–9.

Galtung, Frederick (1994), *Korruption*, Göttingen: Lamuv Verlag.

Gillespie, Kate (1987), 'Middle East response to the US Foreign Corrupt Practices Act,' *California Management Review*, vol. XXIX, no. 4 (Summer), pp. 9–30.

Graham, John L. (1981), 'A hidden cause of America's trade deficit with Japan', *Columbia Journal of World Business*, Fall, pp. 5–15.

Graham, John L. (1983), 'Foreign Corrupt Practices Act: A manager's guide', *Columbia Journal of World Business*, vol. 18, no. 3, pp. 89–94.

Hall, Edward T. (1976), *Beyond Culture*, Doubleday: New York.

Hill, John S., Richard R. Still and Ünal O. Boya (1991), 'Managing the multinational sales force', *International Marketing Review*, vol. 8, no. 1, pp. 19–31.

Hofstede, Geert (1991), *Culture and Organizations: Software of the mind*, McGraw-Hill: Maidenhead, Berkshire.

Jacoby, N. H., P. Nehemkis, and R. Eells. (1979), 'Naivete: Foreign payoffs law', *California Management Review*, vol. XXII, no.1 (Fall), pp. 84–7.

Jefkins, Frank (1989), *Modern Marketing*, 2nd edn, Pitman: London.

Jolibert, Alain and Maud Tixier (1988), *La Négociation Commerciale*, Editions ESF: Paris.

Kaikati, J.G. and W.A. Label (1980), 'American bribery legislation: An obstacle to international marketing', *Journal of Marketing*, Vol. 44 (Fall), pp. 38–43.

Kashani, Kamran (1989), 'Beware the pitfalls of global marketing', *Harvard Business Review*, September–October, pp. 91–8.

Kotabe, Masaaki, Alan J. Dubinsky and Chae Un Lim (1992), 'Perceptions of organizational fairness: A cross-national perspective', *International Marketing Review*, vol. 9, no. 2, pp. 41–58.

Lee, K. H. (1981), 'Ethical beliefs in marketing management: A cross-cultural study', *European Journal of Marketing*, vol. 15, no. 1, pp. 58–67.

Mayo, Michel A., Lawrence J. Marks and John K. Ryans Jr (1991), 'Perceptions of ethical problems in international marketing', *International Marketing Review*, vol. 8, no. 3, pp. 61–75.

McCarthy, E. Jerome (1964), *Basic Marketing: A managerial approach*, Prentice Hall: Englewood Cliffs, NJ.

Ndao, Cheikh Alioune (1985), *Excellences, vos épouses!*, Les Nouvelles Editions Africaines: Dakar.

Péan, Pierre (1988), *L'Argent Noir*, Librairie Arthème Fayard: Paris.

Pinsdorf, Marion K. (1991), 'Flying different skies: How different cultures respond to airline disasters', *Public Relations Review*, vol. 17, no. 1 (Spring), pp. 37–56.

Prus, Robert (1989) *Making Sales*, Sage Publications: Newbury Park, CA.

Rawls, John (1971), *A Theory of Justice*, Belknap Press of Harvard University: Cambridge, MA.

Redding, S. G. (1982), 'Cultural effects of the marketing process in Southeast Asia', *Journal of the Market Research Society*, vol. 24, no. 2, pp. 98–114.

Slatter, Stuart St P. (1987), 'The salesman's job in competitive bidding situations', *Industrial Marketing Management*, vol. 16, pp. 201–5.

Still, Richard R. (1981), 'Cross-cultural aspects of sales force management', *Journal of Personal Selling and Sales Force Management*, vol. 1, no. 2, pp. 6–9.

Taylor, William (1991), 'The logic of global business: an interview with ABB's Percy Barnevik,' *Harvard Business Review*, March–April, pp. 90–105.

Tsalikis, John, Marta Ortiz-Buonafina and Michael S. Latour (1992), 'The role of accent on the credibility and effectiveness of the international business person: The case of Guatemala', *International Marketing Review*, vol. 9, no. 4, pp. 57–72.

Usunier, Jean-Claude and Gérard Verna (1994), *La Grande Triche: Ethique, Corruption et Affaires Internationales*, Editions La Découverte: Paris.

Walter, Ingo (1989), *Secret Money*, 2nd edn, London: Unwin-Hyman.

Zeithaml, Carl P. and Valerie Zeithaml (1984), 'Environmental management: Revising the perspective', *Journal of Marketing*, vol. 48 (Spring), pp. 46–53.

15

◆◆◆

Intercultural marketing negotiations 1

When marketing internationally, negotiation skills are needed. Many agreements have to be negotiated, drafted, signed and finally implemented: sales contracts, licensing agreements, joint ventures and various kinds of partnerships, agency and distribution agreements, turnkey contracts, etc. Negotiation is not only based on legal and business matters, corresponding to the *doing* orientation, but also on the quality of human and social interactions, corresponding to the *being* orientation (section 2.3). Goldman (1994) emphasizes for instance the importance for the Japanese of *ningensei*, which literally translates into an all encompassing and overriding concern and prioritizing of 'humanity' or *human beingness* (see Box 15.2). According to Japanese specialists of international marketing negotiations:

> The North American and U.K. negotiators failed to communicate ningensei at the first table meeting. Rushing into bottom lines and demanding quick decisions on the pending contract they also overlooked the crucial need for ningensei in developing good will ... Hard business facts alone are not enough ... Ningensei is critical in getting Japanese to comply or in persuading Japanese negotiating partners. (Nippon Inc. Consultation, quoted in Goldman, 1994, p. 31)

There are various kinds of 'distances' between the potential partners: physical distance certainly, but also economic, educational and cultural distance, which tend to inflate the cost of negotiating internationally. Negotiations for large contracts may take years, but fortunately not continuously. Most international deals incur transaction costs which are disproportionate to the costs related to domestic deals: people in the domestic market usually share the same language and cultural background which acts as a common knowledge base. For instance, it is much easier within the native cultural setting to guess who will be a good payer, a reliable partner or a trustworthy supplier.

Thus it would be a mistake to go flitting about like a butterfly on the international market: always looking for new partners, new customers and new ventures, without following up. This results in a great deal of 'one-off' business. Business people and companies perform poorly if they do not understand the golden rule of international marketing negotiations which is: have few partners and conduct few negotiations, but

498

make the stakes meaningful. This will enable both parties to build a durable partnership. One should 'marry' well rather than often (section 15.1). This chapter seeks to develop two simple ideas. The first is that trust between buyer and seller is a key variable when structuring and developing any relational exchange. The second is that trust in an international sale or business venture is heavily dependent on culturally coded signs, and may ultimately be withdrawn precisely because these cultural codes have been ignored. These difficulties in interacting, negotiating sales, planning common ventures, working out agreements and achieving them together are deeply rooted in the cultural, human and social, background of business people. They are not related to a superficial variance of business customs.

Simple 'empathy' is not enough for the avoidance of misunderstandings. In fact, people with different cultural backgrounds often do not share the same basic assumptions, as we have shown in Chapters 2 and 3. This may undermine the process of building and maintaining trust between culturally uneven partners (section 15.2). Subsequent sections deal with the various aspects of cultural differences which affect the trust-building process, particularly misunderstandings about personal and institutional credibility (section 15.3); differences in the underlying concept of negotiation: cultural predispositions to integrative negotiation, i.e. the preference for maximizing the common cake before looking at one's own portion, or to a distributive orientation – maximizing one's own portion of the cake, rather than the cake itself (section 15.4); time-based misunderstandings during the negotiation process (15.5); the existence of a common rationality between the parties (section 15.6). Section 15.7 outlines the possibility of differences in outcome orientation and is dedicated to oral versus written agreements as support for trust between the parties. The following chapter complements this one by examining some elements of national negotiation styles.

15.1   The dynamics of trust in relational marketing

The motto of the Deutsche Bank, the largest German bank and a quite successful organization internationally is '*Vertrauen ist der Anfang von allem*': trust is the beginning of everything. Trust is indeed a necessary condition for smooth and efficient business between partners, but is also a highly intangible, volatile asset, difficult to create, easy to destroy. Pursuing the Whorfian perspective of section 12.3, let us look first at how trust is expressed in various languages.

What is trust?

The English concept of *trust* is the reliance on and confidence in the truth, worth and reliability of a person or thing. Reliance is central in the Anglo-Saxon concept of trust, that is why the legal institution of trust has been highly developed in the common law tradition, whereas it was non-existent in the Roman-Germanic tradition up to very recently. The German concept is based on two verbs: *trauen* and *vertrauen*, both of them meaning literally to 'trust'. But in fact the Germans use the first form, *trauen*, mostly in the negative sense, '*Ich traue Dir nicht*' ('I do not trust you'), and the second in the positive sense '*Ich vertraue Dir*' ('I trust you'). The prefix *Ver* indicates a transformation and this informs us on the picture which is behind the German concept of trust: (1) the initial position is distrust and (2) only after a favourable change has occurred can trust be established. The French notion of *confiance*, similarly as in other Romance languages, is based on the Latin *confidentia*, a compound of cum (with, shared) and *fides* (faith, belief): the notion of sharing common beliefs is central to the Latin concept of trust. The Japanese word for trust is *shin-yô* meaning literally: new business; it is based on a compound of *shin*, the word for 'new' when it is used in composites, and *yô* which means literally 'something to do, a business, an errand.'

Assuming that the very concept of trust is the same cross-culturally and that languages only favour a facet of it, we have the following elements:

1. Trust is reliance on and confidence in people, words and things.
2. Trust is inseparable from distrust: since obvious showing of distrust is detrimental to the establishment of trust, every culture has to deal with the paradox of their inseparability.
3. Trust is about sharing common faith, beliefs, possibly education or group membership.
4. Trust is directed to the future and to common achievements, even though this does not deny the value of the lessons of the past.

Trust basically saves transaction costs in interpersonal and interorganizational relationships. The savings result from smooth communication: one does not need to write everything down, to invest in control systems; meetings are quicker: mutual understanding and consensus are reached more easily. But there are major obstacles to the establishment of trust in an *intercultural* perspective: (1) people do not always share the same communication style; (2) they may not share the same beliefs; (3) they do not necessarily agree on what are adequate control systems; and (4) their interpretation of a control system as signalling trust, distrust, or a reasonable combination of both differs. Since the process of trust building and withdrawing is a very dynamic one – it can be killed in some minutes – trust must be seen as an infant to be protected rather than an independent self.

A marriage between buyer and seller: The dimensions of relational marketing

Many successful international marketing partnerships share the following characteristics: (1) a long time span over which transactions occur, (2) a large size as a unit sale (i.e. compared to total turnover) and (3) a long-term relationship established between buyer and seller (Jackson, 1985). These characteristics all fit quite well with the concept of the 'domesticated market' (Arndt, 1979). In this type of market 'transactions are planned and administered, instead of being conducted on an ad hoc basis' (p. 70). Marketing is viewed from this perspective as an ongoing exchange relationship. Exchange is no longer studied as if it were a time-series of independent, discrete transactions. Buyer–seller relationships are seen to extend far beyond the short time horizon of discrete, small-scale transactions.

In industrial markets, relational exchange marketing is almost inevitable, especially at the international level. There is a large world-wide market for international turnkey projects and systems, ranging from the turnkey brewery to the ready-made airport. These contracts are international by their very nature. The contractor (or companies which have jointly created a contracting consortium) and the owner belong to different nationalities. Turnkey operations may even be seen as a continuous sales process when the owner is planning expansion or a new project, subject to the performance achieved by the contractor in the present project. Trust is then an asset of prime importance in that it enables negotiation partners to overcome short-term conflicts of interest, personal confrontations or even communication misunderstandings (Dwyer *et al.*, 1987). This holds true for the negotiation phase itself, that is before signing the contract(s), as well as for the negotiation process during the implementation phase. Different national/ cultural backgrounds are then the source of communication problems and possible misunderstandings.

In relational marketing switching from one supplier to another incurs high transaction costs. This may be contrasted with discrete transactions marketing, which is the case traditionally considered in marketing, applying mainly to consumer goods, with (1) oli-gopolistic markets, where a few vendors face a multitude of buyers, and (2) standardized obligations, which are often embedded in a unilateral contract where price cannot be challenged by the buyer.

Each transaction in relational marketing may be viewed as having its own history as well as encompassing its future, in as far as it may be anticipated by each partner (Macneil, 1980). Future collaboration (new orders, future common ventures, an extension or revamping of the actual plant, etc.) as well as the conditions, atmosphere and end results of the actual co-operation, are dependent on the assumptions each partner makes about the *trustworthiness* of the other party.

One may easily argue that relational marketing is applicable far beyond the domain of industrial and equipment goods. The negotiations of consumer goods companies with their foreign agents, licensees and distributors for making agreements belong to relational marketing. For instance, some of the relations between the Coca-Cola Company and its foreign dealers, or Procter & Gamble and its advertising agencies, have been established for several decades. Even with the individual consumer, discrete transaction marketing is not the only type of possible relationship: one may form a more personalized relationship with individual consumers by establishing contact with them on a more personal basis through distributors and their employees, in order to build long-term consumer loyalty, which is, for instance, largely the goal of the Japanese *Keiretsu* distribution system.

Development stages in the process of relational exchange

There are five main phases in the development of a relational exchange (Scanzoni, 1979): (1) awareness; (2) exploration; (3) expansion; (4) commitment; and (5) dissolution. The practical interest of Scanzoni's model is its validity across cultures. It breaks down the exchange relationship into phases, where trust always appears as the 'central asset'. The first phase – awareness – deals with the recognition of the other party as a feasible partner for exchange. Short distances, whether cultural, geographic or linguistic, facilitate this process. It is easier to trade with 'local buyers' than with 'distant merchants'. The intercultural situation renders this phase more difficult: many deals fail at this level; for instance, when receiving a letter written by a non-native speaker in poor English, most native English speakers will fear further communication difficulties and decide to abandon the project as early as possible, before real costs have been incurred. Case A12.4 (Supreme Canning) illustrates such a failure in the awareness phase. In the second phase – exploration – the exchange relation begins. It remains a tenuous one. Partners are exploring the potential benefits and costs of an exchange. Several means are possible: trial purchase, installing a prototype plant, lending a machine or offering a technical visit to an existing plant. Scanzoni distinguishes five subprocesses which are at work in exploration: attraction, communication and bargaining, power and justice, norm development and expectations development. Most of these subprocesses are subject to a certain cultural variance. For instance, bargaining attitudes, functions and rites vary according to cultures (section 10.2). Moreover the development of common norms is more easily attained if potential partners in the exchange belong to the same cultural background. During the expansion phase partners reap the benefits of their relationship and simultaneously become increasingly interdependent. The subprocesses of the preceding phase are still at work during the expansion. If each party has a strong positive perception of the other party's performance, the motivation to maintain and increase the exchange relationship is strong. This in turn reduces the probability that parties are looking for alternative partners, because of a lack of confidence in the future of the present exchange relationship ('unfaithfulness').

Such a process of exploration has taken place in the case of Euro-Disney (now called Disneyland Paris), between the Disney Corporation and its European partners. Initially the decision was made to transfer the basic successful Disneyland recipe to France, the same amusements, themes and policy guidelines, including the no-alcohol policy. However, while the project was underway, from 1986 to 1992, heavy criticism from some French media called Euro-Disney *'un Tchernobyl culturel'* (a cultural Chernobyl) invoking the risk of cultural invasion, while other parts of the French population were in favour of Euro-Disney. Progressively the park has been Europeanized, emphasizing European characters such as Pinocchio (Italian), Cinderella (French) and Peter Pan (British), as well as European history.

Signing one or more contracts is not a necessary step for the commitment phase. The parties exchange implicit or explicit signs (either written or oral) of their willingness to continue their exchange relationship. One of these signs may be the allocation by both partners of large resources to the joint venture, starting a pilot plant or sharing personnel.

Dissolution is a possibility at any moment of the exchange relationship. It rests on an internal evaluation made by each partner of the costs of discontinuing the exchange. If these costs outweigh the benefits, partners may negotiate the dissolution. These costs are difficult to estimate. The potential benefits of a new exchange relationship are also fairly uncertain and difficult to forecast. Breaking off is a complex process, often related to a crisis initiated by one of the partners. If the other party is willing to enter this separation ritual, dissolution becomes feasible. This 'divorce' is the counterpart of the relational

Box 15.1   *Intercultural discord*

(Soon to be) New Owner: You guys never make decisions in time.

(Soon-to-be) Former Partner: Speedy decisions are not everything. Consensus is more important.

N.O.: Well, just tell the dealers that our products are the best in the world. Tell them that they sell everywhere except here.

F.P.: But the dealers complain that your products are just okay, not great. Even worse, they are not really tailored to the needs or aesthetic preferences of local customers.

N.O.: Nonsense. What customers buy, everywhere in the world, is the physical performance of the product. No one matches us in performance.

F.P.: Perhaps. Still the dealers report that your products are not neatly packaged and often have scratches on the surface.

N.O.: But that has no effect on performance.

F.P.: Tell that to the dealers. They say they cannot readily see – or sell – the performance difference you're talking about, so they have to fall back on aesthetics, where your products are weak. We will have to reduce the price.

N.O.: Don't you dare. We succeeded in the United States and in Europe by keeping our prices at 5% above those of our competitors. If we're having trouble in Japan it's because of you. Your obvious lack of effort, knowledge, even confidence in our products – that's what keeps them from selling. Besides, your parent keeps on sending our joint venture group a bunch of bumbling old incompetents for managers. We rarely get the good people. Maybe the idea is to kill off our relationship entirely so they can start up a unit of their own making imitation products.

F.P.: Well, if you feel that way, there is not much point in our continuing on together.

N.O.: Glad you said that. We'll buy up the other 50% of the equity and go it on our own.

F.P.: Good luck. By the way, how many Japanese-speaking managers do you have in your company – that is, after we pull out all the 'bumbling old incompetents' from our joint venture?

N.O.: None. But don't worry. We'll just hire a bunch of headhunters and get started up in record time.

(Source: excerpt from Ohmae, 1989, p. 148. Reproduced with permission.)

marriage. Ohmae (1989, p. 148) gives a lively example of dissolution of a joint-venture between a US firm (N.O. in Box 15.1) and its Japanese partner (the soon-to-be former partner, F.P., in Box 15.1)

15.2   The influence of culture on marketing negotiations

Culture and negotiation examined by the academic literature

A large part of the academic literature on the influence of culture on international business negotiations uses a comparative and cross-cultural setting (see, for instance, Graham, 1985). Generally, a laboratory experiment (the negotiation simulation of Kelley, 1966) helps in the comparison of negotiations between people of various nationalities.

Nationality is used as a proxy and summary variable for culture. A basic description is made of the cultural traits of a specific nationality in negotiations, which is then contrasted with one or more different national groups. It is the basis for some hypotheses on either the process or the outcome of these negotiations, where the membership of a specific national group is one of the main explanatory variables.

It is advisable to be prudent before directly transposing data on the behaviour or negotiation strategies of people from a particular country, collected during negotiations with their compatriots (intra-cultural). For instance, when Italians negotiate together, or with the French, they may not adopt exactly the same behaviour and strategies as they do when negotiating with Americans. Adler and Graham (1989) address the issue of whether these simple international comparisons are fallacies, when and if researchers are trying to describe cross-cultural interactions accurately. They demonstrate that negotiators tend to adapt their behaviour in intercultural negotiation and do not behave completely as predicted by observations in intracultural settings. They, for instance, show that French-speaking Canadians are more problem-solving oriented when negotiating with English-speaking Canadians than they normally are between themselves. Therefore their behaviour as observed in intracultural negotiations can only serve as a partial basis for the prediction of their style and strategies when negotiating with people belonging to different cultures. Hence the word 'intercultural' in this text directly relates to the study of interaction between people with different cultural backgrounds. The word 'cross-cultural' relates to a research design that is generally comparative but may also be centred on the encounter/interaction.

General influence of culture on business negotiations

Culture has mostly an indirect influence on the outcome of negotiations (see, for instance, the models of McCall and Warrington, 1990 and Graham and Sano, 1990). It works through two basic groups of mediating variables: (1) the situational aspects of the negotiation (time and time pressure, power and exercise of power, number of participants, location, etc.) and (2) the characteristics of the negotiators (especially personality variables and cultural variables). These two groups of factors in turn influence the negotiation process, which ultimately determines the outcome (Jolibert, 1988). However, it is my contention that culture also has an influence on the outcome orientation: certain cultures are more deal/contract oriented whereas others favour relationship development. A census of the impact of culture on international business negotiations is given in Table 15.1. It indicates where in other chapters, especially Chapters 2 and 3, these topics are treated at more length.

An intercultural approach to trust-building in international business negotiations

Trust is the mediating variable in the influence of culture on the process of international business negotiations. Relevant issues for building trust in international business negotiations are as follows:

1. How partners use their own cultural codes, as people and as representatives of organizations, to rate each other's credibility.
2. Their respective preference for the adoption of a 'problem-solving' orientation, embedded in an integrative and collaborative rather than distributive/competitive strategy.

Table 15.1   *The impact of cultural differences on international marketing negotiations*

(1) Behavioural predispositions of the parties	
Concept of the self with others	Impact on credibility in the awareness and exploration phases (Table 3.1 (b) and (c))
Interpersonal orientation	Individualism versus collectivism/relationship versus deal orientation
Ingroup orientation	Similarity/'limited good concept'/See Table 2.2 (a) and (b)
Power orientation	Power distance/roles in negotiation teams/ negotiators' leeway
Willingness to take risks	Uncertainty avoidance/degree of self-reliance of negotiators (Table 3.2 (d))
(2) Underlying concept of negotiation/negotiation strategies	
Distributive strategy	Related to ingroup orientation/power distance/ individualism/strong past orientation
Integrative strategy	Related to problem-solving approach and future orientation
Role of the negotiator	Buyer and seller's respective positions of strength (section 14.2)
Strategic time frame	Continuous versus discontinuous/temporal orientations (Table 2.1 (c) and (d))
(3) Negotiation process	
Agenda setting/scheduling the negotiation process	Linear-separable time/economicity of time/ monochronism/negotiating globally versus negotiating clauses (Table 2.1 (a), (b), (c))
Existence of a common rationality between the partners	Ideologism versus pragmatism/Intellectual styles/ wishful thinking/Table 3.5 points (b), (c) and (d)
Communication	Communication styles (Chapter 12)/degree of formality and informality
Negotiation tactics	Type and frequency of tactics/mix of business with affectivity
(4) Outcome orientations	
Partnership as outcome	Making a new ingroup – marriage
Deal/contract as outcome	Rules between the parties (Tables 3.5; 3.6 and 3.7)/Legal systems
Profit as outcome	Accounting profit orientation (economicity)
Winning over the other party	Distributive orientation
Time line of negotiation	Continuous versus discontinuous/there is no real time line to negotiation

3. How cultural patterns of time affects negotiation phases, scheduling, plans and deadlines.
4. The partners' approaches to formulating problems, identifying relevant issues and alternative solutions, and the extent to which this 'common rationality' is shared by both parties.
5. Differences in communication style and in the degree of formality/informality during the negotiation process.
6. The type of negotiation tactics used and the extent to which certain tactics can be misinterpreted and damage trust.
7. The basis for trust, whether is it oral ('my word is my bond') or written (only what has been laid down on paper and signed is viewed as binding).
8. The attitudes towards possible litigation; some cultures are litigation oriented as a result of the 'get-it-in-writing' mentality.
9. Differences in business ethics concerning illegal payments (see sections 14.5 and 14.6).

15.3 Behavioural predispositions of the parties

Who is seen as a credible partner?

The issue of credibility has been examined already several times in this text. It is a key one in international marketing, depending on which personal attributes in a particular culture provide an individual with credibility for certain tasks and interactions (section 3.1). Triandis (1983, p. 147) has emphasized three dimensions of the self-concept which may have a strong influence on the coding/decoding process of credibility: (1) self-esteem – the extent to which people think of themselves as very good or not too good; (2) perceived potency – the extent to which people view themselves as powerful, able to accomplish almost any task; and (3) perceived activity – the person sees the self as a doer, an active shaper of the world.

Since people generally live in homogeneous cultural settings (i.e. countries or regions within countries with one language, a dominant religion and shared values), they use the same cultural codes. But when people do not share the same codes this may create problems for establishing credibility/trustworthiness. For example, a credible person may be considered by the emitter (coder) to be somebody showing a low self-concept profile (modest, patiently listening to partners, speaking little and cautiously, etc.); if, conversely, the receiver (decoder) considers as a credible person somebody with a high self-concept profile (showing self-confidence, speaking arrogantly, not paying much attention to what the other is saying, etc.), there will be a credibility misunderstanding.

One of the main reasons for the seriousness of the Cuban missile crisis at the beginning of the 1960s was a misinterpretation by the Soviet leader Khrushchev of the credibility of the American president, John F. Kennedy. Kennedy and Khrushchev had held talks in Vienna, after the unsuccessful attack by US soldiers resulting in defeat at the Bay of Pigs. During their meeting, the young President Kennedy recognized that this attack had been a military and political mistake, which he regretted. Khrushchev saw this confession of error as a testimony of Kennedy's frank naivety and lack of character. He therefore inferred that it was possible to gain advantage by installing nuclear missiles in Cuba, which would have been targeted at the United States. This led the world to the brink of nuclear war between the superpowers. The events which followed showed that Khrushchev had been wrong in evaluating Kennedy's credibility. Ultimately, Kennedy showed great firmness and negotiation skill.

Khrushchev's mistake may be explained by differences in cultural coding of credibility. Whereas in the United States, reaching a high position while still young is positively perceived, Soviet people associate age with the ability to carry responsibilities. Moreover, the admission of a mistake or a misjudgement is also positively perceived in the United States. US ethics value frankness and honesty. It is further believed that individuals may improve their behaviour and decisions by taking into account the lessons of experience. On the other hand, in the Soviet Union, to admit errors was rare. It generally implied the very weak position of people subjected to the enforced confessions of the Stalinist trials.

Signs of credibility

Personal credibility is decoded through the filter of numerous physical traits, which are not often considered as they seem to be only appearances or because we tend to use these reference points unconsciously. The credibility signs clearly bear a symbolic dimension: the associative links between personal characteristics and credibility are, in part, fixed arbitrarily by culture. Being tall may, for instance, be perceived as a sign of strength and character. Stoutness may be considered a positive sign for a partner in societies where starvation is still a recent memory. Where malnutrition is a reality for a section of the population, it is better to be fat, that is, well nourished and therefore rich and powerful-looking. Naturally these signs have a relative value: weight, height, age and sex cannot be considered as adequate criteria for selecting negotiators. Furthermore negotiators may in fact be partly aware of or even share the cultural code of their partner. Each of these basic signs plays a role in the initial building of a credibility profile: age, sex, height, stoutness, face, tone and strength of the voice, accent and fluency in a particular language, self-esteem, perceived potency, perceived activity, etc. This profile is a priori because it only influences credibility in early contacts, that is, in the phase of awareness and at the beginning of the exploration phase.

Collective credibility: relating personal trustworthiness to institutional credentials

Collective (company and group) credibility is a complementary issue. Obviously, there are objective elements which permit assessment of the credibility of the firm, such as its balance sheet, annual reports, reference lists, technical specifications and all those elements which identify the financial and technical quality of a potential partner. Data and information increase the objectivity of the exchange relationship, but are not enough.

For instance the Japanese, as well as many Europeans, do not emphasize financial performance measured by profits or dividends as a sign of company credibility as strongly as the Americans do. The Japanese and Europeans tend to place more emphasis on turnover, the company's connection with the government, its social reputation and its history.

As emphasized in the previous chapter, finding the appropriate level to establish contact may be an important issue. In decentralized decision-making societies, it may sometimes be better to contact those people who have the required authority for making decisions, even though they may be at intermediate hierarchical levels (small power distance). In more centralized societies credibility on both sides is established by the top decision-makers meeting. Where committee decision-making is the rule, the firm's credibility must be developed by contacts with many people, since it is often impossible to identify who is the ultimate individual decision-maker. There may be no such person. US or European companies often believe that they have lost a deal negotiated with the Japanese because they do not receive a 'yes' for weeks and sometimes months. During this time, the *ringi* has been at work in the Japanese company. Proposals are circulated among everyone involved in the deal, so that they can discuss it and ultimately affix their own seal of approval. Since (objective) credibility is based on power and decision-making, a capacity to understand the influence process in the other party's decision-making is therefore a key asset for effective negotiation.

In any national environment there are always some institutions which enable potential partners in joint ventures to assess each other as credible (business schools, engineering schools or law schools, professional associations and meetings, clubs, etc.). Laton McCartney (1989), for instance, describes 'The Grove', an annual three-day encampment, organized by the Bohemian Club of San Francisco, which has played a significant role in the growth of the Bechtel empire, the world leader in turnkey operations for many years:

> But the real business of The Grove, where a favorite pastime was figuring out the corporate connections and interlocking directorates of incoming members, was just that: business. Not business by contract or by deal – both of which were barred on The Grove's grounds – but business by sheer association, by men spending time with, getting to know and like each other. 'Once you've spent three days with someone in an informal situation,' explained John D. Ehrlichman, who attended Grove encampments while a chief aide to Richard Nixon, 'you have a relationship – a relationship that opens doors and makes it easier to pick up the phone.' (McCartney, 1989, p. 14)

Interpersonal orientation

The reproach made to western businesspeople by the Japanese, quoted in the introduction of this chapter, illustrates differences in interpersonal orientation. The concept of *Ningensei* (Box 15.2) presented at the beginning of this chapter has to do with the Confucian ethics which favours smooth interactions and the underplaying of conflict to the benefit of social harmony; it is typical of collectivist values of interpersonal relationships. For instance, the interpersonal sensitivity of Japanese people and their sincere interest in foreign cultures and people may make them friendly hosts at business lunches or dinners. As emphasized by Hawrysh and Zaichkowsky (1990, p. 42): 'Before entering serious negotiations, Japanese business-men will spend considerable time and money entertaining foreign negotiating teams, in order to get to know their negotiating partners and establish with them a rapport built on friendship and trust.' But it should never be forgotten that Japanese negotiators remain down-to-earth: they are strongly aware of what their basic interests are.

Ingroup orientation

Concern for the other party's outcome is not necessarily to be found equally across cultures. Cultures place a stronger or weaker emphasis on group membership (the other party is/is not a member of the 'ingroup') as a prerequisite for being considered a trustworthy partner. In cultures where there is a clear-cut distinction between the 'ingroup' and the 'outgroup' (according to age, sex, race or kinship criteria), people tend to perceive the interests of both groups as diametrically opposed. This is related to what has been called the concept of 'limited good' (Foster, 1965).

According to the concept of 'limited good', if something positive happens in favour of the outgroup, the wealth and well-being of the ingroup will be threatened. Such reactions are largely based on culture-based collective subjectivity: they stem from the conservative idea that goods and riches are by their very nature restricted. If one yields to the other party even the tiniest concession, this will directly reduce what is left for the members of the ingroup. The concept of 'limited good' induces negotiators to adopt very

Box 15.2   *The Confucian logic in* Ningensei

Ningensei exemplifies four interrelated principles of Confucian philosophy: *jen, shu, i* and *li*:

1. Based on active listening, *jen* is a form of humanism that translates into empathetic interaction and caring for the feelings of negotiating associates, and seeking out the other's views, sentiments and true intentions.
2. *Shu* emphasizes the importance of reciprocity in establishing human relationships and the cultivation of 'like-heartedness'; in Mastumoto's (1988) words it is 'belly communication' a means of coding messages within negotiating, social, and corporate channels that is highly contingent upon affective, intuitive and non-verbal channels.
3. *i*, also termed *amae*, is the dimension which is concerned with the welfare of the collectivity, directing human relationships to the betterment of the common good. 'The *i* component of *ningensei* surfaces in Japanese negotiators' commitment to the organization, group agendas, and a reciprocity (*shu*) and humanism (*jen*) that is long-term, consistent, and looks beyond personal motivation.'
4. *Li* refers to the codes, corresponding to precise and formal manners, that facilitate the outer manifestation and social expression of *jen, shu* and *i*. The Japanese *meishi* ritual of exchanging business cards is typical of *li* coded etiquette.

(Source: adapted from Goldman, 1994, pp. 32–3)

territorial and distributive strategies. It is a view which clearly favours the idea of the zero sum game, where 'I will lose whatever you may win' and vice versa. In Mediterranean and Middle Eastern societies where the ingroup is highly valued (clan, tribe, extended family), the concept of 'limited good' is often to be found. It slows the adoption of a problem-solving orientation, since cooperative opportunities are simply difficult to envisage.

Power orientation

One must distinguish between the formal power orientation on the one hand and the real power/decision-making orientation on the other. The first has to do with status-showing and how it may enhance credibility, especially in high perceived potency societies. This deals with the kind of meetings, societies, clubs, alumni organizations which assemble potentially powerful people. Belonging to such circles gives an opportunity for social-izing and getting to know each other. The simple fact of being there and a member of a certain *club* is the main credibility message. The signs of formal power orientation differ across cultures; they may range from education and titles (English public schools, French *Grandes Ecoles*, *Herr Doktor*, etc.) to belonging to a particular social class or caste.

Real power orientation is a somewhat different issue. As evidenced by Box 14.2 ('The little man in rags and tatters'), there may be wide differences between formal and actual influence on the decision-making process. When making contacts, in a cross-cultural perspective, people should be aware of the following: (1) status is not shown in the same way according to culture; (2) influential persons are not the same and individual influence is not exerted in the same way; and (3) the decision-making process differs.

Hofstede (1989) in an article about the cultural predictors of negotiation styles, hypothesizes that larger power distance will lead to a more centralized control and decision-making structure because key negotiations have to be concluded by the top authority. And in fact Fisher (1980) notes in the case of Mexico, a typically high power distance country (a score of 81 on Hofstede's scale; see Table 3.3), that one finds a relatively centralized decision-making, based on individuals who have extended respons-ibility at the top of an organization. They become frustrated in front of the Americans who tend to have several negotiators in charge of compartmentalized issues:

> In another mismatch of the systems, the American finds it hard to determine how much Mexican decision making authority goes with which designated authority. There, as in many of the more traditional systems, authority tends to reside somewhat more in the person than in the position, and an organization chart does little to tell the outsider just what leverage – *palanca* – the incumbent has. (Fisher, 1980, p. 29)

Willingness to take risks

Harnett and Cummings (1980), using a risk-aversion scale ranging from 16 to 48, have shown Americans to be risk-takers (31.9) in comparison to the Thais being highly risk-averse (38.2) and the Japanese (34.1) and the Europeans (around 35.7) being in the middle. A high level of uncertainty avoidance is noted by Hofstede as being associated with a more bureaucratic functioning and a lower tendency for individuals to take risks. This may be a problem for business negotiators when they have received a mandate from top management. For instance, the bureaucratic orientation in ex-communist countries has imposed strong government control on industry. As a consequence, Chinese negotiators, for instance, tend not to be capable of individual decision-making. Before any agreement is reached, official government approval must be sought by Chinese negotiators (Eiteman, 1990). The same has been noted in the case of Russian negotiators by Beliaev *et al.* (1985, p. 110): 'Throughout the process a series of ministries are involved. ... Such a process also limits the degree of risk taking that is possible ... the American who does see it from (the Soviet) perspective may well interpret it as being slow, lacking in initiative and unproductive.' Tse *et al.* (1994) confirm this tendency in the case of Chinese executives who tend to consult their superiors significantly more than Canadian executives who belong to a low uncertainty avoidance society.

15.4   Underlying concepts of negotiation and negotiation strategies

Integrative orientation versus distribution orientation

In business negotiations the purchaser (or team of purchasers) and the vendor (or group of vendors) are mutually interdependent while their individual interests clash. The ability to choose effective negotiation largely explains the individual performance of each party on the one hand, and the joint outcome on the other. In pitting themselves against each other, the parties may develop opposing points of view towards the negotiation strategy which they intend to adopt: distributive or integrative.

In the distributive strategy (or orientation), the negotiation process is seen as leading to the division of a fixed 'cake' which the parties feel they cannot enlarge even if they were willing to do so. This orientation is also termed 'competitive negotiation' or 'zero sum game'. It leads to a perception of negotiation as a war of positions – territorial in essence. These are negotiations of the 'win–lose' type: 'anything that isn't yours is mine' and vice versa. The negotiators hold attitudes and objectives that are quasi-conflictive (Dupont, 1994). Interdependence is minimized whereas adverseness is emphasized.

At the opposite end of the spectrum is the integrative orientation (Walton and McKersie, 1965). The central assumption is that the size of the 'cake' (the joint outcome of the negotiations) can be increased if the parties adopt a cooperative attitude. Negotiators may not be concerned purely with their own objectives, but may also be interested in the other party's aspirations and results, seeing them as almost equally important. Integrative orientation has been termed 'cooperative' or 'collaborative'. It results in negotiation being seen as an attempt to maximize the joint outcome. The division of this outcome is to a certain extent secondary or is at least perceived as an important but later issue. Here negotiation is a 'positive sum game' where the joint outcome is greater than zero.

In practice, effective negotiation combines distributive and integrative orientations

Table 15.2 *Dual concern model*

Concern for the other party's outcomes	Concern for one's own outcomes	
	Low	High
High	Yielding	Integrative strategy
Low	Inaction	Contending

simultaneously, or at different stages in the negotiation process (Pruitt, 1981). The 'dual concern model', presented in Table 15.2 (Pruitt, 1983), explains negotiation strategies according to two basic variables: concern for one's own outcome and concern for the other party's outcome. This leads to four possible strategies. According to this model, the ability to envisage the other party's outcome is a prerequisite for the adoption of an integrative strategy.

Factors favouring an integrative strategy

The adoption of an integrative strategy is facilitated by the following:

1. A higher level of aspirations on both sides: the negotiators want to reach a better outcome or are under pressure from their principals who have defined increased outcome objectives while still allowing them explicit autonomy and room for manoeuvre (Pruitt and Lewis, 1975).
2. The ability to envisage the future; this permits the discovery or 'invention' of new solutions, which enables both partners to overcome the problem of the fixed size of the 'territorial cake'.
3. The existence of 'perceived common ground' (Pruitt, 1983); if sufficiently wide, this overlap between the interests of the two parties allows new solutions to be explored.

If one seeks to develop relational marketing, an integrative negotiating strategy is required. The nature of transactions imposes it. Business is fairly continuous and sometimes stretches over several years, and therefore implies a very strong buyer–seller interdependence. The performance level depends largely on the extent and the quality of the collaboration between the partners. In studying the styles of negotiation of industrial purchasers, Perdue *et al.* (1986) have found, on the basis of a sample of 195 industrial purchasers, that the majority of them saw themselves as adopting an integrative strategy towards vendors.

Problem-solving approach

The integrative orientation is directly linked to a problem-solving approach in negotiation (Pruitt, 1983). Problem-solving approach (PSA) can be defined as an overall negotiating behaviour that is cooperative, integrative and oriented towards the exchange of information (Campbell *et al.*, 1988). Fair communication and the exchange of information between negotiators are important. 'Problem-solvers' exchange representative information, that is, honest and objective data. There is no desire to manipulate the partner, as in instrumental communication (Angelmar and Stern, 1978). Empirical studies (experimental negotiation stimulation) have shown that this orientation positively influences the common results of negotiation (Pruitt, 1983). Rubin and Carter (1990), for instance, demonstrate the general superiority of cooperative negotiation by developing a model whereby a new, more cooperative contract provides both the buyer and the seller with cost reduction, compared with a previous adversarial contract. There are, however, some conditions: the first is the availability of cost-related data, the second is the release of the data to the other party during negotiation. The sharing of data is obviously conditioned by culture, language and communication-related issues.

The very concept of PSA is based on culturally relative assumptions:

1. The *doing* orientation is very strong in PSA – to solve a problem is to *do* something – and quite often PSA is posited as the *task*-related part of negotiation.
2. It assumes that both partners are *fair*, an English word untranslatable in many languages – *fair-play* is used as such in French, for instance; 'fair' means something like 'open and honest in communication and interaction' a value which is not shared by many other cultures, as shown in the next chapter on national negotiation styles.
3. A view of *reciprocity*, based on *quick* response to the other party's openings, on a give-and-take basis were concessions on each side are precisely *measured* and balanced.

As noted by Graham *et al.* (1994), the problem-solving approach appears to make sense for the American negotiators, but this framework may not work in all cases when applied to foreign negotiators. Graham *et al.* (1994) developed an empirical comparison across ten countries/cultures (the United States, Anglophone Canada, Francophone Canada, Mexico, the United Kingdom, France, Germany, the former USSR, Taiwan, China, Korea), starting from three rival hypotheses: (1) the PSA framework is universal; (2) there exist variations within the PSA framework when applied to foreign groups; and (3) it does not work at all when applied to non-US negotiators. They show that on average the model works 'differently', and a claim for universality cannot be made. If we think in terms of *ningensei*, it is easy to imagine how, on the one hand, negotiation can be seen universally as problems to be solved, and on the other hand, the ways and means of problem solving may differ: PSA favours task-orientation whereas *ningensei* favours a sense of being on the 'same wavelength', that is, relationship orientation.

Cultural dispositions to being integrative

Even though one may accept the increased effectiveness of integrative strategies, in as far as they aim to maximize the joint outcome, the problem of how this joint outcome is divided between the two sides remains an interesting issue. Three questions then merit consideration:

1. Do the parties tend to perceive negotiations as being easier, and do they tend to adopt an integrative orientation more readily, when they both share the same culture?
2. Do negotiators originating from particular cultures tend towards an integrative or distributive orientation? Furthermore, do negotiators originating from cultures which favour a problem-solving orientation risk seeing their personal results heavily diminished by a distributive partner who cynically exploits their 'goodwill'?
3. Do cultural differences and intercultural negotiation reduce the likelihood of integrative strategy?

Greater difficulties in being integrative in an intercultural negotiation situation than in an intracultural negotiation situation

There is general agreement among the existing literature that the results of negotiation are less favourable when the negotiation is intercultural as opposed to intracultural, all other things being equal (Sawyer and Guetzkow, 1965). Van Zandt (1970) suggests that the negotiations between Americans and the Japanese are six times as long and three times as difficult as those purely between Americans. This increases the costs of the transaction for the American firms in Japan owing to the relative inefficiency of communication. The subjective satisfaction of the negotiators (measured by a questionnaire) in their result tends to be inferior for intercultural negotiation compared to intracultural negotiation (Weitz, 1979; Graham, 1985).

Problem-solving depends on a collaborative attitude which is easier with a partner from the same culture: similarity, according to Rubin and Brown (1975), leads to more trust and an enhanced level of interpersonal attraction (Graham, 1985). As a result, each side considers communication from the other as more representative: in other words, one party perceives that it transmits fairly objective information and does not try to influence the other party, as with instrumental communication.

The hypothesis that the similarity of the parties leads to a more favourable outcome was proposed by Evans (1963). Similarity facilitates awareness and exploration between parties. In fact it is more a question of *perceived* similarity which leads to more cooperative behaviour in negotiation. If this similarity is perceived, but not based on strictly objective indications (such as shared nationality, language or educational background), a dissymetric view of similarity may arise between the buyer and the seller. For instance many business people in the Middle East have a good command of either the English or French language and culture. Middle Eastern businesspeople are often perceived by their American or European counterparts as being similar, whereas they may perceive their western counterparts as different.

The role adopted in negotiation, buyer or seller, combines with perceived similarity: if sellers perceive a greater similarity, this can lead to a stronger problem-solving orientation on their part. Although appealing, similarity-based hypotheses have been poorly validated by the empirical study carried out by Campbell *et al.* (1988). No significant relationship was found among American and British buyer/seller pairs: similarity did not favour problem-solving orientation. In the case of the French and the Germans, the perceived similarity only led to a stronger problem-solving orientation on the part of the seller. However, in Campbell *et al.* (1988), the actual dissimilarity between negotiators was strongly reduced by the fact that all the simulated negotiations were intracultural.

In intercultural terms, the possibility exists of a misunderstanding arising from a perception of similarity which is not shared by both parties. For example, one can imagine a situation where a seller (American, for instance) perceives the buyer as similar (an Arab buyer who is very westernized in appearance, who has a superficial but misleading cultural outlook because of his cultural borrowing). However, the reverse situation does not occur: the Arab buyer is aware that the American seller knows little about the Arabic culture. The seller will in this case have a tendency to take a problem-solving orientation, because of fallacious perceived similarity, whereas the buyer may exploit the seller without feeling obliged to reciprocate and ultimately maximize his personal outcome by adopting a distributive strategy. However, the *dynamics of similarity* (showing to the other side that one understands them and thus lay the foundation for an integrative attitude on both sides) can go the other way round, and *adaptation* can bring a positive result. Harris and Moran (1987, p. 472) cite the case of a US banker from the midwest invited by an Arab sheikh for a meeting in London. The banker demonstrates unusual patience and deep awareness of the other party's power.

> The banker arrives in London and waits to meet the sheikh. After two days he is told to fly to Riyadh in Saudi Arabia, which he does. He waits. After three days in Riyadh, he meets the sheikh and the beginning of what was to become a very beneficial business relationship between the two persons and their organizations began.

National orientations favouring the integrative strategy

The second question concerns the adoption of integrative strategies by some nationalities more than others. Studies tend to show that American businesspeople show trust more willingly and more spontaneously than other cultural groups and have a stronger tendency towards a problem-solving and integrative orientation (Druckman *et al.*, 1976; Harnett and Cummings, 1980). The level of their profits as sellers depends on the buyer responding positively by also adopting a problem-solving approach (Campbell *et al.*, 1988).

American negotiators have a stronger tendency to exchange representative communication, making clear and explicit messages a priority, and to exhibit less suspicion towards the other party than most other cultures (Harnett and Cummings, 1980). This is in line with the American appreciation of frankness and directness (see Chapter 12, explicit communication according to Edward Hall). This is what Graham and Herberger (1983) call the 'John Wayne Style' (Box 15.3). They often meet certain difficulties with cultures who take more time in the preliminaries: getting to know each other, that is, talking generally and only actually getting down to business later. As a result, Americans may not foster feelings of trust in negotiators from other cultural groups who feel it necessary to get to know the person they are dealing with (Hall, 1976).

Box 15.3　*The 'John Wayne Style': just call me John*

Americans, more than any other national group, value informality and equality in human relations. The emphasis on first names is only the beginning. We go out of our way to make our clients feel comfortable by playing down status distinctions such as titles and by eliminating 'unnecessary' formalities such as lengthy introductions. All too often, however, we succeed only in making ourselves feel comfortable while our clients become uneasy or even annoyed. For example, in Japanese society interpersonal relationships are vertical; in almost all two-person relationships a difference in status exists. The basis for such distinction may be one or several factors: age, sex, university attended, position in an organization, and even one's particular firm or company. . . . Each Japanese is very much aware of his or her own position relative to others with whom he or she deals. . . . The roles of the higher status position and the lower status position are quite different, even to the extent that Japanese use different words to express the same idea depending on which person makes the statement. For example a buyer would say *otaku* (your company), while a seller would say *on sha* (your great company). Status relations dictate not only what is said but also how it is said.

(Source: Graham and Herberger, 1983, p. 162. Reproduced with permission.)

Graham and Meissner (1986) have shown in a study comparing five countries that the most integrative strategies are adopted by the Brazilians, followed by the Japanese. On the other hand, the Americans, the Germans and the Koreans choose intermediate strategies that are more distributive. This is consistent in the case of the Germans who are reputed for using the hard-sell approach, where the seller is fairly pushy and adopts an instrumental communication and a distributive strategy (Campbell *et al.*, 1988).

There is no empirical study that has shown, for example, that the Arabs from the Middle East have a tendency to be more distributive than the Americans. Americans tend to see the world as problems to be solved whereas Arabs see it more as a creation of God. Similarly as above for PSA, the concept of integrative strategy is strongly culturally influenced by the American tradition of experimental research in social psychology applied to commercial negotiation. It is based on a 'master of destiny' orientation which feeds attitudes of problem resolution. This presupposes a simultaneous concern for one's own outcome as well as for that of the negotiating partner (the 'dual concern model').

Ignorance of the other party's culture as an obstacle to the implementation of an integrative strategy in negotiation

One of the most important obstacles to effective international business negotiation is the ignorance of all or at least the basics of the other party's culture. This is intellectually obvious, but is often forgotten by international negotiators. It refers not only to the cognitive ignorance of the main traits of the other party's culture, but also to the unconscious prejudice that differences are minor (that is, ignorance as absence of awareness). This favours the natural tendency to refer implicitly to one's own cultural norms, especially for the coding/decoding process of communication.

Lucian Pye (1986), in the case of business negotiations between American and Chinese people, and Rosalie Tung (1984) in US–Japanese business negotiations, note the lack of prior knowledge of the American negotiators about their partner's culture. Before coming to the negotiation table, Americans do not generally read books, nor do they train themselves for the foreign communication style, nor learn about the potential traps which could lead to misunderstandings. As Carlos Fuentes states (in a rather harsh aphorism): 'What the U.S. does best is understand itself. What it does worst is understand others' (Fuentes, 1986). French negotiators also tend to be underprepared in terms of cultural knowledge (see the following chapter on national negotiation styles), whereas the Japanese seemingly try to learn a lot more than the French or the Americans about the other party's culture before negotiation takes place. The negotiation and implementation (which often means ongoing negotiations) of a joint venture may last for several years. In this case, national cultures tend to disappear as the two teams partly merge their values and behaviour in a common 'venture culture'. In order to improve intercultural negotiation effectiveness, it is advisable to build this common culture between the partners/ adversaries right from the start of the negotiations. Adaptation should, however, be made cautiously: it does not mean wholesale adoption of strategies that work for natives, and the advice 'when in Rome do as the Romans do' has to be applied with due caution (Francis, 1991). It means establishing common rules, communication codes, finding people on each side who will act as go-betweens and trying to agree on a common interpretation of issue, facts, solutions and decision-making. This must not be considered as a formal process; it is informal and built on implicit communications. Furthermore, it relies heavily on those individuals who have been involved in the joint venture over a long period of time and who get on well together.

15.5   Time-based misunderstandings in international marketing negotiations

When reading this section, the reader should have in mind time-related cultural differences presented in section 2.2.

A continuous versus discontinuous view of time

Cultures which have a cyclical and integrative view of time will tend to have an underlying concept of negotiation whereby it is only one round of a recurrent relational process, with little sequencing compared with people holding a linear/separable view of time. This is also to be found in the outcome orientation where the time line of negotiation is less important for people with a cyclical/integrative view of time: for them a contract signed is no real reason not to pursue the negotiation process. The *strategic time frame* also depends on temporal orientations: the lack of future orientation, for instance, may be a serious impediment for true involvement of a party.

Time for preliminaries

The role of spending time for establishing personal relationships, especially in Asia and South America, is noted by many authors (Hall, 1983; Pye, 1986; Graham and Sano, 1990; Hawrysh and Zaichkowski, 1990). There are a series of reasons for which a personal relationship is needed: (1) establishing the context of communication (Hall, 1976), acquaintance with the other persons being part of the necessary context; (2) a less strict separation between personal and professional spheres than in the West; and (3) the importance of personal status that causes the need for spending time in exploring who is who with some discretion in order not to offend partners. This is all summed up in Burt's comments (1984, p. 7) that an American negotiator will be well advised to develop personal relations away from the negotiation room: 'The usual intense and rather dry approach to doing business must be supplemented with a social relationship. The Japanese are accustomed to the use of entertainment as a means of becoming better acquainted and of developing goodwill.'

The cultural time concept of Americans, strongly economic, partly explains why spending time for building personal relations is implicitly seen as bad. Time being seen as a resource not to be wasted, spending time on non-business matters, non-task related issues, is experienced as a violation of their cultural norms. What Adler *et al.* (1987) call 'non-task sounding', that is establishing rapport and getting to know each other, the first phase in his four-phase process of business negotiations, not only needs a relaxed sense of economic time but also some past orientation: seeing Japanese shrines, learning the basic about *Zen* or *Ikebana*, the Japanese floral art. The Japanese feel that an understanding of their past is necessary for understanding them as negotiation partners today.

Setting the agenda and scheduling the negotiation process

These tasks are considered by most of the negotiation literature as necessary for the second step in Graham's four-stage model: task-related exchange of information. An agenda is a schedule and list of items to be discussed during the negotiation process. In many cultures the very notion of 'agenda setting' is unheard of: cutting the process into pieces in advance and allocating time lots to each 'task' is at best theoretical. Hall's differences between monochronic and polychronic is highly relevant for the scheduling of negotiation. An agenda oriented negotiation team, basically monochronic, tends to try to negotiate clauses sequentially, whereas the other party, polychronic, may skip from an issue to another, come back to points which had apparently been already settled, because they tend negotiate globally. Graham and Herberger (1983) call it 'One thing at a time': Americans usually attack a complex negotiation task sequentially, that is they separate the issues and try to settle them one at a time.

Managing a temporal clash in intercultural business negotiations

Partners from different cultures may be working together to develop a low-cost operation, or a new R & D project, or distribution and sales facilities, depending on the aim assigned to the joint venture. In such settings, issues to do with time will inevitably arise, both at an everyday level, simply in order to meet at the same time, and at a deeper level, that of assigning a common time frame to business operations. The case in Box 15.4 recounts a stereotypical story which illustrates the clash of temporal cultures both at the individual and at organizational levels.

Different time perspectives, be they organizational or cultural, result in temporal clashes. The conflicts that result from the inability to merge different ways of dealing with time may be located at an individual level, that of business people interacting with foreign partners and negotiating with them. Temporal clash at the level of individual interaction results from differing answers given to the following questions: how is somebody treated when he or she arrives half an hour late for a negotiation session? Do sessions have a finishing time in addition to their starting time? Is time also structured during the meeting by setting an agenda and a definite time limit for discussion on each point?

To illustrate the synchronization problem in negotiation, let us take the example of a French meeting versus a US one (a fairly polychronic versus a fairly monochronic culture; see section 2.2). In France some people come late by quarter of an hour, and some by half an hour. Not only the meeting does not start on time, but those people who were on time have to wait for those who are late. Rarely do people who are late present apologies. Some, not all, simply explain why they were late. It is not rare that, when somebody arrives quite late, most other people stop their discussion and spend five or ten

Box 15.4   *Temporal clash*

Young Mr Johnson, a US (or English) executive, is organising an international meeting: At 1.50 P.M. most participants returned to the meeting room. At 2.05 Johnson started pacing restlessly up and down. Munoz and Gialli were still down the hall making telephone calls. They came in at 2.20 P.M. Johnson said, 'Now, gentlemen, can we finally start the meeting.' The Singaporean and African representatives looked puzzled. They thought the meeting had already started. The first point on the agenda was the time intervals determining bonuses and merits. All except the American, Dutch and other north-west European representatives complained that these were far too frequent. To Johnson and his Dutch and Scandinavian colleagues the frequency was obviously right: 'Rewards must closely follow the behaviour they are intended to reinforce, otherwise you lose the connection.' The manager from Singapore said: 'Possibly, but this go-for-the-quick-buck philosophy has been losing us customers. They don't like the pressure we put on at the end of the quarter. They want our representatives to serve them, not to have private agendas. We need to keep our customers long-term, not push them into buying so that one sales person can beat a rival.'

(Source: Trompenaars, 1993, p. 115. Reproduced with permission)

minutes to explain to the belated what has been said up to now! Moreover, contrary to the US meetings, French meetings are almost never assigned a finishing time. This means that quite often, if there are several successive meetings, the reason why some people arrive late is that the previous meeting was late and finished one or two hours after the (more or less vaguely and implicitly) agreed-upon finishing time.

Time-based tactical moves: exerting time pressures in the bargaining process

Pressure can be exerted on economic-time minded negotiators by postponing the beginning of the negotiation, delaying meetings, making the end of negotiation unknown to them, etc. Cohen (1980) gives a classical example of how the Japanese manipulate their western partner's excessive time consciousness. The Japanese ask him when he is arriving at Tokyo airport:

> 'Are you concerned about getting back to your plane on time?' (Up to that moment I had not been concerned.) 'We can schedule this limousine to transport you back to the airport.' I thought in myself, 'how considerate.' Reaching my pocket, I handed them my return flight ticket, so the limousine would know when to get me. I didn't realize it then, but they knew my deadline, whereas I didn't know theirs. (p. 94)

The place where the negotiation takes place has an obvious influence of time-scarcity. Those who are 'at home' can monitor their regular business tasks while participating in the negotiations. Those who have left their home country to negotiate at their partner's location can be for many reasons, both professional and personal, impatient to go back. *The pressure of 'wasted time'* can be easily used against those who have both an economic pattern of time and are far from their home base.

The expression 'to waste time' has little meaning for many cultures, including the Bantus whose time patterns were described in Reading A2.4. One may lose something tangible, like a ring or a pencil. But in order to waste and lose time, time should be a thing or – at least – it would be necessary to be able to separate time from the events with which it is inextricably bound up. Indeed the Bantus find it difficult to equate abstract time with a monetary unit of measurement. As outlined previously, within their culture Bantu people know nothing comparable to a linear Newtonian time, where events take place. There are events, and each one of these events carries its own desire and its own time. Time cannot be wasted or lost, because time has simply to be lived or experienced, whatever may be the way to experience it. No one can steal time, not even death.

The same quietness in the face of time may be seen in the Orient, compared to the Occidental anguish and guilt about time that might be wasted or lost. Several authors in the field of international business negotiations note that time pressure is strongly felt by American negotiators, whether they negotiate with the Chinese (Pye, 1982) or with the Japanese (Graham, 1981; Graham and Sano, 1990; Tung, 1984). American negotiators are eventually forced to yield by their representation of time as potentially wasted or lost if it is not optimally allocated. When this logic is pushed to its extreme it may result in total inefficiency. People spend their whole time thinking of possible alternative uses of their time and calculating which of these alternatives offers the best marginal return. As noted by Adler (1986, p. 162):

> Americans' sense of urgency disadvantages them with respect to less hurried bargaining partners. Negotiators from other countries recognize Americans' time consciousness, achievement orientation, and impatience. They know that Americans will make concessions close to their deadline (time consciousness) in order to get a signed contract (achievement orientation).

Making plans together: coordinating and planning the common venture

In many international negotiations planning the common venture, the steps of construction of a turnkey plant, or the implementation phases of a joint-venture or licence agreement, need explicit reference to dates, deadlines and the sequencing of interdependent tasks, that is planning. Planning is such a basic function of management that it is extremely difficult to admit that there are other models of time than those on which it implicitly stands. Naturally it would be naive to consider that business people have purely traditional time patterns. In fact, complex patterns of time-related behaviour may be used by people sharing several cultural backgrounds, one of them being the original in-depth background, the other(s) being much more superficial. Furthermore the native cultural background may be undervalued because it is supposed to be 'inefficient' or it is unknown to foreigners. Accordingly, people belonging to non-linear/economic time cultures often have a tendency to imitate the cultural way of life that they tend to favour as the 'best' way. It might result in buying a superb watch as an item of jewellery or a diary because it is fashionable. But the functional behaviour which is in line with the watch or the diary will not be adopted. After these objects have been bought, they lose their cultural value as practical tools of the economic/monochronic/linear/separable time pattern. People involved in such cultural borrowing might prove unable to take any appointment seriously and probably experience difficulties in following any preset schedule.

The fallacy of imported economic time: ideal and actual temporal behaviour

Ideal patterns of time and actual temporal behaviour may differ widely for negotiators who apparently use their partners' time culture rather than their own. Bista (1990), in the case of Nepal, highlights the conflict between time-based behaviour related to foreign education and the traditional influence of fatalistic beliefs on the lack of future orientation and sense of planning:

> Planning involves the detailing of the connections between resources, objects and events, and the determination of an efficient course of action to attain desired results. . . . Control is placed in the hands of the planner. But fatalism does not allow this kind of control, and is inherently antithetical to pragmatic thought. . . . Over the past few decades, many Nepali

students have travelled abroad to study in other countries, and have returned with advanced degrees in various professional capacities. . . . Upon their return many are placed in positions of authority, as they represent the cream of Nepal's manpower resources. Though they may be initially inspired by a high degree of idealism, the new values that they bring back with them immediately confront fatalism and are typically defeated by it. . . . After forty years of planning and an accumulation of foreign trained graduates, Nepal, then, still has little manpower to effectively bridge the disparities between the culture of the foreign aid donors and that of their own. (1990, pp. 137–8)

In everyday management behaviour (appointments, scheduling, meetings) it is quite probable that we face a high level of cultural borrowing: actual time behaviour of economically successful countries like the United States or countries of northern Europe have been imported by other nations as ideal patterns (Usunier, 1990). It is, for instance, very clear that in Latin-European countries, the PERT technique, which is designed for the scheduling of interrelated tasks, has been implemented mostly for its intellectual appeal. PERT is based on graph theory, and has an appealing US 'management science' look. In France, where many managers and top executives have been trained as engineers, there has been a great interest in this scientific management technique. Real project planning in France and Latin-European countries very often works with high discrepancies relative to PERT dates: French people tend to be intellectually monochronic but actually behave in a polychronic manner (Hall, 1983).

Sometimes people even use two completely different systems in parallel. This somewhat schizophrenic situation is most easily recognized by looking at the construction of some turnkey projects in developing countries (Bista, 1990). At the beginning, during the negotiation process and on signature of the contract, everybody seemingly (and also sincerely) agrees about using economic time/monochronic pattern. In fact the partners share the same belief, but as an ideal pattern on one side and as an actual behaviour on the other. There may not even be discussion about it: obviously it is the right way to proceed. But afterwards extreme confusion appears when the project is being implemented.

15.6 Cultural misunderstandings during the negotiation process

Existence of a common rationality between the partners

As explained in section 3.4 people differ in their way of relating thinking to action: whereas ideologists tend to think broadly and relate to general principles, the pragmatist orientation values focusing on detailed issues that are to be solved one by one. Typical pragmatists are the Americans, as noted by Weiss (1987, p. 31), in the case of the GM–Toyota negotiations for their joint venture in California, where 'the Japanese tended to start talks with statements of general principle and usually did not respond to proposals before checking with their headquarters. The Americans preferred specific proposals and responses at the table.'

When negotiating a large contract (for a nuclear plant or a television satellite, for instance), ideologists see arguments in favour of their 'global way of thinking': it is a

Box 15.5   *Cartesian logic in negotiation*

> Rather imprecisely defined, the idea is that one reasons from a starting point based on what is known, and then pays careful attention to the logical way in which one point leads to the next, and finally reaches a conclusion regarding the issue at hand. The French also assign greater priority than Americans do to establishing the principles on which the reasoning process should be based. Once this reasoning process is underway, it becomes relatively difficult to introduce new evidence or facts, most especially during a negotiation. Hence the appearance of French inflexibility, and the need to introduce new information and considerations early in the game. All this reflects the tradition of French education and becomes the status mark of the educated person. In an earlier era observers made such sweeping generalizations as: 'The French always place a school of thought, a formula, convention, a priori arguments, abstraction, and artificiality above reality; they prefer clarity to truth, words to things, rhetoric to science . . .' [Quotation from Zeldin (1977). Reproduced with the kind permission of the publisher.]

(Fisher, 1980, p. 50)

unitary production, it is a complex multipartner business, it often involves government financing and also has far-reaching social, economic and political consequences. Pragmatists, on the other hand, also find many arguments in favour of their way of thinking: the technicalities of the plant and its desired performance require an achievement and deadline orientation (pragmatist values).

Pragmatism is associated with a tendency to look at facts in their details, to measure, to validate empirically. Ideologists on the other hand have a liking for speech, words and ideas. They will be more instrumental communication oriented. In as much as they aim to manipulate other people, ideologists may be as effective as the pragmatists, by influencing their counterparts through nicely worded general communication. In relational marketing, especially in the first two phases of the relational exchange, negotiation between ideologists and pragmatists may create misunderstandings (see Box 15.5) which will be difficult to overcome during subsequent phases.

Indeed, developing common norms will be fairly difficult, although necessary if partners want to be able to predict the other party's behaviour. A frequent comment in such situations will be: 'One never knows what these people have in mind; their behaviour is largely unpredictable.' An American (pragmatist oriented) describes negotiations with the French (more ideologist oriented) in the following terms (Burt, 1984, p. 6): 'The French are extremely difficult to negotiate with. Often they will not accept facts, no matter how convincing they may be.'

Communication

Most of the content of Chapter 12 applies directly to the process of international marketing negotiations. For instance, the role of high context versus low context is to be noted. When messages are exchanged the degree to which they should be interpreted has to be taken into account. For instance, silence is a form of communication for the

Japanese, and Graham (1985) reports twice as many silence in Japanese interaction than American. Westerners often have the impression that they 'do all the talking'. In fact, being ready to try to understand very different styles of communication is a key to better negotiation. This is especially true for non-verbal communication. For instance a lack of eye contact for the Americans is a signal that something is amiss and 'American executives reported that the lack of eye contact was not only disconcerting but reduced their bargaining performance' (Hawrysh and Zaichkowsky, 1990, p. 34).

Negotiators must be ready to hear true as well as false information, discourse based on facts as well as on wishful thinking or pure obedience to superiors. Frankness and sincerity are relative values: they can be interpreted as mere naivety, a lack of realism, or a lack of self-control in speaking one's own mind. Furthermore, waiting for reciprocation when disclosing useful information for the other party makes little sense in an inter-cultural context. Frankness and directness are of substantial value for the Americans and to a lesser extent for the French, but they are not so for Mexicans in formal encounters, nor to the Japanese at any time (Fisher, 1980).

The issue of formality versus informality is a difficult one. Frequently a contrast is made between cultures that value informality (e.g. American) and those that are more formal (most cultures which have long historical roots and high power distance). 'Informality' may be simply another kind of formalism and the 'ice breaking' at the beginning of any typical US meeting between unknown people is generally an expected ritual. More important is to try to understand what kind of formality is required in which circumstance with which people. Out of formal negotiation sessions, people belonging to apparently quite formal cultures can become much more informal. Formalism in communication takes sometimes the form of diplomatic language, a highly coded type of speech, sometimes apparently quite remote from actual reality, known in French as *langue de bois* (literally 'wooden tongue' or 'wood language'). George Orwell in *Animal Farm*, gives a good example of *langue de bois* concerning the pig Napoleon who had taken control of the farm.

> Napoleon was now never spoken of simply as 'Napoleon'. He was always referred to in formal style as 'our Leader, Comrade Napoleon', and the pigs liked to invent for him such titles as Father of All Animals, Terror of Mankind, Protector of the Sheepfold, Ducklings' Friend, and the like. In his speeches Squealer would talk with the tears rolling down his cheeks of Napoleon's wisdom, the goodness of his heart, and the deep love he bore to all animals everywhere, even and especially the unhappy animals who still lived in ignorance and slavery on other farms. It had become usual to give Napoleon the credit for every successful achievement and every stroke of good fortune. You would often hear one hen remark to another, 'Under the guidance of our Leader, Comrade Napoleon, I have laid five eggs in six days'; or two cows, enjoying a drink at the pool would exclaim, 'Thanks to the leadership of Comrade Napoleon, how excellent this water tastes!' (1945, p. 62)

Langue de bois, although a very non-American concept given the emphasis on direct, frank and honest speech in US culture, is practised in many organizations world-wide, either concerning powerful people or groups, or concerning tabooed issues; for instance, a previous failure with a foreign partner that would shed some useful light on actual negotiations.

Negotiation tactics

Graham (1993) has studied the negotiation tactics used in eight cultures, using videotaped negotiations where statements were classified in twelve categories using the framework of Angelmar and Stern (1978). His results show very similar negotiation tactics across cultures, most of them using a majority of tactics based on an exchange of information, either by self-disclosure or questions (more than 50 per cent in all cases). The Chinese are the highest in posing questions which is consistent with the comments of Pye about them: 'Once negotiation begins the Chinese seem passive. They simply ask questions, probe for information, and conceal any eagerness they may feel' (1986, p. 78). On the other hand, the Spaniards are the best at making promises. The proportion of 'negative' tactics, including threats, warnings, punishment and negative normative appeal (a statement in which the source indicates that the target's behaviour is in violation of social norms) is fairly low in all cases, never exceeding 10 per cent of the information exchange. Finally cross-national differences are not great at the level of the type of tactics used, nor at the level of their frequency but rather at the level of how they are implemented.

The use of theatricality, withdrawal threats and tactics based on time, such as waiting for the last moment to obtain further concessions by making new demands, are based in national styles of negotiations which are discussed in the next chapter. Tactics are also related to the ambiguous atmosphere of business negotiations when implied warm human relations are supposed to be mixed with business. This relates to the divide between affective and neutral cultures (Trompenaars, 1993) presented at the end of section 3.5. Negotiations are always interspersed with friendship and enmity, based on personal as well as cultural reasons.

15.7 Differences in outcome orientation: Oral versus written agreements as a basis for trust between the parties

It would be naive to believe that profits, especially future accounting profits for each party, are the only possible outcome of the negotiation process. Other possible outcomes are listed in Table 15.2. The main reason for profits not to be the sole possible outcome is they are not really foreseeable. Basic differences in outcome orientation are generally hidden to the negotiation partners, generating increased misunderstandings. Another reason is that many cultures are more relationship rather than deal oriented: as is described by Weiss (1987) and Hawrysh and Zaichkowski (1990) in the case of the Japanese, and Pye (1986) and Eiteman (1990) in the case of the Chinese, they prefer a gentleman's agreement, a loosely worded statement expressing mutual cooperation and trust between the parties, than a formal western-style contract.

Asymmetry in the perceived degree of agreement

Agreements are generally considered as being mostly written. They are achieved by negotiation and by the signing of written contracts, which are often considered 'the law of the parties'. This is unfortunately not always true. Keegan (1984) points out that for some cultures 'my word is my bond' and trust is a personal matter, which he contrasts with the 'get-it-in-writing' mentality where trust is more impersonal. The former is typical of the Middle East, whereas the latter is to be found in the United States where hundreds of thousands of lawyers help people negotiate written agreements and litigate within the framework of these written agreements

This has to be interpreted: it does not mean that people rely *entirely* on either an oral base (oaths, confidence between people, membership of a common group where perjury is considered a crime) or a written base. Exploring, maintaining and checking the bases for trust is a more complex process (Usunier, 1989). It entails various possibilities:

1. An agreement may be non-symmetrical. A agrees with B, but B does not agree with A. Various reasons may explain this situation: either B wishes to conceal the disagreement or there is some sort of misunderstanding, usually language-based.
2. People agree, but on different bases, and they do not perceive the divergence. They have, for instance, quite different interpretations of a clause or some kind of non-written agreement.

   Although much may be written down, some things will always remain unwritten. What is unwritten may, to one party, seem obviously in line with a written clause, but not to the other. Moreover, if there is no opportunity to confront their interpretations, they cannot be aware of their divergent nature.
3. The agreement is not understood by both parties as having the same degree of influence on:
   (a) the stability;
   (b) the precision and explicitness of the exchange relation.

Written documents as a basis for mutual trust between the parties

There is a fundamental *dialectic in written agreements between distrust and confidence*. At the beginning there is distrust. It is implicitly assumed that such distrust is natural. This has to be reduced in order to establish confidence. Trust is not achieved on a global and personal basis but only by breaking down potential distrust in concrete situations where it may hamper common action. Trust is built step by step, with a view towards the future. Therefore *real trust* is achieved only gradually. Trust is deprived of its personal aspects. Thanks to the written agreement, the parties may trust each other in business, although they do not trust each other as people. Trust is taken to its highest point when the parties sign a written agreement.

On the other hand, cultures that favour oral agreements tend not to hypothesize that trust is constructed by the negotiation process. They see trust more as a prerequisite to the negotiation of written agreements. Naturally they do not expect this prerequisite to be met in every case. Trust tends to be mostly personal. Establishing trust requires that people know each other. That is probably why many Far Eastern cultures (Chinese, Pye, 1982; Japanese, Graham and Sano, 1990; Tung, 1984; de Mente, 1987) need to make informal contact, discuss general topics and spend time together before they get to the point, even though all this may not appear task-related.

Subsequently, the negotiation process will be lengthy because another dialectic is at work. Since people are supposed to trust each other, the negotiation process should not damage or destroy the basic asset of their exchange relationship – trust. They will avoid direct confrontation on a specific clause, and therefore globalize the negotiation process. Global friends may be local foes, provided trust is not lost as the basic asset of the negotiation process.

The ambiguity of the cultural status of written materials as a basis for trust-building between the parties

That one should always 'get-it-in-writing' is not self-evident. The contrary idea may even impose itself ('if they want it written down, it means that they don't trust me'). Regina Traoré Sérié (1986) (quoted in Ollivier and De Maricourt, 1990, p. 145) explains, for instance, the respective role of oral communication (spoken, transmitted through personal and concrete communication, passed through generations by storytellers) and the written materials (read, industrially printed, impersonally transmitted, with no concrete communication) in the African culture.

> Reading is an individual act, which does not easily incorporate itself into African culture. Written documents are presented as either irrelevant to everyday social practices, or as an anti-social practice. This is because someone who reads, is also isolating himself, which is resented by the other members of the community. But at the same time, people find books attractive, because they are the symbol of access to a certain kind of power. By reading, people appropriate foreign culture, they get to know 'the paper of the whites'. As a consequence, reading is coded as a positive activity in the collective ideal of Ivory Coast society, since it is a synonym for social success. This contradiction between 'alien' and 'fetish' written documents encapsulates the ambiguity of the status of books in African society.

Does writing produce irreversible commitments?

In cultures where relationships are very personalized, confidence cannot be separated from the person in whom the confidence is placed. The basis for mutual trust is no longer the detailed written contractual documents, but a man's word which is his bond. It is not 'just any word', but a special kind of word, which is heavily imbued with cultural codes (Hall, 1976). These words as bonds cannot easily be transferred from one culture to another. Adler (1980) describes the case of an Egyptian executive who, after entertaining his Canadian guest, offered him joint partnership in a business venture. The Canadian was very keen to enter this venture with the Egyptian businessman. He therefore suggested that they meet again the next morning with their respective lawyers to fill in the details. The Egyptians never arrived. The Canadian businessman wondered whether caused by the lack of punctuality of the Egyptians, or by the Egyptian expecting a counteroffer, or even the absence of lawyers available in Cairo:

> None of these explanations was true, although the Canadian executive suggested all of them.
> At issue was the perceived meaning of inviting lawyers. The Canadian saw the lawyer's

presence as facilitating the successful completion of the negotiation; the Egyptian interpreted it as signalling the Canadian's mistrust of his verbal commitment. Canadians often use the impersonal formality of a lawyer's services to finalize an agreement. Egyptians more frequently depend on a personal relationship developed between bargaining partners for the same purposes. (Adler, 1980, p. 178).

If agreements are mostly person-based, then their written base may be less important. Thus the demand for renegotiation of clauses by a Middle Eastern buyer in a contract already negotiated and signed, should not be seen as astonishing. It should not necessarily lead to litigation. Behind the demand for renegotiation is the assumption that, if people really trust each other, they should go much further than simple and literal implementation of their written agreements. This leads to the following question: to what extent should the contract signature date be considered as a time line which signals the end of the negotiation?

Written agreements as a time line for negotiations

According to what has been explained above, there are two different ways to look at the influence and function of the written agreement on the time line of the exchange relationship. Those favouring written-based trust-building tend to see a written agreement as a very definite break in the exchange relationship. It completes a phase during which potential relations have been carefully discussed and explored. It establishes a strict contractual code, which has then to be implemented literally. Written words, sentences and formulas have to be strictly observed. If a party feels free to depart from what has been written down, the Damocles sword of litigation will hang over the parties – and nobody likes litigation, supposedly.

Those favouring oral-based, personal trust consider the signing of a written agreement as an important step, but only one of many in a continuous negotiation process. The negotiation process was active before signature and will be active afterwards. A continuous negotiation process, where the contract is only one step. is seen as the best basis for maintaining trust.

As stated by Edward Hall (1960, p. 94):

> Americans consider that negotiations have more or less ceased when the contract is signed. With the Greeks, on the other hand, the contract is seen as a sort of way station on the route to negotiation, that will cease only when the work is completed. The contract is nothing more than a charter for serious negotiations. In the Arab world, once a man's word is given in a particular kind of way, it is just as binding, if not more so, than most of our written contracts. The written contract therefore violates the Moslem's sensitivities and reflects on his honour. Unfortunately, the situation is now so hopelessly confused that neither system can be counted on to prevail consistently.

Different attitudes towards litigation

It is easy to understand that the function of litigation will be different for both sides. Recourse to litigation will be fairly easily made by those favouring written-based agreements as the ultimate means of resolving breaches of contract. The oral and personal tradition is less susceptible to recourse to litigation, because litigation has major drawbacks:

1. It breaks the implicit assumption of trust.
2. It breaches the required state of social harmony, especially in the Far Eastern countries, and may therefore be quite threatening for the community as a whole.

As David (1987, p. 89, author's translation) states:

. . . in Far Eastern countries, as well as in Black Africa and Madagascar . . . subject to the westernization process which has been attempted, one does not find, as in Hinduism or Islam, a body of legal rules whose influence may be weakened by the recognized influence of other factors; it is the very notion of legal rules which is challenged. Despite authorities having sometimes established legal codes, it is well known and seems obvious that the prescriptions of these codes are not designed to be implemented literally. They should only be considered as simple patterns. The judge will be able to moderate their strictness and, moreover, it is hoped that this will not be necessary. The 'good judge', whether Chinese, Japanese or Vietnamese, is not concerned with making a good decision. The 'good judge' is the one who succeeds in not making any award, because he has been skilful enough to lead the opponents to reconciliation. Any dispute, as it is a threat to social harmony, has to be solved by a settlement through conciliation. The individual only has 'duties' towards the society. Recognition of 'subjective rights' in his favour is out of the question. Law as it is conceived in the West is seen as good for barbarians, and the occupation of lawyer, in the limited extent that it exists, is regarded with contempt by the society.

These remarks by a specialist of comparative law give a good idea of the differences of litigation tradition between the Far East and the West. In the field of contracts, the Western saying 'the contract is the law of the parties' dominates the practices of international trade. But this is in part window-dressing. When marketing internationally, a set of written contracts is always signed. This is not to say that people choose either oral or written agreements as a basis for trust. The real question is rather: how should the mix of written and oral bases for trust, as they are perceived by the parties, be interpreted? People do not deal with the real world in the same way. Negotiating together requires changing one's views of reality. Not only differences in rationality and mental programmes, but also differences in time representations, may lead to a partner 'who thinks differently' being considered a partner 'who thinks wrongly'.

The greatest caution is recommended when interpreting the bases of trust, whether written documents or oral and personal bonds. Even in the Anglo-Saxon world, where it is preferred to 'get-it-in-writing', a number of business deals, sometimes large ones – in the area of finance, for instance – are based on a simple telex or fax, or the simple agreement between two key decision-makers. It would be a mistake to believe that personal relationships do not exist in places where written contracts are generally required. Moreover, in cultures where 'my word is my bond', it should never be forgotten that it is difficult to trust somebody who is a member of the 'outgroup', whether on a written or spoken basis. Trust has therefore to be established (and monitored) on both bases, while at the same time keeping in mind a clear awareness of the limits of each.

Questions

1. Discuss the principal foundations of trust and their cultural variability
2. What is the role of time pressure in international marketing negotiations? How can you take advantage of time in the negotiation process?
3. Explain how frankness and directness in marketing negotiations can be diversely interpreted.
4. Why is seeing negotiation as a set of problems to be solved culturally relative?
5. How can the adoption of an integrative strategy be hindered by cultural factors?
6. To what extent is a written and detailed contact the basis of an agreement?
7. Discuss the value of introducing lawyers in intercultural negotiations.
8. Your company has signed for a 10,000-student turnkey university in Saudi Arabia. A number of its facilities are designed for science and engineering schools and the remaining parts of the buildings will be designed for arts. The construction has not yet started. The Saudis send a fax telling you that a 500-student additional business school is now planned and it must be integrated in the construction due to start in two months. What do you do?

APPENDIX 15

———— ♦♦♦ ————

Teaching materials

A15.1   Case: McFarlane Instruments

An American firm, the McFarlane Instruments Company, had delivered approximately US$400,000 worth of instruments to a People's Republic of China government agency. The agency refused to pay for the instruments, so the US company contacted the American Embassy in Beijing for assistance. The American commercial attaché arranged a meeting between the PRC industrial ministry representatives, company representatives, and himself.

In the meeting, the government officials stated that they would not pay because the instruments did not conform to the guarantee of accuracy of plus or minus 0.2 per cent. The US firm found this to be very strange since they had not encountered accuracy problems with their instruments sold in other countries. They finally inquired as to the temperatures at which the tests had been conducted. The Chinese officials indicated that tests had been conducted at 10 °C and at 50 °C.

The American firm replied that international practice and standards called for such tests to be conducted at 25 °C. The instruments were normally used at approximately room temperature. Because of differential expansion and contraction coefficients of the materials in the instruments, use under much lower or higher ambient temperatures resulted in different levels of precision and need for recalibration.

The Chinese officials then produced a copy of the company's brochure which stated the plus or minus 0.2 per cent precision, but did not specify the test temperature. After approximately one hour of discussion, which consisted mainly of each side reiterating its position, the US firm attempted to break the deadlock. While avoiding any admission that the instruments failed to conform to international standards, they agreed to reduce the price by 30 per cent 'in order to maintain good relations'. Their only other choice was to attempt to reclaim the machines, and then attempt to re-export them through potentially difficult Chinese customs administration to the United States or elsewhere. The Chinese officials requested that a written proposal be submitted. This was done and the offer was made valid for a period of sixty days.

Three months later the Chinese government organization rejected the proposal, restating that the instruments did not meet the promised precision. The US firm, after several more attempts at reconciliation, gave up and took back the machines. They now faced the difficult task of obtaining permission to re-export them, and the additional cost of doing that and paying for shipping costs.

Subsequent investigation indicated that the real problem had not had anything to do with the instruments themselves. Between the time the original contract had been signed and the instruments delivered, the currency of the PRC had been devalued. While the contract was written in US dollars, the Chinese organization had been allocated a given amount of the PRC currency, the '*rem min bi*', to pay for it (through the appropriate foreign exchange agency). With the new exchange rate, the Chinese government organization did not have enough money to pay for the instruments. The discount offered by the American company had not been sufficient to make up for the difference in exchange rates. The Chinese found it easier to reject the instruments than to admit what had happened.

(Source: adapted from Albaum *et al.*, 1989, pp. 388–9. Reproduced with the kind permission of the author, George Lee, San Francisco State University.)

Questions

1. How can you determine the real problems which impeded the negotiations? What are they, in your opinion?
2. Would you expect it to be easy to get appointments with Chinese government officials? Why or why not?
3. Would you expect it to be easy to obtain information from Chinese officials? Why or why not?
4. What important lesson for negotiations does this case illustrate? How would you have approached this problem?

A15.2 Negotiation game: Kumbele Power Plant

A consortium, BDH, has been established between a US-based engineering company, a French company belonging to the same sector and a German firm producing heavy industrial equipment. This consortium is in the final phase of negotiations to win a contract for building a turnkey electric power plant. The owner is the National Electricity Authority, a state-owned corporation which holds a monopoly on the transport and distribution of electricity in an English-speaking country in Africa. National Electricity Authority has issued the tender.

The tender procedure was initiated eighteen months ago. At first there were about twenty potentially qualified contractors which submitted bids. Most of them were engineering companies originating from the main industrial countries, and some came from newly industrialized countries such as South Korea, Brazil and Turkey. After a preselection phase, the number of potential contractors was reduced to a short list of five companies or consortia. The final selection process lasted for several months, as bids that were technologically incomparable had to be taken into account.

The consortium created by Brown Engineering Corp. (US), Duponval SA (French) and Horst BauTechnik AG (German) was chosen as the organization with which the final negotiations would take place. But a Japanese competitor has also made a very attractive offer and is equally in a position to supplant BDH, if BDH proves to be too demanding for National Electricity Authority. In fact BDH has a strong reference list, supported by similar plants it has built which are working effectively. Moreover, in addition to its offer, BDH provides a low-rate, long-term financing scheme for the buyer, which has been created by putting together export credits issued by public organizations from the countries of the three members of BDH: US Eximbank for Brown, BFCE (Banque Française du Commerce Extérieur) for Duponval and KfW (Kreditanstalt für Wiederaufbau) for Horst BauTechnik.

The final price has not yet been settled, as there are still some important clauses to be discussed:

1. The supply of basic materials by the consortium, during the start-up of the power plant.
2. The possibility of signing a 'products in hand' contract. A 'products in hand' contract is a particular kind of turnkey operation, where part of the payment by the owner to the contractor is subject to the level of performance reached by the plant. After the start-up phase has been finished and individual pieces of equipment have been shown to work effectively, a phase begins where the contractor is assigned to operations. This means that a management contract has been signed. The variable fee may cover part or all of the turnkey operations as such and/or the management contract. In this case the consortium would agree to sign a management contract to run the operation until it reaches 100 per cent of its target capacity (400 megawatts).

The proposal which served as a starting base for the final bargaining process was priced at US$105 million. Each one of the partners-to-be has naturally retained its right to improve its position, either by obtaining a rebate (the buyer) or by increasing this base price level by astutely negotiating supplementary services (the consortium).

Since the inception of this tender, National Electricity Authority has made it known that the first power plant will be followed by the construction of two similar plants, all this being stated in the ten-year plan for the electrification of the country. It seems very likely that the contractor selected to build the first unit, if effective, will be well positioned for the next two orders which may possibly be placed by direct agreement between contractor and owner, that is, without a competitive bidding procedure.

At the negotiating table are three representatives of the buying organization and three representatives of the BDH consortium, each one an employee of one of the companies:

1. For the buyer:
   (a) Mr Ozuwu, who is in charge of project financing for industrial development at the Ministry of Finance. He might be a useful and even necessary go-between for many red-tape problems related to administrative and financial issues which could arise when completing the project: payments, clearing customs for imported equipment, fiscal and social problems of expatriates, etc.
   (b) Mr Kempele, who is the director in charge of energy at the Ministry of Industry. He is concerned with the coordination of this project with the other industrialization projects being undertaken in the country. There have been many negative experiences of this in recent years: two years ago, some ships with a full load of cement were stranded in the main sea port of the country because there was not enough unloading equipment such as docks and cranes. This caused severe delay on several projects.
   (c) Mr Bura, the third representative, is 38, much younger than both Ozuwu who is about 50 and Kempele who is 60. He has been trained in the United Kingdom and the United States and holds a Master of Science degree in Electrical Engineering. At National Electricity Authority he is in charge of new plants and investment project. He is reputed to be ambitious but also capable and hard-headed. In the long run he is seen as a possible chief executive for National Electricity Authority. Bura has confidence in the country's development projects and in the capacities of local managers to run the new plants effectively.
2. For the consortium:
   (a) Mr Smith, a project manager aged 42, who has worked for many years at Brown, the US member of the consortium. Brown will take charge of the boiler part and the plant monitoring system. Brown is ranked among the leading US engineering companies. It has a high reputation for technical excellence as well as for cost control. Project managers at Brown are partly compensated with a bonus based on the profit generated by the project. A sophisticated cost accounting system monitors actual and forecast costs and margins regularly during the project. When projects are completed after two

to three years or more, final costs are calculated, with a minimal deviation from target costs.

(b) Mr Robin from Duponval SA, a French engineer who has worked for this company for the last ten years. Duponval has already formed several joint ventures with Brown, and Robin knows Smith because they have already worked together. Duponval SA is in charge of civil engineering and the total coordination of the work. This firm has established a good reputation world-wide for meeting delivery times.

(c) Mr Dietermeyer, a Doctor of Law, aged 55, has worked for the last twenty years for Horst BauTechnik. Although he has not been formally trained in engineering, he has built up a good knowledge of industrial engineering on the job. In addition to this he has attended many training sessions which have provided him with an in-depth knowledge of the technologies of a large variety of turnkey plants. He is considered in his company a skilful, experienced and effective business negotiator. His law background is very useful in discussing precise clauses, understanding what is at stake and the possible legal consequences of a specific clause. Horst is in charge of supplying and installing turbo-alternators and all the electrical parts in the plant.

BDH consortium has been chosen as the contractor with which National Electricity Authority is willing to negotiate the final agreement under the supervision of the Ministry of France and the Ministry of Industry. A sum of US$105 million is the starting point for the discussion; until now it has been considered a lump sum for a turnkey operation contract. But things have not yet been fully settled.

The African team wishes to negotiate either a rebate on this price level, arguing that there will be future projects which could be awarded to BDH, or complementary services or guarantees, which could be granted for free. These might possibly be the following:

1. The free supply of materials required for production during the start-up phase, which will last one month.
2. Free technical assistance for the industrial management of the power plant, in order to be able to serve consumers and to manage the electricity distribution network properly.
3. A commitment from BDH to subcontract part of the job locally, especially the less sophisticated part of the civil engineering work.

BDH naturally prefers to maintain its price, for which it had been selected from harsh competition. In fact there were some cheaper competitors, sometimes $15 million less. But neither their reference lists nor their financing deals matched BDH's bid.

To tell the truth, BDH is somewhat worried about the delay penalty clause which National Electricity Authority wants to include. The fine is supposed to be 1 per cent of the total price for each construction month beyond the standard completion time. The consortium foresees that there could be some delay. It fears that it might be difficult to assign clear responsibilities to either the contractor or the owner (or the state authorities of the country, or a large subcontractor, especially if it was a local business). Usually turnkey contracts include a customs franchise for all the equipment imported in order to build the plant. But it is not that rare for customs officers not to apply these rules immediately, and it may delay the customs clearance of these components and equipment, thereby delaying the completion of the plant.

The parties have agreed to discuss the issue of transforming this pure turnkey operation, paid for by a lump sum, into a 'products in hand' contract. Under this scheme, part of the payment will be subject to a variable scale related to the level of capacity reached during the management contract period after the plant has been completed and started up. The possibility of a management contract has been discussed. It will probably be added to the turnkey contract (which includes the construction start-up phase, but no more). This management contract will encompass handling the industrial management procedures, the accounting system, setting salaries, customer service and providing training programmes for local executives. Progressively, local management is supposed to take over the management of the project. The basis on which the variable payment would be calculated has not been clearly settled up to now. This basis could be: the whole amount of the management contract, part of it, or the whole amount of the management contract plus part of the $105 million turnkey project.

The African proposal for this final negotiation includes the following elements:

1. The price of the management contract plus US$10 million (on top of the turnkey price) to become a variable and conditional payment, subject to the capacity level reached within a certain time span. This scheme would extend throughout the total thirty-six months of the management contract period.
2. For this variable part the proposed payment scheme is as follows:
   (a) 15 per cent after six months if the output reaches at least 50 per cent of the target capacity;
   (b) 15 per cent after twelve months if the output reaches at least 60 per cent of the target capacity;
   (c) 15 per cent after eighteen months if the output reaches at least 70 per cent of the target capacity;
   (d) 15 per cent after twenty-four months if the output reaches at least 80 per cent of the target capacity;
   (e) 20 per cent after thirty months if the output reaches at least 90 per cent of the target capacity;
   (f) 20 per cent after thirty-six months if the output reaches 100 per cent of the target capacity.
3. The management contract may grant decision-making powers to the consortium in the following matters: recruiting personnel (workers, not the management), operating the plant and choosing supplies of appropriate quality and price. The selling price of the output as well as the operating costs are to remain the sole responsibility of National Electricity Authority.

The negotiation takes place at the headquarters of National Electricity Authority in Port Kumbele, where the power plant will be built. The talks simply aim at finalizing an agreement for beginning the construction as soon as possible. No detailed agenda has been prepared for the negotiations.

Discussion begins . . .

Recommendations for playing Kumbele Power Plant negotiation game

The objective is to simulate business negotiations for international turnkey operations. It may be played in four half-days, preferably in half-day sessions, with some time between them. Participants should first discuss between themselves as a team in order to prepare their negotiation strategies and tactics. The discussion should be centred on business negotiation. Participants should not discuss technical matters related to the plant: first, the necessary information is not included in the text and, second, it is not meant to be an engineers' discussion.

The intercultural aspect may be adapted according to participants. The characters in the game may easily be changed to women.

This game may be played as a competitive game, where two teams compete for the contract with National Electricity Authority. One team representing BDH and one team representing the Japanese engineering company (let's call it Chikoda) will face the Kumbele team.

Participants should research some information about selling turnkey projects and management services internationally. See for instance Brooke (1985).

A detailed teaching note is available in the instructor's manual as well as personal and team role instructions, a standard contract form and an evaluation sheet for the negotiators.

References

Adler, Nancy, J. (1980), 'Cultural synergy: the management of cross-cultural organizations', in W. Warner Burke and Leonard D. Goodstein (eds), *Trends and Issues in OD: Current theory and practice*, University Associates: San Diego, CA, pp.163–84.

Adler, Nancy J. (1986), *International Dimensions of Organizational Behavior*, PWS-Kent: Boston.

Adler, Nancy J. and John L. Graham (1989), 'Cross-cultural comparison: The international comparison fallacy?', *Journal of International Business Studies*, vol. xx, no. 3, pp. 515–37.

Adler, Nancy J., John L. Graham and Theodore Schwarz Gehrke (1987), 'Business negotiations in Canada, Mexico and the United States', *Journal of Business Research*, vol. 15, pp. 411–29.

Albaum, Gerald, Jesper Strandskov, Edwin Duerr and Lawrence Dowd (1989), *International Marketing and Export Management*, Addison-Wesley: Wokingham.

Angelmar, Reinhardt, and Louis W. Stern (1978), 'Development of a content analysis scheme for analysis of bargaining communication in marketing', *Journal of Marketing Research*, vol. 15, February, pp. 93–102.

Arndt, Johan (1979), 'Toward a concept of domesticated markets', *Journal of Marketing*, vol. 43 (Fall), pp. 69–75.

Beliaev, Edward, Thomas Mullen and Betty Jane Punnett (1985), 'Understanding the cultural environment: U.S.–U.S.S.R. trade negotiations', *California Management Review*, vol. XXVII, no. 2, pp. 100–2.

Bista, Dor Bahadur (1990), *Fatalism and Development*, Orient Longman: Calcutta.

Brooke, Michael Z. (1985), *Selling Management Service Contracts in International Business*, Holt, Rhinehart and Winston: London.

Burt, David N. (1984), 'The nuances of negotiating overseas', *Journal of Purchasing and Materials Management*, Winter, pp. 2–8.

Campbell, Nigel C. G., John L. Graham, Alain Jolibert and Hans Günther Meissner (1988), 'Marketing negotiations in France, Germany, the United Kingdom and United States', *Journal of Marketing*, vol. 52 (April), pp. 49–62.

Cohen, Herb (1980), *You Can Negotiate Anything*, Bantam: New York.

David, René (1987), *Le Droit du commerce international, réflexions d'un comparatiste sur le droit international privé*, Economica: Paris.

De Mente, Boye (1987), *How to do Business with the Japanese*, N.T.C. Publishing: Chicago, IL.

Druckman, D., A. A. Benton, F. Ali and J. S. Bagur (1976), 'Culture differences in bargaining behavior', *Journal of Conflict Resolution*, vol. 20, pp. 413–49.

Dupont, Christophe (1994), *La négociation: Conduite, Théorie, Applications*, 4th edn, Dalloz: Paris.

Dwyer, Robert F., Paul H. Schurr and Sejo Oh (1987), 'Developing buyer–seller relationships', *Journal of Marketing*, vol. 51 (April), pp. 11–27.

Eiteman, David K. (1990), 'American executives' perceptions of negotiating joint ventures with the People's Republic of China: Lessons learned', *Columbia Journal of World Business*, Winter, pp. 59–67.

Evans, Franklin B. (1963), 'Selling as a dyadic relationship: A new approach', *American Behavioral Scientist*, vol. 6 (May), pp. 76–9.

Fisher, Glen (1980), *International Negotiation: A cross–cultural perspective*, Intercultural Press: Yarmouth, ME.

Foster, G.M. (1965), 'Peasant society and the image of limited good', *American Anthropologist*, vol. 67, pp. 293–315.

Francis, June P. (1991), 'When in Rome? The effects of cultural adaptation on intercultural business negotiations', *Journal of International Business Studies*, vol. 22, no. 3, pp. 403–28.

Fuentes, Carlos (1986), cited in 'To see ourselves as others see us', *Time*, 16 June, p. 52.

Goldman, Alan (1994), The centrality of 'Ningensei' to Japanese negotiating and interpersonal relationships: implications for U.S.–Japanese communication,' *International Journal of Intercultural Relations*, vol. 18, no. 1, pp. 29–54.

Graham, John L. (1981), 'A hidden cause of America's trade deficit with Japan', *Columbia Journal of World Business*, Fall, pp. 5–15.

Graham, John L. (1985), 'Cross-cultural marketing negotiations: A laboratory experiment', *Marketing Science*, vol. 4, no. 2, pp. 130–46.

Graham, John L. (1993), 'Business negotiations: Generalizations about Latin America and East Asia are dangerous', *UCINSIGHT*, University of California Irvine, Summer, pp. 6–23.

Graham, John L. and Roy A. Herberger Jr (1983), 'Negotiators abroad: Don't shoot from the hip', *Harvard Business Review*, vol. 61, no. 4, pp. 160–8.

Graham, John L. and Hans G. Meissner (1986), 'Content analysis of business negotiations in five countries', Working Paper, University of Southern California.

Graham, John L., Alma T. Mintu and Waymond Rodgers (1994), 'Exploration of negotiation behaviors in ten foreign cultures using a model developed in the United States', *Management Science*, vol. 40, no. 1, January, pp. 72–95.

Graham, John L. and Yoshihiro Sano (1990), *Smart bargaining: Doing business with the Japanese*, 2nd edn, Ballinger: Cambridge, MA.

Hall, Edward T. (1960), 'The silent language in overseas business', *Harvard Business Review*, May–June, pp. 87–96.

Hall, Edward T. (1976), *Beyond Culture*, Anchor Press/Doubleday: Garden City, NY.

Hall, Edward T. (1983), *The Dance of Life*, Anchor Press/Doubleday: Garden City, NY.

Harnett, Donald L. and L. L. Cummings (1980), *Bargaining Behavior: An international study*, Dame Publications: Houston, TX.

Harris, Philip R. and Robert T. Moran (1987), *Managing Cultural Differences*, 2nd edn, Gulf Publishing Company: Houston, TX.

Hawrysh, Bryan Mark and Judith Lynn Zaichkowsky (1990), 'Cultural approaches to negotiations: Understanding the Japanese', *International Marketing Review*, vol. 7, no. 2, pp. 28–42.

Hofstede, Geert (1989), 'Cultural predictors of national negotiation styles', in Frances Mautner-Markhof (ed.), *Processes of International Negotiations*, Westview Press: Boulder, pp. 193–201.

Jackson, Barbara B. (1985), *Winning and Keeping Industrial Customers: The dynamics of customer relationships*, D.C. Heath and Company: Lexington, MA.

Jolibert, Alain (1988), 'Le Contexte culturel de la négociation commerciale', *Revue Française de Gestion*, November–December, pp. 15–24.

Keegan, Warren J. (1984), *Multinational Marketing Management*, 3rd edn, Prentice Hall: Englewood Cliffs, NJ.

Kelley, Harold H. (1966), 'A classroom study of the dilemmas in interpersonal negotiations', in K. Archibald (ed.), *Strategic Interaction and Conflict*, Institute of International Studies, University of California, Berkeley, CA.

McCall, J. B. and M. B. Warrington (1990), *Marketing By Agreement: A cross-cultural approach to business negotiations*, 2nd edn, John Wiley: Chichester.

McCartney, Laton (1989), *Friends in High Places: The Bechtel story*, Ballantine Books: New York.

Macneil, Ian R. (1980), *The New Social Contract: An inquiry into modern contractual relations*, Yale University Press: New Haven, CT.

Matsumoto, M. (1988), *The unspoken way: Haragei – silence in Japanese business and society*, New York: Kodansha International.

Ohmae, Kenichi (1989), 'The global logic of strategic alliances', *Harvard Business Review*, March–April, pp. 143–55.

Ollivier, Alain and Renaud de Maricourt (1990), *Pratique du marketing en Afrique*, Edicef/Aupelf: Paris.

Orwell, George (1945), *Animal Farm*, Penguin: London.

Perdue, B. C., R. L. Day and R. E Michaels (1986), 'Negotiation styles of industrial buyers', *Industrial Marketing Management*, vol. 15, no. 3, pp 171–6.

Pruitt, Dean G. (1981), *Bargaining Behavior*, Academic Press: New York.

Pruitt, Dean G. (1983), 'Strategic choice in negotiation', *American Behavioral Scientist*, vol. 27, no. 2, pp. 167–94.

Pruitt, Dean G. and Steven A. Lewis (1975), 'Development of integrative solutions in bilateral negotiations', *Journal of Personality and Social Psychology*, vol. 31, no. 4, pp. 621–33.

Pye, Lucian (1982), *Chinese Commercial Negotiating Style*, Oelgeschlager, Gunn and Hain: Cambridge, MA.

Pye, Lucian (1986), 'The China trade: making the deal', *Harvard Business Review*, vol. 46, no. 4, pp. 74–84.

Rubin, J. Z. and B. R. Brown (1975), *The Social Psychology of Bargaining and Negotiations*, Academic Press: New York.

Rubin, Paul A. and J. R. Carter (1990), 'Joint optimality in buyer–seller negotiations', *Journal of Purchasing and Materials Management* Spring, pp. 20–6.

Sawyer, J. and H. Guetzkow (1965), 'Bargaining and negotiation in international relations', in H. Kelman (ed.), *International Behavior*, Holt, Rinehart and Winston: New York.

Scanzoni, J. (1979), 'Social exchange and behavioral interdependence', in R. L. Burgess and T. L. Huston (eds), *Social exchange in Developing Relationships*, Academic Press: New York.

Traoré Sérié, Régina (1986), 'La Promotion du livre en Cote d'lvoire', Paper presented to the conference on 'Marketing and Development', Abidjan (Ivory Coast), December.

Triandis, Harry G. (1983), 'Dimensions of cultural variation as parameters of organizational theories', *International Studies of Management and Organization*, vol. 12, no. 4, pp. 139–69.

Trompenaars, Fons (1993), *Riding the Waves of Culture*, Nicholas Brealey: London.

Tse, David K., June Francis and Jan Walls (1994), 'Cultural differences in conducting intra- and inter-cultural negotiations: A Sino–Canadian perspective' *Journal of International Business Studies*, vol. 25, no. 3, pp. 537–55.

Tung, Rosalie L. (1984), 'How to negotiate with the Japanese', *California Management Review*, vol. XXVI, no. 4, pp. 62–77.

Usunier, Jean–Claude (1989), 'Interculturel: la parole et l'action', *Harvard-L'Expansion*, no. 52, March, pp. 84–92.

Usunier, Jean-Claude (1990), 'Négociation commerciale des projets: une approche interculturelle', *Revue Française du Marketing*, no. 127–128, pp. 167–84.

Van Zandt, H.R. (1970), 'How to negotiate with the Japanese', *Harvard Business Review*, November–December, pp. 45–56.

Walton, Richard E. and Robert B. McKersie (1965), *A Behavioral Theory of Labor Negotiations*, McGraw-Hill: New York.

Weiss, Stephen E. (1987), 'Creating the GM–Toyota joint venture: A case in complex negotiation', *Columbia Journal of World Business*, vol. 22, no. 2 (Summer), pp. 23–37.

Weitz, B. (1979), 'A critical review of personal selling research: the need for contingency approaches', in G. Albaum and G. A. Churchill Jr (eds), *Critical Issues in Sales Management: State of the art and future needs*, University of Oregon: Eugene.

Zeldin, Theodore (1977), *France 1848–1945*, vol. 11, Oxford University Press: Oxford.

16
♦ ♦ ♦

Intercultural marketing negotiations 2: Some elements of the national style of business negotiations

Identifying a set of strategic archetypes used by foreign negotiators may enhance one's negotiating power. For instance, Asians, driven by low self-esteem and perceived potency, may open a negotiation by dwelling on their company's vulnerability, small size and other alleged weaknesses, to swell westerners' confidence and induce them to ask less and yield more. In marketing negotiation the image of the other negotiating party is based on a collection of stereotypes, often meaningful, a portrait of their national culture. This exercise in mutual reflection would have to be reciprocal and particular for each bilateral relationship. It is unlikely, for example, that Germans or Italians would have an identical perception of the French negotiation style. Similarly the view held by the Japanese of Westerners, remarking their lack of *ningensei*, cannot be considered as simply inverse and complementary to the view held by US negotiators of their Japanese counterparts. US negotiators do not complain for the excessive *ningensei* orientation of their Japanese partners! Therefore a matrix would be necessary to effectively describe the negotiating style of a particular country through the perception of other nationalities: for example, the Italian style being defined in terms of how it is perceived by the Americans, the French, etc. However, the use of multiple perspective would be too complex. Because of the necessity to reduce complexity, it must be recognized that archetypes of negotiation styles are most often an average of what is seen through western eyes.

This chapter complements the previous one. It describes some elements of the national or regional style of business negotiation. Taking the risk of what could be termed (western) stereotyping, the salient traits of various 'nationalities' (in alphabetical order) are described: African, American, British, Chinese, French, German, Japanese, Mexican, Middle Eastern and Russian. Section 16.1 describes Oriental, section 16.2 western negotiation style, section 16.3 deals with other areas of the world, and the last section proposes recommendations for effective intercultural marketing negotiations.

540

16.1   Orientals

Chinese style

One of the main experts in business negotiation with the Chinese, Lucian W. Pye (1982, 1986) lists the following factors, which combine to demonstrate that the Chinese are tactical, skilful and fairly tough negotiators:

1. 'As hosts, the Chinese take advantage of their control over the pace of negotiations. First they set the agenda, then they suggest that the Americans start the discussions ... their proposals become the starting point from which all compromise follows' (Pye, 1986, p. 177).
2. The Chinese deliberately adopt a fairly passive attitude, taking care not to show enthusiasm, covering up any feeling of impatience, playing their game impassively so as to force their opponents to be the first to show their hand.
3. They do not shy away from appearing very manipulative: with a view to disconcerting the other side and in the ultimate hope of obtaining further concessions, they will attribute an exaggerated importance to minor details, which in reality are of no consequence to them, or return to discussion of points where full agreement seemed to have previously been reached.
4. The bureaucratic orientation of the PRC is often noted: socialism has imposed strong government control on industry. As a consequence, Chinese negotiators tend not to be capable of individual decision-making. Before any agreement is reached, official government approval must be sought by Chinese negotiators (Eiteman, 1990).
5. Chinese business people tend to overrate the advantage offered by their large population in terms of market opportunities. However, per capita purchasing power remains quite low. The Chinese promote their country as being 'the last big market on the planet' but underestimate the opportunities offered to their foreign partners by other countries (Eiteman, 1990).
6. Like the Japanese, the Chinese are less economic-time minded and less short-term oriented than westerners. 'The Chinese use time shrewdly. If they sense that business people are in a hurry to leave China, they may slow down negotiations and turn the deadline to their advantage' (Pye, 1986, p. 78).
7. Pye also notes the role played by differences of attitude relating to the concept of 'friendship'. Thus it seems that whereas the Americans view friendship in terms of a feeling which rests on a natural mutual exchange, in other words on a principle of reciprocity, the Chinese view friendship in terms of loyalty. The idea is that of a long-lasting obligation:

> What the Chinese neglect in terms of reciprocity they more than match in loyalty. They not only keep their commitments, but they also assume that any positive relationship can be permanent. A good example of this is the number of Chinese who have tried to establish pre 1949 ties with U.S. companies and individuals – as though nothing had happened in the intervening days. (Pye, 1986, p. 79).

Japanese style

Numerous books are devoted to consideration of the Japanese style of negotiation and more generally to the Japanese mentality and style of management. Several major traits can be distinguished:

1. The Japanese are well prepared, particularly from the point of view of familiarity with the culture of the people with whom they are dealing (Tung, 1984a). They are a highly ethnocentric people who are, paradoxically, at the same time very conscious of this ethnocentrism. They are also well prepared as far as definition of their basic interests is concerned and are willing to struggle quite bitterly to defend them.
2. The purchaser's role is predominant. Vendors must be fully aware of this fact and adapt their behaviour accordingly (Graham, 1981).
3. Although at heart they are very sensitive and emotional, they seek to conceal their true emotions as far as possible (Burt, 1984; see also end of section 3.5 and section 12.2). Like all Asians they must not be made to 'lose face': in practice (at the very least) their foreign counterparts should avoid a style of communication that would be resented by the Japanese as being too direct.
4. Within a group of Japanese negotiators it is difficult to determine who really performs what function and who holds what power; it is always unwise to rely solely on 'who says what' as a clear indication of 'who holds power'.
5. Japanese negotiators display quite a high level of tolerance of ambiguity. Whereas ambiguity may be perceived by Americans as a sign of weakness and a lack of masculinity and assertiveness, the Japanese do not see ambivalent behaviour as contradictory to masculinity (Hawrysh and Zaichkowsky, 1990).
6. Japanese people are very long-term oriented. In large companies lifetime employment is the rule. These companies are often backed by large banks which, as the shareholders, do not strive for a quick return. They are more concerned with the soundness of the long-term business strategy of the company to whom they lend. This partly explains why Japanese negotiators do not feel as strongly pressured by time lines as their Western counterparts.
7. Like most Asians, the Japanese tend to prefer an agreement based on trust to a written contract. Even though this agreement may be loosely worded, in their view it is a better expression of the mutual trust that has developed between the parties (Oh, 1986).
8. The empathy of Japanese people may be very high: the interpersonal sensitivity of Japanese people and their sincere interest in foreign cultures and people may make them friendly hosts at business lunches or dinners. As emphasized by Hawrysh and Zaichkowsky (1990, p. 30): 'Before entering serious negotiations, Japanese business men will spend considerable time and money entertaining foreign negotiating teams', in order to get to know their negotiating partners and establish with them a rapport built on friendship and trust. But it should never be forgotten that Japanese negotiators remain down-to-earth: they are strongly aware of what their basic interests are. They are reputed to be tough negotiators.

Middle Eastern style (Arab-Islamic world)

If a 'Middle Eastern style' truly exists, it would display some basic characteristics:

1. The countries considered here are almost exclusively Arab-Islamic countries, except for Iran which is Shiite Islam but not Arab, and Turkey which is Ottoman and Islamic but not Arab and has dominated the Arab world for centuries. Yet it would be a mistake to ignore the enormous diversity of the Middle East. Christian minorities (Lebanese Maronites, Egyptian Copts, Iraqi Nestorians, Armenians, members of the Orthodox churches, etc.) are present almost everywhere and influential in some countries. These religions are in fact fully integrated in the Middle East. It is therefore essential to be fully aware of the fact that a world that is somewhat hastily classified as Arab-Islamic is also composed of Arabs who are not Muslims and Muslims who are not Arabs.
2. The importance of 'concrete territorialities': knowledge of the subgroup to which the negotiator belongs is essential; the relationships between the parties must be explored with great care, to find out who is who and what relationship each negotiator has with the different groups.
3. The role of intermediaries ('sponsors' in Saudi Arabia) is very important. As a result of European colonization over the last two centuries, the majority of 'Middle Eastern' businesspeople speak French or English and understand European civilization; whereas the reverse is rarely true. Intermediaries must be employed for a simple reason: we (the Europeans and Americans) systematically underestimate the cultural divide.
4. It must always be borne in mind that Middle Eastern civilizations were largely the founders of those in Europe. They have left many traces behind, and as far as art and culture are concerned, their influences were dominant for many centuries during the Middle Ages. The pride of the person with whom you are dealing must be – truly – respected.
5. One must expect a great deal of emotion, theatricality and demonstrativeness, interspersed with true pragmatism. The mixture is often bewildering. Friendship is sought, relationships are personalized, and the idea of a cold 'business-like' relationship is difficult to envisage. Once a true friend has been made (which is far from straightforward), the sense of loyalty can be very strong.
6. As has already been emphasized, Islamic values permeate daily life. For example, if the negotiations lead to consideration of a loan and interest rate, although this problem is not insurmountable, a great deal of caution is essential. The question of *riba*, which is usually translated as 'interest', never fails to pose problems for Koranic law and the different legislative assemblies entrusted with its interpretation. These assemblies have been more or less strict in their interpretation of *riba*, which is mentioned several times in the Koran, as being forbidden. Thus specific financial operations, excluding the imposition of a method of repayment for loans which is fixed in advance, have been settled in accordance with Islamic law and on the basis of ancient practices. Rather than loans, they are joint operations where the banker brings the financing and clients their facilities and business talents. *Mudhâraba* corresponds to a project

financing with no recourse for the banker; *musharaka* is similar except that the client brings part of the financing; *murabaha* is a sort of leasing agreement.

16.2 Westerners

American style

The American style is oriented towards several major aspects which are linked to the US national character, namely individualism, with the emphasis on ability, competence, professionalism, decision-making and explicit communication. As a consequence American negotiators usually possess the following qualities: seriousness, pragmatism and accuracy in writing clauses. American negotiators have fairly well-defined autonomy and room for manoeuvre, but clear limits are also set, and they have to report to their principals. In the negotiation process, Americans often consider that decisions have to be made on the spot by the individual who has the most expertise or responsibility in a given area (Beliaev *et al.*, 1985).

1. Professionalism is a quality that is very widely recognized in Americans. In business negotiation, it means careful selection of the negotiators and methodical preparation of files.
2. In their failure to take sufficient account of the culture of other parties (Tung, 1984b), the Americans, like the French, are an 'ethnocentric-missionary' people. They are quite convinced (as are the French) that their system is the 'one best way', and that the other peoples of the world would do well to adopt their system of values and behaviour.
3. A great deal of attention is (pragmatically) paid to precise issues to be debated, to facts and evidence, to an attitude oriented towards matter-of-fact discussions and to a tight negotiation time schedule. This renders them susceptible to becoming irritated by negotiating parties that are more interested in general principles or even logical reasoning (the French, for example; Burt, 1984). This may also lead to their interpretation of the attitudes of their negotiating counterparts who have a non-linear style as delaying tactics. They will resent global negotiation as a way of reconsidering what has already been decided and as a failure to respect preset agenda.
4. A strong positive emphasis is placed on frankness and sincerity; Americans show willingness to make the first move by disclosing their position in the hope (sometimes unfulfilled) that their adversary will do likewise. They are also prepared to adopt the 'John Wayne Style' (Graham and Herberger, 1983; see Box 15.3), by pushing frankness to the bounds of arrogance. This can shock people from cultures where self-assertion must be contained within strict limits.
5. A genuine naivety, ingenuousness and a 'retarded adolescent' style (noted by Margaret Mead) can sometimes lead Americans to choose positions that are very tough because they are – genuinely – disappointed. This occurs mainly when, having demonstrated their – genuine – sincerity, they then feel that they have been badly treated, since their open-mindedness has been taken advantage of. However sincerity

and frankness are by no means universal cultural values, contrary to what a good number of Americans may believe.

6. Equality between purchaser and vendor, and 'let the best man win'. This can surprise people who deal with Americans, since Americans value personal assertiveness and can therefore appear tough: there is little sympathy for anyone who loses. In the US business mentality, no consolation prizes are won by 'losers'.

7. The Americans are supposed to be informal in everyday life. In fact, compared to other peoples, they are formal in different areas. When it comes to negotiating agreements, they are quite formal and anxious about the preciseness and explicitness of written contracts which are therefore drawn up with care. These contracts, the law between the parties, are also the basis for attitudes which are readily oriented towards recourse to litigation and legal battles with the assistance of lawyers.

8. As noted earlier, Americans tend to be short-term oriented. At the end of the Vietnam War, in the US–Vietnamese peace talks in Paris, the Vietnamese were at a time advantage because they had rented a villa with a two and a half years' lease, whereas the Americans rented hotel rooms on a week-to-week basis. The US time pressure in business may be easily explained by the quarterly reporting system to the shareholders and the Stock Exchange. US companies depend more strictly on the financial markets; labour mobility is high. Accordingly people must get quick results, and show a faster return than their foreign counterparts. This 'short-termism' tends to disadvantage them in negotiations.

British style

Together with the French, the British are those who have been most affected by their tradition of diplomatic negotiation. The British Empire and the influence of the United Kingdom have affected the British style. It is characterized by the following:

1. A 'soft-sell' approach which is essential. British coolness is not an empty phrase. An air of confidence, restraint and calm is essential for any negotiators in the position of seller. They must never be seen to be pushy in negotiation.

2. The English have the reputation of being less motivated by money than the Americans; with the relative decline of Great Britain, they are more inclined towards their free time; companies are often full of administrative personnel. This situation has a tendency to slow down the decision-making process significantly (Burt, 1984).

3. The study carried out by Campbell *et al.* (1988), using the vehicle of a simulated negotiation, demonstrates that the factor that has the strongest influence on negotiation in the United Kingdom is the role of negotiator (purchaser or vendor). In the negotiation simulation, British purchasers obtained slightly superior results to vendors of the same nationality. This is consistent with the reputation of the British of having a 'soft-sell' type of approach, where the vendor must take care not to annoy the purchaser by being too pushy, turning up too often, making too many proposals or by adopting an attitude that is too action-oriented.

4. Although seemingly closest to the Americans, the British are not necessarily those who resemble them the most in the field of business practice. They are usually more contextual in communication and indirect, hence a willingness to try to interpret the British position in business negotiation is essential.
5. Language-related issues (the style of writing clauses, for instance) are treated very differently by the British and the Americans. Whereas US people easily accept a somewhat simplified 'international English' that will be used for drafting agreements, the British, like the French, take pride in correct language, and are sensitive to style for style's sake.

French style

1. The French are said to be somewhat difficult to negotiate with. As noted earlier, the French tend to be ideologists and find it difficult to 'accept facts, no matter how convincing they may be. Although they may consider themselves to be experts at negotiating, at times they tend to be amateurish and inadequately prepared' (Burt, 1984, p. 6).
2. The fact that the French are conflict-prone, do not mind confrontation and sometimes even enjoy it, is confirmed by Weiss and Stripp (1985) who describe the French negotiating style as competitive and inherently confrontational. They also tend to use emotional and theatrical ways of behaving in negotiation.
3. In France (as in the United Kingdom) social class remains an important feature of society. Social-status consciousness is very strong in France, as is power distance (see Chapter 3). French negotiators are sensitive to the organizational status of their foreign counterparts, requiring equivalence.
4. France is still one of the most centralized nations in the world, with a very long tradition of Paris-based decision-making (inaugurated by Hughes Capet, in 987!). High-ranking civil servants (*énarques* and *polytechniciens*) have a substantial say in business deals which involve large companies and their subsidiaries.
5. At times, some French negotiators may be resented as arrogant and disdainful: in a very high power distance society, which is at the same time individualistic, power display may be exacerbated, to the detriment of politeness and courtesy.
6. Burt (1984, pp. 6–7) complements his view of the French negotiation style as follows:

> The French seem to enjoy negotiating for its own sake. When they are in the mood sometimes for several days – very little progress is made. Sooner or later though, they tire of the game and want to reach closure. A careful count of the numbers of cigarettes consumed per hour serves as an indication of the restlessness and the willingness to make concessions in order to reach closure. Leisure time and the desire for the 'good life' are key motivators. An awareness of these motivators can be useful in reaching agreement. as is indicated in the following dialogue:
>
> American: 'We need to reach agreement, since I've booked us at (the Frenchman's

favourite restaurant). But we can't go until we reach agreement on these remaining issues.'

    Frenchman: 'I agree. Let's go!'

German style

1. One of the striking aspects of the German national mentality is its relatively high level of uncertainty avoidance (a score of 65 on Hofstede's scale of uncertainty avoidance; see Table 3.3). A key term is *sicher* (sure, safe). The Germans do not like *unsicherheit*, a sense of insecurity which makes them feel uneasy in business, as well as in their whole life. In front of partners who generate such uncertainty, Germans will quickly develop *Mißtrauen* (mistrust). They need to be *versichert*, that is, assured, and this cannot be done through superficial and wordy arguments, but only with hard facts, sound arguments, tests and so on.
2. The German love of formality is one of the first elements that stands out clearly. For example, the title of *Doktor*, even *Professor Doktor*, is a recognized sign of ability and will be employed. Formality and the presence of constraining rules (which are generally respected) in the decision-making process on the German side are characteristics of the German system which seeks to avoid uncertainty (as defined by Hofstede, 1980). These rules are often the end result of a reasonably solid consensus. The respect for accepted rules is more internalized by the Germans than forced upon them.
3. Decisions in a German company are taken at a fairly slow pace. The machine is 'well-oiled', but it is also rather cumbersome. A fairly substantial number of signatures will be required for any final agreement.
4. Great pride is taken in the technical quality of products manufactured in Germany; thus a reaction of disbelief is instinctively provoked when a German is faced with something that originates from abroad and which fails to conform, for example, to the DIN standards. As a result, readiness to participate in detailed discussions with technical experts is essential.
5. German earnestness is no myth. The Germans are people who keep their word, and who will respect the agreement made, whether it takes a written or an oral form. They loathe anything that approaches flippancy, in particular negotiation for negotiation's sake, or indeed the failure to keep to appointments. Germans, when they negotiate with the Italians or the French, often resent their Latin counterparts' unreliability in keeping to their commitments.
6. Explicit communication, and a temporal style that is clearly monochronic. In negotiations, Germans wait for the schedule and agenda to be respected.
7. The role of emotions and friendship (in negotiations) is fairly limited: in the process of negotiations, Germans keep their distance. They feel that a personal relationship could interfere with the result of their work (Schmidt, 1979).
8. There is ambiguity about the perception of Germans by other people: Germans are both admired and disliked. As stated by Barzini (1983, p. 94), this 'has its roots not only in their less amiable traits – arrogance. tactlessness and obtuseness – but also in

their great virtues, their excellence in almost all fields.' Germans should be considered as individuals more than any nationality in the world. This is the best way to avoid negative bias when negotiating with Germans, who, after all, are not personally responsible for every event of German history.

16.3   Negotiation styles in other areas of the world

Black African style

1. Black Africans' love of talking is always amazing for those used to useful speech. Africans simply do not have the same relationship to the universe as Europeans and Americans do. Differences relate to basic concepts such as time and space (see sections 2.2 and A2.4). Poetry has a powerful meaning for Africans. The African is a very verbal person: language (Africans are almost all polyglots) is an instrument for the enjoyment of the pleasure of speaking. As a result, negotiations can sometimes seem to be rather ill-directed, not purely because Africans enjoy debating, but also because they enjoy speaking.

2. There is an absence of a strictly economic individual motivation:

   > Money does not have the same value as in Europe. Westerners are accustomed to an age-old tradition of exchange based on money which has acquired a strong symbolic value as reward for work, as a means of saving, as a measure of personal success and as the fair price of things ... [in Africa] attitudes towards money follow different rules. Money is only a means of obtaining enough for survival and projection of self-image, whereas its other attributes fade into the background ... this money is taken without remorse, and in good humour [the 'baksheesh' that is – see Chapter 14], and usually benefit, not jut the person who receives it but also the whole family. The African system of distribution functions in such a way that money goes to the one who needs it: the employee whose salary does not allow him to live decently, the high-ranking civil servant who supports a large family in the village for example. (Gruère and Morel, 1991, pp. 122–3).

3. The reality of tribes and the group is never to be ignored: during the process of business negotiations, the influence of the family and ethnic background will inevitably make its presence felt, whether it be through the participants or the beneficiaries of its results.

4. The concept of time is simply not the same. This has a direct influence on the progress of business negotiations. As noted by Weiss and Stripp (1985, p. 39) in the case of Nigeria, 'Time is simply considered flexible. Lateness to meetings (even of several hours) is common. In the same vein, the foreigner who hurries through a negotiation – even after a very late start – will often be suspected of cheating.'

5. As Gruère and Morel (1991) emphasize, Black Africa is a mosaic, involving various characteristics of diversity: ethnic, religious (Christianity, Islam, animism) and linguistic. There too, as in the Middle East, a map of the 'human landscape' must be prepared in advance. In the West, we rarely consider people first as members of their tribe. People tend to be considered purely as individuals. The advantage has been the growth in tolerance and the reduction in violence between groups whose identity

conflicts. The disadvantage has been the increase in individual isolation, since individuals are significantly less supported in their personal life by the in-group.

Mexican style

1. As in many South American societies, family and political ties are extremely important for determining individual influence. Strong ingroup orientation is expressed in bonds of loyalty and solidarity among the top people in both business and government. The dominating political party, PRI, is also a structure allowing patronage and networking in the Mexican society, where relationships are a key issue. *Ubicacion*, that is, where one is plugged into the system, is important for determining a negotiator's status (Weiss and Stripp, 1985).
2. As noted earlier Mexico is a high power distance country, ranking second or third highest world-wide, according to the countries considered; as a consequence, decision-making is fairly centralized and 'Mexicans logically prefer to deal abroad at the higher levels of government and business and on a personal and private basis' (Fisher, 1980, p. 28).
3. Personal leverage – *palanca* – is important and influential Mexican negotiators tend to be well positioned in their society, exhibiting their status and stamina.
4. Like most Latins, body language is important: it conveys emotions, especially when trying to persuade the other party. Especially to their American neighbours, Mexicans appear at times overly dramatic, emotional and sentimental. Conversely, Mexican negotiators may resent some of their foreign partners as reserved, inexpressive and cold.
5. Truthful communication is not to be awaited full time from Mexicans and frankness should not be taken for granted. Paz (1962) explains that: 'The Mexican tells lies because he delights in fantasy, or because he is desperate, or because he wants to rise above the sordid facts of his life' (quoted by Weiss and Stripp, 1985, p. 33). The use of instrumental strategies by Mexican negotiators is confirmed by Adler *et al.* (1987). This allows them to increase their profits, by manipulating their negotiation partner.
6. According to Graham (1993), in a comparative study across seventeen countries, Mexicans appeared as competitive negotiators (this being evidenced by a fairly low level of joint profits) and the Mexican buyers were those which obtained the lion's share of the profits with almost 57 per cent of the joint outcome for them, the highest position for buyers out of the seventeen countries.
7. The Mexicans have a relaxed concept of time, expressing a polychronic pattern whereby schedules are not given precedence over relations with people. The *mañana* philosophy of time is based on a strong present orientation, which is detrimental to the accuracy of long-term planning and to real commitment *vis-á-vis* dates and deadlines. As the example of 'ocio' and 'negocio', at the beginning of Chapter 12, has shown, extreme activity, workalcoholism and high time consciousness are not strong values in Spanish-speaking Mexico.
8. Mexicans have a problematic identity problem with their big neighbour, the United States, and there is high sensitivity 'to their perceived dependent relationship with the

United States and their long memory of patronizing and demeaning actions taken by the U.S. as a government, by American companies and by Americans as individuals (Fisher, 1980, p. 40)

9. Although corruption has been combated by public authorities in recent years, bribery remains frequent in Mexico.

Russian style

1. Given the more than seventy years of communist regime, the Soviet system has let some deep imprints on the Russian society. As emphasized in section 7.5, this results in a lack of understanding of basic economic concepts such as that of free-market price, company valuation or balance sheet. The lack of knowledge of the free-market mechanisms is progressively redressed by management education.

2. The low level of individual initiative and the strong aversion for risk-taking are explained by Beliaev *et al.* (1985, p. 105) in the following terms: 'Each negotiator will be well trained in the party discipline; obedient, with a well-developed sense of hierarchy; hard-working and trained for stress, but with narrow horizons; loyal to the state and fearful of mistakes because of the risk of falling to the level of the average Soviet citizen; cautious, tough, and inflexible because of the strictness of their instructions; and willing to subordinate personal life to the demand of the position.'

3. As a result the Soviet style, still a part of the Russian style even after the Communist regime has fallen down, has been described as fairly tough and unilateral. Negotiators tended to make extreme initial demands, to view adversary concessions as weakness, to be stingy in concessions, and to ignore deadlines (Cohen, 1980). On the other hand, the Soviet-style Russians were good payers and did respect contracts which were drafted in a very detailed way.

4. Graham *et al.* (1992) note the consensus of description of the Soviet negotiators as 'competitive' and 'uncompromising'. They show in a laboratory experiment that Russian negotiators tend to prefer a distributive strategy, and this with minimal negative effects on their (Russian) partner's satisfaction, which tends to suggest that such competitive behaviour is considered locally as standard practice.

5. The ethical system of Russians widely differs from that of American according to Lefebvre (1983):

> Something that an American considers normative positive behavior (for example, negotiating and reaching a compromise with an enemy, and even any deal with another individual), a Soviet man perceives as showing Philistine cowardice, weakness, as something unworthy (the word 'deal' itself has a strong negative connotation in contemporary Russian). (Quoted in Graham *et al.*, 1992, p. 396)

6. Communist centralized planning, based on five-year detailed plans, has not infused the Soviets with a sense of economic time which they lack (Beliaev *et al.*, 1985). Given the complexity of co-ordination between government bodies, the Soviet had renounced to meeting exact schedules. This logically, in Russia today, results in a highly present and short term oriented society.

7. Russia is now in a deep transition. The bureaucratic controls have been progressively

relaxed giving birth to a new society with deep contrasts. New entrepreneurs are almost western in style, full of initiative but lacking professionalism and reliability, and may look very far from the Soviet-style described above. However, what has been gained in terms of flexibility is largely compensated by the lack of reliability, opportunistic behaviour and the confusion between business and wild capitalism being largely the rule. Payments incidents and negotiated contracts which are never enforced are now frequent. Many new Russian entrepreneurs do not feel bound by normal business norms and contracts because either they ignore it or they view it as foreign and therefore inapplicable to their context.

16.4 Some basic rules for international marketing negotiations

In short, the international business negotiator, should follow some basic rules:

1. Be well prepared; define in advance your basic interests, objectives and bottom line, and room for manoeuvre. Before participating in a negotiation, learn the basics about the behavioural norms in your partner's culture, especially concerning appointments, punctuality and planning.
2. Take time for adequate preliminaries: getting to know the other party is most often crucial. More time is needed than in domestic business negotiations, since cultural as well as personal knowledge have to be acquired.
3. Be flexible with the negotiation agenda if the other party does not stick to it.
4. If needed, be prepared to renounce a negotiation, because the stakes are too low, or send lower level, less expensive executives. If possible, negotiate at home where you have a competitive advantage over your foreign partner in terms of time control.
5. Be ready for different communication styles and be cautious in interpreting silence, emotionality, threats and any kind of manipulative communication.
6. Never tell the other side when you are leaving because this gives them control over your time.
7. Respect the sensitivities of your partner in the area of (a) personal status and (b) national pride.
8. Allow yourself plenty of time, and even more. Patience is an asset for negotiation and it is destroyed by time pressure.
9. Do not get fooled by the other party seemingly sharing your time pattern: try to set realistic dates and deadlines and plan modestly and realistically. Tight deadlines may result into jumbo delays that ruin the credibility of the whole planning process.
10. Try to balance relationship- and deal-orientation: wait for the negotiation process to extend beyond the signature of the deal.

Questions

1. What sort of cultural misunderstandings could arise from a negotiation between Japanese buyers and French sellers?

2. Discuss the influence of group orientation (as presented in Chapter 2 and illustrated in this chapter for some national groups) on behaviour during the negotiation process.
3. Negotiations between Russians and Chinese: are they easy? Why?
4. Imagine a negotiation between a (stereotypical) Mexican businessman and a (stereotypical) US businesswoman: which cultural misunderstandings may appear between them in the negotiation process?
5. Discuss similarities and differences between US and British business negotiation styles.
6. American business people meet potential Japanese partners in California to discuss a joint-venture project. The joint venture would sell US-made products on the Japanese market. One of the Americans starts the first meeting by saying to his Japanese counterpart: 'Since we are going to work together in the future, we had better get to know each other now. My name is John. What is your name?' Is this address adequate? If so, why? If not, why not?

APPENDIX 16

◆◆◆

Teaching materials

A16.1   Negotiation stimulation: Lump Sum

Emergency meeting of representatives from state assemblies on educational planning for Malaysia

You have been called together in this special emergency meeting to represent the unique interests of your (constituencies) in making an extremely important decision. The future of our (country) may depend on your decision today and the unique opportunity presented to us.

A representative of the (United Nations Special Fund) has today informed me that owing to bureaucratic oversight there is (US$10,000,000) which has not been allocated in the budget for any specific project and which is available for the use (of Malaysia) provided that you can make a rapid decision on allocation of those funds and inform (the Secretary-General of the United Nations in New York) by this afternoon. We have an open telephone line to (the Secretary-General's office) to notify him as soon as a decision is made. The representative apologized for the urgency of this request but the fiscal year for the (United Nations) ends tonight and all funds already appropriated but not allocated to specific projects by that time will revert to the (United Nations General Fund) and will not be available for (Special Fund).

For the sake of speed and the fair allocation of the money, special representatives (from the various state assemblies of Malaysia) have been called together today to draw up a specific allocation of the money. The (United Nations) does not care how the money is allocated but (for the sake of national unity and the good of the whole country) they stipulate *absolutely* that you must come to a unanimous agreement on your decision within the time limit or lose the money. (The United Nations) agrees to abide by whatever allocations you *unanimously* decide on within the next (ninety minutes).

You are already divided into your (six State Assembly) groupings:

1. Sarawak-Sabah.
2. Perak-Penang-Province Wellesley.
3. Kelantan-Trengganu.
4. Pahang-Johore.
5. Negri Sembilan Malacca.
6. Kedah-Perlis.

For the sake of a speedy decision, each group will select its own negotiator and the (six) negotiators will carry out the actual negotiations on allocation of the money.

Because only (two hours) can be allowed to reach a conclusion, we have established a timetable which *must* be rigidly adhered to. You will have adequate time to express the proposal of your delegation, to present your proposal to the group, and to negotiate privately as well as publicly with other delegations towards unanimous agreement. While the actual negotiations will take place through your elected negotiator, you may, if the majority of the delegation is dissatisfied with his performance, replace your representative with someone else selected by the majority of your delegation.

Your timetable is as follows:

1. (*Twenty minutes*): Each delegation will meet together and settle among themselves who will be the negotiator representing them in the negotiations, and draw up specific plans for how the entire ($10,000,000) ought to be divided and allocated according to the needs of the entire (country) and the special concerns of your own (constituency).
2. (*Eighteen minutes*): In the first Negotiation Session, each representative will be given three minutes to report on how his delegation proposes to allocate the money. There will be no discussion among the representatives but each representative will be given an opportunity to explain the merits of his delegation's allocation of the money to the assembled company.
3. (*Ten minutes*): In the first consultation, representatives will go back to their own delegation for ten minutes to consult with them on strategy, presentation and any changes in their proposals they may want to make, and to have private consultation with members of other groups.
4. (*Ten minutes*): In the second Negotiation Session, representatives will present any modifications which may have been made on the basis of having heard the other representatives' proposals or on the basis of the consultations which have just taken place.
5. (*Ten minutes*): In the second consultation, further modifications in each group's proposals can be made. Also, this is the time to consult again with other groups

on any private compromises which may be proposed to secure their cooperation.
6. (*Twenty minutes*): In the third Negotiation Session, representatives will discuss
   and present their final and presumably unanimously agreed upon proposal for
   the allocation of the (US$10,000,000).
   Instructions for the role-play of this simulated situation of conflict among
competing interest groups are available in the instructor's manual.

Alternative seating arrangements for Lump Sum are shown in Figures 16.1 and
16.2.
(Source: adapted from 'Lump Sum: A bargaining simulation game design', by Professor

Figure 16.1   Lump Sum: first seating arrangement.

Figure 16.2   Lump Sum: second seating arrangement.

Marshall R. Singer and Dr Paul B. Pedersen, 1970, Kuala Lumpur, Malaysia, in Weeks *et al.*, 1987. Reproduced with the kind permission of the publisher.)

A16.2   Case: Tremonti SpA

Tremonti SpA was a small company located in the suburbs of Milan. Like many small and medium enterprises in the northern part of Italy, it specialized in special machines and mechanical engineering. Tremonti SpA had developed a sophisticated knowledge in the production of machines for assembling electronic components.

The company had been founded by an engineer, Mr Stefanini, who owned the business and gave it its technological drive. Until now he had always made the choice to invest more money in research and development than in production operations. The company therefore cared more about prototypes than mass production (if that means anything in an industry where world-wide markets rarely exceed tens or hundreds of machines).

A large part of the production was in fact subcontracted. This made factory investments lighter and gave production flexibility in the face of unsteady demand. But subcontracting about 60–80 per cent of the parts and a large amount of the assembly work was not satisfactory in that it made it difficult to follow and monitor production schedules accurately.

The export manager, Mr Lesca, had considerably increased export sales during the last five years. Export sales at Tremonti SpA were 80 per cent of the total corporate sales figure. Clients were mostly located in the United States and in Europe, with a very small proportion in Japan. Lesca's team was composed of two export salesmen, who had a technical background and provided maintenance for machines located abroad, and two English-speaking secretaries who were in charge of export logistics and paperwork.

I

Lesca was worried by a problem with an American customer. The American had already bought one machine from Tremonti SpA and was very satisfied with it. It worked at full capacity, it had been delivered on time and it was reliable. Then he ordered a second machine, which was now in the production process.

Unfortunately, according to the manufacturing department, the production of this machine seemed to be delayed by four to six weeks from the agreed delivery date. Yet the American customer was willing to order a third machine, since the first one had been working satisfactorily for the last six months. He did not know about a possible delay for the second machine.

Lesca wondered what he should do:

1. Should he tell the American customer about the delivery delay of the second machine during his next visit to negotiate the sale of the third machine? The

agreed delivery date of the second machine is six weeks after the next visit of Lesca to his American customer.
2. If yes, how should he announce it?

II

Finally, after the visit had taken place, Lesca was satisfied with the tactics he had adopted. He felt a need to extract some more stable principles out of this communication experience. When flying back from the United States, he wondered how he should have acted with people from the following national/cultural backgrounds: German, Japanese and Saudi Arabian.

III

Demand had been growing quickly. Since Tremonti SpA's machines were up to date and reliable, they were especially sought out. But delivery delays were increasing. A conversation with a German customer, Herr Weisslinger, gave him another opportunity to become aware of the high level of sensitivity of clients to their suppliers meeting delivery dates.

'You Italians,' began Weisslinger, 'you do not really know what a delivery date is. There are huge differences between the delivery date agreed upon when signing the contract and the actual delivery date. And you wait until the last minute to tell us that you won't be able to meet your delivery date. Sometimes you do not even report it and we have to send you a fax to try to find out when the machine will be delivered. Yet it should already have been delivered, and we are not even informed.'

'No, you carry it too far,' answered Lesca. 'I do not believe that we deliberately miss delivery dates. You have to understand: a delivery date is indicative. When ordering, a date is fixed that best suits the client. We indicate the delivery date that we think we are able to meet. Numerous hazards may then occur. Our suppliers and subcontractors do not adhere strictly to their delivery dates, and this causes a large part of our own delays.'

'If I understand you correctly, we have to take things as they are,' said Weisslinger.

'I am afraid so,' replied Lesca. 'I am the personal advocate of our clients within the company. But, you know, my authority is limited, and the Italian national character values deadlines and time precision far less than Anglo-Saxons do. Moreover it is an organizational problem: everybody has to feel committed if we want to achieve a greater respect for delivery dates.' 'Yes indeed,' said Weisslinger, 'I think your machines are of good quality and your maintenance and after-sales service are OK. But your competitors provide equal qualities and they meet their deadlines. We have to make rational choices. You do not meet your delivery dates.'

Mr Lesca is now wondering how he should allocate his efforts. Should he go on playing the role of a 'trade ambassador', trying diplomatically to make the foreign clients accept delays? Should he, on the other hand, spend more time in the company and undertake action to improve the organizational functioning for delivery dates? How should he tackle the issue with Stefanini? Which ways and means would be sufficient to improve the commitment to delivery dates?

IV

Some time after this conversation with Weisslinger, Lesca went to Japan for a business trip, where he had the opportunity to present Tremonti SpA's technical achievements. On his return from Japan, he went to Stefanini's office to discuss the potential of the Japanese market. 'We did place some orders there, but they are small compared with the total Japanese market, and particularly small when compared with the sales we achieved in the United States. I have had preliminary talks with a large electronics company called Nokan. We examined the possibility of a marketing joint venture, which would be responsible for selling and servicing our machines on the Japanese market. It looks fine; but I know that Japanese people are not easy to deal with. They are extremely polite, courteous and gentle, but what are their real intentions? Frankly, I do not trust them. Besides, they have a reputation for ransacking technologies, and it is a fundamental that we protect our knowledge base.' Stefanini wanted to prepare for the negotiation of this marketing joint venture.

He asked Lesca the following questions:

1. 'How can we get information about Japanese culture?
2. 'Which aspects are relevant to our problem?'

References

Adler, Nancy J., John L. Graham and Theodore Schwarz Gehrke (1987), 'Business negotiations in Canada, Mexico and the United States', *Journal of Business Research*, vol. 15, pp. 411–29.

Barzini, Luigi (1983), *The Europeans*, Penguin Books: London.

Beliaev, Edward, Thomas Mullen and Betty Jane Punnett (1985), 'Understanding the cultural environment: U.S.–U.S.S.R. trade negotiations', *California Management Review*, vol. XXVII, no. 2, pp. 100–12.

Burt, David N. (1984), 'The nuances of negotiating overseas', *Journal of Purchasing and Materials Management*, Winter, pp. 2–8.

Campbell, Nigel C.G., John L. Graham, Alain Jolibert and Hans Günther Meissner (1988), 'Marketing negotiations in France, Germany, the United Kingdom and United States', *Journal of Marketing*, vol. 52 (April), pp. 49–62.

Cohen, Herb (1980), *You Can Negotiate Anything*, Bantam: New York.

Eiteman, David K. (1990), 'American executives' perceptions of negotiating joint ventures with the People's Republic of China: Lessons learned', *Columbia Journal of World Business*, Winter, pp. 59–67.

Fisher, Glen (1980), *International Negotiation: A cross-cultural perspective*, Intercultural Press: Yarmouth, ME.

Graham, John L. (1981), 'A hidden cause of America's trade deficit with Japan', *Columbia Journal of World Business*, Fall, pp. 5–15.

Graham, John L. (1993), 'Business negotiations: Generalisations about Latin America and East Asia are dangerous', *UCI Irvine/Research*, pp. 6–23.

Graham, John L. and Roy A. Herberger Jr (1983), 'Negotiators abroad: Don't shoot from the hip', *Harvard Business Review*, vol. 61, no. 4, pp. 160–8.

Graham, John L., Leonid I. Ivenko and Mahesh N. Rajan (1992), 'An empirical comparison of Soviet and American business negotiations', *Journal of International Business Studies*, vol. 23, no. 3, pp. 387–418.

Gruère, Jean-Pierre and Pierre Morel (1991), *Cadres Français et Communications Interculturelles*, Eyrolles: Paris.

Hawrysh, Bryan Mark and Judith Lynn Zaichkowsky (1990), 'Cultural approaches to negotiations: Understanding the Japanese', *International Marketing Review*, vol. 7, no. 2, pp. 28–42.

Hofstede, Geert (1980) 'Motivation, leadership and organization: Do American theories apply abroad?' *Organizational Dynamics* (Summer), pp. 42–63.

Lefebvre, Victorina D. (1983), 'Ethical features of the normative hero in Soviet children's literature of the 1960s–70s', *Studies of Cognitive Sciences*, vol. 20, School of Social Sciences: Irvine, CA.

Oh, T. K. (1986), 'Selling to the Japanese', *Nation's Business*, October, pp. 37–8.

Paz, Octavio (1962), *The Labyrinth of Solitude*, Grove: New York.

Pye, Lucian W. (1982), *Chinese Commercial Negotiating Style*, Oelgeschlager, Gunn & Hain: Cambridge, MA.

Pye, Lucian W. (1986), 'The China trade: Making the deal work' *Harvard Business Review*, vol. 46, no. 4, pp. 75–84.

Schmidt, Klaus D. (1979), *Doing Business in France, Germany and the United Kingdom*, pamphlets published by the Business Intelligence Program, SRI International: Menlo Park, CA.

Tung, Rosalie L. (1984a), 'How to negotiate with the Japanese', *California Management Review*, vol. XXVI, no. 4, pp. 62–77.

Tung, Rosalie L. (1984b), *Business Negotiations with the Japanese*. Lexington Books: Lexington, MA.

Weeks, William H., Paul B. Pedersen and Richard W. Brislin (1987), *A Manual of Structured Experiences for Cross-cultural Learning*, Intercultural Press: Yarmouth, ME.

Weiss, Stephen E. and William Stripp (1985), 'Negotiating with foreign businesspersons: An introduction for Americans with propositions for six cultures', Working Paper no. 85–6, Graduate School of Business, New York University: New York.

Postscript

Globalization as 'modernism' brought to backward nations

As Ernest Dichter emphasized in an article entitled 'The World Customer', which is considered a seminal article in the field of international marketing, particularly as it was the first to picture the phenomenon of the globalization of world markets:[1]

> Only one Frenchman out of three brushes his teeth. Automobiles have become a must for the self-esteem of even the lowliest postal clerk in Naples or the Bantu street cleaner in Durban. . . . Four out of five Germans change their shirts but once a week. (p. 113)

The explanation is to be found further on: 'The fact that 64% of the Frenchmen don't brush their teeth is in part caused by the lack of running water in many communities' (p. 116). The Germans rank first for the 'self-illusions' a nation can have about itself. Dichter proposes the following illustration: 'Germans still refer to themselves as a nation of poets and thinkers; yet the largest selling newspaper, the *Bildzeitung*, has a circulation of 2 million based largely on sensationalism and tabloid treatment of news' (p. 117). According to Dichter (at the beginning of the 1960s) Dutch housewives would use instant coffee accompanied by the verbal protest that instant coffee is used only as an emergency. 'What happens, however, is that the number of emergencies has increased amazingly' (p. 117).

One might think that globalization emerged from the advances in modernity and cleanliness accomplished by these backward people, when they overcame their resistance to change. One may also wonder whether there is any real connection between Goethe, Schiller, Kant or Heidegger on the one hand and the *Bildzeitung* on the other, except the fact that they are all German. It is necessary to highlight the first paradox in this approach: many arguments in favour of the globalization of markets are totally ethno-centric; as such, they are in contradiction with the spirit of globalization, which is based on the rejection of ethnocentrism.

Some true reasons for the globalization of markets

Globalization is, first of all, based on technological advances, which in turn explain globalization on the supply side: economies of scale and experience effects, drastic changes over the past forty years in transportation and also new telecommunications technologies. The globalization of consumers and demand will certainly occur in the future, but it will happen much later than its early defenders imagined. Moreover the process of world-wide globalization of demand may be quite different from what they visualized: a steady extension of the 'American way of life' throughout the world which would contribute to the global happiness of humankind.

But cultural coherence should not be forgotten and marketers still have to be aware of it. Consumers buy meanings, not just products. Meaning is intersubjectively shared in the cultural community. The process of globalization of demand will be long term because of the local nature of culture and its contribution to collective identity. Moreover, this evolution can be achieved only by individuals who *learn*. Learning is a large part of the process of culture. Globalization implies that consumers throughout the world have to borrow foreign ways of life, experience new behaviours and construct shared meanings with people from other cultures. At present, a great many things are shared among the cultures of the world, but just as many remain culture-specific. *Amnesty* International, the practice of *judo*, playing or listening to *jazz*, the *Olympics* and many other cultural artefacts, even though they were born in particular cultures, are probably bearers of future universal values. Obviously each national culture has a specific contribution to make to the movement towards globalization. If there is any true (and sincere) way of being *global* it is not by denying differences, but by being aware and responsive to them.

We face a second paradox, the two sides of which must be constantly kept in mind: on the one hand, lifestyles apparently tend to become global; on the other, the claims for recovering cultural identity are stronger than ever. Numerous peoples who have been denied a sovereign state are demanding their independence as nations, emphasizing the uniqueness of their culture. The concept of a nation-state, although a fairly recent one historically,[2] remains very strong for many individuals. While it is not the only way of protecting cultural identity, it is still the most elaborate and efficient one.

The law of comparative advantage is noted in Chapter 7 for it has almost completely eliminated the concept of culture from international trade theory. One may remark, as Galtung (1990) does, that: 'In short, this "law" [of comparative advantage] is a piece of cultural violence buried in the very core of economics.'[3] Ignoring cultural differences, the law of comparative advantage imposes a paradigm of international trade, which is excessively utilitarian: it assumes the *complete pre-eminence of utility over identity*. Yet real people do not live only with what is useful to them, they also live out of the maintenance and self-actualization of their identity, of which their cultural identity is a significant part. Thus it is necessary to integrate the dimension of culture in marketing strategies and in their implementation, when they focus on international markets.

Designing tailored marketing strategies, and implementing them with respect for the local context

As this book (hopefully) shows: marketing strategies tailored to national/cultural markets are not in contradiction with the choice of a global business strategy. On the contrary, cultural tailoring is a basic element of a global business strategy. The reality of cultural exchanges world-wide is now so complex and so inextricable that any oversimplification is dangerous. Let us take a concrete example: using instant coffee does not imply that one has, once and for all, adopted ready-made standardized consumer goods. Bean coffee and ground coffee have made a tremendous come-back against instant coffee, regaining lost market share in most coffee-drinking countries of the world. No evolution is fixed; consumers change from 'tradition' to 'modernism', but also back to (almost) traditional ways of consuming. Among the segments targeted for an intercultural marketing strategy there will be both transnational market segments and national market segments, to which specific offers will be made. National culture will continue to influence strongly the implementation of marketing strategies, under many aspects: choice of distribution channels and trade partners, setting of prices. sales and marketing negotiations, etc.

This is fortunate because, if cultural differences were to disappear, I suspect that life would be very boring.

Notes

1. I am sorry for the unkind use of certain sentences of this article (Ernest Dichter, 1962, 'The World Customer', *Harvard Business Review*, vol. 40, no. 4, pp. 113–22). It is a superb example of sincere ethnocentrism, as well as of relative lack of long-term vision. The article does, however, contain many insightful remarks.
2. The concept of a nation-state emerged clearly at the end of the seventeenth century and during the nineteenth century. Germany and Italy, for instance, were not united as nation-states before the end of the nineteenth century, under the auspices of Bismarck in Germany and Cavour in Italy. Decolonization was the heyday of the concept of the nation-state: many countries were formed which corresponded neither to a nation, nor to a shared culture among the various groups of citizens, nor even to a geographical unit.
3. Johan Galtung, in an article entitled 'Cultural violence' (1990, *Journal of Peace Research*, vol. 27, no. 3, pp. 291–305), thoroughly defines what the process of cultural violence encompasses. In particular, one section of his article (4.5) argues about the role of Ricardo's doctrine (developed further by Heckscher and Ohlin, and others) as justifying the world division of labour. 'The principle of comparative advantage sentences countries to stay where the production-factor profile has landed them, for geographical and historical reasons' (p. 300). However, marketers are not economists: their pragmatism may induce them to choose *culturally non-violent* marketing strategies, if they prove successful.

Author index

563

Subject index